Group Work with
Populations at Risk

GROUP WORK WITH POPULATIONS AT RISK

Second Edition

Edited by

GEOFFREY L. GREIF
PAUL H. EPHROSS

OXFORD
UNIVERSITY PRESS
2005

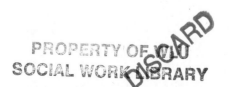

OXFORD
UNIVERSITY PRESS

Oxford   New York

Auckland   Bangkok   Buenos Aires   Cape Town   Chennai
Dar es Salaam   Delhi   Hong Kong   Istanbul   Karachi   Kolkata
Kuala Lumpur   Madrid   Melbourne   Mexico City   Mumbai   Nairobi
São Paulo   Shanghai   Taipei   Tokyo   Toronto

Copyright © 1997, 2005 by Oxford University Press, Inc.

Published by Oxford University Press, Inc.
198 Madison Avenue, New York, New York 10016
www.oup.com

Library of Congress Cataloging-in-Publication Data
Group work with populations at risk /
[edited by] Geoffrey L. Greif, Paul H. Ephross.—2nd ed.
p. cm.   Includes bibliographical references and index.
ISBN 978-0-19-515667-6
1. Social group work. 2. Marginality, Social.
I. Greif, Geoffrey L. II. Ephross, Paul H.
HV45.G73165 2004   361.4—dc22   2003060917

4 5 7 8 9

Printed in the United States of America
on acid-free paper.

Preface
to the
Second Edition

Since the final touches were put on the First Edition in 1996, significant world developments have affected the social work profession and group work. These developments touch all populations, those formerly at risk as well as those who would not have been identified as at risk. Some of these developments are gradual and the result of changes in the way society does business, while others were sparked by specific and horrific events. We have added chapters in this second edition to help readers address these changes.

The internet is one of the gradual developments. The web and email have become a powerful source of information and support, profoundly changing the way that people throughout the world communicate. For people in distress, chat rooms and on-line support groups abound. The understanding of the social work role in mediating these groups is in its beginning but rapidly developing, as is the social work role in on-line counseling. A new chapter, by Andrea Meier, addresses many of the thorny practice issues presented by internet users.

A second development is actually a continuation of a truly American pattern—immigration. Almost one million immigrants enter the United States legally every year. Many of these come from Pacific Rim nations and face difficult assimilation issues. Shoshanna Ringel's chapter describes ways in which social workers can help these new immigrants as well as the family members that preceded them to become acculturated to American society, while also being respectful of the culture in their country of origin.

A third development speaks to communities. With federal funding for Empowerment Zones in the mid-1990s, the importance of involving impoverished communities in solving their own problems was fully embraced. Elizabeth A. Mulroy describes why group work with populations at risk requires vigilance about community and organizational factors that will help guide and shape the direction of social work practice.

When we speak of specific and horrific events that affect the profession and group work, we are referring to violence and hate crimes. The shootings at Columbine High School and the September 11th attacks on the World Trade Center and the Pentagon are two of the most notable. Other hate crimes that targeted specific individuals (for example, in Laramie, Wyoming, and Jasper, Texas) also come to mind. While Columbine and September 11th occurred for different reasons, the treatment of choice for many of the survivors and the families of victims is the same—group work. John Kayser's chapter on group work with victims of school and community violence is a needed addition to any group work textbook. Joan Weiss's chapter, which appeared in the first edition and is retitled "Working with Victims of Hate Crimes," is also of great importance at a time when Americans are being targeted because of their nationality and other identity characteristics.

We have also added a new chapter, a second one by Andrea Meier writing with Edna Comer, on evidence-based practice. Practitioners are increasingly being called upon to prove their interventions are effective. This chapter explains how we can go about the important task of showing that our group work makes a difference. While all of the original authors were asked to address what evaluation measures they use in their practice, this chapter explains from a methodological point of view how to approach this key component of social work practice.

Finally, in addition to the five new chapters that appear here, and a revised introductory chapter from Paul Ephross, the original authors were asked to update their chapters as they saw fit with new literature and new information about practice techniques. Three authors added co-authors. Everyone has updated their national resources (and website addresses—which were absent from the First Edition).

While this is a skills book dedicated to helping practitioners address a variety of populations, the acquisition of group theory should never be given short shrift. Without a grounding in theory, we will not be in a good position to help new client populations as they emerge and need our service. We hope that students, faculty, and practitioners will continue to find the text useful in helping those most at risk.

Baltimore, Maryland   G.L.G.
                                                                          P.H.E.

Preface
to the
First Edition

The genesis of this book was our belief that beginning social workers need concrete suggestions for managing and guiding their forays into group work. Newcomers entering an agency, for example, are often asked to start or take over a group that serves members of a particular population. Where should the worker begin in trying to understand the group's members and their shared condition? Publications about work with the target population may focus on individual needs, policy proposals, social action agendas, or important findings from research. Literature on group work with that population may be available periodically but is not always up-to-date or easily accessible to the worker. It may also not be geared toward guiding a novice through the beginning stages of helping.

Social work with groups has become an orphan in many departments and schools over the last few decades, relegated to part of a practice course or ignored altogether (Birnbaum & Auerbach, 1994). As fewer schools taught group work as a separate subject, fewer group work specialists were developed and the supply of group work teachers, prepared both academically and by practice experience with groups, declined sharply. It is only recently, with the hard work of the Association for the Advancement of Social Work with Groups and recognition by the Council on Social Work Education of the necessity of strengthening education in group work, that the trend toward marginalizing group work has been reversed. The teaching and practice of social work with groups are again starting to proliferate (as they did 50 years ago) both in undergraduate and graduate social work curricula and in the field. This expansion stems from the recognition that group work is often the method of choice to meet the needs of the client and community; is financially viable, given the increased pressure on resources, both organizational and third party; and is often a wise use of the worker's time. Group work can also help meet deeply felt personal and social needs at a time when alienation, a sense of disenfranchisement, and experiences of oppression and fragmentation characterize the lives of many people who seek help from social workers and others.

Learning group work methods in the broadest sense—including the phases of group life, the demands of the worker in each phase, the uses of authority, the opportunities and constraints of agency contexts, and the value of limits, among others—is one important aspect of dealing with the rising demand for groups. Another is learning how to work with the specific population from which group members are drawn. With the rapidly changing nature of practice and its increasing focus on the particular needs of specific populations (a reflection of American society), we believe that proficiency and specificity of skills are in great demand. People seeking help are more likely to be wary consumers. They want to be understood as individuals and will seek help elsewhere if the worker does not help them achieve their goals and reach the outcomes they seek.

The purpose of this book is to provide social workers with a practice-oriented source that describes specific ways of working with a variety of populations in groups. The focus is on populations at risk, those most likely to need social work services in groups. The phrase *at risk* refers to people who have experienced life-changing events; who are at crossroads where prevention would be helpful in staving off undesirable consequences; or who, through their own actions, may represent a risk to others and themselves unless they are helped to change.

To achieve our goal, we approached practitioners who had extensive experience either with populations that have frequently been served by social workers in the past or with populations that we anticipate will need many services in the near future. It is not only their experience that makes these contributors experts; it is also their ability to see themselves in a helping role with the sometimes stigmatized population they serve. Each contributor was asked to write a chapter that would answer the following questions:

1. What does the professional literature say about this population?
2. What particular principles should guide a social worker beginning to work with this population?
3. What common themes have you seen in working with groups composed of members of this particular population?
4. What are some of the methods that you have found successful and that you recommend for working with this population?
5. What evaluation measures are being used to judge whether the members are benefiting from their experiences in these groups?
6. Are there any national sources of information that can be tapped by social workers for further information?

We were especially interested in the common themes that are raised by the groups being served. Social workers often know how to recruit members for groups, screen them, and start the first session. But once all members have introduced themselves, the usual first step, the worker may not know how to proceed. The contributors to this book offer that information by focusing on the areas of concern they have most frequently heard identified by group members. The worker is thus prepared to raise, respond to, or reinforce issues related to potential topics or areas of concern that are known to have been relevant to other such groups.

We begin with an introductory chapter that summarizes the generic practice principles of social work with groups. Then, because it is impossible for one book to encompass all of the populations at risk—our initial survey listed almost 50—the book includes a chapter on each of the following populations: persons being treated for cancer, abused children, parents in the urban public schools, seriously mentally ill people, children of divorce, incarcerated offenders, grieving adults, parents being treated for substance abuse, African-American youth who have had contact with the legal system, gay men, lesbian women, substance-abusing teenagers, men who have committed family violence, HIV-positive men, head-injured people, men who have sexually abused children, noncustodial parents, victims of hate crimes (a growing population), unemployed workers, and workers connected to employee assistance programs. Because of the complexity of the work site, this last chapter presents an overview of groups offered in that setting.

Some contributors have offered detailed explanations of step-by-step programs that they offer. Others are more general in their approach. We believe there is much to be learned from these experts and have left their views and opinions in place, regardless of whether we agree with their point of view. It is our hope that this text well be useful to social workers in a variety of settings and that it will demystify what can be the frightening experience of sitting in a group of strangers and not knowing where to begin.

We would like to thank Renée Forbes for her secretarial assistance, Gioia Stevens of Oxford University Press for her editorial support, and Dean Jesse J. Harris for helping bring about an atmosphere at the School of Social Work, University of Maryland at Baltimore, that makes writing a pleasure. When the entire manuscript had been completed, we realized that we had never decided the order in which the editors should be listed. We flipped a coin to solve this problem. Would that all problems could be solved so easily.

Baltimore, Maryland   G.L.G.
May 1996   P.H.E.

REFERENCE

Birnbaum, M., & Auerbach, C. (1994). Group work in graduate social work education: The price of neglect. *Journal of Social Work Education.* 30(4), 325–334.

Contents

Contributors

STEVEN BALL, ACSW, is a private practitioner and adjunct faculty member at Hunter College School of Social Work in New York.

SARA BONKOWSKI, Ph.D., is a professor at George Williams College, School of Social Work, Aurora University, Aurora, Illinois.

MARGOT BRETON, MSW, is a professor, Faculty of Social Work, University of Toronto.

EDNA COMER, Ph.D., is an assistant professor at the University of Connecticut, School of Social Work, Hartford, Connecticut.

KAY MARTEL CONNORS, LCSW-C, is director of the Care Clinic at the Center for Families, University of Maryland, Baltimore.

BARRY M. DASTE, is a professor emeritus, School of Social Work, Louisiana State University in Baton Rouge.

SHARON S. ENGLAND, MSW, J.D., is a child advocate in Virginia who represents children as a guardian *ad litem*.

BONNIE J. ENGLEHARDT, ACSW, LICSW, is a social group worker in private practice in Needham, Massachusetts.

PAUL H. EPHROSS, Ph.D., is a professor, School of Social Work, University of Maryland, Baltimore.

SUSAN T. FUTERAL, Ph.D., is on the faculty of Towson State University in sociology and is engaged in private practice and consulting.

CHARLES GARVIN, Ph.D., is a professor emeritus, School of Social Work, University of Michigan.

GEORGE S. GETZEL, D.S.W., is a professor emeritus, Hunter College School of Social Work in New York.

MURIEL GRAY, Ph.D., is an associate professor, School of Social Work, University of Maryland, Baltimore.

GEOFFREY L. GREIF, D.S.W., is associate dean and professor, School of Social Work, University of Marlynd, Baltimore.

AMINIFU R. HARVEY, D.S.W., is an associate professor, School of Social Work, University of Maryland, Baltimore.

JOHN A. KAYSER, Ph.D., is an associate professor, Graduate School of Social Work, University of Denver.

MELISSA LITTLEFIELD, Ph.D., is an assistant professor, School of Social Work, University of Maryland, Baltimore.

BENJAMIN LIPTON, CSW, is a private practitioner and adjunct professor at New York University Ehrenkranz School of Social Work.

ANDREW MALEKOFF, MSW, CAC, is associate director of North Shore Child and Family Guidance Center, Roslyn Heights, New York.

ANDREA MEIER, Ph.D., is a research assistant professor, University of North Carolina at Chapel Hill, School of Social Work.

ELIZABETH A. MULROY, Ph.D., is an associate professor, School of Social Work, University of Maryland, Baltimore.

ANNA NOSKO, MSW, is a social worker at Family Services Association of Toronto.

SUSAN RICE, DSW, is a professor, Department of Social Work, and director of the Peace Studies Certificate Program at California State University at Long Beach.

SHOSHANNA RINGEL, Ph.D., is an assistant professor, School of Social Work, University of Maryland, Baltimore.

STEVEN R. ROSE, Ph.D., is a professor, School of Social Work, Louisiana State University in Baton Rouge.

STEVEN STOSNY, Ph.D., is director of CompassionPower, Silver Spring, Maryland.

JOAN C. WEISS, MSW, is executive director of the Justice Research and Statistics Association, Washington, DC.

CAROLYN AMBLER WALTER, Ph.D., is professor and director of the baccalaureate social work program, Center for Social Work Education, Widener University in Pennsylvania.

MARGARET M. WRIGHT, Ph.D., is an assistant professor, School of Social Work and Family Studies, University of British Columbia.

Group Work with Populations at Risk

Introduction

Social Work with Groups: Practice Principles

PAUL H. EPHROSS

This book is about the practice of group work with a wide variety of people who are at risk. The populations are defined by a particular physical or psychological condition, a social identity, an unmet need for a service or form of help, a condition that caused them to be stigmatized or discriminated against by society or social institutions, or by a challenge that arises from their stage of life or personal history. Many are affected by more than one of these factors. What unites the people described in the following chapters is that they share two characteristics. They are at risk for continued, intensified harm, pain, dysfunction, or unmet need. They can also benefit from participating in a group experience through which they can gain skills, understanding, and emotional learnings that can reduce their level of vulnerability.

Each chapter author was asked to note ways in which the particular need of his or her population may necessitate modifications or adaptations of traditional or mainstream social work practice in groups. This instruction, and the chapter authors' responses, suggest that there is a body of knowledge and skills, supported by a cluster of perceptions and attitudes, undergirded by a set of values and commitments about the nature of human beings and society, that constitute mainstream group work. Each chapter assumes that the reader understands the bases of group work and uses those bases as a starting point. The purpose of this chapter is to provide an introduction to concepts that are generic to social group work, including the nature of group experience, values, perceptions, purposes and goals, and methods.

1

Defining *group* is not a simple matter.

The word *group* has met with difficulties of definition, both in the social sciences and in social work literature. In one sense, it is defined by size; i.e., the "small group" or such large units as legislative committees or assemblies. In a second sense, *group* is linked to collectivity. In still another sense, *group* is tied to the term *social*, thereby contrasting the group with individuals. Yet all writers suggest that groups, organizations, and collectivities consist of individuals. (Falck, 1988, p. 3)

THE NATURE OF GROUP EXPERIENCE

Human beings are born into groups, and their lives may be viewed as experiences in group memberships. As Falck has noted:

> Every person is a member. A member is a human being characterized by body, personality, sociality, and the ability to comprehend human experience. Every member is an element in the community of men and women. . . .

He proceeds to characterize a member as a "social being in continuous interaction with others who are both seen and unseen . . . and . . . a psychological being capable of private experience." Falck drew several inferences from the "fact that in speaking of a member one implicitly speaks of others, who are also members."

The term *member* refers to a person who is:

1. A physical being bounded by semipermeable membranes and cavities;
2. A social being in continuous interaction with others who are both seen an unseen . . . and
3. A psychological being capable of private experience.

The fact that in speaking of *member* one implicitly speaks of others, who are also members, leads to the following inferences:

1. A member's actions are socially derived and contributory;
2. The identity of each member is bound up with that of others through social involvement;
3. A member is a person whose difference from others creates tensions that lead to growth, group cohesion, and group conflict; and
4. Human freedom is defined by simultaneous concern for oneself and others . . . (1988, p. 30).

Membership, in this view, is such an essential aspect of humanness that the one is virtually indistinguishable from the other. It is little wonder, then, that groups have been described as microcosms (Ephross & Vassil, 2004), participation in which can lead toward group healing, expanded and enhanced social functioning, learning, the expression of democratic citizenship, the practice of self-determination, mutual aid, mutual support, and progress toward achieving social justice.

What can be mobilized in a group that can give group experiences for change the power to affect the group's members? Northen and Kurland (2001, pp. 25–27) list 10 that they label *dynamic forces* for change: mutual support, cohesiveness, quality of relationships, universality, a sense of hope, altruism, acquisition of knowledge and skills, catharsis, reality testing, and group control. They proceed to make some important observations about these forces:

> Findings from research generally support the importance of these forces in positively influencing the members' group experience. Findings also suggest that some factors are more important than others for different types of groups and even for different members of the same group. . . . Furthermore, these dynamic forces need to be viewed as potential benefits; they are not present automatically in groups but need to be fostered by the practitioner (2001, pp. 26–27)

In this view, though groups are naturally occurring phenomena, the benefits of participation ought not be taken for granted but rather need to be nurtured by the social worker/practitioner.

Other writers may name the influential aspects of group life differently, but they agree both on the power of group experience and generally on the aspects that generate groups' power to affect members. For example, one list highlights nine mutual-aid processes as follows: "sharing data, the dialectical process, entering taboo areas, the 'all-in-the-same-boat' phenomenon, mutual support, mutual demand, individual problem-solving, rehearsal, and the strength-in-numbers phenomenon" (Gitterman & Shulman, 1994, p. 14).

Focusing on "the group as an entity," Garvin developed a classification of the dimensions of group process. . . . [T]hese dimensions are the *(1)* goal oriented activities of the group, and the *(2)* quality of the interactions among the members. This list includes goal determination, goal pursuit, the development of values and norms, role differentiation, communication-interaction, conflict resolution and behavior control, changes in emotions, group culture, group resources, extragroup transactions, group boundaries, and group climate (Garvin, 1987, pp. 113–121).

Henry first notes conflict between those who prefer analytic and organic approaches, respectively, to the question of what goes on in a group. She bases her answers on those identified by many early group work writers. She identifies as important criteria aspects of group life, including group composition and criteria for membership; some level of consensus on group goals; the external structure, which consists of time, space, and size; time, or the time framework within which the group meets; internal structure; cohesion, communication and decision-making; norms, values, and group culture; and group control and influence (1992, pp. 2–16).

GROUP WORK: VALUES AND PERCEPTIONS

Group work is part of social work. As such, it shares many values and perceptions with the entire social work profession.

Northen and Kurland view social work as based on two fundamental values. They are "a conviction that each person has inherent worth and dignity" and "a conviction that people should have responsibility for each other"; the latter, they characterize as "the democratic spirit in action" (2001, p. 16).

On the other hand, it has been pointed out with both truth and wit that contemporary group work stems from a symbolic total of no fewer than three parents (Weiner, 1964). One understands well the permutations and distortions of identity that can arise from interacting with only one or two parents. Imagine those that can arise from interacting with three! The "three parents" referred to are recreation, informal education, and social work. Each has left an inheritance of great value to group work.

From its recreational sources, group work has acquired an understanding of and a respect for the power of participation in activity, only one form of which is talking. Unlike other methods, which assume that talking is the highest form of interaction, group work understands that doing in interaction with others can have wonderful outcomes for individual group members, for groups, and for the society of which the group is part.

Related to this is both a positive valuation and a perception that it is important for people to do, to act, to interact with their environments. Group work has never even seriously considered a view of humans as only passive recipients of external influences. In group work, empowering group members to speak, to express opinions, to interact, to decide, and to act on their external environments are seen as essential purposes, always depending, of course, on the capacities of the group members. While assessment—especially self-assessment—is an important part of groups' lives, social work with groups emphasizes the assessment of strengths in addition to, indeed sometimes instead of, the assessment of weaknesses.

Partly for this reason, clinical diagnoses tend not to be seen as helpful by many group work practitioners. A great deal of practice experience teaches that categorical diagnoses are often inaccurate predictors of how people can and will act in groups. Also, although individual "intake" interviews are recommended by many of the authors in this book, some skepticism about the yield of such interviews may be warranted, primarily because individual interviews do not always predict behavior in a group.

From its early years, group work has valued differences, whether of race, class, sex, ethnicity, citizenship status, religious identity, age, or disability. Much group work took place in agencies and organizational settings identified with minority communities and/or with economically deprived and sometimes societally oppressed communities. Contemporary statements of perspective can be found, for example, in Toseland and Rivas (1998, pp. 131–135) and in Northen and Kurland (2001, pp. 221–237). Among the traditional sources of group work theory and practice, one of the most influential theorists of group dynamics was himself a refugee from totalitarian oppression, and was therefore keenly aware of the potential for bigotry and intergroup violence (Lewin, 1948). A similar perspective can be found in the influential writings of Gisela Konopka (e.g., 1983). An awareness both of women's needs and of various aspects of ethnicity can be found in early writings from the settlement-house field (e.g., Addams, 1909).

As is true of other methods and fields of social work, group workers sometimes work with people with whom they quickly come to feel empathy. Sometimes one feels admiration for group members who struggle with handicaps, who are the victims of injustice, or who face difficult processes of rehabilitation. By contrast, with other populations, it may be difficult or even painful for a worker to attempt to relate helpfully to group members whose past or present behavior is personally abhorrent, or is a reminder of painful experiences in the worker's own life, or violates deeply held personal convictions of the worker. Supervisors, peers, and consultants may all be helpful in dealing with one's feelings about working with such groups.

In the extreme case, it may be impossible for a particular worker at a particular stage of life to work effectively with a particular population. The pain involved may be too great and the blocks to working with a group within the framework of "empathy, genuineness and warmth" (Garvin, 1987, p. 87) or "humanistic values and democratic norms" (Glassman & Kates, 1990, pp. 21–22) too intense. For example, a worker who has recently lost a family member to cancer may not be able, at this time, to work with a group of cancer patients or their relatives. Recognizing such a limitation is a sign of maturity and ethical decision making on the part of the worker and agency, not of incompetence or weakness.

Experience teaches that such situations are rare. Social workers often establish helping, empathic, genuine, and warm relationships with groups whose members have committed deeply antisocial acts. This certainly does not mean that workers approve of these acts. It means that, in groups, members' humanity tends to have more impact on group workers than their past or even present misdeeds and pathologies. The principle of unconditional positive regard for the worth of each person, at the same time that one disapproves of specific behaviors—sometimes stated in a religious context as "loving the sinner even when one hates the sin"— is an important component of group work. So, in a strengths perspective, one builds upon what group members can do and learn to do, rather than upon their limitation and disabilities.

GROUP WORK: PURPOSES AND GOALS

At one level, the purposes of group work are those of the social work profession, given the particular perspectives just sketched, providing the best possible services to clients in order to achieve the three purposes of social work: prevention of dysfunction, provision of resources for enhanced social functioning, and rehabilitation. At a suitably high level of abstraction, it is difficult to argue with these purposes. However, at a higher level of specificity, we have found it useful to take into account the typology of agency purposes and the emphasis on the importance of organizational factors introduced by Garvin (1997).

While emphasizing that no agency can be considered to have only one purpose, this typology views the major categories of purpose as being *socialization* and *resocialization*. Each category contains two subpurposes: *identity development* and *skill attainment* in the case of socialization, and *social control* and *rehabilitation* in the case of resocialization. By emphasizing the importance of agency processes and structure to what happens with groups within that agency, Garvin's discussion, which is based on those of several organizational theorists, provides a useful perspective for the group work practitioner.

Many health care and social agencies seek to sponsor group work programs but are less receptive to the idea that their organizational structure, their emotional climate, how they are perceived by the community, their policies, or even their physical facilities operate in ways that can undercut or oppose the thrusts and objectives of the program. For this reason, conducting a group work program within an organizational context requires a group worker to have a broad vision: one that encompasses the organizational sponsor as well as the members of the groups within the broader context of client systems. In keeping with the general principle that group work always involves work with the group *and* work with the environment, the worker has an ongoing responsibility to address, and sometimes to help the group address, organizational factors such as those mentioned that can interfere with the accomplishment of the group's purposes.

GROUP WORK METHOD: AN OVERVIEW

Alissi (1982) has defined what he referred to as a "reaffirmation of essentials" regarding group work method. It remains a useful platform from which to look at group work methods. He identified relationships, contracts, and programming as essential elements and as elements that distinguish social work with groups from other group methods.

By *relationships,* Alissi meant those that are authentic, that involve an atmosphere in which "genuine feelings can be expressed and shared and by which members can be encouraged to relate in similar ways within as well as beyond the group. . . . The fundamental question to be asked throughout the process is what kinds of relationship are best suited for what kind of ends?" (1982, p. 13).

The worker's relationship with group members and with the group as a whole needs to be simultaneously conscious and spontaneous, a considerable challenge. The principle of conscious use of self—knowing what one is doing and why one is doing it—is basic. The countervailing principle of being oneself, of being spontaneous, of expressing feelings in a warm and accepting way, may seem like a contradiction. In this writer's view, the bridging concept is one of focusing on whose needs are being met primarily. The relationship between worker and group needs to be a disciplined and focused one, and, of course, a nonexploitive one that helps provide an atmosphere of safety, both physical and emotional, within the group.

That exploitation and boundary violations are less often problems in group work than in the one-to-one situation is due to the greater availability of support for group members from each other. This in no way relieves the worker from observing the boundaries set by ethics, by prevailing social standards, and by the sensitivities of the members of a particular group or community.

Alissi's second aspect of method is that of *contracts,* or "working agreements" between worker and group. "Unless members are involved in clarifying and setting their own personal and common group goals, they cannot be expected to be active participants in their own behalf" (1982, p. 13). There is an egalitarian flavor—a sense of worker and members working together to accomplish a common goal that is overt and understood—that distinguishes social work with groups from other therapeutic methods. Naturally, the capacity of group members to understand the common goals often sets significant limitations on this part of group work method.

The third aspect, *programming,* refers to the point made above, about the ability of activities of various kinds, levels of intensity and skills, and activity media to influence both interpersonal and intrapsychic processes within a group. With many of the populations discussed in this book, verbal discussion is not the only medium of communication, and it is often far from the best.

GROUP WORK: SPECIFIC TECHNIQUES

Many of the specific techniques and skills of group work practice are discussed in the chapters of this book as they relate to the population under discussion. As is often the case, terminology can pose a problem. What one author calls *techniques,* another calls *skills, technologies, worker behaviors,* or *interventions.* Despite the popularity of the last term, we think it is limited as a description of what social workers do in groups. Somehow *intervention* connotes entering group process from the outside and therefore portrays the worker as external to the group, at least most of the time. We think that the social worker is best understood as a person who is a member of the group, although a member with a difference: one with a specialized, disciplined, professionally and ethically bounded role. This role is defined in part by the structure and purpose of the sponsoring organization, in part by the personality and style of the worker, and in large part by the needs and developmental stage of group and members.

Many writers have attempted to list techniques. It is often useful to review these lists, both to free one's creativity and to remind oneself of the great range of possibilities open to a worker in a group. Among the useful lists of techniques are those developed by Balgopal and Vassil (1983), Garvin (1987), Northen and Kurland (2001), Glassman and Kates (1990), Brown (1991), Middleman and Goldberg Wood (1991), Bertcher (1994), and Toseland and Rivas (2004). Although Ephross and Vassil's list (2004) was originally intended for use with working groups, its contents are suitable for work with many other kinds of groups as well. Shulman's book on skills of helping (1999) contains a great deal of discussion of techniques.

Brown's list of 11 specific techniques may be particularly useful to beginning workers. Clearly referring primarily to verbal group processes, his typology is organized under three major headings:

Information Sharing
1. Giving information, advice, or suggestion; directing;
2. Seeking information or reactions about (a) individual, group, or significant others, or (b) agency policies and procedures.

Support and Involvement
1. Accepting and reassuring, showing interest;
2. Encouraging the expression of ideas and feelings;
3. Involving the individuals or group in activity or discussion.

Self-Awareness and Task Accomplishment
1. Exploring with the individual or group the meaning of individual or group behavior, as well as life experiences;
2. Reflecting on individual or group behavior;
3. Reframing an issue or problem;
4. Partializing and prioritizing an issue or problem;
5. Clarifying or interpreting individual or group behavior, as well as life experiences;
6. Confronting an individual or the group. (Brown, 1991, p. 113)

Each of these techniques, of course, can be further subdivided and needs to be adapted to work with particular groups at particular stages of development in particular settings.

What may be useful to add to the various lists are some techniques and principles of practice that are so basic that they are often overlooked. The first is the *ability to keep still,* sometimes referred to as the *ability not to interfere with group process and group development.* The problem here is not just that social workers in general and group workers in particular tend to be verbal people, but rather a more serious, more or less conscious misunderstanding of the purposes of helping to form a group. The issue is the locus of the helping dynamic. Contrary to the (more or less conscious) fantasies of beginning group workers, help in groups comes *from the group, not just from the worker.* For the group to develop and to provide members with the support, learning, growth, and healing referred to earlier in the chapter and throughout this book, the group needs "air time," room for members to talk and act, and silences that can represent reflective pause for groups or can stimulate participation by members.

Of course, workers need to be more active at the beginning of groups, with groups whose members have limited capacities, and in particular situations. After a while, though, we offer the following rough estimate: if the social worker is occupying more than 20 percent of the group's talking time—and with some groups even this proportion is high—the situation needs analysis and reflection. This figure, not to be taken too literally, is meant to apply over a period of time. But the technique of *not responding verbally,* which is really an expression of a participative and group nurturing skill, is an important one.

A second technique is that of *summarizing and bridging.* Often akin to the technique of *framing and reframing,* noted by other writers, *summarizing* consists of sharing an assessment of what the group has done and the point it has reached, while *bridging* consists of suggesting the work that lies ahead and assigning it a time frame. Nothing sounds simpler or demands greater concentration from the social worker. Because of the possibility that one may summarize inaccurately, social workers often will "ask" a summary rather than "tell" it, inviting correction and the expression of different views. Some experienced group workers refer to the summarizing-and-bridging process as serving as a road map for the group, helping its members see where it has arrived and where it has to go.

A third important technique is the use of limits. In group life, as for individuals, the absence of limits equals madness. Skill in the use of limits is, in part, the willingness of social workers to accept and feel comfortable with the authority they often have in groups. But skill in the use of limits means much more than comfort with the realities of administrative (and sometimes legal) authority as an internal process within the workers. Its other components include an ability to form clear and easily understood contracts with groups and an ability to help the group focus on why they exist and what they are about. Effective limits are those that have been internalized by group members and those that are defined by the reality of the group's situation, rather than merely those imposed by the social worker or agency, seemingly for arbitrary or irrelevant reasons.

Skilled group workers employ a range of approaches to developing consensual limits. Some people, situations, and matches between workers and groups seem to minimize conflicts about limits; others seem to intensify them. Also, one needs to recognize that there may be situations—as in a group in which attendance is legally mandated, for example—in which simply stating and enforcing a rule is the path to effective limits. One principle to keep in mind is that, for most members, most groups, and most sponsoring organizations, groups are transitory realities. The goal is for members to gain from their group participation knowledge and growth that they can take with them into the other areas of their lives and into future memberships, not merely to become the "best" possible members of the groups in which they participate with professional social work leadership.

Considerations of space limit us to a brief reference to the development of practice theory linked especially to the concept of the stages of group development (Garland et al., 1965, among others). One of the most useful developments is the connection that can be drawn between stage theory and specific worker roles and behaviors in the group. Particularly, one should note that often the worker needs to be considerably more active in the beginning stages of a group than later, when the group has developed some momentum (and some norms and structure) of its own. Schiller (1995) has raised the probability that many groups composed of women go through these steps of group development in a different order than had been described in men or mixed groups.

Let us turn now to some specific considerations about the behavior of the worker. First, the reader should note the use of the singular. In our view, the basis for professional helping in groups is one worker, one group. This is not to imply that there is no place for co-leadership. In an era of concern about resources, for one thing, and given the nature of group work, for another, there needs to be a positive reason for having more than one worker in a group. Several good reasons come quickly to mind. They include:

1. Physical safety. In a group that contains people with a tendency to act out, there may need to be two workers, one of whom can go for help or leave the group with a disruptive member, and the other worker.
2. Situations in which the co-leader is really a trainee. It is often very helpful for a student or an inexperienced worker to co-lead with a senior colleague. At other times, however, students and beginning workers can do very well in a solo worker situation.
3. Groups in which it is important to model differences, whether sexual, racial, ethnic or any other kind. A male-female team may be effective in working with a group of heterosexual couples, for example.

Other situations that justify co-leadership can be described. In the absence of a positive reason, however, solo leadership is much less expensive and causes fewer logistical problems. Of equal importance is the fact that co-leadership can provide a fertile ground for various interpersonal processes that can impede group progress. These can be minimized in a solo worker format. Co-leadership requires planned communication between the workers (Weiss, 1988).

The basic reason for doing group work is the power of the group, *not the worker.* As long as one can keep this point clearly in mind and recognize that the worker in a group is the orchestra's conductor, not its concert master or principal bassist, the use of a solo worker will make greater sense in the absence of a positive reason for having more than one worker.

Various texts are available that supplement the brief overview given in this chapter. Many are listed in the references at the end of this chapter. All agree that no specific technique equals in importance the commitment of a group worker to enabling a group to form, allowing it to operate, and joining with the members in celebrating the individual and group growth which is the raison d'être of group work.

REFERENCES

Addams, J. (1909). *The spirit of youth and the city streets.* New York: Macmillan.

Alissi, A. (1982). The social group work method: Towards a reaffirmation of essentials. *Social Work with Groups.* 5(3), 3–17.

Balgopal, P., & Vassil, T. V. (1983). *Groups in social work.* New York: Macmillan.

Bertcher, H. J. (1994). *Group participation: Techniques for leaders and members* (2nd ed.). Thousand Oaks, CA: Sage.

Brown, L. N. (1991) *Groups for growth and change.* New York: Longman.

Ephross, P. H., & Vassil, T. V. (2004). *Groups that work: Structure and process* (2nd ed.). New York: Columbia University Press.

Falck, H. S. (1988). *Social work: The membership perspective.* New York: Springer.

Fatout, M., & Rose, S. R. (1995). *Task groups in the social services.* Thousand Oaks, CA: Sage.

Galinsky, M., & Schopler, J. (1989). Developmental patterns in open-ended groups. *Social Work with Groups.* 12(2), 99–104.

Garland, J., Jones, H., & Kolodny, R. L. (1965). A model of stages of group development in social work groups. In S. Bernstein (ed.), *Explorations in group work* (pp. 21–30). Boston: Boston University School of Social Work.

Garvin, C. D. (1987). *Contemporary group work* (2nd ed.). Englewood Cliffs, NJ: Prentice Hall.

Garvin, C. D. (1997). *Contemporary group work* (3rd ed.). Boston: Allyn & Bacon.

Garvin, C. D., & Reed, B. G. (1994). Small group theory and social work practice: Promoting diversity and social justice or recreating inequities? In R. R. Greene (ed.), *Human behavior theory: A diversity framework* (pp. 173–201). New York: Aldine de Gruyter.

Gitterman, A., & Shulman, L. (1994). *Mutual aid groups, vulnerable populations, and the life cycle* (2nd ed.). New York: Columbia University Press.

Glassman, U., & Kates, L. (1990). *Group work: A humanistic approach.* Newbury Park, CA: Sage.

Goroff, N. N. (1979). *Concepts for group processes.* Hebron, CT: Practitioners Press.

Henry, S. (1992). *Group skills in social work: A four-dimensional approach.* Pacific Grove, CA: Brooks/Cole.

Konopka, G. (1983). *Social group work: A helping process* (3rd ed.). Englewod Cliffs, N.J.: Prentice-Hall.

Lewin, K. (1948). *Resolving social conflicts.* New York: Harper & Row.

Middleman, R. R. (1982). *The non-verbal method in working with groups: The use of activity in teaching, counseling and therapy* (enlarged ed.). Hebron, CT: Practitioners Press.

Middleman, R. R., & Goldberg Wood, G. (1991). *Skills for direct practice social work.* New York: Columbia University Press.

Northen, H., & Kurland, R. (2001). *Social work with groups* (3rd ed.). New York: Columbia University Press.

Roberts, R. W., & Northen, H. (eds.). (1976). *Theories of social work with groups.* New York: Columbia University Press.

Schiller, L. Y. (1995). Stages of development in women's groups: A relational model, in R. Kurland & R. Solomon (eds.), *Group work practice in a troubled society: Problems and opportunities* (pp. 117–138). Binghamton, NY: Haworth.

Shulman, L. (1999). *The skills of helping individuals, families, groups and communities* (4th ed.). Itasca, IL: Peacock.

Toseland, R., & Rivas, R. F. (2004). *An introduction to group work practice* (4th ed.). Boston: Allyn & Bacon.

Weiner, H. J. (1964). Social change and social group work practice. *Social Work.* 9, 106–112.

Weiss, J. C. (1988). The D-R model of co-leadership of groups. *Small Group Behavior,* 19. pp. 117–125.

PART I

HEALTH ISSUES

Chapter 1

Group Work with Cancer Patients

BARRY M. DASTE AND STEVEN R. ROSE

Cancer is a disease with psychological, physiological, and social consequences for the patients, as well as for their families and friends. The disease can and does strike regardless of sex, socioeconomic background,
race, age, or other demographic factors. The American Cancer Society
estimated that 1,284,900 new cases of cancer would be diagnosed in the
USA for the year 2002 (Jemal et al., 2002, p. 23).

Cancer is a pervasive illness that affects three out of four families
and one out of three individuals in the United States (Taylor et al., 1986).
Although the treatment of cancer has become more successful in recent
years, the emotional impact on individuals and their families is great
(Evans et al., 1992, p. 229). A cancer diagnosis is considered to be one of
the most feared and serious events of an individual's life. It produces significant stress on all individuals involved (Daste, 1990).

Before diagnosis, the individual normally experiences general illness
that progresses to the point where malignancy is suspected. Following
this period of illness, the individual is subjected to numerous physiological tests that determine whether cancer is present. Testing leads to diagnosis. The stages that follow diagnosis include surgery and/or treatment,
through such means as chemotherapy or radiotherapy, evaluation of the
patient's prognosis, and medical follow-up (Gilbar, 1991, p. 293). During
each of the progressive stages of cancer detection, diagnosis, and treatment, cancer patients face a number of questions about their own vulnerability to the disease.

The specific issue patients face include a sense of threat to their
lives, their wholeness of body, sense of self-perception, mental balance,

and social functioning (Gilbar, 1991, p. 293). Patients are often concerned about the implications of the disease for their future quality of life and for relationships with family members and friends. In addition, they normally experience a wide spectrum of emotions, including anger, fear, sadness, guilt, embarrassment, and shame. Young adults may struggle with anxiety about their physical well being, fertility, and raising children (Roberts et al., 1997).

The cancer patient often expresses anger at his or her fate. Anger is also frequently directed at the medical staff, who first inform the patient of the disease or treat the patient over the course of the illness, and at family members who may attempt to protect, coddle, or treat the patient differently than before the diagnosis.

Sadness and depression are common emotions of cancer patients and may arise from many different sources. Resignation about uncompleted tasks or goals may be a cause of sadness for the patient, as well as fear and isolation often resulting from the disease itself. Physical losses associated with specific types of cancer, such as breast, colon, or laryngeal cancer, may promote a feeling of depression. Often the cancer patient is unable to discuss fears and emotions with family members, which may serve to increase the sense of isolation. A number of studies have reported that both self-help and therapy groups designed to treat cancer patients allow them to express fears, in particular the fear of death; such expression has numerous positive effects on the patient's sense of well-being and self-esteem (Ferlic et al., 1978; Spiegel & Yalom, 1978).

If a patient must undergo radical surgical or treatment procedures that leave visible scars or signs of the disease, he or she may be susceptible to feelings of embarrassment or shame. The appliances such as those used with colostomy patients, for example, often have side effects such as odor, which can cause the patient great embarrassment (Gilbar & Groisman, 1992). Other results of the cancer treatment, such as mastectomy or prostate removal, can cause patients to feel less sexually attractive and desirable to their spouses or lovers (Arrington, 2000; Gilbar, 1991).

The changes in bodily function resulting from such procedures also require some adjustment for the patient, as well as for family members and friends. These changes may create major inconvenience in terms of planning for simple day-to-day activities, as well as limiting access to activities in which the person previously participated.

In dealing with the issues and emotions inherent in the diagnosis of cancer, family members and friends of the patient can serve as important sources of support (Palmer et al., 2000). Studies have documented the need for social support both as a means of preventing disease and as a factor in recovery from illness (Taylor et al., 1986).

In some cases, however, family members or friends often become overwhelmed with the patient's crisis and withdraw to protect themselves and deal with their own emotional issues (Daste, 1989). In cases where the supporter and the patient may have had previous relationship difficulties, the supporter may make attempts to rectify the situation for his or her own benefit without considering the needs or wishes of the patient. For example, a spouse who may have been ready to leave a failed marriage may decide to remain in it ostensibly to protect the patient, but in reality to avoid the prospect of facing immense personal guilt. In other situations, family members may attempt to support the patient but may actually contribute to the patient's emotional distress (Daste, 1990). This occurs, for example, when supporters of the patient attempt to treat the patient in the ways they themselves would want to be treated in similar circumstances while ignoring the requests or desires of the patient to be treated as he or she wishes.

There are many issues involving family relationships when cancer develops. Both juvenile and adult cancer patients often do not express fear and sadness with family members because of their desire to protect the family system (Daste, 1990; Price, 1992). Siblings of juvenile cancer patients often experience negative emotions and are not likely to express these emotions to family members (Evans et al., 1992). Kaufman and his colleagues (1992) report that cancer diagnoses in children may exacerbate existing problems in dysfunctional families, and the resulting stress can increase the child's illness.

Support or self-help groups designed to address the specific needs of cancer patients and/or their families allow the patient to receive support and express emotions in a nonjudgmental and safe environment. These groups can provide education about the disease and about methods or techniques the patient can employ to alleviate anxiety, stress, and depression (Forester et al., 1993; Montazeri et al., 2001; Vugia, 1991). Techniques such as visual imagery, self hypnotic therapy, deep muscle relaxation, and systematic desensitization can also help to counteract the side effects of treatment methods like chemotherapy (Forester et al., 1993; Harmon, 1991).

Researchers have concluded that groups that provide intensive group coping skills, such as those discussed above, are far more effective than traditional supportive group therapy (Telch & Telch, 1986). Liebermann (1988) had reported that although client-led self-help groups have not been proved to be an effective means of treatment because research concerning them has not been available, they do appear to have "meaningful roles in helping individuals with psychosocial problems" (p. 168). Other authors maintain that self-help groups are now quite prevalent (Gray & Fitch, 2001).

While much information is available about different types of cancer-focused treatment groups, studies continue to be performed in an attempt to substantiate the effectiveness of one group treatment method over another. Telch and Telch (1986) report that supportive group therapy is the most widely used and most intensively studied form of treatment. Other researchers indicate that while a group may be designed primarily to provide education, psychological intervention is typically needed by group members.

PRACTICE PRINCIPLES

The practice principles that apply to group work with cancer patients are similar to those that apply to group work in general. The variety of issues cancer patients typically face, however, may be quite different from those of other populations and should be kept in mind when composing and facilitating groups. One issue that could have an impact on a treatment group is the treatment status of each group member. Patients who are receiving chemotherapy or radiation therapy are likely to experience such side effects as nausea, pain, or extreme fatigue. These patients may not be able to attend the group regularly during this phase of their treatment or may be disoriented and distracted if they do attend. Contracting with members of these groups requires a lot of flexibility, and contracts should always be tailored to each member. Due to the nature of cancer and the effects it can have on attendance and participation, social workers must be understanding and accepting when members cannot attend or participate. It is also important, however, for the social worker to continually encourage members to attend and participate when they are able to do so. Termination of these groups is often a flexible issue. Again, due to the nature of cancer, people cannot often predict with accuracy when they can continue to attend. Some groups formed specifically for terminally ill cancer patients are open groups and continue to function after the deaths of individual members.

Other factors that are important to group work with cancer patients include stage of the disease, type of cancer, amount of physical distress, age, level and quality of support from family and friends, religious affiliation, probability of psychiatric problems related to cancer, terminal versus non-terminal status, size of the group, and training of the leaders (Daste, 1990).

STAGE OF THE DISEASE

The stage of a patient's disease is important for a number of reasons. First, the issues faced by patients whose cancer is in remission are dramatically different from those of patients who are terminally ill. Patients whose cancer is in remission may be primarily concerned with recurrence of the disease, while patients who are terminally ill are often more concerned about their death, the process of dying, and the implications these events have for their family and friends. Understandably, patients who are dying may feel envious or may even resent those whose prognosis is more hopeful. Simonton and Sherman (2000) have developed a treatment model that addresses various stages of the disease.

DIFFERENCES AMONG AFFECTED GROUPS

Cancer, while having similar implications for all patients, strikes a very heterogeneous group of individuals. Particular types of cancer, such as breast or colon cancer, often have specific implications for group composition. Breast or colon cancer patients often have similar issues and can relate readily to other patients with the same concerns. Breast cancer patients may have issues relating to their sexuality and their perceived loss of femininity that they feel more comfortable discussing with other breast cancer patients. Persons who have had sarcoma of a limb may have lost an arm or a leg due to amputation or may have experienced more limited use of the limb. Issues such as limited mobility will often arise among these individuals.

Issues such as these and many other related concerns need to be kept in mind by the social worker. All such issues are often discussed with patients before they enter a group in order to offset possible problems at a later date.

DEMOGRAPHIC ISSUES

Issues such as age and religious affiliation may have significance for a treatment group. Clearly, pediatric cancer patients require a group setting that is age appropriate and allows them to discuss their own unique concerns. Also, adult patients who are at different stages in life may feel more accepted by those in a similar stage. They may be better able to deal with issues that suit their particular needs. Similarly, religious affiliation can significantly affect the cancer patient's sense of purpose and hope. The religious or spiritual orientation of the patient may influence his or her acceptance of various aspects of the disease. In addition, religion or spirituality of significant others can significantly affect how cancer patients relate to them.

LEVELS OF SUPPORT

Support from family and friends affects the cancer patient's overall sense of support and can be significant in a group setting. Some patients have far more support than others, and this can make those who have less support feel even more depressed and alone in the group. This is often the case in groups where family members and friends are allowed to attend. The social worker should be aware of situations where some patients may not have any supportive family members or friends and other patients seem to have an abundance. One way of warding off this problem is to have separate groups for patients and family members. In fact, some patients may feel more comfortable discussing sexual and other issues among fellow patients without family and friends being in attendance. Well meaning as family and friends may be, there are issues in which their attendance will inhibit discussion. There appears to be a relationship between level of support and benefits from group work. One study showed that peer discussion groups were helpful for women with breast cancer who lacked support elsewhere but were unhelpful for women who had high levels of outside support (Gelgeson et al., 2000).

PSYCHIATRIC COMPLICATIONS

Often as a result of the disease itself, patients develop psychiatric problems (Fawzy et al., 1997). In some cases, psychiatric problems may be present before the diagnosis. These factors should be considered by the social worker who composes and facilitates the group. While there may be psychological issues that will need to be addressed, the appropriateness of including patients with significant psychiatric difficulties should be considered in terms of their ability to interact with other group members and to engage in the group process.

SIZE OF THE GROUP

Group size can have an impact on the effectiveness and level of intimacy within a group. Spiegel and Yalom (1978), in reporting on their group of patients with metastatic carcinoma, noted that the maximum effective size was seven. When the size of the group reached more than eight, the group was divided into two smaller groups (Spiegel & Yalom, 1978). Similarly, in a program designed by Cunningham and his colleagues (1991), educational groups ranged in size from 12 to 15 members, but these groups were later divided into two or more subgroups to facilitate discussion (p. 44). Smaller groups are usually more cohesive and develop closer bonds than larger groups (Daste, 1990). The concept of group size is often related to other issues, such as the presence of supportive family members and friends. As previously mentioned, the appropriateness of having family members present during discussions of subjects that the patients may want to discuss privately should also be considered.

WORKER SELF-AWARENESS

Among the most important issues in group practice with cancer patients is the social worker's own orientation to the disease. Often one of the cancer patient's most pervasive fears is of death and dying. Because of the importance of this issue, it is often necessary for the social worker to address this issue within the group setting. Consequently, the social worker may need to face his or her own feelings regarding death. This is an easy issue to trivialize, and often its full impact does not come until one is faced with it personally. This can be a very lonely time, and the issue becomes an existential one as opposed to an interpersonal one. Even in a group setting, members can feel alone and will require a lot of empathic understanding.

The social worker's interaction with the group should be clearly conceptualized and described in the planning phase of the group. In some groups, the social worker may provide education and/or psychological intervention. The literature is widely divided on what the group facilitator's role should be. In a number of groups studied, the social worker's or facilitator's role is to educate the group members. In other groups, researchers contend that the facilitator should assist the members in expressing their emotions about their disease. Cunningham et al. (1991) note that psychological interventions in cancer groups are becoming increasingly common. However, Vugia (1991) sees the role of leaders in self-help support groups as aiding members while allowing the members to maintain some authority themselves (p. 94).

OPEN VERSUS CLOSED GROUPS

Should groups be open or closed? Opinions vary among professionals in the field. The literature indicates that cancer groups frequently are open, allowing new members to enter at any time (Daste, 1989). Other research concludes that groups should be closed to new members after the first few sessions to enhance cohesion of the group and to "allow progressive work and promote good attendance" (Cunningham et al., 1991, p. 44).

In light of the information presented thus far, the social worker should keep in mind that cancer patients constitute a very heterogeneous group whose needs are vastly different and challenging. It is important to point out that work with cancer patients can be very trying (Daste, 1990). Davidson (1985) notes that the concept of *burnout* is especially applicable to those working in the field of oncology because death and the threat of death create a large emotional burden on these persons.

Persons who work with cancer patients in the group setting should be prepared to discuss such topics as death, dying, disfigurement, pain, and loss of function. Harmon (1991) discusses the experience of one group in which a member died and the leaders of the group consequently attempted to prevent the group from acknowledging or discussing it. Yalom and Greaves (1977) found that in their group, the therapists contributed to superficial group interaction because they felt that such topics might be too threatening for patients when, in reality, they were protecting themselves. According to Fobair (1997), open groups, such as drop-in groups, and closed groups, such as supportive-expressive existentialist groups, span a continuum.

COMMON THEMES

Some of the themes that social workers should keep in mind when working with cancer patients are the following:

1. Fear of death.
2. Fear of disease recurrence.
3. Unique problems related to the long- and short-term effects of treatment.
4. Changes in personal relationships.
5. Economic issues.

There are many other common themes in conducting groups with cancer patients. These include unique problems such as changes in sexual function during treatment, partners' reactions to loss of breasts or scarring, and loss of fertility due to some types of chemotherapy. All of these present some unique difficulties, each of which has interpersonal manifestations that become significant in a group setting.

Fear of Death

The patient's fear of death is considered reasonable given the cancer mortality rates. Although cancer is a more treatable and survivable illness today than in the past, a diagnosis of cancer frequently implies the possibility of death. As noted above, often the patient's family or friends are frightened by the diagnosis and may prevent the patient from discussing the possibility of death. Some authors have reported that patients' anxiety about death was often lessened when they were able to connect on a transcendent or spiritual level (Cunningham et al., 1991, p. 52). Similarly, Spiegel (1992) found that allowing patients to discuss the possibility of death and its attendant anxieties lessened their fear of death and dying (p. 115).

Fear of Disease Recurrence

Most cancer patients experience fear of recurrence. This is especially manifested for varying periods of time following initial diagnosis and treatment. Whenever a new pain occurs, an unexplained lump appears, a cough begins, or one of many other conditions arises, the cancer patient will typically fear the worst. This is perhaps the single most difficult part of coping for those who have had one experience with cancer. It is as if a sword hangs over one's head from the time of first diagnosis until the day one dies, even though the disease may never reappear. The fear of recurrence becomes a focal point, particularly for cancer patients who have survived the initial cancer and are in remission. The fear of recurrence will continue for years.

Long- and Short-Term Effects

Other common themes with cancer patients are the effects of chemotherapy and radiation therapy, both short and long term. Various types of chemotherapy cause hair loss, as does radiation to specific body areas. Nausea and vomiting and the inability to maintain earlier eating patterns become recurrent themes. Many financial issues typically arise as well. In addition to possible loss of income during treatment, the cost of care frequently exceeds insurance benefits. Added to this is the future burden on survivors, who often have extreme difficulty obtaining or transferring insurance plans due to preexisting condition limitations. Cancer patients and survivors also report job discrimination both in hiring and in promotion. Any person who has undergone treatment for cancer is considered legally handicapped and thus has some protection from job discrimination. This does not necessarily prevent it from occurring, however.

Interpersonal Relationships

Cancer patients often find that their interpersonal relationships alter as a result of the disease. Some become distanced from friends and family members. Some face constant questioning from others about the cancer, even when they would rather not talk about it. Some patients find that their choice of partners may become limited, frequently due to fears about the future of the patient. This problem may continue long after the person has survived cancer. Some experience either overprotectiveness or distancing from spouses or lovers. Interpersonal manifestations are multiple and often provide surprises for group members.

Economic Issues

Economic issues become a major concern with many cancer patients. Insurance may become difficult or impossible to obtain following a cancer diagnosis (Nessim & Ellis, 2000). Job discrimination is commonly reported in hiring, as well as in promotions and job assignments. The cost of treatment may create severe hardships. Lost wages often create further difficulty. These are some of the more common themes among group members. Each of them provides bases for discussion in the group.

RECOMMENDED WAYS OF WORKING

As there are so many variables in working with cancer patients, the social worker must be very flexible. This flexibility extends from the initial conceptualization of the group all the way to termination. Perhaps the most important thing to keep in mind is that social workers will be more effective if they structure their groups to best meet the needs of the particular cancer patients and/or cancer survivors they wish to serve. As previously mentioned, people with cancer are very heterogeneous, yet they usually have specific pressing concerns. Rather than lumping everyone with a cancer diagnosis into a large group, it seems far more beneficial to tailor each group to the specific needs of the prospective members. For example, a group for 8- to 12-year-old children who have all had chemotherapy or radiation therapy have very different concerns than a group of women dying of breast cancer. By the same token, a group of people who have been cancer free for 5 years would have a whole different set of concerns.

The agency setting and the population being served will, of course, dictate to a large extent who will be in the group. A large hospital in a major metropolitan area, for example, has far more latitude in terms of numbers and types of groups than a small rural clinic. The agency context may also define other parameters of the group, including size, space considerations, availability of coleaders, advocacy of services, and the availability of ancillary services such as meals on wheels or hospices.

The issue of open versus closed groups again depends on the population being served. Both have advantages and disadvantages. Open groups, for example, allow more utilization, while closed groups provide a more intimate atmosphere and allow for more discussion of sensitive topics.

Length of the group is also population dependent. Many social workers experienced difficulty when they specified a certain number of sessions initially, only to discover later that the members, due to treatment difficulties or other problems, found it difficult to use the preimposed format. Group length often has to be experimented with and tailored to each agency and its population. Many agencies simply offer one large long-term group for all patients and significant others. This approach avoids many selection, time, and member availability issues since the group meets on a regular basis for all who care to attend. However, it also limits the potential that smaller, more carefully planned groups may offer.

A case illustrating one of the problems of a large group open to all is as follows:

> During the weekly meeting of a large support group offered for cancer patients, friends, and families by a metropolitan radiation treatment center, several newly diagnosed persons attended for the first time. It so happened that "John," a regular member, was suffering from a brain tumor and tended to dominate conversations without allowing others to speak. For this reason, the new members, who were uncomfortable

about being there and very much in need of support, were denied an opportunity to participate. Situations such as this are far easier for the social worker to control in a smaller, more carefully selected group.

A coworker pattern is usually considered to be easier on social workers and other professionals, and it has many advantages over an individual worker format, assuming that the coworkers work well together. It allows more individual attention to be given to distraught members, for example, since one worker can attend to the individual while the other attends to the group process. It also doubles the probability that the group can meet if one worker is absent. Coworkers potentially can help each other in providing both technical expertise and emotional support.

A case illustrating how a coworker format might be beneficial is as follows:

> During one of the sessions of a support group for women survivors of breast cancer, "Jackie," who had been doing fine following breast cancer 2 years previously, had just learned that her cancer had recurred. She bravely waited her turn to talk, but finally felt overwhelmed by her fear, jumped up, and ran from the room. One of the coworkers took off after her and spent a lot of time calming her down, as she felt unable to return to the group. The other coworker was able to continue without her.

One key advantage of a coworker pattern with these groups is that it allows the workers to deal with personal crises, which are often severe and require additional attention. If only one worker is present, the group as a whole must wait or must deal with the crises as a whole. In another type of therapy group this might be appropriate, but due to the nature of cancer and the potential for sudden life-or-death issues arising, the fear and panic may be so great that individual intervention is warranted.

EVALUATION MEASURES

Researchers have used many different methods to measure the effectiveness of groups in producing tangible benefits to patients. Currently instruments exist that measure quality of life, body image, self-esteem, support, and perceived personal control over illness (Helgeson et al., 2000). Scales that measure quality of adjustment, stress levels, affect, optimism with regard to disease treatment, and overall sensations of pain, discomfort, and anxiety, as well as other such scales would all be useful in determining the effectiveness of a cancer group intervention (Goodwin et al., 2001).

In a group organized by Spiegel, Bloom, and Yalom (1981), women with metastatic breast cancer were found to have less tension, depression, fatigue, confusion, maladjusted responses, and fewer phobias than their control group counterparts.

In their study of self-perception after surgery with women who had had mastectomy, Clarke, Kramer, Lipiec, and Klein (1982) divided 40 patients into treatment and control groups. Ten weekly group psychotherapy sessions were offered. The authors used Q-sort tests and the Structured and Scaled Interview to Assess Maladjustment. While both groups showed positive change, the treatment group showed significantly greater improvement.

Other studies, such as the one conducted by Kriss and Kraemer (1986), have examined patients periodically over several time periods—for example, three times over 12 months—to determine possible changes following group treatment. Longitudinal studies covering longer time periods are also appropriate in determining changes following group treatment.

One of the difficulties in assessing evaluative research in this area is the great variety of methodology. There are many ways to conduct research in this area, and it should be noted that assessing the outcome accurately is difficult due to the number of variables involved. A lot depends on what the social worker wants to know about the group members. Both quantitative and qualitative measures may be important in assessing changes. Questionnaires and scales measuring such factors as depression, fear, and coping can be administered on a pre- and posttreatment basis. Recording group attendance, degree of participation, and demographic representation by various ethnic, racial, and socioeconomic groups will yield data that may prove useful to the social worker. Research questions should be addressed as early as possible to allow for more potential data.

CLOSING STATEMENT

Even though we are making progress in the diagnosis and treatment of cancer, this diagnosis places a great deal of emotional and physical stress on patients, as well as on their families and friends. This further mandates the need for groups designed to meet the specific needs of this population.

ACKNOWLEDGMENT

We would like to thank Jennifer A. Boice for her assistance in the preparation of this manuscript.

RESOURCES

American Brain Tumor Association
2720 River Road
Des Plaines, IL 60018
(847) 827-9910
Fax: (847) 827-9918
Patient Line: (800) 886-2282
info@abta.org
www.abta.org

American Cancer Society
1599 Clifton Rd NE
Atlanta, GA 30329
Cancer Answer Line: (800) 227-2345
www.cancer.org

American Institute for Cancer Research
1759 R Street NW
Washinton, DC 20009
(800) 843-8114
aicrweb@aicr.org
www.aicr.org

Children's Leukemia Foundation of
    Michigan
29777 Telegraph Road, Suite 1651
Southfield, MI 48034
(248) 353-8222
(800) 825-2536
Fax: (248) 353-0157
leukemiamichigan@voyager.net
www.leukemiamichigan.org

Colorectal Cancer Network
P.O. Box 182
Kensington, MD 20895-0182
(301) 879-1500
Fax: (301) 942-7145
www.colorectal-cancer.net

Federation for Children with Special Needs
1135 Tremont Street, Suite 420
Boston, MA 02120
(617) 236-7210
Fax: (617) 572-2094
fcsninfo@fcsn.org
www.fcsn.org

Foundation for Children's Oncology Group
440 E. Huntington Drive, P.O. Box 60012
Arcadia, CA 91066-6012
(800) 458-6223
Fax: (626) 447-6359
info@ConquerKidsCancer.org
www.nccf.org

Kidney Cancer Association
1234 Sherman Avenue, Suite 203
Evanston, IL 60202-1375
(847) 332-1051
(800) 850-9132
Fax: (847) 332-2978
office@kidneycancerassociation.org
www.kidneycancerassociation.org

National Alliance of Breast Cancer
    Organizations
9 East 37th Street, 10th Floor
New York, NY 10016
(888) 80-NABCO
www.nabco.org

The National Breast Cancer Coalition
1707 L Street, NW, Suite 1060
Washington, DC 20036
(800) 622-2838
Fax: (202) 265-6854
www.natlbcc.org

National Children's Cancer Society
1015 Locust, Suite 600
St. Louis, MO 63101
(800) 532-6459
www.children-cancer.com

National Foundation for Cancer Research
4600 East West Highway, Suite 525
Bethesda, MD 20814
(800) 321-CURE
www.researchforacure.com

National Information Center for
    Handicapped Children and Youth
P.O. Box 1492
Washington, DC 20013-1492
(800) 695-0285 (Voice/TTY)
Fax: (202) 884-8441
nichcy@aed.org
www.nichcy.org

National Ovarian Cancer Coalition, Inc.
500 NE Spanish River Boulevard, Suite 14
Boca Raton, FL 33431
(561) 393-0005
Fax: (561) 393-7275
(888) OVARIAN
NOCC@ovarian.org
www.ovarian.org

Support for People with Oral and Head
   and Neck Cancer
P.O. Box 53
Locust Valley, NY 11560-0053
(800) 377-0928
Fax: (516) 671-8794
www.spohnc.org

REFERENCES

Arrington, M. I. (2000). Sexuality, society, and senior citizens: An analysis of sex talk among prostate cancer support group members. *Sexuality & Culture.* 4(4), 45–74.

Clarke, D. L., Kramer, E., Lipiec, K., & Klein, S. (1982). Group psychotherapy with mastectomy patients. *Psychotherapy: Theory, Research, and Practice.* 19(3), 331–334.

Cunningham, A. J., Edmonds, C., Hampson, A., Hanson, H., Hovanec, M., Jenkins, G., & Tocco, E. (1991). A group psychoeducational program to help cancer patients cope with and combat their disease. *Journal of Mind-Body Health.* 7(3), 41–56.

Daste, B. (1989). Designing cancer groups for maximum effectiveness. *Groupwork.* 2(1), 58–69.

Daste, B. (1990). Important considerations in group work with cancer patients. *Social Work with Groups.* 13(2), 69–81.

Davidson, K. W. (1985). Social work with cancer patients: Stresses and coping patterns. *Social Work in Health Care.* 10(4), 73–82.

Evans, C. A., Stevens, M., Cushway, D., & Houghton, J. (1992). Sibling response to childhood cancer: A new approach. *Child Care, Health and Development.* 18, 229–244.

Fawzy, F., Fawzy, N. W., Hyun, C. S., & Wheeler, J. G. (1997). Brief, coping-oriented therapy for patients with malignant melanoma. In J. L. Spira (ed.), *Group therapy for medically ill patients* (pp. 133–164). New York, NY: Guilford.

Ferlic, M., Goldman, A., & Kennedy, B. (1979). Group counseling with adult patients with advanced cancer. *Cancer.* 43, 760–766.

Fobair, P. (1997). Cancer support groups and group therapies: Part I. Historical and theoretical background and research on effectiveness. *Journal of Psychosocial Oncology.* 15(1), 63–81.

Forester, B. (1993). Group psychotherapy during radiotherapy: Effects on emotional and physical distress. *American Journal of Psychiatry.* 150(1), 1700–1706.

Gelgeson, V. S., Cohen, S., Schulz, R., & Yasko, J. (2000). Group support interventions for women with breast cancer: Who benefits from what? *Health Psychology.* 19(2), 107–114.

Gilbar, O. (1991). Model for crisis intervention through group therapy for women with breast cancer. *Clinical Social Work Journal.* 19(3), 293–304.

Gilbar, O., & Groisman, L. (1991). A training model of self-help groups for patients with cancer of the colon. *Journal of Oncology.* 9(4), 57–69.

Goodwin, P. J., Leszcz, M., Ennis, M., Koopmans, J., Vincent, L., Guther, H., Drysdale, E., Hundleby, M., Chochinov, H. M., Navarro, M., Speca, M., & Hunter, J.

(2001). The effect of group psychosocial support on survival in metastatic breast cancer. *The New England Journal of Medicine.* 345(24), 1719–1726.

Gray, R. E., & Fitch, M. (2001). Cancer self-help groups are here to stay: Issues and challenges for health professionals. *Journal of Palliative Care.* 17(1), 53–58.

Harmon, M. (1991). The use of group psychotherapy with cancer patients: A review of recent literature. *Journal for Specialists in Group Work.* 16(1), 56–61.

Helgeson, V. S., Cohen, S., Schulz, R., & Yasko, J. (2000). Group support interventions for women with breast cancer: Who benefits from what? *Health Psychology.* 19(2), 107–114.

Jemal, A., Thomas, A., Murray, T., & Thun, M. (2002). Cancer statistics: 2002. *Ca— A Cancer Journal for Clinicians.* 52(1), 23–49.

Kaufman, K. L., Harbeck, C., Olson, R., & Nitschke, R. (1992). The availability of psychosocial interventions to children with cancer and their families. *Children's Health Care.* 21(1), 21–25.

Kriss, R. T., & Kraemer, H. C. (1986). Efficacy of group therapy for problems with postmastectomy self-perception, body image, and sexuality. *Journal of Sex Research.* 22(4), 438–451.

Liebermann, M. A. (1988). The role of self-help groups in helping patients and families cope with cancer. *Ca–A Cancer Journal for Clinicians.* 38(3), 162–168.

Montazeri, A., Jarvande, S., Haghighat, S., Vadhami, M., Sajadian, A., Elrahimi, M., & Haji-Mahmoodi, M. (2001). Anxiety and depression in breast cancer patients before and after participation in a cancer support group. *Patient Education and Counseling.* 45(3), 195–198.

Nessim, S., & Ellis, J. (2000). *Can survive: Reclaiming your life after cancer.* Boston, MA: Houghton Mifflin.

Palmer, L., Erickson, S., Shaffer, T., Coopman, C., Amylon, M., & Steiner, H. (2000). Themes arising in group therapy for adolescents with cancer and their parents. *International Journal of Rehabilitation and Health.* 5(1), 43–54.

Price, K. (1992). Quality of life for terminally ill children. *Social Work.* 34(1), 53–54.

Roberts, C. S., Piper, L., Denny, J., & Cuttleback, G. (1997). A support group intervention to facilitate young adults' adjustment to cancer. *Health and Social Work.* 22(2), 133–141.

Simonton, S., & Sherman, A. (2000). An integrated model of group treatment for cancer patients. *International Journal of Group Psychotherapy.* 50(4), 487–506.

Smith, K., & Lesko, L. M. (1988). Psychosocial problems in cancer survivors. *Oncology.* 2(1), 33–44.

Spiegel, D. (1992). Effects of psychosocial support on patients with metastatic breast cancer. *Journal of Psychosocial Oncology.* 10(2), 113–120.

Spiegel, D., Bloom, J. R., & Yalom, I. D. (1981). Group support for patients with metastatic cancer: A randomized outcome study. *Archives of General Psychiatry.* 38(5), 527–533.

Spiegel, D., & Yalom, I. D. (1978). A support group for dying patients. *International Journal of Group Psychotherapy.* 28(2), 233–245.

Taylor, S., Falke, R., Shoptaw, S., & Lichtman, R. (1986). Social support, support groups, and the cancer patient. *Journal of Consulting and Clinical Psychology.* 54(5), 608–615.

Telch, E. G., & Telch, M. J. (1986). Group coping skills instruction and supportive group therapy for cancer patients: A comparison of strategies. *Journal of Consulting and Clinical Psychology.* 54(6), 802–808.

Vugia, H. D. (1991). Support groups in oncology: Building hope through the human bond. *Journal of Psychosocial Oncology.* 9(3), 89–107.

Yalom, I. D., & Greaves, C. (1977). Group therapy with the terminally ill. *American Journal of Psychiatry.* 134(4), 396–400.

Chapter 2

Group Work with Seriously Mentally Ill People

CHARLES GARVIN

This chapter describes ways of providing group services to people who suffer from severe mental illness. The term sometimes used is *chronic mental illness*, although many practitioners do not use the word *chronic* because of the negative picture about recovery that it conveys. The definition of a person with this disability is "an individual who suffers from a major psychiatric disorder such as psychosis, who is so disabled as to have partial or total impairment of social functioning (such as vocational and homemaking activities), and who has had a long or a number of short stays in a mental hospital" (Garvin & Tropman, 1998, p. 277). The psychiatric diagnoses usually assigned to people who are classified as seriously mentally ill are schizophrenia, schizoaffective disorder, bipolar disorder, major depression, severe borderline personality disorder, and severe organic disorder. There are, however, many controversies regarding how to define this population related to the length of time the person is disabled and the degree of disability (Rubin, 1986, p. 10).

Many Americans suffer from severe mental illness; a recent estimate is 1.7 to 2.4 million (Garvin & Tropman, 1998, p. 277). Until the mid-1950s, many people with these diagnoses were confined in mental hospitals. At that time, however, a movement referred to as *deinstitutionalization* became a major determinant of mental health policy. This movement was propelled by the discovery of psychotropic drugs allowing for control of many of the behaviors of mentally ill people that led to their confinement. These include such manifestations of psychoses as hallucinations, delusions, and bizarre behaviors, as well as the mood swings or severe depression found in other types of clients.

Other forces that promoted the declining use of institutional care were humane concerns for the civil liberties of patients and fiscal crises related to the greater costs of institutional compared to community care. Deinstitutionalization was facilitated by the increasing number of community mental health centers designated to care for mentally disabled individuals in the community.

Recent statistics indicate that about 150,000 of the seriously mentally ill are in institutions, about 750,000 are in nursing homes (including about 400,000 who suffer from forms of senility), and between 800,000 and 1.5 million reside in the community and are likely to receive some form of care from community mental health centers (Garvin & Tropman, 1998, p. 277). Hospital stays are likely to be short, due not only to the use of medications and the provision of community-based services but also to the action of insurance providers who limit the amount of hospital care for which they will pay. Social workers are very likely to be the providers of service, and this service is often in the form of groups. Increased resources have been allocated for research and program development in this field, but much more support is required to realize the aims of the deinstitutionalization movement.

The seriously mentally ill have several common characteristics (Gerhart, 1990). These include the following:

- Many suffer from multiple problems. One writer estimated that 50% of mental health clients are or have been substance abusers (Bentley, 2002); another major epidemiological study estimated that 52% of persons with alcohol abuse/dependence had had at least one other psychiatric diagnosis (Robins et al., 1991).
- A severe mental illness limits the ability to cope with stress, and such persons are likely to function poorly under stressful circumstances.
- Many may have deficits in skills needed in daily living, such as preparing food, making purchases, and engaging in social activities.
- Many have difficulty keeping a job and are supported by governmental income maintenance programs.
- Many are a burden on their families because of their unpredictable ways of scheduling their lives, their emotional demands, and the problems they cause when engaging in annoying or inappropriate behavior.
- Many become homeless and live either on the street, in temporary shelters, or in facilities such as foster homes, group homes, or other supervised dwellings. It is estimated that up to one in three individuals who experiences homelessness has a mental illness (Federal Interagency Task Force on Homelessness and Mental Illness, 1992). (Report of the Surgeon General, 1999)
- A growing number are young adults who did not grow up in mental hospitals, as did earlier generations of mentally ill people, and are hospitalized only when they exhibit severe symptoms. Many live

with their families, have never been married, and have at least a high school education. Like other members of their generation, they have been exposed to street drugs and easy access to alcohol. They may engage in aggressive and rebellious behavior that is especially challenging to social workers and other professionals.

Recent studies have sought to identify differences among men and women and among people of different ethnic backgrounds with respect to serious mental illness. According to Gerhart:

> It has been suggested that men tend to develop classic schizophrenic conditions at a slightly higher rate than women, while the latter are more prone to develop schizophreniform conditions. Stressors that cause males to relapse seem to have some connection with their role performance as men, such as criticism of their physical strength or lack of a job, being turned down for a date, and the like. On the other hand, women seem more sensitive to events in their interpersonal relationships. . . . There is evidence that women are significantly more prone to depressive disorders than men. . . . Subsequent investigations concluded that it was not women's roles that caused their depression, but rather the uneven distribution of power between husbands and wives. (1990, p. 30–31)

There is no indication that the rates of severe mental illness differ among African-Americans, Latinos/Latinas, and whites (Gerhart, 1990). People from different cultures, however, may act differently when they suffer from a mental illness. According to Gerhart (1990), for example, "Blacks and Hispanics who suffer from major mood disorders tend to exhibit more hallucinations, delusions or hostility than Whites, whereas the latter show a higher degree of mania, depression, or guilt" (p. 32). She concludes:

> all the research dealing with ethnic and racial differences in the appearance and treatment of mental illness is still in its infancy. Although there is much that we still don't know about this area, the ongoing research reminds us once again of the importance of being sensitive to and knowledgeable about our clients' racial, ethnic and cultural backgrounds. (p. 32)

Much is unknown about the causes of serious mental illness. Nevertheless, the current consensus is that it is a condition produced by the interaction of biological and social circumstances with the evolving personality of the individual. Thus, it is often referred to as a *biopsychosocial* phenomenon. The basis of the biological input is concluded from the genetic, biochemical changes in the brain, as well as from heredity and twin studies. The social basis is determined from studies of the family, peer group, and other socialization circumstances of the individual. The developmental circumstances are elucidated by examining the life history of the individual in relation to coping patterns (Gerhart, 1990, pp. 17–20).

PRACTICE PRINCIPLES

A number of practice principles are typically applied when working with the severely mentally ill in light of the characteristics of this client group. While individual (Bentley, 2002), family (Sands, 2001: 312–320), and group approaches are all utilized, the last are especially prominent. One reason is the deficits in social skills found among these clients; groups provide an excellent way to learn to relate to others by observing and practicing social behaviors. Groups can also be used to simulate a variety of social circumstances such as those found in job, recreational, and family settings. Groups also offer the client an opportunity to learn how others in similar circumstances have coped with a wide range of real-life situations. In addition, groups allow clients to participate at their current level of readiness: some may be highly active socially, while others are passive participants. This makes a group less stressful for some clients than one-on-one encounters in which they feel a strong expectation to participate actively. On the other hand, some clients may be so inappropriate in their behavior, so delusional, or so stressed by the presence of others that they would be highly disruptive if invited to a group session.

A major practice principle for group work with seriously mentally ill clients is to have a good deal of program structure, as an unstructured group may be experienced at best as a waste of time and at worst as highly stressful. Despite this, we have observed many groups led by social workers for these clients in which the only structure is the opening query "What would you like to talk about today?" Some members may prefer this experience to the loneliness and boredom of having no social interaction at all, but this unstructured approach is an invitation to not participate at all, to engage in fruitless complaints about the "system," or to talk in an unfocused manner. A more structured approach involves such things as presenting information, introducing structured exercises, identifying problems to be solved, and posing useful questions.

Another practice principle is to utilize a psychosocial rehabilitation approach more than a psychotherapeutic one. According to Sands (2001), psychosocial rehabilitation encourages people who suffer from severe mental illness to develop to their fullest capacities through learning new skills and through acquiring environmental supports. She states that for the social worker "this means working with the client and community resources to promote the client's physical, psychiatric, and social functioning to the extent possible" (p. 242). She goes on to say that

> Programs of intervention target the individual, family, group, and the social environment. Individual, group, family, or milieu therapy can be utilized to teach individuals skills in activities in daily living (self-care, transportation, laundry), interpersonal behaviors, employment, and problem solving through skills training based on social learning theory (p. 242).

A traditional psychotherapeutic approach, defined as utilizing psychological interpretations and "depth"-oriented questions to enable the client to examine unconscious mechanisms, is not recommended for use with most seriously mentally ill people, either individually or in groups. As Rapp (1985) states: "Psychotherapy and psychosocial services without drugs may be harmful to the chronically mentally ill, not benign. The most prevalent hypothesis is that they overstimulate the client and lead to tension, anxiety, and exacerbation of symptoms" (p. 36). It is possible that some of these clients might benefit from this type of therapy, individually or in groups, after they have recovered sufficiently from their illness and have developed stronger coping abilities, but these will not be the majority. Some clients, however, who are defined as having borderline personality disorder might benefit from psychotherapy because of their greater ability to reflect on their circumstances.

Earlier social workers who thought of severe mental illness as a psychological manifestation produced by traumatic childhood experiences may have favored forms of psychotherapy for these clients. This, however, is not the view of most social workers today who understand the biological factors in severe mental illness. A significant consequence of this increased biological understanding is a movement away from earlier approaches that blamed mothers for acting in ways that promoted such illness or that blamed the family for engaging in communication patterns that "drove some family members crazy."

Another practice principle is to find ways to make each group session a rewarding one. This is because these clients are likely to find sessions anxiety provoking; they also have to make a considerable effort to attend, given the lethargy produced by their illness. They have to look forward with pleasure to attending, especially when they are living in the community. Even hospitalized clients may resist attending group sessions and, when pressured to do so by hospital personnel, may enter meetings with a feeling of anger.

A major way of rewarding members for attending sessions is to use program activities during at least part of each session. Such activities might include the following:

- A game, especially one designed to teach a useful skill. Some workers have invented board games, for example, that help members to formulate individual goals or identify obstacles to obtaining goals.
- A dramatic activity, such as a role play, in which members practice a social skill.
- A musical or craft activity that helps members work together, experience a sense of accomplishment, or express themselves creatively.

Another way of rewarding members for coming to meetings is to make sure that they gain a sense of having accomplished something useful at each meeting. This requires the social workers to think in terms of concrete, short-term goals for each session. Examples of such goals are learning a specific social skill, solving an immediate problem, or creating a tangible product such as through a craft activity.

Another type of practice principle is to respond to a psychotic symptom in ways that help the member to cope with it while protecting other members from some of the anxiety produced by the symptom. One way to help individuals cope with psychotic symptoms is by educating them about such symptoms and labeling symptoms as such. Thus, seriously mentally ill members can be taught that hallucinations, for example, can be produced by their illness, and that they can use this understanding when experiencing such hallucinations to tell themselves that they are experiencing something unreal. They also can be taught that some people can be told about symptoms (e.g., the social worker), while other people should not be told because they may be upset. The worker can also empathize with the fact that hearing voices or seeing strange images can be frightening. At the same time, the worker can reassure other members that he or she understands and is able to deal with psychotic symptoms, and will help them to understand and respond helpfully when a member is experiencing such symptoms.

Groups for the seriously mentally ill are often time limited and have specific purposes and goals. The length of time varies from one or two sessions while a client is in the hospital to several months for those in the community. However, because recovery from mental illness may be slow and because there may be periods of illness for many years, some groups are self-help and support groups in which membership may continue indefinitely, such as Schizophrenics Anonymous and some Alcoholics Anonymous groups attuned to the needs of mentally ill people. Clubhouse-type programs for mentally ill people may sponsor ongoing social activity groups, lunch clubs, and special interest groups.

COMMON THEMES

The above discussion of services to people with serious mental illnesses should suggest to social workers that a number of themes frequently arise in such groups. The following are those that we have encountered.

Stigma

These clients are often avoided, persecuted, and denied their rights by others who become aware of their illness. Actions include being fired from jobs, denied housing, refused entry to educational programs, and other serious consequences of having the label "mentally ill." Members of groups will look for help in deciding how and when to explain their illness, how to pursue their rights in an appropriately assertive manner, and how to find advocates to help them obtain things to which they are entitled.

Coping with Symptoms

The terms *positive symptoms* and *negative symptoms* are often used. Positive symptoms are direct consequences of the illness, such as hallucinations, mania, depression, and confused thought processes. Negative symptoms are behavior deficits due to lack of adequate socialization experiences, such as lack of skill in handling social interactions. Group members will ask for help in coping with positive symptoms and in acquiring the skills to eliminate negative ones.

Housing

As indicated earlier, a lack of adequate low-cost housing severely affects this population. Housing is especially a problem to these clients because they may need support to maintain it once they find it, such as learning to care for an apartment, get along with a landlord, or locate roommates.

Employment

Many of these clients lack employment or employment for which they are adequately compensated. This may be because they have educational deficits, because they cannot tolerate the stresses of jobs for which they were trained, or because of the stigma factor. They may not be aware of vocational rehabilitation services or these may be lacking. They may also require employment in a setting that offers them some form of support or even a so-called sheltered workshop program. Thus, members may ask help from each other in identifying and utilizing employment resources.

Education

Many of these clients have had their education interrupted by episodes of illness. Despite this, they are as likely to be as capable intellectually of acquiring an education as anyone else. The group is a medium in which they can explore educational opportunities, discover how to cope with school, and learn how to utilize resources to maintain themselves in an educational program.

Medication Effects

Clients are likely to bring up issues related to the medications they are taking to control their illness. They may not be compliant with their regimen because of a fear of dependence on medication. They may also experience unpleasant side effects of the medication. The medication itself may not be helpful, and the client may be unsure of how to assess this situation and what to do about it. At times, the social workers and other group members may provide useful information. At other times, the social worker will invite medical experts to attend one or more group sessions.

Family Relations

Two family issues are often brought up in these groups. One has to do with parents and siblings with whom the members have conflicts. Some of these conflicts occur because these family members are severely stressed by the client's symptoms. The other issue has to do with the nuclear families that these clients have created and seek to create. They may, for example, have difficulty acting as a spouse and parent. For these reasons, many programs form groups for family members of persons with mental illness and/or refer them to a major self-help organization such as the Alliance for the Mentally Ill (AMI).[1]

Leisure Time

Many of these clients are unemployed and are not attending an educational program; therefore, time hangs heavily on them. Their solution is often to spend a lot of time watching television or "hanging out" in a public place such as the library or park. A major service that can be provided by the group is to help such clients identify interests that can be satisfied, such as engaging in musical activities, attending sports events, or taking courses that further such interests at places such as the local "Y" or adult education programs. The group can also provide a context for engaging in recreational activities that can then be extended outside of the group.

Problems with the Treatment System

These clients are likely to complain about the way the system reacts to them. Sometimes this is because of the real inadequacies in the system and sometimes it is because of the challenges these clients provide. An additional factor is that these clients may lack the skill to make their needs known. These complaints may concern difficulty in arranging for appointments with professionals, denial of services, frequent changes in professionals, and various forms of prejudice against them. These issues contribute to low self-confidence and self-esteem. The group can help the members come to terms with situations that cannot be changed while seeking changes that are appropriate and possible. On some occasions, group members can join together to engage in social action to change the system.

RECOMMENDED WAYS OF WORKING

Several different approaches to group work with these clients have emerged in response to the needs of different agency contexts and client themes. We will briefly discuss each of these approaches in terms of these conditions.

---

[1] We provide the address of AMI at the end of this chapter.

Group Work: Mutual Aid

Social workers have utilized traditional group work methods with the seriously mentally ill and have reported successful outcomes. Poynter-Berg (1994) reports one such group whose members lived in an institution and were identified as schizophrenic. A major theme of this group was coping with issues of intimacy and loss. The members approached the first session hostile to or suspicious of the group experience. The social worker was not as direct as she thought she should have been in establishing a contract with the members in which the purposes of the group and the anticipated activities were clearly enunciated. Nevertheless, the social worker sought to relate to members' feelings as they acted in hostile or disruptive ways. She also sought to introduce activities that were familiar to the women in the group, particularly craft projects. This led to a greater degree of security based on trust of the social worker and each other. A consequence of this was that as a holiday approached, the members talked with each other about painful feelings the holiday evoked, as indicated in the following record excerpt:

> The group members slowly came into the meeting room. Beverly sat with her back to the rest of the group, muttering an occasional "fuckin' mishugana." . . . The women made their instant coffee and drank it, all silently. They were much quieter and still today than usual; they appeared depressed and showed it by their slouched postures and lowered heads. I felt it might have something to do with feelings about Thanksgiving. I said everyone looked quite sad and wondered if they might want to talk about it. Rhoda furrowed her brows and moved her lips. I asked her if she wanted to say something. She shook her head. Another pause. All kept their heads lowered and Arlene, who usually talks to herself, was silent. I said they may all be having thoughts and feelings that the rest of the group might share with them. Silence. I finally said that sometimes it's hard to talk about things that are painful, like being in the hospital on holidays and maybe feeling lonely. Most of the members reacted to this by moving around in their chairs a little. I said I wondered if they did feel sad about tomorrow being a holiday. Rhoda nodded very slightly to herself, but kept her head lowered and didn't speak. Another lengthy pause, with all the ladies looking up at me briefly but not speaking.
>
> When it was time for the group to end, I commented that sometimes it's very hard to talk, like today—and especially when they might be feeling sad. I said I thought next week would be easier. They all looked up at me, and Rhoda smiled, saying, "have a nice Thanksgiving." (Poynter-Berg, 1994, p. 324)

Task-Centered Group Work

Task-centered group work, like traditional group work, models the process of helping the group to become a mutual aid system in which the members are committed to helping one another. The major difference is that in task-centered work, each member is assisted by other members in defining a personal goal, choosing activities (tasks) to reach the goal, and carrying out these tasks (Tolson et al., 2002). While members are helped to express and cope with feelings, this is done in the context of defining and accomplishing tasks. This is accomplished in a limited time, typically about 12 sessions.

Garvin (1992) reported excellent outcomes in utilizing this model in a community mental health setting serving the seriously mentally ill. He tested this approach with four groups composed of members who wished to enhance their use of leisure time. One group was composed of low-functioning clients, another of somewhat higher-functioning schizophrenic clients, a third of women who were trapped in highly dysfunctional family situations, and a fourth of clients who were also chemically dependent.[2]

The plan for the 12 sessions was as follows:

Meeting 1	Get-acquainted activities
	Orientation to task-centered work
	Clarification of group purpose
Meetings 2 and 3	Determining members' goals
	Discussion of the idea of tasks
Meetings 4 and 5	Selection of member tasks
Meetings 6–11	Working on tasks
	Learning to overcome barriers to accomplishing tasks
Last meeting	Termination and evaluation

During these meetings, the social workers used a variety of program tools to help the members maintain their interest in the group and sustain their motivation to participate. One example was a series of board games devised by the staff. Each game taught members how to accomplish some aspect of the process, such as formulating goals or tasks. In a goal game, for example, members moved their "pieces" around a board and "landed" on a problem area for which they had to formulate a goal.

Social Skills Training

A great deal of development, as well as research on effectiveness, has been devoted to creating models of social skills training for seriously mentally ill clients. Corrigan, Schade, and Liberman (1992), who have been at the forefront of this work, define social skills as representing "a structured application of behavioral learning techniques aimed at helping patients build

[2] This last group was not successful; the groups were formed before much was known about work with the so-called dually diagnosed, and neither of the workers had knowledge about working with that type of client.

a repertoire of skills that improve their ability to function adequately in the community" (p. 95). Their approach involves groups, and excellent materials the social worker can use, such as detailed manuals for practitioners, workbooks for group members, and audiovisual tapes that present models of the skills to be acquired, have been prepared.[3]

Liberman et al. have developed separate modules for a variety of social skills, such as recreation for leisure and medication management. Information on teaching friendship and dating skills is also contained in their text *Social Skills Training for Psychiatric Patients* (1989). These authors suggest the following steps for the group facilitator to use in planning a social skills session:

1. Give introduction to social skills training.
2. Introduce new patients.
3. Solicit orientation from experienced patients who can explain social skills training to new patients.
4. Reward patients for their contribution to the orientation.
5. Check homework assignments.
6. Help each patient pinpoint an interpersonal problem, goal, and scene for this session.
7. Target scene and interpersonal situation for dry run role play.
8. "Set up" the scene.
9. Give instructions for the scene.
10. Run the scene as a dry run.
11. Give positive feedback.
12. Assess receiving, processing, sending skills.
13. Use a model.
14. Ensure that the patient has assimilated the demonstrated skills.
15. Use another model.
16. Give instructions to patient for next rehearsal or rerun.
17. Rerun scene.
18. Give summary positive feedback.
19. Give real-life assignment.
20. Choose another patient for the training sequence and return to step 1.

The following is a brief excerpt of a social skills session reported by Liberman et al.:

> (Karen, at the invitation of the therapist, has been explaining to a new member, Mark, what the members do in social skills training group. The therapist then turns to Ted, who has been in the group for a week, and asks him to add to what Karen has said.)
> *Therapist:* Great, Karen! Ted, would you add to what Karen said?

---

[3] These materials can be obtained from Dissemination Coordinator, Camarillo-UCLA Clinical Research Center, Box A, Camarillo, CA 93011.

(Ted has only been in the group for a week. He often gets angry and upset with other people. He decided to seek social skills training because he recently lost his third roommate in six months and has begun to realize that he alienates other people, including his coworkers. His boss has told him to improve his relations with workmates or else risk being fired.)

Ted: I don't know, Karen described it.

Therapist: Well, can you think of some of the other things we can focus on?

Ted: You mean like solving our problems by looking at alternatives for communicating? And whether or not we look mad?

Therapist: Right, Ted. We concentrate on facial expression and problem solving, too. When you talk to someone, they get a lot if information from seeing the kind of expression on your face. How loud we talk and our tone of voice are really important, too. Ted, how is voice tone different from voice loudness?

Ted: Why don't you pick on someone else?

Therapist: Because you're doing really well. You've only been here a short time, and you've learned a lot. (pp. 84–85)

Inpatient Group Psychotherapy

A major feature of contemporary hospitalization of patients with serious mental illness is that is it likely to be short—perhaps for only a week or two while the patient becomes stabilized after an acute episode. While in the hospital, patients may attend groups on a daily basis. These groups may be very unstructured, and our experience is that they are of limited usefulness. Yalom (1995) has developed and tested an approach he terms *inpatient group psychotherapy*. This approach has two variations, one for high-functioning and one for low-functioning patients. The high-functioning ones are able to make a conscious decision to enter the group, can sustain conversations with other patients that focus on interpersonal behaviors, and can remain in the group for approximately an hour. The low-functioning patients are unable to sustain that much verbal interaction. The structure of groups for the latter patients, therefore, includes more nonverbal activity such as physical exercise.

In the group for higher-functioning patients, the workers ask each member in turn to select a concern (referred to as an *agenda*) that can be worked on in a single session. Examples include telling another group member something about oneself or finding a way of coping with another member's angry response. After social workers have helped each member to chose an agenda for the session, the workers promote group interactions that will allow each member to work on her or his agenda for at least part of the session. Workers must have a good deal of skill in helping members choose a workable agenda and then pursue the agenda as part of the subsequent stage of the group's process.

After the interactional period, workers give feedback to members on how they have worked on their agendas. Yalom also often invites observers (such as interns) to attend and to comment toward the end of the session on the group's process. Members also are given a brief opportunity to react to this feedback on group processes.

EVALUATION APPROACHES

A great deal of research has been conducted to evaluate services to people with severe mental illness; this had to led to the development and testing of a variety of instruments to measure client outcomes. The following are some that can readily be used by social workers:

1. Scale for the Assessment of Negative Symptoms; Scale for the Assessment of Positive Symptoms (Schuldberg, Quinlan, Morgenstern, & Glazer, 1990). These scales are used by practitioners primarily to assess the symptomatology of schizophrenia.
2. Symptoms Checklist (Bartone, Ursano, Wright, & Ingraham, 1989). This instrument is designed to measure the frequency of such psychiatric symptoms as tenseness, depressed mood, and difficulty sleeping.
3. Cognitive Slippage Scale (Miers & Raulin, 1985). This scale is designed to measure the cognitive distortion that is a primary characteristic of schizophrenia.
4. Social Adjustment Scale-Self Report (Weissman & Bothwell, 1976). This instrument helps the social worker to assess how adequate the client is in such areas as housework; employment; dealing with salespeople, neighbors, and friends; schooling; and family relations.

CONCLUSION

Group approaches have a great deal to offer to people suffering from serious mental illnesses. These approaches provide experiences in dealing with relationships through group activities, the possibility for mutual aid as members discover the support they can give and receive, and the opportunity for members to learn vicariously when they are not ready to take a more active role. With the large number of investigations currently underway, the future is bright for the creation of even more useful ways of offering group opportunity to these clients.

RESOURCES

Alliance for the Mentally Ill
2107 Wilson Blvd., Suite 300
Arlington, VA 22201
(800) 950 NAMI
www.nami.org

Center for Psychiatric Rehabilitation
Boston University
Sargent College of Health and
    Rehabilitation Sciences
940 Commonwealth Ave. West

Boston, MA 02215
(617) 353-3549
www.bu.edu/cpr

REFERENCES

Anderson, C. M., Reiss, D. J., & Hogarty, G. E. (1986). *Schizophrenia and the family.* New York: Guilford Press.

Bartone, P. T., Ursano, R. J., Wright, K. M., & Ingraham, L. H. (1989). The impact of a military air disaster on the health of assistance workers. *Journal of Nervous and Mental Disease.* 177, 317–328.

Bentley, K. J. (ed.). (2002). *Social work practice in mental health: Contemporary roles, tasks, and techniques.* Pacific Grove, CA: Brooks/Cole.

Corrigan, P. W., Schade, M. L., & Liberman, R. P. (1992). Social skills training. In R. P. Liberman (ed.), *Handbook of psychiatric rehabilitation* (pp. 95–126). New York: Macmillan.

Dincin, J. (1985). Psychiatric rehabilitation today. In J. P. Bowker (ed.), *Education for practice with the chronically mentally ill: What works?* (pp. 18–31). Washington, DC: Council on Social Work Education.

Federal Interagency Task Force on Homelessness and Mental Illness (1999) *Report of the Surgeon General.* Available online at http://www.surgeongeneral.gov/library/mentalhealth/toc.

Garvin, C. (1992) A task-centered group approach to work with the chronically mentally ill. In J. A. Garland (ed.), *Group work reaching out: People, places, and power* (pp. 67–80). New York: Haworth Press.

Garvin, C., & Tropman, J. (1998). *Social work in contemporary society* (2nd ed.) Boston: Allyn & Bacon.

Gerhart, U. C. (1990). *Caring for the chronic mentally ill.* Itasca, IL: Peacock.

Liberman, R. P., DeRisi, W. J., & Mueser, K. T. (1989). *Social skills training for psychiatric patients.* New York: Pergamon Press.

Miers, T. C., & Raulin, M. L. (1985). The development of a scale to measure cognitive slippage. Paper presented at the Eastern Psychological Association Convention, Boston, March 1985. A copy of the instrument may be found in K. Corcoran and J. Fischer (2000), *Measures for clinical practice: A sourcebook* (3rd ed.), Vol. 2: *Adults* (pp. 193–195). New York: Free Press.

Poynter-Berg, D. (1994). Getting connected: Institutionalized schizophrenic women. In A. Gitterman & L. Shulman (eds.), *Mutual aid groups, vulnerable populations, and the life cycle* (2nd ed.) (pp. 315–334). New York: Columbia University Press.

Rapp, C. (1985) Research on the chronically mentally ill: Curriculum implications. In J. P. Bowker (ed.), *Education for practice with the chronically mentally ill: What works?* (pp. 32–49). Washington, DC: Council on Social Work Education.

Robins, L. N., Locke, B. Z., & Regier, D. A. (1991). An overview of psychiatric disorders in America. In L. N. Robins & D. Regier (eds.), *Psychiatric disorders in America* (pp. 328–386). New York: Free Press.

Rubin, A. (1986). Review of current research on chronic mental illness. In J. P. Bowker & A. Rubin (eds.), *Studies on chronic mental illness: New horizons for social work researchers* (pp. 5–28). Washington, DC: Council on Social Work Education.

Sands, R. G. (2001) Clinical social work practice in behavioral mental health: A post-modern approach to practice with adults (2nd ed.). Boston: Allyn & Bacon.

Schuldberg, D., Quinlan, D. M., Morgenstern, D. M., & Glazer, W. (1990). Positive and negative symptoms in chronic psychiatric outpatients: Reliability, stability, and factor structure. *Psychological Assessment.* 2, 262–268.

Tolson, E. R., Reid, W. J., & Garvin, C. D. (2002). Generalist practice: A task-centered approach (2nd ed.). New York: Columbia University Press.

Weissman, M. M., & Bothwell. (1976) Assessment of social adjustment by patient self-report. *Archives of General Psychiatry.* 33, 1111–1115.

Yalom, I. D. (1995) *The theory and practice of group psychotherapy* (4th ed.). New York: Basic Books.

Chapter 3

Group Work Services to People with AIDS During a Changing Pandemic

GEORGE S. GETZEL

Group work and the acquired immune deficiency syndrome (AIDS) have been closely associated in the first efforts, beginning in the early 1980s, to help people with AIDS (PWAs). The model of group work for PWAs developed then reflected the desperate need to gain social support and to reduce societal isolation.

This chapter reviews the development of group work services to PWAs and suggests a reconsideration of the design and implementation of such services in light of the significant changes that have occurred in the treatment of human immunodeficiency virus (HIV)/AIDS and in the sociopolitical and cultural meanings of the disease. An overview of the biopsychosocial factors that surround HIV/AIDS is presented and is related to the core themes that emerge in a support group's interaction and content. The benefits of the group work experience for PWAs are identified.

Special attention is given to strategies for pregroup planning, the functional characteristics of groups, and the problem-solving process underlying group themes addressed by the group. Guidelines for the social worker's interventions are detailed. Finally, evaluation criteria are suggested.

OVERVIEW

In the more than 20 years since the appearance of AIDS as a major public health problem and the subsequent discovery of HIV, these conditions have significantly entered the everyday lives of people in far-reaching ways (Cox, 1990); (Shilts, 1988; Wright, 2000). Although we may tend to avoid thinking about AIDS and its deadly consequences, growing numbers of people throughout the world are denied that option because their kin, friends, and neighbors infected by HIV become irreversibly ill from AIDS-related symptoms and diseases (Mann, Tarantola, & Netter, 1992; Stine, 2001).

The AIDS pandemic has produced creative and humane efforts to prevent the spread of HIV and to care for PWAs with serious illness and functional impairments. The use of groups with PWAs and with kin, friends, and volunteers caring for them has become an integral aspect of many social service and health care programs (Ball, 1998; Danilos, 1994; Dean, 1995; Edell, 1998; Foster et al., 1994; Hayes et al., 1998; Getzel, 1991a; Lopez & Getzel, 1984, 1987). Beginning with the discovery of the first AIDS cases in New York City, group approaches quickly were picked up by newly developing AIDS community-based organizations in other cities.

No longer can people, even in the most sophisticated developed countries, conceive of AIDS as a disease largely of gay men and intravenous drug users, as was the case when the pandemic was first recognized in the early 1980s (Cahill, 1984). The 1990s has been a period with a significant increase worldwide in the proportion of women, children, and men diagnosed with AIDS where infection is attributed directly or indirectly to heterosexual contact (Mann et al., 1992; Stine, 2001). All sexually active persons and their offspring throughout the world are at risk of developing HIV infection and the breakdown of bodily immune protection.

HIV infection and AIDS have a profound cultural and economic impact on whole societies (Bateson & Goldsby, 1988; Mann et al., 1992; Smith, 2001; Stine, 2001). The HIV disease sequence has a welter of emotional and practical effects on the lives of all involved (Christ et al., 1988; Getzel, 1991b; Getzel & Willroth, 2001). The psychosocial consequences of HIV/AIDS in many respects resemble the reactions of other categories of persons to life-threatening disease. For example, the prospect of being infected with HIV or the knowledge of being HIV positive may be met with denial, which is dangerous if a person has unprotected sex.

All major illnesses with disabling and disfiguring consequences can result in depression and agitation; it is very common for sick persons to feel shame and guilt about becoming sick, resulting in bouts of anger, isolation, and self-loathing. Sontag (1978) noted that historically, serious diseases like cancer and tuberculosis have had complex metaphorical content and values connotations; this has been strongly demonstrated in the case of AIDS. Because the first identified victims of HIV/AIDS were gay men, drug addicts, and poor persons of color in large cities, the stigma attached to persons with the disease has been insidious, resulting in incidents of withdrawal of care by professionals, violation of human rights, and violence against PWAs and their families (Altman, 1986; Bayer, 1989; Smith, 2001; Gant, 2000). The societal problems of homophobia, classism, racism, and sexism are exposed and magnified in the presence of HIV/AIDS.

As we begin the third decade of the AIDS pandemic, knowledge about AIDS and HIV has greatly expanded. Nonetheless, scientists have been unable to create a vaccine to prevent the spread of the virus or to find methods to eradicate it in the human body (Bartlett & Finkbeiner, 2001). A number of useful halfway medical technologies have been developed to temporarily prevent the replication of HIV in infected persons; these antiviral medications have significantly extended longevity but have not altered the disabling course of disease. Antiviral medications also present significant quality of life concerns because of side effects and the uncertain benefits for some individuals (Bartlett & Finkbeiner, 2001).

The extension of life for persons with both HIV and AIDS has increased the prevalence of complications from opportunistic infections. The longer persons live with HIV or AIDS, the more apt they are to develop chronic, persistent, disabling, disorienting, and disfiguring conditions (Bartlett & Finkbeiner, 2001).

A reconfiguration of group work services is required to respond more effectively to PWAs and the evolution of their biomedical treatment. These changes will be described below.

Review of the Literature

From the start of the first AIDS service organizations, support groups were recognized as important normalizing experiences for PWAs and for kin and friends caring for them (Hayes et al, 1994; Lopez & Getzel, 1984; Maasen, 1998) and for volunteers in these organizations (Lopez & Getzel, 1984, 1987; Meier et al., 1995; Moore, 1998; Weiner, 1998). Support groups for professionals working with PWAs were recognized as a necessary resource somewhat later (Cushman et al., 1995; Garside, 1993; Gladstone & Reynolds, 1997; Grossman & Silverstein, 1993). The use of groups to teach HIV prevention has been extensively reported. Peer education is widely employed to teach safer sexual techniques to gay men, women, adolescents, and other populations (Duke & Omi, 1991; Kelly & St. Lawrence, 1990; Palacios-Jimenez & Shernoff, 1986; Ponton et al., 1991; Redman, 1990; Roffman et al., 1997; Subramanian, et al., 1995; Yoakum, 1999).

The literature on group work with PWAs and caregivers, while not large, does point to the widespread use of support groups for special populations in a variety of contexts. Group work models for gay men in community-based organizations have been described in some detail (Gambe & Getzel, 1989; Getzel, 1991a, 1991b; Getzel & Mahony, 1990; Livingston, 1996; Sandstrom, 1996).

Child and Getzel (1989) describe a support group model for poor people in a urban hospital setting that is crisis oriented and capable of serving hospitalized and recently released patients with AIDS, including those with drug histories, women, and gay men of color. PWAs who are intravenous drug users can benefit from group support programs that emphasize harm reduction strategies to curtail the use of drugs while providing social support and guidance about the disease process (Bataki, 1990; Greene et al., 1993; Junturem et al., 1999; O'Dowd et al., 1991). Recently, increased attention has been given to PWAs living in rural areas who are limited in their ability to attend support groups at distant community-based organizations. Telephone support group work models have been developed for both PWAs and caregivers to break down the isolation of PWAs in rural areas also to protect their anonymity (Rounds et al., 1991). Telephone support groups have also been used for parents of children with AIDS (Heckman et al., 1999; Weiner et al., 1993) and for PWAs who are disabled in the terminal phase of the disease process (Ritter & Hammons, 1992). Group work approaches for special populations with AIDS and their caregivers are an increasing source of interest: the homeless (Mancoske & Lindhorst, 1991), family members in rural areas (Anderson & Shaw, 1994), parents of children with AIDS (Mayers & Spiegel, 1992; Weiner, 1998), gay partners of PWAs (Land & Harangody, 1990), and prisoners (Pomeroy et al, 1997; Richey et al, 1997).

Gambe and Getzel (1989) emphasize that groups provide substitutes for weakened or absent social supports in PWAs' lives created by life-threatening disease, the unpredictability of the disease process, and the stigma associated with AIDS. In a similar vein, Getzel and Mahony (1990) identify the themes of loss and human finitude as causing crises in the group and forcing members to confront their personal sense of mortality. The group becomes a context in which to face painful and inchoate feelings of dread, helplessness, shame, and guilt. The social worker's acceptance of members' expressions of vulnerability and the group's constancy permit a sense of security and solidarity when members explore these themes.

PRACTICE PRINCIPLES

Work with PWAs entails a clear understanding of the functions of a support group. Critical to the use of group work with PWAs is effective pre-group planning and formation.

Pregroup Planning

The capacity of groups to meet the needs of PWAs must be clearly understood by the social worker before a group is begun. Groups have the following identified functions for PWAs:

1. Assisting members to find support from peers as a way of accepting their new status as PWAs.
2. Helping members explore ways in which family, friends, and others respond to them differently as PWAs and how to handle issues of intimacy, receiving help, and gaining acceptance.
3. Assisting members to find safe ways to express the sadness, anger, guilt, helplessness, and shame associated with the problem of living with AIDS.
4. Providing opportunities for members to find ways to counter the fright and feeling of powerlessness about death and dying.
5. Helping members examine quality-of-life options (how they want to live and die) prompted by serious illness and a likely death from complication from AIDS.
6. Assisting members with their personal belief systems about being diagnosed with AIDS and facing an uncertain future in a world that is not sympathetic to their plight.

Group Formation and the AIDS Pandemic

Early in the AIDS pandemic, support groups for PWAs consisted of members who had recently become aware of their AIDS diagnosis by becoming seriously ill with *Pneumocystis Cariniii* pneumonia (PCP), discovering a Kaposi's sarcoma (KS) lesion, or developing some other symptom associated with an opportunistic infection. Prior to the development of more effective treatments for these diseases and antiviral medication for HIV, most of the initial cohort joining a group died from complications from AIDS over 1 to 2 years (Gambe & Getzel, 1989). There was a brief early period "of quiet before the storm," soon followed by multiple hospitalizations, near-death experiences, and the appearance of other opportunistic infections such as taxoplasmosis, cytomegalovirus (CMV) infections, tuberculosis, and so forth. All of these illnesses can result in death, but not before causing extreme body wasting, incontinence, mental confusion, blindness, disfigurement, profound neurological impairments, and other dire consequences.

PWAs entering a formed group could see themselves in contrast to very sick members and could be in the group as members died in rapid succession. While this situation was intrinsically frightening and overwhelming, a basis for dropping out of the group, it also provided an opportunity to understand and prepare for the likely biopsychosocial crises to come. Other group members served as models of forbearance and coping. A member could deal with prospective and current quality-of-life issues while providing help to peers. Group members were seen to be in the same lifeboat "until death do them part."

Reconfiguring Group Work Services

While this early model of group support services is still relevant in many respects, it must be adjusted and refined in view of PWAs' increased longevity and the highly variegated cohorts of persons now affected by AIDS in many settings. What was once a single model of group work service has become a series of specialized models that reflect with more precision the disease sequence and medical treatment advances. Three general types of support groups are recommended and principles for intervention specified.

Orientation Support Group

This group's primary focus is assisting members to cope with the issue of recognizing themselves as persons with AIDS. This may also mean coming out of the closet as a gay person or a person with a history of drug abuse.

Understanding the practical and emotional consequences of the disease for the person's future orientation and management of different aspects of everyday life becomes important. Women with children have to consider custody after they die. All persons must consider how they will manage their income and health care now and if they become unemployed or disabled in the future. Guidance about available health and social services and how to use them is an important aspect of group activities.

Depression, guilt, shame, and powerlessness are reduced as group members gain understanding about the similarity of their reactions and their different coping strategies. The orientation support group is comprised of newly diagnosed PWAs; it is time limited (six to eight sessions) and focuses on getting on with life after an AIDS diagnosis. These groups are most effective when sponsored by community-based organizations.

Group homogeneity is an important consideration in the design of orientation support groups. Gay men, male intravenous drug users, women who are nondrug abusers infected by men, and women using intravenous drugs may benefit from homogeneous group composition that allows for more in-depth discussions of members' diagnosis, needed services, and coping strategies. Linguistic barriers and disabling conditions may necessitate special groups led in a foreign language or American Sign Language. Increased sophistication in developing specialized groups also applies to the two support group models that will now be discussed.

Relationship Support Group

This group is needed after the initial shock of the diagnosis has been handled. This model of group support focuses on the significant changes in the quantity and quality of interpersonal relationships that ensue for PWAs after they and other persons in their lives contemplate the current and prospective consequences of the disease. PWAs may see themselves as tainted or, as some PWAs have described it, as "soiled goods." The stigma attached to PWAs is reinforced when other persons, who were previously close, begin to disengage or abandon them. PWAs and others close to them may be troubled by the HIV/AIDS diagnosis and by the disclosure of homosexuality, bisexuality, drug use, or marital infidelity.

Just as PWAs become preoccupied with recurrent death anxiety, persons close to them must contemplate hospitalizations, new symptoms, and dying. Relatives and others may experience feelings of rage and emotional conflict.

Needless to say, if the PWA is presumed to have infected family members, the emotional turmoil and conflict are magnified enormously. Consider the following situation of Mr. A., a 35-year-old man, and his wife of five years.

> Mrs. A. has been previously married. While she is pregnant with their second child, she and Mr. A. discover that Mrs. A's first husband died of AIDs (related to a hidden history of drug abuse). HIV tests are given to Mr. and Mrs. A. and their first child; the results for each of them are positive. Mrs. A. has been recently diagnosed with disseminated tuberculosis and AIDS; it will take over a year of testing to determine if the newborn is HIV infected because the mother's and the child's antibody production must be distinguished.

The need for a variety of health and social services for the A. family now and in the future is apparent. Part of a case plan for Mr. and Mrs. A. can be a relationship support group to address the welter of interpersonal problems they may face. Among the possibilities are a couples support group composed of others in a comparable situation, a women's PWA group composed of women infected by spouses, and a caregiver support group of men caring for women with AIDS.

Relationship support groups explore the current stresses in interpersonal relationships arising from being a PWA or a caregiver. These groups are time limited, with a focus on providing emotional and practical assistance in working out interpersonal conflicts and finding additional sources of support as the mounting demands of self-care and caregiving create stresses for group members. One objective of these groups is to maximize the autonomy and self-determination of the members as they make choices between the demands originating from the disease and those arising from day-to-day living. A group meeting for 8 to 12 weeks is introduced by the social workers, who state that group members will develop the understanding and skills needed to get on with their lives. Throughout this group experience, the social workers reinforce examples of members' resourcefulness in handling AIDS-related problems and making life plans. The social workers state that they believe that living with AIDS means that members get on with their lives, which includes work, friendship, intimacy, and new experiences.

Coleadership should be considered as a way of modeling roles and providing continuity when a facilitator is absent. The group members may recontract for an extension of the group as needed and as resources permit. Emphasis should be placed on enhancing group members' capacity to understand and to manage HIV/AIDS-related problems that typically arise within their kinship and friendship systems. Problems at work may also be discussed.

Relationship support groups require careful intake. The social worker helps the potential group member or couple identify possible interpersonal issues to be addressed in the group. The intake process is expedited when group candidates have first explored interpersonal concerns in an orientation support group. This model of group support can be based in AIDS community-based organizations, mental health settings, family services agencies, child care agencies, and other settings used by and accessible to PWAs, their kin, and others associated with informal caregiving.

Quality-of-Life Support Group

This group is appropriate during periods of serious illness and the end stage of the disease process. It may not address many PWAs' needs until a few years after diagnosis. Life-threatening diseases tend to occur later. PWAs frequently experience an asymptomatic period or a period of less dramatic symptomatic display when AIDs and its life-threatening potential need not occupy exclusively PWAs' cognitive and emotional lives.

A quality-of-life support group provides PWAs with a safe location to discuss their reactions to shortened life. A process of life review, more typically associated with the elderly, occurs in the group. It is occasioned by serial losses in the form of disfiguring symptoms, social isolation and abandonment, deaths of others, mental disorganization, and other disabling conditions. The group gives support and guidance as members confront humiliating, severe symptoms. For example, the group allows members to exchange opinions about undergoing experimental treatments that may cause irreversible side effects. Members can openly discuss issues like HIV dementia symptoms and even use humor to face the affront of baldness caused by chemotherapy treatments.

Particular symptoms of opportunistic diseases may warrant special efforts to develop homogeneous groups. Groups may be composed of PWAs with visual impairments resulting from the activity of a persistent, chronic cytomegaloviral infection that destroys the retina of the eye, or they may consist of members with rapidly progressing and disfiguring lesions of Kaposi's sarcoma, a form of skin cancer. In such groups, members can provide empathetic support and exchange useful information about resources: how to obtain cosmetics to disguise lesions or community resources for mobility training at home. Quality-of-life support groups are found in AIDS community-based organizations, hospitals, long-term care programs, hospices, religious organizations, and local health and social service agencies. Parallel groups of this nature for caregivers are also very useful. Coleadership is strongly recommended to provide continuity of facilitation and emotional support to leaders in these very demanding groups. This support group model is usually opened-end in time. Careful consideration and preparation must be given to the introduction of a new member (Gambe & Getzel, 1989).

COMMON THEMES

Recurrent themes emerge in group discussion and interaction that present the social worker and members with rich opportunities to work together.

An Uncertain Conditioning

Uncertainty occurs in all support groups during different phases of group development. For example, in the beginning phase of the group, members may express deep ambivalence about being in a group for PWAs because they do not understand what AIDS represents to them. Rather than confront the uncertainty of their life course, they protect themselves against death anxiety through simple denial—maybe they really do not have AIDS or perhaps they are not suited for a group of PWAs.

Approach-avoidance behaviors appear in the group. Members join subgroups that are in conflict. Some members only want to talk about cures and treatments for HIV/AIDS and castigate others who want to discuss their fear of becoming sick or the recent deaths of friends from complications of AIDS.

Recommended Ways of Working. There is a great temptation to side with one subgroup; this tendency should be avoided. The social worker should make group conflicts a problem for group members to solve. The social worker should assist group members to explore solutions that might simultaneously address the need to accept the uncertainties of disease sequence and treatment while approaching life without a morbid outlook. Group members share thoughts and problem-solve together. The social workers must walk a fine line, carefully accepting different perspectives offered by conflicting subgroups.

If the social worker is not a PWA or does not have a background similar to that of the members, he or she may become a target of group members' anger for not having to deal with the same life issues.

Case

The following incident occurs at an early meeting of gay men with AIDS after Robert returns to the group when his lover dies from an opportunistic infection:

Members are engaged in an intense discussion of the benefits of combining antiviral medications to halt HIV replication when Robert asks, in an offhanded way, if this discussion is boring to the social worker, since he does not have AIDS. Other group members stop and stare at the social worker, who begins to flush. Looking at Robert and the other group members, the social worker says, "The group seems to be reacting to Robert's important question to me."

In defense of the social worker, another member, John, says that you do not need to have AIDS to lead a group of PWAs. The social worker indicates that this might be so but wonders if Robert and some other group members might feel differently. An intense group discussion ensues in which Robert talks about his anger about the death of his lover and his distrust of anyone who does not have AIDS and has not suffered. Some group members, while defending the social worker, acknowledge their jealousy in their lives toward people who do not have AIDS. Group members, with the help of the social worker, go on to discuss their concerns about how Robert is managing after the death of his lover. The discussion slowly edges back to new treatments as the session ends.

Crisis Situations

Recurrent biopsychosocial crisis situations arise in the PWAs' interpersonal systems that necessitate in-depth attention by the group members. Previous patterns of adaptation and problem solving may no longer be available to PWAs in crisis. Acceptance of powerful emotional displays occurs in the support group. Other members can display a sense of mastery by using their learning from undergoing similar crises to help a peer in active crises.

Recommended Ways of Working. The social worker must see the group members as capable of accepting crisis situations that arise among members, avoiding an overprotective stance. To the extent that the social worker encourages members to discuss how they have handled similar situations, mutual aid will be encouraged, in contrast to flight behavior, in which members give facile advice on a one-on-one basis. It is important to point out themes that reflect emotions and ideas shared by the members. The social worker may also help members reach out to each other as crisis situations arise between sessions, assuming that members agree to this type of support during the group's deliberations.

Case

A crisis situation was revealed in a women's PWA group when Mary, in a tearful, agitated manner, told the other members that she had been diagnosed with cervical cancer and would be hospitalized the next day. Mary told the group that she did not care if she lived or died but felt shame for what would happen to her two young children. Shaking convulsively, May wept, saying that she had not planned for guardianship after her husband had died 6 months ago.

Joan held Mary and the group began telling Mary that they were very worried about her. Tanya said that she used a lawyer from the social work agency when she panicked about going into the hospital. The social worker told the group that it seemed very hard to do a will and make guardian provisions. Joan said that you just don't want to think about dying but that you have to be realistic, concluding, "Better late than never." The group then began a discussion about how, after being diagnosed, they had grown more responsible in thinking about their children.

A Changed Identity

A very strong theme that emerges in groups of PWAs is participants' change of self-image linked to AIDS. For example, receiving an AIDS diagnosis can be seen as a rite of passage. Normalizing and AIDS identity is a way of coping with an otherwise unacceptable condition that others readily see as a death sentence.

Support groups simultaneously normalize the PWA status and provide guidance in understanding this status when representing oneself to outsiders. Strongly associated with a shift of self-definition is a greater capacity to look at the question of mortality and the meaning of a life threatened by AIDS.

Erikson (1964) notes that all stages of the life cycle place demands on the individual to find meaning in life in order to cope with the stresses of existence and reminders of death. Human individuality finds its ultimate challenge when a human being confronts mortality. Identity questions may become exquisitely transparent in the face of death.

Recommended Ways of Working. The group becomes a safe context to discuss concerns and express feelings about the inequity of a life ending too early, unfulfilled goals, unfinished projects, and taking leave of loved ones. With the death of a member, surviving members bear witness to the meaning of the loss and the significance of their own lives. Clearly, the social worker must be prepared to listen and not to quickly reassure. The social worker's guilt and helplessness as a survivor necessitate the presence of supervisory and peer supervision.

Case

After the group discusses the recent death of a member, Greg says to the social workers, "It is your job to remember us after we all die." The social worker, after some hesitation, replies that the deaths of group members sadden him greatly and he feels the heavy burden of loss, yet his is grateful to be part of the group, where he has met so many wonderful men. He can never forget them.

The social worker asks the group members if they have reactions to his outliving them. Some members joke, saying that he had better enjoy himself when they are gone. Paul says that he is jealous of the social worker. Gradually, the subject is adroitly changed by Paul.

EVALUATION APPROACHES

Although difficult, the evaluation of group support models for different population is very much needed. Consumer feedback about short-term support groups is a good way to begin. Measurements of consumer satisfaction, knowledge gained about resources, and the actual use of services and entitlements should be investigated. More traditional measurements of clinical outcomes can be obtained from relationship support groups.

Quality-of-life support groups present serious concerns, and ethnographic approaches should be considered because of the likelihood of physical fragility and HIV-related dementia among members. Since PWAs feel stigmatized and may have histories of stigma, respect for the integrity of their personal boundaries, confidentiality, and autonomy are critical. PWAs should be allowed to tell their stories without prejudice, coercion, or prior interpretation. Telling their stories may represent the human need to be remembered.

RESOURCES

American Foundation for AIDS
   Research (AmFar)
120 Wall Street (13th Floor)
New York, NY 10005-3902
(800) 39-amfar
www.amfar.org

Gay Men's Health Crisis
119 West 24th Street
New York, NY 10011
GMHC Hotline (800) 243-7692 or
   hotline@gmhc.org
www.gmhc.org

National AIDS Hotline (Centers
for Disease Control and
Prevention)
(800) 342-2437 (English)
(800) 344-7432 (Spanish)
(800) 243-7889 (TSS)
www.ashastd.org/nah

National Minority AIDS Council
1931 13th Street NW

Washington DC 20009
(202) 483-6622
www.nmac.org

San Francisco AIDS Foundation
995 Market Street
San Francisco, CA 94103
California Hotline: (800) 367-AIDS or
    feedback@sfaf.org
www.sfaf.org

REFERENCES

Altman, D (1986). *AIDS in the mind of America.* New York: Anchor Books.

Anderson, D. B., & Shaw, S. L. (1994). Starting a support group for families and partners of people with HIV/AIDS in a rural setting. *Social Work.* 39, 135–138.

Ball, S. (1998). A time-limited group model for HIV-negative gay men. *Journal of Gay & Lesbian Social Services.* 8, 23–42.

Bataki, S. L. (1990). Substance abuse and AIDS: The need for mental health services. *New Directions in Mental Health Services.* 48, 55–67.

Bateson, M. C., & Goldsby, B. (1988). *Thinking AIDS: The social response to the biological threat.* Reading, MA: Addison-Wesley.

Bayer, R. (1989). *Private act, social consequences: AIDS and politics of public health.* New York: Free Press.

Cahill, K. M. (1984). Preface: The evolution of an epidemic. In Cahill, K. M. (ed.), *The AIDS epidemic* (pp. 2–6). New York: St. Martin's Press.

Child, R., & Getzel, G. S. (1989) Group work with inner city people with AIDS. *Social Work with Groups.* 12, 65–80.

Christ, G., Weiner, L., & Moynihan, R. (1988). Psychosocial issues in AIDS. *Psychiatric Annals.* 16, 173–179.

Cox, E. (1990). *Thanksgiving: An AIDS journal.* New York: Harper & Row.

Cushman, L. F., Evans, P., & Namerow, P. B. (1995). Occupational stress among AIDS social service providers, *Social Work in Health Care.* 21, 115–131.

Daniolos, P. T. (1994). House calls: A support group for individuals with AIDS in a community residential setting. *International Journal of Group Psychotherapy.* 44, 133–153.

Dean, R. G. (1995). Stories of AIDS: The use of narrative as an approach to understanding in an AIDS support group. *Clinical Social work Journal.* 23, 287–304.

Duke, S. I., & Omi, J. (1991). Development of AIDS education and prevention materials for women by health department staff and community focus groups. *AIDS Education and Prevention.* 3, 90–99.

Edell, M. (1998). Replacing community: Establishing linkages for women living with HIV/AIDS—a group work approach. *Social Work with Groups.* 21, 49–62.

Erickson, E. H. (1964). *Insight and responsibility.* New York: Norton.

Foster, S. B., Stevens, P. E., & Hall, J. M. (1994). Offering support group services for lesbians living with HIV. *Women & Therapy.* 15, 69–83.

Gambe, R., & Getzel, G. S. (1989). Group work with gay men with AIDS. *Social Casework.* 70, 172–179.

Gant, L. M. (2000) Advocacy and social policy issues. In V. J. Lynch (ed.), *HIV/AIDS at year 2000: A sourcebook for social workers* (pp. 197–210). Boston: Allyn & Bacon.

Garside, B. (1993). Physicians mutual aid group: A response to AIDS-related burnout. *Health and Social Work.* 18, 259–267.

Getzel, G. S. (1991a). AIDS. In A. Gitterman (ed.), *Handbook of social work with vulnerable populations* (pp. 35–64). New York: Columbia University Press.

Getzel, G. S. (1991b). Survival modes of people with AIDS in groups. *Social Work.* 36, 7–11.

Getzel, G. S., & Willroth, S. (2001). Acquired immune deficiency syndrome (AIDS). In A. Gitterman (ed.), *Handbook of social practice with vulnerable resilient populations* (2nd ed.) (pp. 39–63). New York: Columbia University Press.

Getzel, G. S., & Mahony, K. (1990). Confronting human finitude: Group work with people with AIDS. *Journal of Gay and Lesbian Psychotherapy.* 1, 105–120.

Gladstone, J., & Reynolds, T. (1997). Single session group work intervention in response to employee stress during workforce transition. *Social Work with Groups.* 20, 33–51.

Goldfinger, S. M. (1990). *Psychiatric aspects of AIDS and HIV infection.* New York: Jossey-Bass.

Grant, D. (1988). Support groups for youth with the AIDS virus. *International Journal of Group Psychotherapy.* 38, 237–251.

Greene, D. C., McVinney, L. D., & Addams, S. (1993). Strengths in transition: Professionally facilitated HIV support groups and the development of client symptomatology. *Social Work with Groups.* 16, 41–54.

Grossman, A. H., & Silverstein, C. (1993). Facilitating support groups for professionals working with people with AIDS. *Social Work.* 38, 144–151.

Hackl, K. L., Somlai, A. M., Kelly, J. A., & Kalichman, S. C. (1997). Women living with HIV/AIDS: The dual challenge of being a patient and a caregiver. *Health and Social Work.* 22, 53–62.

Hayes, M. A., McConnell, S. C., Nardozzi, J. A., & Mullican, R. J. (1998). Family and friends of people with HIV/AIDS support group. *Social Work with Groups.* 21, 35–47.

Heckman, T. G., Kalichman, S. C., Roffman, R. R., Sikkema, K. J., Heckman, B. D., Somali, A. M., et al. (1999). A telephone-delivered coping improvement intervention for persons living with HIV/AIDS in rural areas. *Social Work with Groups.* 21, 49–61.

Juntunen, A., Hwalek, M., & Neale, A. V. (1999). Tracking and interviewing clients at risk for HIV and substance abuse in a Latino community. *Evaluation and Program Planning.* 22, 305–312.

Kelly, J. A., & St. Lawrence, J. S. (1990). The impact of community-based groups to help persons reduce HIV infection risk behaviors. *AIDS-Care.* 2, 25–35.

King, M. B. (1993). *AIDS, HIV, and mental health.* Cambridge: Cambridge University Press.

Land, H., & Harangody, G. (1990). A support group for partners of persons with AIDS. *Families in Society.* 71, 471–482.

Lopez, D. J., & Getzel, G. S. (1984). Helping gay patients in crisis. *Social Casework.* 65, 387–394.

Lopez, D. J., & Getzel, G. S. (1987). Strategies for volunteers caring for persons with AIDS. *Social Casework.* 68, 47–53.

Maasen, T. (1998). Counseling gay men with multiple loss and survival problems: The bereavement group as a transitional object. *AIDS Care.* 10, 57–64.

Mann, J., Tarantola, D. J. M., & Netter, T. W. (1992). *A global report: AIDS in the world.* Cambridge, MA: Harvard University Press.

Mancoske, F. J., & Lindhorst, T. (1991). Mutual assistance groups in a shelter for persons with AIDS. *Social Work with Groups.* 14, 75–86.

Mayers, A., & Spiegel, L. (1992). A parental support group in a pediatric AIDS clinic: Its usefulness and limitations. *Health and Social Work.* 17, 183–193.

Meier, A., Galinsky, M. J., & Rounds, K. A. (1995). Telephone support groups for caregivers of persons with AIDS. *Social Work with Groups.* 18, 99–108.

Moore, P. J. (1998). AIDS bereavement supports in an African American church: A model for facilitator training. *Illness, Crisis & Loss.* 7, 390–401.

Livingston, D. (1996). A systems approach to AIDS counseling for gay couples, *Journal of Gay & Lesbian Social Services.* 4, 83–93.

O'Dowd, M. A., Natalie, C., Orr, D., & McKegney, F. (1991). Characteristics of patients attending an HIV-related psychiatric outpatient clinic. *Hospital and Community Psychiatry.* 42, 615–619.

Palacios-Jimeniz, L., & Shernoff, M. (1986). *Eroticizing safer sex.* New York: Gay Men's Health Crisis.

Pomeroy, E. C., Rubin, A., Van Laningham, L. & Walker, R. J. (1997). "Straight Talk": The effectiveness of a psychoeducational group intervention for heterosexuals with HIV/AIDS. *Research on Social Work Practice.* 7, 149–163.

Ponton, K. E., DeClemente, F. J., & McKenna, S. (1991). An AIDS education and prevention program for hospitalized adolescents. *Journal of the American Academy of Children and Adolescent Psychiatry.* 30, 729–734.

Redman, J. M. (1990). *Women and AIDS: What we need to know.* A workshop manual on educating women about AIDS and safer sex. New Orleans: Planned Parenthood.

Richey, C. A., Gillmore, M. R., Balassone, M. L., Gutierrez, L., Hartway, J. (1997). Developing and implementing a group skill training intervention to reduce HIV-AIDS risk among sexually active adolescents in detention. *Journal of HIV/AIDS Prevention & Education for Adolescents & Children.* 1, 71–101.

Rittner, B., & Hammons, K. (1992). Telephone group work with people with end stage AIDS. *Social Work with Groups.* 15, 59–72.

Roffman, R. A., Downey, L., Beadnell, B., Gordon, J. R., Craver, J. N., & Stephens, R. S. (1997). Cognitive-behavioral group counseling to prevent HIV transmission in gay and bisexual men: Factors contributing to successful risk reduction. *Research on Social Work Practice.* 7, 165–186.

Rounds, K. A., Galinsky, M. J., & Stevens, L. S. (1991). Linking people with AIDS in rural communities: The telephone group. *Social Work.* 36, 13–18.

Sandstrom, K. L. (1996). Searching for information, understanding, and self-value: The utilization of peer support groups by gay men with HIV/AIDS. *Social Work in Health Care.* 23, 51–74.

Shilts, R. (1988). *The band played on: Politics, people and AIDS.* New York: St. Martin's Press.

Smith, R. A. (2001). *Encyclopedia of AIDS: A social, political, cultural and scientific record of the HIV epidemic.* New York: Penguin Books.

Sontag, S. (1978). *Illness as metaphor.* New York: Vintage Books.

Stine, G. J. (2001). *AIDS update.* Upper Saddle River, NJ: Prentice Hall.

Subramanian, K., Hernandez, S., & Martinez, A. (1995). Psychoeducational group work for low-income Latina mothers with HIV infection. *Social Work with Groups.* 18, 53–64.

Wiener, L. S. (1998). Telephone support groups for HIV-positive mothers whose children have died of AIDS. *Social Work.* 43, 279–285.

Weiner, L. S., Spencer, E. D., Davidson, R., & Fair, C. (1993). National telephone support groups: A new avenue toward psychosocial support for HIV-infected children and their families. *Social Work with Groups.* 16, 55–71.

Wright, E. M. (2000). The psychosocial context. In V. J. Lynch (ed.), *HIV/AIDS at year 2000: A sourcebook for social workers* (pp. 18–32). Boston: Allyn & Bacon.

Wyatt-Morley, C. (1997). *AIDS memoir: Journal of an HIV-positive mother.* West Hartford, CT: Kumarian Press.

Yoakam, J. R. (1999). The youth and AID projects: School and community outreach for gay, lesbian, bisexual, and transgender youth. *Journal of Gay & Lesbian Social Services.* 9, 99–114.

Chapter 4

Group Work with Head-Injured People

SUSAN T. FUTERAL

Traumatic brain injury, as evidenced in head trauma patients, is defined as brain damage from an externally inflicted trauma to the head that results in significant impairment to the individual's physical, psychological, and/or cognitive functional abilities (Aliev, 1984). Brain injury is characterized by altered consciousness (coma and/or post-trauma amnesia) during the acute phase after injury (Bakay & Glasauer, 1980), and by neurophysiological sequelae in the recuperative phase (NINDS, 2002). A *coma* is defined as the state of not being responsive or able to be aroused in that the person doesn't open their eyes, speak, or follow commands. *Post-trauma amnesia* is defined as a failure of memory after the injury until continuous recall, sometimes with retrograde amnesia, which is the loss of memory of events for a period of time prior to the injury—Headway, 2003. The duration of the acute phase and rehabilitative phase varies greatly, usually depending on the severity and placement of the injury (Ashley et al., 1994).

There are two distinct types of head trauma or TBI (traumatic brain injury): one is open head injury and the other is closed head injury, each producing serious concerns during the rehabilitation. An open head injury may be sustained when there is intracranial penetration of the head, such as in wartime or street violence, as in a gunshot wound. A closed head injury can be sustained in either of two ways: one is a no-missile injury in which sudden acceleration/deceleration is the primary force, such as in a car accident when one's head hits the windshield such that the brain smashes forward and then backward, rebounding against the walls of the skull, causing damage to both the front and back of the brain; and the second could be from a blow to the head by a blunt instrument, often causing a contra coup lesion, in which there is bruising of the brain tissue in the side opposite to where the blow was struck, resulting in an altered state or total loss of consciousness. There are also persons who suffer from a CVA (cardiovascular accident), stroke, or viral or post-viral syndromes who suffer with symptoms paralleling those of other head trauma patients, and the rehabilitation is similar as well. There are several scales available in the assessment of neuropsychological functioning after the injury. Two of the more common scales are the Glasgow Coma Index Scale and the Ranchos Los Amigos Scale, each rating the individual on various verbal and non-verbal (mostly tactile) responses (Ashley et al., 1997). By definition, a person must lose consciousness for a period of twenty minutes to be diagnosed as "in a coma," and these two scales provide a means for consciousness to be measured.

TBI patients comprise a relatively new population, as many head trauma patients had poor survival rates prior to new medical and technological advances. In the mid-1900s the survival rate from TBI was about 10% for persons with severe head injury, whereas in the twenty-first century, we are witnessing about a 50% survival rate for this same population (Persel & Persel, 2001). The Medical College of Virginia completed a NINDS-funded study (National Institute of Neurologic Disorders and Stroke), which focused on the issues of rehabilitation, citing the fact that medical technology has decreased the number of deaths, but have they increased the number of disabled survivors? This study concluded that aggressive surgical and medical treatments have indeed enabled some patients, who would have otherwise died, to make a good recovery without increasing the proportion of severely disabled patients. Other studies looking at patients with minor head injuries, such as concussions, sports injuries (such as boxing, wrestling, and football) or falls (stairs, ladders, rock climbing), indicate that subtle consequences may be higher in frequency and more lasting than previously believed.

Traumatic brain injury differs in two ways from other types of brain damage (Alzheimer's, Parkinson's, genetic stroke, degenerative, drug and alcohol abuse, etc.). Head trauma happens suddenly, bringing significant change immediately, and the damage is usually diffuse and widespread throughout the brain. The effects, therefore, are multiple. Additionally, damage to the brain can be acquired in the course of what may have been normal development (Maryland Head Injury Foundation, 1985). The success rates of rehabilitation techniques in improving the quality of life, increases in ADLs (activities in daily living), and survival rates for TBI patients are mostly due to better knowledge of the brain, the body's most complex organ. The research is often twofold: one set of researchers studying at the micro level, the localization of brain function, structure, and brain cells; the other set following the patient's progress, comparing it to the premorbid history to predict better physical, psychological, and social recovery (Little et al., 1996). The residual deficits that result from traumatic brain injury may be divided into two areas: medical (or physical) and psychological. The medical deficits may include muscle contractions, bowel and/or bladder dysfunction, and seizures. The psychological deficits may include depression, judgment loss, memory loss, impulsiveness, headaches, and lowered self-esteem.

Head injury is a significant cause of mortality and morbidity. Each year in the United States, 400,000 to 600,000 people suffer severe traumatic head injury. Of these, it is estimated that 100,000 deaths occur, and between 30,000 and 50,000 others are left with disabilities severe enough to preclude a return to normal life (Kraus et al., 1984). Head trauma is the third most common cause of death in persons less than 38 years of age (Maryland Head Injury Foundation, 1990).

Severe head injury occurs with an overall frequency of 24 per 100,000. The peak age range is between 10 and 19 years, with an incidence of 38 per 100,000. Severe head injury occurs two to three times more often in males than females; the largest sex difference is found in the age range of 15 to 24 and accidental falls in children under 15 years (Maryland Head Injury Foundation, 1990).

This chapter describes the effectiveness of social group work with head trauma rehabilitation patients. As head trauma patients have never survived until the past few decades, there is presently no defined therapy aimed at rehabilitating them emotionally (Maryland Head Injury Foundation, 1989). Therefore, this is an area in which social workers can explore, develop, and refine methods for their clients' mainstreaming into society (Gerring, 1986).

CHARACTERISTIC PROBLEMS

Individual and family therapies are often provided for head trauma victims; group treatment is not routinely offered in head trauma facilities. However, studies have shown group treatment to be effective in assisting troubled people to reintegrate into society (Garvin, 1987).

Some of the difficulties that head trauma patients face are readjustment to social, vocational, and educational settings (Maryland Head Injury Foundation, 1989). Feelings of grief over loss of normal bodily functions and limbs may affect their self-esteem throughout the recovery and rehabilitation period (Gerring, 1986). These issues can be approached in group work.

Because of personality traits, learning styles, location and severity of the injury, and time lapse between the impact and the psychological reaction, the recovery rate is different for each individual. Varying degrees of physical, mental, and personality changes occur after a traumatic head injury. Although systematic comparative studies of the consequences of head trauma in adults and children have not been undertaken, evidence suggests that children experience a swifter recovery because of the greater plasticity of the immature nervous system. Determining whether a post-traumatic patient is suffering intellectual impairment as a result of the injury depends on the assessment procedures used in evaluation. A brief mental status examination may suggest normal functioning, whereas more detailed testing may uncover defects of varying degrees.

PRACTICE PRINCIPLES

Limit and Structure

For several reasons, head trauma patients often suffer from cognitive impairments that ultimately affect not only their knowledge and memory but also their decision-making ability. The group worker needs to understand that it is imperative to set limits with the members of the group. They must agree to start and end on time. The group must have structure; a beginning warm-up, a middle period of work, and a final period of sharing. Guidance is paramount, especially during periods of sharing, so that group members do not, intentionally or otherwise, react in such a way to adversely affect the member who has shared.

The phases of the group (the beginning, middle, and final activities) must be communicated to the group members so that they, too, can follow and track their progress. Whereas in other group approaches discussed in this book these phases are not always made explicit, here, with an emphasis on structure, they are openly discussed.

Group Composition

One important feature of any group is homogeneity. Head trauma patients often experience a feeling of isolation, as if they are the only ones going through recuperation. Not only is it wise to provide a support group for these patients, it can also be helpful, at times, to run a multi-family group for their spouses and family members. These people can help enhance the patient's functioning and quality of life.

Worker's Role

As the emphasis is on structure, the worker's activity level needs to be high. The worker may feel that he or she is being condescending by making statements such as "You need to put your coffee down and start the group now," or "It's time to put cigarettes out and come in to start the group now." This can make a worker feel as if she or he is dealing with a grade-school class and not a population of adults.

When working with head trauma patients, one must be very specific. Activities must be clearly organized and defined. This clear sense of guidance makes it easier for the trauma patients to follow through and gives them a feeling of acceptance and security. Group members may feel awkward asking questions, particularly concerning the context of neurophysiological impairments such as aphasias, agnosias, work retrieval problems, and other communication disorders. The worker must be prepared to state the guidelines and goals, the intended climate of the group, and the rules for sharing, participation, and confidentiality. These rules must be adhered to strictly.

Time and Hope

The group worker must take time to process the information conveyed in the group. The events of the lives of group members may seem random, unfair, overwhelming, and confusing. Helping trauma patients cope with their losses and deficits and with their families can become a severe emotional drain. Group workers cannot take all this home every night. They must find a way to leave the stress in the office and be willing to share experiences with coworkers to achieve support.

Yalom (1995) says that instillation of hope is critical to head trauma patients. Research shows about a four-year recovery time. Patients need to know that they can get better and will improve with work.

A group worker should know what other services are being provided for the patient, such as occupational therapy, vocational redirection, job coaching, rehabilitation therapy, family counseling, individual counseling, skilled nursing, home visits, physical and speech therapies, and posttrauma psychological testing. A knowledge of the brain (see Figure 4.1 and Table 4.1) is necessary to understand the nature of the injury. Often head trauma patients have near to full IQ recovery, and this recovery needs to be pointed out to them. Hearing that "you're doing really well in your math class, and we can work together on helping you remember what period of the day you are in" can give a patient's sagging ego the boost needed to continue their progress and show the family members that the patient need not be totally dependent.

Common Themes

A firm but gentle, focused discussion is necessary. Common group themes for discussion include a review and recapitulation of the injury; experiences while in the hospital; ongoing concurrent services; assessing what's helpful and what is not; feelings in one's body, mind, and spirit; and coping with family relationships. Financial stressors created by the injury may not be a motivating theme for change, but group members may want to discuss the realities of their new situation.

This section is divided into two shorter sections in order to gain greater understanding of group themes in practice: one focusing on youngsters and the other on adults.

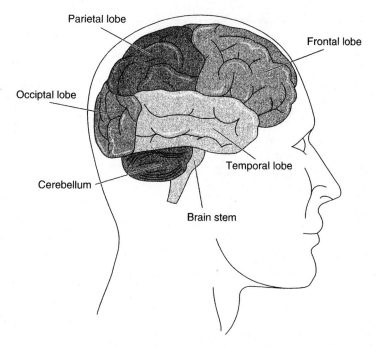

Parietal lobe

Frontal lobe

Occiptal lobe

Temporal lobe

Cerebellum

Brain stem

Figure 4.1 Major Divisions of the Brain

Children and Adolescents

Every year, about 1 in 500 children sustain a head trauma serious enough to require hospitalization, in which boys are twice as likely to sustain a traumatic brain injury (TBI). Approximately 3,000 children and adolescents die from TBI each year; 29,000 are hospitalized each year and 400,000 are treated in emergency rooms each year. Children under age four are mostly injured from falls or child abuse, five- to nineteen-year-olds are most likely injured in motor-vehicle accidents, and fifteen- to nineteen-year-olds have the highest rate of firearm-related injuries. Many children also suffer from acquired brain injury resulting from tumors, strokes, infections, illness, or loss of oxygen. The most common physical changes are fatigue, headaches, seizures, balance problems, and sensory impairments. The neurophysiological sequelae seen most often in children are depression and anxiety, low frustration tolerance, and impulsivity and disinhibition (agitated, aggressive, argumentive), all of which may have an impact on one's education. Some of the common deficits in academic performance are difficulty learning and remembering new things, difficulty integrating new and old learning, difficulty paying attention and concentrating, and difficulties with planning and executing tasks. The executive function in the brain is responsible for problem-solving, organization, recognizing priorities, planning, working towards a goal, and recognition of due dates. Often these students will finish up their homework or class work or group work assignments and forget to turn them in.

Table 4.1 Localization of Brain Function

Cerebral Cortex

Pre-frontal and frontal lobe	Functions	Problems
Located right under the forehead	Consciousness, activity, language	Attention; emotional lability; disinhibition; paralysis; loss of spontaneity; expressive language—Broca's aphasia

Parietal lobe	Functions	Problems
Located near the back and top of the head	Visual attention, touch, manipulation of objects, integration of different senses	Anomia—inability to name object; Agraphia—inability to locate the words for writing; Alexia—problems with reading; Dyscalculia—difficulty doing math; attention deficit; difficulty with hand-eye coordination

Occipital lobes	Function	Problems
Located most posterior, at the back of the head	Vision	Visual deficits; color or movement Agnosia—not recognizing the colors or movements of an object; word blindness

Temporal lobes	Functions	Problem
Located above the ears on the side of head	Hearing, memory, categorization of objects	Prosopagnosia-inability or impairment to recognize familiar faces; difficulty in understanding spoken words—Wernicke's aphasia; memory loss

Brain Stem

	Functions	Problems
Located deep in brain, leads into spinal cord	Breathing, heart rate, swallowing, reflexes, digestion, temperature, blood pressure, sweating, sleeping, and balance-vestibular function	Dizziness and vertigo; difficulty with organization and perception of the environment; swallowing food and water-dysphagia; decreased vital capacity in breathing; problems sleeping

Cerebellum

	Functions	Problems
Located at the base of the skull	Coordination of voluntary movement, balance and equilibrium, some memory	Loss of ability to coordinate fine motor movements such as reaching and grabbing objects; loss of ability to walk; tremors; dizziness; slurred speech; inability to produce rapid movements

Many students with TBI need special education services, Individual Educational Plans (IEP's), medication, and more intensive services (SEW, 2001).

The Maryland Institute for Emergency Medicine studied 230 families of multiple-trauma patients in an attempt to develop an effective treatment modality to help families confronted with the sudden or threatened death of a family member (Epperson, 1977).

Epperson describes six phases following the catastrophic event which the family and the patient must pass through before they are able to reorganize, reintegrate, and regain a homeostatic state: *(1)* high anxiety, *(2)* denial, *(3)* anger, *(4)* remorse, *(5)* grief, and *(6)* reconciliation. These stages are viewed as the phases of recovery. The outcome of this descriptive study offers methods of family intervention for social workers in critical care settings.

Chadwick, Rutter, Brown, Chaffer, and Traub (1981) completed a longitudinal field study comparing 25 children with head injuries to an individually matched group of 25 children with orthopedic injuries, using the WISC Performance and Verbal IQ Scale. Their findings were positive to the extent that post-test measures, compared to the pretest scores obtained one year earlier, showed significant improvement in the head-injured group.

Gerring (1986) examined 52 children and adolescents (2 to 18 years old) who had sustained head injuries and were treated at Johns Hopkins Hospital and the Kennedy Institute. She explored the duration of coma in relation to the early and late cognitive and psychiatric sequelae. Gerring identified a spectrum of behaviors, known as the *disinhibition syndrome,* which refers to the inclusion of inappropriate words or acts, poor judgement, amotivation, apathy, carelessness in hygiene and dress, conceptual disorganization, inattention, hyperactivity, impulsiveness, aggression, hypergraphia, and pica. She also discussed pre-injury psychiatric or behavioral disorders and the role of medication.

Adults

Prigatano, Fordyce, Zeiner, Roueche, Pepping, and Wood (1983) studied the cognitive and personality disturbances following closed head injury in young adults. They concluded that treatment successes were manifested as less personality disturbance and better learning and memory scores after treatment than treatment failures.

Brooks and McKinlay (1983) not only explored the cognitive functioning of head trauma patients but also expanded their research to include personality and behavioral changes that often occur after trauma. They found that teaching the family member or caretaker to recognize and manage personality and behavioral changes in the patient may be a crucial aspect of rehabilitation for this population.

Weddell, Oddy, and Jenkins (1990) evaluated 44 young head-injured adults over a two-year period to monitor their social adjustment. They concluded that "in addition to developing improved retraining techniques for intellectual and personality changes, it may be important to look for better ways of helping patients and their relatives adjust to these residual mental impairments" (p. 26).

In summary, the literature supports the need for rehabilitative group work. The evidence of neurobehavioral and psychological sequelae is present in this population, even two years after trauma. Although it seems that children and adolescents may heal more rapidly than adults (Chadwick et al., 1981; Epperson, 1977), there are still cognitive and behavioral deficits that need to be addressed through further rehabilitation. Head trauma rehabilitation with adults is a complex issue because recovery involves the interdisciplinary treatment team at both the acute and post-trauma stages. The ongoing rehabilitation (Brooks & McKinlay, 1983; Hill, 1984; Prigatano et al., 1983) involves relatives and caretakers to promote stability in the home setting. Overall, there seems to be support for more intense outreach efforts to facilitate the emotional adaptation and social reintegration of head trauma patients.

INTERVENTIONS

Although head trauma is primarily seen in young adults, many young children and adolescents are affected by severe traumatic brain injury through sustained head trauma. In organizing a group, the agency plays a key role. The worker must conform to the rules of the agency, whether in a state-run, an inpatient, or an outpatient setting. The setting itself provides the norms for the climate of the group in terms of promoting a sharing and caring atmosphere. My preference is the closed model, in which the group worker limits the number of participants and follows guidelines for a specific structure, whether a task or behaviorally oriented recidivist model. A closed model does not allow new people to enter the group, a distracting aspect of the open model. A number of self-help groups, such as the 12-step programs, operate on the open model. I have found, however, that in professionally led groups, a closed model is more successful because the social worker sets the guidelines and structure for related expectations of individuals in the group, at a given time, and for a given period. Group phases are easier to monitor, an essential consideration when working with people with severe neurological damage and other at-risk populations.

In the early stages of the group, it is essential for the group worker and coworker to facilitate and develop both short- and long-term goals. A rehabilitative approach seeks to make changes that will alleviate specific handicaps or disabilities to the individual's functioning in his or her social role (Garvin, 1987). Interventions may include therapeutic discussions, education, tutoring, arts and crafts, recreation, sports, politics, religion, sexuality, or other themes.

The goals of the group are to *(1)* maximize the potential of poly-injured clients within the limitations imposed by their injuries; *(2)* help clients readjust both psychologically and socially to their environments; *(3)* help clients deal with their new identities, relearn social skills, maximize their communication abilities, explore new roles, and discover new vocational opportunities; and *(4)* emphasize the clients' functional capacities in the areas of daily living skills, communication, cognition, mobility, and psychosocial awareness, and thereby reestablish their self-esteem (Garvin, 1987).

A case example of a short-term closed group is found at a metropolitan state hospital on the East Coast. The outpatient department for head trauma rehabilitation, termed "The Center for Living," had a multidisciplinary focus. Its purpose was to help recovering head trauma patients adjust and reintegrate into society. There was an equally important support system for family members and significant others. The goal of the group, because of its homogeneity, was to help the patients adjust and reenter, although discussions became intense. The patients in the group were reasonably familiar with one another since they were together for various activities, such as speech therapy, occupational therapy, physical therapy, and job coaching.

None of the members of this particular group was able to work, but they spoke freely about their loss of bodily control—for example, the frustration of a stuttering problem that had not existed before the injury. It was frightening for them to talk about relationships with family members. Many relatives had grieved for them and had been prepared for them to die. When they lived, their relatives were not prepared for the personality changes they experienced. Additionally, the patients did not always realize that they had undergone a personality change. Often they admitted to having a shorter temper or angrier feelings than previously, but they were truly unaware of the significance of the disinhibition syndrome that typically characterizes head trauma rehabilitation patients.

Both of the group workers in this setting were patient and focused. They assured complete safety and confidentiality to the group members. Their participation was geared to helping the members share their feelings and lives with each other. They helped patients cope with recovery issues—the loss of body parts and bodily functions, changes in personality and attitudes—and to understand the grief of their families. By setting clear, concise goals, the members of the group were able to participate in a warm and sharing climate.

A second case example comes from the support group offered at the University of Maryland through the Maryland Institute of Emergency Medical Systems Department. The group's members were former hospital patients who had also sustained closed-head injury. This group did not receive many formal services through the university but were able to spend time sharing their experiences. The goal of this group was to understand the emotional, social, and behavioral impairments resulting from their injuries. The members were able to create a climate of safety. They considered themselves lucky to be able to maintain as healthy a lifestyle as they had. This hospital-based group met in the nurses' station, which provided a warmer atmosphere than might exist in other inpatient settings. This, too, was a closed group, but it continued for several months, in contrast to the 10-week program of the previous example.

This group set the short-term goal of helping its members obtain all of the supportive physical services they might need. Also discussed were job coaching and vocational redirection. The group's long-term goal was to help the members cope with the stress and difficulties of recovery from their injuries. These people were living independently. Although some of them received disability income, they were either employed in some capacity or completing a Department of Vocational Rehabilitation–supported training course to obtain better jobs.

They were determined to enhance the quality of their lives. Nebulous as such a group goal might seem, the members were comfortable with it and with the climate created by the group worker. They felt safe in sharing their limitations, as well as in setting new personal goals as they attained better health and learned to compensate for their new deficiencies.

I found that, above all else, the ability to inspire confidence in the patients, ensure safety in the setting, and demonstrate the reliability of the worker benefited the members as much as the attainment of their personal goals.

EVALUATION

To assess change in a group, the worker must evaluate both the group as a whole and the changes that occur within each group member. The worker will assess the changes in the group by offering feedback to the members as the group moves through various stages. For example, at the first meeting (the beginning/forming stage), after introductions, the group worker can ask questions such as "What brought you to the group?" "How was the injury incurred?" "How do you think the group can/will help you?" and "What goals do you have for yourself?" This will set the stage for participants to state their goals and receive feedback at subsequent meetings. The workers can monitor group participation by asking each participant to offer comments a prescribed number of times per session. Some measures of group participation plot the pattern of group communication by monitoring to whom one speaks. Another group measure involves assessing the roles each participant plays in the group, such as clown, hero, parent, rebel, peacekeeper, antagonist, and so on. As the group worker helps the participants realize their group roles, he or she can help members gain insights to share with their families, as well as their patterns of behavior in the group.

Several methods are available to measure how individuals evolve and improve the quality of their lives, such as behavioral reports, surveys, observations, record reviews, and self-reports. In a behavioral report, someone other than the patient/client completes the instrument measuring a change in the behavior being reviewed. Behavioral reports are used in counseling, speech, and occupational therapy, and may include behaviors such as communication, eye contact, body posture, and clarity of speech. A survey may measure attitudes, personality style, or other aspects of life by having the reporter or investigator complete a series of questions. Observational reports are often used by the social worker to determine progress at home, in the marriage or family, or at work. Items such as concentration level, ability to stay focused, and appropriate speech may be discussed. Record reviews are used most often by the professional staff, an interdisciplinary team that reads the nursing notes and progress notes in the patient's chart to see how the patient is progressing. Issues such as compliance, motivation, goal-directed behavior, and social and emotional growth are usually reviewed. Self-report scales allow patients to report how they view their own behaviors, thoughts, and feelings. Self-respect measures play an integral role in assessing the changes in the patient, particularly when contrasted to the other reports completed by the social worker, interdisciplinary team members, and family members.

In conclusion, it is essential for the group worker to provide a climate conducive to change. The worker must facilitate the change among the group members and assess the change in the quality of life in the group setting, in the natural environment, and within the patients as they become increasingly rehabilitated.

RESOURCES

Traumatic Brain injury; CNS—Centre for Neuro-Skills
Locations in California and Texas
(800) 922-4994
www.neuroskills.com
Offers outpatient, rehabilitation, residential and community services for TBI patients.
Offers manuals, newsletters, new research updates, and continuing education for caregivers and professionals.

National Resource Center for TBI
Virginia Commonwealth University's Medical College of Virginia
Box 98052
Richmond Virginia, VA 23298-0542
(804) 828-9055
www.neuro.pmr.vcu.edu/
Offers treatment, resource lists, new ideas, and services to TBI patients.
Offers training and conferences to caregivers and professionals.

Neuro-Recovery Head Injury Program
5123 North Royal Drive
Traverse City, MI 49684
(231) 935-0388
www.tbiguide.com
Offers literature on coping with common problems.

Traumatic Brain Injury National Data Center
TBI Model Systems
Kessler Medical Rehabilitation Research and Education Company
West Orange, NJ 07052
www.tbiindc.org
Additional locations in California, Alabama, Ohio, and Michigan
Offer services to TBI patients, coordinated neuro and rehab care, and produces innovative research.

Brain Injury Association of America
8201 Greensboro Drive, Suite 611
McLean, VA 22102
(703) 761-0750
www.biausa.org
Family Line: (800) 444-6443

Offers resources, research, publications, prevention and education, and government lobbying (congressional bills affecting TBI patients).

National Institute of Health—BRAIN
P.O. Box 5801
Bethesda, MD 20824
(800) 352-9424
www.ninds.nih.gov/health
Offers resources and information networks.

Brain Trauma Foundation
523 East 72nd Street-8th floor
New York, NY 10021
(212) 772-0608
www.brasintrauma.org
Offers support services to TBI patients.

NARIC—National Rehabilitation Information Center
1010 Wayne Ave.-Suite 800
Silver Spring, MD 20910-5633
(800) 346-2742
www.naric.com
Offers resources and publication to patients and their families.

REFERENCES

Aliev, Z. M. (1984). Characteristics of the clinical course of closed head injury in children. *Soviet Neurology and Psychiatry.* 17, 65–73.

Ashley, M., & Persel, C. (1999). Traumatic brain injury recovery rates in post acute rehabilitation: Spontaneous recovery or treatment? *Journal of Rehabilitation Outcomes Measurement.* 3(4), 15–21.

Ashley, M. J., Persel, C., & Clark, M. (2001). Validation of an independent living scale for post-acute rehabilitation application. *Brain Injury.* 15(5), 435–442.

Ashley, M. J., Persel, C. S., Lehr, R. P., Feldman, B., & Krych, D. K. (1994). Post-acute rehabilitation outcome: Relationship to case-management techniques and strategy. *Journal of Insurance and Medicine.* 26(3), 348–354.

Ashley, M., Schultz, J., Bryan, V., Krych, D., & Hays, D. (1997). Justification of postacute traumatic brain injury rehabilitation using net present value techniques: A case study. *Journal of Rehabilitation Outcomes Measurement.* 1(5), 33–41.

Bakay, L., & Glasauer, F. E. (1980). *Head injury.* Boston: Little, Brown.

Becker, D. P., Miller, J. D., & Ward, J. D. (1977). The outcome from severe head injury with early diagnosis and intensive management. *Journal of Neurosurgery.* 47, 491–502.

Brooks, D. N., & McKinlay, W. (1983). Personality and behavioral change after severe blunt head injury: A relative's view. *Journal of Neurology, Neurosurgery, and Psychiatry.* 46, 336–344.

Chadwick, O., Rutter, M., Brown, G., Chaffer, D., & Traub, M. (1981). *Psychological Medicine,* 11, 49–61.

DeBoskey, D. S. (ed.). (1996). Coming home: A discharge manual for families of persons with a brain injury. Houston, TX: HDI. (Telephone: (800) 321-7037. URL: www.braininjurybooks.com)

Depompei, R., & Cluett, B. (1998). *All about me!* Wolfeboro, NH: L&A Publishing/Training. (For use by elementary school children with TBI.)

Ephross, P. H., & Vassil, T. V. (1988). *Groups that work.* New York: Columbia University Press.

Epperson, M. M. (1977). Families in sudden crisis: Process and intervention in a critical care center. *Social Work in Health Care.* 2, 265–273.

Garvin, C. D. (1987). *Contemporary group work* (2nd ed.). Rahway, NJ: Prentice Hall.

Gerring, J. (1986). The diagnosis, treatment, and rehabilitation of severe closed head injury. Speech presented at the Johns Hopkins University School of Medicine, Baltimore, June 15.

Hartford, M. E. (1971). Groups in social work. New York: Columbia University Press.

Hill, J. (1984). Disorders of memory, language, and beliefs, following closed head injury. *Psychological Medicine.* 14, 193–201.

Kraus, J. F., Black, M. A., & Hessol, N. (1984). The incidence of acute brain injury and serious impairment in a defined population. *American Journal of Epidemiology.* 199, 186–201.

Little, A. J., Templer, D. I., Persel, C. S., & Ashley, M. J. (1996). Feasibility of the neuropsychological spectrum in prediction of outcome following head injury. *Journal of Clinical Psychology.* 52(4), 455–460.

Maryland Head Injury Foundation. (1985). *Maryland Head Injury Foundation Newsletter,* p. 1.

Maryland Head Injury Foundation. (1989). *Maryland Head Injury Foundation Newsletter,* p. 1.

Maryland Head Injury Foundation. (1990). *Maryland Head Injury Foundation Newsletter,* p. 1.

Persel, C. H., & Persel, C. S. (2001). Cornerstones of success: Principles to maximize recovery from brain injury. *Continuing Care.* 20(4), 21–23.

Prigatano, G., Fordyce, D., Zeiner, H., Roveche, J., Pepping, M., & Wood, B. (1984). Neuropsychological rehabilitation after closed head injury in young adults. *Journal of Neurology, Neurosurgery, and Psychiatry.* 47, 505–513.

Special Education Works, Vol. 7, No. 7, March 2001, p. 5.

Weddell, R., Oddy, M., & Jenkins, D. (1980). Social adjustment after rehabilitation: A two-year follow-up of patients with severe head injury. *Psychological Medicine.* 10, 257–263.

Yalom, I. (1995). *The theory and practice of group psychotherapy* (4th ed.). New York: Basic Books.

Chapter 5

Group Work in the Prevention of Adolescent Alcohol and Other Drug Abuse

ANDREW MALEKOFF

The problematic use of alcohol, drugs, and tobacco is unquestionably the nation's number one health problem. While all segments of society are affected, the future of young people is most severely compromised by this epidemic.

A recent study by the University of Michigan (Johnston et al, 2002) found that 54% of American young people in grades 8 through 12 have tried an illicit drug by graduation from high school. Sixty-one percent have tried cigarettes by twelfth grade and almost one-third of seniors are regular smokers. Alcohol use remains widespread, with 80% having consumed more than a few sips by the time they leave high school. Nevertheless, according to one research analyst (Males, 1999), prevalence rates for teenage alcohol and other drug abuse are at record low levels, and young people are in the greatest danger from their parents' addictions.

There are millions of children who grow up in homes with alcohol- and other drug-abusing parents (Hosang, 1995). It has been estimated that approximately one in four children in the United States is exposed to alcohol abuse and/or drug dependence in the family at some point before age 18 (Grant, 2000). These young people are likely to become alcohol or drug abusers themselves without intervention. Parental alcoholism and drug addiction influence adolescent alcohol and other drug use in several ways, including stress and decreased parental monitoring. Negative impaired parental monitoring contributes to adolescents' joining in a peer group that supports drug use. There is a need for an integrated service approach to enhance the lives of these children (Committee on Child Health Financing, 2001).

The pervasiveness of the problem extends well beyond the individual. Alcohol and drug abuse play a major role in "destroying families, crippling U.S. businesses, terrorizing entire neighborhoods, and choking the educational criminal justice and social service systems" (Brandeis University, 1993, summary p. 1). As social workers committed to youth, and to the families and communities in which they live, we cannot escape the need to address the problems of alcohol and drug abuse, regardless of the setting of our work. Where there are people, there is alcohol and drug abuse. Where there are youth, there are youth at risk. The purpose of this chapter is to highlight group work as a protective factor, a powerful preventive tool for youth who show early signs of alcohol and other drug abuse and who are at risk for alcoholism and drug addiction.

REVIEW OF THE LITERATURE

What differentiates people with negative outcomes from those who grow up in similar circumstances and bounce back from great adversity? This question has stimulated much speculation and a dramatic growth of the literature on vulnerability, resiliency and risk, and protective factors (Garmezy, 1991, Garmezy & Rutter, 1983; Glantz, 1995; Goleman, 1987; Landy & Tam, 1998; Rutter, 1979 & 1995; Sameroff, 1988; Schorr, 1989; Werner, 1989, 1990; Werner & Smith 2001; Werner et al., 1998). What differentiates youth who become alcohol and drug abusers from their contemporaries from similar backgrounds who do not? This questions illustrates the special concern of those interested in understanding the relationship between risk reduction strategies and substance abuse prevention (Bernard, 1991; Griffin et al., 2001; Hawkins, Catalano & Associates, 1992; Hawkins et al., 1992; Vega et al., 1993; Werner, 1986).

Risk factors include constitutional (i.e., physiological) deficits and contextual realities (i.e., the physical, cultural, social, political, and economic environments). Examples of risk factors for youth include a history of alcohol and drug abuse/addiction in the family; neighborhood disorganization; being a victim of child abuse; becoming pregnant; having a chronic history of school failure; being economically; disadvantaged; having attempted suicide; and associating with alcohol- and drug-abusing peers.

Protective factors are the individual's constitutional assets (i.e., intelligence, temperament) and family and environmental supports (i.e., a close, lifelong bond with an adult relative or mentor) that have the potential to reduce risk. Hawkins, Catalano, and Associates (1992) emphasize the importance of bonding as a key protective factor:

Antidrug attitudes are strengthened by promoting adolescents' bonds, including relationships with non-drug users, commitment to the various social groups in which they are involved (families, schools, community, prosocial peer groups), and values and beliefs regarding what is healthy and ethical behavior. (p. 27)

Some of the settings in which group approaches have been used to address and/or study the preventive needs of youth at risk include the school (Bilides, 1992; Brown, 1993; Hanson, 1992; Kantor et al., 1992; Perry, et al., 2002; St. Pierre et al., 2001; St. Pierre & Kaltreider, 2001; Shields, 1986; Sussman et al., 1997; Taylor et al., 1999), the public housing development (Schinke et al., 1992), the community mental health center (Malekoff, 1994a), the criminal justice system (Freidman & Utada, 1992; Smith, 1985), and street youth (Unger et al., 1998). Comprehensive approaches have been described by Hawkins et al. (1992) and by Felner, Silverman, and Adix (1991).

Beyond the physical setting of the service are the cultural context of substance abuse (Bachman, et al., 1991; Belgrave et al., 2000; Bilides, 1990; Catalano et al., 1992; De La Rosa & Andrados, 1993; Delgado, 1997; Forgey, 1994; Harachi et al., 2001; Hogue et al., 2002; Myers, 2002; Rich, 2001; Taylor, 2000; Vega et al., 1993; Wallace, 1993) and the family context (Black, 1979; Deckman & Downs, 1982; Efron, 1987; Emshoff, 1989; Gross & McCane, 1992; Johnson et al., 1998; Knight et al., 1992; Treadway, 1989).

A protective network of supports has the potential to increase the individual's resistance to risk, placing him or her in a better position to avoid alcohol and other drug problems. Group work can be an important part of constructing such a network.

PRACTICE PRINCIPLES

Beginning group work with at-risk adolescents requires careful planning, thoughtful programming, and attention to helping the group members to become a system of mutual aid. When combined, these principles set the tone for an experience that provides a sense of order and an opportunity for role flexibility, something often missing in the lives of youth at risk.

Planning

The planning model, as formulated by Kurland (1980, 1982) and further explicated by Northen and Kurland (2001) and Malekoff (1997), identifies seven variables necessary for the formation of successful groups. Careful preparation can make the difference between groups that thrive and groups that fail. The seven variables are:

Needs: What are the needs of prospective members?

Purpose: What are the tentative goals and objectives of the group?

Composition: Who are the potential members?

Structure: What concrete arrangements are necessary to proceed?

Content: What means will be used to enable the group to achieve its purpose?

Pregroup Contact: How will prospective members be recruited?

Agency and social context: What obstacles exist and how might they be overcome?

Good planning is invaluable when working with youth who live in disorganized families and or communities. Consistency, predictability, and structure elude them in their day-to-day lives. *A well planned group experience serves as a counterforce to living in a capricious environment.* What begins as a counterforce can become a protective factor, mitigating against risk and stimulating healthy development.

Programming

Redl and Wineman (1952) describe programming as "activities which require a certain amount of definite planning, on the part of the children themselves, of the adults, or both" (p. 76). Breton (1990) asserts that "the way we structure groups is all-important, for a group can be structured so that the whole person in each member is invited to participate, or it can be structured so that only the troubled, or broken, or hurt parts of the person [are] invited to participate" (p. 27).

Programming is the activity that the group does to achieve its purpose. How programming is determined and implemented can make the difference between a group in which members' strengths are supported (Malekoff, 2001) and one in which deficits (i.e., pathology) are highlighted. In the case of adolescents at risk, it is important for the social worker to structure the group to invite the whole person, to blend discussion and activity with an eye toward promoting competency (Malekoff, 1997).

Mutual Aid

A critical question for all social workers working with groups is "Am I the central helping person here or do I enable others to help one another?" The latter stance, "the valuation of members as helper" (Middleman & Wood, 1990, p. 11) distinguishes social work with groups from other group treatments (with the notable exception of self-help groups, such as Alcoholics Anonymous and Alanon, which are leaderless mutual aid groups). The practice of promoting mutual aid implies faith in the group and its potential to function autonomously. Furthermore, it suggests the social worker's commitment to "learn not only *about* but *from* group members" (Breton, 1990, p. 23). Attention to planning, programming, and mutual aid can lead to the creation of a healthy group environment in which trust is established, various roles are practiced in safety, and reliance on self is broadened to include reliance on others. To structure the group "to invite the whole person," the social worker must have a good understanding of normal adolescent development, the adolescent in the group, the social worker in the group, and the group in context. The following practice principles will address these issues.

1. *Alliance formation with parents and other involved persons and systems is a prerequisite to establishing an engaged group membership* (Malekoff, 1997).

Adolescents cannot be seen in a vacuum. Sanction from parents and cooperation with related systems (e.g., school) are necessary for ongoing work with the group. By establishing working alliances with these significant others, the social worker models collaboration and establishes the groundwork for mediating with the various systems. Working relationships with parents help to reduce the guilt that children often feel about betraying the family. Working relationships with all involved persons and systems help to reduce the possibility that dysfunctional interactions will be extended to the helping system.

In the Youth of Culture Drug Free Club, an after-school program for youth at risk located in Long Island, New York (Malekoff, 1994a; Walthrust, 1992), a well-planned and organized dance for local youth was marred by a post-dance fight in which a youngster was slashed with a razor. The staff team worked closely with parents in the aftermath of the incident. This collaboration, in light of a chaotic and potentially tragic situation, enabled the group members to work through the crisis in a thoughtful manner despite their fear that the club might be terminated.

2. *An appreciation for paradox and an ability to differentiate the words from the music is essential to working with adolescents in groups* (Malekoff, 1994b).

Just below the surface of the strident facade or apathetic veneer that many adolescents project are the deeper meanings that not many adults are privileged to discover. Often the familiar refrain "Leave me alone!" carefully conceals the cry for help. It's not always easy to hang around to hear the music underneath the static of the words. Yet to work with adolescents, one must hang in there. Too many adults have already bailed out.

3. *Cultural awareness and sensitivity are essential for practicing social work with groups in a society of ever-increasing diversity.*

Social workers must be aware of racism, sexism, and homophobia, as well as other cultural issues and values, as well as how they impact on group members and how they have affected their own lives. Bilides

(1990) suggests some guidelines for putting one's multi-cultural awareness into practice with groups. These include the following: "discuss stereotypes at all levels (personal, familial and societal) . . . point out commonalities . . . explore the meanings of words and language . . . recognize and acknowledge your own discomfort about race, color, ethnicity, and class issues" (pp. 51–56).

The Youth of Culture Drug Free Club reflects some of the values suggested above in their choice of club name. A predominantly African-American group, they planned and presented a communitywide "international cultural day" in which they modeled traditional clothing from various cultures. This was a step in the direction of opening the club to members of other groups, including growing immigrant populations from Central America and Haiti.

4. *Use the self and access to childhood memories.*

Awareness of what the group experience evokes in oneself is invaluable, especially with a population in motion. This includes conscious memories of the social worker's earlier years and struggles during adolescence (e.g., personal and/or familial experiences with alcohol and drugs). The feelings that inevitably bubble up in the lively context of the adolescent group must not be ignored. Feelings and experiences can be disclosed at times, using good judgment. For example, the purpose of disclosure should never be to gain the acceptance of the group or to tacitly encourage acting-out behavior for a vicarious thrill. This is where good supervision enters the picture.

5. *Don't go it alone.*

Social workers working with at-risk adolescents in groups need support from colleagues. Too many adults (professional or otherwise) disapprove of the group modality when adolescents are involved. They question the efficacy of the work when confronted with the noise, action, and attitudes that seem absent in the adult group. Colleagues with a track record and an inclination to work with youth can be invaluable partners. This includes good supervision from peers or adults and opportunities for teamwork. Coleadership of groups is an approach that requires adequate time for planning and reflection. Too many human services workers without adequate group training operate under the false assumption that coleadership is better, easier, or less stressful than one-person leadership. Maybe it is, but this depends entirely on the match and on the commitment and honesty that develop in the partnership. Simply throwing workers together to lead groups is to be avoided at all costs.

COMMON THEMES

Groups may be formed specifically for children living in families with a present or past history of alcohol or drug abuse. Other groups may be composed of youth who evidence a variety of related risk factors. Substance abuse prevalence rates (and practice experience) suggest that in either case the social workers must have knowledge of the impact of alcohol and drug abuse (including alcoholism and addiction) on the individual in the family.

What are the implications of growing up in a dysfunctional family? How might these issues influence the individual in the group? How might they affect the group as a whole? (Although the attention there is to substance abuse, these questions may also apply to families in which there is child abuse, domestic violence, or severe mental illness.) The following six themes will address these questions.

1. *Children who grow up in families with alcohol and drug abuse/addiction learn to distrust to survive.*

Attention to the beginning phase of group development is critical in building trust. By exercising anticipatory empathy, the social worker tunes into the experience of the group members, taking an important step in helping to build a safe environment for mutual exchange. At the beginning the social worker allows and supports distance, searches for common ground, invites trust gently, establishes group purpose, facilitates exploration, begins to set norms, and provides program structure (Garland et al., 1965; Malekoff, 1997).

2. *Children growing up in alcohol- or drug-abusing/addicted families become uncomfortably accustomed to living with chaos, uncertainty, unpredictability, and inconsistency.*

It has been said that children growing up under these conditions have to "guess at what normal is." The group experience must provide a clear structure with norms and reasonable limits. Issues of membership (Is it an open or closed group? If it is open, how do new members enter? How do members exit?), space (Is there a consistent meeting place?), and time (Does the group meet at a regular time for a prescribed period?) are all important considerations. Group rituals might be considered to reinforce a sense of order and to establish value-based traditions. For example, in the Youth of Culture Drug Free Club referred to earlier, the members all recite a drug-free pledge at the beginning and end of each meeting.

3. *Denial, secrecy, embarrassment, and shame are common experiences of children who live in alcoholic or addicted families.*

Joining a group of outsiders might in itself be felt as an act of betrayal, a step toward revealing the "family secret." Awareness at this juncture allows the social worker to invite trust gently while paying careful attention to questions of trust and confidentiality throughout the life of the group.

4. *Growing up with the ever-present threat of violence (verbal and physical) contributes to a pervasive sense of fearfulness, hypervigilance, and despair.*

The group can become a place where differences can be safely expressed and where conflicts need not be a matter of life and death. Conflicts can be resolved and differences respected in a thoughtful and increasingly mature manner in the group. The group is a place where members can practice putting a reflective pause between impulse and action and where despair can be transformed into hope.

In response to another violent incident, an interracial murder in the community, the Youth of Culture Drug Free Club organized the largest youth contingent in a March for Unity. Again they acted to replace despair with hope, and an anticipated riot was averted.

5. *Children, who grow up in alcohol- and drug-abusing/addicted families become rigidly attached to roles.*

Many of those growing up in alcohol- and drug-abusing/addicted systems construct a wall of defenses and repressed feelings by adopting rigid family roles (Wegscheider, 1981, pp. 86–149). Accompanying these roles are stultifying family rules, unspoken mandates, such as *don't talk, don't trust, don't feel.* A group experience can provide members accustomed to assuming rigid roles with an opportunity to practice role flexibility, broaden their intra- and interpersonal repertoires, and gain competence in coping with the environment.

In the Youth of Culture Drug Free Club, the members planned a holiday party for themselves and organized a trip to a local nursing home, offering gifts and spending time with an isolated population of AIDS patients. Both activities, the party and the visit, required careful preparation, enabling the members to assume diverse roles and to work in partnership to accomplish the group's goals.

6. *Growing up in an alcoholic or addicted family system leaves youths with little hope that things will ever change.*

The group is a social system that develops a life of its own, marked by a developing history of events and relationships. As in any system, there are decisions to be made, problems to solve, and crises to surmount. If a dysfunctional family system is the primary frame of reference for a young person, he or she may have little experience in successfully resolving conflicts or overcoming obstacles. The group can provide members with a growing sense of confidence that difficult and frustrating circumstances can be overcome. The group worker must be tuned in to the sense of hopelessness that such members bring to the group so as not to become easily discouraged. It cannot be emphasized strongly enough that group work with this population requires hanging in for the long haul and modeling a sense of hope.

One of the activities of the Youth of Culture Drug Free Club is wilderness outings (hiking, canoeing, camping), providing members with multiple obstacles (frustration, fatigue, fear) to confront and overcome. The members learn quickly that surviving in the wilderness requires more than self-sufficiency. They must come to trust and rely on one another to navigate a current or climb a mountain, powerful metaphors for what they face daily. With each trip they experience change as they stretch their limits together, and with each successful journey they increase their appreciation of themselves and their fellow group members. In time the group itself becomes a valuable frame of reference.

RECOMMENDED WAYS OF WORKING

The agency context of the service being offered is a key determinant of the success or failure of the endeavor. In other words, do the values of the agency lead to policies and practices that allow the group to work toward its purpose in a hospitable environment? The answer to this question becomes obvious when arrangements for staffing, space, time, and materials are negotiated. To work effectively with at-risk adolescents, the host agency must sanction the activity in word and deed. The social worker's responsibility is to see to it that the work of the group reflects the stake that the agency and group members have in one another. It is not enough to be available to work with a group. Good planning and sound social work practice often require mediation and advocacy.

The Place of North Shore Child and Family Guidance Center is an alcohol and drug treatment and prevention program for youth and their families. Located in a low-income minority community in Nassau County, New York, The Place's clientele and staff represent a multicultural mix that reflects a growing number of suburban communities. The services of The Place include an intensive after-school program that is a comprehensive blend of group, family, and individually oriented activities. The group program includes services for adults, children, and adolescents; alcoholics and drug addicts; nonaddicted substance abusers; and at-risk, non-substance-abusing significant others (youths and adults).

Some adolescents are seen as referred clients who are admitted to the program following a formal evaluation and case disposition. Others are seen in a variety of after-school programs that do not require a formal clinical evaluation. The Youth of Culture Drug Free Club is an example of the latter. Many adolescents participate in both programs as clients and as community members.

In her landmark work on "breaking the cycle of disadvantage," Schorr (1989) asserts that "most successful programs find that interventions cannot be routinized or applied uniformly. Staff members and program structures are fundamentally *flexible* and *see the child in the context of family and the family in the context of its surroundings*" (p. 257).

Groups at The Place vary in composition, length, and purpose. Content includes psychoeducation, socialization, discussion, counseling, therapy, outings, arts and crafts, cultural awareness activities, and community service. Staff members work in teams. This enables program participants to become engaged with the agency as well as with an individual social worker or counselor. Regularly scheduled team meetings are held for the purposes of case assignment and management, program development, supervision, and skill development.

Family involvement is an important value at The Place. All incoming families with adolescents are assigned to an 8-week multiple-family group program. There are generally four to seven families per group, ranging from 8 to 20+ people. The group's purposes include helping families with drug and alcohol problems to learn from one another, to decrease isolation, and to address the shame that children carry as a secret. These issues are addressed in the service of prevention. The content includes a combination of alcohol and drug education, discussion, role play, and psychodrama. The first two sessions are structured to allow time for the adults and youth to meet briefly in separate groups to identify needs and make connections. The groups are co-led by two or three social workers. The number of workers is determined by group size and by the presence of younger (school-age) children. When the group divides, one of the three workers meets with the children. The different age groups tend to ally, early on, with different workers, who are tuned in to the importance of modeling collaboration as differences arise. The cultural diversity of the staff enriches this process as group members see people of different racial and ethnic backgrounds working together with mutual respect.

The fifth session of one multiple-family group series began with a staff presentation of normal development in the latency and adolescent periods and its relationship to the family life cycle. (Psychoeducation on normal development is of great value for families in which the members have grown accustomed to uncertainty and consequently must guess at what normal is. In the group this process serves to provide support, encourage dialogue, and reduce isolation. When the theme of separation was presented, one of the group members, a Hispanic mother who understands and speaks English but prefers Spanish, addressed the bilingual worker:

> If I may I want to respond to something that the other workers said about separation. In my country [Colombia], it is different. The kids are expected to stay with their families until they marry. If they go to college they stay home. This [discussion] is a problem for us [motioning to her husband, a practicing alcoholic] and upsetting that the children are encouraged to leave.

Once this statement was translated, a lively discussion ensued as the group, consisting of four families of various cultural origins (Columbian, African, Yugoslavian, and Italian), exchanged their feelings about separation. At one point the Hispanic mother's 17-year-old son, who was referred to The Place following a single incident of binge drinking, spoke:

> "I didn't know this." He spoke in short, choppy sentences and was encouraged to elaborate. "Well, now that I know [what she thinks], I'll think about looking into colleges close to home, but I'm not staying there until I got married." Everyone laughed, including the boy's parents. One of the social workers summed up, turning to the boy. "It sounds like you're willing to negotiate with your parents." He acknowledged her comment with a smile.

In this interchange the group was warming up to the meeting, testing the waters, and reestablishing trust. (Remember that distrust is more often than not the norm in these families.) An emotionally charged issue surfaced. Differences along cultural and generational lines were drawn. Respect for differences was modeled by the social worker, who encouraged discussion. Four different cultural groups (one bilingual), four sets of parents (and one grandparent), and four sets of adolescents produced no dire consequences.

All of the adolescents had abused alcohol and/or had tried other drugs on at least one occasion. In all four families the fathers, only one of whom was present, were alcoholic or drug addicted. As is often the case, the adolescents and their presenting problems were the key to getting help. As the session proceeded, separation issues gave way to issues of limits, boundaries, and private space. The adolescents and parents began to draw battle lines as parents revealed their suspicions.

> The group was now heated as the adolescents referred to their parents as "nuts," "stupid," "crazy," and "ridiculous." A 14-year-old girl who had verbally assaulted her mother last week took the offensive again. When one of the social workers reminded her of the rule of not attacking and allowing others to finish speaking, she smiled and said, "Okay, okay." The social workers then asked what a parent should do if she suspects that her child is using drugs? The parents discussed various issues, including the circumstances under which they would search their children's rooms. The mother of the 14-year-old girl then said, somewhat defensively, "People don't know what they would do until it really affects them. I never thought I'd be going through my daughter's room, but I had a feeling and it was right. It was a good thing I followed my instinct because now I can get help." Then for the first time in five meetings, the Hispanic mother spoke in English and directly to the other mother. She exclaimed, "You did right! You did the right thing and I would too, to help my child." This was a moving moment in which a mother who was struggling with an aggressive 14-year-old who abused her in the group setting was supported by others in the presence of her daughter. Returning to Spanish, the Hispanic mother made an impassioned request of the worker: "Please tell her [the girl] if she didn't love her she wouldn't have done this. It is an act of caring, and her daughter is so aggressive. "When this was translated, the 14-year-old girl asked:

"What's 'aggressive' mean?" It was described as "hostile." By this time, the group was becoming very intense as the adolescents were beginning to bond in anger against the parents. As angry glances were exchanged across the generational dividing line, one social worker acknowledged the feeling and suggested an activity to promote empathy. Addressing the 14-year-old but speaking to the group, she explained what a role reversal is and said, "I find it helpful to try this when parents and children are in conflict." She then asked the 14-year-old to "put yourself in your mother's shoes. If you thought your child was in danger, that she might have weapons or drugs in her room, would you search it?" The girl became pensive and clearly thought deeply about this, as did the others, judging from their facial expressions and body language. She finally responded, "Yes, I think I would." It was with this reflection, as the other soaked in her response, that the group moved to an ending. One social worker concluded with a brief restatement of the rules regarding confidentially and repeated that there would be no consequences for what was shared in the group. The 14-year-old girl seemed more relieved than offended by the definition of her behaviour as aggressive and hostile. A limit was being set that perhaps she had been seeking all along.

The illustration of the multiple-family group can be considered in light of the specific group process described or from a metaphorical perspective. In the latter case, the reader might consider the ways in which the family can be brought into the group when it is not part of the group. In either instance, what is clear is that the establishment of trust over time and in each session is essential. While this is true for any group, it is particularly so when distrust becomes the norm for the individual struggling with personal and/or familial substance abuse/addiction. In such families, feelings are often not valued or tolerated, and poor identification and labeling of feelings is a consequence of having little or no practice. The group provides an opportunity to practice these skills with the knowledge that no one will be physically or emotionally destroyed by violent or impulsive acts.

Group work provides people with places in which diversity is tolerated, difference is understood and respected, problems are universalized, and people depend upon one another and not only on the experts. To the extent that this occurs, group work becomes a protective factor in the lives of adolescents at risk.

EVALUATION

According to Muraskin (1993), evaluation for drug and alcohol prevention and treatment programs can be conducted for the following purposes:

To determine the effectiveness of programs for the participants;

To document that program objectives have been met;

To provide information about service delivery that will be useful to program staff and other audiences; and

To enable program staff to make changes that improve program effectiveness.

Categories of outcome measurement for individuals may include the following variables: use of alcohol and drugs, knowledge of alcohol and drugs, attitudes regarding the use of alcohol and drugs, ability to refuse using alcohol and drugs in the face of peer pressure, self-esteem, and a sense of hope. Pre- and posttests can be given to determine changes in attitude and habits. Surveys can be developed for this purpose (see Muraskin, 1993, for several examples). In the case of drug and alcohol use, many programs (e.g., in treatment-oriented and criminal justice settings) use the breathalizer and urine analysis to test for use. Changes in risk and protective status and in level of functioning over time are also variables that can be used to assess change.

Observations of the group members over time, reports from parents and school personnel, and monitoring of academic, social, and extracurricular progress are all important in the process of evaluation. Not to be underestimated is the self-evaluation of the individual, members' evaluations of one another, and the group's evaluation of itself, a standard part of the ending phase of group work.

According to Dryfoos (1993), "prevention programs seem to work best when they address the total life of the young person and focus on the factors that place him or her at risk" (p. 3). In this era of categorical funding for human services, it is not always easy to provide comprehensive services; therefore, collaboration between the various systems that serve youth is essential.

RESOURCES

Al-Anon Family Groups
World Service Office
P.O. Box 862
Midtown Station
New York, NY 10018
(800) 344-2666
www.al-anon.org

Alcoholics Anonymous (AA)
World Service, Inc.
475 Riverside Drive
11th Floor
New York, NY 10115
(212) 870-3400
www.alcoholics-anonymous.org

Institute on Black Chemical
  Abuse/African American Family
  Services
2616 Nicollet Ave. South
Minneapolis, MN 55498
(612) 871-7878
www.aafs.net

Join Together
441 Stuart Ave., 6th Floor
Boston, MA 02116
(617) 437-1500
www.jointogether.org

Nar-Anon Family Group
P.O. Box 2562

Palos Verdes Peninsula,
CA 90274-0019
(310) 547-5800
www.onlinerecovery.org

Narcotics Anonymous (NA)
P.O. Box 9999
Van Nuys, CA 91409
(818) 773-9999
www.na.org

National Association for Children of
   Alcoholics (NACOA)
11426 Rockville Pike, #100
Rockville, MD 20852
(301) 468-0985
www.nacoa.org

National Black Alcoholism and
   Addiction Council
1629 K St. NW. Ste. 450
Washington, DC 20006
(202) 296-2696
www.nbacinc.org

Center for Substance Abuse
   Prevention (CSAP)
www.samhsa.gov/csap
(301) 443-0365

National Clearinghouse for Alcohol
   and Drug Information (NCADI)
P.O. Box 2345
Rockville, MD 20847-2345
(800)-729-6678
www.health.org

National Council on Alcoholism and
   Drug Dependence, Inc.
20 Exchange Place Ste. 2902
New York, NY 10005
(212) 269-7797 or (800) NCA-CALL
www.ncadd.org

National Institute on Drug Abuse Drug
   Abuse Information and Treatment
   Referral Hotline
(800) 662-HELP
www.drughelp.org

Evaluation Resources
1552 University, Ave.
Madison, WI 53726
www.uhs.wisc.edu/wch/WCHDOT/
   Evaluation/reference.htm

Basic Guide to Program Evaluation by
   Carter McNamara
www.mpnp.org/library/evaluation/
   fnl_eval.htm

REFERENCES

Bachman, J. G., Wallace, J. M., Jr., Kurth, C. L., Johnston, L. D., & O'Malley, P. M. (1991). *Drug use among black, white, Hispanic, Native American and Asian American high school seniors* (1976–1989): *Prevalence, trends and correlates* (pp. 1–63). Ann Arbor: Institute for Social Research, University of Michigan.

Belgrave, E., Van Oss Marin, B., & Chambers, D. (2000). Cultural, contextual and intrapersonal predictors of risky sexual attitudes among urban African American girls in early adolescence. *Cultural diversity and ethnic minority psychology.* 6(3), 309–322.

Bernard, B. (1991). *Fostering resiliency in kids: Protective factors in the family, school and community* (pp. 1–27). Portland, OR: Northwest Regional Training Laboratories.

Bilides, D. (1990). Race, color, ethnicity and class in school-based adolescent counseling groups. *Social Work with Groups.* 13(4), 43–58.

Bilides, D. (1992). Reaching inner city children: A group work program model for a public middle school. *Social Work with Groups.* 15(2/3), 129–144.

Black, C. (1979) Children of alcoholics. *Alcohol, Health and Research World.* 1(1), 23–27.

Brandeis University, Institute for Health Policy (1993). *Substance abuse: The nation's number one health problem; key indicators for policy.* Princeton, NJ: Robert Wood Johnson Foundation.

Breton, M. (1990). Learning from social group work traditions. *Social Work with Groups.* 13(1), 21–34.

Brown, M. E. (1993). *Successful components of community and school prevention programs.* National Prevention Evaluation Research Collection, 1(1), 3–5.

Catalano, R. F., Morrison, D. M., Wells, E. A., Gillmore, M. R., Iritani, B., & Hawkins, D. J. (1992). Ethnic differences in family factors related to early drug initiation. *Journal of Studies on Alcohol.* 55(3), 208–217.

Committee on Child Health Financing (2001). Improving substance abuse prevention, assessment, and treatment financing for children and adolescents. *Pediatrics.* 108, 1025–1029.

Deckman, J., & Downs, D. (1982). A group treatment approach for adolescent children of alcoholic parents. *Social Work with Groups.* 5(1), 73–77.

De La Rosa, M. R., & Adrados, J. (1993). *Drug abuse among minority youth; advances in research and methodology.* NIDA Research Monograph 130. Washington, DC: U.S. Department of Health and Human Services.

Delgado, M. (1997). Strengths-based practice with Puerto Rican adolescents: Lessons from a substance abuse prevention project. *Social Work in Education.* 19(2), 101–112.

Dryfoos, J. (1993). Lessons from evaluation of prevention programs. *National Prevention Evaluation Research Collection.* 1(1), 2–4.

Erfon, D. (1987). Videotaping groups for children of substance abusers: A strategy for emotionally disturbed acting out children. *Alcoholism Treatment Quarterly.* 4(2), 71–85.

Emshoff, J. G. (1989). A preventive intervention with children of alcoholics. *Prevention in Human Services.* 17(1), 225–253.

Felner, R. D., Silverman, M. M., & Adix, R. (1991). Prevention of substance abuse and related disorders in childhood and adolescence: A developmental based, comprehensive ecological approach. *Family and Community Health.* 14(3), 12–22.

Friedman, A. S., & Utada, A. T. (1992). Effects of two group interaction models on substance using adjudicated adolescent males. *Journal of Community Psychology.* (Special issue: Programs for Change, Office of Substance Abuse Prevention), 106–117.

Garland, J., Jones, H., & Kolodny, R. (1965). A model for stages of development in social work with groups. In S. Bernstein (ed.), *Explorations in group work: Essays in theory and practice* (pp. 21–30). Boston: Boston University School of Social Work.

Garmezy, N. (1991). Resiliency and vulnerability to adverse development outcomes associated with poverty. *American Behavioral Scientist.* 34(4), 416–430.

Garmezy, N., & Rutter, M. (1983). *Stress, coping and development in children.* New York: McGraw-Hill.

Glantz, M. (1995). *The application of resiliency and risk research to the development of preventive interventions.* Bethsda, MD: National Institute on Drug Abuse.

Goleman, D. (1987, October 13). Thriving despite hardship: Key childhood traits identified. *New York Times,* pp. C1, C11.

Griffin, K., Scheier, L., Botvin, G., & Diaz, T. (2001) Protective role of personal competence skills in adolescent substance use: Psychological well being as a mediating factor. *Psychology of additive behaviors.* 15(3), 194–203.

Gross, J., & McCane, M. (1992). An evaluation of a psychoeducational and substance abuse risk reduction intervention for children of substance abusers. *Journal of Community Psychology* (OSAP Special Issue). 75–87.

Grant, B. F. (2000). Estimates of U.S. children exposed to alcohol abuse and dependence in the family. *American Journal of Public Health.* 90(1), 112–115.

Hansen, W. B. (1992). School based substance abuse prevention: A review of the state of the art in curriculum, 1980–1990. *Health and Education Research: Theory and Practice.* 7(3), 403–430.

Harachi, T., Catalano, R., Kim, S., & Choi, Y. (2001). Etiology and prevention of substance use among Asian American youth. *Prevention science.* 2(1), 57–65.

Hawkins, J. D., Catalano, R. F., Jr., and Associates (1992). *Communities that care: Action for drug abuse prevention.* San Francisco: Jossey-Bass.

Hawkins, D., Catalano, R., & Miller, J. (1992). Risk and protective factors for alcohol and other drug problems in adolescence and early adulthood: Implications for substance abuse prevention. *Psychological Bulletin.* 112(1), 64–105.

Hogue, A., Liddle, H., Becker, D., & Johnson-Leckrone, J. (2002). Family-based prevention counseling for high risk young adolescents: Immediate outcomes. *Journal of Community Psychology.* 30(1), 1–22.

Hosang, M. (1995). Group work with children of substance abusers: Beyond the basics. In M. Feit, J. Ramey, J. Wodarski, & A. Mann (eds.), *Capturing the power of diversity* (pp. 109–114). New York: Haworth.

Johnson, K., Bryant, D., Collins, D., Noe, T., Strader, T., Berbaum, M. (1998). Preventing and reducing alcohol and other drug use among high-risk youths by increasing family resilience. *Social Work.* 43(4), 297–308.

Johnston, L. D., O'Malley, P. M., & Bachman, J. G. (2002). *Monitoring the future: National results on adolescent drug use.* Bethesda, MD: National Institute on Drug Abuse.

Kantor, G., Candill, B., & Ungerleider, S. (1992). Project impact: Teaching the teachers to intervene in student substance abuse problems. *Journal of Alcohol and Drug Education.* 38(1), 11–29.

Knight, A., Vail-Smith, K., & Barnes, A. (1992). Children of alcoholics in the classroom: A survey of teacher perceptions and training needs. *Journal of School of Health.* 62(8), 367–371.

Kurland, R. (1980). Planning—the neglected component of group development. *Social Work with Groups.* 1(2), 173–178.

Kurland, R. (1982). *Group formation: A guide to the development of successful groups.* Albany, NY: Continuing Education Program, School of Social Welfare, State University of New York at Albany and United Neighborhood Centers of America.

Landy, S., and Tam, K. K. (1998). *Understanding the contribution of multiple risk factors on child development at various ages.* Quebec, Canada: Hull: Applied Research Branch, Strategic Policy, Human Resources Development.

Malekoff, A. (1994a). Action research: An approach to preventing substance abuse and promoting social competency. *Health and Social Work.* 19(1), 46–53.

Malekoff, A. (1994b). A guideline for group work with adolescents. *Social Work with Groups.* 17(1/2), 5–19.

Malekoff, A. (1997). *Group work with adolescents: Principles and practice.* New York: Guilford.

Malekoff, A. (2001). The power of group work with kids: A practitioner's reflection on strength-based practice. *Families in Society.* 82(3), 243–249.

Males, M. A. (1999). *Framing Youth: 10 myths about the next generation.* Monroe, MN: Common Courage Press.

Middleman, R., & Wood, G. G. (1990). From social group work to social work with groups. *Social Work with Groups.* 13(1), 3–20.

Muraskin, L. D. (1993). *Understanding evaluation: The way to better prevention programs.* Washington, DC: U.S. Department of Education.

Myers, P. (2002). Pain, poverty, and hope. *Journal of Ethnicity in Substance Abuse.* 1(1), 1–5.

Northen, H., & Kurland, R. (2001). *Social Work with Groups (3rd ed.).* New York: Columbia University Press.

Perry, C., Williams, C. L., Komro, K., Veblen-Mortenson, S., Stigler, M., Munson, K., Farbakhsh, K., Jones, R. M., & Forster, J. (2002). Project Northland: Long-term outcomes of community action to reduce adolescent alcohol use. *Health Education Research.* 17(1), 117–132.

Prothrow-Stith, D., & Weissman, M. (1991). *Deadly consequences.* New York: Harper Collins.

Redl, F., & Wineman, D. (1952). *Controls from within: Techniques for the treatment of the aggressive child.* New York: Free Press.

Rich, J. A. (2001). Primary care for young African American men. *Journal of American College Health.* 49(4), 183–186.

Rutter, M. (1979). Protective factors in children's responses to stress and disadvantage. In M. W. Kent & J. E. Rolf (eds.), *Primary prevention psychology: Social competence in children* (Vol. 3). Hanover, NH: University Press of New England.

Rutter, M. (1984, March). Resilient children. *Psychology Today.* 57–65.

Rutter, M. (ed.) (1995). *Psychosocial disturbances in young people: Challenges for prevention.* New York: Cambridge University Press.

Sameroff, A. (1988, June). *The concept of the environtype: Integrating risk and protective factors in early development.* Keynote address for North Shore Child and Family Guidance Center Conferences, Garden City, NY.

Schinke, S. P., Orlandi, M. A., & Cole, K. C. (1992). Boys' and girls' clubs in public housing developments: Prevention services for youth at risk. *Journal of Community Psychology* (OASP Special Issue). 118–128.

Schorr, L. B. (1989). *Within our reach: Breaking the cycle of disadvantage.* New York: Doubleday.

Shields, S. (1986). Busted and branded: Group work with substance abusing adolescents in schools. *Social Work with Groups.* 8(4), 61–81.

Smith, T. E. (1985). Group work with adolescent drug abusers. *Social work with Groups.* 8(1), 55–64.

St. Pierre, T., Mark, M., Kaltreider, D., & Campbell, B. (2001). Boys' and girls' clubs and school collaborations: A longitudinal study of a multicomponent substance abuse prevention program for high-risk elementary school children. *Journal of Community Psychology.* 29(2), 87–106.

St. Pierre, T., & Kaltreider, D. (2001). Reflections on implementing a community agency–school prevention program. *Journal of Community Psychology.* 29(2), 107–116.

Taylor, A. S., LoSciuto, L., Fox, M., Hilbert, S., & Sonkowsky, M. (1999). The mentoring factor: Evaluation of the across ages' intergenerational approach to drug abuse prevention. *Child and Youth Services.* 20(1/2), 77–99.

Taylor, M. (2000). The influence of self efficacy on alcohol use among American Indians. *Cultural Diversity and Ethnic Minority Psychology.* 6(2), 152–167.

Treadway, D. C. (1989). *Before it's too late: Working with substance abuse in the family.* New York: W. W. Norton.

Unger, J., Simon, T., Newman, T., Montgomery, S., Kipke, M., & Albornoz, M. (1998). Early adolescent street youth: An overlooked population with unique problems and service needs. *The Journal of Early Adolescence.* 18(4), 325–348.

Vega, W. A., Zimmerman, R. S., Warheit, G. J., Apospori, E., & Gil, A. C. (1993). *Risk factors for early adolescent drug use in four ethnic and racial groups. American Journal of Public Health.* 83(2), 185–189.

Wallace, B. C. (1993). Cross-cultural counseling with the chemically dependent: Preparing for service delivery within a culture of violence. *Journal of Psychoactive Drugs.* 25(1), 9–20.

Wegscheider, S. (1981). *Another chance: Hope and health for alcoholic family.* Palo Alto, CA: Science and Behavior Books.

Werner, E. (1986). Resilient offspring of alcoholics: A longitudinal study from birth to age 18. *Journal of Studies on Alcohol.* 44(1), 34–44.

Werner, E. (1989). High-risk children in young adulthood: A longitudinal study from birth to 32 years. *American Journal of Orthopsychiatry.* 59, 72–81.

Werner, E. (1990). Protective factors and individual resilience. In S. Meisels & J. Shonkoff (eds.), *Handbook of early childhood intervention* (pp. 97–116). New York: Cambridge University Press.

Werner, E., Smith, R. S., & Garmezy, N. (1998). *Vulnerable but invincible: A longitudinal study of resilient children and youth.* New York: Adams, Bannaster, Cox Publishers.

Werner, E. & Smith, R. S. (2001). *Journeys from childhood to midlife: Risk, resiliency and recovery.* Ithica, NY: Cornell University Press.

Chapter 6

Common Themes for Parents in a Methadone Maintenance Group

GEOFFREY L. GREIF

People with an addiction to heroin who enter methadone maintenance are often dealing not only with their addiction but also with their role as parents. Although treatment initially must focus on drug-related behavior, other issues may be raised once the patient has been stabilized. Otherwise, the continual stress that so often accompanies an addicted person's life may make maintenance and recovery doubtful. Parents who enter methadone maintenance often have realistic concerns about their children. A parents' group provides an opportunity to address these concerns. In addition, it affords them the chance to redefine themselves not as being drug addicted but rather as parents with drug problems who are getting help for their children. Such a redefinition can provide the basis for a healthier self-concept. This chapter describes some of the issues in working with a parents' group in a methadone maintenance program.

REVIEW OF THE LITERATURE

Perhaps one of the most controversial drug abuse treatment approaches, methadone maintenance has attracted increased interest during the last 20 years with the spread of AIDS. Methadone maintenance offers the chance for people who share needles to cease their high-risk disease-spreading behavior. The benefits can go further. Effective methadone maintenance programs have also been found to curb drug abuse, reduce criminal activity, mortality, and have potentially positive benefits for the members of the addicted person's family (Centers for Disease Control, 2002).

When methadone is dispensed, it is coupled with some form of psychotherapy in most programs. Research on psychotherapy approaches has long shown the potentially beneficial effects of limit setting in structured treatment (McCarthy & Borders, 1985), cognitive-behavioral therapy (Weiner & Fox, 1982), and contracting (Magura et al., 1987) in either reducing drug abuse or facilitating other useful behaviors. Active case management after discharge holds the potential for cementing gains made in treatment (Coviello, et al., 2002).

Despite some evidence of effective treatment, the children of addicts are often at risk for a variety of physical and emotional problems, particularly if they were conceived while the mother was on heroin or methadone (Sinha et al., 2001). These problems can begin prenatally, as the addicted mother is likely to neglect her health. Obstetrical complications are frequent. At birth, these children's head circumferences are smaller and their birth weights are lower. Encephalopathy and seizures have also been noted (Kelly et al., 2000). The neonate's withdrawal from methadone or heroin may continue for months.

A range of symptoms may be present in the newborn. Marcus, Hans, and Jeremy (1984) found that very young children of methadone-maintained mothers exhibited poorer motor coordination and shorter attention spans than a comparison group. Similarly, Bernstein, Jeremy, Hans, and Marcus (1984) reported that a subgroup of the infants exposed to methadone in utero had worse social functioning and a higher level of tension than the comparison group who were not exposed to methadone. Babies of methadone users do have fewer symptoms, though, than babies of heroin users (Sinha et al., 2001). During opiate withdrawal, sleep may be impaired and the infants may suffer from flu-like symptoms, restless and irritable behavior, and sucking and feeding difficulties (D'Apolito & Hepworth, 2000). While the focus here is on heroin, alcohol and cocaine, commonly used by heroin users, have also been found to have negative effects on infants pre- and postnatally (Scherling, 1994).

Symptoms in newborns can have a negative impact on the bonding that normally develops between a healthy newborn and a nonaddicted mother. The mother, seeking a bond and having little tolerance for rejection, may experience failure at her first attempt to connect with the newborn given the symptoms listed above. Unfortunately, the potential problems of these children do not necessarily cease in infancy. They have been known to continue until children reach to age of 6 or older, in part because of a lack of ability to attend to tasks (Deren, 1986). Recent research has begun to question how far-reaching the effects of neonatal addiction are, with some researchers finding that these effects do *not* last into middle childhood.

With the addicted mother (or father), adequate child-rearing behavior is sometimes minimal (Plasse, 2000). Thus, the child may be affected by both the residue of the drug and inadequate parenting (Schuler et al., 2002). Mothers may exhibit low self-esteem, anxiety, and depression (Zilberman et al., 2003), and may not have adequate sources of social support for dealing with a difficult child and their own problems. They also are likely to feel inadequate and to use authoritarian and often ineffective means of parenting (Deren, 1986). Financial stability and safe housing may be issues. On measures of intelligence and personality these mothers, compared with non-drug-addicted mothers, have been found to be less adaptive (Bauman & Levine, 1986). In addition, they often come from dysfunctional families (Deren, 1986) where they had few adequate role models for how to parent.

Other problems that beset the often fragile child include erratic and unpredictable parental behavior and mood swings, absence of consistent parenting, and the shifting of parental responsibility to other adults in the family (often the mother of the addict). When the addicted mother has a low level of tolerance for the demands of parenting, the children may be at higher risk for child abuse (Schuler et al., 2002) and neglect and may not be given the structure needed to cope with their own deficits. The result is a parent with a host of problems attempting to raise a child with potential biological and emotional difficulties.

By treating these drug-dependent parents in a group, some of these issues can be addressed with success (Khantzian, 2001; Plasse, 2000). Group treatment can provide a supportive atmosphere where members can disclose their fears; gain information about normal developmental stages in children, as well as those that often accompany an addicted neonate; and learn how to cope with daily parenting and survival demands, and where, perhaps for the first time, they can experience themselves constructively helping others (Yalom, 1995). Attachment to children is encouraged (Goodman et al., 1999). With a group approach they are learning in vivo many of the give-and-take skills necessary for parenting.

Significant hurdles remain for the group members. They are subsisting on low incomes; often raising children with severe physical, emotional, and legal problems; and living in neighborhoods where drug use is rampant. Therefore, change is measured in terms of years, not weeks or months.

PRACTICE PRINCIPLES

This group, which met over a five-year period and varied in size from four to six members, was racially mixed and had both male and female members. They ranged in age from their mid-20s to their 40s. Members came and went as their status at the drug center changed. Some were removed from the program for noncompliance or drug abuse (as measured by a urine test or for displaying drug-induced or other noncompliant behavior). Others quit the program to try a different kind of treatment or no treatment at all. Some also moved to a different group because of scheduling conflicts. It was an involuntary group in that members had to attend or be reported to their individual counselors for non-compliance.

The members, most of whom had abused a variety of drugs for many years before entering treatment, specifically raised issues concerning their children, who ranged in age from birth to young adulthood. Teenagers, especially daughters, some of whom were being reared away from their mothers, caused the most conflict in the parents. The group met weekly and lasted for an hour (an agency policy), a period of time that occasionally seemed too short. Yet given the short attention span and child care demands of some of the parents, it may have been as long as was possible. A group member was allowed to miss four sessions every 6 months without a physician's note. If there were more absences or continued drug abuse, the member was dropped from the program and detoxified from methadone over a 1-month period.

The group leaders, the author and a full-time female counselor at the agency, used a multimethod approach that was guided by two types of family therapy: structural family therapy (Minuchin & Fishman, 1981) and Bowen family systems (Wylie, 1991). The structural school provided a framework for looking at the parent-child interactions that emphasized the maintenance of boundaries between the two. Families are viewed as dysfunctional when children are pulled into the parental sub-system or when parents are not maintaining a hierarchy in which they are in charge of the children. The focus of many of the interventions in this model is on the present. Group members were asked to review their behavior, with suggestions sometimes given by the leaders and others for possible behavioral changes to try at home during the week. In this way, work that began in the session could be continued throughout the week. This focus on the present provided a way of dealing with crises and emphasized for all parents that their behavior affected and was affected by others in the family.

Bowen's family systems theory provided a framework for teaching about the family of origin. By drawing genograms or family trees, the members examined their own drug histories and behaviors in the context of a family history. The genograms also provided the leader with easy access to important information that might not have emerged during the group process. Members learned that their own behaviors and expectations for their children might have been the result of the family environment in which they were raised. Such an approach provided insight into feelings that might have impeded their attempts to parent. The genogram was also used to focus on strengths. After considering the devastating effect that drugs have had on families, we asked the group members whom they got their strength from in the family and wondered aloud with them how these group members survived when others of their generation were dead.

Contracting played an important part in the group process. The members were expected to follow the rules that had been established concerning confidentiality, supporting other members in the group, and coming to the group one final time before termination. The leaders encouraged group interaction, looked for ways to be supportive, and positively reinforced healthy behavior. The potential for assaultive behavior between members was low, in part because some of them took their methadone just prior to group meetings, which had a temporary narcotizing effect on them.

The group members were seen as having had deficient parenting themselves and as being in need of specific parenting skills. An attempt was made to present information in a way that did not undermine the self-esteem of these parents, who already felt incompetent. Thus, in this long-term group (some members had been attending for over 2 years and had remained abstinent from heroin and other drugs during this period), the emphasis was on accepting the member's behavior, confronting it, relating it to past experiences where appropriate, providing information about child development, and suggesting areas for change. This was done with the context never straying from drug treatment. The impact of long-term substance abuse on relationships was kept at or near the forefront of the discussions.

COMMON THEMES FOR THE MEMBERS

Throughout the course of the group, a number of common themes emerged. These themes fell into two groups: those relating to the behavior and personality traits of the addicted parent (points 1 through 4) and those associated with the challenges of raising children (points 5 through 7). They included (1) difficulty with being consistent and providing structure on a daily basis; (2) inability to parent because of deficiencies in their own upbringing; (3) inability to parent because of guilt from neglecting their children in the past; (4) difficulty in dealing with their own parents, who may have been blocking their attempts to establish parenting relationships with their children; (5) being verbally attacked by their children because of their drug histories; (6) raising adolescents; and (7) dealing with larger systems like the school system and child protective services.

Difficulty with Being Consistent and
Providing Structure on a Daily Basis

Many group members lacked consistency and structure in their own lives. They often lived in chaotic households and neighborhoods where unpredictability and violence were the norm. Providing a predictable, caring environment for their children was difficult. Members came and went in their own homes at odd hours. Discipline was often too harsh or inappropriately lax. If restrictions were placed on the child that were unrealistically punitive, the parent backed away from them as they became difficult for the parent to enforce. At other times, parents forgot what the punishment was supposed to be. If the mother had been on drugs or methadone during pregnancy, the child's development may have been problematic in the early years, further burdening the parent-child relationship.

Inability to Parent Because of Deficiencies in Their Own Upbringing

These drug addicts were often insufficiently parented themselves. Many may have turned to drugs as a result. When they became parents, they had few positive models to guide them in dealing with the normal ups and downs of child rearing. By looking at their family histories, as suggested by Bowen, the group members learned that their way of interacting with their own children might have been similar to how they were raised. One mother, who was abandoned by her father, learned to deal with difficult situations by cutting herself off from people, as her father had done with her. When she needed to intervene in her 14-year-old daughter's pregnancy, her tendency was to remove herself and say that her daughter had to handle it alone. Another parent, ill equipped to manage her own life, became overly responsible (Nelson-Zlupko et al., 1995), trying to raise her own children and also those of a sister. She had difficulty saying no to outside obligations because that was never a role model for her.

Inability to Parent Because of Guilt from Neglecting Their Children in the Past

The group members were often unable to follow through with punishment they established because of the guilt they felt about what their children had experienced at their hands or at the hands of others when they were addicted. A number of these parents neglected their children or turned them over to relatives to raise while they were addicted. As one mother in the group said, "Whenever I punish my daughter, I feel sorry for her because I wasn't there for her [when she was younger]."

Parents struggled with the issue of how involved to be in their children's lives, unsure of whether they were a positive influence and if their children wanted them to be involved. Many of these parents were immobilized when their child was angry at them, even though anger at one's parent is a normal part of growing up. As a reaction, the parents refrained from parenting and instead tried to establish a peer relationship, hoping to get love from the child through friendship.

Difficulty in Dealing with Their Own Parents, Who May Have Been Blocking Their Attempts to Establish Parenting Relationships with Their Children

Drug abuse has been cited as one of the primary reasons for the increase over the last few years in relatives, rather than parents, raising children (Cox, 2002). Often the mother of the addicted parent assumes the primary parenting responsibility if the parent abdicates it. As the parent enters treatment and begins methadone maintenance, he or she reaches a point where there may be a desire to resume parenting responsibilities. Attempts to do so are often blocked by the parent's mother, who does not trust the parent because of past indiscretions. In this situation, the grandmother may be attempting to protect the child. However, she may also have her own need to keep the parent in a dependent position and herself codepenent, a family cycle that may have contributed to the parent's initial addiction.

Being Verbally Attacked by Their Children Because of Their Drug Histories

Some members experienced the verbal, and occasionally physical, wrath of their children because of their past histories of drug abuse. The children may have been responding solely to their own feelings or to feelings generated by their peers, who teased the children about their parent's drug abuse. Being called an addict by one's child often fed into a group member's own insecurity and heightened the imbalance in the parent-child hierarchy, placing the child in a position of greater power. One member stopped disciplining and nurturing her child because of these attacks. Another member (described earlier as having a pregnant 14-year-old daughter) reported that she was not going to advise her daughter to get an abortion even though she thought she should. "I can't tell her what to do," she told the group. "She already says I did stuff to her because of drugs, and I'm not going to be blamed by her later for telling her to kill her baby."

Raising Adolescents

Many addicted parents began taking drugs during their own adolescence. Their psychosocial development may have ceased at that point, resulting in their now responding to situations from an adolescent rather than adult perspective. When their own children reached adolescence, this began a particularly hard period for them for a number of reasons: (1) raising an adolescent may have caused any unresolved issues from their own adolescence to reemerge; (2) many thorny issues, such as sexuality, pregnancy, and sexually transmitted diseases, emerged for the first time in the parent-child relationship; and (3) the way the member handled issues focused on drug and alcohol abuse was important not only from a parent-child perspective but also from the perspective of that member's own abstinence. For example, if a parent tolerated any drug use in his or her own children, did that undermine a policy of abstinence that the parent may have been pursuing in treatment?

Dealing with Larger Systems: The School System

A few of the parents had ongoing contact with the school concerning their children's problems. These were usually behavioral concerns, with children exhibiting short attention spans and disruptive behavior, and sometimes academic concerns. These were serious issues for the parents, who often saw their own histories of school failure being repeated in their children. Their ability to cope with these problems in partnership with the school was often severely compromised by their own histories. They tended to side with their children and to approach the school administration and teachers with an oppositional attitude rather than one of partnership. As a result, problems were often exacerbated when they could have been worked through.

Dealing with the Child Protective Services (CPS) System

Similar authority issues were raised by parents who complained that either their children threatened to call CPS if they disciplined them physically or that CPS was already involved. In one situation, a mother started to beat her 15-year-old daughter for staying out past curfew but was forced to restrain herself when the daughter threatened to call CPS. Parents complained that they were no longer able to "do anything" with their children because of governmental interference.

When CPS was actually investigating a situation, the leaders were occasionally asked to write a letter for the group member attesting to his or her good parenting skills. While we could write that the member was in a group for parents, we could honestly say only that we had not seen the parent interact with the child often enough to make a sound determination as to the parent's competence as a parent. The parents were aware that reports of abusive behavior would have to be reported by us. This may have constrained some of the discussion around child-rearing.

RECOMMENDED WAY OF WORKING

Teaching child development, particularly information relevant to a drug-addicted infant, is important (Edelstein et al., 1990). The group leaders attempted to help the parents internalize structure by providing it themselves through consistent interactions with the members and through educating them. The structural model was used in explaining to group members the need to act in a manner that reinforced their own competence as parents.

In helping parents deal with the ghosts from their own past, we attempted to show group members where their feelings about their parenting abilities originated. More difficult was the task of then convincing them that they were not tied to the past but had a choice as to how they wished to parent in the present and future.

As mentioned, parents felt guilty about the way they had previously treated their child. For the mother who had difficulty punishing her daughter, withdrawal of the punishment could be seen as engaging in enabling behavior and as a reflection of the relationship this mother had with her own mother. Focusing on the gains the parent has made in treatment can help the parent to incorporate a more beneficial self-image. Emphasizing the appropriate building of boundaries and examining past relationships the member had with responsible adults can assist similar parents in deciding where parental and child roles should be kept distinct.

For the parents who struggled with the involvement of other family members, the group leaders' interventions had a dual focus: (1) asserting the importance of avoiding all drugs, as any abuse reinforces the need for intrusion of the surrogate parent, and (2) asserting the importance of responsible behavior, particularly parenting behavior, in other areas of the member's life. Family work was assigned for the members to accomplish outside of the group. When warranted, the group member was asked to discuss with his or her mother (or responsible adult) what behaviors the group member would need to display before that responsible adult would relinquish more control of the child. For the group members, confronting their mothers or fathers on these issues was particularly difficult because of past unresolved conflicts.

Children in these situations are often angry but also frightened about their parents' potential return to drugs. One approach in the group had been for the leaders to reframe the verbal attacks by a child as a call for help or structure and that more, not less, parental involvement may be needed. This combatted the parent's tendency to withdraw, a pattern usually seen in other areas of their lives.

Because of the often overlapping developmental stage of the parent and the adolescent he or she is raising, adolescents pose particular problems. Insight assisted some of the parents here. Helping the group members recognize the overarching themes between their own adolescence and their children's provided them with tools to begin to deal more objectively with the difficulties of this development stage. This theme had to be reconsidered in every group session, as it was the parents with adolescents who tended to have the most severe crises.

Helping parents with school-related problems begins with pointing out to them the potential similarities between their own academic histories and that of their child. Introducing the notion of partnership or "teaming" with the school teacher can place the parent in an executive or parental role, which is more appropriate than reacting to school contacts as if the school is "picking on" their child.

Parents complained about not being able to raise their children the way they wanted to because their children threatened to call CPS. They were supported in their frustration but encouraged to find other ways to discipline that would avoid this potential source of conflict. This opened up an opportunity for discussing discipline in general and searching for alternative, less punitive measures.

Two illustrations show the often divergent reactions when authority systems become part of a parent's life.

> Carly felt unable to control her teenage daughter from the time the girl was quite young. She turned over her rearing to her own parents and assisted them in disciplining. But when the daughter reached her teens and became uncontrollable, Carly's parents called the Department of Social Services for help. The courts also became involved when the daughter committed several petty crimes. Carly supported her parents' decision, feeling that they needed more help with discipline than either she or they could offer.

More complicated is the situation in which intrusion is unwelcome:

> CPS was concerned about Nancy's sometimes neglectful and abusive behavior of her son. Nancy turned over custody of her 8-year-old son to her neighbor, telling CPS that the neighbor was a cousin. She was trying to prevent the child's being placed in foster care, where she would not see him. The neighbor received foster care payments for the son but later refused to return him and lose the payments. Nancy also was frequently at school, fielding complaints about a second child's behavior, and indicated that she often stretched the truth when meeting with school officials.
>
> Nancy wanted the group leaders to testify at a custody hearing that she was fit to regain custody. Social workers are often asked to advocate for clients, but in this situation we did not feel comfortable advocating for her when we believed her to be unfit.

For Carly and Nancy, their erratic, drug-induced behavior contributed to the intrusion of outside systems into their lives. But Carly welcomed it as a needed form of external control, while Nancy resisted it. Diagnostically, the outcomes of their treatment were perhaps predictable. Carly succeeded and Nancy was thrown out of the program for using other drugs.

EVALUATION AND SUMMARY

Measuring change is a matter of parental self-report in terms of both the child's reactions and the group member's parenting behavior, lack of substance abuse (also measured by urine screens), in-group behavior, and lack of trouble with the law. By these criteria, change was noted in some of the group members. For example, one long-term group member (Carly), who never spoke when she was in a previous group that focused on addiction-related problems, became the role model for other members. In this group, she said, she felt more competent. She was appropriately outspoken and established relationships with her children that consistently supported the parent-child boundaries that needed to be drawn. One specific issue she resolved involved her 19-year-old son and his girlfriend, who was pregnant. By role playing the different positions of each of these people (Carly was paying the rent and had the right to set the rules; the girlfriend was feeling unaccepted by Carly and was acting out inappropriately; the son was caught between trying to please the two women), Carly was able to clarify for herself how to approach future conflicts. (Ten years after her involvement in the group, Carly was successfully employed in the school system as a janitor.)

A second group member improved her relationship with her son (age 3) but still struggles with her 15-year-old daughter. What was most effective was teaching her to count to 10 before responding to what she considers the goading of both children. In addition, she was feeling pressured by her mother, in whose house she lived, to toilet train her son. After learning about the normal developmental stages and allowing for other possible deficits that might be related to having a child who was addicted at birth, the member was able to put less pressure on her son and to feel more competent herself.

A third member slowly opened up to the group after being guarded and defensive for the first 4 months of attendance. With her youngest son in a group home for delinquent boys, interventions focused on supporting her attempts to see him and allowing her to vent her frustration at trying to raise him alone. A fourth member showed little improvement and continued to be of great concern to the leaders. A fifth member (Nancy) entered the group as a continual abuser and was detoxed from the program 6 months later because she continued to abuse. A sixth member had to change groups because of child care conflicts.

Work with this difficult population requires a long-term commitment and the establishment of goals that consider the life history of the abuser. Change is slow and incremental. There are nearly as many setbacks as there are signs of positive change. Yet, in a supportive atmosphere, group members can be reparented and helped to be more effective in raising their children.

For an earlier version of this chapter, see G. L. Greif & M. Drechsler (1993). Common issues for parents in a methadone maintenance group. *Journal of Substance Abuse Treatment. 10*, 339–343.

RESOURCES

Centers for Disease Control at
http://www.cdc.gov/idu

National Institute of Drug Abuse
Centers for Substance Abuse
   Treatment
(for treatment referrals)
5600 Fishers Lane
Rockville, MD 29857
(800) 662-HELP
WWW.health.org

*Narcotic Treatment Program
   Directory*
U.S. Department of Health and
   Human Services has nationwide
   inventory of drug programs; see also

National Directory of Drug Abuse
and Alcoholism Treatment And
Prevention Programs.
www.hhs.gov

numerous professional journals are also
available on the topic, including:

Journal of Substance Abuse Treatment
*The American Journal of Drug and
   Alcohol Abuse*
International Journal of the Addictions
Journal of Drug Issues
*Journal of Social Work Practice in the
   Addictions*
Journal of Psychoactive Drugs.

REFERENCES

Bauman, P. S., & Levine, S. A. (1986). The development of children of drug addicts. *The International Journal of Addictions.* 21, 849–863.

Bernstein, V., Jeremy, R. J., Hans, S. L., & Marcus, J. (1984). A longitudinal study of offspring born to methadone-maintained women. II. Dyadic interaction and infant behavior at 4 months. *American Journal of Drug and Alcohol Abuse.* 10, 161–193.

Centers for Disease Control (2002). Methadone Maintenance Treatment Report. February, http://www.cdc.gov/idu.

Coviello, D. M., Zanis, D. A., Welsh, S. A., Alegria-Poyras, M. A., & Alterman, A. I. (2002). Is case management effective in re-engaging discharged methadone maintenance patients in treatment? *Drug & Alcohol Dependence.* 66–S, 338.

Cox, C. (2002). Empowering African American custodial grandparents. *Social Work.* 47, 45–54.

D'Apolito, K., & Hepworth, J. P. (2000). Prominence of withdrawal symptoms in polydrug-exposed infants. *Journal of Perinatal & Neonatal Nursing.* 14, 46–60.

Deren, S. (1986). Children of substance abusers: A review of the literature. *Journal of Substance Abuse Treatment.* 3, 77–94.

Edelstein, S., Kropenske, V., & Howard, J. (1990). Project T.E.A.M.S. *Social Work.* 35, 313–318.

Goodman, G., Hans, S. L., & Cox, S. M. (1999). Attachment behavior and its antecedents in offspring born to methadone-maintained women. *Journal of Clinical Child Psychology.* 28, 58–69.

Kelly, J. J., Davis, P. G., & Henschke, P. N. (2000). The drug epidemic: Effects on newborn infants and health resource consumption at a tertiary perinatal center. *Journal of Paediatrics and Child Health.* 36, 262–264.

Khantzian, E. J. (2001). Reflections on group treatments as corrective experiences for addictive vulnerability. *International Journal of Group Psychotherapy.* 51, 11–20.

Magura, S., Casriel, C., Goldsmith, D. S., & Lipton, D. S. (1987). Contracting with clients in methadone treatment. *Social Casework.* 68, 485–493.

Marcus, J., Hans, S. L., & Jeremy, R. J. (1984). A longitudinal study of offspring born to methadone-maintenance women. III. Effects of multiple risk factors on development at 4, 8, and 12 months. *American Journal of Drug and Alcohol Abuse.* 10, 195–207.

McCarthy, J. J., & Borders, O. T. (1985). Limit-setting on drug abuse in methadone maintenance patients. *American Journal of Psychiatry.* 142, 1419–1423.

Minuchin, S., & Fishman, C. (1981). *Family therapy techniques.* Cambridge: Harvard University Press.

Nelson-Zlupko, L., Kauffman, E., & Dore, M. M. (1995). Gender differences in drug addiction and treatment: Implications for social work intervention with substance-abusing women. *Social Work.* 40, 45–54.

Plasse, B. R. (2000). Components of engagement: Women in a psychoeducational parenting skills group in substance abuse treatment. *Social Work with Groups.* 22, 65–74.

Scherling, D. (1994). Prenatal cocaine exposure and childhood psychopathology: A developmental analysis. *American Journal of Orthopsychiatry.* 64, 9–19.

Schuler, M. E., Nair, P., & Black, M. M. (2002). Ongoing maternal drug use, parenting attitudes, and a home intervention: Effects on mother–child interaction at 18 months. *Developmental and Behavioral Pediatrics.* 23, 87–94.

Sinha, C., Ohadike, P., Carrick, P., Pairaudeau, P., Armstrong, D., & Lindow, S. W. (2001). Neonatal outcome following maternal opiate use in late pregnancy. *International Journal of Gynecology & Obstretrics.* 74, 241–246.

Weiner, H., & Fox, S. (1982). Cognitive-behavioral therapy with substance abusers. *Social Casework.* 63, 564–567.

Wylie, M. S. (1991). Family therapy's neglected prophet. *Family Therapy Networker.* 15, 24–37, 77.

Zilberman, M. L., Tavares, H., Blume, S. B., & el-Guebaly, N. (2003). Substance-use disorders: Sex differences and psychiatric co-morbidities. *Canadian Journal of Psychiatry.* 48, 5–15.

PART II

ADJUSTING TO CHANGE

Chapter 7

Support Groups for Widows and Widowers

CAROLYN AMBLER WALTER

REVIEW OF THE LITERATURE

The loss of a spouse is considered the most stressful life event (Holmes & Rahe, 1967). Furthermore, in many respects, American society is a death-denying culture that views death as an unnatural occurrence rather than as a universal phase of the life cycle. Our society's superficial and often sanitized reaction to death makes it very difficult for a widow or widower to give vent to genuine and, at times, intense expressions of grief. People in general are uncomfortable at the expression of unhappiness and do not want to be reminded of their own mortality (Kinderknecht & Hodges, 1990). Society can also make widowed persons "feel that their behavior is abnormal: society decides when one has grieved long enough, then lets the bereaved know that it is time to bury the dead and get on with the living" (Kinderknecht & Hodges, 1990, p. 47). A support group can combat this insensitive "society schedule" and help bereaved spouses establish their own timetable of grieving.

Many researchers have noted that "preventive intervention early in the bereavement process may lessen the morbidity and mortality associated with the death of a spouse" (Barrett, 1978; Hiltz, 1975; Jones, 1979; McCourt et al., 1976; Rachael, 1977; Yalom & Vinogradov, 1988, p. 420). Bereavement support groups represent an excellent approach to this highly vulnerable population because the small group format can specifically address and lessen the "intense social isolation experienced by most bereaved spouses" (Yalom & Vinogradov, 1988, p. 420). Within the past 8

years, support groups for bereaved spouses have proliferated in many different settings to provide important support for working through the grief
of a loss that is profound and highly stressful, changing life irrevocably
(Kinderknecht & Hodges, 1990; Lewis & Berns, 1975).

PURPOSE OF SUPPORT GROUPS

Although there is some disagreement regarding the efficacy of support
groups as a change agent in the lives of widows and widowers (Levy et al.,
1993; Tudiver et al., 1992); the literature in general supports the usefulness of support groups for bereaved spouses (Barrett, 1978; Folken,
1991; Kay et al., 1993; Kinderknecht & Hodges, 1990; Lieberman, 1989;
Lieberman & Videka-Sherman, 1986; Lorenz, 1998; Rognlie, 1989).
Some authors state that there is a connection between the degree of social engagement and positively perceived change in the bereaved
spouse's functioning (Folken, 1991; Kauffman, 1994; Lopata, 1986, p.
212). The "social linkages" within the spousal bereavement group are
seen as critical factors in positive change; neither time alone nor mere
contact with a self-help group is sufficient to enhance the mental health
of the widowed (Lieberman, 1989; Lieberman & Videka-Sherman,
1986). In self-help groups, the widows who established new social contacts with other widows were the only ones who experienced relief from
their distress (Lieberman & Videka-Sherman, 1986). Therapeutic experiences such as cognitive structuring or affective discharge alone may not
be sufficient to "change the psychological balance incrementally"
(Lieberman & Videka-Sherman, 1986, p. 447). These findings suggest
that for certain bereaved spouses, individual psychotherapy alone may
not be enough to effect change.

Support groups for bereaved spouses have several goals. One is to
assist the members to cope with the pain of grief and mourning (including the "holding on" and "letting go" processes) "by creating a temporary
community in which they [are] deeply understood by peers" (Lorenz,
1998; Yalom & Vinogradov, 1988, p. 443); a second is to help combat the
social isolation that is so pervasive for this population and to provide "consensual validation" for spouses regarding their bereavement experiences
(Yalom & Vinogradov, 1988); and a third is to support members as they
begin to understand the changes facing them as they begin to fashion a
new future for themselves.

Finally, our society encourages and rewards speed and productivity,
and "managed care has further imposed the expectation of quick results
on the healthcare and mental health communities" (Lorenz, 1998). Support groups for widows and widowers can give bereaved spouses the
"space and time for normal healing to occur" (Lorenz, 1998). These support groups can challenge our society's tendency to curtail the grieving
process by encouraging the surviving spouse to move on and live their life

soon after the loss of their spouse. Instead, within a small community of grievers, permission is granted to each bereaved spouse to experience the pain associated with his or her loss.

PRACTICE PRINCIPLES

Norms

Social rules of mourning tend to encourage people to feel that it is appropriate to avoid their grief. Within support groups for bereaved spouses, "Norms (shared agreement among group members) sanction and facilitate the experience of the pain of loss and need to be carefully cultivated and secured in the group process" (Kauffman, 1994, p. 165). The social worker must work to create a group climate that permits the expression of grief (including permission for its prolongation) while encouraging the forging of a new life (Lieberman, 1989; Yalom & Vinogradov, 1988). This is no small task, as bereaved spouses seem to experience a tension between the process of change (the letting go of one's old life and moving forward) and a sense of "devotion or love for the deceased spouse" (Lieberman, 1989, p. 439).

Kauffman (1994), Lawrence (1992), and Folken (1991) consider the critical function of "mirroring" within support groups for widows and widowers. When mirroring occurs, it sanctions grief (mutual and reciprocal recognition of one's grief) and facilitates the release and experiencing of grief. "It provides the sense that one is known by another in the intimacy of pain" (Kauffman, 1994, p. 163). Folken (1991) also discusses the importance of establishing a therapeutic bond between grieving people, which encourages a mutual acknowledgment of suffering and a recognition of differences in ways of coping with grief, and thus supports the effort at recovery. Talking or listening to others talk about their feelings reassures newly bereaved spouses that they are not losing their minds as they learn how bizarre and erratic the grief process can be. Kauffman agrees that "group members frequently discover their own feelings through recognizing the feeling in and through another" (1994, p. 163).

The mirroring function develops when group members feel comfortable with one another. Therefore, early in the group's history, a group climate must be established in which members can share openly with one another. The mirroring process lessens the sense of social isolation and the narcissistic injury associated with the loss of a spouse. The experience of normalization offered by a support group provides a feeling of acceptance that helps the individual to address the stigma associated with being a widowed adult in our society (Lieberman, 1989).

Since research (Lieberman, 1989; Lieberman & Videka-Sherman, 1986) suggests that "members who have made social linkages in the group show higher positive change . . . compared to members who attend meetings only" (Lieberman & Videka-Sherman, 1986, p. 444), norms that develop strong group cohesion through active participation and meaningful interactions among members must be encouraged to develop. Support groups with "high social exchange" characteristics develop a group climate that encourages the expression of a wide range of feelings, both unhappy and happy, and motivates group members to get together outside of the formal meetings. To encourage outside socializing, the worker can suggest that members who so choose meet after the formal group session for coffee at a local restaurant (without the leader).

Role of the Leader

Although social workers may facilitate the process by introducing topics or structured exercises, the most important task is to refrain from interfering with the natural course and currents of the group, and to be attentive to the timing of interventions so as to not inhibit important spontaneous interactions in the group (Kauffman, 1994; Kliban et al., 1984; Lawrence, 1992; Lieberman, 1989; Rognlie, 1989; Yalom & Vinogradov, 1988, p. 424). The most important role of social workers seems to be to "anticipate and facilitate a natural process of self-exploration and change" by staying out of the way or by serving as "gentle midwives" to issues and concerns that emerge spontaneously (Yalom & Vinogradov, 1988, p. 445). In order to be able to help to develop a group climate that provides "a safe space to allow the healing process to unfold" (Lorenz, 1998) the group leader must be able to tolerate intense sadness, which may continue throughout the group's existence. Kauffman (1994) concurs and further suggests that leaders of bereavement groups need to be especially aware of their own reactions to the pain and the meaning of death in order to be able to create a group climate in which grieving can occur.

Lorenz (1998) believes that self-awareness is essential for bereavement group leaders. She suggests that prospective group leaders spend time prior to committing to leading a bereavement group in exploring questions such as, "What losses have I experienced? How many? How recently? How well resolved are they? How do I typically respond to people who are experiencing sadness and emotional pain?" Once the group is underway, the leader needs to monitor his or her own feelings and reactions in order to remain emotionally available to the group members and to the group process.

Structure

While the inclusion of a structured educational format may be an appropriate and helpful part of the design for a support group for bereaved spouses, a word of caution is in order: If the group is too structured, the leader may be playing into his or her own anxiety about grieving and death or allowing the group to play into theirs. "Structuring of bereavement groups often serves the purpose of suppressing the pain of loss and death" (Kauffman, 1994, p. 170). Yalom began his work with bereavement groups by using structured group exercises but soon reported that "the members welcomed a simple forum where they could talk openly and the imposition of structure was thus generally counterproductive" (Yalom & Vinogradov, 1988, p. 426).

However, educational provisions "may be informative in ways that reassure and normalize and may help focus and contain diffuse or marginally conscious grief" (Kauffman, 1994, p. 171). This author has found that a combination approach is particularly helpful. The group can begin with a "go-round" for each member to state where he or she is in the process for that particular session and then follow with some didactic material that can be discussed either in the larger group (if there are eight or fewer members) or in smaller subgroups of three members. The larger group can then reconvene for the last half hour of the session to share material and experiences of the subgroups.

Regarding the use of homework and structured exercises, Rognlie (1989) found that many participants considered remembering their spouses, by sharing photos and experiences, to be the most helpful aspect of the program, while homework was considered the least helpful. Lawrence (1992) and Yalom and Vinogradov (1988) found the use of photos was particularly helpful in facilitating the widow's ability to accept her new reality while relating to the loss she had experienced.

The literature on support groups for bereaved spouses is split on whether groups should be time-limited or open-ended. Yalom and Vinogradov (1988) advocate fairly short-term work with such groups. The advantage of short-term, time-limited groups is that a cohesive group forms more easily with a steady, unchanging membership. Within time-limited groups, the members form a stronger bond and the culture may be safer to introduce (in the later sessions) discussions about the less idealized, more problematic areas of marriage. These areas include "anger at the dead spouse and at oneself for things left unsaid in the marriage, resentment over fixed, restrictive roles, and guilt about new or future relationships" (Yalom & Vinogradov, 1988, p. 431). In addition, termination issues can be handled more directly with the group members as they relate to the grieving process. The literature surveyed indicates that time-limited groups involve 6 to 15 sessions.

However, Kauffman (1994) suggests that the "advantage of an ongoing group is that it can be available to diverse needs over time and see a person through the process, as needed" (1994, p. 171). This quality of open-ended groups mirrors the grieving process, which "flows in fits and starts" with "unanticipated outbreaks of grief and shifts in focus" (p. 171). In open-ended groups, members can choose a short-term experience and stay for 6 to 15 sessions, or they may stay for up to 1 or 2 years. Another advantage of an open-ended group is that the newer members (probably those more newly widowed) who join the group can learn a great deal from those further along in the grieving process. This experience provides hope for the newly widowed (a crucial element to recovery) and an opportunity for the experienced widows and widowers to assess their progress.

Group Composition

It is important to honor the principle of homogeneity in group composition because widowed adults wish to be with others who have had an experience like their own (Kauffman, 1994). However, the common situation of bereaved spouses is "such a powerful commonality that it [the group] is able to incorporate individual differences in background and personality" (Gitterman, 1989, p. 8) without leading to intense interpersonal conflict. Moreover, both the literature (Kauffman, 1994; Lieberman, 1989) and the author's personal/professional experiences suggest that homogeneity in group membership should be preserved for factors such as age and type of bereavement. That is, specific groups should be created for bereaved spouses under age 50, whose tasks and needs may be different from those of widows and widowers over 50. This is particularly true with regard to being a single parent and coping with children who are still living at home. Furthermore, combining men and women in support groups for bereaved spouses seems to be useful in allowing both sexes to begin to relate again to the opposite sex, something very difficult to do following the loss of a spouse.

Termination

As with all groups, termination requires two basic tasks with which social workers must provide help. The first task is to deal with the loss and say good-bye, acknowledging the ending of the group and facing other feelings evoked by termination. In a bereaved spouse group, the issue of group termination evokes powerful feelings related to the loss of the spouse allowing another opportunity to confront the grief. Time must be provided within the group for this process, as it is a most powerful one with this particular population. The second task is to deal with regret over unfinished business and work left undone by the group (Yalom & Vinogradov, 1988). This allows bereaved spouses to cope with the issue of regret over unexpressed sentiments in their marriage. The ending of the group provides an opportunity to acknowledge this reaction. One method that can be used to help this process is to have group members write a letter to their deceased spouses telling them the things that were left unsaid.

With this population, it seems helpful to encourage informal group meetings following termination of the formal group (Lieberman & Videka-Sherman, 1986; Yalom & Vinogradov, 1988). If a group is ongoing, it is important to structure the comings and goings of members and to urge members to let the group know prior to their last session, so that there is time for the group to discuss feelings about the termination.

COMMON THEMES

Loneliness and Isolation

Widowhood is considered the most isolating crisis event associated with marriage. Often the widow/widower is unprepared for the degree of isolation that experienced following the death of a spouse (Kinderknecht & Hodges, 1990; Lopata, 1986). The issue of isolation is a central one to be addressed in a support group for bereaved spouses (Folken, 1991; Kauffman, 1994; Kinderknecht & Hodges, 1990; Lieberman & Videka-Sherman, 1986; Yalom & Vinogradov, 1988).

There are two basic types of loneliness common to bereaved spouses. One involves the "loss of daily intimacies of shared routines and private moments," as well as the loss of family holidays, time spent with children and grandchildren, and sexual and romantic closeness (Yalom & Vinogradov, 1988, p. 435). The other type of loneliness is that of "no longer being the single most important person in someone's life, nor of having a single significant other with whom to share important experiences" (Yalom & Vinogradov, 1988, p. 436). One widow (aged 47 at the death of her husband) lamented, when invited by the group leader to share what members felt was most difficult for them, "I no longer feel special to anyone." The social worker can encourage possible growth for this member with a response such as "If you have felt that special to someone, you obviously made your husband feel special; you can do that again." This turns the passive grief experience of loss into a potential, active growth experience in which bereaved spouses can begin viewing themselves as active persons again. Another aspect of loneliness is the feeling that much of one's history died with one's spouse. Each member has lost the one person who has known him or her over time and who shared the same memories.

While friends and family return to their lives following this loss, widowed spouses must face the task of bereavement, for the most part, by themselves. The phase of disorientation that inevitably follows the loss of a spouse often brings with it the underlying fear that one is "going to pieces." Because of this severe degree of isolation, membership in a support group for widows and widowers can be beneficial. In one group for widows and widowers under the age of 50, a 42-year-old woman remarked, 2 months after the loss of her husband: "I can remember feeling the first break in the severe sense of loneliness and isolation I had been experiencing following the death of my husband during my drive home, after attending the second session of our support group. I knew other people felt the way I did—that I wasn't alone in the world for the first time in a long while."

Coming home to an empty house is one of the most difficult adjustments that widowed adults must make. That night following a support group session was a turning point for this widow in coming home.

Identity Change—We to I

An issue of equal importance facing widowed spouses is the task of establishing a new identity. "To lose a spouse is to lose something of one's self; many spouses experience seeing themselves as "only half a person" following the loss of their husband or wife (Kinderknecht & Hodges, 1990, p. 43). For women, one aspect of formulating a new identity is that of title because many women have been known as Mrs. Somebody. In reorganizing her life the widow must decide what her title will be.

In his research on support groups for bereaved spouses, Lieberman (1989) considers the important task of reconstituting a "coherent and consistent self-concept, including addressing feelings of grief and mourning and integrating these feelings into ongoing psychological portraits of themselves" (p. 206). Issues to be discussed in the support group surrounding this task are *(1)* examining the meaning and importance of the lost relationship; *(2)* addressing the transition necessary for bereaved spouses in negotiating a new role that is not based on a couple relationship; and *(3)* highlighting the problems of loosening/renegotiating old ties with friends and family and developing new social relationships.

One effective exercise is to ask group members to consider the transition from spouse to widow to single adult. Group members are invited to free-associate feelings and thoughts they have about each status, taking each one individually. The group leader writes these reactions on a blackboard or flipchart and then leads a general discussion about the group's reactions.

Another identity issue for both men and women involves their new role within the couple's old circle of friends. When the spouse who is now bereaved was part of a couple, this social network was probably comprised mostly of other couples. It can be painful to be with these friends now, and the bereaved spouse may wonder how he or she will fit in and feel comfortable as a single person in this social network.

Widows who were doing well (Lieberman, 1989; Lieberman & Borman, 1979; Vachon, 1979) displayed an ability to get on with their lives that seemed to involve a shift in identity from wife to widow to woman—a shift that allowed the past to inform the present. This movement was more evident in those who had participated in groups for bereaved spouses than in those who had not (Vachon, 1979). Lopata's (1986) review of the literature suggests that the reconstruction of the self (for widows) "requires communication with others; the women most aware of changes in the self are least isolated. The person can engage in new behavior and observe the self in change, but it is in interaction that this consciousness is crystallized" (p. 213). It seems clear that support groups can aid the widowed adult in this process of reconstruction of self.

Although there have been few documented studies of men's grief following the loss of a spouse, researchers examining gender differences have generally found more similarities than differences (Brabant et al., 1992, p. 35). They found that men, like women, following the death of their spouse experienced a severe loss of their sense of identity. This research seems to refute the notion that the wife is less central to the husband's life than the husband is to the wife's. One man reported: "I thought I was a real individual before she died, but afterwards I realized she was a big part of me" (Brabant et al., 1992, p. 43). In another support group for bereaved spouses, all five men in the group reported a loss of the sense of self. The men in this group experienced their wives as central to their lives and perceived that their identity as a spouse had been critical to their sense of themselves. One 45-year-old widower poignantly said: "I feel like half of me is gone now that my wife is gone—we made all of our decisions together." The restructuring of identity following the loss of a spouse may be as critical for men as for women. This is an important consideration for social workers, who may believe the popular notion that men are protected from the impact of bereavement because their wives are less central to their identities due to the strong presence of a career or work identity prior to the loss of their spouses.

Relationships

The importance of discussing relationships and intimacy is central to the issue of identity change from we to I. Following the loss of a spouse, one of the most significant areas of change is relationships—with friends, immediate and extended family, in-laws, and social networks. For bereaved spouses, particularly in the younger age group (under 60), dating is a very important, difficult, and conflicted issue, made more difficult by all of the changes in social norms and mores within the last 20 to 30 years since these adults last dated.

The issue of loyalty to one's dead spouse also plays a part in the conflict around dating experienced by many bereaved spouses. The idea of loving someone new can evoke a wide range of feelings. In a group for bereaved spouses, some members usually see this desire as a signal of healing and a readiness to move forward; others see it as a betrayal of their marriage, as if loving someone new might somehow invalidate the love they had for their spouse. It is constructive for the worker to help the group understand the fallacy of believing that only a finite amount of love is available. In one group for bereaved spouses under age 50, several new members were sharing their concern about their capacity to ever love another person again. A 32-year-old widow, whose husband had died nine months prior to this session and who had very recently started dating, poignantly told the group that "this capacity comes in time, and what you learn to do is to keep your love for your spouse in a corner of your heart which goes untouched by any new relationship." Other group members compared this experience to the way parents often feel prior to the birth of a second child—"How will I ever love the second child as much as the first?" This comment was discussed by several members after the group session that night as being critical to their beginning to understand the possibility of loving again.

Since this issue is a very sensitive one, if the group is time limited and closed, it is better to introduce the topic of dating after some group cohesion has developed. If the group is open-ended or is an ongoing series (with sessions in the fall, winter, and spring), it is better to introduce this topic near the end, when some members who have dated can share their experiences.

Yalom and Vinogradov (1988) report that the issues of dating and relationships created a major division between the men and women in their support groups. "The men were far more driven to form new relationships," while the women were "more hesitant to become romantically involved with someone new too soon and seemed anxious about the idea of being pursued or, worse yet, being pursuers" (p. 441). In groups with which the author has been involved, this has not been the case.

Time and Ritual

Another important issue related to forging a new life from the old one while coping with the grief process is handling important marker events (such as anniversaries, birthdays, holidays, weddings, and graduations) that were once shared experiences. It is important for group members to share their experiences with regard to how they celebrated these occasions as married persons, and then to hear from "group veterans" how they handled these same marker events as single, widowed adults. At the beginning of each session, members may be encouraged to discuss important events coming up for them. A special session around family holidays on how to cope with the bereaved spouse's reactions can also be included.

Group members can be extremely helpful in sharing how they cope with the anxiety and depression surrounding holidays and may provide ways to ward off intense reactions. One young widow with five children spoke of how she handled the day of the wedding anniversary following the first year of her husband's death. Sandra described her plan of hiring a babysitter and treating herself to a day-long tour of a local arboretum with several friends. When she reported back to the group about her experience, she smiled and said that it had definitely helped her through the day.

The other major marker event is the first anniversary of the death of the spouse. One 55-year-old Protestant widow borrowed from the Jewish tradition and planned an unveiling ceremony at the graveside for close friends and family. In addition to placing the marker at the graveside, this widow shared thoughts from letters she received from many friends and family members following her husband's death. In sharing her experience with the group, she stated emphatically that this process itself helped her to let go of her husband and that life seemed easier afterward.

Another issue related to ritual and coping with marker events is confusion about the proper length of time for the grieving process. It is important to have a discussion early in the group's history about the notion of "shoulds" and how they provide an "invisible burden" for bereaved spouses (Yalom & Vinogradov, 1988, p. 427). When members are invited to share the "shoulds" they carry around, ideas like "one should grieve for a whole year" or "one should (or should not) quickly give away the spouse's clothing" quickly emerge. Discussion centering on the idea that each person establishes his or her own rhythm for grieving usually provides a liberating experience for group members.

Handling Anger and Other Negative Reactions

Handling anger and other negative reactions is often not focused on directly in support groups for bereaved spouses. In the author's experience and according to Yalom and Vinogradov (1988) and Francis (1997), dealing with negative feelings is an important part of the grieving process. However, this is a difficult issue for bereaved spouses, who are often struggling to hold on to the positive aspects of a relationship that they desperately miss. It is difficult to confront the fact that the bereaved are angry at their spouses for "leaving them" or that there are negative aspects of their marital relationship that they must let go of, as well as positive ones. This difficulty is magnified by society's tendency to "sanctify" persons who have died, putting them on a pedestal (Lopata, 1979). Yalom and Vinogradov (1988) found that group members were more able to direct anger toward physicians who had missed a diagnosis or had been insensitive to the needs of the patient and/or family. Expressing anger toward the dead spouse for abandoning the survivor, or for persistent denial while ill, was much more difficult. It is probably most effective to plan a discussion of this topic near the middle or end of a series (if closed ended) or wait until a nucleus of members has formed in an open-ended group.

One exercise that can help bereaved spouses cope with their positive and negative feelings about their marital relationship is having them work in triads, so that each member can role play and/or discuss with a partner two positive and two negative aspects of the marital relationship. After identifying each aspect, it is helpful to have the members say good-bye to that aspect of the relationship with the deceased partner. Some participants in spousal bereavement support groups have commented that progress in the healing process occurs when they can say, "I see this person (spouse) as he really was. I loved him, but I see his . . . weaknesses" (Francis, 1997).

There is also considerable anger that cannot be easily focused— "anger at life, at destiny, at the unfairness of it all" (Yalom & Vinogradov, 1988, p. 442). This can be introduced as a discussion topic, but it flows more easily from group members' comments. There is often new realization that this is an unjust world, and that neither working hard as a couple nor doing good in the world guarantees a protected life.

Taking Responsibility for and Care of Oneself

The death of a spouse confronts the remaining partner with his or her own mortality. While there are usually increased fears about being alone, feelings of abandonment, and concerns about physical safety and health, many bereaved spouses use increased awareness about death in a positive way. "The death of their spouses served . . . to teach them existential responsibility—that they, and only they, have ultimate responsibility for their life and their happiness" (Yalom & Vinogradov, 1988, p. 143). This is a profound statement, and is particularly salient for bereaved spouses who married at a young age and may have viewed their marriage and/or their marital partner as the key to their lifelong happiness. It is not easy to move from feeling abandoned by one's spouse to taking responsibility for one's life.

In the author's experience as a social worker, one of the most helpful techniques is to tell the group members from the beginning (and reinforce it in every session) how important it is to take care of oneself—to discover or rediscover what activities nourish and promote relaxation. It is also important to lead group discussions on this topic so that members can exchange ideas about the range of activities that each finds nurturing. Another method for approaching a session on taking care of oneself is to provide a more didactic review of all the areas that are subject to abuse when an individual experiences prolonged stress and/or mourning and to suggest recommendations for coping with these problems. Topics to be covered can include physical activity, exercise, sleep, nutrition, substance abuse, finances, excessive spending or frugality, social networking, and entertaining (Kliban et al., 1984).

When a review is conducted at the end of a group's sessions, members frequently state that one of the most helpful experiences within the support group was that "I learned to be good to myself" (Kliban et al., 1984, p. 14). Both men and women leave the group with this new learning for their new lives and especially appreciate the social worker's encouragement in this area.

EVALUATION APPROACHES

The literature suggests both informal and formal approaches to evaluation of support groups for bereaved adults. One informal method is to ask group members to summarize at the end of each session and to comment on its negative and positive aspects. Group leaders can complete periodic self-appraisals by using a process log to identify areas for improvement (Heiney & Wells, 1989). They can also evaluate various group processes using predetermined criteria based on the goals and important norms to be established.

A more formal evaluation approach is to use written questionnaires completed by the participants and/or the group leaders. If the group is closed-ended and meets for a defined number of sessions, these questionnaires can be distributed and completed during the final session. If the group is open-ended and ongoing, the questionnaire can be distributed to members during their last session with the group and returned by mail. In either case, questionnaires can also be mailed several months after the members' participation in the group. One questionnaire (Heiney & Wells, 1989) suggests the following questions:

1. Was it helpful to attend a bereavement support group?
2. Would you prefer an ongoing group or a series of 4, 6, 8, or 10 sessions?
3. Was the content applicable to you?
4. What areas of concern were not addressed?
5. Were books and handouts helpful?
6. What was the most helpful aspect of this group experience for you?
7. What was the least helpful aspect of this group experience for you?
8. Would you attend other meetings if it could be arranged?

Folken (1991) mailed a more formal 15-item questionnaire to 137 widowed adults who had participated in meetings within a 2-year period. This survey was conducted to determine if the leaders' perceived benefits coincided with the participants' expectations. These included "1) reaching additional widowed, 2) affording [an] opportunity to interact with a variety of other widowed in a comfortable and caring environment, 3) presenting diversity in ways of coping with grief and chances to evaluate these various methods for personal use, and 4) providing many models of progress through grief" (Folken, 1991, p. 176).

Rognlie (1989) used a more detailed instrument (see the appendix at the end of this chapter) for evaluation of the perceived short- and long-term effects of bereavement support group participation (23 of the 30 members surveyed were widowed spouses). Rognlie mailed the questionnaire and a covering letter to participants who had attended the support groups at least 1 year before completing the questionnaire. After the mailing, the subjects were interviewed by phone, and the responses to the questionnaire were collected and recorded. The questionnaire consists of questions both about the group and about personal issues. "The subjects were asked to evaluate their group experience on a rating scale from 'not helpful' to 'very helpful' as well as to answer more subjective questions in written form" (Rognlie, 1989, p. 43).

CONCLUSION

In conclusion, this chapter has provided a summary of the literature and the author's experiences related to the purposes, practice principles, common themes, and evaluation approaches in designing and leading support groups for widows and widowers. Following is a list of national sources that can be used for further information and services for widowed adults.

RESOURCES

American Hospice Foundation
2120 L ST. NW, Suite 200
Washington DC 20037
(202) 223-0204
www.americanhospice.org

Association for Death Education and
Counseling
342 N. Main St.
Hartford, CT 06117
(203) 586-7503
www.adec.org

National Hospice and Palliative Care
Organization
1700 Diagonal Road, Suite 625
Alexandria, VA 22314
www.nhpco.org

New Beginnings (monthly support
groups for young widows and
widowers, 55 and under)
(216) 383-3737, ext. 3041

Society of Military Widows
5535 Hempstead Way
Springfield, VA 22151
(703) 353-4380

THEOS (They Help Each Other
Spiritually)
Suite 105
322 Boulevard of the Allies
Pittsburgh, PA 15222-1919
(412) 471-7779
www.ncvc.org/gethelp/grief

To Live Again
P.O. Box 415
Springfield, PA 19064
(610) 353-7740
www.eldernetonline.org

Widowed Persons' Services
601 E St. NW
Washington, DC 20049
(202) 434-2260

Widowed Support Group of
Ottawa-Carleton
P.O. Box 16087
Ottawa, ON K2C 3S9
Canada
(613) 723-0010
www.fortnet.org/widownet

WidowNet
widownet.org

REFERENCES

Barrett, C. (1978). Effectiveness of widows' groups in facilitating change. *Journal of Consulting Clinical Psychology.* 46, 20–31.

Brabant, S., Forsyth, C., & Melancon, C. (1992). Grieving men: Thoughts, feelings and behaviors following deaths of wives. *Hospice Journal.* 8(4), 33–47.

Folken, M. (1991). The importance of group support for widowed persons. *Journal for Specialists in Group Work.* 16(3), 172–177.

Francis, L. (1997). Ideology and interpersonal emotion management: Redefining identity in two support groups. *Social Psychology Quarterly.* 60(2), 153–171.

Gitterman, A. (1989). Building mutual support in groups. *Social Work in Groups.* 12(2), 5–21.

Heiney, S., & Wells, L. (1989). Strategies for organizing and maintaining successful support groups. *Oncology Nursing Forum.* 16(6), 803–809.

Hiltz, S. (1975). Helping widows: Group discussions as a therapeutic technique. *Family Coordinator.* 24, 331–336.

Holmes, T. H., & Rahe, R. H. (1967). The social adjustment rating scale. *Journal of Psychosomatic Research.* 11, 213–218.

Jones, D. (1979). The grief therapy project: The effects of group therapy with bereaved surviving spouses on successful coping with grief. Doctoral dissertation. *Dissertation Abstracts International.* 39, 6121–6122.

Kauffman, J. (1994). *Group thanatropics.* In V. Schermer & M. Pines (eds.), *Ring of fire* (pp. 149–173). London: Routledge.

Kay, M., DeZappien, J., Wilson, C., & Yoder, M. (1993). Evaluating treatment efficacy by triangulation. *Social Science Medicine.* 36(12), 1545–1552.

Kinderknecht, C., & Hodges, L. (1990). Facilitating productive bereavement of widows: An overview of the efficacy of widows. *Journal of Women and Aging.* 2(4), 39–54.

Kliban, M., Hanig, F., & Schnitzer-Newson, G. (1984, September). Bereavement counseling in groups. *Caring.* 3(9) 12–18.

Lawrence, L. (1992). Till death do us part: The application of object relations theory to facilitate mourning in a young widows' group. *Social Work in Health Care.* 16(3), 67–81.

Levy, L., Derby, J., & Martinkowski, K. (1993). Effects of membership in bereavement support groups on adaptation to conjugal bereavement. *American Journal of Community Psychology.* 21(3), 361–381.

Lewis, A., & Berns, B. (1975). *Three out of four wives: Widowhood in America.* New York: Macmillan.

Lieberman, M. (1989). Group properties and outcomes: A study of group norms in self-help groups for widows and widowers. *International Journal of Group Psychotherapy.* 39(2), 191–208.

Lieberman, M., & Borman, M. (1979). *Self-help groups for coping with crisis.* San Francisco: Jossey-Bass.

Lieberman, M., & Videka-Sherman, L. (1986). The impact of self-help groups on the mental health of widows and widowers. *American Journal of Orthopsychiatry.* 56(3), 435–449.

Lopata, H. (1979). *Women as widows.* New York: Elsevier North-Holland.

Lopata, H. (1986). Becoming and being a widow: Reconstruction of the self and support systems. *Journal of Geriatric Psychiatry.* 19(2), 203–214.

Lorenz, L. (1998). Selecting and implementing support groups for bereaved adults. *Cancer Practice.* 6(3), 161–166.

McCourt, W., Barnett, R., Brennan, J., & Becker, A. (1976). We help each other: Primary prevention for the widowed. *American Journal of Psychiatry.* 133, 98–100.

Raphael, B. (1977). Preventive intervention with the recently bereaved. *Archives of General Psychiatry.* 34, 1450–1454.

Rognlie, C. (1989). Perceived short- and long-term effects of bereavement support group participation at the hospice of Petaluma. *Hospice Journal.* 5(2), 39–53.

Tudiver, F., Hilditch, J., Permaul, J., & McKendre, D. (1992). *Evaluation and the Health Professions.* 15(2), 147–162.

Vachon, M. (1979). *Identity change over the first two years of bereavement: Social relationships and social support in widowhood.* Unpublished doctoral dissertation, York University, Toronto.

Yalom, I., & Vinogradov, S. (1988). Bereavement groups: Techniques and themes. *International Journal of Group Psychotherapy.* 38(4), 419–446.

APPENDIX: BEREAVEMENT SUPPORT GROUP EVALUATION*

Background Information

Age   Sex
Date client began support group

       1 = Not helpful
       2 = Uncertain
       3 = A little helpful
       4 = Moderately helpful
       5 = Very helpful

1. In general, the support group was: 1 2 3 4 5
2. Learning about the grief process and the
    manifestations of grief was: 1 2 3 4 5
3. Being able to share my feelings with others who
    had gone through something similar was: 1 2 3 4 5
4. The knowledge and/or support of the group
    leaders was: 1 2 3 4 5
5. Making new friends and reaching out to other
    people in grief was: 1 2 3 4 5
6. Talking about the spouse who died was: 1 2 3 4 5
7. Hearing others talk about their feelings and
    experiences was: 1 2 3 4 5
8. Reading, writing and homework assignments were: 1 2 3 4 5
9. The topics covered during the groups were: 1 2 3 4 5
10. Do you feel that participation in a bereavement support group
    made a difference in the way that you dealt with your loss at the
    time? If so, how?
11. Has your past involvement in a support group affected how you
    have dealt with your loss over an extended period of time? If so,
    how? For example has it affected how you deal with stress, eating or
    sleeping patterns, or social interactions?
12. In retrospect, would you have chosen to attend a support group,
    having had the experience? Why or why not?

*From Rognlie, 1989, pp. 51–52.

13. Would you recommend a bereavement support group to a bereaved friend or family member?
14. Have you kept in contact with, or formed friendships with, any of your previous group members?
15. Can you suggest how any benefits of support group interactions could be maintained or increased after the group is over?

Chapter 8

Group Work with Noncustodial Parents

GEOFFREY L. GREIF

Family breakup (and its correlates) looms as one of the major social problems of the last few decades. The number of one-parent families with children under 18 more than tripled between 1970 and 2000, while the number of married-couple families fell slightly (U.S. Bureau of the Census, 2001). Even when children are not involved, divorce is often accompanied by residential and economic instability, loss of key adult relationships, destruction of one's hope of "living happily ever after," and anger, depression, and anxiety (Garvin et al., 1993). When children are present, the tasks associated with coping and the complexity of those tasks greatly increase (Portes et al., 1992).

After divorce or separation, one parent often becomes a visitor in his or her child's life, a role that is not clearly defined. This is more often the father than the mother (Stewart, 2003). The parent usually loses, to varying degrees, some level of input into how that child will be raised and, in many instances, is relegated to having a minimal relationship with the child. Such a person is left in an ambiguous position both as a parent and as an adult trying to establish an identity. Sometimes isolated from friends, family, and other sources of support after the breakup, the noncustodial parent suffers.

Group experience can help reduce noncustodial parents' pain and provide a safe haven for exploring their relationship with their children (Oygard & Hardeng, 2001). This chapter describes a short-term support group for noncustodial parents, detailing common themes that emerged during the course of the group sessions.

REVIEW OF THE LITERATURE

The relationship of noncustodial fathers to their children is not clearly defined and has not been well researched (Greif, 1997). The literature describes noncustodial fathers as struggling with and sometimes failing to maintain a relationship with their children after the breakup of their marriage. Over time, the relationship between the father and his children frequently deteriorates (Aquilino, 1994). Fathers may feel guilt about the failure of the marriage and inadequate as parents. Some fathers, smarting from the failed marital relationship, undergo intense conflict with their ex-wives that affects their ability to coparent (Dudley, 1991). When they have an acrimonious relationship with their ex-wives, it can spill over into their relationship with their children (Arditti & Kelly, 1994) and involve them in ongoing battles. Such stress may cause depression, low self-esteem, and disturbances in work performance and sleeping patterns (Coney & Mackey, 1989; Stone, 2002). Similar problems also persist for fathers who were never married (Fischer, 2002). Of course, not all fathers are negatively affected. Some use the single-parent experience to forge even stronger bonds with their children.

While noncustodial mothers suffer many of the same feelings and stresses as fathers (Depner, 1993; Greif, 1997), they also face additional ones. Women in our society earn less money than men. As they are socialized to be the primary caregivers of children, deviation from that norm often exposes them to disparaging comments from friends and family and creates a sense of failure. Because of the stigma associated with a mother's giving up custody, they are often reluctant to discuss their noncustodial status with others. Some choose to hide this aspect of their lives. Thus many experience guilt, shame, anxiety, and depression (Greif & Pabst, 1988; Rosenblum, 1986) and feel compelled to deal with these issues alone. Group treatment offers both of these populations the opportunity to meet with other parents in a supportive atmosphere where their reactions to being noncustodial can be approached.

PRACTICE PRINCIPLES

Meetings of the group discussed in this chapter were held at a family service agency in Baltimore. Clients were either referred from current caseloads or self-referred from advertisements describing a 4-week support group for noncustodial parents. The coleaders were the author, who was connected to the agency only during the leadership of this group, and a staff member in charge of single-parent issues who was always available to group members. Following a telephone screening interview, a core group was formed for a four-week set of sessions. It was believed that a short-term group would have the best chance of attracting a sufficient number of members. Given the nature of this population, contracting played a large part in the establishment and initiation of the group. Contracting was important for the members because so much of their lives focused on the broken contract of marriage. In addition, many of them had been locked in legal battles concerning child support and visitation. By paying careful attention to expectations about attendance and participation, we believed we would pave the way for a successful group experience. A great deal of time was spent discussing obstacles to attendance (Shulman, 1999). Two people knew each other and were reluctant initially to share personal material; scheduling proved difficult for a few others. Contact outside of the group between members (something we did not discourage) was also discussed at the first session.

The leaders played an active role from the outset in starting and stopping the group and in guiding the discussion. We suggested topics and helped to facilitate discussion. We believed it was especially important to be central to the group, as there were only four sessions. With a longer-term group, we would have considered taking a more peripheral role in the middle stage. Since the group dealt with relationships in the broadest sense, we focused on this aspect of work with these parents. It became the underlying theme that we returned to continually throughout the meetings.

The group was sufficiently satisfying that the members requested two more 4-week sessions. When the group recontracted, we judged that internal leaders had emerged from the group and that we could assume a more peripheral role, except initially when a few new members joined and specific leader-related tasks had to be accomplished. In this way, our roles shifted as the group moved into the later stages of its work.

With new members coming for the second set of sessions, a total of eight members attended at least one set of four group meetings. The typical number per group was five or six members. The members, who were in their mid-30s to mid-40s, were divided evenly between males and females. Their backgrounds varied. Most worked full time, though one of the men lost his job during the course of group meetings. One woman, previously unemployed, began volunteer work at the suggestion of group members. Members' children ranged in age from 5 to 22, and the number of children per parent ranged from two to four. Half of the members were remarried, and two members had children from their new marriage.

Group members varied in the amount and nature of contact they had with their children. Two mothers regularly visited their children but wanted more time because they were unhappy with the way the children were being raised. The other two mothers had little or no contact with their children. One of these mothers ended her marriage and left home; visitation was initiated while the children were living with their father. Over time, the children became verbally and physically abusive to the mother, perhaps as an expression of their anger toward her for ending the marriage. She refused to see them until they began to treat her with respect. When she entered the group, she had not spoken with either child (both were in their teens) for 1 year. The other mother had experienced many ups and downs with her four children (12 to 22 years old); two of them refused to see her, and she refused to see the other two. Substance abuse, psychiatric hospitalizations, the suicide of a 16-year-old daughter, and a suicide attempt by another child made this mother's parenting situation extremely complicated.

The fathers also had difficult family situations. Two of them had children who lived at a great distance; although the children were allowed to visit, they did so only occasionally. Another father had regular visitation, and the fourth father had been rejected by his 22-year-old daughter and his 2-year-old son.

The different marital statuses of the members were not a critical factor in group work. Although the unmarried members seemed more lonely than those who had remarried, remarriage did not provide a buffer from the pain of separation from the children. Those who had remarried usually felt that their new spouses supported them in their feelings toward their children and in their battles with their ex-spouses. In some cases, the new spouses even helped escalate intrafamilial conflict. Remarriage did not seem to enhance members' ability to cope with the problems that brought them into the group.

As might be expected, relations with ex-spouses varied but tended to be acrimonious. Members showed signs of being significantly emotionally attached to their ex-spouses (Masheter, 1990), which made it difficult for some of the parents to separate their anger at their ex-spouses from their need to behave as competent coparents. This confusion emerged in the group. As members discussed their feelings toward their ex-spouses, members of the opposite sex sometimes jumped to the defense of the ex-spouses as the discussion touched on members' vulnerabilities.

COMMON THEMES

Various themes emerged during group work with these parents that could be addressed in future groups serving this population.

Children Rejecting Parents

The most painful issue for parents was their children's actual or perceived rejection of them. In some cases, children refused to see a parent for reasons that members often understood cognitively but found painful nonetheless. In a few instances, children chose to live with the other parent. For mothers, in particular, a child's electing to live with the father was devastating. Often, group members felt rejected when their children did not want to spend their prearranged visitation time with them if it interfered with peer activities. Group members proved particularly helpful to one of the fathers by interpreting his daughter's need to be with adolescent peers as age-appropriate behavior.

A hope frequently expressed by parents who were struggling with feelings of rejection was that their children would some day "return" to them or appreciate them more if they continued to behave in a consistent and caring manner. One mother who had not spoken with her children for a year continued to send them cards and to attend sporting events at their school so that her children would, she hoped, look back on this period in their lives and think more kindly of her. Despite this optimistic attitude, members struggled with deciding at what point their efforts to establish a relationship with rejecting children became self-defeating or too painful to continue. One parent wondered aloud how long he would continue to put himself in such an uncomfortable position.

Parents Rejecting Children

Some parents rejected their children because they felt their children had rejected them. Parents of preadolescents and adolescents in particular felt angry with their children. Rubbed raw by the divorce process and the legal wrangling that accompanied it, some parents were unable to assume an adult, parenting role. They treated their children more like peers or siblings than like children. They had difficulty seeing their children as needy because they themselves were too needy to step back and observe the parent-child dynamics. As a result, opportunities to reestablish contact with their children were often defeated by their own reactions.

Differences between Mothers and Fathers:
Stigma, Money Matters, and Advice

Fathers and mothers tended to differ both in the issues they raised within the group and in their interactions with their children. Chief among these differences was the way in which they explained their noncustodial status to new acquaintances outside the group. As the literature suggests, women were much more apt to deny their noncustodial status. Two of the mothers recounted how they changed the subject or lied when they were asked if they had children. The fathers did not express such tendencies. Because fathers were generally court-ordered to pay child support, they were more likely to express anger about financial matters and having to pay lawyers.

Mothers were more likely than fathers to seek and accept advice from the group and to present themselves in a "one-down" position as the help seeker. Fathers were more likely to intellectualize problems as a defense strategy and to offer advice and assurance. This response was anticipated, given the general finding that women are socialized to seek help from and affiliation with others (Diedrick, 1991). Men, in general, are less likely to seek services and are considered a more difficult population to serve because of their typical defensive posture (Meth & Pasick, 1990).

Holidays and Special Events

A great deal of group time was consumed by discussions of holidays and major life transitions for the children. Mother's Day and religious holidays are typically difficult times for divorced parents. One mother said she planned to spend Mother's Day at work so that she could be alone and avoid others who were celebrating the day. The holiday made her acutely aware of the loss of her role and status. On advice from the group, she spent time with friends instead. Fathers tended to be less affected by Father's Day and to be more adept at shutting out this holiday.

Ceremonies such as school graduation and bar and bat mitzvahs were also upsetting for the parents. Such events typically include many family members, financial expenditures, coordination of celebrations, and a public appearance of the divorced parents in the same place. Many problems surfaced at such times. Participants talked about being snubbed by in-laws, major events being canceled because parents could not make plans together, and stepparents replacing them in key roles. Fathers complained about being asked to pay for these events and then relegated to a supporting rather than a starring role. The children were frequently caught in the middle of such disputes and often withdrew to avoid further triangulation. This was interpreted as rejection by some of the parents.

Grandparent Issues

The support of grandparents, other relatives, and friends can be vitally important when a parent has little or no contact with his or her child. Some parents regressed to a childlike role in seeking reassurance from their parents. Grandparents varied in their reactions to their children and grandchildren. Some were supportive, others refused to become involved, and a small group ignored the parent in the middle (the group member) and sought contact directly with their grandchildren. This left some group members feeling undermined.

Group members who had little visitation time with their children felt caught between their wish to be alone with their children and having their children visit their grandparents. If the grandparents protested about how little time they saw their grandchildren, the parents felt a dual sense of failure. Not only could they not negotiate a relationship with their children, they were hurting their own parents' chances as well. The parents were extremely vulnerable to any criticism from their own parents and often reacted angrily, isolating themselves even more.

Emotional Triangulation

Divorced parents typically struggle to establish clear boundaries with the other parent and the children so that parenting issues can be more easily managed. When emotions are inflamed, this can prove to be a daunting task. Group members described situations in which their parenting efforts were blocked by the custodial parent, a not uncommon occurrence (see, e.g., Gardner, 2003, for a discussion of the Parental Alienation Syndrome). Out of frustration from being unable to parent as they wished, the noncustodial parent typically exploded with anger at either the custodial parent or the child. As a result, the child often felt caught between the parents and believed they were the cause of their fighting. One child reacted by screaming at both parents when all three were on the telephone.

Triangulation also took a different form. Some parents in the group believed that the custodial parents' well-being was too closely tied to their children's affections. The custodial parents were described as having a "stranglehold" on the children's emotions and as using that overly intense connection to paint the noncustodial parent as incompetent or unworthy. At the same time, children were depicted as being unable to make decisions on their own and, conversely, as having too much power over the custodial parent's emotional well-being. In these complex symbiotic relationships, it appeared as though the children were in a lose-lose situation in which they felt they had to align themselves with and be supportive of the custodial parent. They formed the third side of a triangle but felt excluded from the other two sides.

Depending on the emotional maturity of the group member and the behavior of the custodial parent, these thorny relationships were difficult to sort out. The advantage of having a mixed-sex group was that members were able to examine their reactions and to gain insight regarding the behavior of both male and female custodial parents. When contentious relationship issues arose, members encouraged one another to behave in a way that made them feel good about themselves and did the least harm to the children. Such advice was not always acted on. For some members, revenge at any price, even at the child's expense, was the operating principle.

Children's Progress

Paradoxically, parents with the least involvement with their children were often extremely interested in how the children were progressing. On the one hand, they hoped their children's lives were going smoothly. On the other hand, they took a certain amount of pleasure in learning that the custodial parent was having difficulties with the children. From the members' perspective, if the children had little contact with them but were progressing well, then they obviously were of little importance to their children and their role was diminished.

Termination Issues

Group termination was postponed twice because some of the members wanted to recontract for four more sessions. For these parents, termination of the group was closely linked with past losses that permeated their lives. A few members were also coping with the loss of jobs and the actual or impending death of a parent. Because of the multitude of losses in these group members' lives, discussion never strayed far from this topic. We tried to look at loss through a different lens and provide a new way of thinking about it. When parents talked about recontracting, we reframed it as wanting connection rather than avoiding loss.

RECOMMENDED WAYS OF WORKING

The themes discussed above unfolded within the context of the group process. Initially, members found it difficult to trust one another. Villains outside the group were easy to find. Members fed into one another's defenses by denigrating their ex-spouses and, in some cases, their children. Although trading "divorce war stories" was initially soothing and a way of normalizing their experiences, continual focus on these issues would have derailed meaningful group work.

For example, one member's stories about his children indicated a lack of willingness to be vulnerable with them, a pattern that he mirrored with other group members. Another member rarely shared her pain, "reporting" her experiences rather than expressing her feelings in a way that would make it easier for other members to connect with her.

In one extreme situation, a mother who had suffered greatly at the hands of her children considered legally divorcing her children as a way to avoid being hurt by them. She brought the group a book that offered a guide to this type of divorce. As leaders, we believed that these actions displayed the degree to which she had been hurt by her children (one of whom had committed suicide two years prior to her group attendance). We did not attempt to dissuade her from her plan. Rather, we listened and helped her identify her underlying feelings. We stated that this seemed a fairly serious action for her to take but one that we could certainly understand. We asked that she bring the issue back to the group in future weeks so that we could consider it further. She did reintroduce the issue at the next meeting but eventually abandoned the idea. Because she felt supported in her ruminations, she was able to explore her options.

In general, it was easier for members to give support than to ask for it. Although providing support is one of the benefits of the group process, it was especially important for these parents because it reinforced their ability to nurture (a quality that had been questioned by others). Receiving support, however, was much more difficult for them because they perceived it as an admission that they needed help and raised painful questions about whether they deserved to be supported. Admitting their need for support meant that life as a noncustodial parent was somehow deficient, which undermined their defenses.

Member-leader communication differed according to the worker. Both female and male members tended to look to the male worker for advice and approval and, in the case of male members, for camaraderie. Members looked to the female leader for emotional support. When the members were emotionally upset, the female leader's counsel was generally sought.

The group proceeded slowly at first as members sought to justify their interactions with their children. We attempted to provide a supportive atmosphere in which members could feel safe in sharing their doubts and insecurities about themselves. The group focused on members' current experiences and feelings, encouraging members to think about their interactions with their children. Some members responded better to cognitive analysis than they did to emotional content. Leaders were keenly aware of the potential for negative transference. We were reluctant to offer advice during the first few sessions because members might interpret such advice as disapproval. Instead, we offered comments that would encourage members to reflect on their situation and behavior. As the group progressed, we helped members identify painful situations and offered more suggestions when we were confident that they would not be interpreted as criticism.

EVALUATION APPROACHES

Progress was charted through detailed note taking after each group meeting and with follow-up telephone calls three months after the last meeting. Positive change was noted in five of the eight members. Four members used the group to resolve difficulties with their children, and a fifth, the one with the best relationship with his children, appreciated his situation more. Another member remained passive and seemed to receive little benefit from the group experience, and one man, who was an active member, showed no change in his ability to handle his anger toward his children and ex-spouse. Another member's situation deteriorated. She had entered the group feeling the most anger toward her children, had wanted to divorce them, and continued to suffer both in her relationships with them and in her personal adjustment as a noncustodial parent.

In planning services for single parents, social workers need to focus on noncustodial parents. Group work with this population can help ease the difficult divorce-related transitions that adults and children often have to make and can broaden the scope of services offered in the community.

RESOURCES

Parents Without Partners
1650 South Dixie Highway, Ste. 500
Boca Raton, FL 33432
(800) 637-7974.
www.parentswithoutpartners.org

Children's Rights Council
6200 Editor's Park Drive, Ste. 103
Hyattsville, MD 20782
(301) 559-3120
www.gocrc.com

REFERENCES

Aquilino, W. S. (1994). Impact of childhood family disruption on young adults' relationships with parents. *Journal of Marriage and the Family.* 56, 295–313.

Arditti, J. A., & Kelly, M. (1994). Fathers' perspectives of their co-parental relationship postdivorce. *Family Relations.* 43, 61–67.

Coney, N. S., & Mackey, W. C. (1989). Perceptions of the problems of the divorced father. *Journal of Divorce.* 13, 81–96.

Depner, C. E. (1993). Parental role reversal: Mothers as nonresidential parents. In C. E. Depner & J. H. Bray (eds.), *Nonresidential parenting,* pp. 37–57. Newbury Park, CA: Sage.

Diedrick, P. (1991). Gender differences in divorce adjustment. *Journal of Divorce and Remarriage.* 14, 33–45.

Dudley, J. R. (1991). Increasing our understanding of divorced fathers who have infrequent contact with their children. *Family Relations.* 40, 279–285.

Fischer, R. L. (2002). Gaining access to one's children: An evaluation of a visitation program for noncustodial parents. *Families in Society.* 83, 163–174.

Gardner, R. A. (2003). Does DSM-IV have equivalents for the Parental Alienation Syndrome (PAS) diagnosis? *American Journal of Family Therapy.* 31, 1–21.

Garvin, V., Kalter, N., & Hansell, J. (1993). Divorced women: Individual differences in stressors, mediating factors and adjustment outcome. *American Journal of Orthopsychiatry.* 63, 232–240.

Greif, G. L. (1997). *Out of touch: When parents and children lose contact after divorce.* New York: Oxford University Press.

Greif, G. L., & Pabst, M. S. (1988). *Mothers without custody.* New York: Macmillan/Lexington Books.

Masheter, C. (1990). Postdivorce relationships between ex-spouses: A literature review. *Journal of Divorce.* 14, 97–122.

Meth, R. L., & Pasick, R. S. (1990). *Men in therapy: The challenge of change.* New York: Guilford Press.

Oygard, L., & Hardeng, S. (2001). Divorce support groups—How do group characteristics influence adjustment to divorce? *Social Work with Groups.* 24, 69–87.

Portes, P. R., Howell, S. C., Brown, J. H., Eichenberger, S., & Mas, C. A. (1992). Family functions and children's postdivorce adjustment. *American Journal of Orthopsychiatry.* 62, 613–617.

Rosenblum, K. E. (1986). Leaving as a wife, leaving as a mother. *Journal of Social Issues.* 7, 197–213.

Shulman, L. (1999). *The skills of helping individuals, families and groups* (4th ed.). Itasca, IL: F. E. Peacock.

Stewart, S. D. (2003). Nonresident parenting and adolescent adjustment: The quality of nonresident father–child interaction. *Journal of Family Issues.* 24, 217–244.

Stone, G. (2002). Nonresidential father postdivorce wellbeing: The role of social supports. *Journal of Divorce & Remarriage.* 36, 139–150.

U.S. Bureau of the Census. (2001). America's families and living arrangements: June. P20-537. Washington, DC: Government Printing Office.

Chapter 9

Group Work with Children of Divorce

SARA BONKOWSKI

Since 1960 the number of divorces and the divorce rate have more than doubled (Ahlburg & DeVita, 1992). Divorce is far more prevalent in the United States than elsewhere; in 1997, 1.6 million divorces occurred. Between 1970 and 1993, the number of divorced adults nearly quadrupled, while the total number of adults increased by less than half. Divorce affects not only adults but their children as well. The odds of having parents divorce are twice as great today as they were a generation ago; over 1 million children under the age of 18 saw their parents divorce in 1997 (U.S. Bureau of the Census, 1997). Married couples raising their own children have declined significantly since 1970 (U.S. Bureau of the Census, 2001). Estimates are that half of all children will experience the breakup of their parents' marriage (Ahlburg & DeVita, 1992).

Divorce is unlike other seemingly similar life experiences for a child, such as loss of a parent through death, in that divorce is specifically rooted in the failure of the relationship between the mother and father, who model the reliability of love and commitment (Wallerstein, 1991a). Adjustment problems in children of divorce have been documented in several realms—cognitive, behavioral, affective, and physiological (Wallerstein, 1991a)—and spill over into school performance and personal relationships (Frieman et al., 1994). Children in divorced families, compared with those in intact families, show more aggression directed toward authority figures, more difficulty with peers, more learning difficulties, and more school dropout (Furstenberg, 1990). Similar comparisons have found that children of divorce exhibit diminished coping capacity and lower self-esteem (Kurtz, 1994).

135

Social workers and others, concerned with both the immediate crisis and the long-term effect of parental divorce, have responded by designing interventions for children aimed at ameliorating the stress of divorce (Bonkowski et al., 1984; Cowen et al., 1989; Roseby & Johnston, 1997; Rossiter, 1988; Stolberg & Mahler, 1989). Participation in a divorce group with other children can be fun and at the same time can promote general adjustment (Bonkowski et al., 1984; Hett & Rose, 1991). Children in divorce groups have demonstrated a decrease in problematic behaviors and an increase in school performance (Alpert-Gillis et al., 1989).

Thus, the ability to design and lead children's groups is an important professional skill for the social worker providing services for children of divorce. This chapter will discuss practice principles and common themes for group work with children of divorce.

PRACTICE PRINCIPLES

Designing and implementing a divorce group for children requires the social worker to consider several practice principles. Decisions made in one area may affect other decisions, so it is important to clarify the underpinnings of the group.

Who Is the Client: The Child, the Parent, or the Agency/Sponsor?

The first response may be, of course, that the child is the client. However, whenever children participate in a group, their parents must have some involvement; parental participation may include calling a community agency to enroll the child, giving permission to participate in a school-based group, providing transportation to attend the group, and occasionally bringing refreshments. In groups where children are dealing with divorce issues, some parents, especially those in conflict, may want to know what the child is saying to the group; the parent may even attempt to tell the social worker what types of issues to discuss.

The agency sponsoring the group may require some input into the group. For example, a school may decided that only children of divorce who display school problems are eligible for group participation. Some teachers and administrators expect the social worker to provide them with specific information about a group member. If so, the social worker should make it clear at the beginning of the process what can and cannot be shared.

The child and the child's needs must always be paramount. Both parents and administrators should be provided with guidelines clarifying confidentiality and participation. Clear communication regarding boundaries will prevent potential misunderstandings among administrators, parents, and the social worker.

Confidentiality

The children in the group must feel safe and free to participate fully. Confidentiality should be discussed in the first session. Children should know that it is permissible to tell their parents anything they choose, but they should be supported if they prefer not to talk with parents about the group experience. Children of divorce frequently feel powerless; helping them understand their rights gives them more control over their group experience.

All group members must be encouraged not to discuss what other members share. The social worker will guarantee the children confidentiality, explaining the one exception: when there is a danger to the child. The discussion of confidentiality may be the first time a child has been told that she or he has rights. This process will help the child apply the same principles if one parent tries to gather information about the other parent.

Children of Divorce Groups: Prevention or Treatment?

Divorce groups for children, especially in nonclinical settings such as schools, YWCA/YMCAs, and churches, are often conceptualized as prevention groups. The literature has established that children of divorce are at risk of developing many problems (Wallerstein, 1991b); thus, the goal of prevention is to provide groups for children early in the divorce process in the hope of preventing or lessening the impact of family disruption (Kaminsky, 1986).

Many children, however, enroll in groups several years after divorce. Wallerstein (1991b) states that families of divorce remain at risk for several years. Children in these families may have been struggling with such stressful life events as witnessing parental conflict, moving, changing schools, and complying with imposed visitation schedules. As a result of living with these stressors, the child may have taken on adult responsibility or is experiencing intense loyalty splits that can contribute to a range of problems, such as angry acting-out behavior, headaches, stomach problems, withdrawal from childhood activities, and so on. The goal for these children is to provide help that will improve their functioning.

In all likelihood, groups for children of divorce will have members whose parents are just beginning the divorce process and children whose parents divorced long ago. In the group, the children and social worker engage in a process that strengthens all the children. Thus, the categorization of a group as prevention or treatment serves the need of administrative planning; in reality, children's divorce groups are both.

Utilizing Paraprofessional Group Leaders

Many groups for children of divorce are led by professional leaders (e.g., Bonkowski et al., 1984; Cowen et al., 1989; Rossiter, 1988; Stolberg &

Mahler, 1989). Other groups are led by volunteers who have been trained by a professional.

No evaluations have assessed the outcome of groups led by volunteers compared to groups led by social workers. Such comparison studies would provide data to make decisions about the relative importance of the professional background of group leaders. Currently, the demand for groups for children of divorce is so great that social workers may be in a position to design and lead groups or to train and supervise others.

Extent of Intervention

Most divorce groups for children are time limited, ranging from 6 weeks (Hett & Rose, 1991; Rossiter, 1988) to 14 weeks (Pedro-Carroll et al., 1992; Roseby & Johnston, 1997; Stolberg & Mahler, 1989). Some groups have parallel groups for parents (Rossiter, 1991; Stolberg & Mahler, 1989). When the group is completed, the intervention with both children and parents ends. For some children, there is little need for ongoing intervention; others may still have serious unresolved problems. When there is a continuing need for help, the social worker may refer children for more in-depth counseling. However, the termination of a trusting relationship with the group leader marks another loss for the child.

Given the realities of budget and time restraints, there are no easy answers to these ethical and practice concerns. However, the social worker must acknowledge the dilemma and attempt to minimize the loss for the child.

COMMON THEMES

Groups designed for children of divorce should include exercises, experiences, and information that address divorce-related issues. The divorce issues and themes discussed apply specifically to grade school children because divorce groups have been found to be an effective intervention for children between the ages of 6 to 12.

This does not imply that younger children or high school adolescents do not need help at the time of parental separation; however, the cognitive and emotional development of younger and older children have different considerations. For example, pre-school children do not have the cognitive capacity to understand the concept of divorce; they may say the word *divorce,* tell you what it means, and then ask if Daddy is coming home tonight. (See Rossiter, 1988, for a discussion of a preschool group.)

Adolescents often object to participating in a divorce group. They do not want to be labeled or pathologized by the action of their parents. Parents are able to enroll an 8-year-old in a group, but it is much more difficult to force an adolescent to do anything against his will. Teenagers may address divorce-related concerns in a general peer support group at school.

The following themes apply specifically to time-limited divorce groups for children aged 6 to 12.

Feeling Alone and "Different"

Although in any classroom 30%–50% of the children may have divorced parents, many children feel they are the only one with this family situation. Typically, grade school children do not discuss intimate family concerns with their schoolmates. Instead, they interact in the immediate environment, playing ball, borrowing paper, talking about fire drills and the class bully.

The child sitting at the next desk may be in the midst of parental divorce of which her seatmate is totally unaware. Even when children know that another child's parents are getting a divorce, they seldom know how to offer support. Children need trusted adults to help them understand and master loss and stress; children also need to know that other children are coping with sad family changes.

The process and importance of peer support are often cited as an essential group ingredient: helping the child know he is not alone (Hett & Rose, 1991), fostering group support (Pedro-Carrol et al., 1992), being with others who are having similar feelings and experiences (Cantrell, 1986), and offering peer support (Bonkowski et al., 1984).

Child participants are the best spokespersons for the supportive power of the group. Eight-year-old Megan reported, "I love Tuesdays. I get to go to Wendy's group [Wendy was the school social worker]. Amy goes too. I never knew she was divorced. Her dad lives in New Jersey." Megan had felt sad because she was allowed to visit her father only every other weekend. In the group she discovered that other children were also missing their fathers, and in fact they thought she was lucky to see her father so often. Amy, her special friend in the group, was a popular, well-liked classmate; this dispelled some of Megan's fears that other children wouldn't like her if her parents were divorced.

Feeling Worried and Anxious, Not Knowing What Is Going to Happen

"I thought I would have to be on the witness stand," 10-year-old Sammy confided to the group. Sammy had been secretly worried that he would have to be part of a courtroom drama, like many he had seen on television.

Children whose parents are divorcing often know very little about what takes place in a divorce, what types of decisions will be made and by whom, when changes will occur, and, most important, what input they will have. Some children are told in advance by their parents that there is going to be a divorce and may be given an explanation of why the parents can no longer stay married; many children are told nothing.

Children need to be taught that divorce is an adult decision, not something caused by the child. They need to be prepared for the roles of attorneys and judges, and told what a court may be like and the meaning of child support, custody, and visitation. When children understand these concepts they will feel empowered, and divorce will not seem so mysterious. What is unknown to children is most frightening.

In the divorce group, children can learn about the legal process of divorce in an age-appropriate manner. Of course, cognitively, a 12-year-old will understand more than a 6-year-old.

School-age children are often fascinated with the concept of fairness; they argue at recess about fair rules and accuse teachers of not being fair. It seems logical and reassuring that there is someone, a judge, who will make fair decisions about the divorce. It is important for children to understand that their parents may not think that what the judge decides is fair, but that the judge is thinking about all members of the family, and especially about what is best for the children.

Feeling Stuck, Pressured, and Unable to Make Decisions

Children from divorced homes often face situations in which what they want to do or how they feel conflicts with one or both parents. Ginny, a shy second grader, was invited to her first birthday party. Unfortunately, the Saturday of the party was the time she had visitation with her father. Ginny desperately wanted to go to the party, but she did not know if she had any choice. Feeling stuck, she hid the invitation in her backpack.

Generating and exploring various solutions to problems is a process that can be learned. Helping children begin to understand the process of rationally thinking through different options can give them a powerful tool in facing dilemmas that arise during parental divorce.

The extent to which children can master problem-solving skills depends partially on their age. Younger grade school children need to practice very simple solutions to the problem "When you are feeling mad at your mother, what can you do?" Older grade school children can engage in more creative but realistic problem solving, such as using flow charts to trace the results of different options.

Stolberg and Mahler (1989) have developed a systematized approach to teaching problem-solving skills. To help children retain the information presented in the divorce group, they designed *Kidsbook*, a book to take home and apply the skills learned in the group to the home, classroom, and playground.

The group leader can model problem solving when issues arise in the group. Children living in emotionally labile homes may have had little experience watching adults calmly discuss options.

Not Understanding and Acknowledging
Ambivalent Feelings

Adults often have difficulty accepting the ambivalence present in any intimate relationship. It is no wonder, then, that children experiencing the collapse of their parents' marriage will not understand the range of conflicting feelings they experience, especially when the feelings are emotional opposites such as anger and love.

Ralph admired his father, emulating his interest in baseball. During the time his parents were divorcing, Ralph witnessed his father physically hurting his mother; now he felt rage toward the loved, admired father. Ralph shut down emotionally because he could not allow himself to feel both love and hate for his father. After the group leader helped him express how much he missed and loved his father, and how he hated him for hurting his mother, Ralph's previous outgoing personality gradually returned. Encouraged by Ralph's understanding that he could have both of these feelings, other group members began to share their feelings.

The expression of feelings may temporarily make the child feel sad, angry, and so on. However, in the long run, it is healthier for the child to express and acknowledge the pain and ambivalence of parental divorce than to freeze emotional responses.

Needing Encouragement and Modeling to Promote
Communication with Important Others

Promoting clear communication is the goal of many social work interventions, and it is important for children of divorce to be able to communicate with others about their needs, feelings, and wishes related to parental divorce. The most important people the child communicates with are her parents, but under some circumstances the child may need to communicate with attorneys or judges.

Elaine was a valuable member of her sixth-grade volleyball team. The volleyball games were played on Saturday mornings, but every other Saturday she was with her father, who elected not to take her to the games. Afraid that she would hurt his feelings, Elaine had been unable to tell her father that she wanted to go to the games.

In the divorce group, she practiced telling her father exactly how she felt and asking him to take her to the volleyball games. Much to Elaine's relief, her father responded by telling her how much he appreciated her letting him know about the games and stating that he had been unaware of their importance. He began taking her to volleyball on the Saturdays she was with him.

Communication is not only talking. Children can communicate through writing letters, drawing pictures, making a tape, or writing a story. After identifying their feelings, children can decide how to communicate those feelings to their parents. (This process links the identification of feelings, problem solving, and communication.)

An important caveat needs to be included in a discussion of communication. In some instances, it may be dangerous for a child to communicate feelings and wishes to a parent. The parent may react with anger or disbelief, use the child's feelings in the divorce battle, or ignore expressed wishes. The social worker should help the child realistically assess the possible outcomes of communication.

Children should be aware that communicating clearly does not guarantee an outcome. For example, a child may tell his father that he does not want to visit. The father may respond that he understands his wishes but that the child will still have to visit.

Children from intact families do not get all of their wishes either. They too must do things they do not want to do. It is never desirable for a child to be in charge of his parents, but it is important for parents to listen and consider the child's feelings. The lack of power children have in divorcing families is often frustrating for both the children and the social worker; all parties can be empowered by communicating this frustration.

Experiencing Low Self-Esteem

Parental divorce and the accompanying stress often weaken the child's ability to maintain a good self-image. "If my family is having these awful problems, we must not be a very good family and I must not be a very likable person" is the child's reasoning.

The social worker may want to include group exercises that specifically identify the child's strengths and interests (Bonkowski et al., 1984). During divorce and in a divorce group, there will be a focus on divorce. But children are much more than part of their parents' divorce; it is important to value and acknowledge the whole child—soccer player, dog lover, potential veterinarian, comedian, and so on.

Needing Fun

Divorce is not fun for anyone. But children need to have fun, to laugh, to be silly. Children and their social worker can have fun at the group meetings. This does not mean that difficult topics or unpleasant feelings are ignored; in fact, the group gives children a safe place to face these topics and feelings.

However, every group meeting must include some fun time, such as telling jokes, playing a guessing game, or discussing Halloween costumes. Social workers dealing with children need to be able to play, to value nonverbal experiences, and to tolerate being touched, hugged, and kissed.

RECOMMENDED WAYS OF WORKING

Group activities, the length and number of sessions, and the number of adult leaders will vary depending on the ages and number of children in the group, available resources, specific population characteristics, and the leader's interests and strengths. However, there are general guidelines that will aid in planning the group.

First, in the writer's opinion, having more than one adult leader will benefit both the children and the leaders. Children are energetic and often demand individual attention. When two adults are available, there is always one to keep the group focused and the other to respond to the unexpected. If it is not feasible to have two social workers, then college students or adult volunteers can be utilized.

Each session should have specific objectives, with activities designed to help achieve these objectives. Art projects, role plays, puppetry, film strips, letter writing, games, making a video, singing, story telling, and relaxation exercises are examples of techniques that can be used to meet specific group objectives.

For example, if the group objective is to help the children understand divorce, the children can take turns playing the role of a mother or father telling their children (played by the other group members) what divorce is and why the parent is getting a divorce. Another method of addressing the same objective is to have the children paint a picture of divorce. After completing the pictures, the group can discuss their artwork, highlighting different ideas and feelings.

Tried-and-true program activities can be used in subsequent groups. But when the composition of the group varies, the social work leader should be flexible and free to change exercises, using activities that will be most effective with a specific group.

If time and resources allow, providing a snack—an apple, a fruit drink, cookies—is nurturing and can build cohesion. Feeding the children helps them feel cared for and important. For some, this may be the only time in the week they feel special.

The most emotionally laden divorce content should be discussed in the middle third of the sessions. For example, if the group is to meet for 8 weeks, weeks 4, 5, and 6 are the best times to deal with potentially charged issues. In the first few sessions, getting acquainted, building trust, and introducing problem solving are safe objectives. The final sessions, designed to help the children leave the group feeling whole and hopeful, can examine self-esteem and termination.

Termination is a sensitive issue for children of divorce, as they are facing many changes and losses in their lives. Making memory books, exchanging phone numbers, and taking a group picture are concrete ways of helping the child take some of the group with him.

EVALUATION APPROACHES

Evaluation of interventions provides social workers with needed knowledge of what works and with whom. Several methods have been utilized to evaluate the effectiveness of groups for children of divorce.

When the group is in progress, the group leader can evaluate each session and the overall group experience (Bonkowski, et al., 1984). These evaluations are usually qualitative, providing clinical and descriptive data (e.g., Were the children engaged in the session? Did the planned activity result in meeting the group's objective?)

Data assessing the child's behavior and adjustment before and after the group meetings can be gathered from the children (Pedro-Carrol et al., 1992), parents (Alpert-Gillis et al., 1989; Bonkowski et al., 1984), and teachers (Alpert-Gillis et al., 1989; Cowen et al., 1989). Drawing on information from several sources provides the social worker with multidimensional measures that help answer the question "Did participation in the group facilitate adjustment to parental divorce?"

Brown, Portes, and Christensen (1989) stress the need to tie specific interventions to known risk factors and then to assess the effectiveness of such interventions with controlled studies. Grych and Fincham (1992) challenge the social work practitioner to strengthen the link between theory and research. For example, critical areas that still require research are the following: What process promotes positive change and adjustment? What interventions can ameliorate the effect of divorce for children known to be most at risk (boys, early elementary school children, and children exposed to parental violence)?

Although empirical evaluation is crucial, the evaluation often most meaningful to the practitioner comes spontaneously from the children. Ten-year-old Jeff, at first a reluctant group member, said, "I don't want these meetings to be over. I really like coming."

RESOURCES

Parents Without Partners
401 N. Michigan Ave.
Chicago, IL 60611
(312) 644-6610
www.parentswithoutpartners.org

Rainbows
2100 Golf Rd. #370
Rolling Meadows, IL 60008
(800) 266-3206
www.rainbows.org

REFERENCES

Ahlburg, D., & DeVita, C. (1992). New realities of the American family. *Population Bulletin.* 47(2), 1–44.

Alpert-Gillis, L. J., Pedro-Carroll, J. L., & Cowen, E. L. (1989). The Children of Divorce Intervention Program: Development, implementation, and evaluation of a program for young urban children. *Journal of Consulting and Clinical Psychology.* 57, 583–589.

Bonkowski, S. E., Bequette, S. Q., & Boomhower, S. (1984). A group design to help children adjust to parental divorce. *Social Casework.* 6, 131–137.

Brown, J. H., Portes, R. P., & Christensen, D. N. (1989). Understanding divorce stress on children: Implications for research and practice. *American Journal of Family Therapy.* 17, 315–325.

Cantrell, R. G. (1986). Adjustment to divorce: Three components to assist children. *Elementary School Guidance and Counseling.* 15, 163–173.

Cowen, E. L., Hightower, A. D., Pedro-Carroll, J. L., & Work, W. C. (1989). School-based models for primary prevention programming with children. *Prevention in Human Services.* 7, 133–159.

Frieman, B. B., Garon, R., & Mandell, B. (1994). Parenting seminars for divorcing parents. *Social Work.* 39, 609–613.

Furstenberg, F. F., Jr. (1990). Divorce and the American family. *Annual Review of Sociology.* 16, 379–403.

Grych, J. H., & Fincham, F. D. (1992). Interventions for children of divorce: Toward greater integration of research and action. *Psychological Bulletin.* 111, 434–446.

Hett, G. G., & Rose, C. D. (1991). Counselling children of divorce: A divorce lifeline program. *Canadian Journal of Counselling.* 25, 38–49.

Kaminsky, H. (1986). The divorce adjustment education and support group for children. *Conciliation Courts Review.* 24, 45–49.

Kurtz, L. (1994). Psychosocial coping resources in elementary school-age children of divorce. *American Journal of Orthopsychiatry.* 64, 554–563.

Pedro-Carrol, J. L., Alpert-Gillis, L. J., & Cowen, E. L. (1992). An evaluation of the efficacy of a preventive intervention for 4th–6th grade urban children of divorce. *Journal of Primary Prevention.* 13, 115–129.

Roseby, V., & Johnston, J. R. (1997). *High conflict, violent, and separating families: A group treatment manual for school-age children.* New York: The Free Press.

Rossiter, A. B. (1988). A model for group intervention with preschool children experiencing separation and divorce. *American Journal of Orthopsychiatry.* 58, 387–396.

Stolberg, A. L., & Mahler, J. L. (1989). Protecting children from the consequences of divorce. *Prevention in Human Service.* 7, 161–176.

U.S. Bureau of the Census, 1997, as cited in www.divorcemagazine.com.

U.S. Bureau of the Census, 2001. American families and living arrangements. *Current Population Reports.* p 20–537. Washington, DC.

Wallerstein, J. S. (1991a). The long-term effects of divorce on children: A review. *Journal of the American Academy of Child and Adolescent Psychiatry.* 30, 349–360.

Wallerstein, J. S. (1991b). Tailoring the intervention to the child in the separating and divorced family. *Family and Conciliation Courts Review.* 29, 448–459.

Chapter 10

Group Work with Elderly Persons

SUSAN RICE

WHO ARE THE ELDERLY?

The purpose of this chapter is to provide the beginning group worker with an understanding of doing social group work with elderly clients. The demographics of the elderly population in this country and others dramatically demonstrate that the aging population is growing. In the United States, the older population, as a proportion of the total population, has tripled in this century (Administration on Aging, 2002). Between 2000 and 2050, the population that is 65+ is expected to more than double. Additionally, the population that is 85+ is expected to triple. Therefore, there is a compelling need to provide effective, user-friendly group work services to the elderly in order to enhance both the quality and the span of their lives.

There is a second compelling need for a social worker to provide effective groups for the elderly: One of the primary problems of elderly clients is isolation. What better method is there than working with people in groups to combat this daily dilemma?

REVIEW OF THE LITERATURE

What defines an "elderly" population? A variety of definitions have been used, focusing on the difference between the "young-old" and the "old-old" (Neugarten, 1975). Most recently (Kart & Kinney, 2001) the National Institute on Aging has been trying to understand the distinctions among the "old-old" group, suggesting that people 75–84 years old (the elderly), are different from those people 85 years old and over (the very old or the oldest old). This chapter will address the distinction between the two groups in the discussions of practice principles and themes.

Why do people age? The aging process apparently involves failure of the surveillance, repair, and replacement process typical of a young body (McInnis-Dittrich, 2002). The body loses the ability to replace cells that compose most of its tissues. The immune system loses the ability to eliminate cancerous cells. Tissues that are damaged in daily life can no longer be repaired. When all of these processes occur, senescence appears, causing the organism to deteriorate and eventually die. This accounts for the physical and mental deterioration that occurs in old age, although for many people it does not happen fast enough to cause severe functional problems before some dramatic disease or occurrence causes immediate death.

Just as significant as the real changes that take place in an older person are the perceived changes, those largely due to the ageism that permeates our society. *Ageism* refers to the prejudices and stereotypes attributed to older persons based solely on their age (Butler et al., 1998). These stereotypes are usually negative and convey an attitude that older adults are less valuable as human beings, thus justifying inferior or unequal treatment of them. We begin to develop these attitudes early in life, as we see parental, media, and social attitudes towards elderly persons. And just as society treats older people as different and less human, older people treat themselves that way. When an older person has a physical complaint, he or she will often say, "So, what can a doctor do about it? I'm getting old." When that message is reinforced by the medical profession, the individual starts to believe it, and no longer thinks of the body as something that he controls. When a person forgets the house keys and says "I must be getting senile," and the reply is "It happens to everyone over 60," the individual believes that her memory is failing and that there is nothing she can do about it. It is apparent how easily people, and the support systems around them, slip into a mindset that allows deterioration to occur without being concerned about the changes that are atypical and are causing that individual great trouble in functioning.

One method of assisting the elderly is to provide social support, often correlated with reducing health and mental health problems (Jacobs et al., 2002). Social support groups are an effective way of providing this support. Senior citizen centers, in which older people find a network of peers with whom they can share common ground, are one common source of these groups. The elderly find companionship, use time productively and satisfactorily, make contributions, discover new interests and skills, and rediscover and maximize old ones (Gitterman & Shulman, 1994). This chapter uses the mutual aid model to explore the practice principles, themes, and ways of working with older people.

PRACTICE PRINCIPLES

Group work practice has been defined in a number of ways. In working with the elderly, the large majority of groups function most effectively using the mutual aid model of practice, developed and elaborated on by Gitterman and Shulman (1994) and first described by Schwartz (1961). The mutual aid model states that clients have difficulties that arise from three interrelated problems of living: life transitions, environmental pressures, and maladaptive interpersonal processes. Using the mutual aid process to address these problems gives each member of a group the ability to help every other member. The purpose of the leader in such a group is to be a mediator, facilitating the engagement of individual members with the group as a whole. The mutual aid model allows older people to function in a way that draws on their strengths and allows them maximum freedom in determining the scope and course of the group.

How do these general practice principles fit group work with elderly clients? Most social work practitioners envision a model of social work (Toseland & Rivas, 2001) practice (individual or group) that includes a focus on assessment, planning, contracting, building rapport, direct action, indirect action, evaluation, and termination. Each phase needs to be modified to fit the needs of groups composed of elderly clients. In all phases of practice, the level of the social worker's activity is high, perhaps higher than in working with younger clients. The reasons for this are numerous. Many elderly clients have had minimal exposure to the world of social work. They have more or less adequately resolved their own problems throughout their lives, counting on informal support systems to help them through hard times. As people reach their 80s and 90s, those informal systems disappear. The individual is left to flounder and often seeks social work services for the first time, not really knowing what to expect. The worker's job is then to model what a social group worker does by being active in the group from the very beginning. For example, in assessment, the social worker is often trying to understand the degree to which group members are willing to provide mutual aid and to share their solutions to a problem. The worker needs to demonstrate actively how the mutual aid process takes place. The worker does this by drawing on his or her knowledge of each member's experience and encouraging that member to share that experience with the rest of the group. The worker also encourages all members to see the similarities among them and tries to help each client understand the source of his or her discomfort.

Contracting is often done on an informal basis in support groups for the elderly because the themes of groups are so amorphous. In general, when a younger client or a client with a concrete need contracts for services (or a worker offers services), there is a fairly clear understanding of what the agency is prepared to offer and what the client wants to receive. Groups with clear contracts include those where clients want to learn to be better parents or where older people are learning to deal with insulin-dependent diabetes in order to manage their illness effectively. However, social support groups are often seen as a forum for clients to adjust to losses or changing life situations. That rubric could fit almost everyone, and so, in practice, the contract becomes a statement of allowing members to decide, as they participate in the group, what the benefits might be and what they might want to focus on.

Such informality also provides a safety net that allows fearful, timid clients to "try out" the group without being committed to one specific goal for change in their lives. Informality does not necessarily mean lack of clarity. Shulman (1999) describes contracting as clarifying the worker's purpose and role. He stresses the importance of eliminating jargon in contracting and urges workers to state clearly what they can offer. For example, in a group that has been formed to help frail elderly clients to continue living independently in the community, a leader might say, "This group will be a place where you can explore the feelings you have about living alone or feeling isolated some of the time." Each client is then free to pick up on that theme in whatever way seems appropriate.

There is a general belief (Corey & Corey, 2002) that older people need support and encouragement more than they need confrontation. The goal of group work with the elderly is less oriented toward radical personality change than it is toward making life in the present more meaningful and enjoyable. The social worker, for example, is more likely to be an advocate for the group that needs help with transportation (indirect intervention) than he or she is to empower the members to either work out the transportation problem as a way of building strength or to empower them to advocate for themselves (direct intervention). This is a fine distinction because sometimes one does want older people to see the extent to which they can remain powerful (Hopps & Pinderhughes, 1999). Often, however, workers try to make it easier to attending the group as part of the goal of offering a service that will enhance the quality of members' lives.

The general theme of learning to resolve conflict is related to this goal. Many theorists (Kottler, 2001) agree that conflict is an integral part of group development and allows members to become intimate and work together more beneficially. For older people, conflict is often seen as threatening to the relationships they are taking significant risks to build. Learning skills of conflict resolution can allow true intimacy to develop in groups, facilitating the mutual aid process.

Termination is an area that needs to be planned carefully in groups with older people. Termination is important both in the here and now and also because of the memories the experience evokes for clients in relation to past terminations in their lives (Shulman, 1999). For people who are seeing friends, family members, and acquaintances die on a regular basis, all endings take on an especially poignant meaning. In fact, many elderly clients will bluntly say that they do not want to become close to other group members "because they're only going to die anyway." Nevertheless, those who run groups and those who attend them believe that the benefits of being close to people, and feeling supported in one's efforts to improve one's quality of life, outweigh the pain involved in separations and endings.

Social workers need to make group endings (and endings of individuals who leave a group) positive and honest, allowing the expression of a wide range of feelings. For example, when a person drops out of a group because he or she becomes too ill to attend, it is useful to encourage the rest of the group to write to the member or pay a visit to the member's home or the hospital to provide closure. This is not only helpful to the individual but also provides a reassuring message to the rest of the group: My absence is important, and people care about what happens to me. Similarly, when a group ends, the members need to be helped to express the importance that it has had in their lives, as well as frustrations about what was not accomplished in the group. Social workers also need to be aware of their own feelings about endings in order not to ignore what group members need to express and explore.

COMMON THEMES

The most common themes encountered in groups for the elderly are loneliness, social isolation, loss, poverty, the feeling of rejection, the struggle to find meaning in life, dependency, feelings of uselessness, hopelessness, and despair, fears of death and dying, grief over others' deaths, sadness over physical and mental deterioration, depression, and regrets over past events (Corey & Corey, 2002).

If this seems like a list of negative, depressing concerns, one can turn to an emphasis on the wellness model of aging (Rowe & Kahn, 1998; Sheehy, 1995), which says that the norm is very different from that of people who are struggling. However, as discussed above, it is difficult to age without struggling. One of the themes mentioned is a pervasive sadness related to physical and mental deterioration. When I first began writing about aging, I authored a chapter in a book that focused on sexuality and intimacy in women as they age (Rice, 1990). When my own parents (who were in their early eighties at the time) read it, their reaction was, "What garbage! When you physically ache when you wake up in the morning, it's hard to believe this stuff." At the time, I shrugged off that sentiment, and said to myself, well, they never were very romantic. Since then, they have died. However, last year, when I was asked to write a revision of the article, I read it over and I was horrified by own naïveté. The revised version of the article, while still holding onto a basic optimism, is much more realistic about the ravages of physical change, and how it affects people in a very real sense (Rice, 2001).

We need to keep the wellness model of aging in mind so that we do not stereotype all older people as invalids. But we also need to appreciate the degree to which physical changes affect mental status and emotional involvement in different situations. A balance needs to be achieved between focusing on positive and negative themes. Some groups promote activities that emphasize the positive, and others plan activities that allow safe expression of negative feelings. For example, music can be used to enhance the psychological, emotional, and physical well-being of people (Bright, 1997). It has been maintained (Hanser & Clair, 1995) that music focuses on elders' strengths and abilities rather than their disabilities. Similarly, it is felt that the mind and the body operate as one, so that when feelings and experiences are expressed through art, the body is affected as well (Kaplan, 1998). The fact is that the efficiency of the human body does decline gradually with age (Hayflick, 1994). Ironically, what people are most aware of first are the cosmetic changes associated with aging, such as gray hair, wrinkles, and a widening pelvis. These are the changes that make people feel that they are getting old, although they do not relate to physical functioning at all.

Mental functioning is perhaps the essence of who we are, and when one sees one's own functioning deteriorating, or sees it in others, the effects are devastating. Alzheimer's disease causes cruel changes in a person's personality and cognitive abilities that effectively isolate the person from everyone. It is estimated that 4 million people suffer from Alzheimer's disease, and by 2030 this number is expected to climb to 14.5 million as the baby boomer population ages (Hamdy & Turnbull, 1998). Group work services to such clients can have a number of beneficial effects (Gallagher-Thompson, 1994) including a chance to foster peer experiences and emotional support, stimulating and encouraging the functioning of all remaining intellectual and social capacities, affirming a sense of individual identity, eliminating frustrating expectations, and replacing them with supportive social and group controls. While this chapter focuses on the elderly as clients, it is important to note that groups for caregivers can also help relieve the tension and strain that tear families apart as they watch a loved one, previously capable, competent, and intelligent, deteriorate.

Loneliness and Social Isolation

The themes discussed in this section are framed by gender and are all related, as more older people are female than male, females tend to live alone more than males, people who live alone also have lower incomes than other older people and have more chronic health problems that make it harder for them to remain independent. As people age, the male–female ratio steadily drops. In 1999, in the 55–64 age group, the ratio was 92–100, but in the 84 years and over group, the ratio was 49–100 (U.S. Census Bureau, September 2000). More than one-third of all elderly people live alone. Among people who are over 85 years old, only 49% of men and 12% of women still are married and live with a spouse. (U.S. Census Bureau, September 2000). Ethnic differences also exist. The percentage of non-

Hispanic whites over age 75 is still larger than either non-Hispanic blacks, or people of Hispanic origin (28% as compared to 22% and 18%, respectively) (U.S. Census Bureau, September 2000). However, since the minority elderly population is now increasing more rapidly than the white elderly population, those numbers will also change.

Income also changes with gender, age, and living arrangements. Five and one-half million (10.1%) people over 55 years of age were "poor" in 1998; when the 75 years and over group is examined, the rate goes up to 12%. Older women, in general, have a higher poverty rate than older men; at 75, 15% of women live in poverty, as compared to 7.5% of men. (U.S. Census Bureau, September 2000). In general, the economic situation of the elderly population is expected to improve, but the exception will be elderly people living alone. African-American and Hispanic women may be particularly at risk (Ozawa, 1995).

Therefore, it is no surprise that loneliness, social isolation, and poverty are common themes in groups composed of elderly clients. Social isolation is known to contribute to higher rates of substance abuse and suicide (Gomberg & Zucker, 1998; Lindesay, 1997), and group work interventions can directly address this phenomenon and impact the populations involved (McInnis-Dittrich, 2002). Feelings of uselessness, hopelessness, despair, and regrets over past events are also the foci of many discussions in social support groups. Retirement represents a significant milestone for older people. Particularly for men in our society, there can be a loss of meaningful job roles, productivity, and relationships that have been central throughout adult life (Carter & McGoldrick, 1999). (Again, there is a link with poverty because retirement usually is associated with a reduction of family and/or individual income.)

One way to conceptualize these feelings is through the work of Erik Erikson. Erikson (1963) describes the last two developmental stages of life—generativity versus stagnation and ego integrity versus despair—as two sides of a coin. *Generativity* refers to the concern about establishing and guiding the next generation. When one feels that one has not been instrumental in this process, either through one's own children, or by giving to society in a larger way, a pervasive sense of stagnation occurs. *Ego integrity* is the sense that one has accepted "one's one and only life cycle as something that had to be and that, by necessity, permitted of no substitutions" (Erikson, 1963, p. 268). If one cannot feel that way about one's life, despair is the result. If one looks back at one's life and blames oneself for the paths not taken, the overall feeling is one of making wrong choices. The elderly often struggle with these issues in groups.

Fears About Death and Dying and Grief Over Others' Deaths

Death and dying remain a taboo subject in our society. Many people cannot (or will not) openly discuss these significant issues, although they secretly harbor strong feelings about them. Death remains a hidden secret, as eroticized as it is feared (McInnis-Dittrich, 2002). We focus instead on concrete issues such as relieving specific ailments. Meanwhile, the controversy rages about how death should occur and how much control we should have over it. When Daniel Callahan wrote about rationing health care for the elderly (1987; 1996), some critics were afraid it would be used to support "killing off" old people by refusing them medical care (Abels & Rice, 1990). When Derek Humphry published *Final Exit* (1991), a suicide manual of sorts geared to people with terminal illnesses, it became an immediate best-seller and made people fear that suicide would become acceptable. What does this do to the older person who is seeing people die constantly? This theme recurs in groups, although it is rarely brought up unless the group worker is willing to facilitate the sharing of painful and risky feelings related to the topic.

RECOMMENDED WAYS OF WORKING

First, in order to work with clients, we need to reach them. A sobering fact is that for most types of social work services, including group work, minorities are served less often—not because there are fewer potential clients for a given service but because of perceived and actual barriers to receiving that service. For example, many concrete services specifically developed for the elderly (homemaker services, home health care, congregate meals) are used primarily by Caucasian elderly, despite the fact that older persons of color have needs that are typically two to three and a half times as great (Davis, 1998). Successful attempts to increase minority representation in client groups include efforts to have minority staff (speaking one's own language or coming from one's own culture provides familiarity that makes accepting help much easier), as well as training workers to be sensitive to cultural differences. Since in our country minority status is often tied to lower income, accessibility issues need to be addressed too, including transportation, cost of services, and flexibility of hours.

In developing groups of clients, it is important to pay attention to issues of homogeneity and heterogeneity (Corey & Corey, 2002). In general, groups need to have maximum homogeneity in terms of degree of vulnerability and capacity to tolerate anxiety. In other words, the ego strength of all members needs to be at similar levels. On the other hand, maximum heterogeneity in participants' conflict areas and patterns of coping allows input of new ideas and perspectives on the situations that clients face. Regardless of the themes discussed, this balancing rule between difference and similarity will allow participants to use the mutual aid model to share with each other.

These themes can be incorporated in most groups that allow clients to determine the focus of the discussion. For 5 years, this author directed a weekly support group for members of a retirement community. Pairs of undergraduate students facilitated weekly support groups that lasted for a full academic year, and combined small-group discussions and programs with occasional large-group workshops and potluck dinners (Black et al., 1994). These groups were ongoing, in the sense that many members stayed with the groups from year to year, but the student workers changed every September. As people grew older and frailer, there was a fairly high degree of turnover among the group members, and ways of working with them needed to change while maintaining the initial purposes of the group.

For example, the potluck dinners were initially a wonderful opportunity for members to demonstrate their culinary skills and to "give," in a concrete way, to their friends and to the student workers. Over time, the participants' cooking abilities faltered as their vision, hearing, and health deteriorated. It was decided to cater the main dish for the potluck dinners, and the members brought desserts to share. Even with dessert, however, we saw a gradual change from the "famous homemade recipe for brownies" to boxes of cookies that were store bought. This change saddened those staff who had been with the group from the beginning. However, it was a wonderful example of changing the parameters of the situation so that the members could still enjoy the essence of the program. Most recently, the potluck dinners were changed to potluck luncheons because more members were having trouble getting out at night even within their gated community.

Workers must be sensitive to the environmental changes that need to be made to allow the substantive work of the group to continue. The purpose of the potluck dinners has remained constant: They combat the social isolation and loneliness of the members (about 70% of whom live alone) and allows them to feel part of a community and a family.

In addition, workshops held twice each semester gave members specific skills to improve their ability to function within the group. For example, this author held a three-hour workshop on conflict resolution skills, including teaching "I-messages," discussing innate styles of conflict (turtles or sharks), and demonstrating skills of negotiation and mediation. A presentation of these skills coupled with an opportunity to discuss the feelings attached to them primed members to use them outside of the group.

In addition to retirement communities, groups for the elderly can be located in institutions. In contrast to retirement communities, where residents live independently in whatever manner they choose, institutions provide the assistance needed for their residents to perform the tasks of daily living at the cost of lessened freedom. In an examination of institutions, Schmidt (1990) begins by describing people's feelings about them. "Most elderly persons entering a home for the aged view this move as their last one. But, whatever sense of loss they may feel, they are concerned also with the life they can make there. Thus, homes for the aged become laboratories of human behavior as residents deal with change on a scale for which their previous lives have not prepared them" (p. 1).

Reminiscing groups can be utilized in both community and institutional settings to assist clients to "relive, re-experience, or savor events of the past that are personally significant" (Burnside & Schmidt, 1994, p. 164). Reminiscence can increase morale, self-esteem, and life satisfaction, as well as help clients feel an increased sense of control over their environment. For younger social workers, it can be a way to learn about the past and gain a deeper understanding of their clients as they hear about the experiences that brought their clients to the present. Group members feel an increased sense of understanding and support for other members as they realize the depth of the commonality of their experiences.

Programming (using an activity to further a major goal for the group) can also be used in beneficial ways. In one group session, the worker brought in the game "Trivial Pursuit" (immensely popular at the time). The game consists of a board, dice, and cards with questions on them, asking for answers about different topics including science, nature, history, entertainment, arts and leisure, and sports. The usual game is played by competing against each other (individually or in teams), and trying to win by being the first to answer questions correctly in each category. The rules were modified for this group by abandoning the board, the dice, and the competitive aspect of the game. Instead, the worker read a question and all group members tried to answer it, often asking each other questions about their personal circumstances during the event in question. For example, to the question of when a baseball player broke the world record, the answer came via a path that included deciding if it was before or after World War II, where each group member had been during those years, and what they were doing. There was no score keeping, and no winner or loser. The group spent as much time as they wanted on one question, and it ended when the right answer was given or the group as a whole gave up. The entire session utilized only four or five cards from the game, but the group emerged with a sense of closeness and cohesiveness that had not been present before.

EVALUATION MEASURES

How does one know when a group is successful? Much has been written about single-subject design and about the importance of every practitioner's evaluation of his or her own practice (Bloom et al., 2003; Nugent et al., 2001). This emphasis exists because we need to know if the money spent on a resource is effective and if the interventions we are using are helpful. To evaluate social support groups for older people, one of the most effective ways is to go to the source—the consumer.

In most groups, sessions end with a 1-minute evaluation. This evaluation consists of three questions: What was the most helpful thing that happened for you here today? What was the least helpful thing that happened for you here today? What would you suggest that we do differently next time? If the clients are able to write, this can be done on a sheet that is handed to each member. If writing is too burdensome, the clients can answer these questions quickly in a round-robin format.

More formal evaluations can be done at the quarter point, midpoint, and/or endpoint of a time-limited group. Clients can be asked about their overall satisfaction, about the effectiveness of specific techniques or sessions, and about how the enjoyment of their group is related to the goals they wanted to reach.

With all evaluation, the introduction is crucial to its success. If the worker asks for feedback in a way that implies that only positive feedback is welcome, that may be what he or she will get. If the members think that the continuation of the program is riding on their feedback, it will be greatly distorted. Allowing time for critique and change sends a welcome message to participants. It puts them in control of their group and enables them to make it the best it can be. With groups of elderly persons as with other groups, evaluation can be an ongoing part of group work that contributes to the group's overall effectiveness.

RESOURCES

Administration on Aging
Center for Communication and
  Consumer Services
330 Independence Avenue SW, Room
  4656
Washington, DC 20201
(202) 619-7501
www.aoa.gov/NAIC/

Alzheimer's Association
919 N. Michigan Avenue, Suite 1100
Chicago, IL 60611
(800) 272-3900
(312) 335-9602
www.alz.org

American Association for Retired
  Persons
601 E Street NW

Washington, DC 20049
(800) 424-3410
www.aarp.org

Association for the Advancement of
  Social Work with Groups
University of Akron
Akron, OH 44325
(800) 807-0793
www.aaswg.org

National Institute on Aging
Building 31, Room 5C27
31 Center Drive
MSC 2292
Bethesda, MD 20892
(301) 496-1752
www.nia.nih.gov

REFERENCES

Abels, P., & Rice, S. (1990). Stop the world, I want to get off: Rationing health care for the elderly. *Social Thought.* 16, 41–47.

Administration on Aging (2002). Older Population by Age: 1900 to 2050. Available at www.aoa.gov/aoa/stats/AgePop2050.html

Black, J., Kelly, J., & Rice, S. (1994). A model of group work in retirement communities. In I. Burnside and M. Schmidt (eds.), *Working with older adults: Group processes and techniques* (3rd ed.), (pp. 240–249). Boston: Jones and Bartlett.

Bloom, M., Fischer, J., & Orme, J. (2003). *Evaluating practice: Guidelines for the accountable professional.* Boston: Allyn and Bacon.

Bright, R. 1997. *Wholeness in later life.* London: Jessica Kingsley Publishers.

Burnside, I., & Schmidt, M. (eds.) (1994). *Working with older adults: Group processes and techniques* (3rd ed.). Boston: Jones and Bartlett.

Butler, R. N., Lewis, M. I., & Sunderland, T. (1998). *Aging and mental health: Positive psychosocial and biomedical approaches* (5th ed.). Boston: Allyn and Bacon.

Callahan, D. (1987). *Setting limits: Medical goals in an aging society.* New York: Simon and Schuster.

Callahan D. (1996). Limiting health care for the old. In T. L. Beauchamp and R. M. Veatch (eds.). *Ethical issues in death and dying,* (pp. 441–443). Upper Saddle River, NJ: Prentice Hall.

Carter, B., & McGoldrick., M. (1999). *The expanded family life cycle: Individual, family, and social perspectives* (3rd ed.). Boston: Allyn and Bacon.

Corey, G., & Corey, M. (2002). *Groups: Process and practice* (6th ed.). Monterey, CA: Brooks/Cole.

Davis, K. (1998). Managed care, mental illness, and African Americans. In G. Schamess and A. Lightburn (eds), *Humane managed care?* (pp. 51–64). Washington, DC: National Association of Social Workers.

Erikson, E. (1963). *Childhood and society.* New York: W.W. Norton.

Gallagher-Thompson, D. (1994). Direct services and interventions for caregivers. In M. H. Cantor (ed.), *Family caregiving: Agenda for the future,* (pp. 102–122). San Francisco: American Society on Aging.

Gitterman, A., & Shulman, L. (eds.). (1994). *Mutual aid groups and the life cycle* (2nd ed). New York: Columbia University Press.

Gomberg, E. S. L., & Zucker, R. A. (1998). Substance use and abuse in old age. In I. H. Nordhus, G. R. VandenBox, R. S. Bera, & P. Fromholt (eds.), *Clinical geropsychology* (pp. 189–204). Washington, DC: American Psychological Association.

Hamdy, R. C., & Turnbull, J. M. (1998). Alzheimer's disease: An overview. In R. C. Hamdy, J. M. Turnbull, J. Edwards, & M. M. Lancaster (eds.), *Alzheimer's disease: A handbook for caregivers* (3rd ed.), (pp. 1–7). St. Louis, MO: Mosby

Hanser, S. B., & Clair, A. A. (1995). Retrieving the losses of Alzheimer's disease for patients and care-givers with the aid of music. In T. Wigram, B. Saperston, & R. West (eds.), *The art and science of music therapy: A handbook* (pp. 342–360). Chur, Switzerland: Harwood Academic.

Hayflick, L. (1994). *How and why we age.* New York: Ballantine.

Hopps, J., & Pinderhughes, E. (1999). *Group work with overwhelmed clients.* New York: The Free Press.

Humphry, D. (1991). *Final exit: The practicalities of self-deliverance and assisted suicide for the dying.* Eugene, OR: Hemlock Society.

Jacobs, E., Masson, R., & Harvil, R. (2002). *Group counseling: Strategies and skills* (4th ed.). Monterey, CA: Brooks/Cole/Thomson Learning.

Kaplan, F. F. (1998). Scientific art therapy: An integrative and research-based approach. *Art Therapy: Journal of the American Association of Art Therapy.* 15(2), 93–98.

Kart, C., & Kinney, J. (2001). *The realities of aging: An introduction to gerontology.* Boston: Allyn and Bacon.

Kottler, J. (2001). *Learning group leadership: An experiential approach.* Boston: Allyn and Bacon.

Lindesay, J. (1997). Suicide in later life. In I. J. Norman and S. J. Redfern (eds.). *Health care for elderly people* (pp. 63–174). New York: Churchill Livingstone.

McInnis-Dittrich, K. (2002). *Social work with elders: A biopsychosocial approach to assessment and intervention.* Boston: Allyn and Bacon

Neugarten, B. (1975). The future and the young-old. *The Gerontologist.* 15, 4–9.

Nugent, W., Sieppert, J., & Hudson, W. (2001). *Practice evaluation for the 21st century.* Monterey, CA: Brooks/Cole (Wadsworth Press)

Ozawa, M. (1995). The economic status of vulnerable older women. *Social Work.* 40, 323–333.

Rice, S. (2001). Sexuality and intimacy for aging women. In J. Dianne Garner and S. Mercer, (eds.), *Women as they age* (2nd ed.). New York: Haworth Press.

Rice, S. (1990). Sexuality and intimacy for aging women. In J. Dianne Garner and S. Mercer (eds.), *Women as they age.* New York: Haworth Press.

Rowe, J., & Kahn, R. (1998). *Successful aging.* New York: Pantheon Books.

Schmidt, M. G. (1990). *Negotiating a good old age: Challenges of residential living in late life.* San Francisco: Jossey-Bass.

Schwartz, W. (1961). The social worker in the group. *The Social Welfare Forum.* New York: Columbia University Press.

Sheehy, G. (1995). *New passages: Mapping your life across time.* New York: Random House.

Shulman, L. (1999). *The skills of helping individuals, families and groups* (4th ed.). Itasca, IL: F. E. Peacock.

Toseland, R., & Rivas, R. (2001). *An introduction to group work practice* (4th ed.). Boston: Allyn and Bacon.

United States Census Bureau, September (2000). The Older Population in the United States: Population Characteristics. Washington, DC: U.S. Department of Commerce.

Chapter 11

In-Person Counseling and Internet Self-Help Groups: Synthesizing New Forms of Social Work Practice

ANDREA MEIER

For people confronted with life-changing situations, the internet can be a valuable portal to information and self-help resources to help them cope. Social workers can help clients benefit from the social support and social learning that internet self-help groups offer. When they help clients learn how to use these "cyber support" resources effectively, social workers are writing a new chapter in the profession's history of using the mutual aid of groups for individual growth and collective empowerment (Association for the Advancement of Social Work with Groups, 1999).

Based on that history, social workers should be leaders among the caregiving professions in exploring how to integrate internet therapeutic and support groups into clinical practice. In fact, few are doing so. Social workers have many legitimate reasons for being cautious about adopting this new intervention technology. Research on internet-mediated (IM) therapies, including on-line self-help groups, is only in an early stage of development. We do not know much yet about which types of IM groups are most suitable for which consumers, or how to design such groups to maximize their benefits.

There are many deterrents to offering online therapeutic groups as part of a clinical practice. There are no well-tested practice models to guide practitioners' treatment decisions about how to use them. Few social work schools offer systematic training in organizing and facilitating therapeutic on-line groups.[1] Ethical standards for IM practice in all the helping professions are in flux. Professional associations have responded with a global policy to the effect that practitioners must take "reasonable steps to ensure the competence of their work and to protect patients . . . and others from harm" (American Psychological Association, 1997). Social work licensing boards have, for now, taken a conservative stand: "Social work practice takes place where the consumer is located, and licensing boards should have jurisdiction over any social worker providing services to the citizens the board is supposed to be protecting" (Association of Social Work Boards, 2002). This current policy position makes it impossible for social workers to take advantage of the "boundarylessness" of cyberspace for delivering therapeutic services. The insurance companies, such as the one that provides professional liability coverage for NASW, will cover in-state e-therapy services, albeit reluctantly.[2] The few clinicians in private practice who are willing to take the risk of offering e-therapy services must do it on a fee-for-service basis; third-party payers do not reimburse for these services (Dunaway, 2000).

Since there are so few models of professionally facilitated internet groups, this chapter describes ways social workers can help their clients benefit from the myriad on-line self-help groups that already exist (Meier, 2000). In face-to-face counseling sessions, practitioners can help their clients identify on-line self-help that might meet their needs, and then work with them to integrate their group experiences with the rest of their lives. (The discussion that follows assumes that readers have at least some experience with e-mail and the World Wide Web.)

Social workers need to see the internet as part of their clients' social environments and consider how clients can benefit by establishing relationships and participating in communities in cyberspace. The first section of the chapter contains a brief developmental history of internet self-help groups as a backdrop to the discussion on current practice. The second section presents an ecological framework that sketches out how the characteristics of IM communication can affect clients' internal awareness and their relationships with the people they interact with online. Although there has not been much research on internet self-help groups, the third section summarizes the evidence of the benefits and limitations of this kind of social support. To begin filling the gap in practice models for IM therapeutic groups, the final section proposes a practice model that can guide social workers when they work in person with

[1] A few organizations have begun to offer on-line training in "e-counseling" for clinicians with a master's degree and above (see, for example, http://www.etherapytraining.com/). There is, however, no formal credentialing service to certify the quality of these training programs.

[2] Eric Marine, Vice President, Claims Development, American Professional, Inc., personal communication, April 11, 2002.

clients who are already involved with internet self-help groups or would like to join one.

A DEVELOPMENTAL HISTORY OF
INTERNET SELF-HELP GROUPS

Not long after personal-computer users began to go on-line in 1976, users began to invent ways to interact in groups. The first groups were local e-mail "bulletin board systems" (BBS). It is likely that some of these were small, informal support groups (Ainsworth, 2001). Over the past three decades, groups of all kinds have proliferated in cyberspace. Beginning in 1979, The Source and Compuserve, the first national commercial internet services, enabled personal computer users to communicate with each other nationwide. Not long afterward, formally organized, independent on-line support groups started to become popular (Ainsworth, 2001).

Since then, many individuals and groups have recognized how the internet could eliminate geographic barriers that prevent people from coalescing around shared concerns (Meier, 2000). Many of the on-line self-help groups have been started by people who are coping with problems and could not find a satisfactory local face-to-face support group they could join. Others may have joined face-to-face groups first but discovered that they needed ongoing support between meetings.[3] With the expansion of the World Wide Web, national support organizations have developed their own websites to provide current information and support by sponsoring internet self-help groups. For example, one of the world's most famous self-help organizations, Alcoholics Anonymous, went on-line in 1996 (Online Intergroup of Alcoholics Anonymous, 2002).

AN ECOLOGICAL VIEW OF THE
INTERNET SELF-HELP GROUPS

When working with clients who are getting on-line support, practitioners should keep in mind the physical and social contexts of IM interactions. To go on-line, users must be at some kind of computer with internet capability.[4] Typically, they are alone in their rooms, but some may use computers in sites where other people are present, such as cyber cafés, classrooms, Boys and Girls Clubs, or community technology centers. When

---

[3] Karyl Chastain Beal, founder of Parents of Suicides international virtual community, personal communication, November 11, 2002.

[4] While most people access the internet through a computer and modem, a small but growing number of users have wireless access through handheld computers (e.g., Palm Pilots and other "personal data assistants," [5%], web-enabled cell phones [4%], or other messaging devices [1%]) (Rainie & Packel, 2001). In this discussion, we assume clients will access the internet the "traditional way," using a desktop or laptop computer with dial-up, DSL, or cable modem.

other people are around, they can be distractions or prevent internet users from having the privacy they need to write openly to their groups.

People do more than coexist with their physical environments, they interact with them. In the case of internet self-help groups, the internet is the medium through which all member interactions take place. Practitioners who understand the basic concepts of communication theory will be better able to assist clients in understanding and managing their on-line group experiences.

The Internet as a Communication Channel

Social psychologists have studied how these channel characteristics can affect the ways internet users function in their on-line social networks and the groups that are embedded in them. In this section, we will briefly describe those interactions as they are mapped out in Figure 11.1.[5] To begin with, there must be a "sender" who is the source of the message (signal) and a receiver whose goal is to reconstruct the sender's messages. Second, there must be a some kind of medium, a "communication channel," through which the sender's message can be transmitted (Shannon, 1948). Communication channels vary in the amount of data that can be transmitted per unit time. This characteristic is called "bandwidth." The more data transmitted, the greater the bandwidth needed. For face-to-face communication to occur, the brain uses lots of "bandwidth" to receive messages that are sent simultaneously through all the sensory channels. In IM communication, different types of messages require different amounts of bandwidth. Messages containing numbers and text require the least. Messages containing audio or video data require much more; multimedia communication over the internet requires the greatest amount of bandwidth.

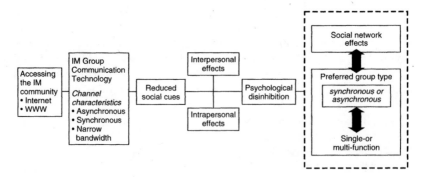

Figure 11.1 Integrative Framework of IM Communication and IM Support Groups

[5] For a more extensive discussion of this integrated conceptual framework, see Meier (2004).

Communication is also affected by the timing of message sending and receiving. When message senders and receivers do not have to be present at the same time, this is called *asynchronous communication.* On the internet, email communication, usenet and listserv groups, and web discussion forums are familiar examples of asynchronous communication in which messages are stored in a dedicated computer for recipients to retrieve at their convenience. With synchronous communication, message senders and receivers must be present at the same time, as in face-to-face communication. Instant and chat groups are examples of synchronous internet communication.

Intrapersonal Effects

Once they log on, users' intrapersonal and interpersonal behaviors are affected by the internet channel. Computer monitors are similar to television screens; both have low-level stimuli and "light-through" effects that can be mesmerizing (Hill, 2002). With restricted bandwidth, users can be anonymous and invisible to each other. In combination, the effects of the computer monitor and internet-related reductions in social cues can have a psychoactive effect that enhances users' awareness of their thoughts and feelings and alters their moods (Greenfield, 1999). They can become intensely engaged in their online transactions, tuning out cues and stimuli from their local, "real world" environments. Social psychologists refer to this type of behavior as *deindividuation* (Siegel et al., 1986).

Interpersonal Effects

People who participate in on-line self-help groups are geographically distant from the other members in their groups. They must construct mental images of other group members based on incomplete information and come to terms with the fact that they may never meet them in person. Reduced social cues also affect how internet users interact with one another and how they behave in groups. Invisibility and anonymity can reduce users' presentation anxiety, especially for those living with stigma (Mickelson, 1997). Internet users can control how much information they reveal about themselves and the timing of those disclosures. When in states of internet-induced "boundarylessness," users are more likely to idealize or project onto the people they communicate with (Colon, 1997; Walther, 1996). Incomplete information and delayed feedback can make it harder to develop realistic impressions.

Psychological Disinhibition

Social psychologists have argued that internet-induced weak social ties and reduced social cues can combine to produce *disinhibition*—the constellation of behaviors associated with internet use. These include: emotional regression, projection, weakened boundaries, and feelings of safety due to anonymity and invisibility. These conditions prompt some users to disclose sensitive details about their lives much sooner than they would in face-to-face transactions. The same factors elicit emotional regression in its creative and destructive forms. As a creative state, regression enables people to be playful (including experiments in gender and other identity shifts), nonconformist, and altruistic. As a destructive state, it can lead to impulsive and hostile acts, such as rapidly escalating verbal attacks ("flaming") (Finn, 1996), or gender and other forms of harassment (Bell & de La Rue, 1995).

Social Network Effects

Internet users have access to a diverse array of communities in cyberspace (Rheingold, 2000). By going on-line, they extend their social networks. They establish "weak ties" to people outside of their intimate social networks. These new contacts possess new information and hold different perspectives than do families, friends, and coworkers who live nearby (Walther & Boyd, forthcoming). As a result, users may become less dependent on the support and opinions of intimates in their networks with whom they have "strong ties." The social distance and anonymity of internet interactions can also make it easier for Internet users to disclose information that might be too embarrassing to reveal to people whom they see every day.

On-line Group Preferences

How people participate in internet communities depends on the power of their computers, modem speeds, and bandwidths of their internet service providers. People who have older, less powerful computers will find communicating through asynchronous channels (text-based e-mail) easier because it requires less bandwidth. People who prefer the graphical interface of the World Wide Web will need more powerful, faster computers that can manage the greater bandwidth requirements.

Each type of internet communication channel requires different cognitive and interpersonal skills to communicate in groups. Clients may prefer one kind of group over the other. Asynchronous online groups (newsgroups, listservs, and web forums) encourage members to be more reflective. They can write as much as they want in their e-mail posts without interfering with other members' messages. In synchronous chat groups, interactions occur in "real time." Members' comments appear word-by-word on screen like a play script. To participate effectively, members must be able to type and express themselves quickly in writing.

Other members can interrupt the previous "speaker" in midsentence whenever they want and start a new comment.

Most internet groups are "single-function," operating on only one channel (Finfgeld, 2000). With the expansion of the web, support organizations began to sponsor web portals linking users to both web discussion forums (asynchronous) and chat support groups (synchronous) on the same subjects. Resources at the end of this chapter show a list of national support organizations with websites where clients can choose between either kind of group or alternate between them to get the kind of support that best matches their needs at any given time.

DEMOGRAPHICS OF THE INTERNET

The Pew Internet and American Life Project (Fox, 2002) has been conducting systematic surveys of how the technology is being used and its social impacts. Based on those surveys, Pew estimates indicate there are nearly 149 million internet users in the United States who have access to the internet from work or home or both (Rainie & Packel, 2001). Until about two years ago, the the typical internet user was a college-educated white man between the ages of 30 and 65, who lived in an urban area, was fully employed, and received an income of over $50,000. In 2001, the Pew surveys began to detect important changes in the internet user demographics. More women, children, and minorities, and people with incomes under $30,000 are gaining access at an increasing rate (Rainie & Packel, 2001). The number of activities that users did while on-line has also increased.

Pew's data also indicate that the population of internet users now resembles the overall population of the United States. Women have achieved parity with men in their use of the internet. In the overall population of English-speaking internet users, Asian-American men and women have the highest rate of daily internet use (75%) followed by white Americans (58%), Hispanics (48%), and African Americans (39%). In the general population, younger adults (ages 18–29) are most likely to be using the internet.

There are still differences in internet access among population groups related to income and age (Rainie & Packel, 2001). Although people with incomes less than $30,000 represent the most rapidly growing group of new internet users, people with incomes above $75,000 are much more likely to have access. There has also been substantial growth in the number of adults in the 50 to 64 age group with internet access, but seniors aged 65 years and older were the least likely to report using the internet. The internet has had much less penetration in rural than in urban areas, largely because fewer people in rural areas use computers (Lenhart, 2000). Yet even among groups who currently do not have internet access, 41% reported that they probably or definitely plan to go on-line (Lenhart, 2000).

Internet Use Patterns

People use the internet most often to send email (93%). More than 85% use internet "search engines" (such as Google, Yahoo, MSN.com and AOL.com)[6] to find information. Nearly a quarter of all users (23%) have used the internet to get information about a mental health issue such as depression or anxiety. Nearly a fifth of all users (18%) have gone on-line to get information about a concern they felt was too sensitive or embarrassing to discuss in person. A quarter of all internet users report that they have participated in chat or on-line discussion groups. A smaller group (9%) have participated in an online support group. While participation in on-line support groups is less common than many other internet uses, 9% of the internet-using population in the United States represents over 13 million people who have had experience with internet support groups.

In sum, these data vividly illustrate why social workers must pursue ways to incorporate the resources of the internet into their face-to-face work with their clients if they want their profession to stay socially relevant. The increasing diversity and dynamism of the population of American internet users mean that social workers are likely to have clients who use the internet. Practitioners must make the effort to understand the role that the internet plays in their lives. Furthermore, consumers are accessing the internet using a variety of different technologies and locations. Social workers must understand how these channels and settings affect consumers' use of and experiences with the internet. Finally, many users view the internet as an important way to obtain information and social support, including participation in on-line self-help groups. Social workers need to understand how the different IM communication channels affect group behavior. They must also craft practice models for integrating consumers' on-line help-seeking and support experiences with their in-person helping relationships.

Who participates in on-line self-help groups? The people who participate in on-line self-help groups are a subset of a much larger community of internet users. Many of the people who seek out IM self-help groups never participate in face-to-face individual therapy or therapeutic groups because they are unwilling or unable to do so (Suler, 1999). There have not been any systematic surveys to find out how many people who are receiving face-to-face counseling or group services are also participating in on-line self-help groups.

---

[6] Search engines are specialized programs for the World Wide Web that enable users to use key words as descriptors to find websites containing information on specific topics.

RESEARCH ON THE BENEFITS AND LIMITATIONS OF INTERNET SELF-HELP GROUPS

Researchers of on-line therapeutic groups have been unable to keep up with the burgeoning number and types of groups. Relatively few studies have been done, and those are scattershot across populations and problem conditions. Of the 16 articles reviewed for this chapter, seven investigated usenet groups; six were studies of listservs or bulletin board groups; two investigated web forums; one study compared a chat group, a listserv group, and a face-to-face group. All 16 studies were exploratory; researchers used diverse research designs to collect data. Eight used qualitative methods, three used surveys, two used mixed methods (surveys and qualitative methods).

Investigators have studied asynchronous on-line support groups for people who were living with chronic or life-threatening physical conditions such as cancer (Weinberg et al., 1995), amyotrophic lateral sclerosis (Feenberg et al., 1996); HIV (Gustafson et al., 1994); miscellaneous disabilities (Braithwaite et al., 1999) and diabetes (Loader et al., 2002). Other studies have examined group processes in support groups for people with emotional difficulties such as obsessive compulsive disorders (Stein, 1997), depression (Salem et al., 1997), eating disorders (North, 1998), sexual abuse (Finn & Lavitt, 1994), survivors of alcoholic families (Phillips, 1996), and recovering drug addicts (King, 1994). There have also been studies of support groups for older adults (Wright, 2000) and caregivers of people with mental illness (Peron, 2002).

Several researchers have compared how problem themes were discussed in different kinds of groups. McKenna and Bargh surveyed members of usenet support groups that addressed concerns about marginalized identities, some discussing visable stigmas (obesity, stuttering, cerebral palsy, and baldness) and others that discussed drugs, homosexuality, and sexual bondage (McKenna & Bargh, 1998). Miller and Gergan (1998) explored how suicidality was discussed in groups for recovering alcoholics, child abuse survivors, and parents.

The small sample sizes, coupled with diverse target populations, problem conditions, and research designs used in these studies, make it impossible to compare across studies or generalize from their findings. Taken together, however, the findings suggest a range of potential benefits and limitations of on-line self-help group support.

Benefits

Internet groups have the advantage of being convenient and accessible (Finn & Lavitt, 1994; Phillips, 1996). The technology enables people who are unable or unwilling to attend a face-to-face group to interact with each other. Thus, geographically distant from each other, people who suffer from rare diseases, or who are homebound due to illness or caregiving responsibilities, can now benefit from group support. In IM groups, members are invisible and can choose how much to disclose to each other. People who suffer from stigmas may be attracted to these groups because of the control they have over their self-presentation (King, 1994; Kummervold et al., 2002; Radin, 2001). Some researchers have also suggested that IM self-help groups could be used to supplement face-to-face groups (King, 1994)

Internet self-help groups can be significant sources of social support. Members frequently offer each other information and advice (Braithwaite et al., 1999; Fernsler & Manchester, 1997; Loader et al., 2002; Peron, 2002). Members can vent about their problems and have their feelings validated by others (Braithwaite et al., 1999; Fernsler & Manchester, 1997; King, 1994; Loader et al., 2002; McKenna & Bargh, 1998; Miller & Gergan, 1998; Reid, 1998; Salem et al., 1997). Many members who participate in these groups feel less isolated and more hopeful (Finn & Lavitt, 1994; King, 1994; North, 1998; Weinberg et al., 1995). Sometimes, the support members receive from the group may spur them to social action (Kummervold et al., 2002; McKenna & Bargh, 1998).

Limitations

There are three main types of limitations ascribed to internet self-help groups. The first category includes problems arising out of the need to rely on telecommunications technology to communicate. Participation in internet self-help groups is limited to users who have access to computers, modems, and internet services, and are competent navigating in cyberspace (Phillips, 1996). This means that participants need the resources to gain access to computers. They must also be literate and be able use a computer to express themselves in writing. They must be able to weather the frustration and confusion of inevitable computer and internet crashes that disrupt or delay message transmissions.

The informality of internet self-help groups and the restricted social cues caused by IM communication can also limit the quality of the support members receive. Many people seek out on-line groups for information about ways to deal with problems, but the information they receive from other members may not be accurate (Finfgeld, 2000). Most internet self-help groups have open membership and are ongoing; consequently, there can be a high level of turnover among members (Cummings et al., 2002). Discussions can be superficial (Finn & Lavitt, 1994). In large groups, members who have unrealistic expectations about the group may be frustrated because they are unable to get their needs met for emotional support. Because IM communication promotes psychological deindividuation and disinhibition, social controls can be weaker than in face-to-face groups. In conflict situations, some members may "flame," expressing hostility or becoming verbally abusive in ways that would other emotionally fragile members in the group (Finn & Lavitt, 1994).

Leadership in internet self-help groups is unregulated. Members may have unrealistic expectations about the group leader's role and skills (Holmes, 1997a, 1997b). In peer-led groups, members in leadership roles may not be trained in group facilitation and not know how to intervene if problems arise. Finally, because many on-line self-help groups are run by volunteers, they may dissolve with little warning if the group's list-owner decides that it takes too much time and energy. If this happens, group members who have come to rely on it for companionship and other support may feel bereft.

The third type of limitation includes problems that can arise when members' lives in the "virtual world" are not well integrated with their lives in the "real world" (Suler, 2000). In a few cases, users may start to compulsively overuse the internet, creating problems in their marriages, family life, and work because they spend so much time on-line.[7]

When this occurs, internet users may find their on-line relationships more rewarding than those they have with their families, friends, and coworkers. If they are newly introduced to the internet, they may spend so much time on-line participating in their cyberspace communities that they reduce their participation in their face-to-face social networks (Kraut et al., 1998). Some clinicians have experessed concern that people may become so dependent on the support of their on-line communities that they delay seeking professional help when they need it (Finn, 1996). Despite these potential risks, internet users appear to believe that the advantages outweigh the risks and are "voting with their fingers" by seeking out IM self-help groups.

INTERNET SELF-HELP GROUP
STRUCTURE AND DEVELOPMENT

The structure of IM self-help groups depends largely on whether members use a synchronous or asynchronous channel to interact. Asynchronous groups (listservs, newsgroups, and Web discussion forums) can be large, ranging from a few to several hundred members, because members do not have to take turns "speaking." Synchronous chat groups are time-limited. Generally, they have to be relatively small (under 10 members) to insure that everyone has a chance to contribute during a session.

Group Composition

Internet self-help groups usually allow open membership. Members self-identify with the problems addressed by the group, but no one follows up

---

[7] There is no classification for internet addiction yet in the DSM-IV-TR, but psychologists have noted similarities between compulsive internet use and compulsive gambling (Greenfield, 1999).

to insure that members are who they claim to be. In internet self-help groups, members generally assume that people are who they claim to be and that they share the group's common interests and concerns. Occasionally, people may set out to deliberately create false impressions about their backgrounds and life situations (Donath, 1999), but there are no data on how often this happens.

Participation Levels

In internet self-help groups, a few core members typically provide most of the commentary (Cummings et al., 2002). There is no way to enforce norms for participation. Because IM communication allows people to be invisible, active participants often know little about the much larger group of unseen "lurker" members who follow the e-mail discussion but rarely post comments themselves. In chat groups, a list of onscreen aliases of members who have logged onto the group is displayed on the monitor, but members are not obligated to write any messages.

Although a majority of members may lurk most of the time, this is not necessarily just social loafing (Roy et al., 1996). New members may lurk to learn group norms, to observe how the group functions, and to become acquainted with other members' personalities and concerns. By lurking for a while, new members can be more informed and adept when they finally join the discussion. Some members in crisis may be too overwhelmed to compose messages, but find comfort and hope by reading others' accounts of their life challenges and how they coped.

Group Development

Fluctuations in internet self-help group membership makes these groups resemble large, single-session, face-to-face "drop-in" support groups (Steinberg, 1999). The lack of consistent participation results in greater diversity in members' emotional neediness and coping skills, and their capacity to do the "work" needed to achieve group cohesion. Although active core members may establish strong emotional bonds, most of these groups do not become very cohesive. Invisibility, anonymity, and physical distance make it difficult to enforce conformity and contribute to the leveling of status differences.

Unfacilitated internet groups have unpredictable life cycles. When members are anonymous and invisible to each other, they may be less invested in keeping their groups going. If the core members decide to spend their time doing something else, it is unlikely that lurking members will step in to fill their roles. Groups that are very active at one point in time may go inactive a few weeks later. Social workers need to warn clients about the possibility that their groups could dissolve, and, if they do, help them cope with their feelings of frustration and abandonment.

Social workers need to draw on research, practice wisdom, and their own experiences with the internet to develop strategies for: *(a)* assessing whether or not their clients are using the internet; *(b)* how they are using it when they are; and *(c)* helping them access internet self-help resources if they need them. Once clients are able to go on-line, practitioners need to continue working with them in face-to-face sessions to help them integrate their "virtual" and "real-world" lives (Suler, 2000).

COMBINING INDIVIDUAL COUNSELING AND INTERNET SELF-HELP GROUPS: A NEW PRACTICE MODEL

Currently, there are no evidence-based practice guidelines for combining internet self-help groups and face-to-face individual treatment. The practice model is based on best practices for individual and group interventions and communication theory. It maps out what social workers should do at each phase of treatment, starting from the initial assessment through to termination (see Figure 11.2).

Assessment

Social workers are not trained to ask clients about their internet use and experiences as part of the initial assessment process. As a result, they may only learn about clients' internet experiences—or their interest in using the internet—after treatment is well underway. If they ask, social workers may find that a surprising number of their clients have access somewhere to computers and internet services. Sometimes, clients who want

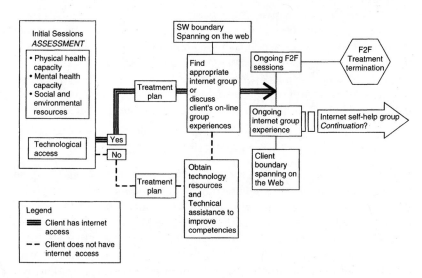

Figure 11.2 Practice Model: Treatment Map

to use the internet do not have access to the technology but would like help to obtain it.

The internet demographic trends described previously signal to social workers that they should assume that their clients are using the internet—or at least, rule it out. If they discover that their clients are already going on-line, practitioners need to know how clients' internet experiences fit in with their other life domains. If their clients do not currently have internet access, social workers can inquire whether they are interested in learning how to use the internet and would like help in getting access.

To obtain this information, social workers need to modify their biopsychosocial assessment routine. They will need to probe further to discover whether clients have the physical, cognitive, expressive, and interpersonal capacities to interact competently on the internet. Mental health assessments should assess whether and how the psychoactive effects of internet use might strengthen or weaken clients' hold on reality, as well as identify appropriate types of on-line self-help groups.

Technological Assessment

The technological assessment should determine whether the clients have access to the internet and for how long. If they do, the assessment would also determine the number of locations and how much technical assistance is available in those locations. For clients with internet access, this stage of the assessment would also explore their patterns of internet use (email and web), experiences establishing and maintaining relationships via email, and their experiences with and preferences for different kinds of on-line groups.

Where clients do not have access but do want it, social workers' case-management efforts could focus on locating community access sites and volunteers who could provide training and technical assistance. Alternatively, the social worker could seek donors who could supply computers and modems, and, if needed, subsidized internet services. Once clients who are new users go on-line, social workers need to monitor their use patterns and how they are coping with technological problems.

Finding a Good Self-Help Group

If clients are new to the internet, they may need help finding a good group. As part of their ongoing resource-seeking strategies, social workers who specialize in specific at-risk populations may want to scan the internet periodically for groups addressing those problems. To help clients be resourceful, social workers should also work with clients to teach them how to find groups for themselves. Practitioners should discuss with clients what their goals are for joining an internet self-help group and also tell them about local face-to-face groups that address the same issues.

Using web search engines, it is relatively easy to find information about IM self-help groups on any topic, including the number of subscribers (see Resources). If their clients are inexperienced internet users, social workers need to warn them the number of subscribers is not a reliable indicator of group functioning. Some groups have an internet "presence" and a long list of subscribers, but few members regularly post messages. Groups can be established technologically but never attract a sufficient number of members to be viable. New members who sign on may discover that the groups are moribund and there is very little activity. Unfortunately, there is no good way to assess group functioning without joining.

When referring clients to 12-Step and other face-to-face self-help groups, social workers would offer information about how a self-help group works. Likewise, social workers need to help clients understand how internet self-help groups work. They should discuss with clients how to find out about the group's norms as laid out in "Frequently Asked Questions" (FAQ) documents[8] or other orientation messages, and whether, in fact, the group adheres to them. Clients need to know the steps for withdrawing from the group if they decide it is not helpful.

Protecting Confidentiality

Because people typically use their computers in private, they may believe that messages sent to internet groups are private and will be kept confidential, too (American Association for the Advancement of Science, 1999). While the sheer volume of messages protects internet user privacy, social workers are ethically obliged to inform clients of the risks to confidentiality when they communicate on-line (NASW, 1999). For example, systems operators at any computer node in the internet telecommunications system can intercept messages. Employers have the right to review all messages sent through their worksite computers or internet systems. Members of self-help groups may forward messages without permission to people outside the group. Given all these opportunities for violations of privacy, clients should be forewarned, and periodically reminded, that they should absolutely not write anything in an on-line communication that they do not want others to know.

Treatment Plans

When social workers negotiate treatment plans with internet-using clients in face-to-face sessions, they should also contract when and how

---

[8] An FAQ is an on-line document created for on-line groups that contains a statement of the group's purpose, anecdotal history, and "netiquette." Its purpose is to anticipate new members' questions, so that the more senior members of the group do not have to repeatedly address the same queries. FAQs may be sent out automatically when a member subscribes to an on-line group or be posted on the sponsor's website.

they will discuss clients' experiences with the internet and internet groups. These discussions should be seen as part of a larger exploration of clients' engagement in their social networks. Here the treatment model would be roughly similar to working with clients who are in one-to-one counseling along with a face-to-face self-help group (Nowinski et al., 1992). In their face-to-face sessions, discussions should cover information clients have received from their groups, what they are learning from their groups' process, and the extent to which they are applying that information or suggestions to their "real world" lives.

Storm King, a clinical psychologist and researcher, has proposed using client participation strategically by moving clients through more than one group. A client who is socially phobic, for example, could be encouraged to join an on-line group that discussed a hobby or other safe topic as a way of learning how to carry on a conversation (King & Moreggi, 1998). When the client has become comfortable with internet-mediated communication and desensitized to presentation anxiety with this type of interaction, he or she could then be encouraged to join a self-help group on social phobias. Although no systematic research has been done on this kind of intervention strategy, it is a good example of the variety of ways internet self-help groups could be used as interventions.

Middle Stage

Once a client has been successful in getting on-line and is regularly participating in the group, those experiences become part of the ongoing therapeutic discussion. Clients may ask for clarification of information offered by other group members or want to discuss how it might apply to their situations. Sometimes the clients receive information in their groups that is inaccurate (Klemm & Nolan, 1998; Winzelberg, 1997). In-person sessions can be used as opportunities to identify and correct such errors. Social workers can inquire about their clients' positive and negative experiences in the group, or those that were particularly meaningful or troubling (King & Moreggi, 1998). Clients can also bring in the texts of those messages to review and discuss. They may wish to consult about alternative ways to respond to messages, or their feelings about messages that they composed before posting them.

Social workers also need to monitor whether and how clients' internet use patterns change significantly over time. Have other family members begun to criticize them about their internet use? Do clients discuss their internet group experiences with their families and friends? Do they discuss their families and work experiences with other members in their internet groups? (Greenfield, 1999; Grohol, 1998). If clients begin to show signs of compulsive internet use, social workers should explore the reasons for these behaviors and suggest shifting to off-line sources of support.

Termination

Ideally, clients leave their self-help groups because they decide they no longer need them. Internet groups, however, can also dissolve because the list owner or other key members withdraw. Alternatively, clients may decide to drop out because their groups do not address their needs or have become dysfunctional. Social workers should discuss with clients whether they want to join other internet self-help groups. Alternatively, clients may want to think about how to apply what they learned through their on-line experiences to a face-to-face group. If clients are reaching the end of their face-to-face sessions, social workers can help them examine how their participation in the internet group can serve as a source of continuing support.

Evaluation

Since social workers are not running these internet groups, they cannot evaluate them directly. What they can do is help clients assess group cohesion, the accuracy of information exchanged, and the extent to which they are able to draw on group experience to become more resourceful in the real world.

NATIONAL RESOURCES

The national support organization websites listed at the end of this chapter can serve as resources for social workers. These sites offer up-to-date, evidence-based information about physical and behavioral health problems, current treatments, and other support resources. These websites usually include organizational contact information and email links for users to interact with the sponsors, their web masters, and list owners. Social workers can contact these website staff members to determine the extent to which sponsors monitor their groups. Practitioners may want to join specific groups for a while to learn about participants' concerns and strengths before advising clients to do so. Technically, anyone can join publicly accessible internet groups, but group members may object to having "outsiders" (people without the shared problem) in the group. As a professional courtesy, social workers should contact web masters/list owners of a group they are interested in and find out if the organization has policies governing professional observers.

CONCLUSION

This description of combined in-person counseling and internet self-help groups takes advantage of existing resources and builds social worker and client capacity. As with all social work practice, readers should continue to draw on their own practice wisdom, seek client feedback, and consult with other experienced social workers when they apply these ideas and models in their own work settings. Our hope is that readers will come away appreciating how the internet is transforming the helping professions and curious about how they could use the technology to help their clients.

RESOURCES*

ADHD On-line Community
http://www.adhd.com/talk/talktoc.html

Alanon Family Group Online
http://www.12stepforums.net/alanon.
   html
Al-Anon, ACOA-ACA, Alateen
   meetings, and general 12-Step
   support chat.

Alcoholics Anonymous
http://www.aa-intergroup.org/
   directories/email.html

American Cancer Society
http://www.cancer.org/

Asthma and Allergy Foundation of
   America
http://www.aafa.org/reflections/

Child and Adolescent Bipolar
   Foundation
http://www.bpkids.org/

Council for Equal Rights in Adoption
http://www.adoptioncrossroads.org/
For people who were adopted who are
   searching for their birth families.

Family Caregiver Alliance
http://www.caregiver.org/

GrandsPlace
http://www.grandsplace.com/
For grandparents and special others
   raising children

Listservs
http://www.lsoft.com/lists/listref.html
Up to date list of all publically
   accessible IM groups run on
   listserv software.
http://www.liszt.com/dir/?cid-0
Search engine for a wide variety of
   support groups for disabilities,
   health and mental health
   problems, family challenges.
   Enter "support" in the list directory
   search box.

Multiple Sclerosis Foundation
http://www.msfacts.org/forums.htm

Narcotics Anonymous Online
   Resources
http://na.basicwebpage.org/

Newsgroups
http://www.tile.net/news/
http://www.cyberfiber.com/
Groups are listed alphabetically by
   name, and searchable by key word
   descriptors.

Pain management (Dannemiller
   Memorial Educational
   Foundation)
http://www.pain.com/forumchat

Parents of Suicides
http://www.angelfire.com/mi2/
   parentsofsuicide/index.html

---

* Not a complete list.

REFERENCES

Ainsworth, M. (2001). *Internet Therapy Guide: E-Therapy: History and Survey.* Metanoia. Retrieved October 31, 2001, from the World Wide Web: www.metanoia.org/imhs/history.htm.

American Association for the Advancement of Science. (1999). Ethical and legal aspects of human subjects research on the internet (Report of a Workshop: June 10–11, 1999. Washington DC). Author. Retrieved November 9, 2000, from the World Wide Web: http://www.aaas.org/spp/dspp/sfrl/projects/intres/report.pdf.

American Psychological Association. (1997). *APA statement on services by telephone, teleconferencing and Internet: A statement by the Ethics Committee of the American Psyhcological Association.* American Psychological Association. Retrieved October 15, 2001, from the World Wide Web: http://www.apap.org/ethics/stmn01.html.

Association for the Advancement of Social Work with Groups, I. (1999). *Standards for Social Work Practice with Groups. Retrieved August 2, 2000 from the World Wide Web:* http://www.aaswg.org/standards.htm. Association for the Advancement of Social Work with Groups, Inc. Retrieved, from the World Wide Web:

Association of Social Work Boards. (2002). *Association Report: Social Work Online: Are we ready?* Retrieved November 21, 2002, from the World Wide Web: http://www.aswb.org/members_rept3.shtml

Bell, V., & de La Rue, a. D. (1995). *Gender harassment on the Internet.* Georgia State College of Law. Retrieved November 22, 2002, from the World Wide Web: http://www.gsu.edu/%7Elawppw/lawand.papers/harass.html

Braithwaite, D. O., Waldron, V. R., & Finn, J. (1999). Communication of social support in computer-mediated groups for persons with disabilities. *Health Communication. 11,* 123–151.

Colon, Y. (1997). Chattering through the fingertips: Doing group therapy online. *Women and Performance.* Retrieved July 8, 1997, from the World Wide Web: [Available online: http://www.echonyc.com/~women/Issue17/public-colon.html]

Cummings, J. N., Butler, B., & Kraut, R. (2002). The quality of online social relationships. Communications of the ACM 45(7), 103–108.

Donath, J. (1999). *Identity and deception in the virtual community.* Routledge. Retrieved November 22, 2002, from the World Wide Web: http://smg.media.mit.edu/people/Judith/Identity/IdentityDeception.html.

Dunaway, M. O. (2000). *Assessing the potential of online psychotherapy.* Mental Health Infosource. Retrieved November 18, 2000, from the World Wide Web: http://www.mhsource.com/pt/p001058.html

Feenberg, A. L., Licht, J. M., Kane, K. P., Moran, K., & Smakith, R. A. (1996). The online patient meeting. *Journal of Neurological Sciences.* 139 (supplement). 129–131.

Fernsler, J. I., & Manchester, L. J. (1997). Evaluation of a computer-based cancer support network. *Cancer Practice.* 5(1), 46–51.

Finfgeld, D. L. (2000). Therapeutic groups online: The good, the bad and the unknown. *Issues in Mental Health Nursing.* 21, 241–255.

Finn, J. (1996). Computer-based self-help groups: On-line recovery for addictions. *Computers in Human Services.* 13(1), 21–41.

Finn, J., & Lavitt, M. (1994). Computer-based self-help for survivors of sexual abuse. *Social Work with Groups.* 17(1), 21–46.

Fox, S. (2002). Pew Internet Project data memo: Search engines. *Pew Internet and American Life Project*. Retrieved November 1, 2002, from the World Wide Web: http://www.pewinternet.org/reports/toc.asp?Report=64

Greenfield, D. N. (1999, August 20). The nature of Internet addiction: Psychological factors in compulsive Internet use. Paper presented at the American Psychological Association, Boston, MA.

Grohol, J. (1998). Re: Internet Addiction [long]. Message posted to research@cmhcsys.com

Gustafson, D. H., Hawkins, R., Boberg, E., Bricker, E., Pingree, S., & Chan, C. (1994). The use and impact of a computer-based support system for people living with AIDS and HIV infection. *Proceedings of the 18th Annual Symposium on Computer Applications in Medical Care*. 18, 604–608.

Hill, D. (2002). *Computer-mediated therapy: Possibilities and possible limitations*. Psy Broadcasting Corporation. Retrieved August 23, 2002, from the World Wide Web: http://www.psybc.com/library_cyber.html

Holmes, L. (1997a). *The pros and cons of support groups for trauma survivors*. Retrieved April 4, 2002, from the World Wide Web: http://mentalhealth.about.com/library/weekly/aa091597.htm

Holmes, L. (1997b). *The pros and cons of support groups for trauma survivors—Part 2*. Retrieved April 4, 2002, from the World Wide Web: http://mentalhealth.about.com/library/weekly/aa092297.htm

King, S. (1994). Analysis of electronic support groups for recovering addicts. *Interpersonal Computing and Technology*. 2(3), 47–56.

King, S., & Moreggi, D. (1998). Internet therapy and self-help groups—the pros and cons. In J. Gackenbach (ed.), *Psychology and the Internet: Intrapersonal, interpersonal and transpersonal implications* (Vol. 1998, pp. 77–106). New York: Academic Press.

Klemm, P., & Nolan, M. T. (1998). Internet cancer support groups: Legal and ethical issues for nurse researchers. *Oncology Nursing Forum*. 25(4), 673–676.

Kraut, R., Lundmark, V., Patterson, M., Kiesler, S., Mukopadhyay, T., & Sherlis, W. (1998). Internet paradox: A social technology that reduces social involvement and psychological well-being? *American Psychologist*. 53(9), 1017–1031.

Kummervold, P. E., Gammon, D., Bergvik, S., Johnson, J. A., Hasvold, T., & Rosenvinge, J. H. (2002). Social support in a wired world: Use of online mental health forums in Norway. *Nordic Journal of Psychiatry*. 56(1), 59–65.

Lenhart, A. (2000). Who's not online: 57% of those without Internet access say they do not plan to log on. *Pew Internet and American Life*. Retrieved November 1, 2002, from the World Wide Web: www.pewinternet.org

Loader, B., Muncer, S., Burrows, R., Pleace, N., & Nettleton, S. (2002). Medicine on the line? Computer-mediated social support and advice for people with diabetes. *International Journal of Social Welfare*. 11(1), 53–65.

McKenna, K. Y. A., & Bargh, J. A. (1998). Coming out in the age of the Internet: Identity "demarginalization" through virtual group participation. *Journal of Personality and Social Psychology*. 75(3), 681–694.

Meier, A. (2000). Offering social support via the Internet: A case study of an online support group for social workers. In J. Finn & G. Holden (eds.), *Human services online: A new arena for service delivery* (pp. 237–266). New York: Haworth Press.

Meier (forthcoming). Group work with technology-mediated groups. In C. D. Garvin, L. Gutierrez & M. J. Galinsky (eds.), *Handbook of Social Work with Groups*. New York: Guilford Publications.

Mickelson, K. D. (1997). Seeking social support: Parents in electronic support groups. In S. Kiesler (ed.), *Culture of the Internet.* Mahwah, NJ: Laurence Erlbaum Associates.

Miller, J. K., & Gergan, K. J. (1998). Life on the line: The therapeutic potentials of computer-mediated conversation. *Journal of Marital and Family Therapy.* 24(2), 189–202.

NASW. (1999). *Code of ethics.* National Association of Social Workers. Retrieved from the World Wide Web: http://www.socialworkers.org/pubs/code/code.asp.

North, C. L. (1998). Computer-mediated communication and social support among eating disordered individuals: An analysis of the alt.support.eating-disord news group. *Dissertation Abstracts International Section A: Humanities-and-Social-Sciences.* 58(12-A), 4496.

Nowinski, J., Baker, S., & Carrol, K. (1992). *Twelve Step Facilitation Therapy Manual* (Vol. 1). Washington DC: U.S. Department of Health and Human Services; Public Health Service; Alcohol, Drug Abuse, and Mental Health Administration; and the National Institute on Alcohol Abuse and Alcoholism.

Online Intergroup of Alcoholics Anonymous. (2002). *Purpose and structure of the Online Intergroup.* Retrieved November 22, 2002, from the World Wide Web: www.aa-intergroup.org

Peron, B. (2002). Online support for caregivers of people with a mental illness. *Psychiatric Rehabilitation Journal.* 26(1), 70–77

Phillips, W. (1996). *A comparison of online, e-mail and in-person self-help groups using Adult Children of Alcoholics as a model.* Rider University Psychology Department. Retrieved April 29, 1999, from the World Wide Web: www.rider.edu/users/suler/psycyber/acoa.html

Radin, P. A. (2001). "Hello, my friends": Social capital and transformations of trust in a grassroots breast cancer Website. Unpublished dissertation, University of Washington, Seattle, WA.

Rainie, L., & Packel, D. (2001). More online, doing more: 16 million newcomers gain Internet access in the last half of 2000 as women, minorities and families with modest incomes continue to surge online. *Pew Internet Project.* Retrieved May 19, 2001, from the World Wide Web: *http://www.pewtrusts.com/pdf/vf_pew_internet_population_report.pdf.*

Reid, E. (1998). The self and the Internet: Variations on the illusion of one self. In J. Gackenbach (ed.), *Psychology and the Internet* (pp. 29–60). New York: Academic Press.

Rheingold, H. (2000). *The virtual community: Homesteading on the electronic frontier.* Cambridge, MA: MIT Press.

Roy, M. C., Gauvin, S., & Limayem, M. (1996). Electronic group brainstorming: The role of feedback on productivity. *Small Group Research.* 27(2), 215–247.

Salem, D. A., Bogat, G. A., & Reid, C. (1997). Mutual help goes on-line. *Journal of Community Psychology.* 25:(2), 189–207.

Shannon, C. E. (1948). A mathematical theory of communication. *Bell System Technical Journal.* 27, 379–423 and 623–656.

Siegel, J., Dubrovsky, V., Kiesler, S., & McGuire, T. W. (1986). Group process in computer mediated communication. *Organizational Behavior and Human Decision Processes.* 37(157–187).

Stein, D. J. (1997). Psychiatry on the internet: Survey of an OCD mailing list. *Psychiatric Bulletin.* 21, 95–98.

Steinberg, D. M. (1999, October). Group work practice with odd ducks: Mining for mutual aid in single-session, open-ended, and very large groups. Paper presented at the XXI Annual Symposium of the Association for the Advancement of Social Work with Groups, Denver, CO.

Suler, J. (1999, January 2001). *Psychotherapy in cyberspace: A 5-dimensional model of online and computer-mediated psychotherapy.* Retrieved May 14, 2001, from the World Wide Web: http://www.rider.edu/users/suler/psycber/therapy.html.

Suler, J. (2000, January 2000). *Bring online and offline living together: The Integration Principle.* Retrieved November 9, 2000, from the World Wide Web: http://www.rider.edu/users/suler/psycyber/ethics.html.

Walther, J. B. (1996). Computer-mediated communication: Impersonal, interpersonal and hyper-personal interaction. *Communication Research.* 23, 3–43.

Walther, J. B., & Boyd, S. (forthcoming). Attraction to computer-mediated social support. In C. A. Lin & D. Atkin (eds.), *Communication technology and society: Audience adoption and uses of the new media.* New York: Hampton Press.

Weinberg, N., Uken, J., Schmale, J. D., & Adamek, M. (1995). Therapeutic factors: Their presence in a computer-mediated support group. *Social Work with Groups.* 18(4), 57–69.

Winzelberg, A. (1997). The analysis of an electronic support group for individuals with eating disorders. *Computers in Human Behavior.* 13(3), 393–407.

Wright, K. (2000). Computer-mediated social support, older adults, and coping. *Journal of Communication.* 50(3), 100–118.

Chapter 12

Group Work with Asian-American Immigrants: A Cross-Cultural Perspective

SHOSHANNA RINGEL

INTRODUCTION AND LITERATURE REVIEW

Social work has had a long tradition of group work practice with diverse immigrant communities, starting before Jane Addams's Hull House in Chicago during the 1890s and continuing up until the present day. Group work practice with immigrants started in the settlement houses, which were located in poor urban neighborhoods where most of the new immigrants initially settled. At the time, the new immigrants came from European countries such as Italy, Germany, Greece, Poland, Russia, and Ireland. The settlement houses usually provided services to young boys, according to Reid (1981), as those boys were the most frequent visitors. Untrained volunteers initially led group work with these first-generation immigrants. As the settlement houses and club activities began to expand, however, trained social workers became the group leaders (Reid, 1981). These early groups helped the immigrant boys acculturate into the American mainstream, and the settlement houses also served as a social center for their parents. Similar settlement houses and neighborhood centers continue to provide services today for many diverse communities. While this chapter will focus on specific issues of cross-cultural group work with Asian Americans from East Asia—primarily China, Korea, and Japan—the chapter will begin by briefly addressing the universal themes that all immigrants experience in order to maximize its relevance for practitioners.

181

An important aspect of the immigrant experience is the development of a bicultural identity, or "the ability to move freely between one's ethnic community and the larger culture" (Chau, 1990, p. 2), which helps maintain the immigrants' self esteem and facilitates their integration into the dominant culture. The immigrants' ethnic identity, meaning the attitudes, values, and behaviors that are shared by a group within a culture (Uba, 1994), is closely linked to their attainment of a bicultural identity, and it has also been found to be positively correlated with self-esteem (Phinney, 1989, 1990). Therefore, the process of ethnic identity formation and the related degree of acculturation are both important factors that affect the immigrant's level of stress, self-esteem, and social relationships.

Significant aspects of the acculturation process are the economic hardships and the experience of racism and oppression that are common to the immigrant experience. Racism and oppression can especially affect adolescents who are more exposed to the dominant culture through the educational system (Huang, 1997), but it plays a part in many immigrants' lives and thus may also become an important issue in the group process (Comaz-Diaz & Jacobsen, 1991; Sue & Sue, 1990). Finally, the experience of multiple losses is universal for all immigrants, such as the immigrant's inevitable loss of family members who remain in the native country, of community, of profession, and of home and native land (Grinberg & Grinberg, 1989).

While immigrants have continued to come to the United States in steadily growing numbers, the immigrants' countries of origin have, for the most part, changed. Currently some of the fastest-growing immigrant communities in the United States are from Asia (Kitano & Daniels, 1995). Asian immigrants come from varied cultures that have different languages, religions, histories, and cultural values. Most have come from China, Korea, Japan, India, Pakistan, Vietnam, Cambodia, Laos, and the Philippines. Recent statistics from the Immigration and Naturalization Service (2002) cite that there were over one million legal immigrants entering the United States. Of this group, 56,426 immigrated from the People's Republic of China, 53,154 from the Philippines, 35,531 from Vietnam, and 20,742 from Korea. The majority of Asian Americans are foreign-born, and therefore their cultural differences and level of acculturation play an important role in their group process (Sue & Sue, 1990). While some Asian communities have immigrated voluntarily, others, including immigrants from Cambodia, Vietnam, and Laos, came to the United States as refugees and thus have unique needs and experiences. Therefore, group work with Asian immigrants can be extremely complex because Asians can come from vastly heterogeneous cultures with many intergroup differences. These differences may be religious, historical, and/or cultural. For example, while the major Japanese religions are Buddhism or Shintoism, most Korean immigrants in the United States are Christian, and Chinese immigrants who have lived under Communism since the early twentieth century typically do not practice a particular religion. Historically, Japan, China, and Korea have had significant military and political conflicts, and therefore immigrants from these countries, especially those of the first generation, may feel uncomfortable in Asian groups of mixed ethnicity. An additional difficulty for the practitioner is that there is currently limited empirical literature on group work with this population (Chen & Han, 2001; Leong, 1992).

Despite the wide variance in East Asian cultures, there are certain characteristics and experiences that are shared by most East Asian immigrant communities. Many East Asian cultural traditions, values, and social mores are radically different from our own Western traditions. Research findings indicate, for example, that there is a strong stigma associated with mental illness and therefore an underutilization of mental health services in the Asian community (Atkinson et al., 1998; Kitano & Daniels, 1995). Somatization of mental health problems is a culturally specific behavior. Rather than admitting to depression, anxiety, or stress, for example, Asian clients are more likely to refer to somatic symptoms such as a stomachache or headache (Sue & Morishima, 1982; Uba, 1994).

The Eastern social paradigm of familial and communal interdependence and harmony, hierarchical structure, and respect for authority may conflict with the Western paradigm of individuality, independence, autonomy, and egalitarian relationships (Yamamoto & Acosta, 1982). In addition, Asian cultures emphasize a respect for privacy, thus clients may find it difficult to seek help from outsiders or to talk about their problems to non–family members (Narikiyo & Kameoka, 1992; Lee, 1996). Therefore, a group process may be a difficult undertaking for Asian clients because talking publicly about oneself to perceived outsiders is considered inappropriate from a cultural perspective (Yu & Gregg, 1993). While educational and vocational problems are socially accepted, psychological problems are not, and consequently Asian clients will find it easier to focus initially on educational or professional difficulties, or in fact may prefer to resolve their problems on their own. Because of these complex factors, group work with Asian immigrants presents a difficult challenge for the Western group leader.

Finally, an important difference between Asian and Western cultures is the Asian emphasis on nonverbal communication systems, unlike the Western culture, which is highly verbal (Roland, 1991; Sue & Sue, 1990). Consequently, silence, eye contact, physical distance, and other nonverbal signals constitute a subtle and highly developed form of communication in Asian cultures, and have to be carefully attended to and understood by the group leader.

PRACTICE PRINCIPLES

Role of the Leader

The leader's cultural competence and their awareness of their own ethnic identity development is an important aspect of their leadership role (Chen

& Han, 2001; Yu & Gregg, 1993). It is preferable that, especially with first-generation immigrants, the group leader shares the same or similar cultural background as the group members or speaks their native language so that she or he can inspire trust and relate to their immigrant experience. Most social workers, however, are of European descent and come from the mainstream American culture (Pack-Brown, 1999; Yutrzenka, 1995). Thus, group work with immigrants often entails a cross-cultural process between group members and the group leader. The group may therefore become a "microcosm of society" (Hurdle, 1990) as group members' experiences with racism and oppression may be projected onto the group leader. Consequently, in order to facilitate a safe multicultural environment, it is important for the group leader to address feelings of bias and discrimination as soon as they arise in the group. In order to create this safe environment, the group leader should be culturally competent. The requisite skills for cultural competence include *(1)* the leader's awareness of their personal values and biases, *(2)* their understanding the world-view of culturally different clients, and *(3)* their developing appropriate intervention strategies and techniques (Lum, 1999).

Several authors recommend using a stage model of ethnic development for both the group leader and the group to see if they are placed within the same ethnic developmental stage (Leong, 1992; Tsui, 1997). According to Phinney (1990), ethnic identity development begins with the precontact phase, where few cross-cultural contacts have been made, and then progresses to the dissonance phase, wherein there are more inter-ethnic contacts, and the individual feels dissonance with the dominant culture due to discrimination or oppression. The third phase includes either immersion, when the individual submerges into the dominant cultural values, or marginality, when the individual isolates herself from both her native culture and the dominant culture. The fourth phase is introspection, where reflection on one's cultural conflicts leads to reconciliation between both native and majority cultures. The final stage is integration, or the acquisition of an inner sense of security about one's ethnic identity and a positive view of the dominant culture. The group leader's awareness of both their own ethnic identity process and the group's ethnic identity stage at any given point may prevent discord, denial, conflict, and distrust in the group. In addition, the leader's self-awareness may also help them empathize with the group members' struggles and identity conflicts (Comaz-Diaz & Jacobsen, 1991; Hurdle, 1990). This author, for example, used her own experience as an immigrant to empathize with her Asian group members' struggles. Another clinician used his relationship with his Chinese mother-in-law to relate to his Asian clients' outsider experience.

One important goal in the group is to facilitate the members' bicultural skills and their acculturation process. It is important, therefore, that the leader find out whether group members are first-, second- or third-generation immigrants in order to evaluate their level of acculturation to the American culture. Clearly, second- and third-generation immigrants are more acculturated than first-generation immigrants (Atkinson et al., 1998; Atkinson et al., 1993). The leader can use members' issues of cultural miscommunication and misinterpretation to teach them new relational skills, and, in a multicultural group, the group process can be used as a vehicle for developing multicultural relationships and communication skills for the group members (Hurdle, 1990).

Group Structure

Most Asian cultures are hierarchical and encourage a strong respect for authority figures. Therefore, the group members may view the leader as an expert from whom they can seek advice, direction, and problem-solving (Tsui, 1997). Thus, a structured group with clearly defined tasks, purpose, and agenda will be more relevant for the Asian group members, at least initially, than a more reflective, process-oriented group with ambiguous goals (Brinson & Lee, 1996; Tsui, 1997). This may change, however, as group members become more comfortable with each other and with the leader, and/or as they become more acculturated. Therefore, it is important for the group leader to take on a more directive role initially, but as the group process unfolds, the leader can also encourage group members to speak up. This more task-oriented, structured approach may clearly pose a dilemma for the Western group leader who may prefer a more fluid, collaborative group process throughout.

Chen and Han (2001) suggest that the highest risk for dropping out is in the initial "forming" stage of the group. During this stage, concerns about the expression of feelings, self-disclosure, expectations of leadership, tolerance of ambiguity, and handling of culturally different communication styles are predominant themes. Asian immigrants may initially prefer to discuss more practical concerns, such as academic difficulties and professional problems, rather than their personal feelings, which they would rather keep to themselves. For example, one Vietnamese group member dropped out after her first session after she had disclosed to the group her anger with her adoptive American mother. This may have resulted from her feeling that she had broken a powerful cultural taboo. The fear of being shamed or of "losing face" and being rejected are also strong cultural characteristics that may cause members to drop out from the group.

Group Composition

In deciding on group composition, the leader should take into account the members' level of acculturation; e.g., whether they are first- or second-generation immigrants, as well as their language skills. More acculturated Asian immigrants are more likely to be willing to expose themselves and to talk about personal problems and may feel more at ease in a heterogeneous group (Leong et al., 1995). An additional consideration is whether the group should be ethnically homogeneous or culturally diverse. An ethnically heterogeneous group can benefit the participant's increased multicultural awareness and reduce stereotypes and prejudice (Chen & Han, 2001; Merta, 1995). It can also result, however, in increased anxiety concerning the exploration of ethnic issues (Yu & Gregg, 1993). A homogeneous group, on the other hand, can become more cohesive and allow for more comfort with the exploration of problems, as Asian immigrants may be more likely to express their difficulties and personal experiences in a homogeneous group (Leong, 1992; Yu & Gregg, 1993). A homogeneous group, however, may risk being more superficial and less creative as group members are not exposed to a diversity of cultural perspectives (Tsui, 1997).

While literature regarding the impact of gender differences on group composition with Asian immigrants was not found, it may be preferable to establish gender-specific groups with first-generation immigrants because of the widely divergent gender roles in Asian cultures. Women may feel safer and more at ease in an all-women group, especially one organized around a common topic. For example, some successful women's groups this author was familiar with included an adjustment and socialization group for Cambodian immigrant women, a support group for academic problems for female Japanese university students, and a support group for Chinese mothers of chronically mentally ill young adults.

Termination

Termination may bring up intense issues of grief, loss, and abandonment for first-generation immigrants and refugees who have already experienced a great deal of traumatic grief and loss in their lives (Nicholson & Kay, 1999). During the termination phase, the group leader should help the members to express and address these issues. Chen and Han (2001) suggest that during termination it is important for the group leader to help the members handle their unresolved issues and their "separation anxiety" and to transfer their group experiences to their daily life (Corey, 2000; Vasquez & Han, 1995). The group leader should also allow members to express any unfinished business about cultural issues and conflicts. Finally, it is important to ascertain whether members have social supports, people with whom their new insights and behaviors can be maintained, especially when these new behaviors are not culturally syntonic and may therefore meet with resentment or criticism from family members and friends.

COMMON THEMES

Acculturation

As previously discussed, issues related to the acculturation process are a common group theme, especially with first- and second-generation immigrants. Stress, low self-esteem, and intergenerational conflicts among second-generation adolescents and their more traditional first-generation parents may accompany the acculturation process. Consequently, it is an important issue for both immigrant adolescents and adults. Finally, in group work with adolescents, identity conflicts and the process of ethnic identity formation may become a predominant theme in the group. For example, one therapist described a poignant identity struggle for second-generation Chinese immigrants, who went back to China to find their roots and realized at that point how different they were from the native Chinese. Consequently, they experienced a serious identity crisis.

Intergenerational and Gender Conflicts

While gender roles and social relationships in the West are generally egalitarian, traditional Asian cultures adhere to more disparate gender roles and a more hierarchical and patriarchal social structure. Traditionally, men are at the head of the household, while women play a traditional social and familial role, and children are expected to comply and defer to all adults in order to maintain familial harmony (Lee, 1996; Queener & Kenyon, 2001). When these traditional mores come in contact with the American culture, familial and intergenerational conflicts may ensue. This can happen when women have to enter the job market to help support the family, and when children who are exposed to the American culture through education start behaving in Westernized cultural patterns. Consequently, familial, intergenerational, and internal conflicts stemming from the contact between two conflicting cultural paradigms are all common group themes. These gender and intergenerational conflicts may also present a dilemma for the Western group leader, who typically comes from a paradigm of gender equality, egalitarian social roles, and an emphasis on independence and individuation from the family of origin. It is important that he/she be aware of these frequently conflicting cultural paradigms and be careful of imposing his/her own cultural values on group members.

The Experience of Migration and Loss

The issue of migration and loss is an important underlying dynamic of the immigrant and refugee experience (Bilides, 1991; 1999; Grinberg & Grinberg, 1989; Nicholson & Kay, 1999). This includes the loss of supportive social networks, the loss of family and friends, the loss of a home, the loss of a way of life, the loss of employment, and the loss of a national and "territorial identity" (Breton, 1999). Loss is an inherent dynamic, especially for refugees who may have experienced civil wars, natural disasters, violence, and economic hardships. Narrating these experiences and sharing them with the group are thus important components of the healing process. In the context of group work with Asian refugees, specific immigrant groups may include Cambodians, Vietnamese, Hmong, and Chinese immigrants who have experienced the Cultural Revolution.

Racism and Oppression

Lum (1999) and Pinderhughes (1984) emphasize the political and social dimension of cross-cultural counseling. New immigrants frequently experience poverty, marginalization, and powerlessness, both as minorities in their native countries and as refugees in the United States. The group leader's presence as a representative of the majority culture naturally raises issues of power and powerlessness that may have an impact on group interactions. Therefore, it is important that the group leader attend to potential cultural differences, stereotyping, and biases, coming both from the leader and from among group members. This is especially true in a heterogeneous, multi-ethnic group, and these issues should be addressed directly as soon as they come up (Bilides, 1991). Racial stereotyping of Asians can be extremely subtle. Such stereotyping may include Asian immigrants being cast as the "model minority" (Uba, 1994), and having high academic and professional expectations placed on them (or conversely, being resented for their high achievements). Another common assumption may be that all Asian women are shy and submissive.

RECOMMENDED WAYS OF WORKING

Verbal and Nonverbal Communication

Understanding verbal and nonverbal communication is an important dimension of group work with Asian immigrants, especially when the leader and the members come from different cultural paradigms, and when English is the group members' second language. Unlike the highly verbal Western tradition, in East Asian cultures nonverbal communication and silence are highly developed (Itai & McRae, 1994; Morris & Robinson, 1996). These differences in modes of communication can typically result in mistaken assumptions and consequent misunderstanding. Nonverbal signals can have different meanings in Western and Asian cultures. For example, silence may mean a hesitation to disagree with the leader or to express anger, rather than compliance. Smiling may mean deference, rather than happiness, and direct eye contact is considered rude in Asian cultures, whereas it is appropriate in the West (Sue, 1990; Tsui, 1997). A qualitative study of Western therapists working with Asian immigrants conducted by this author (Ringel, 2000), revealed that therapists who are not familiar with Asian communication systems may erroneously view their Asian clients as non-communicative, overly concrete, or passive-aggressive in their behavior. Therefore, it is important that the group leader be attuned to cultural differences in order to understand the meaning of the Asian members' verbal and nonverbal communications.

Expressing Feelings

Asian cultures emphasize the indirect expression of feelings, and public displays of emotions are at odds with the Asian worldview, which values social and collective harmony. The disclosure of familial conflicts to non–family members may imply a "loss of face" for the Asian group members (Pearson, 1991). Therefore, it is not advisable that group leaders encourage members to share their personal feelings or discuss personal conflicts too early in the group process. One way to encourage members to express feelings at a later group stage is to normalize their feelings by explaining them as a common part of the cultural adjustment process, in order to minimize their shame and embarrassment. One therapist told a story that illustrates this point well. When he was treating patients in a mental hospital in Beijing for issues related to traumatic loss, some became highly emotional. While this Western therapist saw this as a breakthrough in the treatment, his Chinese colleagues viewed these displays of feelings as "drama" and didn't consider it helpful or productive for the patients. More concrete and pragmatic issues, such as academic or professional difficulties, may be more comfortable topics for the group members to begin with. Eventually, however, as the leader's credibility is established and group members feel more at ease with each other and with the group process, they may start sharing personal feelings on their own (Nicholson & Kay, 1999; Yu & Gregg, 1993).

Problem Solving, Structure, and Psycho-Education

Because of their deference to authority and their more hierarchical cultural model, the group members will often look, at least initially, for the leader to provide structure, to initiate the group process, and to be the expert who can provide advice and problem-solve (Pearson, 1991). Another important function of the group is to provide a psycho-educational component in order to help members understand the different aspects of American culture, and to educate them about specific problems in negotiating it (Nicholson & Kay, 1999; Queener & Kenyon, 2001; Rittner & Nakanishi, 1993). The idealization of the group leader and the expectation that they function as a mentor-teacher is based on strong cultural traditions, especially in the Japanese culture. Consequently, the group members' apparent "compliance" and their reluctance to challenge their group leader may stem from a desire to protect the leader from a loss of face. In return, they may expect the leader to take care of them. Eventually, as group members establish trust with the leader and feel more at ease with other group members and with the group format, they will start to take the initiative and to feel more at ease with a less structured group process.

Dealing with Conflict

Unlike Western culture, Asian cultures, based on a Confucian philosophy, emphasize social and interpersonal harmony and the avoidance of conflict at all costs. Consequently, the Asian group members will often not admit to conflict, and will do their best to avoid direct disagreements both with the leader and with other group members (Pearson, 1991). As stated previously, silence may be one indication of the group members' reluctance to voice disagreements. Therefore, in the early stages of the group, the group leader should avoid direct confrontation, which can be seen as a negative behavior by the group members (Leong, 1992). One skillful way to work with this cultural dynamic of conflict avoidance was illustrated by several experienced clinicians who stated that they invited their clients to disagree with them openly by making intentional mistakes (Ringel, 2000). The group leader can also demonstrate and model modes of empathic and constructive confrontation (Chen & Han, 2001, 1995; Corey, 2000). Finally, the consensus among several clinicians who have worked with Asian clients is that group members will be more likely over time to openly express their disagreements with the leader or with others in the group (Ringel, 2000).

Leader's Self-Disclosure

The leader's appropriate self-disclosure may help group members feel more trust and familiarity with the group leader, and thus be more willing to be open and to share their own personal experiences. One group leader, for example, who ran a support group for Chinese parents of chronically mentally ill young adults, disclosed to the group that she had just adopted a Chinese girl. While she told this writer that during the first two years of the group there was little group interaction, and members usually waited for her to initiate discussion, following her disclosure the group members became much more interactive, open, and engaged with each other. Another group leader who ran a drop-in group for Chinese immigrants encouraged his group members to express their feelings and normalized them by sharing his own experience of loneliness and isolation during an extended stay in China. Others agree that the Asian group members may feel more at ease with a Western group leader when the leader discloses their own cultural identity and acculturation experiences with the group (Rittner & Nakanishi, 1993).

Familial and Communal vs. Individualistic Perspective

Asian cultures emphasize a familial and communal paradigm, rather than a Western individualistic, autonomous perspective. Therefore, members' family problems can be experienced as personal conflicts, and disagreements with family members can cause serious psychological problems such as anxiety and depression. These conflicting Asian and Western agendas may present a serious dilemma for second-generation Asian immigrants, who are more likely to be influenced by Western culture, and who may therefore feel conflicted between their desire to achieve autonomy and independence and their loyalty to their family. The group leader, therefore, has to be sensitive to the importance of family and community for the Asian members' self-concept, and to be careful not to encourage "individualistic" solutions that may cause serious familial and interpersonal conflicts (Leong, 1992).

Evaluation

The literature about group work with Asian immigrants is limited, and therefore there are only two general recommendations for an evaluative process. The first is to use both the participants' verbal self-report and a Lickert scale–type questionnaire at the end of the group to assess whether the goals of the groups have been achieved. These goals typically include issues related to cultural identity, developing trust among group members, self-acceptance, and learning to strategize in the real world (Queener & Kenyon, 2001). Questions can assess the group members' satisfaction with the content of the group, the activities of the group, and the group leader. A second evaluative method may be the use of measurements that reflect the group purpose, such as self-esteem and empowerment, at the beginning and the end of the group in order to assess the group's impact on its members' personal characteristics. While an evaluative discussion is always an option, the group leader has to consider cultural factors that may influence the members' openness, such as their deference to the leader, their desire to protect the leader, and their potential reluctance to voice any criticism.

CONCLUSION

While this chapter focused primarily on the complexity and challenges of group work with Asian-American immigrants, it is likely that many of the issues and dilemmas that have been raised here will be relevant for group work with other immigrant groups. In light of the cultural, social, economic, and other unique challenges that immigrants face, it is clear that the leader's cultural competence constitutes their most important professional attribute in a cross-cultural group process. This includes the leader's awareness of his/her own biases and assumptions, respect for cultural differences, understanding of his/her own ethnic identity, and ability to use culturally specific interventions.

In any group work practice the needs and goals of the group members should be of primary consideration. Nevertheless, group work with immigrants is an experience of mutual enrichment, growth, and development for both the group members and the group leader. The group leader can help the group members become empowered, develop new coping skills, and learn to navigate successfully in a new and unfamiliar environment. On the other hand, the group members can help the leader broaden her or his knowledge and understanding of new cultural paradigms and lead to questioning familiar belief systems, as well as developing authentic curiosity and novel ways of perceiving the world.

RESOURCES

Asian Human Services, Inc.
4753 N. Broadway
Suite 700
Chicago, IL 60640
(773) 728-2235
www.asianhumanservices.org

Cambridge Hospital
1493 Cambridge St.
Cambridge, MA 02139
(617) 665-1000
www.challiance.org

REFERENCES

Atkinson, D., Morten, G., & Sue, D. W. (1998). *Counseling American minorities.* New York: McGraw-Hill.

Atkinson, D., Thompson, C., & Grant, S. (1993). A three-dimensional model for counseling racial and ethnic minorities. *The Counseling Psychologist.* 21, 257–277.

Bilides, D. (1991). Race, color, ethnicity and class: Issues of biculturalism in school-based adolescent counseling groups. *Social Work with Groups.* 14(1), 43–57.

Breton, M. (1999). The relevance of the structural approach to group work with immigrant and refugee women. *Social Work with Groups.* 22(2/3), 11–29.

Brinson, J. A., & Lee, C. C. (1996). Culturally responsive group leadership: An integrative model for experienced practitioners. In H. Forester-Miller & J. A. Kottler (eds.), *Issues and challenges for group practitioners* (pp. 43–56). Denver, CO: Love.

Chau, K. (1990). Introduction: Facilitating bicultural development and intercultural skills in ethnically heterogeneous groups. *Social Work with Groups.* 13(4), 1–5.

Chen, M., & Han, Y. (2001). Cross-cultural group counseling with Asians: A stage-specific interactive approach. *Journal for Specialists in Group Work.* 26(2), 111–128.

Comaz-Diaz, L., & Jacobsen, F. (1991). Ethnocultural transference and counter-transference in the therapeutic dyad. *American Journal of Orthopsychiatry.* 6(3), 392–402.

Corey, G. (2000). *Theory and practice of group counseling* (5th ed.). Belmont, CA: Wadsworth.

Grinberg, L., & Grinberg, R. (1989). *Psychoanalytic perspectives on migration and exile.* New Haven, CT: Yale University Press.

Huang, L. (1997). Asian American adolescents. In E. Lee (ed.), *Working with Asian Americans* (pp. 175–185). New York: Guilford Press.

Hurdle, D. (1990). Ethnicity and biculturalism. *Social Work with Groups.* 13(4), 59–70.

Immigration and Naturalization Service (2002). *Annual report: Legal immigration, fiscal year 2001.* August, No. 7. Washington, DC: Department of Justice.

Itai, G., & McRae, C. (1994). Counseling older Japanese American clients: An overview and observations. *Journal of Counseling and Development.* 72, 373–377.

Kitano, H., & Daniels, R. (1995). *Asian Americans: Emerging minorities.* Englewood Cliffs, NJ: Prentice Hall.

Lee, E. (1996). Chinese families. In M. McGoldrick, J. Giordano, & J. Pearce (eds.), *Ethnicity and family therapy* (pp. 249–267). New York: Guilford Press.

Leong, F. (1992). Guidelines for minimizing premature termination among Asian American clients in group counseling. *The Journal for Specialists in Group Work.* 17(4), 218–228.

Leong, F., Wagner, N., & Tata, S. (1995). Racial and ethnic variations in help seeking attitudes. In J. Ponterotto, M. Casas, L. Suzuki, & C. Alexander (eds.), *Handbook of multicultural counseling* (pp. 415–438). CA: Sage Pubs.

Lum, D. (1999). *Culturally competent practice: A framework for growth and action.* Pacific Grove, CA: Brooks/Cole.

Merta???, R. J. (1995). Group work: Multicultural perspectives. In J. G. Ponterotto, J. M. Casas, L. A. Suzuki, & C. M. Alexander (eds.), *Handbook of multicultural counseling* (pp. 567–585). Thousand Oaks, CA: Sage.

Morris, J. R., & Robinson, D. T. (1996). A review of multicultural counseling. *Journal of Humanistic Education and Development.* 35, 50–60.

Narikiyo, T., & Kameoka, V. (1992). Attributions of mental illness and judgments about help seeking among Japanese-Americans and White American students. *Journal of Counseling Psychology.* 39, 363–369.

Nicholson, B., & Kay, D. (1999). Group treatment of traumatized Cambodian women: A culture-specific approach. *Social Work.* 44(5), 470–479.

Pack-Brown, S. P. (1999). Racism and White counselor training: Influence of White racial identity theory and research. *Journal of Counseling and Development.* 77, 87–92.

Pearson, V. (1991). Western theory, Eastern practice: Social group work in Hong Kong. *Social Work with Groups.* 14(2), 45–59.

Phinney, J. (1989). Stages of ethnic identity development in minority group adolescents. *Journal of Early Adolescence.* 9, 34–49.

Phinney, J. S. (1990). Ethnic identity in adolescents and adults: Review of research. *Psychological Bulletin.* 108, 499–514.

Pinderhughes, E. (1984). Teaching empathy: Ethnicity, race and power at the cross-cultural treatment interface. *The American Journal of Social Psychiatry.* 4(1), 5–12.

Queener, J., & Kenyon, J. (2001). Providing mental health services to Southeast Asian adolescent girls: Integration of a primary prevention paradigm and group counseling. *Journal for Specialists in Group Work.* 26(4), 350–367.

Reid, K. (1981). *The history of the use of groups in social work.* Westport, CT: Greenwood Press.

Ringel, S. (2000). The effect of culture on the working alliance between Asian American clients and Western therapists. Unpublished dissertation. Northampton, MA: Smith College School for Social Work.

Rittner, B., & Nakanishi, M. (1993). Challenging stereotypes and cultural biases through small group process. *Social Work with Groups.* 16(4), 5–23.

Roland, A. (1991). The self in cross-civilization perspective. In R. Curtis (ed.), *The relational self* (pp. 160–180). New York: Guilford Press.

Sue, D. W. (1990). Culture-specific strategies in counseling: A conceptual framework. *Professional Psychology: Research and Practice.* 21(6), 424–433.

Sue, S., & Morishima, J. (1982). *The mental health of Asian Americans.* San Francisco: Jossey-Bass.

Sue, D., & Sue, D. W. (1990). *Counseling the culturally different.* New York: Wiley & Sons.

Tsui, P. (1997). The dynamics of cultural and power relations in group therapy. In E. Lee (ed.), *Working with Asian Americans: A guide for clinicians* (pp. 354–363). New York: Guilford Press.

Uba, L. (1994). *Asian Americans: Personality patterns, identity, and mental health.* New York: Guilford Press.

Vasquez, M., & Han, A. (1995). Group interventions and treatment with ethnic minorities. In J. F. Aponte, R. Y. Rivers, & J. Wohl (eds.), *Psychological interventions and cultural diversity* (pp. 109–127). Boston: Allyn & Bacon.

Yamamoto, J., & Acosta, F. (1982). Treatment of Asian Americans and Hispanic Americans: Similarities and differences. *Journal of the American Academy of Psychoanalysis.* 10, 585–607.

Yu, A., & Gregg, C. (1993). Working with groups: Asians in groups, more than a matter of cultural awareness. *The Journal for Specialists in Group Work.* 18(2), 86–93.

Yutrzenka, B. A. (1995). Making a case for training in ethnic and cultural diversity in increasing treatment efficacy. *Journal of Counseling and Clinical Psychology.* 63, 197–206.

PART III

VIOLENCE: VICTIMS AND PERPETRATORS

Chapter 13

Working with Victims of Hate Crimes

JOAN C. WEISS

Incidents of harassment, intimidation, assault, or vandalism can be particularly traumatic and have long-lasting effects when directed against people because of their race, ethnicity, religion, sexual orientation, or disability. The terms *hate crime, bias crime, and ethnoviolence* are used interchangeably to describe such incidents. This chapter will provide social workers with an understanding of the nature of such incidents and their effects on victims.

Knowledge of hate crimes is critical for all group work, because any group may contain members whose experiences of hate crimes may affect their reactions and behaviors to a wide range of issues and actions, as well as to other people, both in and out of the group. In communities dealing with intergroup tensions and incidents, there may be a clear need for a group for victims of hate crimes. Hate crimes can occur in neighborhoods or workplaces, such as when an individual or family is the first of a minority group to appear on the block or in the office; in public places; or when someone is attacked just walking down a street.

A group format is particularly suited to this population for several reasons. All members of a family are affected when one member has been victimized, so group work with one or more families may be indicated. Also, when one person in a community has been targeted, such as for racial reasons, there are frequently others who have had similar experiences. Furthermore, seldom is there only one isolated incident; victims often have experienced numerous incidents over time. Perhaps most important, being a victim of violence stigmatizes and isolates individuals.

Sharing the experiences and ways of coping in a group format can be cathartic and healing, and can provide a support network for the future.

REVIEW OF THE LITERATURE

Although victimization based on someone's race, ethnicity, religion, or sexual orientation is not a new phenomenon, it is only during the last 20 to 25 years that social workers have worked with groups whose primary characteristic is their members' experiences of hate crimes.[1] Prior to that, people who were victimized because of their group identity, rather than for any act they committed, turned to institutions representative of these groups for support. African Americans could count on support from the NAACP or local churches; Jews turned to the Anti-Defamation League or the American Jewish Committee, and so on. Informal support often came from family members and neighbors.

In 1979, police departments began keeping records of "bias crimes" or "hate crimes." The Boston and New York City departments were two of the first in the country to do so and had departments designated to handle such crimes, and others followed suit. In Maryland, Montgomery and Baltimore counties were two jurisdictions whose police departments began keeping such records early. Each assigned community relations specialists to deal with the problems of investigating hate crimes and their impact both on the victims and on the communities involved.

Local and state human rights agencies began working with victims of hate crimes and began formal efforts to provide support to victims. Programs that agencies developed included those designed to train citizens to respond to victims in their communities. The "Network of Neighbors" and "Network of Teens," created by the Commission on Human Relations in Montgomery County, Maryland, to provide support to adults and youth who are victimized, are examples of programs that have been replicated in other jurisdictions. Training on issues of victimization and in basic skills of support is available to people who join the groups.

National organizations that tracked racially and religiously motivated incidents as well as neo-Nazi, Ku Klux Klan, and other hate group activity included the Southern Poverty Law Center and its affiliate, Klanwatch, in Alabama, and the Anti-Defamation League in New York. In 1985, the first national organization devoted exclusively to research, education, and training on the problem of "ethnoviolence"—a term it coined for hate crimes—was established in Baltimore. The National Institute

---

[1] While the information contained in this chapter is relevant to persons victimized because of disability as well, historically the terms *hate crime* and *bias crime* have not included disability, and therefore less information with that as a special focus is available.

Against Prejudice and Violence conducted the first nationwide study of incidents of ethnoviolence and their effects on victims.[2]

National attention to the problem of hate crimes, and the efforts of a coalition of many organizations representing a wide range of minority populations and civil rights groups, led to the passage of the Hate Crime Statistics Act of 1990 (Public Law 101–275). The law required the Attorney General of the United States to compile data and publish a summary of crimes that "manifest evidence of prejudice based on race, religion, sexual orientation or ethnicity" for five years, beginning in 1990. Bias against persons with disability was added to the Hate Crime Statistics Act in 1994, and in 1996, the sunset clause was removed from the original statute, mandating the permanent collection of hate crime data.

While the nationwide data on hate crimes do not accurately represent the prevalence of the problem, they do reveal a widespread phenomenon that warrants serious attention. The Uniform Crime Reporting Program of the FBI is responsible for maintaining the data collected under the Hate Crime Statistics Act, and began collecting national data on hate crimes in 1991. In its report *Hate Crime Statistics 2001*, the FBI indicated that 11,987 law enforcement agencies (of almost 17,000 that report to the FBI), representing 85% of the U.S. population, had reported 9,730 bias-motivated criminal incidents. These incidents involved 12,020 victims and 11,451 total offenses. Almost 68% of the offenses were crimes against individuals; the rest targeted businesses, religious organizations, and other institutions. Racial bias was the motivation in 45% of the incidents, and religion in almost 19%. Sexual orientation was the motivation in 14% of the incidents. Of the rest, 22% were motivated by the ethnicity or national origin of the victim, of whom 28% were Hispanic (with the rest designated as "other"). Incidents based on disability, first reported in the FBI report for 1997, constituted less than .4%. Of the racial incidents, 66% were antiblack; 20% were antiwhite. The rest were directed against Asians/Pacific Islanders, American Indians/Alaskan natives, or multiracial groups. The majority of the incidents motivated by religious bias were directed against Jews (57%); anti-Islamic bias accounted for 26%. There were 10 murders, 4 rapes, 941 aggravated assaults, 1,795 simple assaults, 3,563 acts of intimidation, and 3,607 property crimes (FBI, 2002).

Official statistics understate the problem of hate crimes, because many victims of hate crimes do not report their experiences to police. Reasons for not reporting vary. For immigrant groups, there is often a language barrier and, for some, a fear of police. In some communities, victims do not trust the police. For other victims, the level of frustration with the inability of police to apprehend perpetrators convinces them that reporting an incident will not accomplish anything. Fear of having

[2] The National Institute Against Prejudice and Violence closed in 1995; some of its work has continued under the name The Prejudice Institute.

their privacy compromised inhibits some victims, including many gays and lesbians. In cases of assault where the perpetrator is known, there is frequently fear of retaliation. In addition to non-reporting by victims, official statistics are low because police do not always accurately identify or record the motivation in a bias incident.

Information from organizations that represent victimized populations further illuminates the problem. The Anti-Defamation League, which documents anti-Semitism, publishes an annual audit of incidents reported to its offices around the country. In 2000, they recorded 1,606 incidents against Jews in 44 states and the District of Columbia. Fifty-five percent of the incidents were harassment, assault, or threats; 45% were acts of vandalism (Anti-Defamation League, 2001). The American-Arab Anti-Discrimination Committee, in its report of hate crimes against Arab Americans for 1998–2000, notes that such incidents are not distinguishable in the FBI reports of hate crimes. The Committee documents several dozen incidents of physical and psychological attacks for the period reported, which does not include incidents experienced by Arab Americans in the wake of the terrorist acts of September 11, 2001. In fact, the incidents counted as anti-Islamic in the FBI report cited above represented an increase from 28 in 2000 to 481 in 2001 (FBI, 2000; FBI, 2001).

The National Coalition of Anti-Violence Programs published a report, "Anti-Lesbian, Gay, Bisexual and Transgender Violence in 2001" based on incidents monitored by a network of 26 anti-violence organizations across the country. For 2001, 1,887 incidents directed at 2,210 victims were reported. They included 12 murders, 82 sexual assaults/rape, and 732 assaults or attempted assaults; the majority of the rest were intimidation or verbal harassment (National Coalition of Anti-Violence Programs, 2002).

In its sixth annual report of violence directed at Asian Pacific Americans, the National Asian Pacific American Legal Consortium documented 429 reported anti-Asian incidents, including 110 aggravated or simple assaults. In the report the Consortium states that under-reporting of hate crimes continues to be a serious problem, which is compounded by the fact that community groups that collect information from victims who are reluctant to report to the police were forced to scale back their efforts due to insufficient resources (National Asian Pacific American Legal Consortium, 1999).

Little is known about victims of hate crimes, their responses to incidents, and the impact of victimization on their lives. There are anecdotal reports that have been collected over the years, and some research. The reactions to being targets of hate crimes are both similar to and different from those of victims of random acts of violence. On the one hand, the feelings of victims of hate crimes are common to victims of crime in general: anger, fear, vulnerability. Many crime victims experience psychosocial adjustment problems, including disorientation, fear, helplessness, anger, and depression (Davis, 1987; Office for Victims of Crime, 1994; Resick, 1987). Furthermore, being victimized by crime sparks fear of further victimization, often resulting in changes in behavior (Skogan, 1987).

As with other crime victims, the seriousness of the crime does not necessarily determine the extent of reactions of a victim of ethnoviolence (Ehrlich, Larcom & Purvis, 1994). That is, someone who is the victim of repeated harassment where there is no physical injury may take longer to recover emotionally and return to a normal pattern of activities than someone who is the victim of a serious physical assault. The duration of reactions and level of life disruption depend on a host of factors, including the social context of the incident, the meaning of the incident to the victim, the availability of a network of support, and the individual's coping mechanisms.

On the other hand, being targeted for who one is rather than for something one has done creates fears and feelings that separate victims of hate crimes from victims of random violence. Research findings indicate that victims of ethnoviolence do suffer more in response to incidents of comparable violence than do victims of random crimes (Ehrlich et al., 1994; Iganski, 2001; McDevitt et al., 2001). If one is convinced that being a victim was a coincidence of time and place, at least one can try to avoid those circumstances. But correctly believing that one is being attacked for how one looks, or for one's identity in a given group, can create an ongoing level of fear that one is forever at risk.

In 1986, the National Institute Against Prejudice and Violence conducted a pilot study of the effects of hate crimes on minority group members. Ten focus groups were convened around the country, and victims, identified through police departments, human rights organizations, and community leaders, were interviewed using open-ended questions. Crimes the victims had experienced included physical assault; harassment and threats by mail, telephone, and in person; vandalism of their homes; and symbols or slogans of hate on their property. The costs to victims can be emotional, physical, and financial, and the effects can be long-lasting. The most prevalent reaction was one of anger toward the perpetrator (68 percent), followed by fear for the safety of their families (51 percent). Over one-third indicated feelings of sadness. Behavioral changes were also reported by one-third of the victims. Actions taken by victims included moving, reducing social interactions, taking security measures, and purchasing guns, both for increased safety and in preparation for retaliation if attacked again. Almost one-third of the victims never reported their experiences to the police (Barnes & Ephross, 1994; Ephross et al., 1986; Weiss, 1990).

The first national study designed to assess the prevalence and impact of ethnoviolence and other forms of victimization was also conducted by the National Institute Against Prejudice and Violence in 1989. Telephone interviews, using a stratified random sample, were completed with 2,078 respondents. To determine how the experience of being victimized in general compared with being victimized because of prejudice, interviewers asked subjects about symptoms they experienced that are associated with stress. A comparison of four groups of respondents—non-victims, victims of group defamation, victims of random crimes, and victims of hate crimes—revealed that victims of ethnoviolence experienced the greatest number of negative psychophysiological symptoms as well as the most social and behavioral changes of any group. (Examples of psychological and psychophysiological symptoms included feeling depressed or sad, feeling more nervous than usual, having trouble sleeping, and feeling very angry. Social and behavioral changes included items such as: "moved to another neighborhood"; "tried to be less visible"; "bought or started carrying a gun"; "took a self-defense class".) The study concluded that victims of ethnoviolence exhibited more symptoms with greater frequency than did victims of random violence (Ehrlich et al., 1994).

A more recent study was conducted in Boston from 1992 to 1997, to compare the impact of aggravated assault in bias-motivated cases and non–bias-motivated cases. The researchers found that bias crime victims were more likely to be attacked by a *group* of attackers than nonbias victims, and bias crime victims were significantly less likely to have a prior relationship with the offender. Nearly all bias assaults were committed by strangers, and most of those victims reported that the assault was an unprovoked attack. Whereas the victims of nonbias assaults could foresee how they could prevent such crimes in the future by changing their behavior, bias crime victims expressed feelings of frustration and felt powerless to protect themselves in the future. On measures of post-event stress, bias victims had a higher incidence of adverse psychological sequelae than the non-bias control group on all 19 of the items measured. Bias victims also felt less safe after the crime and suffered more health problems (McDevitt et al., 2001).

PRACTICE PRINCIPLES

Maintain Objectivity and Balance

In working with victims of hate crimes in groups, it is critical that social workers be in touch with (1) their own personal experiences with ethnoviolence that might affect the way they view others' experiences and (2) prejudices that might interfere with working with such victims. While this principle applies under all circumstances, working with victims of hate crimes calls for a particular combination of skills:

> A worker must be empathic and sensitive to the pain, yet maintain sufficient detachment to be effective. . . . Maintaining this delicate balance can cause a worker considerable stress. Additional strain often derives from the inherent limits of the situation: legal remedies are often infeasible or unenforceable. The perpetrator is nameless and faceless, official response sometimes denigrates the experience, and the ultimate

enemy—the conditions and institutions that breed the isms in society—seem undefeatable (Weiss & Ephross, 1986, p. 134).

Understand Intergroup Relations

It is critical for the social worker not only to have a general understanding of the history of minority groups and their interactions with each other, but also to have a clear sense of the intergroup factors that exist in the community in which one is working. This is true in general, but particularly so for those dealing with hate crimes. Isolated incidents can lead to widespread intergroup conflict, and lower levels of harassment can escalate into more violent acts (Iganski, 2001; Levin & Rabrenovic, 2001; McDevitt, et al., 2001; Wessler & Moss, 2001). The stereotypes minority groups have about each other, and the possibility of competition between victim groups, can interfere with the goals of the group. The social worker must understand the history and current state of black–Jewish relations, for example, or the feelings of other minority groups regarding the apparent success of Asian American immigrants. Current events also have an impact. Events like the terrorist acts of September 11, 2001, created thousands of victims and also had a ripple effect, resulting in crimes directed at those perceived as Muslim and Arab American and, hence, connected somehow to the terrorism. Other factors that exist in the group, often as silent contributors to tension, are race/ethnicity and social class, the interplay of which influences reactions such as resentment and lack of empathy and must be understood.

Focus on the Present and on the Individual

The issues surrounding intergroup relations and the historical factors affecting victims' feelings demand that the social worker acknowledge the impact of the past. Racial/ethnic group histories can become a major force to be contended with in victim groups, and can be used by group members to avoid dealing with the current victimization issues. Victims may want to talk about historical events that affected their families and are recalled by the current incidents. Without minimizing the impact of history, the social worker must help the individual and the group stay focused on the effects of recent events and how they affected the victim. It is important that group members be helped to see the costs and benefits of identifying themselves as victims, and the positive results that could result from their gaining a feeling of empowerment.

COMMON THEMES

Fear

The fear connected with hate crimes often affects not only the individual victim, but the family and community as well. An underestimated aspect of hate crimes is the ripple effect on the community. One case the author dealt with involved a black family who had a cross burned on their lawn. They had a young daughter and, after the incident, were very fearful that the unknown perpetrator would attack again. Overly cautious behavior began to govern their lives. They would no longer allow their daughter to walk to her friends' houses on the same block alone, for fear that she might be in danger. Worse, families in the neighborhood—well-meaning and supportive on the surface—would not let their children visit the home of the victim family, for fear that their children might be in danger if another, more serious, incident occurred while they were visiting.

Fear associated with having been targeted for attack can manifest itself in the group. Individuals may be highly suspicious of others and be reluctant to trust the social worker, or, if it was a racial incident, any members of another race, for example.

Anger

Many victims of hate crimes are angry. The anger is directed not just toward the perpetrator, whether known or unknown. Frequently, there is a great deal of anger toward the police. The rate of arrest for crime is low to begin with, and extremely low in cases of property crime where the perpetrator acted under cover of darkness, without witnesses. Victims often feel frustrated by the lack of resolution and afraid of the nameless, faceless enemy, about whom they can do nothing. That frustration is often directed at the police and other aspects of the criminal justice system. Anger and frustration may also be directed at the social worker and other members of the group.

Members must be given an opportunity to vent their feelings and have them validated by others in the group, lest they turn the anger toward themselves. A major goal of the group is to help the victims move beyond their anger so that they can deal with the aftermath of incidents constructively and have their daily routines return to normalcy.

Physical and Psychological Symptoms and Behaviors

Like other types of victimization, hate crimes can result in a wide range of physical and psychological symptoms. Examples of physical symptoms are changes in sleep patterns (difficulty falling asleep, waking frequently during the night), weight loss or gain, onset or exacerbation of back pain or other ailments, and development of nervous tics. Psychological symptoms may include fear of all strangers who look like the perpetrator (or imagined perpetrator), being particularly jumpy in response to unexpected noise, or acting suspicious of everyone, including friends and acquaintances if the act was committed by a stranger ("How do I know whom I can trust?"). Changes in behaviors include resuming or increasing smoking or drinking, changing routes walked or driven to work, changing jobs, moving, staying home, or becoming particularly protective of children. Some symptoms may manifest themselves in ways victims may be unaware of. Conversely, victims can blame their victimization for things that occur in their lives that may or may not be connected to the victimization. A critical role for the social worker in working with groups of victims of hate crimes is to facilitate discussions of symptoms and behaviors that are problematic for the group members, and help them separate the ones related to the victimization from the ones that need other types of attention.

Dealing with Legal Issues and the Criminal Justice System

It is important that the social worker be able to serve as an advocate for the victims, and make appropriate referrals to legal resources, while maintaining clear boundaries. Hate crimes may or may not be crimes by legal definition. Some victims, for example, may be suffering because of repeated verbal harassment where there is no legal recourse because the incidents did not qualify as crimes. In some cases, the victim may be working with the police to identify perpetrators; in others, there may be no leads to the perpetrators. In still other cases, the victims may be loath to report the victimization to police either because of fear (as in the case of illegal aliens who are victims) or because of past experience leading to the conviction that the police cannot do anything (Doerner & Lab, 1995). Issues and concerns frequently arise that are related to working with the criminal justice system. Victims worry, "Will I be in danger if I identify the perpetrator or testify at a trial? Will my family? Can the police protect me? What will happen during the trial? Who will pay for the damage to my property?"

As with all groups, members can benefit a great deal from each other's experiences. Social workers should be knowledgeable about the laws that apply both in the state and the local jurisdiction in which they work, and be able to answer basic questions. While it is appropriate for the social workers to be advocate, and identify appropriate resources and information within the criminal justice system that might be helpful to clients, they should not give advice on whether to press charges or take particular actions that the police or others might recommend; instead, they should facilitate group members' own decision-making processes.

Continued Interaction with an Offender/Perpetrator

When the incidents have occurred in the workplace or when the perpetrator is someone the victim comes into contact with regularly, such as a next-door neighbor, victims need guidance on how to handle unavoidable interactions and how to avoid confrontations. These incidents often take the form of persistent harassment, sometimes in subtle ways over a long period, and are designed to force the victim to quit a job or move. Victims of such acts need help in assessing the possible ramifications of taking formal actions to stop the perpetrators. Discussion of the pros and cons of such actions, and of how best to handle interactions with the perpetrators, often forms a significant part of group's content and consciousness.

RECOMMENDED WAYS OF WORKING

Agency Context

One type of agency particularly well suited for groups of victims of hate crimes is a local human rights (or human relations) agency that traditionally deals with cases of discrimination in housing, employment, and public accommodations. Some human-relations commissions have a community relations component that specializes in intergroup conflict in the community. School systems, also used to dealing with intergroup tension, can also provide the official context for such groups, particularly when juveniles are involved, either as victims or perpetrators. Mental health associations or interfaith organizations often have programs designed to promote positive intergroup relations, and can provide a setting for groups of hate crime victims.

Time Frame

Groups of hate crime victims need immediate crisis counseling and help in dealing with the immediate aftermath of the incident. It is important to provide assistance within a few days so that the immediate fear of danger can be addressed. Although there is no reason that groups of victims should not meet for a long period (12 months or more), and the group members could certainly provide support for each other through the often grueling aspects of arrest and trial, if they occur, the most critical time is the first few weeks following an incident. A short-term group (8 to 10 weeks) can frequently address the most critical issues.

Open versus Closed Groups

While either type can be used, there are several advantages to an open group when working with victims. One never knows when support for victims will be needed, and it is better for a victim to have immediate access to an ongoing group, and deal with problems of acceptance and entry, than to have to wait until a new group starts. Incidents, with or without physical harm, should be treated as crises initially. Also, victims at different stages can help each other, not only with emotional support, but also with practical advice (such as dealing with the police and other aspects of the justice system).

Co-Leadership Involving a Team with Different Races, Ethnicities, or Orientations

Victims of hate crimes are often more wary of other groups after an incident. While a co-leadership team can represent only a few categories, it is frequently advantageous for such a team to work with a victim group. Co-leaders can diffuse the fear and distrust that might exist toward a particular person who might look like the perpetrator. Also, co-leaders can model openness about racial or other sensitive issues. Because white social workers feel less successful when working with minority group members than do minority social workers (Davis & Gelsomino, 1994), and groups of hate crime victims may be composed entirely or primarily of members of minority groups, a co-leadership team may contribute to the success of the group.

WORKING WITH THE ENTIRE FAMILY WHEN THE VICTIM IS A CHILD

Sometimes the group consists simply of the family. An important issue when a child is attacked, either in the neighborhood or in school, is that of parents becoming overprotective. In some cases, the children want to return to normal routines, which may make parents uneasy. Parents sometimes want the child to change schools or stop walking to school, when the child is worried more about the stigma attached to those behaviors than to any danger. In other cases a child who has been harassed or intimidated is too ashamed to tell parents and is worried about their reaction, particularly if the parents have shared stories of their own experiences. The social worker can help family members separate the realities from the fears, and help the parents and child sort out what is relevant from the past and what needs to be addressed now.

DEALING WITH LANGUAGE BARRIERS

An inadequate command of the English language coupled with cultural differences may prevent some victims of hate crimes from reporting incidents or participating in programs of support. Studies by service providers have pointed to the language barrier as one factor that makes access to services difficult for some minority groups (Browne & Broderick, 1994). Provision of service may be complicated by relationships within a family where children are fluent in English and serve as interpreters for parents. In such cases, the children may be more comfortable dealing with the authorities and the justice system, while the parents are distrustful and anxious. There are several ways to address the language barriers. One is for materials providing helpful information and resources to be printed in as many languages as possible for a given community. Another is to limit some groups to a particular victim population and arrange for an interpreter to work with the social worker if a social worker who speaks the language of the victims is not available or trained to work with groups. In addition, social workers can train bilingual members of the victim community to serve as facilitators in self-help groups. Of course, attempts by the worker to gain even minimal command of other languages are helpful and appreciated by group members.

MEDIATION BETWEEN THE VICTIM AND THE OFFENDER

Ad hoc short-term groups can be an important tool of social workers dealing with hate crimes. Mediating the conflict between the victim and the offender can be the purpose of such a group, particularly when there is continued interaction between the victim and the offender through work, school, or neighborhood contact. Critical group work skills are required for effective mediation. Following is a case study of a successful use of mediation:

> A 16-year-old white youth assaulted a black youth the same age on a basketball court during an informal after-school game, calling him names such as "dirty nigger." The fight was stopped by a school official. Police were not called because there were no serious injuries and no weapon was involved. Because a racial epithet had been used, however, and officials learned that the white youth had been harassing the black youth for some time, they contacted the local human-relations commission and asked for assistance. There was fear that the tension between the youths would spill over to other students and become more violent. The community relations specialist, a white female social worker, had the school arrange a meeting with both youths at the school one evening. Each student was required to bring one parent. The social worker brought a black male police officer experienced in community relations work. No school official was permitted to participate. Over the course of two sessions of two hours each, the black student had a chance to talk about his feelings about being called racist names and being attacked. The white student expressed no remorse at first, only anger toward the black student, who had teased him for months because he was very small in stature. When the black student realized how painful the white youth's experience of being small was for him, and had been for years, he was able to forgive the assault. The mediation was followed up by periodic contacts for the rest of the school year; the intervention was successful in averting what could have been an explosive situation.

EVALUATION APPROACHES

There have been no rigorous evaluations of work with groups of hate crime victims. It is not difficult to evaluate their impact, however. The primary purpose of such groups is to help victims express and work through the psychological and psychophysiological symptoms they experience, and empower them to make critical decisions relevant to the criminal justice system if that is relevant, and about choices they need to make (such as whether to move, change jobs, etc.).

One way to evaluate the effectiveness of the group experience is to have members fill out questionnaires at the inception regarding the nature of the incident, symptoms they are experiencing, concerns they have, and decisions they would like to make. They could then complete another questionnaire at the termination of their time in the group to determine how much they felt they had accomplished.

With juveniles, both they and their parents could fill out relevant questionnaires. Follow-up could be done with them as well as with their teachers, if the victimization was affecting classroom performance and/or behavior.

CONCLUSION

Groups offer particular advantages for work with victims of hate crimes. Working with such groups calls for sophisticated knowledge both of the issues involved and of group work skills. Social workers must have a clear understanding of the manifestations of victimization based on race, religion, ethnicity, sexual orientation, or disability in order to determine whether crises in the group are related to group process, the stage of development, or to individuals' experiences of trauma.

Knowledge about hate crimes is also valuable for social workers called on to work with other types of groups. Interorganizational task groups or committees created to address the issue of violence in schools, workplaces, or communities would benefit from social workers' knowledge of hate crimes and the ways it affects both individuals and the groups to which they belong.

RESOURCES

American-Arab Anti-Discrimination
  Committee
4201 Connecticut Avenue, N.W.,
  Suite 300
Washington, DC 20008

(202) 244-2990
www.adc.org

Anti-Defamation League
823 United Nations Plaza

New York, NY 10017
(212) 885-7700
www.adl.org

National Asian Pacific American Legal
Consortium
1140 Connecticut Avenue, NW
Washington, DC 20036
(202) 296-2300
www.napalc.org

National Association for the
Advancement of Colored People
(NAACP)
4805 Mt. Hope Drive
Baltimore, MD 21215
(877) NAACP-98
www.naacp.org

National Coalition of Anti-Violence
Programs
c/o New York City Gay and Lesbian
Anti-Violence Project

240 West 35th Street, Suite 200
New York, NY 10001
(212) 714-1184
www.avp.org

Southern Poverty Law Center
400 Washington Avenue
Montgomery, AL 36104
(334) 956-8200
www.splcenter.org

The Prejudice Institute
2743 Maryland Avenue
Baltimore, MD 21218
(410) 243-6987
www.prejudiceinstitute.org

U.S. Department of Justice
Community Relations Service
600 E Street, NW, Suite 6000
Washington, DC 20530
(202) 305-2935
www.usdoj.gov/crs

REFERENCES

American-Arab Anti-Discrimination Committee (2001). *1998–2000 Report on hate crimes and discrimination against Arab Americans.* Washington, D.C.

Anti-Defamation League (2001). 2000 audit of anti-Semitic incidents. New York.

Barnes, A. J., & Ephross, P. H. (1994). The impact of hate violence on victims: Emotional and behavioral responses to attacks. *Social Work.* 39(3), 247–251.

Browne, C., & Broderick, A. (1994). Asian and Pacific Island elders: Issues for social work practice and education. *Social Work.* 39(3), 252–259.

Community Relations Service, U.S. Department of Justice. (2001). *CRS Bulletin— Hate crime: The violence of intolerance.* Washington, DC.

Davis, L. E., & Gelsomino, J. (1994). An assessment of practitioner cross-racial treatment experiences. *Social Work.* 39(1), 116–123.

Davis, R. C. (1987). Studying the effects of services for victims in crisis. *Crime and Delinquency.* 33(4), 520–531.

Doerner, W. G., & Lab S. P. (1995). *Victimology.* Cincinnati: Anderson Publishing Co.

Ehrlich, H. J. (1990). *Campus ethnoviolence and the policy options* (Report No. 4). Baltimore, MD: National Institute Against Prejudice and Violence.

Ehrlich, H. J. (1992). *Campus ethnoviolence: A research review* (Report No. 5). Baltimore, MD: National Institute Against Prejudice and Violence.

Ehrlich, H. J., Larcom, B. E. K., & Purvis, R. D. (1994). *The traumatic effects of ethnoviolence.* Baltimore, MD: The Prejudice Institute.

Ephross, P. H., Barnes, A. J., Ehrlich, H. J., Sandnes, K. R., & Weiss, J. C. (1986). *The ethnoviolence project pilot study.* Baltimore, MD: National Institute Against Prejudice and Violence.

Federal Bureau of Investigation, U.S. Department of Justice. (1991). *Training guide for hate crime data collection.* Washington, DC.

Federal Bureau of Investigation, U.S. Department of Justice. (2001). *Hate crime statistics, 2000.* Washington, DC.

Federal Bureau of Investigation, U.S. Department of Justice. (2002). *Hate crime statistics, 2001.* Washington, DC.

Herek, G. M., & Berrill, K. T., eds. (1992). *Hate crimes: Confronting violence against lesbians and gay men.* Newberry Park, CA: Sage Publications.

Iganski, P. (2001). Hate crimes hurt more. *American Behavioral Scientist.* 45(4), 626–638.

International Association of Chiefs of Police. (2000). *Responding to hate crimes: A police officer's guide to investigation and prevention.* Alexandria, VA.

Levin, J., & Rabrenovic, G. (2001). Hate crimes and ethnic conflict. *American Behavioral Scientist.* 45(4), 574–587.

McDevitt, J., Balboni, J., Garcia L., & Gu, J. (2001). Consequences for victims: A comparison of bias- and non–bias-motivated assaults. *American Behavioral Scientist.* 45(4), 697–713.

National Asian Pacific American Legal Consortium. (1999). *1998 audit of violence against Asian Pacific Americans: Sixth Annual Report.* Washington, DC.

National Coalition of Anti-Violence Programs (2002). *Anti-lesbian, gay, bisexual and transgender violence in 2001.* New York.

Pincus, F. L., & Ehrlich, H. J. (1994). *Race and ethnic conflict: Contending views on prejudice, discrimination and ethnoviolence.* Boulder, CO: Westview Press.

Strom, K. (2001). *Hate crimes reported in NIBRS, 1997–1999.* Washington, DC. Bureau of Justice Statistics, U.S. Department of Justice.

Weiss, J. C. (1990) Violence motivated by bigotry: "Ethnoviolence." In *Encyclopedia of Social Work, 18th ed., 1990 supplement* (pp. 307–319).

Weiss, J. C., Ehrlich, H. J., & Larcom, B. E. K. (1991–92). Ethnoviolence at work. *Journal of Intergroup Relations.* 18(4), pp. 21–33.

Weiss, J. C., & Ephross, P. H. (1986). Group work approaches to hate/violence incidents. *Social Work.* 31(2), pp. 132–136.

Wessler, S., & Moss, M. (2001). Hate crimes on campus: The problem and efforts to confront it. Washington, DC.: Bureau of Justice Assistance, U.S. Department of Justice.

Chapter 14

Group Work with Women Who Have Experienced Abuse

MARGOT BRETON AND ANNA NOSKO

This chapter discusses specific aspects of group practice with women who have experienced abuse in their relationships with male partners. This practice is based on a recognition of the women's strengths and of their competence to identify what they want and what they need, as well as the competence of practitioners to activate the mutual aid dynamics of groups. One mutual aid group is used to illustrate various points: it is sponsored by the Family Services Association of Toronto (which has sponsored such groups for over a decade) and will be referred to as the *FSA group.* It meets in a multiservice center that has a full health clinic, a full legal clinic, and a counseling unit; the coleaders of the group are in the counseling unit. Working out of a multiservice center helps the group leaders maintain a broad perspective on the context of the group and on the members' issues and needs. It also allows them to keep in mind that, when dealing with a social problem such as violence against women, interdisciplinary cooperation is essential to providing effective services, as research findings indicate (see, e.g., Horton & Johnson, 1993; Edelson & Eisikovits, 1996).

The female coleaders of the FSA group have worked for 10 years with women who have experienced abuse. They have learned that it is best if the decision on whether the group should remain open or closed is not predetermined before the group begins to meet but rather is made by the coleaders and the group members together. Although the FSA group has a limit of 12 members, the group may be closed when, after several weeks, there is a core of seven or eight members, and both the workers, and the members agree that the size is right for a productive group. If the membership drops off, then the members can be asked how they feel about allowing more women into the group. Their answer has always been that they want more women in their position to benefit from the group experience. Whether the group is short- or long-term is negotiated between the women and the agency—the number of women awaiting entry into the group being one of the most important determining factors for reopening the group.

Even though the cost of having two workers exceeds that of having only one, experience has shown that the increment in benefits of having a coleader is greater than the increment in costs because coleadership *(1)* provides the women with a model of a relationship based on equality, respect, and caring; *(2)* demonstrates to the women that two people can be different and yet can accept their differences, work together, accommodate, and adapt to each other; *(3)* offers the workers the opportunity to debrief after the sessions, which lessens the probability of burnout, always high in work with this population, as studies have shown (see, e.g., Horton & Johnson, 1993); and *(4)* becomes a support system for the workers (Chataway & Nosko, 1989).

The major reasons for working with the women *in a group* are that *(1)* groups offer a warm, accepting, and caring milieu in which the women can feel secure and appreciated—the tendency of professionals in responding to the plight of women who have experienced abuse is to consider them *deviant* for staying with the abusers (Saunders, 1993; Peled et al., 2000): other women "in the same boat" do not have that tendency; *(2)* groups provide the ideal structure for consciousness raising, that is, for dispelling a number of false perceptions (including that of being alone with the particular problem and/or that of being somehow responsible for the violence they experience), as well as for instilling new perceptions (such as that of connecting their personal situations with the structural/political conditions that affect them collectively) (see Profitt, 2000); and *(3)* groups are the most efficient venue for accessing information on how other women handle their situations and on what they have done or are doing to change these situations. Sharing such information is one of the aspects of mutual aid groups most highly valued by the women. As Killilea (1976, p. 72) noted: "what constitutes 'help' is often a new definition of the problem and specific information about practicalities learned through experience and shared with others because it 'works'."

REVIEW OF THE LITERATURE

Knowledge of wife assault is evolving, and perhaps because this is a relatively new field of study, many myths still abound (Saunders, 1993; Peled et al., 2000). Compounding the problem, the etiology of female battering is difficult to explore, for the privacy of the family, traditionally paramount in most societies, is respected both legally and socially. This hampers the work of researchers who wish to conduct empirical studies of spouse abuse (Horton & Johnson, 1993). Furthermore, some of the earlier work in the field is being challenged, if not discredited. For example:

> Clinical lore of a decade ago presented similar profiles of the offender and victim. They were both said to be form violent homes, to be isolated, to be deficient in communication skills, and to have low self-esteem. Recent reviews of empirical studies make it clear that it is the offender who differs most from the norm. Hotaling and Sugarman (1986) reviewed controlled studies of husband-to-wife violence. Out of 15 risk factors reviewed, the men had nine, including nonassertiveness, alcohol abuse, and a propensity to abuse their children. The women, on the other hand, had only one risk factor: a greater likelihood of having witnessed violence between their parents. (Saunders, 1993, pp. 209–210; see also Holtzworth-Munroe et al., 1997b).

The early literature on female spouse abuse presents issues from a psychological/victim perspective, viewing the women as pathological; for example, the concept of masochism assumes that women enjoy suffering (see Gelles, 1979, on this point). The literature then moves from pathology to social and structural issues; for example, social learning theories postulate that one learns to be a victim first through intergenerational transmission of violence and then through rigid sex role definitions (Eisikovits et al., 1998). This theory of learned helplessness assumes that women do not learn the skills necessary to leave abusive situations (see Mahoney, 1994). Social interaction theory views men as attempting to gain control over their spouses through various means, including the use of violence; this is deemed particularly relevant where there is a threat from female competence (Holtzworth-Munroe et al., 1997b). Resource theories connect abuse to economic issues, surmising that a woman's greater status and resources undermine the man's traditional role as breadwinner, with violence seen as a way to regain control (Holtzworth-Munroe et al., 1997b). Sociocultural theories view violence as endemic to society and therefore as normal (Straus, 1980). The structural/political approach (Holtzworth-Munroe et al., 1997a; Pahl, 1985), adopting a historic overview, examines how social institutions, over the millennia and in all societies, condone a husband's authority over his wife and support laws such as the "rule of thumb" in England, whereby a husband could hit his wife with a stick no wider than his thumb. (For an excellent and comprehensive review of the early literature, see Health and Welfare Canada, 1989.)

More recent studies focus on women who cope with abusive situations (Baker, 1997; Lampert, 1996; Nurius et al., 1992) or have successfully ended them. For example, Horton and Johnson (1993), and Baker (1997) document the tremendous investments women make to end the abuse in their lives. This new research recognizes women's strengths and resourcefulness. Building on this research, it is important to look for new solution. Until recently, one of the most common approaches to the problem of spouse abuse was to enjoin women to leave their spouses. Yet research indicates that the majority of women return to their partners (Holtzworth-Munroe et al., 1997a; Horton & Johnson, 1993; Worth & Jiggeman, 1996). This information challenges the field to find out from the women themselves what it is they want changed. It also indicates that it is time to develop practice principles that build on the strengths and resourcefulness of women who have experienced abuse (Edelson & Eisikovits, 1996; Goldberg Wood & Roche, 2001; Peled et al., 2000).

Before discussing these principles, we want to make a point about the use of theories in the kind of group practice we advocate. Practitioners should not focus on theories that purport to explain wife assault or women battering but should listen to the women themselves as *they* explain their reality. In other words, it is essential to stop looking at the women through the lenses of theories. A change of theoretical lenses does not suffice, for these lenses always distort. It is not a question of adopting a particular clinical or political stance or theoretical perspective, whether it represents the latest research or the latest fad, because the women and their experiences (recognized as diverse; see, e.g., Nurius et al., 1992) simply do not fit neatly within any one theory. The leaders of the FSA group, instead of teaching the women, as they used to do, about the theory of learned helplessness for example, now ask them if that theory applies to them. Some say yes and others no, and the leaders, willing to learn from the women, treat the answers as information that becomes a learning tool for everyone in the group. This in no way implies that practitioners do not have a very important leadership role to play in a group, nor that they can ignore the latest research and theories. It simply emphasizes that they need to subordinate the theories to what the women identify as their reality.

PRACTICE PRINCIPLES

The practice principles that should guide social workers beginning with a group of women who have experienced abuse are essentially the same as those principles guiding all practice that is focused on strengths and competence and is empowerment oriented (see, e.g., Breton, 1994, 2002; Brun & Rapp, 2001; Saleebey, 1997). Such practice demands that from the outset the workers *demonstrate respect for the women*. This first principle is operationalized through the following actions and attitudes: *(1) let each woman tell her story* and encourage her to use her new-found voice to "name [her] world" (Freire, 1993, p. 159); *(2) believe the women*, their stories, and what they understand as the facts. In other words, accept their representation of their situation as "legitimate knowledge" (Weick,

1997, p. 23), and do not assume that the women have low self-esteem (Saunders, 1993). A rather telling and funny dialogue took place in the group one day:

> *Woman:* I have no self-esteem.
> *Worker:* What does self-esteem mean to you?
> *Woman:* I don't know, really.
> *Worker:* Well then, maybe you have some.
> *Woman:* Well, yeah . . .

This interchange emphasizes the need for workers to have a sense of humor, which, as Malekoff (1994, p. 7) points out, refers to "the ability to see the humor in a situation or exchange and the capacity not to take oneself too seriously." This "in no way refers to making light of deadly subjects as an end in itself. What it implies is a flexibility of mind and spirit and the faith and trust that the group can and will, with a little assistance, move through the humor in a growth inducing way" (p. 8); *(3) facilitate the process of consciousness raising:* (a) affirm the actual and potential competence and strengths of the women, emphasizing "how they have survived thus far" (Goldstein, 1997, p. 32) and using their stories and their "own knowledge of their lives . . . as a natural resource" (Weick, 1997, p. 24); (b) confront the oppressor within (Freire, 1993) and challenge negative self-images and self-evaluations; (c) help the women to identify, as they become aware of the patterns in their stories, the common social, political, economic, and cultural contexts of their situations. This last guideline should not be construed as a license to proselytize and to impose the workers' belief system or values on the members. On the contrary, it is up to the women themselves to choose what to do with the awareness they develop of the interconnection of issues. The workers should inform them of various alternatives, including some form of social action, but the choice remains the women's.

Thus the second principle, which flows from the first, is that workers *base all interventions on member self-determination.* To make this operational requires that the workers *trust the members.* In a group, one major manifestation of the workers' trust is the emergence of a mutual aid system, for this happens when workers trust the members to help one another. From the very beginning of the group, as the women tell their stories, each woman realizes that hearing the stories of others makes her feel less alone and better about herself. When the workers acknowledge that the women are indeed the experts at helping each other, the process of mobilizing and supporting their competence and strengths can begin.

Self-determination also requires that workers *identify what the women want.* As Rapp (1997, p. 48) states unequivocally: "if client self-determination is to be taken seriously, the client's desires must be given absolute primacy." This may cause problems for workers when a group member chooses to stay with an abusive partner, but it is *not* the workers' prerogative to dictate what another person should want. Challenging, discussing, confronting—those behaviors are in the workers' rightful domain; pretending to know what is best for other people is not. It is important to signal here that the notion of contracting, as a formal mechanism to ensure self-determination and to establish the specific conditions under which the group will operate, may not always be relevant to work with a group of women who have experienced abuse; it may have to be abandoned if the women interpret it as a constraint that locks them into a situation and once again makes them feel controlled. What is essential is to be accountable to the women; how this accountability plays itself out will vary, depending on a number of factors, including the cultural background of the women and their individual motivations, including their distrust of would-be helpers, their fear of failure, and their aversion to risk taking (Breton, 1985).

To be accountable and to base interventions on self-determination means that workers are guided by a third principle, that of *individualization.* Pray (1991) makes a strong case that this principle is given lip service more than genuinely honored in traditional problem-focused and pathology-centered social work approaches. A renewed and vigorous interpretation of the principle, one that is congruent with a focus on strengths, competence, and empowerment, demands that workers *(1) eschew preconceived plans and solutions,* generic goals, and all other forms of "homogenization of clients" (Rapp, 1997, pp. 51–52)—*and of groups,* we hasten to add. This suggests a flexible approach to group structure. As indicated above, choosing an open or closed format, for example, will depend on the needs of the group at various points in its evolution. Individualization also suggests that the process of termination be left to the women to determine and be individually tailored; each member's termination should occur when she has achieved the goals she has set for herself and does not believe the group can be of further help.

Individualization further requires that workers *(2) reject labels,* such as "abused women" and "abused women's group"; this implies seeing the women as whole persons, not just as victims. The idea is to reject the connotation of passivity that pervades the label of "victim" without rejecting the fact of victimization/oppression. The intention is to always put the accent on the women as active subjects, not as passive objects. Thus the reference to the members of the FSA group as "women who have experienced abuse" provides them an opportunity to take back some control over their lives by identifying the abuse as something *they* experienced, and not primarily as something *others* perpetrated against them. Workers who forget that women who have been victimized "above all are whole human beings with the same potential and aspirations as anyone else . . . further victimize them" (Breton, 1990, p. 26; see also Saleebey, 2001).

Seeing the women as whole persons demands that workers *(3) promote a group context and encourage group programs in which the women can demonstrate and share their specific strengths,* showcase their talents, and acknowledge their abilities, including their ability to empathize, nurture, and comfort each other, and practice and develop their skills. The group should enable the women to translate into action their changing ways of thinking and feeling about themselves (see Pollio, 2000).

However, like all human beings, the women need ongoing support networks, not only to sustain their present strengths and to maintain changes already achieved, but also to develop potential strengths and continue to make changes, a condition of survival and growth in this world. Although women who have experienced abuse usually need the support of a professionally led mutual aid group for a relatively long period of time, their relationship with the group and the workers eventually ends. The workers, knowing that the group's support is time limited, have the responsibility to ensure postgroup support that will endure over time.

Therefore, the last principle is that workers *make maximum use of natural supports in the community.* This entails that workers *(1) perceive the community as a resource* (Sullivan, 1997), identifying natural helpers and natural resources such as recreation centers, libraries, and Ys, informing women about these people and resources, and connecting them to each other if the women so wish. The principle also demands that workers *(2) maximize the potential support in the women's environment,* modifying existing structures or creating new ones to meet the members' needs (Wood & Middleman, 1989). Where personal natural support networks are nonexistent, workers encourage group members to see themselves as the first links in a new natural support system, one that exists outside of the group and will continue to exist once they leave the group (Breton, 1985). Finally, workers will be required to *(3) create partnerships in the community* (Breton, 1994, and forthcoming). By acknowledging community strengths, and by accepting collaboration as partners with natural helpers and with normal community services and institutions, workers facilitate the women's perception of being not only members of a group but also members of a community, and thus facilitate their integration into that community.

COMMON THEMES AND HOW TO DEAL WITH THEM

Workers need to be prepared (tuned in) to pick up on themes that regularly come up in groups of women who have experienced abuse. An important one to emphasize from the very beginning is that of *power.* For example, assuming that the members cope with their situations, and expecting that they will share how they cope, harnesses the positive interactional energy of the group. The workers presume that each woman has some power and that together the women have greater power. Starting from a proactive position (namely, a position that postulates that the women already have strengths) lays a foundation for them to acknowledge the choices they make and to move toward different choices. This proactive stance is illustrated when workers ask "What are you doing to keep yourself safe?" instead of "Are you keeping yourself safe?"

Assuming that the women have *choices* creates an atmosphere of respect and encourages the women to see themselves as capable and open to yet other choices:

> *Barbara:* You know, I really don't want to leave my husband because I love him. I've invested too much for too many years to go—
>
> *Tina:* Me too. For thirty years I looked after him and raised my children so they would have a mother and father, but my job is done and I don't need to take it anymore.
>
> *Karen:* I have left many men, and I still haven't learned how to find a good man; do they exist?
>
> *Heddy:* If they abuse you, get rid of them, find someone else.

Many significant themes emerge from each interchange among the members. The workers keep a list of these individual "strands" and re-thread them through the discussions. The women themselves then weave these strands into a coherent and resilient tapestry in which they are high-lighted and from which radiates the support they get from and give each other.

One of these other significant themes is *safety*. It needs to be kept in the foreground of the group. The workers approach it from the perspective that each woman is responsible for her safety and that of her children, which again presumes that each woman is capable and competent. The concern for their children often motivates the women to do something about the violence they experience:

> *Jan:* I won't let my child suffer like I did.
>
> *Heddy:* It's not fair to the children. They shouldn't have to suffer from seeing all this abuse. I worry about how it is affecting them.

This concern is well founded; a Canadian national survey indicates that children witnessed violence against their mothers in almost 40% of marriages with violence (Rodgers, 1994; see also Holtzworth-Munroe et al., 1997c). The theme of safety thus expands into the theme of *love for their children,* and the women move from considering their own experiences to reflecting on the different experiences they want their children to have. Workers who trust that it is the members who know best what will help them to reach their goals support the transformations or evolutions of themes.

The theme of safety also involves a consideration of *violence* per se and an examination of its possible sources. This often leads to exploring the *resources available* to do something about violence. These resources include knowledge of the legal system and of various social agencies, the role of the police and of one's physician, and so on. At this point, the women have an opportunity to share their experiences about resources and to pursue the themes of their *right to protection under the law* and their *right to access community resources,* the themes of the *adequacy of*

services offered and of the *cultural and societal biases* influencing the reactions of police and physicians, as well as other related themes. As research indicates (Horton & Johnson, 1993, p. 490), "Clinicians' advocacy
and educational roles are important factors in stopping the cycle of
abuse."

It can be argued that *mutual aid* with its "strength in us" dynamic,
constitutes the leitmotif or dominant theme that recurs throughout the
duration of the group. For example, Miller (1991, p. 199) believes that
one of the strengths women possess is being relational, that is, being
adept at "using one's power to help another . . . increasing the other's
resources, capabilities, effectiveness and ability to act." The mutual aid
system of the group encourages and buttresses this relational strength or
competence. As members explore themes important to them, they experience positive human relations:

> *Susan:* I feel so comfortable talking about how I feel. If I'm disappointed
> with myself, I don't fear being judged or put down here, like I do by
> my husband.

The sense of acceptance and of respect is also achieved through another
mutual aid dynamic; the dialectical process that recognizes diversity and
differences along with the common ground:

> *Tina:* You young women should save yourselves, don't wait till you are old
> like me.
> *Susan:* Tina, you give me hope that it is never too late to change.
> *Worker:* Each one of you has much to share; you can help each other in dif-
> ferent ways.

Themes provide a "mirror" in which each woman sees part of herself
or her issue (Alonso & Rutan, 1988). For example, as Mary tells Jane to
stand up for herself (the theme of *assertiveness*), she also sees this advice
reflected back to her. In this way, many topics that are perceived as threatening or painful to broach are made safe because they are accessed indirectly. When the theme of abuse is activated and women *choose* to talk
about their experience, or even when only one woman, at a particular
point, chooses to talk, all the women become part of the disclosure; each
woman need not directly disclose all the specific details of her situation because it is captured in the stories of others—hence the group mirror.

Any time the group discusses one of the themes, new knowledge is
gained. The group workers' role is to monitor these themes, label them,
reintroduce them when appropriate, add information that may be helpful, expand, and connect them. For example, when the women talk about
how they have been trying hard to get their husbands to change, the
workers raise the point that they are presently focusing on changing the
other, yet earlier they had agreed that one can only change oneself. This
comment connects the discussion to earlier themes (those of *responsibil-*

ity and *change*) and challenges the women to look in a direction in *which they have more control and choice.*

EVALUATION APPROACHES

Evaluating the progress made by the abused women in the group would enhance the process through which they acquire a voice, as suggested by all empowerment research (Bartle et al., 2002). This demands that the women participate in planning the evaluation, that is, in deciding what will be evaluated and how. Indeed, if the purpose of research is to provide useful information, "not just for professionals, but for their clients" (Holmes, 1997, p. 159), then the participation of the women as partners in the evaluation is imperative. In a collaborative approach to the evaluation process, the members become research participants whose stake in the research is fully recognized (see, e.g., Lee, 2001).

As early as possible, therefore, and with the encouragement and help of the workers, the members should consider how the evaluation could "authenticate the resources and transformation capacities" that they have as individuals and as a group (Saleebey, 1997, p. 178) and how it could help them "to redefine their experience of the world, [and] to act within it from a position of greater human potential and power" (Holmes, 1997, p. 164). Empowerment research challenges the traditional assumption that what is important in the evaluation process is how the *professional* judges if there is change. In their study of women who have ended abuse, Horton and Johnson (1993, p. 491) recognize the inherent limitations of self-reporting but conclude that "Nevertheless, the women . . . were 'experts' on wife abuse. Researchers' tasks are to summarize the data victims provide, explore their strategies for ending abuse, and report what works and does not work" (see also Edelson & Eisikovits, 1996).

In the FSA group, the workers no longer use formal evaluation measures to assess the women's progress. The women do this themselves in an ongoing way, every time they meet and throughout their meetings. For example, as she arrived one day, Lisa told the workers that her ex-boyfriend had been phoning her frequently during the past week, and she didn't know if she should let him come back. Her dilemma was brought up in the group, and as she discussed with other women what she should do, she evaluated the changes she had made thus far. She then admitted that to maintain the progress she had made, she would have to be very careful about not being enticed back into the relationship by her expartner's sweet words. To help her chart her progress, she employed an unorthodox but effective measure of progress used repeatedly in the group: "the garbage collection day" metaphor. The women had decided that each week, in the group, they have the opportunity to throw out old, use-less ideas and behaviors to make room for new ones. As they help each other to discard their "garbage," they are conscious of making choices, making progress, and moving forward. This is, for them, a meaningful and valuable evaluation process. The more garbage they throw out, the more progress they make.

Evaluation of progress is essential in groups of women who have ex-perienced abuse, but it is more significant *for the women* and more sup-portive of the changes *they* want when it is incorporated in the group's life and becomes a natural feature of the work that goes on in the group. An ongoing parallel process of evaluation must take place between the work-ers, not only for them to fully understand what is happening in the group, but so that the group never suffers from unresolved issues arising within the coleaders subgroup (Nosko & Wallace, 1992).

CONCLUSION

The group practice presented in this chapter is driven not by the pre-ferred ideologies and theories of professionals, but rather by what the group members say they need and want. The principles discussed above should help practitioners who work with women who have experienced abuse to listen to what the women say and pay heed to their voices. This, as pointed out earlier, does not mean that workers cannot challenge the women, or cannot plan or prepare for the group, but simply that they should not pre-determine what the work of the group will be or what changes the women will seek in the way they conduct their lives and/or in the way social systems limit their lives. When practitioners believe in, and take into account, the strengths that individuals bring to groups and fur-ther develop in and through groups, the possibilities for all kinds of changes are as vast as the human spirit that characterizes women who have experienced abuse and are willing to work together in a group to overcome these experiences.

RESOURCES

Sources of information for social workers who wish to begin a group of women who have experienced abuse exist at the national, provincial/state, regional, and local levels. A good place to start is the local Family Services Association, where a list of other relevant resources may be available. Municipal libraries are also a good source of information, though in some rural areas, women's shelters may be the best resource.

Canada
National Clearinghouse on Family
  Violence
Family Violence Prevention Division
Health and Welfare Canada
Government of Canada
Ottawa, Ontario, K1A 1B5
(613) 957-2938 or 800-267-1291
Telephone Devices for the Deaf (613)
  952-6396 or 800-561-5643

www.hc-sc.gc.ca/hppb/family
  violence/index.html

United States
National Coalition Against Domestic
  Violence and National Domestic
  Hotline
(800) 799-7233
www.ncadv.org

REFERENCES

Alonso, A., & Rutan, S. (1988). The experience of shame and restoration of self-respect in group therapy. *International Journal of Group Psychotherapy.* 38(1), 3–14.

Baker, P. L. (1997). And I went back—Battered women's negotiations of choice. *Journal of Contemporary Ethnography.* 26, 55–74.

Bartle, E. E., Couchonnal, G., Canda, E. R., & Staker, M. D. (2002). Empowerment as a dynamically developing concept for practice: Lessons learned from organizational ethnography. *Social Work.* 47(1), 32–43.

Breton, M. (1985). Reaching and engaging people: Issues and practice principles. *Social Work with Groups.* 8(3), 7–21.

Breton, M. (1990). Learning from social group work traditions. *Social Work with Groups.* 13(3), 21–34.

Breton, M. (1994). Relating competence-promotion and empowerment. *Journal of Progressive Human Services.* 5(1), 27–44.

Breton, M. (2002). Empowerment practice in Canada and the United States: Restoring policy issues at the center of social work. *Social Policy Journal.* 1(1), 19–34.

Chataway, C., and Nosko, A. (1989). Group work with abused women. Paper presented at the 11th Annual Symposium of the Association for the Advancement of Social Work with Groups. Montreal, October.

Edelson, J. L., & Eisikovits, Z. C. (eds.) (1996). *Future intervention with battered women and their families.* Thousand Oaks, CA: Sage Publications.

Eisikovits, Z., Buchbinder, E., & Mor, M. (1998). What it was won't be anymore: Reaching the turning point in coping with intimate violence. *Affilia: Journal of Women and Social Work.* 13, 411–434.

Freire, P. (1993). *Pedagogy of the oppressed* (20th anniversary ed.). New York: Continuum.

Gelles, R. J. (1979). *Family violence.* Beverly Hills, CA: Sage Publications.

Goldstein, H. (1997). Victors or victims: Contrasting views of clients in social work practice. In D. Saleebey (ed.), *The strengths perspective in social work practice* (pp. 27–38). New York: Longman.

Health and Welfare Canada (1989). *Family violence: A review of theoretical and clinical literature.* Catalogue No.: H21-103/1989E.

Holmes, G. E. (1997). Social work research and the empowerment paradigm. In D. Saleebey (ed.) *The strengths perspective in social work practice* (pp. 158–168). New York: Longman.

Holtzworth-Munroe, A., Bates, L., Smutzler, N., & Sandin, E. (1997a). A brief review of research on husband violence: Part 1. Maritally violent versus nonviolent men. *Aggression and Violent Behavior.* 3, 65–99.

Holtzworth-Munroe, A., Smutzler, N., & Bates, L. (1997b). A brief review of research on husband violence: Part 3. Sociodemographic factors, relationship factors, and differing consequences of husband and wife violence. *Aggression and Violent Behavior.* 3, 285–307.

Holtzworth-Munroe, A., Smutzler, N., & Sandin, E. (1997c). A brief review of research on husband violence: Part 2. Psychological effects of husband violence on battered women and their children. *Aggression and Violent Behavior.* 3, 179–213.

Horton, A. L., & Johnson, B. L. (1993). Profile and strategies of women who have ended abuse. *Families in Society: The Journal of Contemporary Human Services.* 74, 481–492.

Killilea, M. (1976). Mutual help organizations: Interpretations in the literature. In G. Caplan and M. Killilea (eds.) *Support systems and mutual help: Multidisciplinary explorations.* New York: Grune and Stratton.

Lampert, L. B. (1996). Women's strategies for survival: Developing agency in abusive relationships. *Journal of Family Violence.* 11, 268–289.

Lee, J. A. B. (2001). *The empowerment approach to social work: Building the beloved community.* New York: Columbia University Press.

Mahoney, M. R. (1994). Victimization or oppression: Women's lives, violence and agency. In M. A. Fineman & B. Mykitiuk (eds.), *The public nature of private violence* (pp. 59–92). New York: Routledge.

Malekoff, A. (1994). A guideline for group work with adolescents. *Social Work with Groups.* 17(1/2), 5–19.

Miller, J. B. (1991). The development of women's sense of self. In J. V. Jordan, A. C. Kaplan, J. Baker Miller, J. P. Stiver, & J. L. Surfey (eds.), *Women's growth in connection: Writings from the Stone Center* (pp. 11–26). New York: Guilford Press.

Nosko, A., & Wallace, R. (1992). Female and male coleadership. Paper presented at the 14th Annual Symposium of the Association for the Advancement of Social Work with Groups. Atlanta.

Nurius, P. S., Furrey, J, & Berliner, L. (1992). Coping capacity among women with abusive partners. *Violence and Victims.* 7(3), 229–243.

Pahl, J. (ed.) (1985). *Private violence and public policy.* London: Routledge & Kegan Paul.

Pollio, D. E. (2000). Reconstructing feminist group work. *Social Work with Groups.* 23(2), 3–18.

Pray, J. E. (1991). Respecting the uniqueness of the individual: Social work practice within a reflexive model. *Social Work.* 36, 80–85.

Profitt, N. J. (2000). Survivors of woman abuse: Compassionate fires inspire collective action for social change. *Journal of Progressive Human Services.* 11(2), 77–102.

Rapp, C. A. (1997). The strengths perspective of case management with persons suffering from severe mental illness. In D. Saleebey (ed.), *The strengths perspective in social work practice.* New York: Longman.

Rodgers, K. (1994). Wife assault: The findings of a national survey. *Juristat: Service Bulletin.* 14(9). Ottawa: Statistics Canada. Catalogue 85-002 ISSN 0715-271X.

Saleebey, D. (ed.) (1997). *The strengths perspective in social work practice.* New York: Longman.

Saleebey, D. (2001). The diagnostic strengths manual. *Social Work.* 46(2), 183–187.

Saunders, D. G. (1993). Woman battering. In R. T. Ammerman & M. Hersen (eds.), *Assessment of family violence. A clinical and legal sourcebook* (pp. 208–234). New York: Wiley.

Sullivan, W. P. (1997). Reconsidering the environment as a helping resource. In D. Saleebey (ed.) *The strengths perspective in social work practice.* New York: Longman.

Weick, A. (1997). Building a strengths perspective for social work. In D. Saleebey (ed.), *The strengths perspective in social work practice.* New York: Longman.

Wood, G., & Middleman, R. (1989). *The structural approach to direct practice in social work.* New York: Columbia University Press.

Wood, G. G., & Roche, S. E. (2001). Representing selves, reconstructing lives: Feminist group work with women survivors of male violence. *Social Work with Groups.* 23(4), 5–23.

Chapter 15

Group Treatment of Intimate Partner Abusers

STEVEN STOSNY

Intimate partner abusers, who every year injure at least 1 million women (Bureau of Justice Statistics, 1995), constitute one of the most difficult populations served by social workers in terms of cooperative participation in treatment (Bennett & Williams, 2001; Faulkner et al., 1991; Stosny, 1994). Although predominantly court ordered into counseling, their attendance is inconsistent, with 40%–60% dropping out long before completion. Even more disheartening, over one-half of the completers of the most often used group treatment model are likely to reabuse within a year (Harrell, 1991; Stosny, 1995). The factors contributing to this formidable resistance have much to do with why intimate partner offend in the first place. Primary among these are deficits in affect regulation that produce an inability to process guilt, shame, and abandonment anxiety. In treatment sessions abusers tend to convert these vulnerable feelings into anger, just as they do at home. The difference lies in the behavioral enactment of the anger. In the group room it looks like resentful (and superficial) compliance or numb, seemingly indifferent, withdrawal. But at home it generates patterns of abusive control of loved ones, enforced by periodic episodes of violence (Dutton, 1998).

EMPIRICAL AND CLINICAL FINDINGS

The link between violence in childhood and violence against one's intimate partner in adulthood has been well established in the empirical literature (Dutton, 1998; Stith & Farley, 1993). This connection has been most often explained from a perspective of social learning theory; that is, behaviors reinforcing violence as an acceptable means of prevailing in a dispute are modeled at vital learning stages in the early lives of abusers. Unfortunately, social learning theory offers little help to clinicians treating spouse abusers, who will be hard put to find one who does not abhor and condemn the violence of his childhood, much less find it acceptable. From a clinical standpoint, violence in childhood is less significant for what it teaches the male child about interpersonal conflict resolution than for what it prevents him from learning about himself, that is, that he is valuable, acceptable, powerful, and lovable. In other words, violence in childhood inhibits development of a tolerable sense of self.

Attributions and Locus of Control

Abusive men tend to see themselves as powerless victims forced into abusive behavior. Afflicted with an external locus of control and a tendency to make external causal attributions, they tirelessly blame their behavior on family members, on the broad social context, or on the specific situations in which the abuse occurred (Bograd, 1988; Dutton, 1986; Eisikovits, et al., 1991; Flournoy & Wilson, 1991; Rouse, 1984; Sapiente, 1988). Obviously, this has grave consequences for the acceptance of personal responsibility for abusive behavior and for motivation to change (or even participate) in treatment.

Sense of Self and Self-Esteem

Virtually every published study of abusers notes their low self-esteem. Many have related intimate partner abuse to a poor sense of self (Dutton, 1998; Neidig et al., 1986; Rosen, 1991; Stosny, 1995), some concluding that abusers often feel inadequate and dissatisfied with themselves (Dutton, 1998). One group of deficits seems virtually universal, not only in male heterosexual abusers but in gay and lesbian partner abusers as well. These can be understood as *attachment deficits* (Dutton, 1998; Hanson et al., 1997).

The term *attachment deficits* refers to the inability to form and maintain viable attachment bonds. It includes doubts about one's capacity to love and be loved, to trust and be trusted, to feel compassion and be worthy of compassion, to maintain interest in a significant other as an autonomous person, and to hold the interest of another autonomous person. The evidence seems overwhelming that intimate partner abusers, regardless of sexual orientation, exhibit great difficulties in intimacy, trust, mutuality, compassion, jealousy, fear of abandonment, and fear of engulfment; that is, fear that the self will diminish or disintegrate in sustained proximity to another (Barnett & Hamberger, 1992; Crawford & Gartner, 1992; Dutton, 1998; Murphy et al., 1992; Stosny, 1995).

Doubts about one's status as an attachment figure tend to flood the self with the disorganizing experience of guilt, shame, and fear of abandonment. With little internal regulatory skill (the result of a diminished sense of self and an external locus of control), abusers blame these feelings on their spouses, which allows them temporary pain relief and empowerment through anger arousal (Dutton, 1998; Stosny, 1995). Of course, the more they blame their internal experience on their spouses, the more powerless over their own feelings they become. This pervasive sense of powerlessness exacerbates the external locus of control and explains the high level of anger widely observed in intimate partner abusers (Barnett & Hamberger, 1992; Dutton, 1998; Stosny, 1995).

THE ETHICS OF TREATING COURT-ORDERED CLIENTS

Empowerment or Brainwashing?

The treatment of court-ordered clients raises important ethical considerations for clinicians. The urgent need to protect victims of abuse creates the risk of misusing power and authority to impose the majority's familial values on a minority. Abusers are ordered into treatment to help keep them from breaking the law, not to become spouses who conform to the values and preferences of therapists or their agencies, no matter how humanitarian and nobly egalitarian these may seem. For this compelling ethical reason, treatment should avoid the temptation to espouse particular familial values and should strive instead to nurture moral agency, that is, to help clients build the self-regulatory skills necessary to make moral judgments and act on them with integrity. Fortunately, the nurturance of moral agency is not only an ethical pursuit for clinicians, it has tremendous therapeutic value for clients. Moral agency is the product of a powerful—that is, compassionate—sense of self. The topic of morality becomes therapeutic when used overtly in treatment to enhance rather than impugn the self (Gilbert, 1994; Stosny, 1995). In simple behavioral terms, this constitutes an operant conditioning model, emphasizing that as a function of the internal reward of the survival-based need to form attachment and social bonds (Bowlby, 1969, 1973, 1980), people like themselves more when they experience compassion than when they don't; genuine self-esteem depends on our capacity for compassionate morality, at least toward loved ones. In this context, clients experience moral reasoning as therapeutically empowering rather than as a source of guilt and shame. They realize the hope of transcending a powerless abusive past by growing into the genuinely powerful condition of moral agency.

PRACTICE PRINCIPLES AND SPECIAL CONSIDERATIONS IN TREATING INTIMATE PARTNER ABUSERS

There is widespread agreement that structured groups constitute the treatment of choice for intimate partner abusers (e.g., Edleson & Tolman, 1992; Pence & Paymar, 1993). *Structured* simply means that the content and time agenda of the group are developed in advance rather than emerging from the dynamics of the group itself. Most clinicians agree that lack of structure, particularly in the beginning phases of the group, risks allowing the anger and deviant morality of many group members to establish group norms. The male bonding noted by several authors (Edleson & Tolman, 1992; Harrell, 1991; Stosny, 1995) tends to form around the lowest common denominator, which, in the case of spouse abuser groups in the beginning phases of treatment, is perceived victimization by wives (and women in general) and by a court system unfairly biased in favor of women. For that reason, it may be advisable to forbid early discussion of the court system or of individual court cases. I find it more efficient, and safer for victims, to remove the need for such distorted thinking through therapeutic enhancement of the self than to spend time and effort confronting these highly defended but relatively superficial outposts of the client's meaning system.

Virtually every form of group treatment has currency in the clinical literature. Closed groups offer stability to clients who have suffered lifelong difficulties in forming and terminating bonds, which would only be exacerbated by members constantly joining and leaving the groups. Edelson and Syers (1990, 1991) and Gondolf (1999) found no difference in outcome between short- and long-term groups but did find that clients were more likely to complete the former. Coleaders of mixed gender model a healthy balance of power and authority between the sexes. It is especially useful to model disagreement-resolution techniques between the coleaders, at least one of whom should, if possible, match the social class or ethnicity of the group.

The safety of clients and victims is a crucial consideration for this vulnerable population, with the following points of paramount importance: *(1)* give clients and their spouses a written emergency plan with hot line numbers; *(2)* avoid interventions that stimulate guilt, shame, and abandonment anxiety before affect-regulation techniques are learned (this may take discipline on the worker's part, but victims will pay for any unregulated guilt, shame, and abandonment anxiety that unskilled clients take home from the sessions); *(3)* don't let any client go home upset without making every attempt to help him resolve his distress; call him at home to be sure he stayed calm during the drive; *(4)* secure a contract in which clients agree to avoid discussing hot issues until they have learned emotional regulation techniques; *(5)* follow up with dropouts; *(6)* administer the Conflict Tactics Scale (see the Evaluation section of this chapter) to spouses quarterly for the first year following treatment.

Inevitably, countertransference lurks in the shadows when treating abusive populations. If you cannot "hate the sin and love the sinner," this is not the area of social work in which you can be of help. These men have difficulty distinguishing behaviors from the self, which makes the possibility of behavioral change seem obscure to them. They need therapists to help them make this crucial distinction. Treatment that reinforces their self-concept as "bad boys" will make it more likely that they will do bad things. Rather, workers should try to come up with at least one characteristic to admire in each client at the beginning of treatment. That one element of admiration will likely be at the heart of the client's capacity to change abusive behavior. Clients need us to ally with that part of their consciousness that does not want to abuse loved ones.

While it is important that clients remain ever cognizant of external motivations to desist from abuse (legal sanctions and group disapproval), they need ultimately to develop the internal motivation of prosocial behavior: the feeling of well-being stimulated by the experience of compassion. To fully understand how this works, ask yourself why you do not beat up people you love. Is it because you fear going to jail or worry about what others might think of you? Your desisting from violence probably runs much deeper. At bottom, you know that you will not like, value, and respect yourself if you injure people you love, and that you will like, value, and respect yourself if you experience compassion for them. This self-destructive element of attachment violence and contrasting self-building nature of compassion for loved ones must be internalized by clients if they are to remain abuse free.

MIXING VICTIMS WITH PERPETRATORS IN GROUP

Whether to include spouses in abuser groups is an issue of controversy in the clinical literature. Some argue that it places the woman in jeopardy should she say something in group to embarrass her abuser (Edleson & Tolman, 1992). This is certainly true in couples counseling and in unstructured couples group treatment (Stosny, 1995). But this particular risk disappears in highly structured groups in which clients' verbal participation is minimal before emotional regulation techniques are learned. More important, when the victim is part of the group, the entire membership is invested in her well-being, which serves as a potent deterrent to abuse. Best of all, an incomparable mechanism of change occurs frequently in mixed groups when an abuser finds himself experiencing compassion for another man's wife who bears, he realizes, the same scars from subtle and overt abuse as he has caused his own spouse.

Some feminist writers loathe the inclusion of women in abuser treatment groups because it seems to blame the victim (e.g., Bograd, 1984). This view must be taken seriously. Whether in mixed or segregated groups, abusers and victims alike must be reminded often that *nothing* a partner does justifies abuse; victims can do nothing to cause their abuse or be worthy of blame for it. Even abusive behavior in retaliation for perceived abuse is unjustified and only does greater damage to the attachment bond. Receiving this empathic message on the level of a group theme, with spouses present, has more symbolic and literal power than hearing it in segregated abuser and offender groups.

Blaming the victim constitutes a serious argument against ordering victims into treatment. But as long as their participation is completely voluntary, it becomes a cruel kind of revictimization to deny them the same treatment as their abusers. Before we opened the Compassion Workshop to the spouses who wanted it, I had countless complaints about the unfairness of excluding victims from what seemed to them to be obviously beneficial to their husbands. As one woman expressed it, "I get beat up and he gets all this great stuff!" Actually, on the deepest level, the treatment needs of perpetrators and victims are quite similar, insofar as both need help in the area of toxic blame. The abuser blames his internal state on the victim, rendering himself powerless over his own experience, while the victim internalizes blame for the internal state of the abuser, rendering herself powerless to heal her own wounds. Treating them jointly has the advantage of helping them internalize responsibility for their own experience and for no one else's. The therapist helps clients establish boundaries by pointing out the liberating power that responsibility for one's own thoughts, feelings, and behavior gives to each individual, while blame creates nothing but a painful void of powerlessness waiting to be filled with anger and self-contempt.

KEY ISSUES AND COMMON THEMES

The primary theme of abuser groups must be the safety of everyone in the family, as described above. Crucial to the issue of safety is client skill in affect regulation. Spouse abusers require training in affect regulation before they are given any opportunity to ventilate anger in group. (Ventilation of anger has been shown in numerous studies to increase anger; see, e.g., Bushman et al., 1999; Lewis & Bucher, 1992.) Once safety issues are thoroughly discussed and affect regulation techniques mastered (after four weeks or so of practice), *power* emerges as the most common group theme. Many abusers have been socialized to confuse destructiveness with power, resulting in endless power struggles created by their attempts to exert power over others. Discussion must bring out the fact that internal power (over one's own thoughts, values, feelings, and behavior) entails the ability to resist destructive impulses; *genuine power is constructive.* Now interpersonal power can be reframed as empowerment, that is, helping loved ones to find mutually beneficial solutions rather than coercing them to accept one's own solutions. This no-lose notion of empowerment departs drastically from the no-win nature of power struggles, in which the seeming winner of the dispute inevitably pays with future displays of resentment and hostility from the loser.

Other key themes for group discussion include personal responsibility, masculinity, intimacy, communication skills, resentment, forgiveness, and relapse prevention. Responsibility for one's behavior must be framed as a form of personal power; in contrast, blame renders one completely powerless (if my bad feelings are my wife's fault, I'm utterly powerless over them). Many abusers are insecure about aspects of their masculinity. Anger and anxiety regulation are keys to the success of expanding this theme to include related issues of intimacy and communication skills. When feeling more in control of emotions, clients tend to be far less rigid about their masculinity. Resentment is another theme that requires special attention. Fear of their own anger forces many abusers to drag long chains of resentment of loved ones into treatment. A good way to approach the theme is through its opposite: forgiveness. Once again, with emergent skill in emotional regulation, clients are better able to appreciate that there is far more power in forgiveness than in resentment.

In the final phase of the group, relapse prevention is the major theme. Clients should be given a checklist of early warning signs of relapse, such as returning to pretreatment levels of social isolation and feeling an urge to control their spouses or to spy on them. The return of jealous or envious feelings can presage relapse, as can a series of stressful life events, increased irritability, anger in traffic, and trouble sleeping. The relapse package should include prevention strategies and support numbers to call if the clients' risk of relapse begins to increase.

THE COMPASSION WORKSHOP

This highly structured group treatment has been developed over 10 years of work with more than 5,000 abusers. Because abusers have trouble regulating the internal penalties of threatened attachment bonds, namely, guilt, shame, and abandonment anxiety, the treatment emphasizes the great reward for enhancement of attachment bonds: well-being and increased self-esteem. In fact, compassion serves a dual function: as an incompatible response strategy for the dissipation of anger arousal (Baron, 1984; Stosny, 1995) and as a self-enhancing mechanism; clients simply like themselves better when they experience compassion for loved ones. The treatment is based on the assumption that human beings attempt to exert power and control over others when they feel powerless themselves. In other words, the rush of arousal in exerting power over others fills in gaps in the sense of self, providing a temporary illusion of wholeness and personal power. The Compassion Workshop eliminates the exertion of power and control over loved ones by reducing the need for it through enhancement of the self, particularly the sense of power over one's internal experience. The mechanism of enhancement is the development of self-regulatory skills that lead to moral agency.

The skill-building centerpiece of the Compassion Workshop is the five-step emotional regulation technique HEALS, an acronym for the letters of the word HEALING: Explain to yourself which is the deepest of the core hurts you're feeling (unimportant, disregarded, accused-guilty-mistrusted, devalued, rejected, powerless, unlovable); Apply self-compassion to heal the core hurt; Love yourself by feeling compassion for loved ones; Solve the problem.

HEALS uses self-compassion to reduce the guilt, shame, and rejection anxiety that tend to encapsulate abusers in a narcissistic shell. While locked within narcissistic shells, abusers remain insulated from accurate processing of the social cues that normally mediate aggressive impulses. This allows the abusive impulse to gain temporary empowerment qualities through emotional arousal as internal controls, under the painful assault of shame, weaken, permitting full objectification of the victim as nothing more than a source of negative affect. The application of HEALS to the arousal itself breaks the narcissistic shell, allowing the abuser to take the perspective of the potential victim, which stimulates pain-relieving, prosocial compassion.

Through rigorous practice, the development of self-regulatory skills internalizes the sense of personal power, usually within 3 or 4 weeks. Now clients are able to learn interpersonal empowerment techniques to avoid power struggles at home. By this time, they understand the interrelated well-being of attachment figures: that we cannot hurt or diminish those we love without hurting or diminishing ourselves. Thus the goal of conflict resolution is not to "win the dispute" (for that means creating resentment and hostility), but rather to have everyone in the dispute come out feeling important, valuable, acceptable, and lovable. In role play, clients experience the greater power of self-enhancement available through empowerment of loved ones.

The last of 44 required homework assignments (for abusers, not victims), the Statement of Compassion, provides abusers with a way of making a clear demarcation between the self-destructive styles of thinking, feeling, and behaving of the past and the self-building styles they've learned in the present. Completion of the assignment promises to close the door on the past and open the door to the future. The letter should serve as a kind of blueprint for reversing periods of relapse. The content must recount the steps of the client's recovery, including what needs to be done to advance recovery. One objective of the assignment is to create a document that can be read during vulnerable periods in the future, to tell clients what to do for renewed progress and inspire them to fulfill their emerging identity as compassionate persons. Clients tend to hate this exercise when it is first assigned, but the vast majority find it a wonderfully healing process in the doing. On the final day of treatment, clients read their letters aloud. It's a powerfully moving session, especially if the wives are present. Other group members are asked to give feedback on how well the letter meets the requirements and objectives of the assignment.

Case

Gary was court ordered into treatment following the most acute of a long series of violent abuses of his wife Sharon. Gary's violence typically occurred as a result of his jealousy. Virtually every time they went to a party Gary accused Sharon of "coming on" to any man with whom she casually spoke. Gary's interpretation that his wife caused his painful feelings rendered him powerless over them; he was like a robot responding to whatever button Sharon might inadvertently push. He continually exerted power over his wife to control her behavior, lest she make him feel emotions that he could not handle. When she inevitably rebelled against his pervasive distrust and his stranglehold on her autonomy, Gary enforced his desperate control with violence.

Through treatment, Gary understood that his jealousy came from his own deep belief that he was defective as an attachment figure and, at least some of the time, unlovable. (If we believe ourselves unworthy of love, we cannot fully believe those who say they love us; they *must* want someone else.) Of course, the more Gary hurt the person he loved, the more unworthy of love he felt. In learning to use compassion for himself and his wife as an incompatible response to anger and aggression, he began to heal the wounds that made him feel unlovable.

To stress once again the critical importance of teaching affect regulation techniques before any discussion of anger and jealousy, by the end of treatment Gary was certain that, had we asked him to talk about jealousy before he learned HEALS, he would have fallen into the trap of trying to force his wife to regulate his vulnerable feelings. Her inability to do so would have resulted in more violence. In the 3 years following treatment, Gary and Sharon have lived completely free of violence.

EVALUATION

An ethical imperative for workers who treat abusers requires careful and continuous evaluation of outcome effectiveness. The Conflict Tactics Scale (Straus et al., 1996) is an accessible, easy to administer, widely used instrument to measure verbal and physical aggression in intimate relationships. In the Compassion Workshop, we give these scales to victims every four months for a year following treatment. We ask them to keep logs of any verbal abuse and urge them to call us between scheduled contacts if physical abuse threatens to recur. In stark contrast to the predominant treatments that focus exclusively on stopping abusive behavior, the Compassion Workshop boasts a 68% completion rate, with completers remaining 86% violence free and 71% emotional abuse free at one year of follow-up, based on reports of victims (Larson, 1997; Stosny, 1995). It's unwise to rely on the report of abusers for evaluation purposes. They have great interest in lying, particularly after treatment, when re-abuse likely means jail time. Because many victims decide to stay with their spouses in the often illusory hope that treatment will be effective, the historical success rate of the treatment should be made available to them from the beginning. In addition, victims should know of the post-treatment assessment of their abuser's risk factors. These should include a standardized measurement of self-esteem, the depth and breadth of the client's written or verbal accounting of strategies to avoid abuse, and the therapists' assessment of the abuser's improvement in perspective taking, compassion for self and loved ones, validation of the emotional experience of self and loved ones, and the development of an emotional vocabulary adequate for the regulation of complex emotional experience.

CONCLUSION

Intimate partner abusers constitute one of the most difficult treatment populations. They suffer grave difficulties in regulating guilt, shame, and abandonment anxiety, in which they abound, as a result of their inability to form viable attachments with others. Afflicted with an external locus of control and external causal attributions, they see themselves as powerless victims. Structured groups that provide self-enhancement through basic emotional regulation and interpersonal skills for attachment relationships seem the optimal treatment. But clinicians must resist the temptation to impose their own family values on court-ordered abusers and should instead help them to achieve moral agency. Rigorous evaluation of treatment efforts is an ethical imperative in this vulnerable population, as are protocols for relapse prevention.

RESOURCES

Batterer Intervention State
Standards
2627 N. East St.
Lansing, MI 48906
(517) 482-3933
http://www.biscmi.org/other_resources/
state_standards.html

Call to protect: Wireless phones for
Domestic Safety
888-901-7233
2555 Bishop Circle West
Dexter, MI 48130
http://www.wirelessfoundation.org/
02call/index.htm

Community United Against Violence:
Same Sex Domestic Violence
415-333-HELP
160 14th St.
San Francisco, CA 94103
http://www.xq.com/cuav/domviol.htm

Compassion Power
19908 Dunstable Circle
Germantown, MD 20876
compassionpower.com
(301) 528-9977

Ending Men's Violence National
Referral Directory
RAVEN
P.O. Box 24159

St. Louis, MO 63130
(314) 725-6137
www.soros.org/crime/DVDir-state

Institute on Domestic Violence in
the African-American
Community
877-NIDVAAC
290 Peters Hall
1404 Gortner Ave.
St. Paul, MN 55108
http://www.dvinstitute.org

National Domestic Violence Hotline
(800) 799-7233
(address varies by state)
http://www.ndvh.org

REFERENCES

Barnett, O. W., & Hamberger, L. K. (1992). The assessment of maritally violent men on the California psychological inventory. *Violence and Victims.* 7(1), 15–28.

Baron, R. A. (1994). Reducing organizational conflict. An incompatible response approach. *Journal of Applied Psychology.* 69, 272–279.

Baumeister, R. (1997). *Evil: Inside human violence and cruelty.* New York: W. H. Freeman & Co.

Bennett, L., & Williams, O. (2001). Controversies and recent studies of batterer intervention program effectiveness. Paper published by Violence Against Women Online Resources: www.vaw.umin.edu/finaldocuments/Vawnet/AR_bip.htm.

Bograd, M. (1984). Family systems approaches to wife battering: A feminist critique. *American Journal of Orthopsychiatry.* 54, 558–568.

Bograd, M. (1988). Feminist perspectives on wife abuse: An introduction. In K. Yllo & M. Bograd (eds.), *Feminist perspectives on wife abuse* (pp. 11–26). Newbury Park, CA: Sage Newbury.

Bowlby, J. (1969). *Attachment and loss, Vol. I: Attachment.* New York: Basic Books.

Bowlby, J. (1973). *Attachment and loss, Vol. II: Separation: Anxiety and anger.* New York: Basic Books.

Bowlby, J. (1977). The making and breaking of affectional bonds: I. Etiology and psychopathology in the light of attachment theory. *British Journal of Psychiatry.* 130, 201–210.

Bowlby, J. (1980). *Attachment and loss, Vol. III: Loss, depression and sadness.* New York: Basic Books.

Bureau of Justice Statistics Special Report: Violence against women: Estimates from the redesigned survey (NCJ-154348), August 1995, p. 3.

Bushman, B. J., Baumsieter, R., & Stack, A. D. (1999). Catharsis, aggression and persuasive influence: Self-fulfilling or self-defeating prophecies? *Journal of Personality and Social Psychology.* 76(3), 367–376.

Crawford, M., & Gartner, R. (1992). Women killing: Intimate femicide [sic] in Ontario, 1974–1990. Toronto: Women's Directorate, Ministry of Social Services.

Dutton, D. G. (1998). *The abusive personality.* New York: Guilford.

Edelson, J. L., & Tolman, R. M. (1992). *Intervention for men who batter: An ecological approach.* Newbury Park, CA: Sage.

Eisikovits, Z. C., Edelson, H. L., Guttman, E., & Sela-Amit, M. (1991). Cognitive styles and socialized attitudes for men who batter: Where should we intervene? *Family Relations.* 40, 72–77.

Faulkner, K. K., Cogan, R., Nolder, M., & Shooter, G. (1991). Characteristics of men and women completing cognitive/behavioral spouse abuse treatment. *Journal of Family Violence.* 6, 243–253.

Gilbert, P. (1994). Male violence: Toward an integration. In J. Archer (ed.), *Male violence.* London: Routledge.

Gilligan, J. (1996). *Violence.* New York: Gossett/Putnam.

Gondolf, E. W. (1999). MCMI results for batterer program participants in four cities: Less "pathological" than expected. *Journal of Family Violence.* 14(3) 331.

Hanson, R. K., Cadsky, O., Harris, A., & Lalonde, C. (1997). *Correlates of battering among 997 men: Family history, adjustment, and attitudinal differences. Violence and Victims,* 12, 191–208.

Harrell, A. (1991). Evaluation of court-ordered treatment for domestic violence offenders. Washington, DC: The Urban Institute.

Larson, E. L. (1997). An evaluation of the compassion workshop, a group program for perpetrators of domestic violence. Thesis, unpublished: University of Maryland, College Park.

Lewis, W. A., & Bucher, A. M. (1992). Anger, catharsis, the reformulated frustration-aggression hypothesis, and health consequences. *Psychotherapy.* 29, 385–392.

Murphy, C., Scott, E., Meyer, S., & O'Leary, K. D. (1992). Emotional vulnerability patterns in partner assaultive men. Paper presented at a symposium of the 1992 American Association of Behavioral Therapy convention, Boston, MA.

Neidig, P. H., Friedman, D. H., & Collins, B. S. (1986). Attitudinal characteristics of men engaged in spouse abuse. *Journal of Family Violence.* 1, 223–233.

Pence, E., & Paymar, M. (1993). *Education groups for men who batter: The Duluth model.* New York: Springer Publishing.

Rosen, I. (1991). Self-esteem as a factor in social and somatic violence. *British Journal of Psychiatry.* 158, 18–23.

Stith, S. M., & Farley, S. C. (1993). A predictive model of male spousal violence. *Journal of Family Violence.* 8, 183–201.

Stosny, S. (1994). "Shadows of the Heart": A dramatic video for the treatment resistance of spouse abusers. *Social Work.* 39, 686–694.

Stosny, S. (1995). *Treating attachment abuse: A compassionate approach.* New York: Springer Publishing.

Straus, M. A., Hamby, S. L., Boney-McCoy, S. and Sugarman D. B. (1996). The revised Conflict Tactics Scales (CTS2): Development and preliminary psychometric data. *Journal of Family Issues.* 17, 283–316.

Chapter 16

Group Work with African-American Youth in the Criminal Justice System: A Culturally Competent Model

AMINIFU R. HARVEY

There is no wealth where there are no children.
—African proverb

There is national concern about the plight of African-American males in the United States. Gibbs (1989) is so alarmed that she discusses the possibility of this population's extinction. Kunjufu (2001) states that the plight of the African-American is so serious that America is faced with a state of emergency. Central to this concern is the large number of African-American boys who endanger their lives or their prospects for a physically, mentally, spiritually, and economically healthy life by their involvement in criminal activities (Wilson, 1990).

African-American boys between 14 and 18 years of age are a significant percentage of the youths involved in the juvenile justice system (Wilson, 1994). Their offenses include selling drugs, rape, armed robbery, auto theft, burglary, and a host of other crimes. These crimes are destructive to the boys, their families, and their communities. The youths are either sentenced to serve time in institutions or are put on probation. A disproportionate number of African-American youths are sentenced to institutions (Wilson, 1994). Because of this discriminatory practice, the juvenile justice system is exploring alternative methods of intervention and supervision.

The purpose of this chapter is to address issues of working with groups of African-American boys involved in the juvenile justice system. One effective program based on small groups of African-American boys 14 to 18 years of age who are on probation will be described.

REVIEW OF THE LITERATURE

There is a scarcity of social work literature on group work with African-American youth. Two articles were located (Franklin, 1989; Lee, 1989). Franklin points out that the issue of respect is significant in the lives of African-American youths and must be addressed in the context of the group. He also states that the group can serve as an "alternative peer reference group" (p. 330) to counteract negative peer influences and provide support in the face of adversity. Lee (1989) presents a group work model that is school based but has applicability to other settings. This model reinforces the approach for working with African-American males presented later in this chapter. Lee's model is not gender specific; it can be generalized to males or females. He contends that a concentrated effort is needed to develop comprehensive interventions that reflect the needs and contemporary realities of black youths. He further states that it is important to create methods of incorporating African-American culture into the helping process because culture-specific approaches have the potential to transform basic aspects of African-American life generally ignored or perceived as negative into positive psychoeducational experiences. Lee contends that "in order to maximize the effectiveness of cultural specificity in the helping process, emphasis should be placed on group approaches to guidance and counseling with Black youth" (p. 294). Harvey and Coleman (1997) present an agency's comprehensive program from an Afrocentric perspective based upon one author's work with African-American youth. Harvey and Rauch (1997) present another description of this same agency's group work with this population.

Non-social work publications contain material on risk factors, resiliency factors, and concepts for interventions pertaining to African-American male youths. Kunjufu (1985) identifies the following factors that enable African-American youths to overcome the negative influences of inner-city life: strong family background, positive peer pressure, social survival skills, participation on athletic teams, high teacher expectations, low student-teacher ratio, and religious participation. Similarly, Lewis and Lewis (1984) identify effective mental health prevention programs for African-American families and children as those that help them in developing satisfying relationships, acquiring effective cognitive problem-solving skills, managing personal stress, and maintaining positive self-concepts. Hill (1972), in his seminal work on the strengths of African-American families, identifies the following resiliency factors: strong achievement orientation, strong work orientation, flexible family roles, strong kinship bonds, and strong religious participation.

It is recognized that high-risk behaviors are significantly interrelated, especially among youths (Penkower et al., 1991). According to Dryfoos (1990), one in four young people in America "do it all" and are in jeopardy of not growing into responsible adults unless immediate interventions occur. This is more likely to happen among those with low self-esteem, low educational aspiration, low social skills, and low social approval (Botvin & McAlister, 1981; Millman & Botvin, 1983).

Through a complex system of formal and informal networks rooted in family life and ongoing socialization processes, families, adult relatives, and communities traditionally maintained effective social control and instilled common values in their members (Kornhauser, 1978; Sampson, 1987). Marital and family disruption, predominance of streetcorner peer groups, and decline of formal and informal social controls have all contributed to the demise of traditional constraints on the behavior of adolescents (Krohn, 1986). By the 1980s, as children approached adolescence, there appeared to be a progressive decline in the influence of parents and adults and a corresponding increase in the impact of peer networks (Glynn, 1981; Hare & Hare, 1985). Winbush (2001) tries to counter these phenomena with his guide for parents for raising healthy black boys. Kunjufu (2001) also provides a list of what he calls solutions to the problem.

While parents and adult networks tend to hold values, norms, and attitudes that discourage criminal behavior (Wills & Vaughan, 1984), street peer groups that are prone to antisocial behavior may encourage criminal behavior (Skogan, 1986). Due to what has been characterized as "adolescent egocentrism" (Elkind, 1978), adolescents tend to have a heightened sense of self-consciousness concerning their appearance, personal qualities, and abilities. The combination of adolescent egocentrism and the increased influence of street gangs tends to promote substance abuse and other criminal behaviors among many inner-city youths. This is particularly true among inner-city African-American boys, for whom the "street culture" is a major institution comparable to the family, the school, and the church (Perkins, 1986). The more such traditional institutions in the African-American community abdicate their responsibility for socialization of their children, the greater the influence of the street gangs (Harvey, 1988).

Research reveals that several problem behaviors appear to be caused by the same underlying factors (Jessor, 1982). For this reason, it is suggested that prevention programs be developed that target the underlying determinants of several theoretically and empirically related problem behaviors (Botvin, 1982; Swisher, 1979). This assumes that an effective treatment program should aim at promoting youths' general personal and social competence, vocational aspirations, and self-esteem, thereby affecting the factors that underlie many types of delinquent behaviors.

Perkins (1986) states that an Afrocentric cultural approach is needed to deal effectively with the antisocial behavior of high-risk African-American youth and to outline a youth rites-of-passage program. Warfield-Coppock and Harvey (1989) describe various rites-of-passage programs across the nation targeted at African-American boys and girls. According to them, the rites-of-passage approach is based on African and African-American cultures, which seek to restore traditional social constraints on the behaviors of African-American youths, help them to develop their emotional and cognitive abilities in a constructive fashion, and prepare them to become responsible members of society.

An Afrocentric Approach

An Afrocentric approach to the delivery of psychosocial educational treatment services is based on a humanistic and naturalistic orientation. An Afrocentric view recognizes that African-American culture is a nexus between Western culture and traditional African culture. It is within the African culture—a holistic and naturalistic orientation to the world—that the value system and behavioral patterns of African-Americans have their roots. The philosophical concepts work in conjunction with the natural order, working toward such principles as balance in one's environment; family/personal life, and a multifunctional, discretionary, harmonious approach to life rather than a one-dimensional, predetermined, conflictual approach. The Afrocentric approach incorporates the individual, the family, and the community as an interconnected unit, so that any intervention must include interactions with all three entities. This approach recognizes the presence of spirituality (Pinkett, 1993) and interconnectedness (Richards, 1989) in the African-American community and that these characteristics are key in understanding the psychosocial dynamics of the African-American community, family, and individual in order to develop and implement appropriate, effective interventions.

The goal of the Afrocentric approach is to facilitate the development of persons who are aware and who can operationalize their sense of unity or collective, extended selves (Nobles, 1976). The desired outcome is to influence families and persons to cooperate; to understand and respect the sameness of self and of other persons; and to have a strong sense of responsibility for the well-being and harmonious interconnection between self and others (Nobles, 1976).

The Nguzo Saba ("Seven Principles" in Kiswahili) are employed as a value system to foster and evaluate these outcomes. The Nguzo Saba created by Karenga (1965) are as follows:

Umoja/Unity. To strive and maintain unity in the family, community, nation, and race.

Kujichagulia/Self-Determination. To define ourselves, name ourselves, and speak for ourselves instead of being defined and spoken for by others.

Ujima/Collective Work and Responsibility. To build and maintain our community together, and to make our brothers' and sisters' problems our problems and to solve them together.

Ujamaa/Cooperative Economics. To build and own stores, shops, and other businesses and to profit from them.

Nia/Purpose. To make our collective vocation the building and developing of our community in order to restore our people to their traditional greatness.

Kuumba/Creativity. To do always as much as we can, in the way we can, to restore our people to their traditional greatness.

Imani/Faith. To believe in our parents, our teachers, our leaders, our people, and ourselves, and in the righteousness and victory of our struggle.

Another goal of an Afrocentric psychosocial program is to provide principles (Harvey, 1988) (and to assist in their internalization) by which youths and families can become constructive contributors to their community through appreciation of themselves and their culture.

Principles of Afrocentricism

The principles of Afrocentricism (called RIPSO) are the seven Rs: responsibility, reciprocity, respect, realness, restraint, reason, and reconciliation; three Is: interconnectedness, interdependence, and inclusivity; three Ps: participatory, patience, and perseverance; three Ss: sharing, sacrifice, and spirituality; and three Others: cooperation, discipline, and unconditional love. These principles are universal principles of successful Afrocentric people.

PRACTICE PRINCIPLES

The philosophical orientation of the social worker is critical. The social worker should view the youths as being misdirected and victims of a system that discriminates and has intentionally denied African-Americans access to their cultural identity (Akbar, 1991; McRoy, 1990; Polite & Davis, 1999). It is important for the social worker to hold the belief that the youths are capable of change when involved in a program designed to reduce the factors that place them at risk. These programs should be formulated from a group work perspective since African-American youths move through adolescence in peer groups. For these youths, group intervention must provide a positive perspective on African and African-American culture, assist them in developing their own African-American group identity, and provide them with tools to deal with the oppressiveness of white supremacy (Welsing, 1991; Wilson, 1990; Winbush, 2001; Wright, 1984).

To establish rapport and connectedness, it is important for the youths to believe that the social worker is truly interested in them and is not working with them only because required to do so. The youths will usually state the latter belief directly or indirectly. It has been effective to employ the analogy of Michael Jordan, who enjoys playing basketball but at the same time is paid to do so. We explain that this is similar to why we choose this work: that we work with them both out of a concern for their well-being and because we enjoy it.

With African-American youth, it is necessary to place the group within the program rather than label the program a "group." Many youths have been placed in psychotherapeutic groups in institutions and believe that being involved in a group implies that something is innately wrong with them or that they are crazy.

If the service is being provided by an agency contracted with the court system, it is important to establish a referral process that connects the youth, the group leaders, the youth's parents (guardian or another family member), and the probation officer. This process enables the youth to experience connectedness between the agencies and to know from the very beginning that the probation officer and the social worker will be in contact with each other and are working together as a team. Connecting with the family early in the referral process demonstrates respect for the rights of the family and establishes a cooperative relationship. Many families have control and influence over the behavior of their children and want to work with the social worker to promote the well-being of their children.

There are issues that African-Americans will not raise but will discuss if the group leaders introduce them. These include issues of skin color (Harvey, 1995), body type, sexual identity, and inter/intraracial identification. The latter include the negative perceptions that white supremacy promulgates about African-American youths.

In working with African-American youths, it is critical for the social worker to respect their opinions and their right to voice their opinions, even when these differ from the opinions of the social worker. This does not mean agreeing with their opinions but rather giving them the opportunity to develop and express their ideas. It also means that it is the worker's responsibility to challenge their opinions but not to use the authority of the worker's position to impose views.

The worker gains respect by skillfully handling differences that arise. The youths will assess whether the social worker remains "cool" (Majors & Billson, 1992) or is easily intimidated. The youths give respect based on the social worker's ability to handle situations, not because of the social worker's professional degree or authority provided by the job title.

Structure is important, and each session needs to be planned. Nevertheless, the social worker must be flexible enough to focus on the concerns the youths might have during each session, such as a friend's being shot either by another youth or by the police.

These youths want the group leaders to be "real." Thus, it is critical that the group leaders self-disclose appropriately (Yalom, 1995) in a manner that demonstrates familiarity with the African-American culture and community.

The transformational process is greatly enhanced when the group leaders are African-American, as they act as positive same-race role models. The lack of positive African-American role models is one factor in African-American youths being at risk. This lack of same-race role models has been critical in fostering a sense of hopelessness in African-American boys.

COMMON THEMES

The following questions and themes are consistently raised by African-American youths:

- "Why should I change my behavior when I see adults involved in illegal activities?" Youths state that the only thing wrong with their behavior is that they were caught. The task is to help them respect moral and upright behavior.
- "What are the alternatives to violence?" Youths state, "If I don't fight back, my peers will think I am a punk and abuse me on a regular basis." Also, people respect you on the street only if you "kick their ass." People think you are a punk if you try to work out conflicts verbally.
- "How do I maintain my self-respect and moral upbringing without being a social isolate and without being perceived as vulnerable to the violence of other youths?" This is important, as many of the youths' parents stress morality, a characteristic of African-American culture. There is a tension between the morality and materialism of American society that creates conflicts in family values.
- A reputation for being "cool" is important (Majors & Billson, 1992) for self-protection. If you do not display any affect or emotion, people cannot read you and thus hesitate to challenge you physically or mentally. Being cool also attracts females to you because it implies that you are street smart and not a nerd.
- Issues pertaining to male-female relationships: sex and respect for females and nonviolent behavior toward females. Many youths perceive male-female relationships from a superior-inferior paradigm rather than a harmonizing, diunital paradigm (T'Shaka, 1995).
- Issues of respect from police officers whom youths perceive as harassing them, being dishonest, and violating the law. Police are perceived as the enemy. A dilemma for these youths is how to interact

with police, who at times do harass them, so that they do not become victims of police brutality.

- Critical to this population are issues of racism: how to deal with the reactions of white people to them in stores and on public transportation, as well as the racism of teachers and school administrators.
- Lack of cultural identification and racial appreciation, and lack of knowledge of the African and African-American heritage. Central to this issue is how to be successful, yet remain connected to the African-American community (Hines, Gracia-Preto, McGoldrick, Almeida, & Weltman, 1993) and not "become white." Sometimes being white erroneously means being a good student, speaking proper English, or pursuing activities such as tennis.

RECOMMENDED WAYS OF WORKING

The MAATIAN Youth Group Model

Given a social environment where children are physically violent to other children (Wilson, 1991) and are seduced or forced into selling and taking drugs, it is essential for children to be involved with a group that operates out of a positive frame of reference, with guidance from well-trained social workers. The goal of the group is to assist youth in developing the emotional strength to become self and community advocates guided by the MAATIAN principles of truth, justice and righteousness (Obenga, 1995). This is accomplished by providing youth with higher values to employ as life guidelines (Nguzo Saba) and a support group of peers who can assist each other in self-evaluation and provide emotional and physical support to do the right thing.

The group helps youth develop interpersonal skills, fostering new relationships and building a positive self-concept. The emphasis is on youths interacting with youths to develop constructive lifestyles and positive solutions to life problems, as well as to recognize their personal and cultural strengths and abilities. The small-group model employed is a youth rites-of-passage model, a group model many African-American practitioners advocate (Hare & Hare, 1985; Long, 1993; Perkins, 1986; Warfield-Coppock, 1990; Warfield-Coppock & Harvey, 1989).

When a referral for the rites-of-passage Program is received from the court, the probation officer and the group leaders coordinate a meeting with the youth and a parent/guardian. At this meeting the program is explained, including the parent's/guardian's participation in a parenting skills group.

The youths participate in an orientation entitled "Brotherhood Training," which lasts for 8 weeks. This prepares them for the sacredness of the transformation of the rites of passage. During this phase the youths are oriented to the group process, the Nguzo Saba, and the Afrocentric principles; at this time, the group is accepting new members while others are dropping out. At the end of this 8-week period the youths, who are called *preinitiates*, participate in a weekend retreat focusing on cultural and personal survival and enhancement of the community. At the end of the weekend, 15 youth are selected to become initiates based on an evaluation conducted by the coleaders and a group of older male adults called *Elders*. Youths who pass the evaluation are called *Initiates*. *Initiates* are required to take an Initiates' Code of Conduct Oath and to participate in a sacred initiation ritual in which they pledge to uphold the Nguzo Saba, receive an African name based on the day of the week on which they were born (Assem & Dodson, 1994), and are given a special identifying symbol to be worn at all group sessions. At this point in the group process, membership is closed. The group develops a sense of we-ness; its members are integrated into the group, trust each other, and are ready to work.

The group meets once a week for 90 minutes. Each participant is expected to participate in a unity circle as part of the opening group ritual. All members hold each other's hands, and one member reads a spiritually oriented text followed by the pouring of a libation (respect for the community of ancestors). Water, a symbol of life, is poured into a group-owned plant, a symbol of growth and transformation, as names of ancestors are called out loud by the members.

Each group is co-led. The leaders have included social workers, as well as a person with a master's degree in African-American studies, an artist, and a person with expertise in music and the theater. Group meetings are supplemented by follow-up home visits with the family, focusing on the impact of the program on the youths' overall development. The group incorporates creative intervention techniques such as music (use of rap songs to analyze life or create songs as a project), films, videos, and audiotapes. African-American guest presenters are invited to conduct meetings on specific topics, called *modules*. All aspects of the group are structured to develop an appreciation for African and African-American culture. The following is a list of possible modules: Principles and Guides for Living, Win-Win Relationships, Entrepreneurial Development, Personal Development and Self-Control, Mental Health Issues (Skin Color, Negative Names, Body Type), Meditation for Self-Development and Self-Control, African-American Culture and Heritage, African Culture and Heritage, Male-Female Relations, Fatherhood, Motherhood and Marriage, Male and Female Health Issues, Teenage Pregnancy, HIV/AIDS and Sexually Transmitted Diseases, Oppression and Racism, Alcohol Abuse, Tobacco and Other Drug Use, Date Rape and Incest, and Family Violence.

Each module consists of four to six sessions. The first session includes a presentation by a person of African descent who is knowledgeable concerning the topic area. The second session consists of a discussion of the information contained in the topic and how it relates to the youth's life. In the remaining sessions, the youths develop a project related to the topic to demonstrate transformation on the cognitive, emotional, spiritual, and behavioral planes. The variation in sessions allows flexibility in creating the project. Adolescents receive a certificate for the completion of the module at a small ceremony. A youth who misses a session has a follow-up meeting with the probation officer, a home visit, and a letter mailed to the parent/guardian. If an Initiate is consistently disruptive or noncooperative, he is presented to his peers, who recommend how he should reconcile with the group.

At the completion of all the modules, each youth conducts a self-evaluation and is evaluated by his peers, the group leaders, and the elders in order to pass into the final phase: a transformational weekend. During this experience, the Initiates are expected to demonstrate all they have learned and prepare for their rites ceremony.

On successful completion of the transformational weekend, Initiates participate in a final transformation ceremony. It is at this ceremony, to be witnessed by family, friends, court personnel, agency staff, its board of directors, and the general community, that the youths demonstrate specific knowledge, attitudes, and skills indicative of maturation. They announce their sacred name (based on their personality) received at the transformational weekend, to the public, and receive a symbol and a certificate of sacred transformation. Each family who participates in the program will also receive a certificate of transformation. The Initiates, in conjunction with the group leaders, plan and implement the ceremony, allowing the adolescents to experience kuumba (creativity), ujima (collective work and responsibility), and other principles of the Nguzo Saba.

CASE STUDIES: APPROACHES TO DEALING WITH COMMON THEMES

Case 1

The issue of respect for females is critical in the development of African-American males, especially since there has been an influx of antifemale rap videos and T-shirts targeted to the African-American community. In this particular session, an African-American transit policewoman was invited as a guest. The youths discussed how they handled relationships with their female peers. One youth stated that if a woman doesn't do as you say or dates someone else, you should "kick her ass." The officer asked how the group members would feel if someone "kicked their sister's or their mother's ass." The youths reacted angrily, stating they probably would retaliate. Then the worker asked if they should not respect every woman as their mother or sister. Some youths agreed and others tried to explain the difference, but it was evident that they were now beginning to question their value system.

The session continued, with the group leaders raising the issue of spirituality. Emphasizing that each person is unique, has a special reason to be here, and is a reflection of the Creative Force, the leaders asked how one could justify oppression against a woman. This helped the youths to consider alternative methods of dealing with confrontational situations. It also allowed the group leaders to pursue the emotions the youths were experiencing. They reported being angry because they had been treated with disrespect. When probed, they acknowledged that they were hurt emotionally. They also stated that if they did not respond physically, their friends would think they were punks. At that point, the group leaders had them participate in a role play to experience alternative behaviors, thoughts, and emotions.

Case 2

White (1984) contends that the issue of racial identity in African-American youth is crucial to the development of a positive self-concept that includes appreciation of and identification with African-American culture. A number of Afrocentric techniques are employed to facilitate this development. For example, youths are provided with biographies of African-American personalities and are asked to select a person they admire. Each youth is presented with a challenging situation and is asked to think, feel, and behave like the African-American personality he admires in order to resolve the problem. The purpose of this exercise is to enhance the Initiate's ability to employ high-level principles in his thought process, to feel the emotions of a constructive African-American, and to behave in a positive manner in challenging situations.

Some youths react to the infusion of African and African-American culture by stating that they are not African. The group leaders take this opportunity to explain the importance of the rituals, their history, and the role Africa has played with its well developed cultures, such as the Mali and Songhai (deGraft-Johnson, 1986), in world development. The group leaders show videos and films concerning the culture. Many African-American youth use the word *nigger* as both an affective and a derogatory term when addressing their peers. Harvey (1995) explains this as the "paradox of blackness": The oppressor's definition is employed to define one's culture in both positive and negative terms simultaneously because the oppressed culture has not defined itself based on its own world view. In this situation, the history of the term is provided and the paradox is explained. Then the youths are guided through a relaxation exercise to allow them to "feel" their physiological reaction to the world. The youths almost always state that the word creates funny feelings in their stomachs. Then they ask them to use the term *brother* affectionately. They respond that the new term "feels good."

Outcomes

Following group participation, it is anticipated the youths will experience:

- Increased appreciation of the African and African-American heritage and culture.
- Reduction in repeated criminal activity.
- Enhanced positive engagement with their family and community.
- Increased school attendance.
- Improvement in school grades.
- Increase in employment for youth of appropriate age.
- Increased sense of self-worth.
- Increased sense of respect for self, family, and community.

EVALUATION

The participants are evaluated through a process evaluation and a final evaluation. Their degree of participation and transformation while in the program are evaluated. The seven principles of African life (Nguzo Saba) Assessment Scale is employed by the Council of Elders in evaluating the development of the youths. Each youth must score at least a 3 out of 5 points on each dimension of the Likert-type scale in order to graduate from the program.

Preliminary results indicate that over 80% of the youths who complete the orientation phase of the program complete the entire program. Family members report an increase in school attendance, in obeying curfews, in performing household chores, and in showing respect. When the youths are asked what they learned from the program, all of them report that they learned to respect themselves and appreciate their heritage.

RESOURCES

African-American Males Leadership
   Institute, Inc.
P.O. Box 32025
Baltimore, MD 21208
410 602-8058
AAMLI@aol.com

African Rites of Passage United
   Kollective
P.O. Box 10586
Atlanta, GA 30310
(404) 456-7525

Black Family Institute
14849th St.
Oakland, CA 94607
(510) 836-3245

Office of Juvenile Justice and
   Delinquency Prevention
1810 7th St. NW
Washington, DC 20531
(202) 307-5911
www.ojjdp
nejrs.org

The National Rites of Passage
Institutes
2749 Woodhill Rd.
Cleveland, OH 44104
(216) 791-9378
esi@Ritesofpassage.org
www.ritesofpassage.org

The Urban Institute
2100 M St. NW
Washington, DC 20037
(202) 833-7200
www.urban.org

U.S. Department of Health and
Human Services
Public Health Services
Substance Abuse and Mental
Health Services Administration
Center for Substance Abuse
Prevention
5600 Fishers Lane, Rockwall II
Rockville, MD 20857
(301) 443-0353
www.us.dhhs.gov

REFERENCES

Akbar, N. (1991). *Visions for black men.* Tallahassee, FL: Mind Productions and Associates.

Assem, K., & Dodson, J. (1994). Strengthening the African-American family: The birth to re-birth life cycle. In G. R. Preudhomme & K. Assem (eds.), *National public policy institute* (pp. 6–15). Detroit: National Association of Black Social Workers.

Botvin, G. J. (1982). Broadening the focus of smoking prevention strategies. In T. Cotes, A. C. Petersen, & C. Perry (eds.), *Promoting adolescent health: A dialog on research and practice* (pp. 137–148). New York: Academic Press.

Botvin, G. J., & McAlister, A. (1981). Cigarette smoking among children and adolescents: Causes and prevention. In C. B. Arnold (ed.), *Annual review of disease prevention* (pp. 222–249). New York: Springer.

deGraft-Johnson, J. C. (1986). *African glory.* Baltimore: Black Classic Press.

Dryfoos, J. (1990). *Adolescents at risk: Prevalence and prevention.* New York: Oxford University Press.

Elkind, D. (1978). Understanding the young adolescent. *Adolescent.* 49, 127–134.

Franklin, A. J. (1989). Therapeutic interventions with black adolescents. In R. L. Jones (ed.), *Black adolescents* (pp. 309–337). Berkeley, CA: Cobb & Henry.

Gibbs, J. T. (1989). Black adolescents and youth: An update on an endangered species. In *Black adolescents* (pp. 3–27). Berkeley, CA: Cobb & Henry.

Glynn, T. J. (1981). From family to peer: Transitions of influence among drug-using youth. In D. Lettieri & J. Ludford (eds.), *Drug abuse and the American adolescent* (pp. 57–81). DHHS Pub. No. (ADM) 81-1166. Washington, DC: National Institute on Drug Abuse.

Hare, H., & Hare, J. (1985). *Bringing the black boy to manhood: The passage.* San Francisco: Black Think Tank.

Harvey, A. R. (1988). Extended family: A universal and naturalistic salvation for African Americans (pp. 11–19). In *Proceedings of The Black Task Force on Child Abuse and Neglect.* New York: Black Task Force on Child Abuse and Neglect.

Harvey, A. R. (1995). The issue of skin color in psychotherapy with African Americans. *Families in Society: The Journal of Contemporary Human Services.* 76, 3–10.

Harvey, A. R., & Rauch, J. B. (1997). A comprehensive Afrocentric rites of passage program for black male adolescents. *Health & Social Work.* 22(1), 30–37.

Harvey, A. R., & Coleman, A. A. (1997). An Afrocentric program for African-American males in the juvenile justice system. *Child Welfare: Journal of Policy, Practice and Program.* 76(1), 197–211.

Hill, R. B. (1972). *The strength of black families.* New York: Emerson Hall.

Hines, P. M., Gracia-Preto, N., McGoldrick, M., Almeida, R., & Weltman, S. (1993). Intergenerational relationships across cultures. In J. B. Rauch (ed.), *Assessment: A sourcebook for social work practice* (pp. 371–394). Milwaukee: Families International.

Jessor, R. (1982). Critical issues in research on adolescent health promotion. In T. Coates, A. C. Petersen, & C. Perry (eds.), *Promotion of adolescent health: A dialog on research and practice* (pp. 447–465). New York: Academic Press.

Karenga, M. (1965). *Kwanzaa: Origin, concepts and practice.* Los Angeles: Kawaida Publications.

Kornhauser, R. (1978). *Social sources of delinquency.* Chicago: University of Chicago Press.

Krohn, M. (1986). The web of conformity: A network approach to the explanation of delinquent behavior. *Social Problems.* 33, 81–93.

Kunjufu, J. (1985). *Countering the conspiracy to destroy black boys,* Vol. II. Chicago: African American Images.

Kunjufu, J. (2001). *State of emergency: We must save African American males.* Chicago, Illinois: African American Images.

Lee, C. C. (1989). Counseling black adolescents: Critical roles and functions for counseling professionals. In R. L. Jones (ed.), *Black adolescents* (pp. 293–308). Berkeley, CA: Cobb & Henry.

Lewis, J. & Lewis, F. (1984). Prevention programs in action. *Personnel and Guidance Journal.* 62, 550–553.

Long, L. C. (1993). An Afrocentric intervention strategy. In L. L. Goddard (ed.), *An African-centered model of prevention for African-American youth at high risk* (pp. 87–92). CSAP Technical Report No. 6. Rockville MD: U.S. Department of Health and Human Services.

Majors, R., & Billson, J. M. (1992). *Cool pose: The dilemma of black manhood in America.* New York: Lexington Books.

McRoy, R. G. (1990). A historical overview of black families. In S. M. L. Logan, E. M. Freeman, & R. G. McRoy (eds.), *Social work practice with black families: A culturally specific perspective* (pp. 3–17). New York: Longman.

Millman, R. B., & Botvin, G. J. (1983). Substance use, abuse, and dependence. In M. D. Levine, W. B. Carey, & A. C. Crocker (eds.), *Developmental-behavioral pediatrics* (pp. 683–708). Philadelphia: W. B. Saunders.

Nobles, W. W. (1976). African consciousness and black research: The consciousness of self. In L. M. King, V. Dixon, & W. Nobles (eds.), *African philosophy: Assumption and paradigms for research on black persons* (pp. 163–174). Los Angeles: Fanon Center.

Obenga, T. (1995). *A lost tradition: African philosophy in world history.* Philadelphia: Source Editions.

Penkower, L., Dew, M. A., Kingsley, L., Becker, J. T., Satz, P., Scherf, F. W., & Sheridan, K. (1991). Behavioral, health, and psychosocial factors and risk for HIV infection among sexually active homosexual men: The multi-center AIDS cohort study. *American Journal of Public Health.* 81, 194–196.

Perkins, U. E. (1986). *Harvesting new generations: The positive development of black youth.* Chicago: Third World Press.

Pinkett, J. (1993). Spirituality in the African-American community. In L. L. Goddard (ed.), *An African-centered model of prevention for African-American youth at high risk* (pp. 79–86). CSAP Technical Report No. 6. Rockville, MD: U.S. Department of Health and Human Services.

Polite, V. C., & Davis, J. E. (eds.). *African American males in school and society: Practices and policies for effective education.* New York, Columbia University: Teachers College Press.

Richards, D. M. (1989). *Let the circle be unbroken.* Trenton, NJ: Red Sea Press.

Sampson, R. J. (1987). Urban black violence: The effect of male joblessness and family disruption. *American Journal of Sociology.* 93, 348–382.

Skogan, W. (1986). Fear of crime and neighborhood change. In A. J. Reiss & M. Tonry (eds.), *Communities and crime* (pp. 203–229). Chicago: University of Chicago Press.

Swisher, J. D. (1979). Prevention issues. In R. L. Dupont, A. Goldstein, & J. A. O'Donnell (Eds.), *Handbook on drug abuse* (pp. 423–435). Washington, DC: National Institute of Drug Abuse.

T'Shaka, O. (1995). *Return to the African mother principle of male and female equality,* Vol. 1. Oakland, CA: Pan African Publishers and Distributors.

Warfield-Coppock, N. (1990). *Afrocentric theory and applications: Adolescence rites of passage,* Vol. I. Washington, DC: Baobob Associates.

Warfield-Coppock, N., & Harvey, A. R. (1989). *Teenage pregnancy prevention: A rites of passage resource manual.* Washington, DC: MAAT Institute for Human and Organizational Enhancement.

Welsing, F. C. (1991). *The Isis papers: The keys to the colors.* Chicago: Third World Press.

White, J. L. (1984). *The psychology of blacks: An Afro-American perspective.* Englewood Cliffs, NJ: Prentice Hall.

Wills, T. A., & Vaughan, R. (1984). *Social support and smoking in middle adolescence.* New York: Academic Press.

Wilson, A. N. (1990). *Black-on-black violence: The psychodynamics of black self-annihilation in service of white domination.* Bronx, NY: Afrikan World Infosystems.

Wilson, A. N. (1991). *Understanding black adolescent male violence: Its remediation and prevention.* Bronx, NY: Afrikan World Infosystems.

Wilson, A. N. (1992). *Awakening natural genius of black children.* Bronx, NY: Afrikan World Infosystems.

Wilson, J. J. (1994). Disproportionate minority representation. *Juvenile Justice.* 2(1), 21–23.

Winbush, R. A. (2001). *The warrior method: A parent's guide to rearing healthy black boys.* New York: Harper Collins Publishers.

Wright, B. E. (1984). *The psychopathic racial personality and other essays.* Chicago: Third World Press.

Yalom, I. D. (1995). *The theory and practice of group psychotherapy* (4th ed.). New York: Basic Books.

Chapter 17

Group Work with Sex Offenders

PAUL H. EPHROSS

Social workers are frequently called on to provide group treatment to change the behavior of sex offenders. One can acquire the label of sex offender in a variety of ways: most commonly, one is found guilty in court of violating a law against a particular sexual behavior. These prohibitions are of several types. One, often viewed as archaic by social workers but still on the books in many jurisdictions, prohibits a particular form of sexual expression, without regard for the consenting nature of the act or the relationship between the adult partners. The fact that laws banning normative behaviors—oral sex, in private, between adult partners married to each other, for example—are still on the books makes for rueful comments on late-night television programs and produces cartoons of the "believe it or not" genre. Less amusing is the fact that selective prosecution, or the threat of it, is sometimes used to discredit persons who express and promulgate views seen as undesirable by people in politically or socially powerful positions.

In this chapter, however, the term *sex offender* refers to two other types of persons: *(1)* those who have coerced others into participating in sexual activities through either force or the threat of force and *(2)* those who have engaged in sexual activities with partners who are incapable of giving informed consent. Children and adolescents under the legal age of consent and persons of diminished capacity, regardless of age—such as mentally retarded people and mentally ill people—illustrate categories of forbidden partners, while rapists and perpetrators of child sex abuse form part of the coercive cohort. In recent years, there has been a growing awareness of adolescents as sexual abusers of younger children and as perpetrators of sexual coercion on other adolescents.

While technically one must be adjudicated as such in order to be known as a sex offender, in fact there may be as many persons unknown as known who have carried out or perpetrated the same destructive and illegal behaviors. Judging from studies of the prevalence of rape and the behaviors of rape victims, for example, even today only about one-half—in the past, even fewer—of rapes committed in this country are reported to the police or to any other official agency (Bureau of Justice Statistics, (2002)). The true prevalence rates of sexual coercion and abuse are unknown, in part because of the peculiar and confusing mixture of attitudes towards (1) sex and sexuality in general and (2) deviant, coercive, and illegal sexual activities that characterize American culture and its various subcultures at the end of the twentieth century. It is important to try to understand these attitudes and perceptions before we can analyze in any depth the issues involved in group treatment of sex offenders.

"THAT SUBJECT"

One of the world's most distinguished, if often controversial, scholars of human sexuality, writing in 1994, bluntly characterized contemporary American culture as "taboo-ridden [and] antisexual." In the same discussion, he characterized sexual identities that differ in any way from society's prescriptive norms as "unspeakable monsters." He notes, "Being literally unspeakable, an unspeakable monster is not spoken of" (Money, 1994, p. ix). Many writers have commented on how difficult it is for Americans to talk about sex in general and their own sexuality in particular. Although some may think that men find it easier to talk about sex than women, a noted authority on male sexuality states, "men have been, and to a large extent still are, extremely secretive about their sexuality . . . other than . . . bits of bravado, most men simply don't talk about sex to anyone" (Zilbergeld, 1999, p. 4). Allgeier et al. (1999) point out that our cultural norm of segregating the "sexual" from the rest of our experience begins to be taught in infancy. Some observers find the roots of widespread inability to communicate about sex even with a partner in common childhood experiences:

> As children, most of us were discouraged from saying much about sex and many never learned the terminology to describe their sexual anatomy. . . . So, part of the hesitancy people have in talking about sex . . . is actually a carryover from these childhood taboos (Masters et al., 1986, p. 259)

One can relate the difficulties of talking about sex to the ambivalence about sexual experience that is reflected in the culture of our society. Carole Vance has noted, with regard to women's experiences:

> The tension between sexual danger and sexual pleasure is a powerful one, in women's lives. Sexuality is simultaneously a domain of restric-

tion, repression and danger as well as a domain of exploration, pleasure, and agency (1984, p. 1).

Small wonder, then, that discussions about sex, especially about feelings, experiences, fears, perceptions, doubts, and joys, are viewed as potentially dangerous. In addition, to the extent that they are pleasurable, that very pleasure may be experienced as illicit.

Sex is difficult to talk about even for people whose sexual behavior and identities have been labeled as normal. How much more difficult, then, is it for people whose sexual behavior has been labeled as actually or potentially criminal? The stigmas associated with being labeled abnormal, criminal, evil, and, if the victim is a child, unnatural as a man or woman (Scaveo, 1989) combine for a convicted sex offender. Few identities are as universally despised as that of a sexual abuser of children. In prison, the known abuser of children is often at risk of being physically attacked, or worse, by other inmates. Neither murder nor treason, robbery nor criminal conspiracy carries the perceived loathesomeness that attaches to sexual abuse of children and certain other sexual offenses. The sex offender, then, faces a difficult task while carrying multiple stigmas: to admit to oneself and others the nature of the offense and to participate in discussion of feelings, alternatives, reasons, cognitive and emotional triggers, related to sex—a subject difficult and dangerous to discuss at best.

Difficulty communicating about sex is not restricted to people of lower educational or social classes. The title of this section, "That Subject," was the term used by a senior, highly regarded female educator to characterize the topic of a graduate student's thesis research in a school of social work. The student, a gifted researcher, was studying women's experiences of orgasm: "that subject," as the professor described it. The student produced a study that made a genuine contribution to the research literature on an important topic. In general, and with apologies to a few exceptional people within the profession, one cannot describe social work as having distinguished itself in the front rank of the sexual revolution, nor even in promoting healthy and open discourse on sexual subjects. At times, social workers have been willing to discuss sexual pathology but not sexual normality—sexual harassment, for example, rather than the sexuality of organizational life. For the most part, one looks in vain for positive, affirmative discussions of sexual expression in the literature of our profession.

While the dominant culture of the United States is ambivalent about sexuality at best and antisexual at worst, there is great variation among various American subcultures, whether defined by religion, national origin, or race. It is a curious fact, remarked on by behavioral scientists for many decades, that there is generally a sexual aspect to racism (Bettelheim & Janowitz, 1964, pp. 287–88). Sexual superiority is attributed to the oppressed group, and this attribution plays a part in the self-justifying ideology of the dominant group. It is partly for this illogical reason, perhaps, that minorities of color and certain immigrants have at times been viewed as sexual athletes, and thus simultaneously as both desirable and fearsome. Sexuality is one of the topics about which it is often difficult to communicate across ethnic/racial/cultural barriers of difference.

Another factor that makes sexual discussion, and especially discussion about paraphilias, difficult is the issue of counter-transference. Sensitivity and strong feelings about sex, sexual behavior patterns, paraphilias, and punishments for unusual sexual activities are widespread in our society. Feelings of both repulsion and attraction can easily be mobilized by working with sex offenders. The group setting, as always, provides a measure of protection, but only a measure.

One of the factors that make communicating about sex difficult, both in groups and in other interpersonal settings, is the choice of vocabulary. There is an uncommonly wide range of terms available for English speakers to use about sex, virtually all of it unacceptable for some people for various reasons. Professionals often escape to the use of multisyllabic medical terms of ancient Latin or Greek heritage. Besides communicating a vague sense of disapproval, such words are often unknown to ordinary people. For example, the word *coitus,* a more or less standard medicolegal term, is hardly ever heard in spoken English and is therefore unknown to many people. The word *fuck,* which is known to everyone, is unacceptable-to-offensive to virtually everyone. Social workers are often concerned about "lowering" themselves by using street language to describe sexual activities. This is a legitimate concern, as is the fear that clients simply do not understand the language that social workers feel is more appropriate. Given this question of words and its importance in relation to communication, I suggest here three guiding principles:

1. Ask group members which terms they use and feel comfortable with. Either use their terms or explain why you prefer to use other terms. Let them practice using the new ones together with you. The object is effective communication; there are no *good* or *bad* terms.
2. Be sure that you (and group members) understand the meaning of terms. There is probably no subject on which more deliberate obfuscation is employed in the choice of words. Be sure, to the point of being boring, if necessary, that you understand the behaviors to which words refer. "We . . . you know . . . did it . . . we had relations" sounds behaviorally specific. Sometimes it is not. Ask questions. Men who have sex with other men may or may not identify themselves as homosexual, depending on the specific roles taken during particular sexual activities and on ethnocultural definitions (Doll et al., 1992; see also Chapter 20, this volume).
3. Watch out for your own assumptions that may get in the way of your understanding the words that others are using. This is especially true when (a) group members' age- or sex-specific expectations are

different from the social worker's or (b) when the abusive, coercive, or paraphilic behaviors are so distasteful to the worker that a sensation of horror replaces a desire for effective listening. This aspect of working with sex offenders in groups will be discussed below under "Practice Principles."

Sexual fantasies, sometimes bizarre, often accompany racist perceptions and attitudes, as has been noted. These aside, several subcultures and cultural groups in American society are less sex negative, or erotophobic, than is the culture as a whole. Among these are communities defined by race, by culture and language, by being foreign born or native born of foreign parents, and by ethnic identity. There is also abundant evidence that views on the nature of male and female sexuality, and on the nature and origins of heterosexuality and homosexuality, vary by social class and have varied over time, reflecting and responding to other societal changes (D'Emilio & Freedman, 1988). To take just one example, living quarters and standards of past generations and past centuries allowed for, or required, much less privacy for most Americans than is thought necessary by contemporary middle- or working-class standards. Not only birth and death, but also many other behaviors, including sexual behavior, were more visible to others in the household simply because people lived closer together.

At present, communicating about sex has been made more difficult by the imposition in some professional settings of political limits to discourse focusing on the "discomfort" of anyone present. Certain words and concepts, in this view, are so offensive that they should be banned from civilized discourse. Since sexual topics, almost by definition, can be guaranteed to make someone uncomfortable in a social context that is ambivalent about sex, these topics become doubly taboo because of the possibility that whoever introduces them will be viewed as a harasser by those who experience discomfort. Certainly whatever discomfort is introduced into a treatment group for sex offenders by a discussion of sexual subjects and specific sexual behaviors should be recognized, but this should hardly serve as a justification for avoiding such charged and supercharged topics.

We have been discussing difficulties in communicating about sex, especially about deviant sexual behaviors. By now, the reader may wish to protest that contemporary American society is obsessed with sex—that sexuality, sometimes of the most primitive and evident sort, is displayed daily and nightly on television and in other mass media, on advertising billboards, and in the lyrics of popular songs. This obsession should not be viewed as a sign of growing openness and greater comfort with communicating about sex, but rather as the opposite. It is precisely the potential titillation and inherent discomfort accompanying sexual display and images that give TV images and billboard illustrations dramatic power. Sex as tenderness, as communication, as love, as communication and closeness between two people is rarely portrayed. The concomitants of sexual activity, such as pregnancy, sexually transmitted diseases, sexual dysfunction, and various other aspects of human sexual behavior are just now becoming visible in the mass media in the first decade of the twenty-first century. In their own way, the mass media of our society are just now beginning to stop treating sex as an "unspeakable monster."

COMMON GROUP THEMES

What makes these observations relevant to the task of treating sex offenders in groups? First, not only the group but also the worker(s) is doing something that is relatively deviant in our society, namely, legitimating group members' talking about their own sexual behaviors, sometimes in an explicit and detailed way. The worker needs to anticipate and develop comfort with the fact that *resistance in such groups takes many forms*, often including intense fantasizing about the worker. The worker's own sexual experience, motivation for working with a group of sex offenders, and feelings toward the group members may become, for a time, common topics of conversation both inside the group and in the group's interstices—before and after meetings, for example. Some of these issues may be projections of group members' discomfort, guilt, shame, and fears elicited by being in an offenders' group and the process that brought them there. Other comments and discussions may be part of the process of *testing the worker,* a process that is universal in such groups, in this writer's experience.

There are various theories about the origins of destructive sexual behaviors that violate laws and the rights and needs of other people. Regardless of their theoretical orientation, however, a wide range of researchers and practitioners, from a variety of professional backgrounds, agree on the importance of group experience and group treatment for sex offenders (Haugaard & Reppucci, 1988; Ingersoll & Patton, 1990; Maletzky & McGovern, 1990; O'Donahue & Letourneau, 1993). Writers differ as to *whether group treatment should be the primary treatment of choice,* long-term, supplemented by individual therapy on a diminishing frequency basis, which would be the first choice of this writer. Some treatment programs employ two forms of group treatment: one for offenders only and one for couples or, in some cases, entire families formed into groups.

There are biases built into most social workers' education, and perhaps into our culture in a broader way, that tend to prejudice therapists and, through them, clients in favor of individual therapy as being deeper and more effective—in short, better. Such an assumption, often unexamined, characterizes many treatment programs. Assertions are blithely made about readiness for group treatment, who can and who cannot be treated in groups, the issue of confidentiality, the unbearable strains supposedly placed not only on group members but also on group therapists, and other reasons why group treatment can work as a supplement to individual therapy but not as the primary modality for service delivery. The suggestion here is that if a reader is faced with some of the projective rationalizations cited, an appropriate response is to smile and ask calmly for the research findings that support such anti-group treatment views. None will be cited, for there are none that support such views. A good follow-up for social workers of the individualistic heresy is to prescribe a careful reading of Falck (1988).

Most sex offenders have violated both the legal codes and the civilized norms of sexual interaction. They have also demonstrated an inability to understand the concepts of individual boundaries and rights. *These represent failures of learning, either from socialization in general or from interpersonal and group experiences in particular. Group experience is the primary setting in which such failures can be remedied through new learnings.* As one participates as a social worker in treatment groups with sex offenders, one is frequently struck by the lack of empathic ability, in the literal sense of being unable to take or understand others' roles, that many group members display. One may also observe a woodenness and lack of skill in understanding any aspect of others' communications beyond the literal.

As mentioned above, there are two routes to membership in sex offenders' groups. The first is adjudication. In effect, those found guilty of sexual offenses are given the "choice" of attending a treatment program or going to prison. For such group members, and for groups composed entirely of such (actually) involuntary members, the *fact that membership is involuntary is a major issue with which the group must deal if it is to form in any genuine sense.* Confidentiality, at least within the group, is less of an issue since the facts of the members' deviant sexual activity are known, at least to the court and, often, the correctional system. With regard to the outside world, *confidentiality is a major issue, especially if reports of group attendance and/or participation need to be made to a court, a parole officer, or another official.*

Nor are issues of authority resolved by one discussion, even an extensive one. Issues of authority, the involuntary nature of the group, and the power that the court or social agency has over members in terms of compelling attendance tend to resurface repeatedly. If the group is having the desired effect, each resurfacing of this concern will be a bit less intense and the group members themselves will be able to reassert the group's purpose and the group's contract progressively more easily as time goes on.

The second route to membership is a voluntary one, undertaken by the group member without the coercion of the court, even though fear of being arrested and prosecuted is often a strong motivating factor for seeking treatment. For such members, confidentiality is an overwhelming concern. The sexual behaviors involved may have been hidden—may still be, for that matter—from significant others in the group member's life. Often, such *group members express such an intense terror of exposure* that one cannot help wondering whether this "coming out" is something that some people both fear and want, even though the latter desire may well be unconscious.

There is no lack of evidence that victims of sex offenders can suffer serious, long-term harm. Lives can be blighted and sexual activity turned from the natural route to connectedness with a loving partner and expression of one's deepest impulses, as it should be, to an area of life poisoned by fear and degradation (see, e.g., Allgeier et al., 1999; Donaldson & Cordes-Green, 1994; Haugaard & Reppucci, 1988; Mandell & Damon, 1989, pp. 1–4; Roth, 1993). Nonetheless, *denial remains a prominent theme for many sessions of many sex offenders' groups.* This denial takes several forms. One is that the person has been wrongly accused and wrongly charged. Either the act of which the member is accused did not take place or it did not take place in the manner described. The group member is, according to this pattern, the real victim: being set up by a vengeful spouse, being persecuted by the police, wrongly accused in an atmosphere of hysteria.

Another variation is that the offender hasn't done anything that others do not do. The main difference is that the offender got caught. Group members will sometimes seek to get confirmation by going around the group and interrogating others—sometimes including the worker—about their sexual activities. Again, often there is said to be a villain in the piece: the spouse, a relative of the victim, a misunderstanding and unsympathetic bystander, a nosy neighbor, or some other person who butted in.

One of the most disturbing versions of denial places the major blame on the victim. The rape victim was seductively clothed and "was just asking for it." The stepdaughter was flirtatious: "The kid just came over and sat right down on my lap." Without in any way questioning the fact that children, especially adolescents, can be seductive, and that some victims of sexual assault wear short skirts, it is very important that these behaviors be reinterpreted in the group as *not* being invitations to coercive, illegal, and destructive sexual activity. "I couldn't help myself" is an avoidance of responsibility and a copout. It is often a false, *post facto* rationalization.

Substance abuse and dependence and their role in the offending behaviors are often the "uninvited guests" in offenders' treatment groups. Patterns of dealing with this content vary widely. The substance use may be part of what is denied. Alternatively, it may be used as a justification and explanation for the behavior. "I was really stoned out of my mind and barely remember what happened" is a characteristic presentation from this stance. The message of the group needs to emphasize the issue of responsibility with regard to the substance use as well as the sexual behavior. Experience has taught this writer of the truth of the position generally taken by experts in substance abuse: unless the abuse/addiction is being treated effectively, by whatever means, treatment for other pathologies is usually wasted. Gains dissolve into the pattern of abuse or addiction.

"I/a man/someone like me/a person of my background/she gotta have it" is another characteristic theme. Often this is combined with accusing the worker—or other members—of not being able to understand because they are so different from the group member talking. The essence of the group's message, and the worker's, should be that sexual drives, urges, and appetites are strong, real, and natural, but need to be and can be under the conscious control of their owners. A great deal is yet to be learned about what Money (1986) has called *lovemaps,* the patterns of sexual attraction that each person develops. The *DSM-IV, TR,* the *Diagnostic and Statistical Manual* edition 4, Text Revision (2000), of the American Psychiatric Association clearly identifies various paraphilias as disorders. The culture of victimhood however, is not helpful for sex offenders, whether individually or in groups, since it relieves one of responsibility for one's actions. In the short run, such a stance is countertherapeutic. In the long run, it holds out only the "hopes" of death or incarceration for life, since it denies the possibility of change that is, at least partly, under the individual's control.

Several of these themes are alternative forms of a presentation for self as *helpless* in the face of internal and external sexual cues. Altering and reversing this view of one's own sexuality and sexual appetites is the major task of these treatment groups. Support, skill teaching, learning alternative ways of structuring time, and, strangely enough, legitimating a healthy frequency and intensity of sexual activities with an appropriate and consenting partner are other positive outputs of treatment groups. Why is legitimating sexual activity needed? Although one should always be aware of the dangers of stereotyping, a surprising proportion of sex offenders view sexual activity as illicit, as needing to be imposed on others by force or other coercive means. The concept of their being viewed as sexually desirable is mind-boggling.

Case

Neal was attending the group as part of a plan worked out with the state's attorney's office after having admitted to an incestuous relationship with his daughter, who had been in his custody, from ages 11 to 14. (The daughter had been removed to another state by her grandparents, with whom she now was living.) Neal told the group that something unexpected had happened to him this past week. He had been advertising a room in his house since he needed the money and had three extra bedrooms. About two months ago, a woman named Sybil had rented the room. She seemed a pleasant enough person who paid her rent on time, but conversation between the two of them had been limited to brief inquiries about using the washing machine and where to get one's shoes fixed. The other night, Sybil, who is 28, knocked on his bedroom door and asked whether he would like some company. This led, the following night, to the two of them going out to dinner and then "'making love,' as she likes to call it." In the group discussion, Neal revealed that he had never before had a sexual experience with a woman older than 18, the age his wife had been when she left him. Group members interrogated Neal thoroughly to make sure that the activity had been voluntary, and combined congratulating him with sympathy and warnings about how he needed to learn to treat Sybil.

PRACTICE PRINCIPLES

In working with sex offenders, it is particularly important to avoid going to extremes: being seduced into accepting the group members' views of the world or viewing the group members as loathesome and less than human. Either set of perceptions and attitudes on the part of the worker is both unhelpful to the group and poses a serious danger of burnout for the worker. One worker said that working with groups of offenders had the danger of turning her into a "prohibitionist," an antisex erotophobe.

Worker boundaries need to be kept. Testing of the worker may include inquiries about the worker's own sexual past and present. One needs to be both transparent as to one's feelings and responses in the group and reserved with regard to a sphere of privacy in one's own life. Perhaps most difficult, one needs to feel legitimated in both spheres as a worker.

It is useful to provide some structure for group meetings. For long-term, open-ended groups, one fruitful technique is to "bridge" from one meeting to another. This involves using some time—say, the last 5 or 10 minutes of a meeting—to summarize learnings from this meeting and to plan together the content, or at least the starting points, of the next meeting.

Shorter-term groups and groups with fixed life spans—say, 12 meetings over 12 weeks—can be problematic in treating sex offenders. These groups often move slowly for quite a while. Members need to get involved in looking at attitudes and behaviors they may have learned over a long period of time or even an entire lifetime. Genuine change is rarely dramatic but needs to be processed over time. Sometimes membership is not under the worker's control.

In a group that meets within a correctional facility, for example, a person may have completed the term of a sentence, or may have been released on parole, and may leave the group as a result. Generally, however, it is good practice to contract with members for participation in the group as a relatively long-term commitment that will pay long-term rewards to the member and to the group as a whole.

As a worker/therapist, one should mistrust sudden conversions, protestations of "seeing the light," and professions of virtue. There is what may be called a *culture of conning* that surrounds many inpatient and outpatient correctional processes, and those noted here are among the classic signs that this culture is at work.

Violence is absolutely antithetical to group work and group process. As a worker, you should share with the group what your response will be should any violence be threatened or undertaken. You should make the necessary administrative and logistical arrangements to act on your statements and should do so at the first hint that interpersonal violence is even being seriously contemplated.

Cotherapy is sometimes very productive, as with a mixed-sex coleadership team with sexually assaultive men. However, coworking takes careful thought, attention, and follow-through. Unless you have a positive reason for coworking (see Introduction, this volume), a solo worker format is recommended.

Do not, under any circumstances, make "deals" with group members, no matter how innocent they may appear. Subgroups or entire groups may participate in a "splitting" process in which an attempt is made to split the worker from the sponsoring organization. Don't be seduced into doing this. If you have tensions or problems with the organization, find productive means for dealing with them but leave them outside of the group.

Do be creative with program techniques, discussion starters, and ways of posing problems for the group to consider. Often newspaper articles, television stories, or readily available video clips do well and introduce a productive note. As noted above, sex is often hard to talk about, and deviant and criminal sex harder yet.

EVALUATION

Groups for the treatment of sex offenders have objectives that are unique to groups of this type, objectives shared with some other types of groups, and objectives shared with groups in general. The evaluation plan should be discussed and requisite permissions obtained at the time a member joins the group, if it is an open-ended group, or at the time the group begins, if it is a closed-ended group.

The unique objective is the prevention of repeat offenses, and every treatment group should be evaluated in terms of success in achieving this objective. It will generally be necessary to obtain information from other sources in addition to group members' reports. Permission to get this information from, for example, police records will need to be obtained from voluntary group members; those adjudicated are generally viewed as having waived their right to privacy with regard to criminal conduct or have signed such a waiver as a condition of having been released on parole or placed on probation. Family members, those sharing living quarters, and friends may also serve as sources of information, although discretion must be used and permission obtained, in most cases, to use these sources.

As with other types of treatment groups, pre-during-post measurements may be sought in an attempt to accomplish two purposes. The first is evaluation of the effectiveness of the group. The second is the stimulus it provides to members to reflect on their experiences in the group and on their meaning.

This writer is committed to the value of feedback *during* the sessions because it can be useful to the worker and the group members in modifying the content, process, or time allocations of the group. All too often, the post measurements provide feedback that, were there time to act on it, would have made the group more meaningful, effective, or satisfying to its members. When these data are available in an organized way only when the group has finished or is about to finish its life span, the most one can do is seek to apply the knowledge gained to future group experiences.

Experience with both structured and precoded questionnaires, on the one hand, and with less structured one-page questionnaires with four to five questions and space for comments, on the other, have demonstrated both that each kind can furnish valuable information and that each kind can be sabotaged. Clearly there are situations—when one is taking part in a study involving many groups, for example—in which structured instruments, tested for validity and reliability, are preferred. What is most important, however, is the willingness of the worker—and, where appropriate, the group—to *listen to and hear* the data and the feedback they provide.

RESOURCES

Justice Research and Statistics
   Association
www.JRSA.org
Provides links to resources including
   state agencies which conduct
   programs for juvenile sex offenders

Peace and Healing
www.peaceandhealing.com

State of Colorado; *See* North Cottage
   Program for Sex Offenders
www.doc.state.co.us

REFERENCES

Allgeier, R., Allgeier, A. R., & Allgeier, E. R. (1999). *Sexual interactions* (5th ed.). Lexington, MA: D. C. Heath.

Barnard, G. W., Fuller, A. K., Robbins, L., & Shaw, T. (1989). *The child molester: An integrated approach to evaluation and treatment.* New York: Brunner/Mazel.

Bettelheim, B., & Janowitz, M. (1964). *Social change and prejudice, including dynamics of prejudice.* New York: Free Press.

Bureau of Justice Statistics, US Dept. of Justice (2002). *Crime and the nation's households, with trends, 1994–2000.* Washington, DC: Government Printing Office, Sept. (NCJ 194107)

Bureau of Justice Statistics, US Dept. of Justice (2000). *Sexual assault of young children as reported to law enforcement: Victim, incident and offender characteristics.* Washington: Government Printing Office, July.

Conrad, P., & Schneider, J. W. (1992). *Deviance and medicalization: From badness to sickness* (expanded ed.). Philadelphia: Temple University Press.

D'Emiio, J., & Freedman, E. G. (1988). *Intimate matters: A history of sexuality in America.* New York: Harper & Row.

Diagnostic and statistical manual of mental disorders. (4th ed., Text Revision) (DSM-IV). (2000). Washington, DC: American Psychiatric Press.

Doll, L. S., Petersen, L. R., White, C. R., Johnson, E. S., Ward, E. W., & the Blood Donor Study Group. (1992). Homosexually and nonhomosexually identified men who have sex with men: A behavioral comparison. *Journal of Sex Research.* 29, 1–14.

Donaldson, M. A., & Cordes-Green, S. (1994). *Group treatment of adult incest survivors.* Thousand Oaks, CA: Sage.

Falck, H. S. (1988). *Social work practice: The membership approach.* New York: Springer.

Haugaard, J. J., & Reppucci, N. D. (1988). *The sexual abuse of children.* San Francisco: Jossey-Bass.

Horton, A. L., Johnson, B. L., Roundy, L. M., & Williams, D. (eds.) (1990). *The incest perpetrator: A family member no one wants to treat.* Newbury Park, CA: Sage.

Ingersoll, S. L., & Patton, S. O. (1990). *Treating perpetrators of sexual abuse.* Lexington, MA: D. C. Heath.

Maletzky, B., & McGovern, K. B. (1990). *Treating the sexual offender.* Newbury Park, CA: Sage.

Masters, W. H., Johnson V. E., & Kolodny, R. C. (1986). *Sex and human loving.* Boston: Little, Brown.

Money, J. (1986). *Lovemaps: Clinical concepts of sexual/erotic health and pathology, paraphilia, and gender transposition in childhood, adolescence and maturity.* New York: Irvington.

Money, J. (1994). *Reinterpreting the unspeakable: Human sexuality 2000.* New York: Continuum.

O'Donohue, W., & Letourneau, E. (1993). A brief group treatment for the modification of denial in child sexual abuses: Outcome and follow-up. *Child Abuse and Neglect.* 17, 299–304.

Pithers, W. D., Kashima, K. M., Cumming, G. F., & Beal, L. S. (1988). Relapse prevention: A method of enhancing maintenance of change in sex offenders. In A. Salter (ed.), *Treating child sex offenders and victims: A practical guide.* Newbury Park, CA: Sage.

Roth, N. (1993). *Integrating the shattered self: Psychotherapy with adult incest survivors.* Northvale, NJ: Jason Aronson.

Rutan, J. S., & Stone, W. N. (1993). *Psychodynamic group psychotherapy* (2nd ed.). New York: Guilford Press.

Salter, A. C. (ed.). (1988). *Treating child sex offenders and victims: A practical guide.* Newbury Park, CA: Sage.

Scaveo, R. R. (1989). Female adolescent sex offenders: A neglected treatment group. *Social Casework.* 70, 114–117.

Shaffer, J., & Galinsky, M. D. (1989). *Models of group therapy* (2nd ed.). Englewood Cliffs, NJ: Prentice-Hall.

Vance, C. S. (Ed.). (1984). *Pleasure and danger: Exploring female sexuality.* Boston: Routledge & Kegan Paul.

Whitaker, D. L., & Wodarski, J. S. (1988). Treatment of sexual offenders in a community mental health center: An evaluation. *Journal of Social Work and Human Sexuality.* 7, 49–68.

Zilbergeld, B. (1999). *The new male sexuality.* Rev. ed. New York: Bantam Books.

Chapter 18

Group Work with Sexually Abused Children

SHARON S. ENGLAND AND
KAY MARTEL CONNORS

Although not all sexually abused children and adults who were molested as children will experience emotional, physical, and sexual problems, those who do require professional intervention and treatment. Group work has become the most common form of treatment, if not the treatment of choice, with this population, especially with child victims (Faller, 1988, p. 377; Mandell & Damon, 1989, p. 2; Sturkie, 1992, p. 332).

DEFINITION OF CHILD SEXUAL ABUSE

Child sexual abuse can be defined as the commission of a sex act on a child under 18 years of age by an adult (and in some cases an older child). The abuser may be a family member, a trusted adult, or a stranger. The abuse can be contact or non-contact behavior, such as using children in pornography. Contact behavior includes non-genital and genital contact and intercourse. Child sexual abuse may be situational or chronic; physical violence may or may not occur (Milner, 1998, p. 149–150).

REVIEW OF THE LITERATURE

The impact of child sexual abuse has been the subject of much study and research. Accordingly, there now is abundant literature available to beginning social workers exploring the causes, characteristics, and treatment of this complex social problem. Finkelhor (1986) reports that the evidence "conveys a clear suggestion that sexual abuse is a serious mental health problem, consistently associated with very disturbing subsequent problems in a significant portion of its victims" (p. 152) Sexually abused children's vulnerability to mental health disorders is often compounded by poor attachments, parental stress and mental illness, and other socioeconomic risk factors (Trowell et al., 2002). Externalizing behaviors associated with the impact of sexual abuse include aggression, oppositional behaviors, conduct disorders and delinquency; while internalizing behaviors include anxiety, depression, withdrawal and posttraumatic stress disorder. In addition, low self esteem and interpersonal relationships are often problematic (Valle & Silovsky, 2002).

In attempting to explain this complex social problem and its sequelae, researchers have investigated differences in factors, such as abuse (e.g., duration, severity), family (e.g., maternal mental health), socioeconomic risk factors (e.g., poverty), and child characteristics (e.g., age, gender). One of the most interesting factors influencing adjustment outcomes is children's cognitions, including attributions associated with the abuse and children's use of coping strategies (Valle & Silovsky, 2002). Children may attribute sexual abuse to internal or external factors, including attributions such as self-blame and responsibility, lack of control and the dangerousness of the world. In an effort to negate long-term mental health and adjustment problems, group therapy can have an impact on these cognitive factors by setting forth treatment goals to increase self esteem, reduce isolation, strengthen coping skills, and promote attachment behaviors (Connors & Schamess, 1999).

Despite the enormous needs of this population, Friedrich (1990) reports that much of the treatment of child sexual abuse "is frequently relegated to a continually changing group of novice therapists" (p. 277). Therefore, it behooves beginning group leaders to prepare and to obtain as much guidance as possible before attempting to conduct groups or any other type of treatment with sexually abused children. Sources that discuss the history, dynamics, characteristics, impact, cultural variations, and treatment of child sexual abuse include Finkelhor (1986, 1995), Friedrich (1990), Kilpatrick (1992), Milner (1998), O'Donahue and Geer (1992), and Renvoize (1993). Resources that address group work with sexually abused children include Berman (1994, 1999), Crisci et al. (1997), DeLuca et al. (1999), Faller (1988), Friedrich (1990), Mandell and Damon (1989), Sgroi (1982), Sturkie (1992), and Hack et al. (1994). Beginning group leaders will find that child sexual abuse prevention curricula, including those of Harms and James (1983) and Schonfield (1984), also are good sources for assistance in leading groups of sexually abused children.

Trauma researchers have noted reductions in post-traumatic stress symptoms during group work as well as after group treatment (Trowell et al., 2002). Although proponents of group work have not yet agreed on the best approach, both cognitive-behavioral and supportive groups have been effective. In preparing for group work with sexually abused children, social workers should incorporate a developmental approach that includes interventions that focus on the impact of the traumatic experience(s) (retelling the trauma story), the management of traumatic reminders (coping with traumatic triggers and flashbacks) and coping with secondary adversities (e.g., removal from home, maternal response, etc.) (McFarlane, 1996).

Conducting groups with sexually abused children is very demanding and challenging. Social workers planning to conduct such groups must possess great creativity, initiative, and persistence. Since group work with children requires interaction with child participants, their caretakers (parents, guardians, or foster parents), and other professionals, social workers also must become skilled in working with several different client populations and with colleagues.

PRACTICE PRINCIPLES

Several social work practice principles are particularly relevant when conducting groups with sexually abused children. They include empathetic response, self-awareness, contracting, use of authority, dealing with issues of confidentiality, and handling termination.

Empathetic Response

In working with sexually abused children, social workers must create a trusting and safe "holding environment" that contains destructive behaviors while allowing the working-through of very difficult feelings such as anger, fear, rejection, shame, and guilt (Rice-Smith, 1993). Empathy and acceptance are key elements in creating this safe space for child victims. Social workers must develop the capacity to feel deeply what the children are feeling without losing their own perspective (Compton & Galaway, 1989). Empathy enables social workers to join with their clients by better understanding them and communicating to the clients acceptance of their world view. In therapeutic groups, social workers communicate empathy for clients' explicit and implicit feelings. Acceptance of clients' thoughts and behaviors enables them to remember and recount their trauma story in the presence of a "compassionate other" who bears witness to the feelings of powerlessness, helplessness, hopelessness, betrayal, and stigmatization (Heiman & Ettin, 2001).

Self-Awareness

In all social work practice, social workers must constantly strive to maintain objectivity and to identify any personal biases that could have a negative impact on their clients. This is especially true when working with sexually abused children.

Social workers treating this population must recognize their attitudes regarding sexual abuse of children and their own sexuality (Einbender, 1991, p. 115; Faller, 1988, p. 5; Friedrich, 1990, p. 278). Unresolved issues or possible past sexual victimization can interfere with social workers' ability to objectively evaluate their capacity to conduct groups with sexually abused children. Social workers should consult with a supervisor or colleague for help in determining whether they should practice with this population.

Sexual acting-out and the use of childish, sexually explicit, or vulgar language by sexually abused children are common. Often social workers experience discomfort when listening to children discuss their sexual victimization in graphic detail. They must control their inadvertent responses of shock, amusement, and/or disapproval, which can inhibit group discussion.

Conducting groups of culturally diverse children requires group workers to be sensitive to and respectful of different cultures. Man Keung Ho (1992) reports that "Minority clients initially experience difficulty in talking about personal and family problems in a group setting and in front of a stranger who is the group therapist. However, group interaction and group therapy, if properly provided, may have advantages that individual and family therapy do not" (p. 178).

Social workers should not assume that all children will share information that they perceive as unique to their circumstances—as the following example, brought to our attention, illustrates:

> One African-American child told her new African-American therapist that she believed her abuse stemmed from the fact [that] she was darker-skinned than her sister. This revelation led to a discussion of the child's body image and racism. When asked why she had not said this before, the child said she didn't believe her previous white social workers would understand.

Resources that provide social workers with help in treating diverse populations include Devore and Schlesinger (1987), Ho (1992), Lynch and Hanson (1992), and Vacc et al. (1988). Finally, social workers must avoid recreating their child clients' family dynamics. Often children in sexually abusive families have been socialized to consent to, or forced to accept, conduct that was contrary to their best interests. Therefore, social workers should consider the ramifications of asking children to participate in unusual activities, such as interviews with the media or confronting perpetrators. Children's assent may reflect their eagerness to please their social workers rather than comfort with, or willingness to participate in, such activities.

Contracting

Contracting with child clients, their caretakers, and other service providers is invaluable in group work. Contracts provide everyone with clear expectations regarding the purpose of the group, meeting schedule, attendance, transportation, and group rules. Written contracts created and signed by each party facilitate compliance.

Prior to the first group meeting, group workers should interview each child and caretaker if possible. To establish a basis on which to build trust and rapport with children, group workers should use this initial meeting to clarify the purpose and goals of the group. In the authors' experience, children often are given vague or no reasons for attending groups. Sometimes referring social workers may not have had time to explain the group's purpose adequately, or the explanation may have been given long before the group began. Caretakers, wishing to avoid a child's discomfort or refusal to attend, may be uncomfortable or reluctant about discussing the reason for the child's referral to the group. Therefore, it is advisable for group leaders to regularly review and clarify the purpose during subsequent group sessions as well.

As the group will become an important source of support to children, consistent attendance is critical. Group leaders should discuss the children's transportation at this introductory meeting. Various methods should be considered, including coordinating a carpool with other social workers, asking an outside funding source to finance a bus service, providing bus tokens for older children, and arranging for caretakers to transport their own children. The last method is generally used when parents' groups are held simultaneously with the children's.

Group leaders should help groups establish rules at the first group meeting. To facilitate adherence to rules, children should be encouraged to participate in this process. Generally, children will make many suggestions. The rules can then be written down and posted in the group room.

Use of Authority

Social workers must consider their use of authority with this population and take the time necessary to help children overcome their natural resistance in groups rather than force them into uncomfortable situations. To promote group cohesion and trust, all children should be informed and willing participants.

Sexually abused children may have maladaptive control issues that cause them to challenge social workers' exercise of authority. Researchers identify lack of controllability as a defining element of the traumatic experience (Carlson & Dalenberg, 2000). Often, offenders have used and abused their position of authority to gain control over and sexually assault these children (Groth, 1982, p. 224). In the authors' experience, children will generalize this misuse of authority to their social workers and expect them, too, to abuse their authority.

This testing of authority provides an opportunity for constructive learning for the group members. Social workers should anticipate these challenges to their authority and respond so that children can experience authority in a more appropriate manner. First, group leaders must make the limits of their authority clear. At a minimum, children should be told that they will not be permitted to hurt themselves or another group member, nor will they permitted to break or destroy any of the toys or equipment in the playroom.

Second, group leaders should identify and tolerate healthy challenges to their authority even if these challenges frustrate previously planned clinical interventions. These concessions may include allowing children to change a group topic, avoid a group activity, skip a meeting, or even leave the group. Often children who are beginning to experience empowerment through the treatment process will test both their ability to exert control over their own lives and their social workers' promise of support by withdrawing from the group or other forms of treatment. Invariably, these children can be dissuaded more effectively from leaving treatment with sensitive guidance and patience than by an overt refusal. In the authors' experience, children who are permitted to exercise control in these areas do not withdraw permanently from the group or treatment.

Finally, social workers should consider these dynamics before recommending that a child be court-ordered to attend a group. Group members require a high degree of trust and comfort to discuss their sexual abuse experiences. Such discussions do not occur easily. When children are coerced into attending groups, they can become resistant. As a result, other members may become inhibited, fearing that the resistant member will not respect their revelations and keep them confidential.

Dealing with Confidentiality

It is unrealistic and erroneous to tell children that everything they say is confidential. It is important, however, for children to know which information will be shared with their caretakers and other professionals. Group leaders should tell all children that if they say anything indicating that they may be or have been abused or hurt again, either by themselves or by others, their group leaders will take action to protect them. This statement should be made in the initial interview and reiterated throughout the life of the group. If a child's statement must be revealed, group leaders should inform the child of the decision and the reasons.

In the authors' experience, this message does not inhibit children's discussion or revelations. Children will continue to reveal important information, counting on social workers to act responsibly and to take protective action on their behalf. When social workers give unrealistic assurances of confidentiality or fail to take protective action, children can be harmed and their trust irrevocably broken.

Depending on the caretakers' status as parents, guardians, or foster parents, they and the children should be informed about what they can expect to learn from their child's group participation. Group workers should discourage caretakers from questioning children about group discussions and activities. Group workers also should tell children how to handle unwanted questions from caretakers and other children. They should reiterate the importance of the group as a safe haven from parental intrusion and emphasize other group participants' need for confidentiality with members and caretakers.

Handling Termination

Termination issues in groups should be handled with the utmost concern and attention. Group therapists must not only pay attention to the structured activities planned for the end of group, but to the process as well. Sexually abused children often have experienced many abrupt and traumatic endings in their lives. They may have been removed from their homes on disclosure of the sexual abuse. Parents or other family members accused of the abuse may have been incarcerated or forced to leave the home. There may have been little or no opportunity to say goodbye to family members or neighborhood friends. The reality of these traumatic, abrupt endings in these children's lives should be considered in determining guidelines for group termination. Failing to do so can hinder children's social adjustment and progress in treatment.

In one group consisting of latency-aged sexually abused girls, the group leaders failed to address termination issues. The group was open-ended, with no planned termination. As members grew too old for the group they left, sometimes abruptly. The group leaders failed to address the needs of both the girls departing and those left behind. Members perceived the departures as a rejection. When asked to draw pictures of their group, girls included former group members who had left months earlier while omitting new members. These girls leaving the group felt no sense of completion. Recognizing that the group was exacerbating the girls' chaotic lives, the group leaders attempted to redefine these endings. But the poorly handled departures proved to have a more lasting impact than the subsequent intervention. Finally, the group leaders closed entry into the group and began to work on termination issues with the remaining members. Eventually, the group was disbanded.

Social workers conducting groups with sexually abused children should provide a well-defined termination process. "Sensitivity to the process allows the healing power of the group to be harnessed" (Heiman & Ettin, 2001). Short-term or time-limited structured groups, with or without closed membership, can facilitate this process. By making group termination an expected and positive outcome, social workers can help children plan more thoroughly for endings. They can encourage children to explore their feelings about the group's conclusion and their past unhealthy departures.

COMMON THEMES

Several common themes have been observed in treating sexually abused children. The seven themes discussed below are not an exhaustive list.

Social workers should be aware that traumatized children have difficulty putting feelings into words. Instead, they are prone to acting out their feelings and are often unable to resort to language and attachment behaviors that promote flexible and adaptive coping strategies (van der Kolk, 1994).

Fear

Fear has been identified in both empirical and clinical literature as the most common effect of child sexual abuse (Berliner, 1991, p. 99; Finkelhor, 1986, p. 149; Porter et al., 1982, p. 117). Typically, children fear repeated abuse, the consequences of sexual activity, and retaliation and separation from their families (Johnson, 1991, p. 279; Porter et al., 1982, p. 117; Sturkie, 1992, p. 333).

It is important to help children distinguish between realistic and unrealistic fears. Children's fears are reasonable when the perpetrator has continued access to the child, the child is not believed or supported by a caretaker, or the child is exposed to unsafe situations. If these conditions exist, social workers must advocate for changes in children's environment and/or for caretakers' participation in treatment. Otherwise, progress in group or any other treatment is unlikely.

Diane, Mary, and George participated in a child sexual abuse treatment program, along with their mother. Their father, who had molested and seriously beaten the children several times, had been convicted and incarcerated. The children revealed that their mother punished them by sending them to the "ghost room," the room where the abuse frequently had taken place. The group leaders alerted the mother's social workers to persuade her to use another means of discipline.

Anger

Anger is another common reaction to child sexual abuse (Finkelhor, 1986, p. 149). Often children express anger toward the caretaker who had not protected them from the abuse or who had not responded protectively after the abuse was revealed. "Many victims say little initially because they are afraid to confront their own anger and unsure of their ability to handle their feelings. They compensate by being unassertive and by saying as little as possible" (Porter et al., 1982, p. 121).

It is critical to give children permission and opportunities to identify and work through this anger in order to make progress in other areas of treatment. Groups can provide a safe forum to express and explore these angry feelings. "This process can be facilitated by the use of exercises that make the feelings concrete and direct them at an appropriate target, after they are identified" (Porter, 1986, p. 56). Techniques such as role plays, punching bags, letter writing, and art therapy are particularly helpful in helping children ventilate and examine their feelings.

Guilt

Guilt and shame are frequent reactions to child sexual abuse (Finkelhor, 1986, p. 149; Porter, et al., 1982, p. 115). Children may perceive themselves to be responsible for the sexual abuse, its disclosure, and the resulting family disruption.

> Mary, age 13, was blamed for her grandfather's incarceration and subsequent fatal heart attack. Eight-year-old Vicki believed herself to be an unfit "parent" who caused her five siblings to be placed in three different foster homes. Vicki's father forced her to adopt her deceased mother's parental and marital role. Disclosure occurred when neighborhood children saw Vicki's father raping her through the bedroom window. Cindy, age 10, felt shame for experiencing pleasure during oral sex with her aunt.

Unfortunately, children's guilty feelings often are aggravated by their family's, community's, and professionals' attitudes and responses. "Amazingly, the perpetrator's assertion that a seductive child is responsible for the sexual behavior is often given credence by judges, attorneys, police officers, physicians, social workers, and the like" (Porter et al., 1982, p. 115). Some children, however, will need help to identify "appropriate guilt feelings" when they have used their "favored position" to manipulate and behave inappropriately toward others (Porter et al., 1982, p. 117).

In the author's experience, the belief that sexually abused children are irrevocably damaged and without innocence is a prevalent attitude. The mere statement that "it's not your fault" does little to extinguish these children's guilty feelings. Addressing this normalization of children's guilt is most appropriate for a group setting, where children can receive constant and consistent reassurance from their peers through group discussion and structured activities.

Depression

Depression, suicide, and self-mutilation have been observed in both sexually abused children and adults (Beitchman et al., 1992; Pisaruk et al., 1992; Young, 1992). Young reports that self-abuse may occur when survivors believe they cannot trust their own bodies because they feel vulnerable or shame or because they felt some pleasure while the abuse was occurring. Social workers should evaluate all children in treatment for child sexual abuse for possible depression and suicidal ideation.

> Sarah, 11, who was forced to perform oral sex on her mother, slashed at her wrist with a pen knife, put broken glass in her mouth, threatened to swallow the pieces, and kept several doctors, nurses, and social workers at bay before she was finally hospitalized. Eight-year-old Michah, who was sexually abused by her mother's three boyfriends, reported to her group that she planned to jump out of her second-story window onto

the concrete pavement below. Terry, six years old, lay down in the middle of a busy street in an attempt to kill herself.

Inability to Trust

Sexually abused children's impaired ability to trust themselves, adults, and other children has been reported in the clinical literature (Einbender, 1991, p. 115; Mandell & Damon, 1989, p. 1; Porter et al., 1982, p. 121). Social workers often are viewed with suspicion rather than seen as a source of protection and support.

Often this impairment of trust is manifested by children's frequent testing of social workers' trustworthiness, which may be confused with challenges to social workers' authority. Group leaders' cancellation of group sessions, broken promises, and alliances with other children or authority figures can be viewed as rejections and evidence of group leaders' untrustworthiness.

Einbender (1991) reports that "sexually abused children often take longer to form a trusting relationship with the therapist that is secure enough to allow them to begin to explore the actual abuse" (p. 115).

Anxiety Regarding Legal and Court Intervention

It is important that social workers dealing with sexually abused children understand both the criminal and civil legal systems. Often children will require assistance in understanding both the purpose and the outcome of legal intervention. Children may experience fear or anxiety about testifying in court, retaliation by the perpetrator, not being believed, being on trial themselves, or embarrassing questions on the witness stand (O'Donohue & Geer, 1992, vol. 2, p. 298).

By contrast, some children demand to have "their day in court" and become angry if they are not allowed to testify at trial or at sentencing. Green (1992) reports that testifying in court has potential advantages, including giving children an active role in mastering the trauma, offering children a chance to be believed and to see justice work, and providing children a constructive outlet for their anger (p. 298).

Children also may feel dejected after completion of the court process, despite the outcome. Sometimes, at the conclusion of court intervention, social workers, investigators, police, and prosecutors may discontinue or curtail their services to children, thus leaving the children to cope with the aftermath of court intervention alone.

Delayed Development and Socialization Skills

Finally, many sexually abused children experience significant delays in their development and socialization skills (Friedrich, 1990, p. 25; Mandel & Damon, 1989, p. 1). As a result, children's communication, negotiation, and play skills can be hampered. These delays can thwart the development of rapport, cohesion, and trust among the members and, consequently, the promotion of group goals.

Therefore, "intervention must also be geared to the enhancement of age-appropriate skills" (Mandel & Damon, 1989, p. 2). But social workers' premature intervention in group members' interactions and conflicts may deny children critical learning experiences. Group workers must strike a delicate balance between doing too much or too little when helping children overcome these developmental delays and acquire appropriate socialization skills. Intervention must be constructive, without denying group members opportunities to work out conflicts and to learn cooperative play and negotiation skills on their own.

RECOMMENDED WAYS OF WORKING

Establishing a Group Within an Agency

Group work can occur in almost any agency setting. Conducting groups within agencies typically is fraught with difficulties, however. Besides having to convince sometimes-skeptical administrators about the value and effectiveness of group treatment, social workers must struggle to ensure that adequate space and supplies are available. These efforts to establish or fortify an existing group within an agency can be just as important as the clinical techniques used during each group session.

The availability of a regular group room to promote privacy, consistency, and access to art and play supplies to encourage group interaction and communications is important in promoting rapport and trust among the members. Unfortunately, such resources and supplies are often difficult to obtain in agencies with budget and space limitations. Social workers' initiative and ingenuity are essential to overcoming these obstacles.

> In one urban agency, group leaders effectively advocated the conversion of a staff room to a child's play room. They negotiated for the exclusive use of the room for evening group sessions, while agency social workers were given daily access to conduct child interviews. Another group leader got several donations from community toy and art stores. The result: an exceptionally well-stocked playroom well beyond the agency's limited budget.

Group Structure

The developmental age of the members and the purpose of the group are critical in determining the structure of the group. Younger children require less autonomy and are generally more comfortable with a structure similar to a school setting that provides order and consistency. Agendas that include time for free play, organized group play, a snack, and group discussion can be used. Adolescents require more autonomy and should be encouraged to participate in determining the group's structure and activities.

Groups designed to provide children intensive therapy or long-term support usually are longer and open, allowing old members to leave and new ones to enter. As previously discussed, group leaders should take special care to address children's termination and separation issues. Also, new members should be added in pairs or threes to reduce possible discomfort and the feeling of not belonging.

Educational groups and groups formed for child abuse prevention, parenting, teenage sexuality, socialization and play skills, and so on can be shorter-term, with closed membership. These groups are usually more structured, with specific information to be conveyed and discussed at each meeting.

The size of the group also is determined by such factors as the developmental age of its members. Younger groups should be smaller, with six to eight children. Adolescent groups can be larger, with 10 members being the upper limit. These numbers can be increased if there are co-leaders.

Group leaders also must consider the composition of their groups. They must be careful to distinguish between children's chronological age and developmental age.

> Yvonne, a physically mature 12-year-old, had been sexually abused by her mother's boyfriend and sexually active with neighborhood boys for over a year. Her placement in a latency-aged group was fraught with difficulties. Yvonne wanted to discuss her sexual experiences with her boyfriend, while the other members could not comprehend why anyone would engage in sex willingly. Group leader suggested an early graduation for Yvonne and transferred her to the older adolescent group.

Group leaders can successfully combine latency-aged boys and girls in a group setting. Such a mixture provides many positive experiences for both sexes. Boys, who generally are more reticent about discussing their sexual victimization, often become less reluctant on listening to girls describe their experiences. Girls, whose most significant contact with older boys and men has been abusive, are provided an opportunity to experience males in more positive ways.

> Rose, eight years old, was sexually assaulted by a neighborhood boy. She declared that she did not trust boys and was afraid to even touch them. This announcement led Tom, also eight and a typically disruptive and inattentive group member, to offer to shake Rose's hand. Although Rose initially refused, Tom continued thoughtfully to offer his hand throughout the meeting. Eventually, Rose accepted his gesture. This interchange led to a discussion of Rose's diminished aversion to boys and recognition of Tom's persistent efforts to comfort and nurture another group member.

In the author's experience, the combination of boys and girls in one group makes it important to have both a male and a female co-leader. Group leaders should be prepared, though, for the children's tendency to sexualize the relationship between the leaders.

> When setting the table for a snack, the group members consistently seated the two group leaders together. When asked why, the children said they thought the leaders would want to be together since they were married or boyfriend and girlfriend. In other groups, children frequently asked if the group leaders were dating or married.

The decision on whether the group should be co-led is important. There are both advantages and disadvantages. Co-leaders can give each other support and encouragement and an opportunity to talk over the group process with another colleague. Continuity problems are reduced when one leader is absent. Also, having two observers reduces the likelihood of missing important interchanges among the members.

When groups are co-led, however, leaders can dominate the group process and the service is more costlier. Social workers should carefully analyze their ability to conduct a group with each other. Dissension or personality conflicts between group leaders will be readily apparent to members and can dramatically impair group effectiveness. Yet if the group leaders are aware of possible conflicts and willing to examine them constructively, they can provide excellent opportunities to model conflict-resolution behavior for the group members.

Group Techniques

Once group leaders establish the group and an agenda has been set, the first task is to help group members develop rapport, trust, and cohesion. Activities designed to address children's impaired communication and negotiation skills are particularly helpful.

Ice-breaking games are great for a first group. Young children especially enjoy name games that make the chore of learning new names fun. One favorite is a circle game in which the children and social workers sit in a circle and introduce themselves. The first child says his name; the next says her name and the one before her's; then the next child says his own name and the two before his; and so on. The game can be varied by the child's adding an adjective or animal name with the first letter of the child's name. Names such as Tiger Tim, Shining Sheryl, and Lovable Larry create both a sense of fun and camaraderie among the members as they try to help each other remember the names.

Older children respond well to activities designed to ease their anxiety about the group in more sophisticated and direct ways. Children anonymously write notes that answer the following questions: How do you feel about being in this group? What is one thing you like about this group? What is one thing you do not like about this group? Invariably, the children find that their concerns and fears are quite similar, thus universalizing their experience and building cohesion among them.

Art activities provide excellent opportunities to encourage group cohesion and beginning socialization skills. Group leaders can use art activities inexpensively. If resources are limited, paper and crayons can suffice. One author made frequent use of art activities to facilitate cohesion and discussion in younger children's groups. Initial activities should be simple and require minimal verbal interaction. Subsequent activities should become progressively more involved, requiring more demanding interaction.

Group finger painting is an excellent technique to encourage cohesion and communication at a nonverbal level. The children stand around a table where one large sheet of paper with finger paints is placed. They are told not to talk. As the children design the finger painting, they have fun and experience closeness in a nonthreatening manner. The final product, signed by each member, can be hung in the group room. When group ends, portions are given to each member as a keepsake.

At the next session, a variation on the finger painting, a group collage—a common school activity that requires more verbal interaction, planning, and cooperation—can be used. Children can cut pictures from magazines and paste them on posterboard. To complete the activity, children must negotiate how the space will be used and what media to include in the collage. Invariably, the pictures and captions chosen by the children express volumes about the children's personal issues. The collage can be used to facilitate difficult discussions through the life of the group or can be combined with other techniques, such as Richard Gardner's The *Mutual Story-Telling Technique* (1975, p. 101).

Body tracings, in which the group leader traces the children's bodies as they lie down on long pieces of paper, also can facilitate difficult discussions about sexuality and body image. After children color their tracings, their observations often provoke discussions of many topics, such as virginity, puberty, diseases, medical exams, homosexuality, and pregnancy. Children also use the body tracings to depict their interests in sports, dance, and careers. One boy's body tracing led him to reveal that he had been sexually abused by a woman, not a man, as had been suspected.

> Rose, identified earlier, colored her body entirely in white crayon with a bright red heart that presented a strikingly vulnerable appearance and caused many comments. This tracing prompted Rose to identify her fear of boys, which inspired Tom to offer to shake her hand.

Art activities also can be helpful in encouraging children to discuss their relationships with each other and helping social workers assess the group's development progress. Members can be asked to draw a picture of the group or a picture of the group doing something.

> Nine-year-old Lea was drawn with two mouths in one member's group picture, with an extra-large mouth in another's, and with no mouth in a

third's. When the children were asked why this was so, they readily pointed out that Lea talked too much. A constructive discussion then followed on how Lea's monopolizing of the meeting prevented the other members from talking. The discussion concluded with Lea asking the other girls to tell her when she starts talking too much.

A common attribute of a beginning group is one-upmanship. Often the children describe their sexual abuse experience in a storylike manner, followed by a presentation of the next child's ordeal. This pattern results in superficial discussions. In response, group leaders and children have developed the *stop-name-card game.*

Children are each given a card that they can throw in the center of the table when they want to raise an issue. Before another member can raise a similar or new topic, the current speaker must have finished his or her turn and received appropriate responses from the other members. If a child throws in a card prematurely, the group leaders throw out a red stop card, showing that it is not time to move on to a new person or topic. Eventually, the children ask to have their own stop cards so that they can identify when other members are interrupted prematurely. The result is more meaningful and insightful discussions regarding each child's issue and group process.

A common technique used in groups with older sexually abused children is *letter-writing.* This technique is best presented spontaneously as a solution for children who have trouble talking about their sexual abuse. Members write letters to their perpetrators or nonsupportive caretakers and express their feeling about their abuse. The children can then read their letters aloud, have another member read them silently or aloud, send them to their perpetrators, and/or destroy them.

Role-play is an excellent technique to help children of all ages to express their anger, practice interaction with parents, or cope with anxiety about testifying in court. In one latency-aged girls' group, the leaders attempted to use an "alter-ego" role-play in which a leader planned to whisper responses to a group member while she role-played a conversation with her "mother." As the group leader was awkwardly describing the role-play to the children, Sally jumped up and exclaimed, "I know what you mean." Sally went on to show the technique the social worker was attempting to describe and then chose the most reticent group participant for the role-play.

Eleven-year-old Lorraine was an extremely quiet, timid group member who rarely spoke. Although Lorraine's mother had kicked her boyfriend, the abuser, out the house, Lorraine was angry with her for allowing another boyfriend to move in. As Sally whispered into Lorraine's ear, Lorraine became stronger and more assertive. Within minutes Lorraine was pounding her hand on the table, expressing for the first time, in a raised voice, her anger toward her mother. Following this meeting, Lorraine, with her social worker, confronted her mother. Lorraine also became a less shy and more vocal group member.

Videotaping group members for clinical purposes also can be valuable. One author videotaped a group session to facilitate a discussion of group interaction. This activity led to the identification of a group scapegoat and a productive exchange about how group members can use other members as scapegoats to avoid painful discussions.

> Sally, the helpful child in the previous example, was frequently disruptive. She would often leave the group circle, wander throughout the room, or go to the blackboard and draw. The other children frequently complained about Sally's thus interrupting a valuable discussion of another's child's experiences. Sally behaved in her usual manner in the video. On viewing the video, the children recognized how they actually encouraged Sally to behave badly while complaining about her to avoid painful emotions and discussions. Sally, embarrassed by her behavior, asked the other group members to help her change.

Bibliotherapy, in which children read books or short stories on child sexual abuse or other problems, can be very helpful. Books that focus on child sexual abuse prevention also are beneficial, especially since many of these children have a high risk of future abuse. (A bibliography is provided at the end of this chapter.)

EVALUATION APPROACHES

A review of the literature reveals that many researchers evaluate groups' effectiveness by investigating the amelioration of or reduction in post-traumatic stress symptoms (Trowell et al., 2002; Deblinger, 2001). Although researchers don't always agree on the best method of group treatment—e.g., cognitive-behavioral or supportive—there is some evidence that treatment of young sexual abuse victims is recommended to help reduce current symptoms, as well as prevent potential difficulties (Deblinger, 2001).

Several methods can be used to assess the effectiveness of group intervention. The authors used art, group activity, and group observation to determine the children's progress in treatment. In each short-term closed group, the children were asked to paint their self-portraits at the beginning of the group and again at the end. Each time this was done, both the group leaders and the children noted the marked difference between the portraits.

> Eight-year-old Danny compared his obviously distorted and depressed first portrait with his happier and smiling second portrait and said, "Oh, that one [the first self-portrait] was because of what happened to me [sexual abuse] and how sad I was; the other [second self-portrait] was because I was happier, 'cause I was in group and I got to talk about

everything." Another child had painted bars over his first self-portrait as a symbol of protecting himself from his incarcerated father. His second, healthier portrait had no bars and showed him smiling.

Another technique used to evaluate change and progress in short-term, closed groups was *the group members' session.* To encourage the development of children's communication and cooperative play skills, members were asked to plan the last group session. The only condition was that the session should reflect what the children had learned in the group. Group leaders set aside 10 minutes of several preceding groups so that the children could plan this session without their participation. Generally, this activity was a huge success. Each time, the children planned a well-organized group session that accurately reflected the objectives of the group.

Invariably, the children chose to give a performance, such as a play or puppet show that demonstrated what they had learned in the group. The children's caretakers were invited to this session, which included a graduation ceremony, a display of artwork and projects, and refreshments provided by the group leaders and the children.

Many of the techniques and activities discussed above also provide opportunities to assess the children's progress and group development. Children's spontaneous gestures to help one another are the most significant and positive behaviors social workers can observe in the group. Midway through the group, the children started bringing in special snacks or birthday cakes for each other. Children made extra puppets or projects for times when they thought others would not have one.

Children also would comfort and encourage fellow members during difficult discussions or in anticipation of court hearings. Such conduct shows that group members have attained a healthy degree of trust and cohesion. It also shows an improvement in the children's self-esteem, confidence, and ability to nurture and be nurtured.

CONCLUSION

The authors have found conducting groups with sexually abused children to be a professionally rewarding experience. Group work is one of the most effective treatment modalities for addressing the needs of this vulnerable population. Children who refuse to speak of their abuse and consequently thwart clinical intervention disclose their victimization more readily within groups and experience relief on meeting and hearing from other children with similar experiences. The discovery that they are not alone, combined with the opportunity to help other children, provides group members the most significant curative experience of all.

Although group treatment is an effective aspect of the treatment plan for sexually abused children, social workers will include other interventions as well. Sexually abused children benefit from a combination of individual or family therapy, in addition to collateral social work interventions such as advocacy, referral, and case management (De Luca, 1999).

NATIONAL RESOURCE

National Resource Center on
  Child Sexual Abuse of the
  National Center on Child
  Abuse and Neglect
www.ojjdp.ncjrs.org

REFERENCES

Beitchman, J. H., Zucker, K. J., Hood, J. E., DaCosta, G. A., Akrnan, D., & Cassavia, E. (1992). A review of the long-term effects of child sexual abuse. *Child Abuse and Neglect*. 16, 106–107.

Berliner, L. (1991). Cognitive therapy with a young victim of sexual assault. In W. N. Friedrich (ed.), *Casebook of sexual abuse treatment* (pp. 93–111). New York: W. W. Norton.

Berman, P. (1999). Sexually abused preteen girls. In C. Schaefer (ed.), *Short-term psychotherapy groups for children: Adapting group processes for specific problems* (pp. 139–182). New Jersey: Jason Aronson.

Berman, P. (1994). *Therapeutic exercises for victimized and neglected girls: Applications for individual family and group psychotherapy*. Florida: Professional Resource Press.

Bonanno, G. A., Noll, J. G., Trickett, P. K., Keltner, D., Puttman, F. W., LeJeune, J., & Anderson, C. (2002). When the face reveals what words do not: Facial expressions of emotion, smiling, and the willingness to disclose childhood sexual abuse. *Journal of Personality and Social Psychology*. 83, 94–110.

Carlson, E. B., & Dalenberg, C. J. (2000). A conceptual framework for the impact of traumatic experiences. *Trauma, Violence & Abuse*. 1, 4–28.

Compton, B. R., & Galaway, B. (1989). *Social work processes*. California: Brooks/Cole Publishing Company.

Connors, K. M., & Schamess, G. (1999). Traumatized and neglected children. In C. Schaefer (ed.), *Short-term psychotherapy groups for children: Adapting group processes for specific problems* (pp. 219–248). New Jersey: Jason Aronson.

Crisci, G., Lay M., & Lowenstein, L. (1997). *Paper dolls and paper airplanes: Therapeutic exercises for sexually traumatized children*. Indianapolis: Kidsrights.

Deblinger, E., Stauffer, L. B., & Steer, R. A. (2001). Comparative efficacies of supportive and cognitive behavioral group therapies for young children who have been sexually abused and their nonoffending mothers. *Child Maltreatment*. 6, 332–343.

DeLuca, R. V., Grayston, A. D., & Romano, E. (2000). Sexually abused boys. In C. Schaefer (ed.), *Short-term psychotherapy groups for children: Adapting group processes for specific problems* (pp. 183–218). New Jersey: Jason Aronson.

Devore, W., & Schlesinger, E. G. (1987). *Ethnic-sensitive social work practice.* Columbus, OH: Merrill.

Einbender, A. J. (1991). Treatment in the absence of maternal support. In W. N. Friedrich (ed.), *Casebook of sexual abuse treatment* (pp. 112–136). New York: W. W. Norton.

Faller, K. C. (1988). *Child sexual abuse: An interdisciplinary manual for diagnosis, case management, and treatment.* New York: Columbia University Press.

Finkelhor, D. (1984). *Child sexual abuse: New theory and research.* New York: Free Press.

Finkelhor, D. (1986). *A sourcebook on child sexual abuse.* Thousand Oaks, CA: Sage.

Finkelhor, D. (1995). The victimization of children: A developmental perspective. *American Journal of Orthopsychiatry.* 65, 177–193.

Friedrich, W. N. (1990). *Psychotherapy of sexually abused children and their families.* New York: W. W. Norton.

Friedrich, W. N. (ed.) (1991). *Casebook of sexual abuse treatment.* New York: W. W. Norton.

Gardner, R. A. (1975). *Psychotherapeutic approaches to the resistant child.* New York: Jason Aronson.

Green, A. H. (1992). Application of psychoanalytic theory in the treatment of the victim and the family. In W. O'Donahue & J. H. Geer (eds.), *The sexual abuse of children: Clinical issues* (Vol. 2, pp. 285–300). Hillsdale, NJ: Erlbaum.

Groth, N. A. (1982). The incest offender. In S. Sgroi (ed.), *Handbook of clinical intervention in child sexual abuse* (pp. 215–239). Lexington, MA: Lexington Books.

Hack, T. F., Osachuk, T. A. G., & DeLuca, R. V. (1994). Group treatment for sexually abused preadolescent boys. *Families in Society.* 75, 217–228.

Harms, R., & James, D. (1983). *Talking about touching.* Seattle: Seattle Institute for Child Advocacy, Committee for Children.

Heiman, M. L., & Ettin, M. F. (2001). Harnessing the power of the group for latency-aged sexual abuse victims. *International Journal of Group Psychotherapy.* 51, 265–280.

Ho, M. K. (1992). *Minority children and adolescents in therapy.* Thousand Oaks, CA: Sage.

Johnson, T. C. (1991). Treatment of a sexually reactive girl. In W. N. Friedrich (ed.), *Casebook of sexual abuse treatment* (pp. 270–290). New York: W. W. Norton.

Kilpatrick, A. C. (1992). *Long-range effects of child and adolescent sexual experiences: Myths, mores, and menaces.* Hillsdale, NJ: Erlbaum.

Lynch, E. W., & Hanson, M. J. (eds.) (1992). *Developing cross-cultural competence: A guide for working with young children and their families.* Baltimore: P. H. Brookes.

McFarlane, A. C. (1996). Traumatic stress in childhood and adolescence: Recent developments and current controversies. In B. van der Kolk, A. C. McFarlane, & L. Weisaeth (eds.), *Traumatic stress: The effects of overwhelming experience on mind, body and society* (p. 331–358). New York: Guilford Press.

Mandell, J. G., & Damon, L. (1989). *Group treatment for sexually abused children.* New York: Guilford Press.

Milner, J. S. (1998). Individual and family characteristics associated with intrafamilial child physical and sexual abuse. In P. K. Trickett & C. J. Schellenbach (eds.), *Violence against children in the family and the community* (p. 141–170). Washington, DC: American Psychological Association.

O'Donohue, W., & Geer, J. H. (eds.) (1992). *The sexual abuse of children: Clinical issues* (vols. 1 and 2). Hillsdale, NJ: Erlbaum.

Pisaruk, H. I., Shawchuck, C. R., & Hoier, T. S. (1992). Behavioral characteristics of child victims of sexual abuse: A comparison study. *Journal of Clinical Child Psychology.* 21, 16–17.

Porter, E. (1986). *Treating the young male victim of sexual assault: Issues and intervention strategies.* Syracuse, NY: Safer Society Press.

Porter, F. A., Blick, L. C., & Sgroi, S. M. (1982). Treatment of the sexually abused child. In S. G. Sgroi (ed.), *Handbook of clinical intervention in child sexual abuse* (pp. 109–145). Lexington, MA: Lexington Books.

Renvoize, J. (1993). *Innocence destroyed: A study of child sexual abuse.* New York: Routledge.

Rice-Smith, E. (1993). Group psychotherapy with sexually abused children. In H. I. Kaplan & B. J. Sadock (eds.), *Comprehensive group psychotherapy* (pp. 531–550). Baltimore: Williams & Wilkins.

Schonfield, M. (1984). *Talking about touching with preschoolers: A personal safety curriculum.* Seattle: Seattle Institute for Child Advocacy, Committee for Children.

Sgroi, S. M. (ed.). (1982). *Handbook of clinical intervention in child sexual abuse.* Lexington, MA: Lexington Books.

Sturkie, K (1992). Group treatment of child sexual abuse victims: A review. In W. O'Donohue & J. H. Geer (eds.), *The sexual abuse of children: Clinical issues* (Vol. 2., pp. 331–364). Hillsdale, NJ: Erlbaum.

Trowell, J., Kolvin, T., Weeramanthri, H., Sadowski, M., Berelowitz, D., D. Glasser, & Leitch, I. (2002). Psychotherapy for sexually abused girls: Psychopathological outcome findings and patterns of change. *The British Journal of Psychiatry.* 180, pp. 234–247.

Vacc, N. A., Wittmer, J., & Devaney, S. (1988). *Experiencing and counseling multicultural and diverse populations.* Indianapolis: Accelerated Development.

Valle, L. A., & Silovsky, J. F. (2002). Attributions and adjustment following child sexual and physical abuse. *Child Maltreatment.* 7(1) pp. 9–25.

van der Kolk, B. A., & Fisler, R. E. (1994). Childhood abuse and neglect and loss of self-regulation. *Bulletin of the Menninger Clinic.* 58, 145–168.

Young, L. (1992). Sexual abuse and the problem of embodiment. *Child Abuse and Neglect.* 15, 98–99.

SELECTED BIBLIOGRAPHY

Aho, J. S., & Petras, J. W. (1985). *Learning about sexual abuse.* Hillsdale, NJ: Enslow.

Dayee, F. (1982). *Private zones.* New York: Warner Brothers.

Gordon, S. (1985). *When living hurts.* New York: Union of American Hebrew Congregations.

Gordon, S. (1992). *A better safe than sorry book.* Buffalo, NY: Prometheus Books.

Krause, E. (1983a). *For Pete's sake, tell.* Oregon City, OR: Krause House.

Krause, E. (1983b). *Speak up, say no.* Oregon City, OR: Krause House.

Loontjens, L. (1984). *Talking to children/talking to parents about sexual assault.* Santa Cruz, CA: Network Publications.

MacLean, J. (1987). *Mac.* Cambridge, MA: Houghton Mifflin.

Mazer, N. F. (1988). *Silver.* New York: Morrow Junior Books.

Chapter 19

Group Work with Offenders

MARGARET M. WRIGHT

Social work with offender populations is a challenge to the beginning worker. One of the first hurdles that the worker must face is the "lock them up and throw away the key" attitude of some of the most vocal members of the public and the tendency of politicians to take on this theme as their electoral rallying cry and an easy way of garnering votes. This hostile attitude is sometimes present in the institution among staff and administrators. Social workers are often viewed as being naïve and easy prey for manipulative inmates who are looking for ways to increase their privileges and speed up their release. The challenge for the social worker is to demonstrate clearly to all segments of the institution, both staff and inmates, that he or she has a valuable service to provide that does not minimize the inmates' responsibility for their behavior. Some re-search indicates that prison wardens in the United States are receptive to the rehabilitative ideal within a controlled environment (Cullen et al., 1993). This reflects research into attitudes of the public:

> It is often said that Americans are a punitive people, but it also seems that we are a people who see the wisdom of providing even those who have victimized others with the opportunity and help to pursue pro-ductive lives. (Cullen, Skovron, Scott, & Burton, 1989)

The social work service can be seen as credible when presented as a concrete effort to help inmates confront the issues, over which they have control, that resulted in their imprisonment.

The population of offenders in prisons is very difficult to categorize. It is generally accepted that most offenders come from disadvantaged backgrounds and tend to be the poorest citizens of the area in which they reside (U.S. Department of Justice, 2002). The ethnic or racial composition of offenders reflects the degree of representation of the ethnic and racial groups among the poor in the community from which the offenders originate. Specific population groups, then, differ depending on the area from which the prison derives its catchment. Most inmates are poorly educated, and may have not had a stable employment pattern (Adler et al., 2000).[1] One clear characteristic of most prison inmates is that most of them are male (Griffiths & Verdun-Jones, 1994). The management of men and women in prisons differs considerably because of the clearly different issues presented by the gender of the offender.

Male offenders' issues are usually depicted as relating to substance abuse (alcohol and/or drug abuse), aggression and assaultive behavior, impulsivity and poor frustration tolerance, poor education and work skills, and employment record. Problems in relationships with family members or social isolation resulting in the absence of any significant attachment to another person also exist.

Female offenders frequently have issues related to substance abuse as well as poor education and work skills, but one of the primary concerns for many female offenders is the problems related to their role as mothers (Baunach, 1992). A Canadian study of women inmates serving sentences of more than 2 years shows that two-thirds of them are mothers and that, of these, two-thirds have been single parents for at least part, if not all, of their children's lives (Shaw, 1992). They are trying to cope with maintaining contact and relationships with children who are in the care of relatives or social agencies and who do not understand why their mothers have left them.

The prison environment has been described by many writers (e.g., Goffman, 1973; Sykes, 1958). It is consistent with Goffman's descriptions of asylums and is similar to other total institutional environments. It is potentially a more oppressive environment for both inmates and staff then some other total institutions because of the traditional focus on the prison as a paramilitary structure in which inmates are kept against their will by the superior physical force of their keepers. This involuntary environment has not traditionally had any component of helping in the way that other total institutions, like hospitals for the mentally ill, have had. While the effect on keeping people against their will may be the same, the message sent to the inmates is different and much more obviously oppressive in the prison context.

One of the major issues/problems in prisons is the violence or the threat of violence that is part of the fabric of prison life. In most judicial jurisdictions, the population of inmates assigned to or choosing to live in protective custody (apart from other inmates and usually alone for up to 23 hours a day) has become a significant management problem because

---

[1] This good basic text is useful to the beginning worker in this field. Also useful is James C. Hackler (2003). Canadian criminology: Strategies and perspectives. Toronto: Prentice Hall, Allyn and Bacon Canada.

of their increasingly large numbers. Those inmates who do not choose to enter protective custody usually have to accept a lifestyle that involves violence in the conduct of everyday life, an "attack or be attacked" mentality (McCorkle, 1992). Not all prison environments have the same level of inmate subculture and violence or staff control. There is a wide variety of possible prison environments, ranging from relatively open, community-focused, minimum security, or halfway house environments to maximum security, closed institutions in which the presence of mechanisms for physical restraint like mace, batons, or other weapons is obvious. Each level of security presents its own challenges and opportunities to the social worker. Work in the most secure institutions presents the greatest number of limitations to the social worker in terms of group programs because mobility and potential interaction among the inmates are severely limited. According to Griffiths and Verdun-Jones (1994, p. 500), these limitations may be due to the level of acting out of the inmates. This conclusion is questionable because of the custom of putting protective custody offenders who may otherwise present the lowest risk for acting out in maximum security. The inmates' need may be great, but support for social work intervention, particularly in groups, is likely to be low on the list of institutional priorities. Social workers are more likely to work in medium and minimum security institutions simply because the emphasis on physical security is reduced and the opportunities for inmates to interact are greater.

PRACTICE PRINCIPLES

The social worker who hopes to provide a group work service to inmates has to take the environment into account in constructing and operating the group. The environment is the immediate context in which the inmate lives. The staff who work in the prison are also part of the inmate's social context. The social worker cannot work in isolation from other staff in the institution and must attempt to develop positive relationships with custodial/correctional staff, as well as with nurses, teachers, administrators, and as many staff as possible in order to have the greatest possible impact on the environment, which consists of much more than the physical structure of the facility.[2] Social group work (in fact, all social work) should be an authentic experience (Lang, 1978; Papell & Rothman, 1980), and any attempt to ignore the reality of the social context will, at best, result in an artificial attempt to intervene with people for whom the environment is very important.

The inmates in correctional institutions usually attempt to construct their own reality in opposition to the one imposed on them by the official

---

[2] Middleman and Goldberg-Wood's (1991) quadrant model is useful in thinking about working with clients within this context.

institution. As noted earlier, this subculture has a hierarchical form in which the physically strong and the most antisocial are at the top and the physically weak and most intellectually and emotionally vulnerable are at the bottom. The values of this subculture are not compatible with prosocial functioning, but are strongly held and often supported within the prison by the staff, who believe that allowing this system to exist will keep the prison under control. When these values are shared by the inmates and the staff, the result is an understanding that the victims or potential victims of violence will be isolated and the belligerents will have the highest level of privilege. This contradicts the stated purpose of prisons, which is to sanction and/or rehabilitate the aggressor in order to protect the victim and possible future victims. The social worker cannot operate groups or any other programs that support these subcultural values but must recognize and confront their existence on a daily basis. The strength of the subculture in any given institution will affect the social worker's ability to form and guide authentic empowering group experiences for inmates. These prison realities make the contracting process an indispensable part of the social worker's intervention. Inmates must have a clear understanding of what is involved in the group and an awareness of how the group will fit into the institutional milieu. Will membership in the group enhance their lives in the institution or will it put them at risk?

At the point of contracting, it is important to recognize that the members of the group may be quite skeptical about the group's usefulness to them. They may be even more skeptical about the usefulness and trustworthiness of the worker. The worker will have to recognize and address these doubts.[3] What in some settings may be signs of lack of motivation to change in a prison environment may simply be a reflection of the inmate's response to the involuntary nature of the setting and the implications that has for involvement with a social worker (Behroozi, 1992).[4] In beginning a group within a correctional environment, the worker must acknowledge that the activity of the group is taking place in an authority-focused setting and that there are limits to what the group can do based on the limits of members as inmates in an institution. The worker must help the members identify the limits imposed by the setting and articulate them explicitly. The worker must also make it clear that although the limits are significant, there is a lot that the group can do. For example, although women inmates cannot be with their children in the community, they can discuss the problems they share as mothers in prison. They can help each other to explore new ways of dealing with the questions their children ask during visits and discuss how to prepare themselves and their

[3] For a thorough discussion of the issue of gaining the trust of clients, see J. A. Jones and A. Alcabes (1993), *Client Socialization: The Achilles Heel of the Helping Professions* (Westport, CT: Auburn House).

[4] See Behroozi (1992) for a schema of pregroup and group behaviors suggested for social workers dealing with involuntary clients.

children for their return to the community. The focus of the social workers is on what can be done in the present context of the prison to prepare the inmates for the future context of their home community. Part of the purpose of contracting is to let group members know what skills and strengths of the worker will enable the members to explore issues that they need to work on. The members need to decide as a group what their focus will be.

Confidentiality

In order to create a sense of safety, the group worker must state that personal disclosures will not be shared inappropriately with inmates and staff who are not part of the group. Providing this assurance is not easy for the worker in a prison because of the emphasis on security and the inmate's environment. The worker must emphasize to the members of the group, both in pregroup interviews and in the first session, the importance of keeping confidences within the group and the damage that can be done to individuals and to the group as a whole if confidences are violated. The worker's own ability to maintain confidentiality must also be made clear. The worker must make a commitment not to talk about the group to other staff without the inmates' permission but must also admit the responsibility to inform other staff members about disclosures that may signal a potential for suicide in a member, a potential for one member to possibly assault another inmate or a staff member, or to inform other authorities about confessions of child abuse. New workers may be concerned that an admission of limits to the ability of the worker to maintain confidentiality may damage the worker's relationship with the group. In fact, honest acknowledgment of the reality that many inmates are already aware of usually enhances the worker's credibility. In keeping with concerns about confidentiality, the worker should caution group members against sharing areas of vulnerability without thinking and should help them to make careful, informed, and deliberate decisions about sharing this information. The worker should encourage group members to take their time in developing their comfort with and their position in the group. The worker should not tell the members *not* to use or invest in the group but should tell them to go slowly and to develop their relationships as group members gradually, rather than expecting to make disclosures and develop closeness immediately.

Composing the Group

Given the power of the environment discussed above, it is important for the social worker to think carefully about the composition of the group. Klein (1972, chapter 2) discusses some key considerations in the selection of members for a group. The emphasis is on balance and compatibility. The group members may not have many things in common, but they must at least have a common goal and some complementary characteristics in terms of similar life experiences or behavioral attributes (Bertcher & Maple, 1985). In a correctional institution, one of the main things that people have in common is their status as inmates. For this reason, it is useful to think about forming the group from the living unit on which the inmates are held. Because of the size of some living units, this may mean that the group would be a subset of the living unit composed of people who have a similar identified need. Groups based on living units ensure that offenders in the group have the same security status and, generally speaking, the same behavioral capacity in terms of their overall relationship to the institution. When the group is composed on this basis, the potential for rivalries based on differing levels of privilege or risk is minimized. In addition, their presence on the same living unit allows the inmates to develop their relationships outside of the group more completely if they choose to. They have the opportunity to discuss issues raised in the group outside of meetings without concern about violating the confidentiality of the group. The group is thereby a more real or authentic experience because it is relevant to their lives, rather than existing for 1 or 2 hours a week apart from their other realities.

Even though the residents of the same living unit share similar security issues, they may not share the same desire to make changes in their lives. For this reason, the social worker should screen potential group members closely for their motivation to make use of a group. As mentioned earlier, the issue of motivation to change is complex in the prison environment. The worker must not confuse motivation with level of difficulty; that is the worker must not assume that the inmates with the best social skills who can easily articulate reasons for being in the group are necessarily more motivated than inmates who experience more difficulty in presenting themselves succinctly and who express more concern about their ability to change. Many inmates who genuinely want to make changes find it difficult to do so without the guidance of a group and may appear at first to be resistant or hesitant because they are unsure about what is possible. The more articulate inmates can sometimes be those who are not interested in change but rather in using the group to improve their chances for parole or to increase their privileges within the institution. The social worker should attempt to determine the level of need of the inmate for the group and should attempt to group inmates accordingly.

Open or Closed Group

Both open- and closed-ended groups are possible and desirable in correctional settings. The group structure will vary depending on the purpose of the group. Some purposes can be met without developing a high level of cohesion among the members and therefore can be carried out in an open-ended format. These tend to be groups in which the social worker is attempting to provide an educational service that also gives the members a chance to become comfortable enough to ask questions and to solicit advice from both the social worker and other group members. In constructing a group on these lines, the social worker should be clear as to what he or she wants to accomplish and should not expect a high level of cohesion or intimacy to develop among the members (Lang, 1987; Schopler & Galinsky, 1984; Sulman, 1987).

If the social worker wants to create a group atmosphere in which the members can safely discuss deeply felt personal struggles and challenges, the worker must recognize that an open-ended group is generally not capable of providing that opportunity. This is particularly true in the correctional institution. The worker needs to develop a climate of safety in order to facilitate successful work at this level. There are some notable exceptions to this general observation, which usually characterize groups that consist of a small number of inmates sharing a common residence (unit or halfway house) where the turnover of inmates is usually low and where the social worker uses the principles of the mainstream model mentioned earlier (Wright, 1993). The worker must determine to what extent a closed-ended group is possible in his or her setting. Can a group of 10 or 12 inmates meet together regularly for a significant period of time without fear of losing much of the membership to parole, discharge, or transfer to another institution? The worker will need to be familiar enough with the setting, and with the policies and practices concerning the transfer of inmates, to be able to ensure stability of membership.

COMMON GROUP WORK THEMES

Substance Abuse

Many studies of prisoners indicate that substance abuse is reported by 75–80% of them. This may include alcoholism, drug abuse, or both. Some offenders are incarcerated because of drug abuse but many have been convicted of robberies committed to obtain money to buy drugs. Group work with substance abusers can take the form of structured group interaction with education about the risks of drug abuse. However, most prisoners are already experiencing the consequences of drug abuse, and want and need an opportunity to explore alternatives, share their fears, and talk about the lifestyle they have developed around their addiction. While it is not necessary to structure a closed group experience in order to provide education, it may be necessary to ensure a closed-group opportunity for the exploration and integration of the information and in which the difficult concept of changing the drug or alcohol lifestyles can be addressed. Peat and Winfree (1992) studied the progress of drug-addicted inmates and found that they performed better and reported more success in a therapeutic prison community, that is, on a unit devoted to the treatment of such addicts, rather than when worked with in open-ended groups.

They maintain that the closed unit was the only way in which the effects of the subculture could be counteracted or negated. When a therapeutic milieu and even a closed group are not possible, it is important, as noted above, to attempt to control the intake and exits from the group so that the opportunity exists to develop a level of trust and openness.

Relationship Issues

Some offenders have families that they have left behind when they entered prison. Many other offenders have burned their bridges in terms of family and other relationships and are searching for reasons for their failure in this area. Groups dealing with relationship issues should be conducted separately for these two populations. Inmates who are experiencing family and/or marital separations will not have much in common with those who are having problems finding positive relationships nor will they have much tolerance for them. Men, and especially women, who have spouses and children who visit them, frequently experience a great deal of guilt about being incarcerated and fear that they will lose their families as a result. These people need a group to share their experience of this difficult life situation and to gain mutual support.

Those inmates, usually young men, who have difficulty forming and maintaining relationships often exhibit a wider range of difficulties. They are usually more unsocialized and antisocial in a variety of ways, and may require life and social skills training before they can begin to deal with more complex relationship issues. For these men, the worker will need to provide a higher degree of structure than might otherwise be required in group work with inmates. Some individual work may be necessary before group membership is possible. A clear educational format in which a certain degree of didactic instruction and dyadic practice/role play are provided will be necessary. This is a group in which coleadership is advisable because of the demanding nature of the inmate client whose unsocialized behavior is demonstrated in an inability to sustain focus in a group. Such groups often resemble groups of latency-age children who require activities as well as opportunities for talk and sharing.

Aggression Management

Some inmates identify themselves as having problems with their tempers and/or are described as being assaultive or explosive by people in the community or in prison. Unfortunately, these offenders have often used their aggression as a method of coping both inside and outside prison. Some of them may be the same inmates who identify themselves as having problems in developing close relationships with others. They will need to explore their use of violence as a means of coping with perceived threats or getting what they want. They need to explore the effects of violence on their own lives and on the lives of those with whom they attempt to become close. Structured anger management techniques are important to incorporate into this group, but they will not be sufficient. These inmates need opportunities to share their histories of powerlessness and their own feelings of vulnerability and threat so that they can experience openness without threat and have opportunities to practice anger management and conflict resolution techniques outside of a structured group. As noted above, they may need some individual work prior to being referred to group. This individual work could focus on reducing their anxiety about joining a group by using systematic desensitization techniques through which they can learn to improve their listening skills before becoming group members.

Abuse

Issues of abuse are evident in inmate populations, both perpetrators and victims. Although there is some debate about the long-term effects of abuse on eventual criminality, Widom (1989a, 1989b, 1989c, 1989d, 1999, & 2000), in a series of studies on the methodological weaknesses in research into the possible link between child abuse and the development of adult pathology, found a higher rate of delinquency and adult criminality in a study of individuals who were abused as children than in a nonabused control group. Scudder, Blount, Heide, and Silverman's (1993) work supports Widom's conclusions. Dutton and Hart (1992) found that in inmates who reported having been abused as children, there was a significant correlation between the type of crime they committed and the kind of abuse they had experienced. Dutton and Hart recommend that consideration be given to providing treatment for the posttraumatic stress disorder symptoms that these inmates may exhibit. Those who have been abused and have not become abusers should not be put into groups with abusers. Female survivors of abuse should not be put into cocorrectional or coeducational situations with men with whom they may feel at risk. It may be most efficacious to put men who have been abused and are abusers in groups separate from others in order to explore how both of these complex areas interact in their particular circumstances.

Men who are abusive need to discuss their experiences of abuse as children, but the primary focus of any group with this population must be on their responsibility for the abuse and their plans for ensuring that they will not be abusive in the future. Goldberg-Wood and Middleman (1992) have described a process for working with men who batter that incorporates challenges to the men's view of women as chattel and that allows the men to make changes in their perceptual and value systems. Their model is also valuable, with some modifications, for work with men who sexually abuse both women and children. Social workers who are attempting to provide service to male abusers should always have information from sources other than the offender about the nature of the abusive behavior and, if possible, the degree of harm done by him. These men will usually minimize both their responsibility for the abuse and the harm done. Good assessment increases the worker's effectiveness (Becker & Quinsey, 1993; Mair, 1993). Several helpful texts focus on relapse prevention (e.g., Laws, 1989; Wilson, 1992). However, many of these groups do not allow the group to develop in the way the mainstream model of social work with groups suggests is possible and necessary. These approaches can be useful if the worker incorporates a social group work approach. Some education is necessary with abusive men, especially input that challenges their notions of patriarchy and examines concepts of male socialization. The idea of biology as destiny, and the resultant excuses and sense of entitlement that these ideas foster, must be challenged. But these men must also have the opportunity to develop as a group and to explore the meaning of their behavior to themselves and to others.

Women who have been incarcerated for offenses involving child abuse and neglect need to be approached differently in groups than men who commit similar or other acts of abuse (Breton, 1979; Butler & Vintram, 1991; Home, 1991; Lewis, 1992; Lovell et al., 1992). They have had different socialization and life experiences and react differently to being convicted of child abuse. Breton (1979) describes the ways in which these women need to be "nurtured" in order to be helped to change abusive patterns.

Coping with Stigma

Most inmates raise issues at some point related to the label that they carry as identified criminals. They present this label as an impediment to any change in behavior that they may wish to make regarding both personal relationships and job opportunities. They need group experiences in which they can share their fears and needs in terms of strategies to deal with the label they have earned through deviant behavior in the past. The group experience gives them the chance to talk about common concerns while attempting to achieve a common solution to a problem that inmates have always shared.

Discharge Planning

The issue of stigma may be addressed on its own in a specifically formed group or it may be discussed in groups on discharge planning, one of the most frequently identified needs of prison inmates. Although inmates should be encouraged to think about planning for their discharge from the time of their admission, a group dealing with this issue should be composed of inmates who are reasonably close to discharge. In this way, the focus of the group can be real and immediate. As well, group members can be encouraged to think about community services or groups that may be helpful in their reintegration. Members can also be supported in efforts to arrange appointments with these resource services prior to their discharge, or supported for temporary absences from the institution close to the time of discharge, or encouraged to arrange appointments soon after their release.

As noted earlier, this group could be either open- or closed-ended. If it is open-ended, the turnover of members should not be so great at any one time that the group repeatedly has to spend a great deal of time dealing with issues of trust.

Identity

Depending on the demographics of the prisoners in the group, the social workers may deal with issues of race and culture in all group interactions. In some institutions, the prisoners may belong to different racial groups and may benefit from specialized services. Usually the racial groups present will consist of several cultural subgroups, so the group should not be considered homogeneous. There will probably be a common ground on which to meet, however, since the experience of oppression and the history of the group may be unifying themes. For example, native inmates in many Canadian prisons come from a range of tribal groups but they have as shared themes the history of native spirituality and practices that have a common core, although they may vary. These are self-help groups in terms of their organizational style. Institutional social workers are directly involved in these group programs. The groups are guided by members of Native Sons organizations from the community. The role of the social worker is to develop and maintain links with these community organizations so that they come into the prison to provide the service.

AIDS

In the past few years, one of the biggest new issues in dealing with prison populations was that because of the significant number of inmates with a history of intravenous drug use, they are at high risk of contracting and/or passing on the human immunodeficiency virus (HIV). This makes social work intervention important in a number of ways. First, social workers should work with health care professionals and community AIDS organizations to develop and deliver educational programs that help inmates and correctional staff understand how AIDS is transmitted and what precautions they should take with respect to drug use and sexual practices. Second, social workers should work with inmates who are HIV positive to provide both education and support. Groups are useful in both of these situations. Education about AIDS presented in groups allows the group members to discuss their fears and misconceptions and to have them addressed. Group work with inmates who are HIV positive can provide them with mutual support in what is a difficult life circumstance in any environment, but one that is further complicated by the fact that the prison environment is even more afraid of and hostile to them than many communities would be. As well, these individuals do not have ready access to AIDS support groups and to supportive family and friends.

Working with Female Offenders

As noted at the beginning of this chapter and as alluded to above, female offenders as a group may have some problems in common with male offenders, but generally the approach to meeting their needs has to be different (Adelberg & Currie, 1993; Axon, 1989; Gelsthorpe & Morris, 1990). Women are frequently attempting to cope with issues related to their children. They are concerned about what is happening to their children while they are incarcerated and about how their children perceive them as inmates or as bad mothers who have deserted them. They are also worried about the staff of the social agencies concerned with their children. They feel powerless and without sufficient resources to cope with the day-to-day reality of prison and the pressures created by their children and other family members. These women need to explore their feelings, to provide support for each other, and to discuss how to cope with and reduce their feeling of powerlessness.[5] Some women who have been abused will display self-mutilating behavior while incarcerated. Both the women and the institutional staff will need considerable help in dealing with this issue positively.[6]

Women who have been prostitutes may need to come together in groups to identify and work on the issues that this occupation has created for them. A feminist perspective should be used in work with all women but is imperative in this type of group (Moyer, 1992). Women need to enter groups without feeling that they will be judged as "bad women." They may be especially sensitive to male workers because of their experience with the sexuality of some males. Social workers should take this into account in planning any intervention.

RECOMMENDED WAYS OF WORKING

As noted above, the social worker must always consider the correctional environment as part of the client "package."

Case

Male offenders of a correctional center asked for a group to talk about issues concerning relationships with women. In the third

---

[5] Judith Lee's 1994 book *The Empowerment Approach to Social Work Practice* (New York: Columbia University Press) is particularly useful in work with women in these circumstances.

[6] Any social worker dealing with incarcerated women should read the 1991 biography of Marlene Moore by Anne Kershaw and Mary Lasovitch, *Rock-a-Bye Baby: A Death Behind Bars* (Toronto: McClelland & Stewart). This work is particularly helpful in educating workers about self-mutilation behaviors.

group session, one member brought up concerns about his performance in sexual relationships with women. Another member, a leader on the living unit, expressed disapproval about discussing this material in front of the female social worker. The disgruntled member refused to participate and sat in stony silence, nonverbally disapproving of the group members' attempts at discussion. All efforts on the part of group members to address his silent control of the process failed. Finally, he announced that he would not be returning. The social worker met with the inmate alone after the group session. She indicated that there was no possibility of a male worker replacing her and that the group was important to the members. She was careful to discuss the fact that any influence that he brought to bear on the remaining members of the group living on the unit might seriously damage the usefulness of the group. He agreed to come back for the next session, explain his position, and attempt to reassure the group members that he would not make fun of them or otherwise harass them about their continuing membership. After he did so, the members appeared to be reassured both by the fact that he was no longer there and by his stated intention to respect their group. In the next two sessions, group members dealt directly and indirectly with issues of trust. The worker recognized the need for the group to deal with these basic forming issues and did not push the group. In the third session after the crisis, the members once again began to discuss concerns about sexuality. The remaining sessions were characterized by increasing openness and comfort in dealing with sensitive relationship issues.

The success of the group was determined by the worker's handling of the threat posed by the disgruntled inmate and by her understanding of the importance of the feeling of safety to the members. Safety and competence are primary issues for inmates in groups. Workers must always keep them in mind.

Lee (1994) has developed a useful framework for assessing the client that is particularly appropriate for the correctional setting, which she titles "Assessment for Empowerment" (pp. 143–145). The social work role in correctional facilities is to help the client group to become socialized to the possibility of positive, satisfying nonexploitive, relationships. As noted above, to do this, the worker must overcome the skepticism of both inmates and correctional officers. To be genuinely helpful, the social worker must help clients develop skills that will help them reach their fullest potential. This will involve the use of currently popular empowerment approaches summarized as follows:

> social work practice with groups encompasses both intervention within the group and intervention outside the group, i.e., that the group is both a context and an instrument of change involving actions by the group and its members inside group meetings as well as actions by the group

and its members in situations outside the group. (Moore & Starkes, 1992, p. 183)

However, the worker must use considerable judgment and careful planning in deciding what form that empowerment takes. Advocacy for and empowerment approaches with inmates should not set up the inmates or allow them to set themselves up for failure or punishment. On the other hand, approaches that do not include empowerment treat inmates as incapable of positive and reasonable social action.

Case

Women in a local jail were concerned because the director did not allow many community leaves. They discussed their anger about the difficulty of achieving these privileges, and one particularly angry inmate advocated a hunger strike as a way of "getting back at" the director. Other women jumped on the bandwagon and began to plan the protest. The social worker leading the group asked the members to pause and think about the possible negative consequences to them of this course of action. After they listed several, she guided them into a discussion of what other courses of action might be more effective. They concluded with a general discussion about how to get what they wanted in prison in ways that did not make them more vulnerable.

Training is necessary to help inmates overcome their sense that lawful or traditional ways of trying to solve problems do not work for them. They will need to practice empowerment strategies within institutions, but they must be helped to choose and plan strategies that have a very high probability of success. The social worker must have a very good working knowledge of the particular correctional environment in order to know what these opportunities might be.

Group workers like Lee (1982, 1989, 1994; and in Schwartz, 1978), Breton (1979, 1985, 1989), Jacobs (1964), and Brooks (1978) give graphic examples of the effectiveness of the social group work method in helping people to take an active part in decisions that affect them. Giving inmates the opportunity to experience relationship building and decision-making successes while they are in the institution helps them to feel better about their chances for achieving similar success in the community when they are released and lifts some of the depression that is a constant reality for them as prisoners. Middleman and Goldberg-Wood's structural model of social work, originally described in 1974 and further developed in subsequent publications (Goldberg-Wood & Middleman, 1989, 1991, 1992; Middleman & Goldberg-Wood, 1991), helps the worker to keep his or her focus on the clients as whole persons who are capable of self-determination while still keeping the reality of their limitations in view.

EVALUATION APPROACHES

Social workers in correctional institutions are always faced with the problem of determining success or failure in their work with clients in almost life-or-death terms. The traditional test of success with offenders is whether or not they offend again. This information may tell the social workers something about the offender's experience of incarceration in general, but the absence of a return to jail does not necessarily entitle the social workers to claim that his or her group was a success. Nor is a return to jail an indication of a group's failure. Research into correctional treatment indicates that many factors have to be taken into consideration (Gendreau & Andrews, 1990). The worker must then decide how to judge the utility of the intervention for the members of the group. One way of doing this is through a qualitative[7] study of the life of the group. An analysis of the group's progress may tell the worker whether or not the group was able to do the work for which it contracted. Did the members use the group in a meaningful way? Did they discuss the issues that they agreed to at the outset of the group? Did all members make use of the group? Was there a high dropout rate? Did the group end prematurely? Did the members express satisfaction with the group while it was meeting? In addition to a qualitative analysis of the group's ongoing functioning, the social worker can conduct exit interviews with the participants to learn about their experience with the group. The worker can also give the group members a written questionnaire before the group begins, asking for their expectations of the group, and another questionnaire at the end asking whether the original expectations were met. The questionnaires may be anonymous so that the fear of consequences can be minimized if members have negative feedback about the group experience. As well, the social worker should ask front-line correctional staff for their impressions of the usefulness of the group, either at the end or while it is still ongoing. Some front-line workers may not support the notion of rehabilitation of inmates and may feel that groups are useless in general, but many correctional officers will provide concrete feedback on whether or not the inmate's behavior has been influenced by the group experience.

CONCLUSION

When all is said and done, prison inmates are people who have come from a variety of communities and who may have been engaged in social work interventions in other settings. The primary challenge of the social worker in a prison environment is to come to grips with the fact that this

---

[7] For those workers who feel pressure to use only quantitative models of evaluation, Ann Hartman's editorial "Many Ways of Knowing" in *Social Work* (1990) will be useful.

environment is a "shadow client" that must be worked with concurrently as the social worker works with the person. There can be no success without a clear acknowledgment of this reality.

ACKNOWLEDGEMENT

I would like to thank members of the social work department of the Ontario Correctional Institute for their suggestions about what should be included in this chapter.

RESOURCES

Social workers should use as many local organizations as are available to them. For example, most communities now have AIDS organizations that will provide support to inmates who are HIV positive and education to others. The following national organizations may be helpful in providing workers with local city or province/state groups that could be helpful.

Canadian Association of Elizabeth Fry
  Societies (CAEFS)
Association Canadienne des Sociétés
  Elizabeth Fry (ACSEF)
701-151 Slater Street
Ottawa, Ontario K1P 5H3
Tel. (613) 238-2422
Fax.: (613) 232-7130
Email: CAEFS@web.ca
http://www.elizabethfry.ca/

John Howard Society
809 Blackburn Mews
Kingston, Ontario
Canada K7P 2N6
Tel: (613) 384-6272
Fax: (613) 384-1847

Email: national@johnhoward.ca
http://www.johnhoward.ca/

National Institute on Drug Abuse
6001 Executive Boulevard,
  Room 5213
Bethesda, MD 20892-9561
Email: Information@lists.nida.nih.govA
http://www.drugabuse.gov/

National Prison Project
733 15th Street, NW
Suite 620
Washington, DC 20005
Tel.: (202) 393-4930
Fax: (202) 393-4931
·http://www.aclu.org/issues/prisons/
  npp_mission.html

REFERENCES

Adelberg, E., & Currie, C. (eds.) (1993). *In conflict with the law: Women and the Canadian justice system.* Vancouver: Press Gang.
Adler, F., Mueller, G. O. W. & Laufer, W. S. (2000). *Criminology.* New York: McGraw-Hill.
Axon L. (1989). *Model and exemplary programs for female inmates: An international review.* Ottawa: Solicitor General of Canada.

Baunach, P. J. (1992). Critical problems of women in prison. In I. Moyer (ed.), *The changing role of women in the criminal justice system. Offenders, victims and professionals* (pp. 99–112). Prospect Heights, IL: Waveland Press.

Becker, J. V., & Quinsey, V. L. (1993). Assessing suspected child molesters. *Child Abuse and Neglect.* 17, 169–174.

Behroozi, C. S. (1992). A model for social work with involuntary applicants in groups. *Social Work with Groups.* 15, 223–238.

Bertcher, H. J. (1994). *Group participation: Techniques for leaders and members.* Thousand Oaks, CA: Sage.

Bertcher, H. J. & Maple, F. (1985). Elements and issues in group composition. In M. Sundel, P. Glasser, R. Sarri, & R. Vinter (eds.), *Individual change in small groups* (pp. 186–208). New York: Free Press.

Breton, M. (1979). Nurturing abused and abusive mothers: The hairdressing group. *Social Work with Groups.* 2(2), 161–174.

Breton, M. (1985). Reaching and engaging people: Issues and practice principles. *Social Work with Groups.* 8(3), 7–21.

Breton, M. (1989). The need for mutual aid groups in a drop-in for homeless women: The sistering case. In J. A. B. Lee (ed.), *Group work with the poor and oppressed* (pp. 47–59). New York: Haworth.

Breton, M. (1991). Toward a model of social groupwork practice with marginalized populations. *Groupwork.* 4(1), 31–47.

Brooks, A. (1978). Group work in the Bowery. *Social Work with Groups.* 1(1), 53–63.

Butler, S., & Wintram, C. (1991). *Feminist groupwork.* Newbury Park, CA: Sage.

Cullen, F. T., Latessa, E. J., Burton, V. S., Jr., & Lombardo, L. X. (1993). The correctional orientation of prison wardens: Is the rehabilitative ideal supported? *Criminology.* 31(1), 69–92.

Cullen F. T., Skovron, S. E., Scott, J. E., & Burton, V. S., Jr. (1989). Public support for correctional treatment: The tenacity of rehabilitation ideology. *Criminal Justice and Behavior.* 17, 6–18.

Dutton, D. G., & Hart, S. D. (1992). Evidence of long-term, specific effects of childhood abuse and neglect on criminal behaviour in men. *International Journal of Offender Therapy and Comparative Criminology.* 36(2), 129–137.

Gelsthorpe, L., & Morris, A. (Eds.). (1990). *Feminist perspectives in criminology.* Philadelphia: Open University Press.

Gendreau, P., & Andrews, D. A. (1990). Tertiary prevention: What the meta-analyses of the offender treatment literature tell us about "what works." *Canadian Journal of Criminology.* 32, 173–184.

Goffman, E. (1963). *Asylums: Essays on the social situations of mental patients and other inmates.* New York: Doubleday.

Goldberg-Wood, G. & Middleman, R. R. (1989). *The structural approach to direct practice in social work.* New York: Columbia University Press.

Goldberg-Wood, G., & Middleman, R. R. (1991). Advocacy and social action: Key elements in the structural approach to direct practice in social work. *Social Work with Groups.* 14, 53–63.

Goldberg-Wood, G., & Middleman, R. R. (1992). Recasting the die: A small group approach to giving batterers a chance to change. *Social Work with Groups.* 15, 5–18.

Griffiths, C. T., & Verdun-Jones, S. N. (1994). *Canadian criminal justice.* Toronto: Harcourt Brace.

Hackler, J. C. (2003). *Canadian criminology: Strategies and perspectives.* Toronto: Prentice Hall, Allyn and Bacon Canada.

Hartman, A. (1990). Many ways of knowing. *Social Work.* 35(1), 3–4.

Home, A. M. (1991). Mobilizing women's strengths of social change: The group connection. *Social Work with Groups.* 14, 153–154.

Jacobs, J. (1964). Social action as therapy in a mental hospital. *Social Work.* 9(1), 54–61.

Jones, J. A., & Alcabes, A. (1993). *Client socialization: The Achilles' heel of the helping professions.* Westport, CT: Auburn House.

Kershaw, A., & Lasovitch, M. (1991). *Rock-a-bye baby: A death behind bars.* Toronto: McClelland & Stewart.

Klein A. F. (1972). *Effective groupwork: An introduction to principle and method.* Bloomfield, CT: Practitioners Press.

Lang, N. (1988). Social work practice in small social forms: Identifying collectivity. *Social Work with Group.* 9(4), 7–32.

Laws, D. R. (1989). *Relapse prevention with sex offenders.* New York: Guilford Press.

Lee, J. A. B. (1982). The group: A chance at human connection for the mentally impaired older person. *Social Work with Groups.* 5(2), 43–55.

Lee, J. A. B. (1994). *The empowerment approach to social work practice.* New York: Columbia University Press.

Lee, J. A. B. (ed.) (1989). *Group work with the poor and oppressed.* New York: Haworth Press.

Lewis, E. (1992). Regaining promise: Feminist perspectives for social group work practice. *Social Work with Group.* 15, 271–284.

Lovell, M. L., Reid, K., & Richey, C. A. (1992). Social support training for abusive mothers. *Social Work with Groups.* 15, 95–108.

Mair, K. J. (1993). The nature of the act: A neglected dimension in the classification of sex offenders. *British Journal of Criminology.* 33, 267–275.

McCorkle, R. C. (1992). Personal precautions to violence in prison. *Criminal Justice and Behavior.* 19(2), 160–173.

McCormick, R. E., & Visano, L. A. (1992). *Canadian penology: Advanced perspectives and research.* Toronto: Canadian Scholars Press.

Middleman, R. R., & Goldberg-Wood, G. (1991). *Skills for direct practice social work.* New York: Columbia University Press.

Moore, E. E., & Starkes, A. J. (1992). The group in institution as the unit of attention: Recapturing and refining a social work tradition. *Social Work with Group.* 15, 171–192.

Moyer, I. L. (1992). *The changing roles of women in the criminal justice system.* Prospect Heights, IL: Waveland Press.

Papell, C. P., & Rothman, B. (1980). Social group work models: Possession and heritage. In A. Alissi (ed.), *Perspectives in social groupwork practice* (pp. 66–77). New York: Free Press.

Peat, B. J., & Winfree, L. T. (1992). Reducing the intra-institutional effects of "prisonization": A study of a therapeutic community for drug-using inmates. *Criminal Justice and Behavior.* 19(2), 206–225.

Scudder, R. G., Blount, W. R., Heide, K. M., & Silverman, I. J. (1993). Important links between child abuse, neglect and delinquency. *International Journal of Offender Therapy and Comparative Criminology.* 37(4), 315–323.

Schopler, J. H., & Galinsky, M. J. (1984). Meeting practice needs: Conceptualizing the open-ended group. *Social Work with Groups.* 7(2), 3–21.

Schwartz, W. (1978). Rosalie. *Social Work with Groups.* 1(3), 265–278.

Shaw, M. (1992). Issues of power and control: Women in prison and their defenders. *British Journal of Criminology.* 32(4), 438–452.

Sulman, J. (1987). The worker's role in collectivity. *Social Work with Group.* 9(4), 59–67.

Sykes, G. (1958). *The society of captives: A study of a maximum security prison.* Princeton, NJ: Princeton University Press.

U.S. Department of Justice. (1988). *Report to the nation on crime and justice.* Washington, DC: U.S. Government Printing Office.

Widom, C. S. (1989a). Child abuse, neglect and violent criminal behavior. *Criminology.* 27(2), 251–271.

Widom, C. S. (1989b). Child abuse, neglect and adult behavior: Research design and findings on criminality, violence and child abuse. *American Journal of Orthopsychiatry.* 59(3), 355–366.

Widom, C. S. (1989c). Does violence beget violence? A critical examination of the literature. *Psychological Bulletin.* 106(1), 3–28.

Widom, C. S. (1989d). The cycle of violence. *Science.* 244, 160–165.

Widom, C. S. (1999). Posttraumatic stress disorder in abused and neglected children grown up. *American Journal of Psychiatry.* 156(8), 1223–1229.

Widom, C. S. (2000)???. Understanding the consequences of childhood victimization. In R. M. Reece (ed.), *The treatment of child abuse* (pp. 339–361). Baltimore, MD: Johns Hopkins University Press.

Wilson, P. (ed.). (1992). *Principles and practice of relapse prevention.* New York: Guilford Press.

Wright, M. M. (1993). Family-like group in a correctional setting. *Social Work with Group.* 16(4), 125–135.

PART IV

GAY MEN AND LESBIAN ISSUES

Chapter 20

Group Work with Gay Men

STEVEN BALL AND BENJAMIN LIPTON

In the history of social group work with gay men, as in the history of all mental health services to this population, the past three decades have witnessed a dramatic shift from a pathological stance that once regarded homosexuals as mentally ill to an affirmative model that assists gay men and lesbians in asserting their equal, healthy, and ethical place in society (Abelove; 1993; Gonsiorek, 1985; Isay, 1996). Currently, gay affirmative psychotherapy regards homophobia—anti-homosexual attitudes and behaviors (O'Hanlon et al., 1997)—rather than homosexuality as the major pathological variable affecting the mental health of this population (Margolies et al., 1987; Meyer, 1995). Since the psychosocial issues facing all gay men are the result of adapting to an environment that has denied them recognition and acceptance, groups serving this population can provide a healing antidote to a lifelong history of deprivation. The developmental process of growing up in an environment hostile to homosexuality creates a stigmatized identity for all gay men. As a result, it is essential that workers understand the overriding psychosocial factors arising from homophobia that inform individual responses to particular environmental stressors and life issues. Societal homophobia, internalized homophobia, stigmatization, coming out, gender role conflicts, familial and social relationships, and the impact of AIDS inform the process of all group work with gay men, regardless of the specific commonalities around which these groups may be organized. While the psychosocial needs and experiences of gay men are as diverse as those of any other minority group, this chapter will provide essential clinical information about the above issues that can inform practice with more specific subgroups of the population in a variety of social service settings.

REVIEW OF THE LITERATURE

Any overview of the social service and mental health literature on gay men must be understood within the rapidly changing social context of the past three decades (Abelove, 1993; Duberman, 1991; Isay, 1996; Signorile, 1997; Stein & Cohen, 1986). The response of social workers to those with a same-sex orientation reflects a historical progression from pathology to ambivalence across all mental health professions. Prior to 1973, when the American Psychiatric Association officially declassified homosexuality as pathological, gay men were considered mentally ill or perverse because of their sexual object choice. While a small but dedicated group of influential practitioners to this day remain committed to labeling homosexuality an illness (Bieber, 1962; Nicolosi, 1991; Socarides, 1978), growing numbers of gay and lesbian mental health practitioners, including many social workers (Deyton & Lear, 1988; Getzel, 1998), have united with an increasingly vocal and organized gay community in leading the way toward dismantling homophobic myths and creating a psychosocial model for healthy homosexuality. By openly challenging traditional models of pathology and exposing their lack of empirical support (Friedman & Downey, 1993), these men and women have paved the way toward developing an alternative, affirmative practice base for working with gay and lesbian clients.

Practitioners began developing a significant body of literature on the theory and practice of gay affirmative counseling and psychotherapy prior to the onset of AIDS in the early 1980s (Bell & Weinberg, 1978; Cass, 1979; Coleman, 1982; Gonsiorek, 1977). During this same period, psychotherapy groups for gay men primarily came out of the private practices and agency work of increasing numbers of openly gay mental health practitioners who were responding to the long-suppressed needs of their clients. As late as 1980, however, there was only one published article on generic group work with gay men, an outcome study of a short-term group conducted in Australia (Russell & Winkler, 1977). Subsequent reviews of the literature on group psychotherapy with this population by Conlin and Smith (1985) and by Schwartz and Hartstein (1986) reveal that they are the only articles of their kind that specifically address the role of group work in fostering psychosexual maturation in gay men rather than focusing on a particular psychosocial stressor affecting this population. Their articles document the process of groups designed to support, value, and integrate the gay identity by fostering disclosure of sexual orientation, providing opportunities for emotional intimacy, and confronting both external stigmatization and internalized homophobia.

How can we account for the gap in the literature on general group work with gay men over the past decade? We believe there are at least three related reasons. First, many social workers conventionally think of first contacts as individual, often relegating group treatment to a secondary or auxiliary position in treatment. Initial developments in gay affirmative psychotherapy seem to reflect this pattern. Second, at the historical moment when mental health agencies were beginning to sanction the use of affirmative models for group work with gay men, the biopsychosocial crisis of AIDS necessitated an immediate shift in treatment to this population (Caputo, 1985; de la Vega, 1990; Nichols, 1986; Shernoff, 1991). As clients and workers began to view the ongoing external and internal stressors of being self-identified as a gay man through the lens of the human immunodeficiency virus (HIV), the literature on practice with gay men focused on AIDS-related issues of immediate concern and provided a new context in which to understand gay identity development (Cadwell et al., 1994; Isay, 1989; Odets, 1994). Third, self-help has always been a necessary and essential part of the gay experience in a heterosexist, homophobic environment and consistently filled the gap in social services long before mainstream professionals formally responded by incorporating services into their organizations and documenting their work with contributions to the literature (Eller & King, 1990). The most powerful example of this process was the rapid and comprehensive organization of the gay community in response to AIDS when their needs were not addressed by social service agencies.

While much remains to be written about groups for gay men that do not specifically focus on AIDS issues a few resources have begun to emerge (Ball, 1998; Getzel, 1998). Nonetheless, the literature on AIDS-related group work provides an invaluable resource not only for understanding HIV issues but also for understanding deeper conflicts about being gay that will inform the process of working with any group of gay men (Tunnell, 1994). Regardless of the particular focus of any group, whether related to AIDS or not, what is most crucial is the opportunity to build social supports and interpersonal connections. *Homosocialization*, defined as building relationships with other gay men, is essential to the healthy integration of a homosexual identity and the discovery of positive gay role models (Isay, 1989). In their discussions of their work with gay populations, Hetrick and Martin (1987), Conlin and Smith (1985), and Schwartz and Hartstein (1986) all suggest that commonly shared issues arising from stigmatization such as social, cognitive, and emotional isolation—the negative outcomes of stigmatization—can best be coped with by creating opportunities for socialization with peers. Despite increasing visibility of gay people and debates in public law and social policy, recent research continues to uphold these earlier findings (Frable et al., 1998; Frable et al., 1997; Greene, 1996; Igreja et al., 2000; Lambda Legal Defense and Education Fund, 1999; Meyer, 1995). Since gay men are one of the few minorities denied the opportunity to identify with others like them because of both the absence of identifying factors and the oppression of a homonegative environment, group work with this population takes on ever-increasing importance in the lives of its members.

PRACTICE PRINCIPLES

Based on the pervasive impact of stigmatization and homonegativity on gay male development, as well as the need for homosocialization to mitigate the influence of these factors, the following practice principles and procedures should guide a social worker in beginning group work with the population.

Level of Worker Activity Inside and Outside of the Group

The worker's role in any group for gay men extends far beyond facilitating the group process. When developing a group for gay men, the need for outreach and psychoeducation can be guaranteed. Those most in need of a gay men's group may be the hardest to reach, as they remain unaffiliated with the gay community or unacknowledged within it, as in the case of HIV-negative men and gay men living with chronic illnesses other than HIV (Ball, 1998; Lipton, 1997, 1998; Odets, 1994). Outreach to the larger, nonspecifically gay environment away from traditional resources for membership such as community centers, bars, and social clubs may provide new awareness not only to those isolated men who could benefit from a gay group but also to the nongay community at large about issues confronting gay men.

While a secondary gain may be public education about the realities of gay life, an essential task of a social worker leading a gay men's group is to educate the staff of his or her social service agency about gay men. In-service training in addition to individual interactions will increase understanding about gay men and their particular issues as well as the potential for referrals. The combined acknowledgment of the community and the agency positively influences the functioning of the group, as potential members see the group as an acceptable and accepted source of support and a safe place to explore their concerns.

When the group process moves from the stage of pregroup formation to the beginning phase of group work, the social worker's role as an educator continues. Not only must the worker lend a vision and contribute data to the group as it begins to take shape, but throughout the life of the group he or she must continue to provide resources, conceptual frameworks, interpersonal modeling, and general education to counter the cognitive and experiential deficits that result from growing up in an environment void of gay role models and gay affirmative information. Implicit in a social worker's vision of the group must be the awareness that a gay person's stigmatization stems from a society—and a gay community—that often dictate a rigid repertoire of physical and social expressions that may impair healthy psychosocial development.

The Group as a Basic Resource

While the leader is initially responsible for guiding the development of group norms and modeling adaptive interpersonal relating, the goal of these interventions is to help group members see themselves as a source of support for each other and to develop a sense of belonging. Gay men enter groups with a legacy of isolation. Historically, societal groups have been sources of persecution for this population that reinforce a feeling of powerlessness rather than resources for affiliation and validation. When the group recognizes and employs their communal resources for support, group members can begin to counteract their collective history of disenfranchisement. Groups offer an opportunity to clarify emotional priorities and increase their capacity for building cohesive interpersonal networks. To this end, the social worker must consistently introduce, model, and reinforce group norms that invite the group to join with the leader as a basic resource for answers, empathy, and conflict resolution.

Boundaries and Confidentiality

A powerful effect of homophobia and stigmatization has been the internalization by many in the gay community of a narrow sense of identity organized around sex rather than sexual orientation. This reality makes group contracting around the issues of interacting both within and outside of the group of paramount importance in developing an environment of safety and trust. Often group members initially alternate between expressions of excitement and pleasure resulting from identification among members, and fear that the group will become yet another sexualized experience and lose its credibility as a safe space for exploring feelings. To foster and preserve a safe environment, the role of sex within the group process must be addressed from the outset. While setting limits for socialization may include members' abstaining from having sex with each other, it is particularly important in a group where sexual identity is an essential commonality to help members explore how sexual involvement between them would affect the ability of the group to function successfully. A social worker's initial interventions must reflect and normalize sexualized interactions such as flirting among members while helping the group to identify the role of these interactions in defending against emotional intimacy. Modeling an inquisitive stance toward the role of sexuality in initiating relationships in the group empowers members to begin to question what modes of socializing will best fit their needs and help them to realize their treatment goals.

Since gay men have historically had to respond to rather than determine the social norms, boundaries, and limits established by a heterosexual culture, social workers must recognize the interplay between the opportunity for self-determination and the fear of acquiescing to the restrictive norms of a dominant culture. It is the authors' experience that even in large cities that offer some sense of anonymity within the gay community, members may share some past or present social connection to other members. As a result, restricting socialization to the group may, on the one hand, not meet the needs of isolated gay men who would benefit from outside social support and, on the other hand, fail to mesh with the social reality of men already socialized within the gay community. While the group may recognize the need for guidelines on sexual interactions among members, efforts to restrict outside socialization, a common limit in many models of group work, need to be explored, contracted, and recontracted throughout the group process.

All of the principles discussed above must be founded on a firm commitment to the guiding group work principle of confidentiality. The leader must actively address the place of confidentiality in the group process and in outside contacts in order to establish a feeling of safety, particularly for those who have yet to speak openly about their sexual orientation. An ongoing exploration of this principle may provide a powerful opening to discussions of stigmatization and shame.

COMMON THEMES

While the themes discussed in this section will assume varying degrees of priority in groups organized around any number of commonalities, including coming out, substance abuse, sexual abuse, parenting, couples, bereavement, HIV status, aging, and socialization, they may also serve as the target issues for which groups for gay men are developed.

Homophobia

The socialization of every gay man involves exposure to homophobia. The literature refers to the subsequent internalization of the social animosity that a gay man experiences (Hetrick & Martin, 1987) as *internalized homophobia* and widely supports the view that the external and internal impacts of the resulting stigmatization must be addressed in treatment (Hetrick & Martin, 1987; Isay, 1989; Margolies et al., 1987; Silverstein, 1991; Tunnel, 1994). Homophobia frequently manifests itself alongside heterosexism, the culturally conditioned bias that heterosexuality is superior to other sexual orientations (Gonsiorek, 1985; Sears & Williams, 1997).

Homophobia manifests itself in a variety of ways, both blatant and subtle, internal and external, within the gay community and in society at large. It is essential to understand, first, that recognizing homophobia is not equal to eradicating it and, second, that one's some-sex orientation does not preclude homophobic beliefs and behaviors. Within the group process, homophobia may present as fear of disclosure in general; fear of disclosing one's sexual orientation; fear of commitment to the group; discomfort with more open group members or leaders; generalized rejection of heterosexuality; and denial of social differences between gay and heterosexual men. While some of these manifestations may on the surface seem far from homophobic, exploration of feelings will most often unearth negative attitudes and beliefs about what it means to be a gay man.

Stigmatization and Shame

As previously noted, stigmatization is the inevitable result of developing within a homophobic environment. Stigma is the precursor to shame in the psychosocial development of every gay man (Cadwell, 1992; Cain, 1991; Cornett, 1993). As members begin to share life histories, whether anecdotally in support groups or more formally in psychotherapy groups, common themes of rejection, isolation, violence, and abuse will often surface. This retelling of the impact of stigmatization will frequently find its complement in the current group process. Isensee (1991) and Cornett (1993) carefully outline the process by which shame interferes with interpersonal relating and fosters the development of a false self. Since the legacy of shame leads gay men to embrace negative stereotypes about their potential for developing lasting and important relationships, members may initiate a self-fulfilling prophecy that often results in treating one another in the same hostile/rejecting ways in which they fear being treated themselves.

Coming Out

As a gay man begins to integrate his sexuality, the impact of homophobia and stigmatization on gay male development necessitates a process that the literature defines as coming out—an ongoing developmental process of gay identity formation organized around revealing and accepting one's sexual orientation. Of seminal importance to the coming-out literature have been Coleman's (1982) five-stage model, which describes a developmental process from before coming out to integration, and Cass's (1979) six-stage model, which leads from identity confusion to identity synthesis as the gay man works to synthesize his sexuality with his self-concept. For a recent review of the coming-out literature that also provides new insight into the impact of HIV on gay male development, see Linde (1994) and Martin & Hunter (2001).

In order to understand the impact of any life crisis or stressor around which a group for gay men has been formulated, it is necessary to recognize the impact of coming out on each of the group members and on the group process as a whole (Cass, 1979). As stereotypes and dormant issues of homophobia, self-definition, and self-acceptance are activated by the diverse psychosocial issues and stages of members, a group organized around any task can offer a powerful experience on the coming-out continuum for those just beginning the process, as well as for those more openly identified as gay. Initial movements toward coming out in this society are often limited to sexual experimentation and sexualized socialization in bars, dance clubs, and parties. There are few opportunities to attend to the powerful emotions that generate and are generated by the coming-out experience. Whether beginning to come out or already identified as gay, gay men often arrive at a group with a lack of knowledge related to the diversity of gay lifestyles, range of social outlets, and ways of relating to others like themselves. A gay men's group can serve not only as an emotional anchor to explore turbulent feelings to self and others in regard to a specific common issue. It can also be a window on the diversity of the gay experience as one begins to identify more openly as a gay man and/or to expand one's understanding of what it means to be gay.

AIDS/HIV

In the third decade of the AIDS epidemic, HIV remains a central and consistent stressor in the daily lives of gay men, regardless of their HIV status (Cadwell et al.; see also Chapter 3, this volume). HIV is not only a health issue; it is a mental health issue that may further exacerbate existing stressors related to family, friends, relationships, life choices, and a sense of the future. Agencies may organize groups for gay men presenting with any number of HIV-related issues: HIV status, serodiscordant couples, care partners, risk reduction and prevention, early adjustment, bereavement, or substance abuse. Social workers providing group services to gay men within social service organizations will likely find themselves leading HIV-related groups.

Regardless of the particular task around which a social worker organizes a group for gay men, and regardless of whether or not the group task is itself specific to HIV, this concern will undoubtedly appear as a recurring theme in the group process. Any gay man will have to redefine his sense of self in a world of ongoing HIV-related trauma. Isensee (1991) outlines five areas in which AIDS continues to affect gay men: the trauma of a potentially life-threatening illness, hypervigilance, survivor guilt, effects on sexuality, and the impact of catastrophic loss. Now, more than a decade later, these issues continue to remain salient for many gay men. The uncertainty of both diagnosis and prognosis for all gay men, whether HIV positive or HIV negative, whether tested for HIV antibodies or untested, whether symptomatic or asymptomatic for AIDS, often leads to ongoing anxiety and depression. Such anxiety may manifest itself in hypervigilance—a preoccupation with any signs of illness at the expense of more productive and fulfilling activities of daily living. Anxiety may also manifest itself unconsciously as survivor guilt, a complex process through which one maladaptively manages overwhelming feelings of loss and abandonment by acting out a variety of more or less overtly self-destructive behaviors (Odets, 1994).

Emotional conflicts stemming from the trauma of HIV often affect the self-care behaviors of gay men. The legacy of homophobia and stigmatization prior to the AIDS epidemic already complicated their sex lives as feelings of shame frequently shrouded sexual behaviors in secrecy. As gay men struggle with shame, survivor guilt, and internalized homophobia, they may play out conflicting feelings in unsafe sexual practices or feelings of fear in abstinence. Additionally, challenges to HIV medication adherence can become entangled in psychological struggles that both predate and relate to one's status as HIV-positive. These issues require support and exploration toward empowering men to care for themselves most effectively. In an environment in which the link between sex and survival has been turned upside down, groups for gay men may offer invaluable forums for normalizing fears, clarifying values, disseminating information, and building a community of concern to mitigate against overwhelming feelings of confusion and isolation that might otherwise lead to self-destructive behavior. To this end, social workers must be willing to take on a psychoeducational role on the issues of safer sex and treatment adherence. Workers must not only respond to requests for information and discussion but also initiate them. When necessary, they must be prepared to make direct interventions to clarify and confront maladaptive defense structures of members and foster effective problem-solving skills.

Family Issues

As in group work with any population, the group process recapitulates for each gay member the family dynamics that he brings to the group (Yalom, 1995). For gay men who have most often grown up hiding their true selves from their families of origin, this aspect of the group process can prove either particularly traumatizing or extremely empowering. Even in families that appear to function well and attend to the psychosocial needs of all members, apparent attunement can mask underlying, unintentional emotional abuse. As the family fails even to consider the possibility that a son, brother, or father may be gay, the gay member remains silenced by shame, guilt, and secretiveness. If the group process recreates this experience for its members by failing to reach for and affirm self-disclosure and self-reflection about being gay, then the group will perpetuate emotional trauma. If, on the other hand, members are made aware of the dynamic of familial recapitulation in the group process and helped to use it to create new scripts of acceptance and affirmation, then the group can be an important place for developing and consolidating feelings of empowerment (Cornett, 1993; Isay, 1996).

For many gay men, particularly those who came of age in the period preceding public debate about the place of gay men within social structures, their definition of family has been expanded to include families of choice in addition to families of biological origin. Families of choice often develop during the initial stages of the coming-out process, as gay men have had to look outside of their families for acceptance and affirmation, as well as for affiliation with other gay men. Interdependent groups of gay men develop out of this search and provide each other with the physical and emotional caring that heterosexuals can usually expect from their families of origin. For some gay men, families of choice may even replace their families of origin as the primary reservoirs of emotional security. When working with gay men, it is essential to value and respect the place of these families within the lives of group members and to assess the roles that a member may play within his family of choice. Often these roles coincide with earlier roles played out in a member's family of origin and provide helpful information toward understanding the interpersonal dynamics that a member may bring to the group. A social worker must also be alert to the devastating impact of multiple losses and continual grieving on this system of psychosocial support since the beginning of the AIDS epidemic.

Gender Roles

Popular gay culture seems to have evolved, at least in part, in reaction to the collective childhood trauma of gender role nonconformity (Friedman, 1988). Literature on gay male development (Isay, 1989; Schwartz & Hartstein, 1986) suggests that such trauma may begin with a prehomosexual boy's relationship with his father. Emotional distance and unavailability of fathers often develop out of the father's conscious or unconscious homophobia and contribute to poor relations between these men and their gay children. Early negative relationships with fathers then are reinforced as developing gay men continue to interact with heterosexual males in larger social circles. Teased and ostracized for not taking part in traditionally masculine social and sexual pursuits, gay adolescents and younger men often develop feelings of shame and insecurity for failing to fit into heterosexual definitions of masculinity. In keeping with theories of oppressed populations, gay men may defend against these feelings by identifying with the same stereotypical images of traditional masculinity that oppress them. Unfortunately, identification with traditional masculine gender roles creates significant problems with building intimacy, trust, and a willingness to depend on other men.

Since many gay men come to groups with scarred self-images and difficulty relating openly to other men, an important task of any social worker will be to foster interdependence and group cohesion by exploring and normalizing an expansive, inclusive definition of masculinity unimpaired by traditional limitations. The group leader can employ basic, supportive social work skills to help members identify their feelings and learn to hear each other in increasingly empathic ways. The particular tasks of any group for gay men may allow members to peel away layers of maladaptive, rigid identifications in search of more fluid, emotionally responsive, true selves.

Relationships and Intimacy

Men who choose membership in a gay men's group desire relationships with other gay men. Often men may want to use the group either to find a romantic partner or to explore difficulties in their already existing partnerships. While the impulse to fall in love and partner exists for heterosexual as well as gay men, a social worker must be sensitive to the particular difficulties confronting single and coupled group members. Living within a homophobic society excludes gay men from the legal, religious, financial, and social structures that affirm and sanctify heterosexual coupling. Nevertheless, surveys of gay men demonstrate that more than half of them are involved in ongoing partnerships (Peplau, 1991).

To provide help in this area of psychosocial development, social workers must come to understand the ways in which both societal oppression and the characteristics of same-sex relationships impact on gay male couples and on gay men looking for a partner. For example, in contrast to the accepted heterosexual model of monogamy, many male couples in durable, committed relationships distinguish between emotional and sexual fidelity (Johnson & Keren, 1996). As members of a culture steeped in heterosexual norms, social workers must reflect carefully on their heterosexist biases and strive not to assign pathology or dysfunction to gay couples. A group leader must transfer these challenges to group members as well, reinforcing hope by presenting the group as a model for the potential in each member to build intimate relationships. At the same time, the social worker must identify the negative impact of internalized homophobia, heterosexist assumptions, and misleading stereotypes on the process of building intimacy in the group and help the group to reflect on how each of these affects external partnerships or efforts to establish them.

Ethnocultural Diversity

Contrary to prevalent stereotypes, racial, cultural, and ethnic diversity impact on the development and functioning of individual gay men (Fukujama & Ferguson, 2000; Greene, 1996). Just as the white, middle-class male does not represent all of American society, a social worker must recognize that the most easily identifiable gay men do not represent the population in all of its complexity. Since the majority of the literature on gay men is based on samples of white, middle-class men, neither the theory nor research that has resulted is necessarily relevant to all subgroups of the gay population. The marginalized place of ethnic and racial minorities within the literature on gay men parallels the social realities of minority populations not only within society at large but also within the gay community. Being gay does not preclude one from experiencing or fomenting ethnocultural prejudice. It is imperative for a group leader to recognize the additional stigmas of discrimination based on race, gender, age, or ethnicity that many men must carry.

Social workers must help group members to articulate and validate their particular ethnocultural experiences and conflicts in relation to their sexual orientation. For example, African-American gay men may experience identity conflicts as they search for a healthy place amid two problematic environments: their homophobic African-American heritage, on one hand, and the racist white gay culture, on the other (Adams & Kimmel, 1997; Crisp, 1998; Martinez & Sullivan, 2000). Carballo-Dieguez (1989), Colon (2000), Diaz (1997), Pares-Avila (1994), Rodriguez (1996), and Chan (1989) explore similar difficulties that arise from the interplay of race, ethnicity, and sexual orientation for Latino and Asian-American gay men. A group leader can help clients develop effective coping strategies for traversing seemingly exclusive cultures and provide a safe place for ventilating painful feelings of alienation from one or both groups.

In addition to ethnocultural factors, age affects one's identity as a gay man. Since AIDS began to take its toll on the lives of gay men, the concept of longevity has undergone radical redefinition. After the deaths of thousands of gay men from AIDS, men in their 40s and 50s are joining those in their 60s, 70s, and 80s in the developmental tasks of survivorship as they work through issues of loss and strive for regeneration (Rofes, 1996). As they tackle these difficult tasks, middle-aged and older gay men must develop an identity outside of a mainstream gay culture that lauds youth and pays little regard to its older members or to the realities of aging (Adams & Kimmel, 1997; Behney, 1994; Herdt et al., 1997; Kooden & Flowers, 2000; Rosenfeld, 1999). It is ironic that so many younger members in groups for gay men lament the scarcity of role models, while the culture in which these men are trying to find a place continues to marginalize older gay men. These men, the first generation to have had the possibility of living as openly gay for most of their adult lives, are invaluable and overlooked resources for the younger generation.

RECOMMENDED WAYS OF WORKING

The authors' clinical and anecdotal experiences reveal that many gay men continue to mistrust mental health providers, particularly in nongay settings. Such mistrust underscores the marginalized place of gay men within the mental health system, the need for outreach to the gay community, and the ways in which unattuned social work agencies and workers might reinforce injurious feelings of difference, isolation, and invisibility among gay people. To this end, the following section will provide information on effective ways of addressing the needs of this population through group work.

Pregroup Interview

The pregroup interview, an essential procedure for composing all groups, is particularly charged for gay men. It must initiate a process of attunement. For an individual whose identity and way of relating to his environment rest on anticipated rejection, the pregroup interview must set a tone of acceptance as the social worker actively normalizes a gay identity. As social workers attend to the psychosocial assessment of a prospective group member, including a determination of his developmental stage in the coming-out process, the worker must demonstrate real knowledge and awareness of gay issues and the gay community. At the same time, the worker who is less informed about these subjects must acknowledge his ignorance and demonstrate a willingness to learn more about them from sources *outside* of the group so as not to reinforce or repeat negative experiences of members requiring them to confront homophobic misinformation from the group leader (Kus, 1990). Clients must be informed about the diversity of membership and told that the group will not focus on labels or definitions, but instead on their own needs regarding their concerns about being gay and how it may relate to the specific focus of the group.

Member Selection

Groups for gay men must affirm inclusion. As a social worker evaluates an interviewee's appropriateness for group membership, he or she must guard vigilantly against recapitulating a lifelong process of rejection and exclusion from social group participation. Excluding gay men from groups designed specifically for them may not only perpetuate feelings of isolation but may actually leave the client isolated from specific gay services, particularly in geographic areas where there are few alternative resources for this population. Since many agencies do not offer a wide variety of group services to gay men, social workers may find themselves leading groups that must address myriad divergent needs. As a result, the major criteria for membership should be an expressed desire to be a group member and a willingness to commit to the group process. For groups that do not require specific inclusion criteria, only those who are unable to acknowledge consciously that they are attracted primarily to other men to satisfy their sexual and affectional needs, or who are actively psychotic or antisocial in personality, should be excluded (Getzel, 1998).

The question of whether or not to include bisexual clients in groups for gay men often depends on the specific focus and setting of the group. If the group is a more general therapy group, then including bisexual men may prove very helpful in fostering acceptance of diversity and recognition of the complexity of sexual identity. Similarly, in a coming-out group, one could include bisexual men because they share issues with gay men regarding accepting their desire for members of the same sex. In fact, many men who later identify as gay prefer to label themselves bisexual when they first begin to integrate their same-sex object choice (Isay, 1989). If, however, group cohesion is organized around a particular issue or theme not focused on identity formation, then including bisexual men may prove counterproductive to the group task. In an HIV-negative men's group, for example, including bisexual men may create scapegoating and divert the group's process away from the established group focus. At the same time, the limitations of agency provisions and geographic realities may require the group leader to adjust inclusion criteria for the needs of a bisexual client.

Self-Disclosure and Modeling

The social worker's disclosure of his or her own sexual orientation is essential to creating an affirmative environment in which clients can explore their sexuality. Cornett (1993) and Frommer (1994) suggest that clients enter treatment with an inherently nonneutral, heterosexist assumption of a social worker's orientation. As a result, they believe a gay social worker should disclose this information when asked by the client and after a careful exploration to determine its meaning for the client in treatment. They contend that gay leaders provide invaluable opportunities for positive gay role models in a world where too few exist (Isay, 1996). Failure to self-disclose as a gay leader at the beginning of the group experience forsakes an invaluable opportunity to model an affirmative stance toward homosexuality in the service of establishing a trusting environment and building cohesion. Conlin and Smith (1985) believe that gay social workers leading groups for gay men should be in the late stage of their coming-out process. Such leaders may be more able to tolerate the often powerful and ambivalent feelings of those members who remain at earlier stages in the process and reflect to the group more subtle manifestations of homophobia in the group process.

The issue of self-disclosure for heterosexual social workers leading groups for gay men has not been adequately addressed in the literature. Gay affirmative theory seems to be moving toward asserting the value of gay clients receiving treatment from gay practitioners (Ball, 1998; Isay, 1989). However, the reality of human resources within social service agencies requires that heterosexual social workers also provide services to gay clients. The question of self-disclosure remains for heterosexual leaders, but the dynamics are significantly different. Particularly in short-term, problem-focused, and support groups, persistent focusing on the group leader who does not disclose may well sidetrack or derail the necessary tasks of the group and permit the development of maladaptive defenses against group affiliation and intimacy. In any group, a heterosexual social worker must have become a social anthropologist prior to beginning work with the group. He or she must not only identify his or her own homonegative attitudes, beliefs, and behaviors, but also must develop a firm understanding of and belief in the complexity of gay culture and life experiences.

While self-disclosure is important, how one handles disclosure is as important as the act of disclosing itself. The tension between offering a supportive, positive environment for self-exploration, on the one hand, and impinging on a client's ability to verbalize any and all feelings of shame and self-doubt, on the other, must inform the social worker's process of disclosing his or her sexual orientation to group members. The social worker who does not remain keenly aware of his or her own internalized homophobia may shut the door on more helpful explorations of shame and guilt and the healthy desire of members to identify with the gay group leader as a positive role model or a heterosexual leader as a genuinely informed and nurturing influence.

Case

A heterosexual female social worker experienced in group work with gay men was assigned to lead a coming-out group in the absence of openly gay staff at the university counseling service where she worked. After the second group session, the group fell into several weeks of very little activity in spite of the worker's skilled efforts to elicit participation. Long periods of silence were followed by occasional bickering and apologies between members. After 5 weeks, two members had dropped out of the group and those remaining began to express feelings of hopelessness. The worker's supervisor stated that these dynamics were not unusual in the beginning stages of group work and focused on processing the worker's anxiety about her difference from group members. Nonetheless, after reviewing the group process of the preceding weeks, the social worker suggested to the group in the next session that their disappointment and difficulty in moving forward was related not only to her gender difference but also to her perceived sexual orientation as heterosexual.

The group immediately responded. Several members finally expressed feelings of mistrust, anger, and disappointment that the leader was not a gay man. The social worker validated their concerns and managed to redirect the group's anger away from each other and toward her. Her ability to remain supportive and empathic during this period in the group process helped move the group to a new level of openness, understanding, and cohesion.

After many weeks, group members expressed idealized feelings toward the social worker and expressed surprise that they could experience her as particularly nurturing. One client joked, "You must be a lesbian." The group immediately picked up on this theme and demanded an answer, which the leader agreed to provide after the group explored their thoughts and fantasies on the subject. When the social worker finally acknowledged her heterosexuality, the members were able to explore more fully both their heterophobia and their homophobia within a safe environment.

Group Prospectus

A social worker, and sometimes an agency or another sponsoring organization, must decide whether a group should be open or closed and short or long term, based on the group's task and setting. To hasten acceptance within an nongay identified agency that has not previously had a gay-related group, a worker should structure the group to imitate the prevailing model for group work in the agency in order to integrate and normalize the group within the agency culture. These efforts not only elicit acceptance by staff and administration, but also suggest to gay clients that the agency provides a safe place to discuss and explore their sexual orientation.

Case

An openly gay social worker in a continuing day treatment program recognized the need for a gay men's group after several clients confided feeling isolated and unable to express themselves openly in groups, the primary treatment modality at the agency. The worker confronted agency homophobia by educating the staff about the needs of gay and lesbian clients and documenting clients' concerns. The executive director ultimately overrode the worker's immediate supervisor and sanctioned the group.

Initially, the group was composed of clients who had been attending the treatment program for some time. The group process seemed to parallel long-standing institutional beliefs that the group did not belong in the treatment program. Members projected powerful feelings of internalized homophobia onto each other and prevented group cohesion by verbally attacking each for coming out to community members outside of the group. One member stated, "I didn't come to this place to work on my sexual orientation or identity stuff I came here to deal with my psychiatric problems."

As some of the more hostile, intensely homophobic clients left the group, new clients who had entered treatment after the gay group had already been integrated into the agency began contributing more to the process. Members developed greater social relatedness as they began to see themselves not only as part of an affirming gay subgroup, but also as people integrated and accepted by the rehabilitative community. To date, the group has been ongoing for 4 years.

Whether homosexual or heterosexual, a social worker leading groups for gay men must be gay affirmative; cognizant of the powerful impact of homophobia on oneself and on one's clients and willing to address the issue directly; sensitive to the diverse experiences of gay and bisexual men; vigilant against subscribing to destructive stereotypes; and open to exploring both heterosexuality and homosexuality without permitting personal ideology or identity to contaminate professional explorations. In the authors' experience, coming out professionally not only enhances one's self-esteem and professional identity, but also may be a primary step toward helping an agency respond to the emotional needs of its gay, lesbian, and bisexual clients and staff. Hiring motivated, openly gay social workers may increase interest in and attention to the particular needs of gay men while providing essential role models for an all too often silenced, shamed, and ignored population. Armed with awareness, acceptance, and a genuine desire to be helpful, social workers working with gay men can create precious spaces in which these individuals can work toward developing self-esteem, integrating their sexuality, and building emotionally intimate relationships with their peers.

EVALUATION APPROACHES

Outcome measures for clients in gay men's groups remain anecdotal. To date, no instruments directly addressing the outcomes of work with this population in groups have been developed for public use, although instruments for addressing individual problems such as low self-esteem or homophobia could certainly be incorporated into an outcome study of group work with gay men. As in most group work, eliciting outcome information is an essential component of termination. Statements about improved psychosocial functioning seem to be the best barometer for determining the effectiveness of the group. Desire for continued affiliation with other gay men; a sense of belonging both within the gay community and within the larger social environment; improved social and intimate relationships; and diminished homophobic statements and behaviors all would testify to positive outcomes. As men in these groups learn to celebrate their everyday heroism and hard-earned strengths in living as openly gay, hopefully they will carry their resilience outside of their groups, use it to expand on previous roles, and adopt a more affirmative sense of themselves.

RESOURCES

For the most part, mental health services for this population are provided at the local and regional level. To locate these services in a particular region, we suggest consulting the Gay Yellow Pages, which can be found in many bookstores and libraries.

American Civil Liberties Union/
Lesbian and Gay Rights Project
132 West 43rd Street
New York, NY 10036
(212) 944-9800
www.aclu.org
The ACLU provides legal services
aimed at advancing the rights of gay
men and lesbians and educating the
public about discrimination.

Gay Asian Pacific Support Network
(GAPSN)
PO Box 461104
Los Angeles, CA 90046
www.gapsn.org
GAPSN is a source of support and
information for gay, lesbian,
bisexual, and transgender people of
Asian/Pacific Islander descent.

Gay and Lesbian Alliance Against
Defamation (GLAAD)
150 West 26th Street
New York, NY 10011
(212) 627-1398
www.glaad.org
GLAAD promotes visibility of
the gay and lesbian community
and organizes grass-roots
responses to homophobia in
the media.

Gay, Lesbian and Straight Education
Network (GLSEN)
121 West 27th Street, Suite 804
New York, NY 10001
(212) 727-0135
www.glsen.org
GLSEN is a national alliance with
regional offices and local chapters
that advocates for the dignity and
respect of all students regardless of
sexual orientation.

Gay Men of African Descent
(GMAD)
103 East 125th Street, Suite 503
New York, NY 10035
(212) 828-1697
www.gmad.org

The mission of GMAD is to empower
gay men of African descent through
education, advocacy, health and
wellness, prevention, and social
support.

The Hetrick Martin Institute
2 Astor Place
New York, NY 10003
(212) 674-2400
www.hmi.org
The Hetrick Martin Institute
provides comprehensive social
services, high school education,
and referrals for gay and lesbian
adolescents.

Lambda Legal Defense and Education
Fund
666 Broadway
New York, NY 10012
(212) 995-8585
www.lambdalegal.org
Lambda is an organization of gay men
and lesbians providing political advocacy and legal services to gay men
and lesbians.

Llego
1420 K Street NW, Suite 200
Washington, DC 10005
(202) 408-5380
www.llego.org
Llego is a national organization
whose mission is to effectively
address issues of concern to lesbian,
gay, bisexual, and transgender
Latinas/Latinos at local, state,
regional, national, and international
levels.

Parents and Friends of Lesbians and
Gays (P-FLAG)
P.O. Box 27605
Washington, DC 20038
(202) 638-4200
www.pflag.org
With chapters throughout the
country, P-FLAG is an invaluable
resource for information and
support for gay people and their

families and friends, particularly those struggling with coming out.

Pride Institute Hotline
800-54-PRIDE
(612) 934-7554 (within Minnesota)
www.pride-institute.com
The Pride Institute provides residential chemical dependency programs as well as referral to local resources.

Senior Action in a Gay Environment (SAGE)
208 West 13th Street
New York, NY 10011
(212) 741-2247
www.sageusa.org
SAGE provides services and socializing for older gay men and lesbians. The New York office may provide referrals to services throughout the nation.

REFERENCES

Abelove, H. (1993). Freud, male homosexuality and the Americans. In H. Abelove et. al. (eds.), *The lesbian and gay studies reader* (pp. 381–393). New York: Routledge Press.

Adams, C. L., & Kimmel, D. C. (1997). Exploring the lives of older African American gay men. In B. Greene (ed.), *Ethnic and cultural diversity among lesbians and gay men: Psychological perspectives on lesbian and gay issues*, vol. 3 (pp. 132–151). Thousand Oaks, CA: Sage Publications.

Ball, S. (1994). A group model for gay and lesbian clients with chronic mental illness. *Social Work.* 39 (1), 109–115.

Ball, S. (ed.) (1998). *The HIV-negative gay man.* New York: Harrington Park Press.

Behney, R. (1994). The aging network's response to gay and lesbian issues. *Outword,* Winter, pp. 2–5.

Bell, A. P., & Weinberg, M. S. (1978). *Homosexualities: A study of diversity among men and women.* New York: Simon & Schuster.

Bieber, I. (1962) *Homosexuality: A psychoanalytic study.* New York: Basic Books.

Cadwell, S. A., Burnham, R. A., & Forstein, M. (eds.), *Therapists on the front line: Psychotherapy with gay men in the age of AIDS* (pp. 453–471). Washington, DC: American Psychiatric Press.

Cadwell, S. (1992). Twice removed: The stigma suffered by gay men with AIDS. *Smith Studies in Social Work.* 61 (3), 236–246.

Cain, R. (1991). Stigma management and gay identity development: *Social Work.* 36(1), 67–73.

Caputo, L. (1985). Dual diagnosis: AIDS and addiction. *Social Work.* 30(4), 361–363.

Carballo-Dieguez, A. (1989). Hispanic culture, gay male culture, and AIDS: Counseling implications. *Journal of Counseling and Development.* 68(1), 26–30.

Cass, V. (1979). Homosexual identity formation: A theoretical model. *Journal of Homosexuality.* 4, 219–235.

Chan, C. (1989). Issues of identity development among Asian-American lesbians and gay men. *Journal of Counseling and Development.* 68(1), 16–20.

Coleman, E. (1982). The developmental stages of the coming out process. In J. C. Gonsiorek (ed.), *Homosexuality and psychotherapy: A practitioner's handbook of affirmative models* (pp. 31–43). New York: Haworth Press.

Colon, E. (2001). An ethnographic study of six Latino men. *Journal of Gay and Lesbian Social Services.* 12(3–4), 77–92.

Conlin, D., & Smith, J. (1985). Group psychotherapy for gay men. In J. Gonsiorek (ed.), *A guide to psychotherapy with gay and lesbian clients* (pp. 105–112). New York: Harrington Park Press.

Cornett, C. (ed.) (1993). *Affirmative dynamic psychotherapy with gay men.* Northvale, NJ: Jason Aronson.

Crisp, D. (1998). African American gay men: Developmental issues, choices and self-concept. *Family Therapy.* 25(3): 161–168.

De la Vega, E. (1990). Considerations for reaching the Latino population with sexuality and HIV/AIDS information and education. *SIECUS Report.* 18(3), 1–8.

Deyton, B., & Lear, W. (1988). A brief history of the gay/lesbian health movement in the U.S.A. In M. Shernoff & W. Scott (eds.), *The sourcebook of lesbian/gay health-care,* (2nd ed.) (pp. 15–19). Washington, DC: National Lesbian/Gay Health Foundation.

Diaz, R. (1997). Latino gay men and psycho-cultural barriers to HIV prevention. In M. Levine and P. Nardi (eds.), *Changing times: Gay men and lesbians encounter HIV/AIDS* (221–244). Chicago: University of Chicago Press.

Eller, M., & King, D. (1990). Self help groups for gays, lesbians and their loved ones. In Kus, R. (ed.), *Keys to caring* (pp. 330–339). Boston: Alyson Publications.

Frable, D. E. S., Platt, L., & Hoey, S. (1998). Concealable stigma and positive self-perceptions: Feeling better around similar others. *Journal of Personality and Social Psychology.* 24(4), 909–922.

Frable, D. E. S., Wortman, C., & Joseph, J. (1997). Predicting self-esteem, well-being, and distress in a cohort of gay men: The importance of cultural stigma, personal visibility, community networks, and positive identity. *Journal of Personality.* 65(3), 599–624.

Friedman, R. C., & Downey, J. (1993). Psychoanalysis, psychobiology and homosexuality. *Journal of the American Psychoanalytic Association.* 41(4), 1159–1198.

Frommer, M. S. (forthcoming) Homosexuality and psychoanalysis: Technical considerations revisited. *Psychoanalytic Dialogues.* 4.

Fukuyama, M. A., & Ferguson, A. D. (2000). Lesbian, gay and bisexual people of color: Understanding cultural complexity and managing multiple oppressions. In R. Perez & K. DeBord (eds.), *Handbook of counseling and psychotherapy with lesbian, bay and bisexual clients* (pp. 81–105). Washington, DC: American Psychological Association.

Getzel, G. (1998). "Group Work with Gay Men and Lesbians." In G. Mallon (ed.), *Foundations of social work practice with gay men and lesbian women* (pp. 131–144). New York: Haworth Press.

Gonsiorek, J. (1985) *A guide to psychotherapy with gay and lesbian clients.* New York: Harrington Park Press.

Gonsiorek, J. (1977). Psychological adjustment and homosexuality. *JSAS Catalog of Selected Documents in Psychology.* 7, 45 (MS No. 1478).

Greene, B. (1996). Lesbian and gay men of color: The legacy of ethnosexual mythologies in heterosexim and homophobia. In E. D. Rothblum & L. A. Bond (eds.), *Preventing heterosexism and homophobia: Primary prevention of psychopathology.* Vol. 17 (59–70). Thousand Oaks, CA: Sage Publications.

Hays, R. B., Turner, H., & Coates, P. (1992). Social support, AIDS-related symptoms, and depression among gay men. *Journal of Consulting and Clinical Psychology.* 60, 463–469.

Herdt, G., Beeler, J., & Rawls, T. W. (1997). Life course diversity among old lesbians and gay men: A study in Chicago. *Journal of Gay, Lesbian and Bisexual Identity.* 2(3/4), 231–246.

Herek, G. M. (1990). Illness, Stigma and AIDS. In P. T. Costa, & G. R. VandenBos (eds.), *Psychological aspects of serious illness: Chronic conditions, fatal diseases, and clinical care* (pp. 107–149). Washington, DC: American Psychological Association.

Hetrick, E. S., & Martin, A. D. (1984). Ego-dystonic homosexuality: A developmental view. In E. S. Hetrick & T. S. Stein (eds.), *Innovations in psychotherapy with homosexuals* (pp. 2–21). Washington, DC: American Psychiatric Association Press.

Hetrick, E. S., & Martin, A. D. (1987). Developmental issues and their resolution for gay and lesbian adolescents. In E. Coleman (ed.), *Integrated identity for gay men and lesbians* (pp. 25–43). New York: Harrington Park Press.

Igreja, I., Zuroff, D., Koestner, R., & Saltaris, C. (2000). Social motives, social support and distress in gay men differing in HIV Status. *Journal of Research in Personality.* 34(3), 287–304.

Isay, R. (1989). *Being homosexual: Gay men and their development.* New York: Farrar, Straus & Giroux.

Isay, R. (1996). *Becoming gay: The journey to self-acceptance.* New York: Pantheon Books.

Isensee, R. (1991). *Growing up gay in a dysfunctional family.* New York: Prentice Hall Press.

Johnson, T. W., & Keren, M. S. (1996). Creating and maintaining boundaries in male couples. In J. Laird & R. Green (eds.), *Lesbians and gays in couples and families: A handbook for therapists* (pp. 231–239). San Francisco: Jossey-Bass Publishers.

Kooden, H., & Flowers, C. (2000). *Golden men: The power of gay midlife.* New York: Avon Books.

Kus, R. (1990). *Keys to caring.* Boston: Alyson Publications.

Lambda Legal Defense and Education Fund (1999). *State-by-state sodomy law update.* New York.

Lewes, K. (1988) *The psychoanalytic theory of male homosexuality.* New York: Simon & Schuster.

Lewis, J. (1999). Status passages: The experience of HIV-positive gay men. *Journal of Homosexuality.* 37(3), 87–115.

Linde, R. (1994). Impact of AIDS on adult gay male development: Implications for psychotherapy. In S. A. Cadwell, R. A. Burnham, Jr., & M. Forstein (eds.), *Therapists on the front line: Psychotherapy with gay men in the age of AIDS* (pp. 453–471). Washington, DC: American Psychiatric Press.

Linn, G. L., Lewis, F. M., Cain, V. A., & Kimgrough, G. A. (1993). HIV-illness, social support, sense of coherence, and psychosocial well-being in a sample of help-seeking adults. *AIDS Education and Prevention.* 4(3), 254–262.

Lipton, B. (1998). The psychosocial impact of colon and rectal disease on gay men. *Seminars in Colon and Rectal Surgery.* 9(2), 149–154.

Lipton, B. (1997). Responding to non-HIV invisible chronic illness within the gay male community. *Journal of Gay and Lesbian Social Services.* 7(1), 93–98.

Margolies, L., Becker, M., & Jackson-Brewer (1987). Internalized homophobia: Identifying and treating the oppressor within. In Boston Lesbian Psychologies Collective, *Lesbian psychologies: Explorations and challenges* (pp. 229–241). Chicago: University of Illinois.

Martin, J., and Hunter, S. (2001). Lesbian, gay, bisexual and transgender issues in social work: A comprehensive bibliography with annotations. Alexandria, VA: Council on Social Work Education.

Martinez, D. G., & Sullivan, S. C. (2000). African American gay men and lesbians: Examining the complexity of gay identity development. In L. A. Letha (ed.), *Human behavior in the social environment from an African American perspective* (pp. 243–264). Athens, GA: University of Georgia Press.

Meyer, I. H. (1995). Minority stress and mental health in gay men. *Journal of Health and Social Behavior.* 36 (March), 38–56.

Nichols, S. E. (1986). Psychotherapy and AIDS. In T. S. Stein & C. J. Cohen (eds.), *Contemporary perspectives on psychotherapy with lesbians and gay men* (pp. 209–239). New York: Plenum Press.

Nicolosi, J. (1991). *The reparative therapy of male homosexuality: A new clinical approach.* Northvale, NJ: Jason Aronson.

Odets, W. (1994). Survivor guilt in seronegative gay men. In S. A. Cadwell, R. A. Burnham, Jr., & M. Forstein (eds.), *Therapists on the front line: Psychotherapy with gay men in the age of AIDS* (pp. 453–471). Washington, DC: American Psychiatric Press.

O'Hanlan, K., Cabaj, R. B., Schatz, B., Lock, J., & Nemrow, P. (1997). A review of the medical consequences of homophobia with suggestions for resolution. *Journal of the Gay and Lesbian Medical Association.* 1(1), 25–40.

Paradis, B. A. (1993). A self-psychological approach to the treatment of gay men with AIDS. *Clinical Social Work Journal.* 21(4), 405–416. Washington, DC: American Psychiatric Press.

Pares-Avila (1994). Issues in the psychosocial care of Latino gay men with HIV infection. In S. Cadwell & R. Burnham, Jr. (eds.), *Therapists on the front line: Psychotherapy with gay men in the age of AIDS* (pp. 339–362). Washington, DC: American Psychiatric Press.

Peplau, L. (1991). Lesbian and gay relationships. In J. Gonsiorek & J. Weinrich (eds.), *Homosexuality: Research implications for public policy* (pp. 177–196). Newbury Park: Sage Publications.

Pillard, R. (1999). The causes of homosexuality are probably genetic. In M. E. Williams (ed.), *Homosexuality: Opposing viewpoints* (pp. 27–34) San Diego, CA: Greenhaven Press.

Rodriguez, R. (1996). Clinical issues in identity development in gay Latino men. In C. Alexander (ed.), *Gay and lesbian mental health: A sourcebook for practitioners* (pp. 127–157). New York: Haworth Park Press.

Rofes, E. (1996). *Reviving the tribe: Regenerating gay men's sexuality and culture in the ongoing epidemic.* New York: Harrington Park Press.

Rosenfeld, D. (1999). Identity work among the homosexual elderly. *Journal of Aging Studies.* 13(2), 121.

Ross, M. R. (1990). The relationship between life events and mental health in homosexual men. *Journal of Clinical Psychology.* 46(4), 403–411.

Rotheram-Boerus, M., Hunter, J., & Rosario, M. (1994). Suicidal behavior and gay-related stress among gay and bisexual male adolescents. *Journal of Adolescent Research.* 9, 498–508.

Russell, A., & Winkler, R. (1977). Evaluation of assertiveness training and homosexual guidance service groups designed to improve homosexual functioning. *Journal of Consulting and Clinical Psychology.* 45(1), 1–13.

Sandstrom, K. (1996). Searching for information, understanding, and self-value: The utilization of peer support groups by gay men with HIV/AIDS. *Social Work in Health Care.* 23(4), 51–74.

Savin-Williams, R. (1994). Verbal and physical abuse as stressors in the lives of lesbian, gay male, and bisexual youths. *Journal of Consulting and Clinical Psychology.* 62, 261–269.

Schoenberg, R., & Goldberg, R. S. (eds.) (1985). *With compassion towards some: Homosexuality and social work in America.* New York: Harrington Park Press.

Schwartz, W. (1985). The group work tradition and social work practice. *Social Work with Groups.* 8(4), 7–27.

Schwartz, R., & Hartstein, N. (1986). Group psychotherapy with gay men. In T. Stein and C. Cohen (eds.), *Contemporary perspectives on psychotherapy with lesbians and gay men* (pp. 157–177). New York: Plenum Press.

Sears, J. T., & Williams, W. L. (eds.) (1997). *Overcoming heterosexism and homophobia: Strategies that work.* New York: Columbia University Press.

Shernoff, M. (1991). Eight years of working with people with HIV: The impact upon a therapist. In C. Silverstein (ed.), *Gays, lesbians, and their therapists* (pp. 227–239). New York: W. W. Norton.

Shulman, L. (1984). *The skills of helping individuals and groups.* Itasca, IL: F. E. Peacock.

Signorile, M. (1997). *The Signorile report on gay men: Sex, drugs, muscles and the passages of life.* New York: Harper Collins.

Silverstein, C. (ed.) (1991). *Gays, lesbians, and their therapists.* New York: W. W. Norton.

Socarides, C. (1978). *Homosexuality.* New York: Jason Aronson.

Stall, R. (2002). Access to health care among men who have sex with men: Data from the Urban Men's Health Study. *Advancing gay and lesbian health: A report from the gay and lesbian health roundtable.* Los Angeles, CA: Los Angeles Gay and Lesbian Center.

Stein, T. S., & Cohen, C. J. (eds.) (1986). *Psychotherapy with lesbians and gay men.* New York: Plenum Press.

Tunnel, G. (1994). Special issues in group psychotherapy for gay men with AIDS. In S. A. Cadwell, R. A. Burnham, Jr., & M. Forstein (eds.), *Therapists on the front line: Psychotherapy with gay men in the age of AIDS* (pp. 453–471). Washington, DC: American Psychiatric Press.

Wagner, G., Brondolo, E., & Rabkin, J. (1996). Internalized homophobia in a sample of HIV+ gay men, and its relationship to psychological distress, coping, and illness progression. *Journal of Homosexuality.* 32(2), 91–105.

Yalom, I. (1985). *The theory and practice of group psychotherapy* (3rd edition). New York: Basic Books.

Chapter 21

Group Work with Lesbians

BONNIE J. ENGLEHARDT

The purpose of this chapter is to acquaint social workers with the important issues facing lesbian women and to promote social group work as the
primary modality offered to the lesbian client. Lesbians are at risk in our
heterosexist, misogynist, homophobic society. They cannot participate
fully in our societal institutions and are denied social acceptance. It is
therefore imperative to include this chapter in a social work textbook focusing on at-risk populations. Previously, little nonheterosexist material
was available for new workers. An *Annotated Bibliography of Gay and
Lesbian Readings*, edited by Judith A. B. Lee, under the sponsorship of
the Commission on Lesbian Women and Gay Men of the Council on
Social Work Education, was published in 1991. It was developed out of
the Council's mandate "to build knowledge about diversity and its commitment to oppressed groups" (p. i). The introduction of this second
edition states, "it represents approximately a twenty-year survey and review of the literature with an eye toward what is genuinely helpful to minorities of sexual orientation" (p. v), noting that previously articles had
been written in "medical language with words like 'deviance,' 'perver-
sion,' 'ego dystonic homosexuality,' 'developmental arrest,'" and other pejorative terminology.

As clinical social workers, we cannot support any implication that the
primary cause of lesbians' difficulties in adjusting to their sexual identity
is intrapsychic. The primary obstacles for any minority group today originate in the dominant culture and interaction with it. Saulnier (2000) provides a practice example of the need "to examine the power of words by
analyzing the social production of lesbianism." A group facilitator of a lesbian support group states:

"I wanted us to look at lesbianism not just as a personal phenomenon but as a social phenomenon . . . people still deal with stigma and that's a major issue in terms of educating and having support groups— to talk about the stigmatization—There's always going to be a need for someone to understand the powerful effect of growing up in a culture that's your culture but from which you are banished" (Saulnier, 2002, p. 15).

Social workers have written about the effects of racism, classism, sexism, and ageism on our clientele, but this chapter deals with homophobia stemming from our heterosexist society. Herek (1986), looking at the social psychology of homophobia, defined heterosexism "as a world-view, a value system that prizes heterosexuality, assumes it is the only appropriate manifestation of love and sexuality, and devalues homosexuality" (p. 924). Homophobia is defined as the "prejudice, discrimination, and hostility directed at gay men and lesbian women because of their sexual orientation" (Ellis & Murphy, 1994, p. 50). It should be noted that the experience of homophobia linked with sexism is unique to the lesbian culture and that lesbians of color often experience the triple threat of racism, sexism, and homophobia.

As social group workers, we favor group work as the primary modality offered to the lesbian client, whether or not the leader is a lesbian. Group work provides a connection with other lesbians in a safe, partially controlled environment and places responsibility for the evolution of the content and process on the members, not the leader. This allows the diversity needed for individual lesbians, who might be lost in their own identity crises, to appreciate that there are many right choices about how to live one's life as a lesbian. It diffuses the power of the leader and clarifies the need for variety in the role modeling available to women entering the lesbian community. It is an invaluable experience to be in the company of lesbian women talking about their lives because, for all of us, the *invisibility* of the lesbian lifestyle is prominent. In groups, lesbians can gain a perspective on how their choices are similar to or different from those of other lesbians, thereby acquiring more knowledge of what is the norm of lesbian life.

It is important to understand that there is no unified lesbian community, only many distinct lesbian communities. There is no typical lesbian, but rather many unique lesbian women who have developed individually into the type of lesbian that they are today. Good social work practice entails getting the particulars from any lesbian about her own development as a lesbian without making *any* assumptions. It is empowering to an individual to experience her own journey as being a valid developmental process without trying to impose a societal stereotype, a social work definition, or a lesbian community mandate. Having established that no one person, process, or experience is typical, we can then proceed to look for the commonalities. There are no universal paths to lesbian iden-

tity development, but coming out or disclosure stages have been noted in
the literature (Lehman, 1978; Roth, 1985; Roth & Murphy, 1986). Five or
six stages are usually noted including disclosure to self, significant family
members, and intimate others, disclosure at the workplace and in social
networks, and identification with the lesbian label and community.

Social workers must be cognizant of the lesbian client's intrapsychic
and sociopolitical issues in order to help her decide whether her presenting problems are primarily:

- intrapsychic issues, and a therapy group is needed;
- related to her coming-out process, and a group focused on self-
  acceptance and disclosure strategies is appropriate;
- isolation-based issues so that a support group is needed to connect
  her to the lesbian subculture;
- issues of oppression and discrimination, so that an action-oriented
  empowerment group would be helpful;
- a combination of these situations requiring more than one type of
  group intervention.

Social workers need to provide opportunities for lesbian women to
find their natural processes of self-disclosure and disclosure to others
without stigmatization. We need to be able to differentiate the more vulnerable women who could become marginalized during the coming-out
process. Even though there is debate about whether lesbianism is caused
or created—predetermined genetically or chosen as a preference—
everyone does agree that the lesbian woman has to continue to make the
choice of self-disclosure or disclosure to others every day. A safe group
environment is especially helpful for this process. A group may be composed entirely of lesbian women and formed with this awareness in mind
or it may contain lesbians, with or without the knowledge of the nonles-
bian members.

The phrase *lesbian women* is used by Murphy (1992) "to affirm the
use of the terms gay and lesbian as *adjectives* rather than as *nouns* to highlight that sexual orientation is only one aspect of an individual's life AND
to emphasize that lesbian women may have more in common with heterosexual women than with gay men" (p. 242). As noted above, only for
the lesbian is the experience of homophobia linked with sexism. While
this double identity may allow some lesbians to feel comfortable in all-
women's groups or in all-gay groups, in my experience this does not work
for all lesbian women. For example, it is not uncommon for lesbian fem-
inists to feel alienated in a group of heterosexual women even though
they identify with the women's movement. Similarly, women who identify
strongly with the gay rights movement may resent having to deal with
gender differences with their male brothers.

LesBiGay is a term used to affirm the range of possible gay individuals including gay men, bisexual women and men, and lesbians. *LBGT* is
a term used to affirm the range of options including lesbians, bisexuals,

and gay and transgendered individuals. The understanding that coming out is a process and is on a spectrum is only now being written and codified so that all persons can be informed of the various life issues affecting lesbians. It should be noted that the mainstream culture's understanding of the lesbian experience has been gained primarily through observation of the gay male lifestyle and lesbian rock stars.

There have always been lesbians who identified with a wide spectrum of the lesbian community and those who identified with only a small part. The paths of many sub-communities never cross: the sado-masochistic community, the radical lesbian socialists, the bar crowd, the suburban book clubs, the "jocks," the gay professional network, the feminist woman-identified lesbians who may or may not have had sexual relations with a woman. Oppression and the resultant invisibility keep these communities separate and isolated. Social group work is the best vehicle to help an individual find her place in this possibly confusing spectrum of options.

COMMON THEMES

The themes that regularly arise in groups designed for lesbian women will now be considered.

Management of Oppression, Stigma, and Difference

Gay adults often describe themselves as having felt "different" from other children. The factors leading to a sense of difference are diverse. . . . In boys these tend to be aesthetic and intellectual; in girls, they are athletic. Beginning in children, many gay and lesbian people have feelings of shame at being considered deviant, as well as feelings of self-hatred because they identify with those who devalue them. Such feelings arise from identification with the aggressor, a mental mechanism experienced by many victims of abuse. (Friedman & Downey, 1994, p. 926)

The management of shame, self-hatred, and internalized homophobia is required for every lesbian. Internalized homophobia is experienced as internalizing the prejudicial, pejorative views of the homosexual held by the dominant society. Marginalized lesbian women are especially vulnerable because they lack a positive gay identity. Psychologically vulnerable women, teenage girls, and elderly women may resort to alcohol and drug abuse, and there is a higher tendency toward suicide, especially for teenagers (Friedman & Downey, 1994, p. 926). Saulnier (1997) has written of the role of alcohol in the lesbian community and the part that the recovery movement has played in the socialization process for many lesbians. Many of my lesbian couple clients have stressed how significant a source of comfort and support their 12-step programs are for their relationship health. Work performance and career advancement can be seriously impaired by internal and external dilemmas with the development of a lesbian identity. Social group workers must be prepared to deal with despair, alienation, rage, loss, anger, and hostility and to help clients turn these feelings appropriately outward to injustices in the dominant culture.

Invisibility of the Lesbian Woman's Experience

The reality of oppression leads to the invisibility of the identified lesbian woman in our society today. In the lesbian community, the formation of an identity is much more difficult when subcommunities are divided and invisible to each other. Because of the limited number of visible role models, the lesbian subculture has had difficulty developing a nonstigmatized identity. In the dominant culture, confusion can develop and stereotypes can prevail. Lesbians themselves tend to underestimate the complexities of the invisibility factor and the toll it takes on their psychological development.

Safety and Vigilance Issues

Many lesbians have experienced gay bashing ranging from verbal harassment to physical assault. The threat of physical and emotional harm is a powerful determinant of lesbian women's mental health. The actual experience or the veiled threat can dictate constrictiveness, hiddenness, and paranoia or a reactive, self-conscious, or overexpressive behavior pattern. Sometimes mental health professionals have judged these behaviors to be adolescent and acting out rather than seeing them as coping mechanisms for dealing with harassment, assault, and persecution.

It should be noted that the humiliation, shame, and lack of empowerment that physical and sexual abuse survivors experience prevents them from easily acknowledging their difficulties with their own safety. The social group worker needs to create a structure that acknowledges the appropriateness of their dilemma and a language for the entire group to use in negotiating trust and emotional closeness.

Lesbian Relationships and Sexual Expression

Lesbian sexuality and sexual behavior in long-term relationships are more frequently written about than perhaps other aspects of lesbian life. Loulan observed that "frequency of sex among lesbian couples drops off dramatically after the first year" and that "it's so much easier to become passionate about the things we don't like about each other. But who would want to have sex with someone who is critical?" (1987, pp. 103, 117). There appears to be a high correlation between a lesbian's satisfaction with her relationship and satisfaction with her sex life. "Even with infrequent sex, it seems that a woman remains satisfied with her sex life because she feels loved" (Loulan, 1987, p. 202). Murphy hypothesized that "although internalized homophobia affects the sexual relationships of both gay and lesbian couples, the differences in amount of sexual activity and sexual exclusivity may be seen as reflections of gender socialization" (1994, p. 21). "Lesbian women report that they are happy with their amount of sexual activity and that they have more affectionate and non-genital sexual contact than heterosexual and gay male couples" (Murphy, 1994, p. 22).

The goal of the social group worker is to reduce the stigma of discussing lesbian sexuality and to increase the ability of the client to develop her own norms. In groups the worker must take an active stance, leading conversation and providing information on sex. Bibliotherapy and structured group exercises can help reduce anxiety for everyone.

The value of lesbian couples' groups is immeasurable; because there is little visible role modeling, however, the fear of being seen as "abnormal," "not good enough," or an "immature couple" is great. Good preparation is needed, and a focused educational format with enough time for telling the couple's "story" is optimal.

Living with Dignity as a Declared Lesbian Woman

No one can deny the stress of living as a member of a minority group in an oppressed subculture; physical, psychological, emotional, and spiritual stressors continually occur. Managing conflictual inner and outer messages is the accepted reality for all lesbians.

By the time one goes through the coming-out stages, makes peace with one's losses and gains, and accepts a lesbian identity usually a very strong personal sense of self has developed. The lesbian woman today has gifts to give to the general culture, especially in the area of building self-esteem. Brown, a lesbian ethicist, states: "three intertwined themes I see as defining, cross-situationally, the experience of being lesbian and gay: *biculturalism*, with its requirements of juggling, balance and living in and with ambiguity; *marginality*, with its perspective that is both outside and from within; and *normative creativity*, the ability to create boundaries that will work where none exist or may be only partially suited to the task" (1990, p. 2). Examples of courage and perseverance are found particularly in multiply-oppressed lesbians. "A number of clinicians have suggested that the cultural expectations of Asian, African-American, Latino/Latin and Jewish gay men and lesbian women present them (and the couples in which they are members) with unique stress. . . . Although each community offers some support, each has its own expectations and demands which often conflict with each other. The tension of living in these three communities, in all of which one feels marginalized, adds to identity difficulties" (Murphy, 1994, p. 25).

Although it is not always clear to a lesbian woman whether it is better for her physical health (raises risk to assault and harassment) or her economic health (creates the risk of job discrimination, eviction, and loss of family support) to disclose fully her sexual orientation, living as a declared lesbian has may advantages. One's psychological well-being is greatly enhanced by a reduction of ambivalence and inner anxiety. Removing from one's mind and emotions the constant quandary of when to "come out" frees a significant amount of life energy for other purposes.

PRACTICE PRINCIPLES

Sensitize Your Organization as Well as Yourself

The Council on Social Work Education Curriculum Policy statement states:

> Special Populations: The social work profession, by virtue of its system of ethics, its traditional value commitments, and its long history of work in the whole range of human services, is committed to preparing students to understand and appreciate cultural and social diversity. The profession has also been concerned about the consequences of oppression. . . . The curriculum . . . should include content on other special population group . . . in particular, groups that have been consistently affected by social, economic and legal bias or oppression. Such groups include those distinguished by age, religions, disablement, *sexual orientation*, and culture. (Council on Social Work Education, 1982, cited in Gochros, 1984, p. 154; emphasis added)

This policy statement means that your social work agency and your social work training/placement should be sensitive to the issues of gay and lesbian populations and that you will not be alone in trying to create opportunities to serve these populations in your agency. Do not be surprised, however, if that is not so. There are many inherent difficulties even in discovering these populations in your caseload. Although it is always supportive to provide opportunities for clients to come out on intake forms or management information systems (MIS) data sheets, do not underestimate the fear of discrimination and homophobia that might prevent a client from choosing to be open early in the intake process. Attention needs to be paid to a range of options guided by the client's needs and preferences. Some clients prefer to include their sexual orientation on the intake sheet, some prefer to speak of it in person, and some are reluctant to bring it up at all.

Saulnier (2002) has examined the issue of mental and physical health care providers becoming more *lesbian affirmative*. "Being *lesbian sensitive* meant that providers were able to place a lesbian's concerns or problems in their sociopolitical context . . . *lesbian sensitivity* . . . is seen "as almost a mirror-opposite of heterosexism. Lesbians are visible; their partners are included in care. Instead of ignorance, practitioners have up-to-date knowledge. Positive images replace negative stereotypes." *Les-*

bian affirmative practitioners actively reach out and take special care to make lesbians feel like an important part of their practice (p. 362).

Develop Comfort with Learning from Group Members

Do not overstate your knowledge or competencies to your clients or supervisors. It is important, when appropriate, to be a beginner about subculture issues, to ask thoughtful questions, and to seek advice about how to prepare for your role as group leader. You may also need to be prepared to clarify to the group your own sexual preferences, or to talk about sexual practices or ask questions that might imply sexual practices. Don't let feelings of shame or embarrassment stop you. Consult with a knowledgeable person and reveal your lack of knowledge of the lesbian woman's experience. Be direct and share concerns that you feel might be limiting your effectiveness with your clients. Do not rely on the clients as your primary source of information; our work is a partnership, and you must supply your own knowledge and experience.

Communicate Your Positions on Issues

For the most part, lesbians appreciate heterosexuals taking the initiative to bring up the subject of gayness, especially in positions that have a possibly negative effect on the status of the lesbian (job or work settings, authority settings like schools, physicians' offices, etc.). A gay-positive atmosphere or environment can be created in which diversity and differences are affirmed. Taking definite stands on antigay jokes and antigay literature is noticed especially in the workplace. Many persons have come to understand gayness through a family member, a close business/work relationship, or a homosexual encounter. While all social workers should be encouraged to work with lesbians in groups, I believe that specialized knowledge, training, and empathetic connection are vital for building trust and being effective.

Lesbians come in every size, shape, and color; variety is the norm. Many women defy the lesbian stereotype. The social group worker's responsibility is to program opportunities to discuss discrimination, stereotypes, and prejudice. Encouraging group interaction and direct feedback to each other is invaluable helping the individual lesbian understand how she is perceived by others.

Because lesbians are a hidden minority, it is very important to always assume that someone in your group is a lesbian; has a lesbian mother, sister, aunt, or child; or could be developing any of these options. It is equally important to assume that your boss, your secretary, or your mail carrier is possibly a lesbian or has a lesbian relative. In this way, you will open your eyes to the difficulties or knowing who is actually a lesbian. You will hear antigay jokes and know that someone who is listening is unable to speak out against the ignorance being displayed because of fear of declaring her identity. As you take the subject of lesbianism seriously, you will begin to experience the internal struggles of trying to decide when and where to tackle persons on their homophobia.

You must appreciate the burden of managing the dominant culture's constant and intrusive influence on the lesbian's life. An excerpt from an anxiety reduction group for lesbians follows:

> *Beth:* You don't know what is real or not; are you being paranoid or would my supervisor tell our boss that I'm gay just to further her career? I can't take the chance; I change all of my pronouns, don't let my lover call me at work, and I don't know what I will do when the baby is born. I run out at break and all her because her workplace is much more accepting; they know that she is a lesbian and pregnant. But she doesn't want me to come to her work parties because she thinks that I look too "butch" and that her staff might be uncomfortable with me or with us both present and acting like a couple.
>
> *Yvonne:* Do you think that you look too butch? Could you grow your hair a little longer and that might help? You probably wouldn't be wearing your work boots at the party either, right?
>
> *Beth:* I don't think that I look butch at work. Most of the workers in my department are men, and we all dress casual; my supervisor is almost the only one in the entire company that wears a dress. I'm afraid that I can't really change how I look that much—sort of androgynous, I hope. To try and change my looks and personality—now that would really make anxious. Do I really have to look different to feel less anxious?
>
> *Group worker:* How have others in the group dealt with these issues? Do you sometimes wonder if you are being paranoid? The presence of homophobia in our workplace is very real, but I would like us to focus here on sharing your tips and strategies for managing this multidimensional dilemma.

By acknowledging both the reality of the homophobia/heterosexism and the need to be proactive, the group worker encourages members and emphasizes the need to be proactive. Thus, the group worker encourages members to develop resilient behaviors. Be aware, however, that as some group members share examples of courageous behaviors, some clients are inspired but others may feel depression and anxiety.

Set Clear Guidelines and Contract for Them

A common experience in lesbian group life is having couples begin to form sexual relationships (subgroups) and the difficulties that occur for those who are being left out, that is, not chosen. Although group workers usually develop 'rules' at the beginning of groups against involvement with a member of the group, this continues to occur. The experience of intimacy and closeness in the company of other lesbians in a safe setting is almost overwhelming for some women, and no amount of discussion in advance will deter from them acting on their sexual feelings. The author has found it useful to encourage the group to articulate these issues in the first two sessions, focusing on the experience of being in the group and eliciting feelings about both situations: getting sexually involved and not getting sexually involved. Role playing can be a useful tool, utilizing warmups of inclusion/exclusion or "what if" scenarios—What would happen to our group if sexual feelings are acted upon by _____ and _____? Encouraging women to get together in small groups only outside the group can also act as a deterrent. Making agreements to share all contacts outside the group immediately, including phone calls, will make the information available to all members of the group and avoid surprises. It is the group's responsibility, along with the worker, to manage the balance of intimacy, intensity, sexuality, and appropriate boundaries.

RECOMMENDED WAYS OF WORKING

Use of Time and the Program

Due to a lack of "visibility" and "role modeling" within the dominant culture for lesbians, it is very important to create opportunities within group structures to provide remedial experiences.

The importance of allowing sufficient time for women to tell their stories cannot be underestimated; to share with other lesbian women and with other lesbian-affirmative women the secret experiences of everyday life is very empowering. Groups often provide a way to have the first contact with a declared lesbian or with the lesbian community; often individuals are encouraged by case workers to sign up for a coming-out group or an informational lesbian consciousness group. The worker may have assessed with her client that she is ready to begin contact with other lesbians in the process of clarifying her sexual identity. It is very important for the group leader to screen potential group members to determine what phase of the process they are in; if possible, it is best for the group worker to know the range of experiences that members might have had so that all aspects can be included within the norm. Examples include a 50-year-old woman, married, with three children, who has had a 48-year-old lover, married, with two children, for 12 years; a 27-year-old woman who has never had a sexual relationship with anyone but has had a best friend since college whom she loves and lives with; an 18-year-old woman who has had three short-term relationships with women, but none of whom call themselves lesbian. The program would need to be structured to discuss choice of partners, labels to be considered for oneself, the role of children in the woman's life, and the struggle between the sexual self (perhaps just flowering) and the parental and career roles. Because of the nature of some of the issues involved, I believe that coming-out groups need to be run by lesbian group workers. More needs to be known about the special role of a worker who shares the characteristics of the group being served. Perhaps more could be learned by looking to the substance abuse field, the sexual abuse field, or the disability field. Any group leaders, however, might find themselves in a position to help a client engage in these dilemmas; therefore, I consider it important to discuss them. Any worker can support the healthy aspects of the choice and look for any dysfunctional responses (always looking through the lens of oppression and prejudice).

In the author's experience, short-term groups work best when the purpose is educational or when everyone in the group has one or two pivotal life experiences in common (e.g., being Hispanic, being a mother, being an executive). The formation of a long-term group lends itself to the inclusion of more differences and allows interests to evolve as cohesion is built as part of the group process. The use of program materials can always be used to add variety; for example, an all-white able-bodied mothers' group can learn from a videotape featuring Asian women, disabled women, or gay men in nurturing or mothering roles. Books, videotapes, and audiotapes are wonderful resources for showing healthy role models and helping lesbian women to visualize how their behavior might change. These resources are available from gay and lesbian organizations locally and nationally; catalogs are also available if you live in an inaccessible area.

The use of activities to enhance communication nonverbally and to focus communication verbally has been documented by Middleman (1980) and Lynn and Nisivoccia (1992). Creating a genogram, especially noting to whom one has disclosed one's lesbianism, provides a rapid connection for most people to their problems with the coming-out process and to the issue of shame. By adapting anxiety and depression scales, as well as attitude and fear surveys that have been used to help focus symptoms and to show change, you can help group members focus on how much of their current anxiety and depression appears to be rooted in homophobia. Sometimes it is especially useful to have the group create the instrument together. Collages of society's view of the lesbian lifestyle, created by clients at home and presented to the group, can be very evocative.

Coleadership is never my first choice of leadership model for women's groups. Although traditionally it has been used in special circumstances where it has served a particular purpose (e.g., to allow a trainee to gain experience with a difficult population, to provide male-female balance), I have not found the usefulness of the method to outweigh the difficulties of trying to coordinate two leadership styles into one leadership role for a group. The primary exception that I have encountered concerns groups where physical safety and controls are needed and where emotional expressions of the group (sexual abuse or domestic violence) are best shared by two leaders.

Ethical Behaviors and Boundaries

Ethical behavior and appropriate boundaries are expected from all social group workers working with groups but are especially important in working with an invisible and marginalized community group. Relationships that meet the *worker's needs* and are not focused on those of the lesbian client are inappropriate and harmful. More has been written about female sexual abuse perpetrators (Gartrell, 1994) and lesbian domestic violence (Morrow & Hawhurst, 1989). More attention is needed to these issues because of many lesbians' and professionals' denial and avoidance. Sexual behavior and a sexual relationship is never appropriate between member and group worker; it can be especially destructive in group situations when a secret is being kept by one member of the group and the worker. Sexualizing and flirtatious behavior is destructive in group situations because of the power imbalance between worker and member; it also creates specialness and competition among members. Supervision and consultation should always be sought for help in tricky multiple relationship areas, especially if you have any doubts about whether your behavior is in the best interests of the member and the group.

Initial Screening Session

If possible, an initial individual screening session is always useful. Gathering data on the following is useful:

- The individual's knowledge of the coming-out process and where she is currently on the continuum.
- Her current coping skills and social support network.
- How shame and internalized homophobia have been addressed. Ask directly: "How have you handled your internalized homophobia and your experiences of shame?"
- Whether alcohol and substance abuse have been part of the client's life and the family history in regard to alcohol, drugs, violence, and neglect.
- How the client is managing the balance between privacy, disclosure to self, and disclosure to others. This question should always be asked.

In addition, be conscious of the complexities of multiple oppressions. If you are working with a disabled lesbian woman, you may need to get additional information through self-help groups or disability literature. If you are working with a member of another culture, knowing the customs of dealing with privacy and sexuality will help the communication.

Aligning Yourself with the Member's Perspective

It is crucial to assume that the client is doing the best she can in the coming-out process. It is not wise to push a client to come out, both because the outcome can be so variable and because the choice is better made when the client feels ready and able. With a client who says that she is being persecuted or could be persecuted, always start by believing the statement because so little validation is available for her position within the dominant culture. Even liberal colleagues and the social work community can do harm at times by not believing the client's experience.

Help with Planning

An important practice principle is to help members realize that they need a *plan* to deal with their families of origin and with their created families. Too often clients sink into despair because they feel they have to take care and be supportive of their families while their families are processing their own losses and expressing dismay about the client's lesbian identity. The members of the group can give reasons for the correctness of the decision and can also reflect on how difficult it is to hear about anger and emotional turmoil when the woman wants her family of origin to be happy and eager to meet her new lover. Having definite plans for holidays that work for the lesbian woman is crucial. Holidays can be traumatic for lesbians, whether they have declared their status to their families or not. For example:

> *Member:* Even though my mother knows that I am in a relationship now, she still hasn't asked Judy to come to our house for Thanks-giving dinner yet. How long should I wait before I say something? I asked my sister, Kate, and she said that probably since this is the first Thanksgiving since Dad's death, I shouldn't push it. I feel confused because I don't want to upset my mother's holiday, but it is my life, too, and we [she and her lover] have so little time together that I would hate to spend the holiday apart. We have been together for five years, and we have spent the last year coming out in many more places and feeling good about our relationship, and it feels like a step backward.
>
> *Worker:* Could anyone else share how you planned their first few family encounters with your new partner? Did you involve your siblings and friends in the planning or did you do it primarily alone?

Talking about all of the possibilities in a group of individuals who have experienced many of these options is invaluable to the lesbian woman's learning experience of herself and her motives. Understanding that a range of options is available may be new information for her. It is more effective to have members describe how they have handled or would handle this situation than to have the individual social worker work through this with the lesbian client.

EVALUATION MEASURES

One positive outcome of the managed-care movement in mental health has been the emphasis on outcomes and outcome research. At first, it was difficult to change my language and perceptions from intuitions and feelings to numbers and points on a scale. My evaluative expressions of the individual's experience in the group used to be that "she is stuck," "making progress," "having a hard time," and "feeling safe enough to work on her issues." The group evaluative statements used to include "group is stuck," "group is developing leadership," and "group went well tonight." Now I am able to change most of the language on goals, progress, and stuckness into scales for the individual in the group. More techniques are needed to help us evaluate group progress.

It is helpful to utilize specific behavioral terms for goals, group activities, and homework or activities that clients do outside the group. We attempt to develop statements for how they will know when they have reached their goals before the group begins. Group feedback and anecdotal evidence are still the primary tools used to evaluate effectiveness. I often use the next to the last session to evaluate and encourage members to give each other feedback as well. We compare the pregroup goals and the postgroup evaluation, and members are often extremely insightful about the changes made during the life of the group.

RESOURCES

For up-to-date information, see *Journal of Gay and Lesbian Psychotherapy*, published by Haworth Press. Also look for the *Gay Yellow Pages*.

Alternative Family Matters
P.O. Box 390618
Cambridge, MA 02139
(617) 576-6788
www.alternativefamilies.org

Children of Lesbians and Gays
   Everywhere (COLAGE)
3543 18th St. #1
San Francisco, CA 94110
(415) 861-5437
www.colage.org.

Disabled Womyn's Educational
   Project—Dykes, Disability and Stuff
P.O. Box 8773
Madison, WI 53708
(608) 256-8883

Gay and Lesbian Parents Coalition
   International (GLPCI)
P.O. Box 50360
Washington DC 20091
(202) 583-8029
www.glpci.org

Lesbian Connection
Helen Diner Memorial Women's
   Center

Ambitious Amazons
P.O. Box 811
East Lansing, MI 48826
(517) 371-5257

Lesbian/Gay Bisexual Committees
   (NASW)
750 First Street, NW
Washington, DC 20005
(202) 408-8600 x 276
www.naswdc.org

Parents and Friends of Lesbians and
   Gays (P-FLAG)
1726 M Street NW, Suite 400
Washington DC 20036
(202) 467-8180
www.pflag.org

Senior Action in a Gay Environment
   (SAGE)
305 Seventh Ave at 28th St.
16th Floor New York, NY 10001
(212) 747-2247
www.sageusa.org

REFERENCES

Brown, L. S. (1990). *Making psychology safe for gays and lesbians.* Paper presented at the 98th Annual Convention of the American Psychological Association, Boston.

Ellis, P., & Murphy, B. C. (1994). The impact of misogyny and homophobia on therapy with women. In M. Merkin (ed.), *Women in context: Toward a feminist reconstruction of psychology* (pp. 48–73). New York: Guilford Press.

Friedman, R., & Downey, J. (1994). Homosexuality. *New England Journal of Medicine.* 331(14), 923–930.

Gartrell, N. (1994). Boundaries in lesbian therapist-client relationships. In B. Greene & G. Hereck (eds.), *Lesbian and gay psychology,* Vol. 1 (pp. 98–117). Thousand Oaks, CA: Sage Publications.

Gochros, H. L. (1984). Teaching social workers to meet the needs of the homosexually oriented. *Journal of Social Work and Human Sexuality.* 2(2/3), 137–156.

Herek, G. (1986). The social psychology of homophobia: Toward a practical theory. *Review of Law and Social Change.* 14(4), 923–934.

Lee, J. A. B. (ed.) (1991). *An annotated bibliography of gay and lesbian readings.* New York: Cummings & Hathaway.

Lehman, J. L. (1978). What it means to love another woman. In G. Vida (ed.), *Our right to love* (p. 25). Englewood Cliffs, NJ: Prentice Hall.

Loulan, J. (1987). *Lesbian passion.* San Francisco: Spinsters, Inc.

Lynn, M., & Nisivoccia, D. (1992). *Activity groups: Integrating the "doing" with special populations.* Paper presented at the 14th Annual Symposium of the Association for the Advancement of Social Work with Groups, Atlanta.

Middleman, R. (1980). *The non-verbal method in working with groups: The use of activity in teaching, counseling and therapy.* Bloomfield, CT: Practitioner Press.

Morrow, S. L., & Hawhurst, D. M. (1989). Lesbian partner abuse—implications for therapists. *Journal of Counseling and Development.* 68(1), 58–62.

Murphy, B. C. (1991). Coming out of the classroom closet. In K. Harbeck (ed.), *Educating mental health professionals about gay and lesbian issues* (pp. 229–246). New York: Haworth Press.

Murphy, B. C. (1994). Difference and diversity: Gay and lesbian couples. *Journal of Gay and Lesbian Social Services.* 1(2), 5–31.

Roth, S. (1985). Psychotherapy with lesbian couples: Individual issues, female socialization and the social context. *Journal of Marital and Family Therapy.* 11(3), 273–286.

Roth, S., & Murphy, B. C. (1986). Therapeutic work with lesbian clients: A systemic therapy view. In M. Ault-Riche (ed.), *Women and family therapy* (pp. 78–89). Rockville, MD: Aspen Press.

Saulnier, C. F. (1997). Alcohol problems and marginalization: Social group work with lesbians. *Social Work with Groups.* 20(3), 37–59.

Saulnier, C. F. (2000) Incorporating feminist theory into social work: Group work examples. *Social Work with Groups.* 23(1), 5–29.

Saulnier, C. F. (2002). Deciding who to see: Lesbians discuss their preferences in health and mental health care providers. *Social Work.* 47(4), 355–365.

PART V

SCHOOLS, THE WORKPLACE, AND THE COMMUNITY

Chapter 22

Group Work with Urban African-American Parents in Their Neighborhood Schools

GEOFFREY L. GREIF

It is well known that inner-city youth, particularly minority youth, are an at-risk population. Poverty, inadequate housing, and racism (Vera & Vera, 2002), when combined with an environment rife with drugs and crime (Williams et al., 2001), make life a difficult trek in the early years. The school systems, often underfunded in major cities due to a shrinking or static tax base, can be ill equipped to meet the educational, much less the emotional, needs of children. Parents and parent figures are also affected by these problems, as well as by the high unemployment rate. Their own resources are sorely depleted. A feeling of powerlessness, a traditional target of social work practice (Cox, 2002), abounds. A cycle is maintained in which parents with diminished resources are raising children in great need. Finally, traditional attempts to assist minority clients often fall short because of a lack of understanding of the culture (Boyd-Franklin, 2003), a lack of resources, and a failure to focus on strengths and a family's resilience (Seccombe, 2002).

   This chapter describes a parenting support group in three different Baltimore city public schools in a neighborhood that has historically been underserved. Dominated by housing projects and young families, the area is frequently described as one of the worst in Baltimore in terms of crime rate and poverty. This chapter describes the group and the parenting issues that members bring to the group. Discussion of how these issues are handled is included.

REVIEW OF THE LITERATURE

As low-income African-American families have historically received few or no services (Kalyanpur & Rao, 1991), group work, based on the concept of mutual aid (Shulman, 1999), provides a forum for parents to join together and help each other. Here the suggestions emanating from the group will be consistent with the neighborhood's and culture's style of parenting. Group work also has the potential to reduce the isolation so often felt by these parents while providing education and support (Gitterman, 1989). The benefits of groups also include experiences of universality, the instillation of hope, and the feeling of greater strength in numbers. Rehearsal of new parenting behaviors can be attempted, and parents may gain insight into their own approaches to the children they are raising (Cox, 2002; Shulman, 1999). A parenting group can also help parents deal with any personal problems they may be experiencing like depression, which can affect their ability to parent and their child's well-being (Sagrestano et al., 2003).

The social worker as a partner in the school setting is a well-established role, whether functioning as an employee or as a consultant. Leading parent groups to provide both intervention and prevention (see, e.g., O'Donnell et al., 1995) is clearly part of the social work function. Not much has been written, though, about group work specifically with African-American parents. Literature on work with the African-American family in general has suggested the importance of relationship building, focusing on strengths, keeping interventions concrete, and gathering information about who is considered part of the family (Boyd-Franklin, 2003; Hines, 1989).

The notion of family, particularly for a white worker, often needs to be broadened to include those living in the home rather than only those related by blood (Mosley-Howard & Evans, 2000). In addition, as Proctor and Davis (1994) indicate, if the worker is of a different race (as is the case with this group leader and these parents), issues of difference cannot be ignored and the worker must show his or her skill, concern, and ability to offer meaningful help during the group meetings.

PRACTICE PRINCIPLES

This group is given the name "Help! My Kids Are Driving Me Crazy!" The title was picked to convey with humor what parents frequently experience while raising their children. A more straightforward title might have been more threatening. The group is held in several public elementary schools in downtown Baltimore. The attendees are usually mothers and occasionally grandmothers, great-grandmothers, and fathers. It is a 60-minute drop-in group set up to provide mutual aid (see Shulman, 1999), with parents encouraged to help each other. In addition, it functions as a socioeducational group. As Radin (1985) states, such groups can be educative in format, place the worker on a more equal footing with the clients, and are based on nonpathological assumptions. Philosophically, the group is driven by the notion that parenting is a developmental process and that each new stage of a child's growth may pose difficulty for both the child and the parent. The group can help ease that transition by providing support and education about normal stages of development. These parents are also buffeted by the stresses inherent in their environment and by larger social institutions, like Child Protective Services, the Housing Authority, or the Department of Social Services. While these institutions are designed to benefit the parents, they are often perceived as unresponsive and intrusive. Thus the group also deals with issues impinging on the family from the outside.

While long-term supportive work is the major purpose of the group, some parents attend only one or two sessions. For this reason, each group should be a learning and supportive experience in itself. Some sessions address a specific topic that is planned in advance, while others have an open format. The members are encouraged to share concerns about their children and are asked to keep confidential all information they hear from other members.

The leader's level of participation is an important component, particularly when working with a client population from a different racial and economic background. Too much input too early in the group process might be construed as controlling. Yet it is also standard practice for a leader to be active at the beginning of a group in order to establish group structure and allay normal anxiety. There was a beginning period at the first school when the members and worker sized each other up. An African-American co-leader from the parent body, a key person in the success of that particular group, was more active at the beginning. With the parents (the author is white), once the worker was accepted by the group, it was important to be active, as he had been incorporated into the group as a parent and as a person with expertise, the "doctor" from the university. The danger of taking a peripheral role during the middle phase of group work, a role often suggested in the literature on group therapy, is that the leader is perceived as withholding or rejecting. The standard approach was modified. Once the leader was accepted, an active role was assumed and parent issues were both discussed by the leader *and* turned back on the group. It became possible to be active during all phases. The leader also met occasionally outside of the group for consultation with parents who did not feel comfortable using the group to discuss their issues. While this approach theoretically might have undermined the work of the group, given the drop-in nature of the group it was seen as accommodating the needs of the parents.

The groups, which have been conducted for different lengths of time since they started in 1990, were set up to meet weekly or monthly (depending on the school). The parents and leader agreed to meet for a certain period of time, and then stop and determine if they wished to continue. This held the parents and worker to a joint commitment and, depending on the culture of the school, proved effective most of the time.

COMMON THEMES

A number of issues have surfaced at various schools during the years the groups have been in existence. These tend to center on the following themes: disciplining the difficult child; dealing with the noncustodial parent who visits sporadically (usually the father and sometimes the mother if a grandmother was attending the group); managing intrusive grandparents; being triangulated between a child and Child Protective Services; keeping children safe in the neighborhood; enhancing self-esteem; dealing with stress; and giving a child what he wants when there is little money.

Disciplining the Difficult Child

Perhaps foremost in concern among the parents is unhappiness with the behavior of their children. It is this problem that initially drives parents to attend these groups. Complaints range from the mundane to the extraordinary, from normal developmental concerns to examples of extreme behaviors and exposure to traumatic events that strain the limits of current social work thinking.

Parents raise routine concerns about children who will not sit still during dinner, who do not finish their homework, who balk at doing chores, and who ignore them. They raise more troublesome complaints about teenagers feeling unsafe in schools and getting into fights, dropping out of school, and of running the streets until late at night. Occasionally, striking concerns are brought up. One parent worried about what to tell her five-year-old daughter who had seen a dead body in a dumpster. She also wanted assistance in dealing with the same daughter following sexual abuse by a seven-year-old neighborhood boy. The question of how to handle the parent of the boy after the boy was reported to the police was also raised. One great-grandmother did not know what to do about her great-grandson, who, at the age of 10, often stayed out all night without her knowing his whereabouts.

Underlying these concerns and, in some cases, instigating them is a sense the parents have of feeling totally overwhelmed by their environment. Poverty, unsafe housing, unsafe neighborhoods, inadequate resources, and sometimes their own history of school failure and having been inadequately parented combine to drain the parents of the ability to cope. Their own needs are so great that marshalling strength to cope with the environmental pressures on their children is nearly impossible.

Dealing with the Noncustodial Parent Who Visits Occasionally

Many parents (usually mothers) are raising children alone. As such, their lives often remain entwined with those of the father or fathers of their children, particularly if the father shows an interest in his offspring. Visits pose a problem for two reasons: Some fathers say they will visit and do not. When they do visit, they often have more control over the children than the mother.

As with many separations and divorces, the logistics of contact between the noncustodial parent and the child can be problematic. Even in the best of situations, schedules get lost, communication is confused, and last-minute cancellations wreak havoc on long-standing plans. In these families, where some children have been the product of brief relationships, commitments are kept less often. Thus, promises to visit end up being hollow, leaving the custodial parent to deal with the upset child whose father did not stop by to take the child for a ride he had promised.

Group members also raise the problem of having less control over the child than the father seems to have. Whether married or single parents, mothers complain that their attempts to discipline fall short, while all the father has to do is "raise his voice," "stamp his feet," or "shout once" and the children fall into line. The seeming power of the father poses a triple threat to the mother: making her feel incompetent, reinforcing the importance of men over women in her community, and angering her, as she is the one who usually spends the most time with the child.

Occasionally it is the grandmother raising her daughter's child who discusses this issue. In these situations, the grandmother may complain about her daughter's lack of concern and sporadic involvement or, as just discussed with regard to fathers' visits, that when the daughter does visit, she spoils the child.

Managing Intrusive Grandparents

Many group members live with their parents due to financial constraints and the unavailability of child care. These situations lead easily to disagreements over how to parent. Group members sometimes feel undercut by their parents, who invoke certain rules because it is their home. The members, having few options about where else to live, are caught between succumbing to their parents' suggestions about how their grandchildren should be raised and wishing to follow their own rules.

Being Caught Between a Child and Child Protective Services

Parents of older children often feel undermined in their attempts to discipline their child when the child threatens to call 911 or Child Protective Services if the parent is on the verge of physically punishing the child. At times this may be appropriate from the child's perspective. As indicated by the parents, though, it is used even for minor acts of discipline.

For the parents, this tips the balance of power in the home and is an example of the state intruding on their family. For some parents, it creates the feeling that life has changed from the time when they were young and parents were in charge of their children.

Keeping Children Safe in the Neighborhood

One of the larger problems in these neighborhoods is the safety of the streets. Members often lament that they were able to play outside until nighttime when they were young, whereas their own children cannot. Yet keeping the children inside in a small apartment or house, especially on a hot evening, poses other problems and adds to the general level of stress in the home.

Enhancing Self-Esteem

Some parents have been exposed to other parent education programs in the schools. Chief among these programs' goals is the enhancement of self-esteem. A few group members are able to relate their feelings as parents to their feelings about themselves as people and raise this as a topic for discussion in the groups. This can sometimes be effectively linked to their own upbringing.

Dealing with Stress

Parents are constantly bombarded by the chaos in their neighborhoods. They complain that they are stressed out and unable to meet the continuing needs of their children. An ongoing theme is the request for information about how to deal with this stress. In some cases, helping the parent deal with anxiety will also help reduce anxiety in the child (Wood et al., 2003).

Giving a Child What He Wants When There Is Little Money

Parents on limited incomes are often scraping the bottom of the barrel by the end of the month to make ends meet. Giving a child even a small bonus for good behavior or a good school performance can be a financial stretch. Finding enjoyable family activities like a visit to a fast food restaurant or a movie is frequently out of a parent's range. As a result, chances to celebrate in a way that is meaningful for a child are few. This makes the parent feel incompetent as a provider and nurturer.

RECOMMENDED WAYS OF WORKING

The approaches used with these group members must be consistent with their culture and cognizant of their inherent strengths. Suggestions for interventions that are outside their resources will not be successful or accepted and may well be experienced as destructive.

Giving instruction about child development is the first stage in helping parents to discipline more effectively. Parents of very young children often interpret rambunctious behavior as disobedience rather than normal exuberance and get into battles with their children. For example, the 18-month-old who looks at the parent and then throws food on the floor is not trying to anger the parent. Messy rooms are not meant to be disrespectful but rather are a reflection of the child's feelings about himself or herself and a lack of interest in cleanliness. In most cases, the instruction comes from the group members themselves, and not from the leaders. For some members, depending on their acceptance or rejection of authority, this may make the information more palatable. It also gives a sense of competence to the provider of the information.

More serious discipline issues are usually handled in two ways. First, the group provides specific suggestions. If these fall short, as sometimes occurs, or if the group is put off by the difficulty of the issue, the leader and coleader step in. If a diagnostic assessment of the parent has not been made in advance, a few questions about the context of the problem (e.g., who is in the family and who is affected by the problem) sometimes clarify the picture. Family system strengths are often the focus of the questioning. The questions asked include "What has worked for you in the past?" and "Give me other examples of successful coping." Ideas from structural family therapy (Nichols & Schwartz, 2001) are often applied. In addition, rituals are prescribed that are intended to enhance enduring family patterns and build closeness (Mackey & Greif, 1994). Encouraging parents to read to their children every night, have a special pizza night once a week, or have a "choose a TV show" night introduces structure to families that often live in chaos. While these rituals do not deal specifically with the discipline problem, they do build family strength and set the stage for solving the problem. Concepts underpinning short-term therapy are also applied (Nickerson, 1995), with an eye toward providing a different view of the problem. The role of the leader tends to become more central the more serious the problem. Yet the group, when it is working well, provides support around these intractable problems that can touch a reserve of strength in the parent.

Inadvertently, the timing of some disciplinary interventions may be fortuitous. Something that failed once may work again a year later. The parent who comes occasionally, gets a little information, and does not come back is reminded of that information when he or she sees a sign advertising the group, even if the parent chooses not to return. Over the course of many years of working in the same school, the mere presence of the group, even for one-time attendees, becomes a reminder of suggestions for change.

Dealing with the noncustodial parent, particularly a man, requires an acknowledgment of the differential status men hold in this community, where women so frequently are in the majority. While ventilation is helpful, unless a context and limits for group discussion are set, members tend to spiral off into diatribes about men that are ultimately unproductive. Helping to set the context can include leading discussions about the role of men in the parents' lives when they were younger and focusing on the current precarious position that men occupy in many communities.

Group members often believe that the visiting father should be treated harshly, perhaps reflecting the members' own feelings of anger and helplessness. Ideally, the group can be helped to reach the conclusion that, for most fathers, involvement is a positive experience when it is regulated. If the father visits and undermines the authority of the mother, both parents should be encouraged to work together on setting rules for the child. Often this does not work, though, and the influence of the outside father becomes something that the custodial parent and her children have to learn to live with. In that case, the mother is assisted to view the father's involvement in a way that does not get her so upset. This can include discussing what other behaviors surround the visit that the mother can better understand and change. For example, the mother who finds herself screaming at the father the minute he walks in will be asked to anticipate his visit with a different reaction. The purpose is to handle the visit in a way that makes her feel more in control.

In dealing with intrusive grandparents, we return to the ideas of structural family theory. Boundary issues are emphasized at the same time that group members are asked to explore any unresolved problems they may have with their own parents that affect how they themselves parent. The advantage of the group is that grandmothers caring for grandchildren are also present, giving an intergenerational perspective to the discussion. Sometimes when a mother or grandmother sees the conflict from the other's perspective, change can occur.

When group members believe that their attempts to parent are being impeded by a child's threat to call Child Protective Services, we sympathize with them by saying, "It must be hard to be unable to parent the way you want to." The underlying interventions must speak to two themes: helping the members find a way of parenting that will work for them (i.e., increasing their sense of competence) and acknowledging the interference of other institutions in their lives. The first theme is approached by returning the question to the group of what solutions they have found for the particular problem. Then the discussion can turn to other ways in which the members feel that outsiders are interfering, including referring to the group leader as a potential outsider. This sometimes opens up issues about being referred by the school principal to the parenting group and the members' reactions to that suggestion.

When safety concerns keep children cooped up in their homes, suggestions about alternative modes of entertainment in Baltimore are usually given by other group members. The discussion then evolves into how life has changed since the members were young. By broadening the question, members can then be asked to discuss how they can recapture part of their past that they enjoyed. These discussions usually occur as parents exchange ideas about how to improve their position on public housing lists so that they can move to a safer neighborhood sooner. For some, a move is the best intervention.

Self-esteem is built within the group process. By supporting the parents' effective attempts to parent and by parents finding ways to help other group members, self-esteem does increase. Breaking down parenting into small steps helps the parents gain a sense of control. If the group provides helpful suggestions that are put into action, the members often feel better. Some parents are unreachable through the group. The task here is to prevent them from discouraging members working toward change.

Stress is handled the same way. Parents are encouraged to find a small thing they can accomplish that will make their lives more pleasurable. Stress often seems to loom over these parents as a mountain that they can never scale. Telling parents that they have the right to have time for themselves, by asking a trusted neighbor to watch their children one day in exchange for their watching the neighbor's children the next, and stating that they should be allowed to take a shower or bath without interruption provides solace to some parents.

Stress is also handled by helping the parent feel more competent, an issue related to self-esteem.

> One parent whose young daughter was sexually abused by another neighbor's child had also observed a dead body in a trash dumpster adjacent to their high-rise development. As the child was significantly traumatized and then retraumatized by the second event, the mother wanted assistance in dealing with the child's nightmares and increasingly uncontrollable behavior.
>
> Borrowing from structural family theory, we tried to place the mother in charge of the situation by increasing her feeling of competence. The belief was that if the mother felt more competent, the child would feel less upset. (The child was also in occasional individual treatment related to the sexual trauma.)
>
> We asked the mother to read to her child at bedtime. If she could find books about children successfully coping, so much the better. We also asked her to involve her daughter in other activities where the mother was clearly the expert, like cooking and game playing. The hope was that such activities would enhance the role of the mother and show the child that the mother was competent. The intervention succeeded in reducing the child's nightmares but was less successful with the discipline problem.

Finally, we try to help parents discuss money management. Groups whose members receive welfare do not meet when checks arrive. Such groups are often poorly attended because parents are making purchases. By the end of the month, little money is left. Parents who can begin to use money more effectively are not bereft the final week of the month when the child wants change for a candy bar. Money management also shows the child that the parent will be consistent in meeting the child's needs, a message that all children need to hear.

EVALUATION AND CONCLUSION

It must be noted that despite the examples given of successful group interventions, some problems presented by the group members are unsolvable in the group context. They push the limits of social work practice because of the extreme nature of the situation and the lack of resources available to families. Some members with intractable problems drop out of the group, perhaps believing that another attempt to help them has failed. Unfortunately, the net result is to reinforce their sense of helplessness.

The success of the drop-in group is judged by the answers to three questions: (1) Do parents return?, (2) Do the parents who attend even one session appear to get something out of it (a subjective assessment, as paper-and-pencil tests appear to scare off potential attendees)? and (3) Does the principal think it is working? Some parents do return, depending in part on the culture of the school. In two of the three schools, the group has been successful with returning parents; in the third school, where attendance is low, the parent-school liaison reports that the parents still request the group. Parents do tend to leave after each session, saying that they enjoyed the meeting. For some principals, the mere presence of the group is a statement that the school is trying to meet parents' needs. As long as the group may be constructive, the principals of all three schools are happy to sponsor it, though support from one school to the next tends to vary.

Empowering disadvantaged parents through group work can be a key element in any plan to improve the situations of at-risk children. By assisting those who want help and building on their strengths, greater parenting competence may develop throughout the community.

ACKNOWLEDGMENTS

Versions of this chapter appear in G. L. Greif (1993). A school-based support group for urban African American parents. *Social Work in Education, 15,* 133–139; G. L. Greif (1994). Using family therapy ideas with parenting groups in schools. *Journal of Family Therapy, 16,* 199–207; and J. Mackey & G. L. Greif (1994). Using rituals to help parents in the school setting: Lessons from family therapy. *Social Work in Education, 16,* 171–178.

RESOURCES

Educational Resources Information Center
Clearinghouse on Disabilities and Gifted Education

1920 Association Drive
Reston, VA 20191
http://www.ericec.org

Home and School Institute
1500 Massachusetts Ave., NW
Washington, DC 20002
(202) 466-3633

National Black Child Development
   Institute
1023 15th St. NW, Suite 600
Washington, DC 20005
(202) 387-1281
http://www.nbcdi.org

REFERENCES

Boyd-Franklin, N. (2003). *Black families in therapy: A multisystems approach,* 2nd edition. New York: Guilford Press.

Cox, C. B. (2002). Empowering African American custodial grandparents. *Social Work.* 47, 45–54.

Gitterman, A. (1989). Building mutual support in groups. *Social Work with Groups.* 12(2), 5–21.

Hines, P. M. (1989). The family life cycle of poor black families. In B. Carter & M. McGoldrick (eds.), *The changing family life cycle: A framework for family therapy,* 2nd ed. (pp. 513–544). Boston: Allyn & Bacon.

Kalyanpur, M., & Rao, S. S. (1991). Empowering low-income black families of handicapped children. *American Journal of Orthopsychiatry.* 61, 523–532.

Mackey, J., & Greif, G. L. (1994). Using rituals to help parents in the school setting: Lessons from family therapy. *Social Work in Education.* 16, 171–178.

Mosley-Howard, G. S., & Evans, C. B. (2000). Relationships and contemporary experiences of the African American family: An ethnographic case study. *Journal of Black Studies.* 30, 428–452.

Nichols, M. P., & Schwartz, R. C. (2001). *Family therapy: Concepts and methods.* Boston: Allyn & Bacon.

Nickerson, P. R. (1995). Solution-focused group therapy. *Social Work.* 40, 132–133.

O'Donnell, J., Hawkins, D., Catalano, R. F., Abbott, R. D., & Day, L. E. (1995). Preventing school failure, drug use, and delinquency among low-income children: Long-term intervention in elementary schools. *American Journal of Orthopsychiatry.* 65, 87–100.

Parsons, R. J. (1991). Empowerment: Purpose and practice principle in social work. *Social Work with Groups.* 14(2), 7–21.

Proctor, E. K., & Davis, L. E. (1994). The challenge of racial difference: Skills for clinical practice. *Social Work.* 39, 314–323.

Radin, N. (1985). Socioeducation groups. In M. Sundel, P. Glasser, & R. Vintner (eds.), *Individual change through small groups,* 2nd ed. (pp. 101–116). New York: Free Press.

Sagrestano, L. M., Paikoff, R. L., Holmbeck, G. N., & Fendrich, M. (2003). A Longitudinal examination of familial risk factors for depression among inner-city African American adolescents. *Journal of Family Psychology.* 17, 108–120.

Shulman, L. (1999). *The skills of helping individuals, families and groups,* 4th ed. Itasca, IL: F. E. Peacock.

Seccombe, K. (2002). "Beating the odds" versus "changing the odds": Poverty, resilience, and family policy. *Journal of Marriage and Family.* 64, 384–394.

Vera, E., & Vera, J. A. (2002). Undoing racism in America: Help from a black church. *Journal of Black Studies.* 32, 389–404.

Williams, J. H., Pierce, N., Young, N. S., & Van Dorn, R. A. (2001). Service utilization in high-crime communities: Consumer views on supports and barriers. *Families in Society.* 83, 409–417.

Wood, J. J., McLeod, B. D., Sigman, M., Hwang, W-C., & Chu, B. C. (2003). Parenting and childhood anxiety: Theory, empirical findings, and future directions. *Journal of Child Psychology and Psychiatry.* 44, 134–151.

Chapter 23

Group Work with Victims of School and Community Violence

JOHN A. KAYSER

A variety of group work approaches has been developed to prevent community violence and to intervene with victims who have been directly or indirectly injured. The purpose of this chapter is to describe these approaches as a guide for practitioners. Groups also have been used extensively in the treatment of perpetrators of violence. While acknowledging that the line between "victim" and "aggressor" often is a thin one, the present chapter's primary focus is on group work with victims of community violence.

REVIEW OF PROFESSIONAL LITERATURE

Definitions

The term *community violence* arose in the early 1990s through the efforts of the U.S. Surgeon General and the Centers for Disease Control and Prevention (CDCP) to reframe as a society-wide health concern the violent behaviors of individuals that heretofore had been the primary concern of the criminal justice and mental health systems (CDCP, 1993; Rosenberg & Fenley, 1991). According to Shahinfar, Fox, and Leavitt (2000), community violence is defined as "the presence of violence and violence-related events within an individual's proximal development, including home, school, and neighborhood; it may involve direct or threatened harm, be witnessed or experienced, and involve known or unknown perpetrators" (p. 115). These authors suggest that community violence

361

differs from other types of violence in that: *(a)* it is *pervasive*, permeating all micro-systems levels, such as home, school, work, and surrounding community; and *(b)* it is *chronic*, characterized by cumulative, repeated exposure to such violent acts as shootings, stabbings, rapes, and beatings. It may also include robbery, kidnapping, school violence, domestic violence, illegal drug activities, child abuse, sexual abuse, hate crimes, homicide, suicide, etc.; *(c)* it is *random*, presenting a constant threat to community members' safety and security; and *(d)* it is *alienating*, isolating individuals from their community and sources of social support. The predatory nature of some community violence acts (e.g., using physical intimidation, threats, or actual harm to take something of value) increases victims' feelings of vulnerability and fear, and fuels their lack of trust in others (Goguen, 2000).

Community violence may result in *physical* and *psychological trauma*. *Physical trauma* refers to a serious and critical bodily injury, wound, or shock resulting from an external source such as physical assault, gun shooting, or stabbing, etc. It is estimated that physical trauma is the leading killer of Americans under age 45 (Silverman, 1986). The effects of physical trauma can be devastating, in that injuries can destroy health, lives, and livelihoods (Bradford, 1999). *Psychological trauma* refers to an experience that is emotionally painful, distressful, or shocking, which often results in lasting mental and physical effects (National Institute of Mental Health, 2001). A *traumatic event* is any critical incident that causes people to experience unusually strong emotional reactions that have the potential to affect their ability to function at work, at home with family members, or in other areas of their lives (Waldrop, 2001). The event or events may be time-limited, or their impact may be ongoing.

Rates of Exposure

More than 20,000 Americans die from homicide annually; two million more are injured through violent conflicts; and more than 11 million Americans aged 12 years and older experienced violence or personal theft (Juhnke & Osborne, 1997). Although violent crime rates in general and incidents of nonfatal youth violence significantly declined between 1991 and 1997, violence remains a major public health issue because of its tremendous impact on the individual, the family, and the community (Brener et al., 1999). Homicide is the second leading cause of death among 15- to 24-year olds, and, within that age range, the leading cause of death for African Americans, the second leading cause of death for Hispanic Americans, and the third leading cause of death for Native Americans (National Center for Injury Prevention and Control, 2001). Numerous self-report surveys among youth both nationally and in major U.S. cities continue to indicate unacceptably high percentages of children and adolescents who have witnessed violence; have been threatened, physically intimidated, or assaulted; or who have brought weapons (e.g., a gun, knife, or club) to school for protection (Dulmus & Wodarski, 2000; Gabarino & Kostelny, 1997; Shafinfar et al., 2000). The impact of chronic, cumulative exposure to violence, which frequently affects low-income urban neighborhoods, is particularly problematic (Ceballo, 2000; Gabarino & Kostelny, 1997; Timnick, 1989).

Community violence is not confined to poor urban neighborhoods, however, as can be seen by the number of high-profile, multiple-victim school shootings that have occurred in middle-class suburban and rural areas in the late 1990s. For example, in one of the group crisis debriefing sessions attended by this author following the 1999 Columbine High School shooting, in which 13 students and one teacher were killed along with two dozen wounded, it was estimated that there were over 10,000 *direct and secondary victims* of this one event in the Denver metropolitan area alone. (This figure was derived by estimating a minimum of five additional people affected, such as family members, and peers, for each of the approximately 1,870 students and 95 teachers and staff members at Columbine that day). Similarly, Paine and Sprauge (2002) reported that the Springfield, Oregon, school shooting in 1998, in which two students were killed and 25 others wounded, affected all of the 11,000 students and 1,200 employees of the Eugene-Springfield school district. In addition, the sniper shootings in Maryland and Virginia in 2002 closed down schools and affected businesses and communities in the area for weeks. As these incidents ripple throughout the nation, obviously the number of people affected by community violence occurrences is much, much higher.

PRACTICE PRINCIPLES

Establish Groups as a Major Component in Community Planning Efforts

No single approach to community violence is sufficient, and multiple strategies must be employed (Fraser, 1995). *Group work approaches should form a core component of comprehensive, community-based programs dealing with violence prevention and intervention* (Cannon & Gingerich, 2002; Goldstein & Conoley, 1997; Paine & Sprague, 2002). Group work appears to have important advantages over other forms of crisis counseling or psychotherapy. In the views of Ceballo (2000) and Klein and Schermer (2000), many individual and family therapists often ignore or underestimate the impact of clients' exposure to violence; choosing, instead, to direct greater attention to intrapsychic or family issues. Groups, in contrast, can be consciously constructed with a violence prevention or intervention focus, specific to particular populations (e.g., AIDS victims, war refugees, gang members, victims of juvenile violence, sexual abuse victims), or events (e.g., work-place violence, school shootings, rape) (Ceballo, 2000; deYoung & Corbin, 1994; Gabriel, 1996; Hopps & Pinderhughes, 1999; Kinney, 1995; Murphy et al., 1997; Ying, 2001). For many group members whose lives contain daily encounters with violence, conflict, and anger, the group experience may be the one consistent place where they feel safe (Levinsky & McAleer, 1994).

One daunting challenge to community planning efforts is that many people who experience trauma like community violence never seek or receive services of any kind. Indeed, the people most likely to benefit from a group experience (i.e., those with no previous exposure to trauma and violence, and who have fewer sources of social support) apparently are those *least likely* to make use of this experience (Ursano et al., 2000). For example, the CDCP conducted a randomly dialed telephone survey of 3,512 respondents in Connecticut, New Jersey, and New York between October and December 2001 regarding the psychological and emotional effects of the September 11th attacks on the World Trade Center (Melnik & Baker, 2002, September 6). The study indicated that although 75% of respondents reported having emotional problems after the attack, only 12% received some form of help. Of those seeking help, family members and friends were the main source (36%). Women were more likely than men to obtain help.

Given the sheer number of people affected by community violence, a comprehensive community-based plan should include a wide variety of group experiences. These would include:

Prevention groups designed to decrease school and community violence by strengthening empathy, emotional responsiveness, and affectional bonds among members; promote understanding and tolerance of individual and group differences; teach improved help-seeking behaviors, increased communication and conflict-resolution skills; teach about the impact of gangs, guns, and weapons on a community; and reduce members' reactivity to violence, potential for withdrawal, and/or reenactment of aggression and violence (Callaway, 2003; Glodich & Allen, 1998; Murphy, et al., 1997). Prevention groups typically are time-limited, lasting eight to 12 sessions.

Immediate crisis response groups run by mental health professionals specially trained in trauma, designed to: help participants exposed to violence process and debrief the traumatic events or experiences, and identify and refer those at risk of developing a trauma-related dysfunction or disorder for mental health assessment and intervention (Dattilio & Freeman, 2000; Juhnke & Osborne, 1997; Mitchell & Everly, 2000). Crisis groups typically are one-time efforts, usually beginning 24 to 72 hours after an episode of acute violence, although some approaches involve additional sessions, including booster sessions six months after the initial group intervention. Group size may accommodate up to fifty people at a time (Juhnke & Osborne, 1997).

Spontaneous informal groups (e.g., neighborhood support groups, work peer groups, adolescent "groups on the go") run or co-facilitated by natural helpers or paraprofessionals designed to: share stressful experiences; get feedback about their reactions from peers, obtain empathy, support, and validation; problem-solve; and regain a sense of safety and control (Jagendorf & Malekoff, 2000; Ursano et al., 2000). As Gabarino and Kostelny (1997) point out, however, there are drawbacks to using natural helpers to run peer groups. Some experiences may be regarded as "too terrible to talk about," especially with family members (Raphael & Wilson, 2000). Furthermore, natural helpers' degree of comfort in directly discussing traumatic events and their own previous history of victimization will influence their ability to respond appropriately (Ursano et al., 2000). Advanced training of and/or consultation given to natural helpers by the trained professionals appear crucial for success. These groups typically are of short-term duration.

Ongoing groups for survivors, usually begun days or weeks after a major disaster or violent event, designed to: alleviate suffering and promote a return to healthy functioning by normalizing stress reactions; allow time for mourning and grieving; restore a sense of control over certain aspects of the environment; process anger and rage at the perpetrators; build mutual aid and support to help combat feelings of depression, vulnerability, and helpless; and begin the process of rebuilding one's life (Ceballo, 2000; Dembert & Simmer, 2000; deYoung & Corbin, 1994). Typically, these are long-term closed groups, lasting many months.

Follow-up support groups, designed to deal with the long-term impact of community violence, also are essential (Dembert & Simmer, 2000). For example, in the academic year following the Columbine shootings in Colorado, the local district, in conjunction with community mental health agencies, the dean of the School of Social Work at the University of Denver, and the department heads of other professional helping disciplines in several area colleges and universities, developed a year-long *clinical consultation pro-bono project*. This project was designed to link the school district's mental health staff (school social workers, school psychologists, and school counselors) with approximately 50 community-based educators and practitioners in social work, psychology, nursing, and psychiatry. Although primarily designed to assist the school staff in assessing and responding to the mental health needs of students and their families, the consultation groups provided a crucial experience in mutual aid and support for participants themselves, many of whom were struggling to return to normalcy.

In the consultation group run by this author, which included personnel from Columbine and several nearby feeder schools, participants were concerned about being branded permanently as "fragile trauma victims" by the school administration, as well as being blamed by the media, parents, lawmakers, and the public for not preventing the tragedy that eventually erupted. These concerns remained active long after the actual events had transpired. As revealed in a recent follow-up story in the *Denver Post,* three years after the Columbine school shootings, 60% of the teaching and support staff employed at Columbine in 1999 subsequently left through retirements, transfers, or forsaking public education altogether (Curtin & Aguilera, 2002). Many continue to struggle with the long-term impact of those events.

Forming Groups and Selecting Group Members: Situational, Developmental, Cultural, and Mental Health Considerations

Witnessing, experiencing, or responding to violence and victimization of one's self, a family member, or a peer typically are deeply distressing events. A person-environment lens (Fraser, 1995; Wilson & Sigman, 2000) is useful in conceptualizing violence and the complex, interacting situational, developmental, cultural, and mental health considerations that must be addressed when practitioners begin to form groups and recruit members.

Situational Factors. When forming groups to respond to acute episodes of or chronic exposure to violence, it is important to distinguish between *direct victims,* persons directly injured by violence, and *secondary victims,* who include witnesses and bystanders, employees at a worksite, first responders (i.e., police, firefighters, paramedics), family members, stakeholders (those who knew victims), and others connected to the event or people involved (Kinney, 1995). Generally speaking, the more direct the exposure to the traumatic event, the greater the risk for emotional harm (National Institute of Mental Health, 2001).

   Individuals in each category require a different group experience, with their own unique format and structure that best suits their needs for process and recovery. Several authors suggest that iatrogenic effects may occur when individuals with different degrees of exposure are brought together in the same group (Ceballo, 2000; Regher & Hill, 2000). As Raphael and Wilson (2000) observe: "Some [individuals] whose exposure has been minor may be traumatized by vivid accounts of those more intensely involved" (p. 4). Group practitioners, therefore, need to develop a screening process to select the individuals most appropriate for the type of group being organized.

Developmental Factors. An individual's cognitive style, pre-event resiliency (i.e., ego strengths and adaptation abilities), available social supports, and the nature of injury or harm will influence his or her subjective reaction to violence (Fraser, 1995). Developmentally, children and adolescents are at particular risk for developing academic difficulties, emotional and behavior problems, and trauma-related symptoms following exposure to violence (Dulmus & Wodarski, 2000; Hopps & Pinderhughes, 1999; Shahinfar et al., 2000). Children witnessing violence are more likely to develop internalizing problems (depression, anxiety, social withdrawal, etc.); whereas, children who were attacked or injured by violence are more likely to develop externalizing problems (e.g., aggression, conduct problems, delinquency) (Shahinfar et al., 2000).

Violence not only adversely affects children's sense of safety, it may interfere with their development of attachment to adult caretakers and other responsible figures of authority, their ability to process painful emotions, and their development of an internalized conscience. Children in the pre-operational stage of cognitive development (approximately ages two to seven years old), where egocentric thinking is predominant, may believe that they have done something to cause the violence, or that they should have done something to prevent the violence from occurring.

An extensive review of the group therapy literature conducted by Glodich and Allen (1998) stressed the important role groups can have in preventing the *reenactment* of violence among children and adolescents exposed to various types of trauma, thus forestalling the movement from "victim" to "perpetrator." Authorities differ, however, in their opinions of whether children should be encouraged to speak directly about trauma-related incidents from their past. Ceballo (2000) cautions against direct exploration with elementary school–aged children, recommending instead that discussions about neighborhood violence occur in *displacement;* that is, "one step removed from personal experience" (p. 402). In this approach, group practitioners help normalize and universalize the experience by discussing what "most children or adults would feel" when encountering violence. These techniques help prevent traumatizing some children whose exposure to violence is less severe than that of other members in the group.

A different view is taken by Murphy, Pynoos, and James (1997), who developed a combined approach of individual treatment, group psychotherapy, and therapeutic mentoring to help children chronically exposed to urban violence. These authors note that children typically respond to invitations to discuss their experiences in one of three ways: *(a)* sharing minimal details or facts, without processing any deeper thoughts and feelings; *(b)* responding competitively, by sharing "war stories" about their traumatic experiences, without the accompanying appropriate feelings of sadness, anger, or fear; or *(c)* responding anxiously and avoidantly, by seeking to distract themselves and other group members from further discussions of the topic. By drawing attention to when these behaviors occur in the group, practitioners help individual members and the group as a whole develop greater ability to tolerate direct discussions of traumatic experiences, eventually leading to the reintegration of painful feelings into their conscious awareness.

DeYoung and Corbin (1994), also noting the resistance of young adolescent girls to direct discussions about past sexual abuse trauma, developed a guided exercise that facilitates the telling of these stories. The exercise begins and ends with affirmations reinforcing the idea that each person is in charge of how much or little she shares; that it is the perpetrator's behavior, not the victim's, that is shameful; and that nothing the victim did caused the abuse to happen. Following this is a series of questions that an individual completes (prior to the group session), asking what the participant anticipates in telling her story and what she expects or needs from the group in hearing it. Next, a series of guided questions focus on eliciting the details of the abuse—who did it, how many times, how it felt, what the perpetrator told the victim, what her parent(s)' reaction to the abuse was, what eventually happened to the perpetrator, and what future hopes or aspirations the victim has. Sharing the responses to the guided exercise with other group members then provides her the needed structure and safety for the group format.

All three of these approaches, despite their differences, agree that processing underlying feelings and emotional reactions to violence is a crucial component in helping children and adolescents resume the course of their normal development. The advantage of groups is that individual members' emotional needs can be met in a more egalitarian way through mutual aid and support with peers and caring adults.

Cultural Factors. Silove (2000) notes that: "an equivalent term for trauma does not exist in the lexicons of many cultures, even though other concepts such as suffering, grief, and injustice invariably do" (p. 339). Indeed, critics have argued that trauma is a social construction of Western models of medicine and science, that have tended to frame exposure to violence in the language of psychopathology (particularly emphasizing symptoms of Post-Traumatic Stress Disorder [PTSD]) and therefore may not be appropriate to apply to people from non-Western cultures (Abueg et al., 2000). Perren-Klingler (2000), however, makes a different observation: "All societies have recognized the damaging influence of traumatic experiences on the mental health of [their] members. Closer questioning has shown that most cultures have come up with appropriate interventions for working through and integrating what has happened" (p. 50). The important point in this debate is that *group interventions must be adapted to the specific culture and environmental circumstances in which they are to be deployed* (Raphael & Wilson, 2000). Several corollaries of this practice principle emerge from this discussion:

Being a member of a minority cultural group in America may place a person at higher risk for trauma-related symptoms than his/her white counterparts (Abueg et al., 2000). Acute episodes of violence take place in the context of prior exposure to ongoing chronic forms of social oppression and economic disadvantage for many people of color and other marginalized groups. Group work is the intervention of choice with oppressed populations (Hopps & Pinderhughes, 1999). "It is critical for the [group] social worker not only to have a general understanding of the history of minority groups and their interactions with each other, but also to have a clear sense of the intergroup factors that exist in the community in which one is working" (Weiss, 1997, p. 126).

Perception of events and interpretation of traumatic reactions will vary depending upon the culture of those affected. Similarly, cultural beliefs, traditions, and rituals also will be critical in helping individuals work through and integrate their experiences (Perren-Klingler, 2000). Incorporating cultural language and rituals regarding loss, mourning, and death into group interventions may be particularly helpful.

Trauma professionals in charge of psychological debriefing or other group crisis intervention approaches typically are outsiders to the indigenous cultural groups and communities in which they work. Furthermore, outside professionals may symbolize to indigenous community members the historic oppression from a dominant culture or country previously involved in colonization or enslavement of the indigenous people (Abueg et al., 2000). In order to be effective, outside professionals may need to gain credibility by partnering with a cultural expert—a representative of the affected group—who understands the cultural norms (Raphael & Wilson, 2000). The outside professionals' work in the indigenous community should be time-limited, ending at the point in which the community reestablishes its ongoing functioning.

Selection of group members should give consideration to matching the cultural diversity of the general school or community populations from which the group is drawn. As Rose (1998) notes, "cultural factors are sometimes a source of homogeneity. As a source of heterogeneity, however, a diversity of cultural factors in composition provides members with an opportunity to relate to peers from dissimilar backgrounds" (p. 37).

Mental Health Factors. The most frequent mental health diagnoses associated with traumatic events are Acute Stress Disorder (ASD) and PTSD (Abueg et al., 2000). The diagnostic criteria for ASD, for symptoms lasting two days to one month, and PTSD, for symptoms lasting beyond one month, include "persistent, distressing, and intrusive recollections of the trauma, numbing of responsiveness to the environment, avoidance or escape in the presence of trauma-related cues, and a variety of autonomic, dysphoric, or cognitive symptoms" (Muran & DiGiuseppe, 2000, p. 151). In order for ASD to be diagnosed, three of five dissociative symptoms (de-realization, depersonalization, dissociative amnesia, subjective sense of numbing, and reduction in awareness of surroundings) must be present in the immediate aftermath of the trauma. In diagnosing PTSD, the core symptoms are re-experiencing, avoidance, and hyperarousal (Klein & Schemer, 2000). Community violence associated with civil and political unrest or criminal intent, such as the 1995 bombing of the Murrah Federal Building in Oklahoma City, "may be marked by a quicker onset of posttraumatic symptomatology, more intense and dramatic shock, rage, and grief experiences as well as significant physiological manifestations of acute stress such as stroke or headache" (Abueg et al., 2000, p. 252).

Group interventions for victims of community violence should be based on a mental health risk-assessment model. Abueg, Woods, and Watson (2000) have developed a three-tier hierarchical model of risk assessment to aid practitioners in delivering appropriate group interventions to individuals exposed to natural or manmade disaster traumas:

The first tier is the *low-risk category* into which the majority of disaster survivors fall. Because of their inherent resilience and available sources of social support, most need only a modest amount of intervention, if any. According to Stuhlmiller and Dunning (2000), "most persons suffering acute trauma spontaneously remit in symptomatology within six months with or without any formal intervention" (p. 15). Individuals at low risk are able to express their feelings of loss and engage in the process of grief and mourning. Group interventions with low-risk individuals would include (prior to the event) disaster planning, and afterwards, psychoeducational presentations on ASD and PTSD, and critical incident stress debriefing and critical incident stress management (discussed below), as needed.

The *moderate-risk category* includes individuals showing a clinically significant dysfunction, such as ASD, PTSD, depression, ruminative or obsessive disorder, or other forms of psychopathology. Group interventions would include cognitive-behavioral therapy, social skills training, stress inoculation, arousal reduction, and dissociation management.

The *high-risk category* includes individuals with severe dissociation symptoms, profound numbing, acutely suicidal ideation, complex PTSD symptoms, active drug or alcohol abuse, or history of drug dependence. Interventions include environmental change (e.g., removal to safety; providing food, clothing, shelter), hospital-based treatment, and group interventions designed to prevent trauma-relapse and victimization repetition.

It is important to note, however, there have been several significant challenges to the psychopathological conceptualizations of trauma reactions and PTSD symptoms. Critics argue that these conceptualizations divert attention from individuals' resilience, coping, and adaptation; reify stress reactions into a mental health disorder without either an adequate theoretical explanation or empirical validation that they are such a disorder; and ignore the positive, growth-producing effects that frequently occur when individuals successfully cope with a traumatic experience (Raphael & Wilson, 2000; Stuhlmiller & Dunning, 2000; Violanti et al., 2000). Indeed, in group work conducted with people who have experienced extreme events, there must be an acknowledgement of the physical and emotional devastation extreme events can bring about—yet group members' attention eventually must also be turned to their own resilience and the exceptions to the trauma symptoms (Juhnke & Osborne, 1997; Woodcock, 2001).

COMMON THEMES

At the risk of blurring the distinctions among the many different types of groups developed to respond to community violence, the following discussion is an amalgamation of themes across group types and populations. Themes are examined within the overlapping theoretical frameworks for the *phases of trauma recovery* (Kinney, 1995) and *stages of group development* (Dembert & Simmer, 2000). While by no means identical, these two frameworks have some rough parallels with each other.

"Safety and Control". The initial phase of trauma recovery is characterized by reactions of shock, horror, and disbelief (Kinney, 1995), as individuals attempt to process extreme events outside the realm of their previous personal experiences (in the case of acute trauma episodes). For individuals chronically exposed to violence, their firsthand experiences with death and injury may be considerably more extensive, but often they have had little previous opportunity to process their reactions in an appropriate manner (Ceballo, 2000; Timnick, 1989). Initial themes at the beginning stage of group development typically center on whether the group is a safe place to be together and talk about the things that have happened—both the good and the bad. As group members introduce each other and help establish group rules, they begin to create a sense of safety and control. Group rules may include decisions about who can participate, the length of time the group is intended to meet, confidentiality, and how the group will handle individual members who become overwhelmed in talking about their experiences. Ceballo (2000) notes that children exposed to chronic violence may add the rule "no weapons brought to group" to further reinforce their sense of safety and control.

"So Many Thoughts and Feelings". The second stage of trauma recovery is characterized by individuals experiencing the gamut of emotions and thoughts as they attempt to accommodate their experiences into their existing cognitive schemata or worldview (Kinney, 1995). Emotions may range from numbing to intense anxiety, fear, terror, anger, guilt (at surviving), remorse, and grief. Cognitions may range from confusion, to intrusive thoughts and images, to obsessive ruminations on the same events over and over again. Desire to place blame, seek revenge on perpetrators, or express feelings of betrayal and abandonment at not being protected

from harm are common. Feelings of sadness, mourning, and loss over the death of a loved one also predominate (Dembert & Simmer, 2000).

In the middle phase of group development, group facilitators strengthen group cohesion by normalizing common themes and reactions among group members, while also pointing out the uniqueness of each person's individual viewpoints. Themes typically focus on identifying, naming, validating, and expressing these distressing feelings, and on differentiating situations, thoughts, and feelings from each other (Ceballo, 2000; Hopps & Pinderhughes, 1999). In addition, dealing with members' cognitive distortions about their personal responsibility for being victimized and/or their potential for becoming violent themselves is critical. For example, some middle school students who knew the Columbine High School shooters worried that because they liked the same kind of music and video games as the two teenage killers, they would become the victims of other students' and parents' wrath, or feared that they would, themselves, subsequently become violent (Kayser et al., 2001). Similarly, a persistent theme for many group members is the loss of confidence in their ability to cope, and feeling inadequate or ineffective in their role (e.g., spouse, parent, breadwinner, classmate, coworker, etc.) (Dembert & Simmer, 2000). Feelings of being out of control, or of having no control over one's life, may be marked.

"Coping and Reintegration". The third phase of trauma recovery focuses on developing effective coping strategies to deal with the distressing thoughts and feelings, and the restoration of functioning and equilibrium (Kinney, 1995). Themes in this phase typically center on the realization that group members can begin to rebuild their lives, even while recognizing that their lives will never be the same as they were before the violence occurred (Dembert & Simmer, 2000). Highlighting strengths, resilience, and pre-existing coping strategies are important (Juhnke & Osborne, 1997; Woodcock, 2001). In the ending phase of group, practitioners need to recognize that, for some members, there is no final closure to the traumatic event, because their lives have been inalterably changed. Providing concrete, tangible reminders of the group experience (e.g., handing out diplomas and bravery awards, developing a group newsletter that summarizes each person's story) are ways of bringing the group experience to an end (Ceballo, 2000).

METHODS

Because of the wide popularity and use of Critical Incident Stress Debriefing (CISD) in immediately responding to natural as well as manmade disasters (such as community violence), this section will examine its methodology in greater detail. A contrasting debriefing method, placing greater emphasis on resilience and strengths, also will be discussed.

Seven Phases of CISD

CISD is a specific method of psychological debriefing developed by Mitchell (1983), originally for emergency personnel, but now applied to a diverse client group including "college students, educational systems, law enforcement, health care systems, nursing personnel, military personnel, physician assistants, and physicians" (Harbert, 2000, p. 400). It is a group process, drawing on crisis intervention and psychoeducational theory and techniques, designed to facilitate psychological closure to a traumatic event (Mitchell & Everly, 1997). CISD groups may begin as soon as 24 hours after a traumatic event has occurred. Usually, three team members facilitate the group: a mental health professional with specific expertise in trauma, and two peers from the group, all of whom have had training in the CISD method. It is a one-time group experience, typically lasting upwards of three hours, intended for homogenous groups who experienced a traumatic event (Harbert, 2000). CISD is one component of Critical Incident Stress Management (CISM), a more extensive, systematic approach to responding to traumatic events.

Introductory Phase. The opening phase orients participants to the debriefing process. Several important rules are established. First, only persons directly involved in the violent episode may participate—all others are asked to leave. Often a sense of group unity results from this rule. Second, all participants must stay for the entire debriefing, and no one is allowed to leave and not return. (Brief individual bathroom breaks are allowed, and team members provide assistance to anyone temporarily overwhelmed by recalling the traumatic experiences.) Participants are told that their active presence and participation are needed in helping others, and their absence may hinder others' recovery. Third, that what is said in the group is to remain confidential, so no notes or recordings are made of the session (Harbert, 2000). In addition, the expectation for participation is reinforced by informing members that the debriefing may be helpful to them by learning that others share similar feelings and thoughts about what has occurred, and that a discussion of these in a group format can promote a more accurate understanding of the violent episode and its surrounding circumstances (Juhnke & Osborne, 1997).

Fact Phase. This phase begins with a statement from the debriefing team leader that, since the team was not present when the episode occurred, it is important to gather as many facts as possible about what actually happened. Each group member is asked to introduce herself or himself, stating where she or he was when the disaster occurred, what her or his job or role was, and to describe what occurred to the best of that person's ability (Dembert & Simmer, 2000; Harbert, 2000). Emphasis is placed on just accounting the facts, without pushing members to describe their feelings. When emotions and signs of PTSD are expressed, team leaders emphasize that such reactions are not unusual for those who have experienced trauma or violence, and outline some of the ways those feelings can be addressed—both later within the debriefing experience itself, and afterwards through individual counseling (Juhnke & Osborne, 1997).

Thought Phase. This phase is a transition phase, leading from a description of facts toward the processing of intense affective responses (Juhnke & Osborne, 1997). The team leader begins by asking each member what his or her predominant thought was "once they got off the 'autopilot' mode of operating or functioning" (Harbert, 2000, p. 402). Because thoughts are internal members may react intensely, sharing not only cognitions but also affective responses such as anger (including anger at other members in the group and/or debriefing team members), fear, sadness, depression, and guilt. Team debriefing members provide support and understanding to group members by validating and normalizing their reactions as typical responses to trauma and violence (Juhnke & Osborne, 1997).

Reaction Phase. This phase focuses on the affective domain. Questions asked by the team leader include: "What is the worst thing about this incident for you personally?" "What bothered you the most or caused you the most pain?" "If you could change one thing about this experience, what would it be?" Rather than structure the group in a round-robin response format as in the previous phases, anyone who wants to speak may do so (Harbert, 2000). "Too much conversation by the team tends to detract from the affective responses and dilute the group process. Therefore the focus should be kept on group members' discussion of their reactions to the event" (Juhnke & Osborne, 1997, p. 70). This phase is often the most difficult for participants, as they wrestle with their own emotions and react to the emotions of others. Particularly for men, who often have difficulty acknowledging and expressing feelings of helplessness and sadness, the debriefing experience gives permission to share these feelings within a supportive group atmosphere (Dembert & Simmer, 2000).

Symptom Phase. In this stage, participants are helped to move away from sharing their intense affective reactions and back into the cognitive domain, in a conscious effort to restore people to the cognitive level by the time the debriefing ends (Harbert, 2000; Juhnke & Osborne, 1997). This phase begins when the debriefing team asks members to describe any symptoms—physical, cognitive, emotional, and behavioral—they experienced while responding to or in the immediate aftermath of the traumatic events. According to Mitchell and Everly (1997), many participants are reluctant to mention symptoms out of fear that their reactions are, or will be judged to be, abnormal. These fears are lessened as participants come to realize that others have experienced similar reactions.

Teaching Phase. Having elicited a variety of symptoms, the debriefing team then moves to an educational phase, which "demystifies the event and the reactions of participants" (Harbert, 2000, p. 403). Information is presented on a variety of topics, such as: stress reactions; coping and survival techniques—including self-care; and reintegrating with friends, family, and coworkers (Dembert & Simmer, 2000). The information is specifically tailored to the symptoms described by participants in the preceding phase. Information also is elicited from group members regarding what they have found helpful in lessening the symptoms of stress, so that members can experience giving care to and receiving care from fellow group members.

Reentry Phase. The final phase focuses on summarizing the debriefing experience, with all debriefing team members contributing their thoughts and feelings—communicating respect, encouragement, support, and appreciation to the group members (Harbert, 2000). There also is an opportunity to answer any last questions from members, and provide final directions about steps to be taken in the future, as members return to their daily routines and everyday lives (Dembert & Simmer, 2000).

Solution-Focused Debriefing

Juhnke and Osborne (1997) have developed an alternative debriefing approach, incorporating both the CISD phases and techniques from solution-focused therapy. These authors note that, in the traditional CISD single debriefing session, participants are left to care for themselves after the session has been concluded, and therefore they may not be adequately prepared to deal the emergence of PTSD-like symptoms emerging several weeks after the event. Solution-Focused Debriefing (SFD) begins where CISD leaves off. Two additional weekly group follow-up sessions are scheduled beyond the initial CISD debriefing session, each lasting one to two hours. SFD has two discernible phases:

Exploration of the Exceptions. In the first follow-up SFD session, team members ask participants to focus on times when they are not experiencing stress- or trauma-related symptoms or reactions. Participants also are asked to share what they need to do to continue their improvement process. A variety of techniques from solution-focused therapy is employed at this point, such as: identifying positive changes already occurring; focusing on cognitive decisions regarding improvement, rather than dwelling on external forces or dynamics; identifying common elements in symptom-free times; reminding members of past success in coping with other distressing events; encouraging members to "do something different" when existing coping strategies are not working; and using scaling techniques to help participants identify the degree of improvement since the previous session.

Consolidation Phase. The final follow-up SFD session focuses on achieving a more clearly delineated endpoint with participants by identifying and completing any unfinished business left over from the two previous sessions. Group members are invited to share what the debriefing experience has been like for them, and to address how they plan to use this experience over the next several weeks. Group members also are asked for their views on how the debriefing experience could be improved: "sharing ideas and suggestions promotes a sense that participants are giving something back to the counselors and to those who may need such services in the future" (Juhnke & Osborne, 1997, p. 75).

EVALUATION APPROACHES

Part of the difficulty in measuring the impact of community violence is that, even if people have experienced highly stressful events, they may also have positive, growth-producing experiences as well. Multiple measures, therefore, should be employed in order to understand both the nature and impact of the stressful event and the types of adaptation and growth that may have resulted from the experience. It especially is important to differentiate the impact of a single traumatic event from that of multiple traumas and from the accumulated risk of lifetime exposure. According to the PILOTS database (Published International Literature on Traumatic Stress) maintained by the National Center for PTSD (a division of the Veterans Administration), the two most frequently used measures to evaluate PTSD are the Impact of Event Scale (Zilberg et al., 1982) and the Beck Depression Inventory (Beck & Beamesderfer, 1974). The Impact of Events Scale assesses the experience of post-traumatic stress for any specific lifetime event. The Beck Depression Inventory is a client self-reporting scale that assesses the presence and severity of cognitive, affective, motivational, vegetative, and psychomotor components of depression (Regehr & Hill, 2000). Both measures have acceptable reliability and validity and have been used in hundreds of studies.

In addition to these two, the National Center for PTSD's website summarizes a large number of specialized trauma evaluation instruments, including structured clinical interviews, client self-reporting measures, and clinician-administered scales, for both adult and child or adolescent clients (www.ncptsd.org/treatment/assessment/index.html).[1]

One final note regarding evaluation of group methods for interventions with victims of trauma exposure: The CISD debriefing model, although widely utilized, has been criticized on a number of grounds. First, although originally designed to respond to secondary trauma experienced by emergency and rescue personnel, it now is being used with popula-

---

[1] Interested clinician-researchers are referred to Stamm's (1996) *Measurement of stress, trauma, and adaptation,* and E. Carlson's (1996) *Trauma research methodology,* both published by the Sidran Press, for detailed discussion of research design and measurement issues. Another on-line resource that examines measures of traumatic stress and secondary stress can be found at Idaho State University, Institute for Rural Health's website (www.isu.edu/~bhstamm/tests.htm).

tions and in settings far beyond its original purposes, including with direct victims themselves (Raphael & Wilson, 2000; Violanti et al., 2000). The single-session approach and lack of planned follow-up may be particularly problematic for direct victims of violence experiencing ongoing stress- or trauma-related symptoms. Second, and more important, controversy has occurred about the efficacy of crisis-debriefing group approaches. As Regehr and Hill (2000) note, "initial reports of the efficacy of crisis debriefing groups have relied on anecdotal evidence, client satisfaction surveys, and clinical impressions of group leaders" (p. 71). Although the satisfaction of group members participating in crisis debriefing sessions is typically quite high, the anticipated reductions in symptoms of anxiety, PTSD, and depression have not been found in several outcome studies (Regehr & Hill, 2000). Critics have suggested that CISD has taken on the appearance of a "social movement" among adherents, who steadfastly believe in its efficacy, despite the lack of underlying empirical evidence (Raphael & Wilson, 2000; Violanti et al., 2000). In response, proponents counter that improvements have been noted in research on employee functioning after participating in CISD sessions following a traumatic incident, including reduced use of sick leave and a correspondingly higher number of days employees are at work as scheduled (Mitchell & Everly, 2000). It seems safe to say that the final word on the effectiveness of this approach has not yet been spoken.

CONCLUSION

One lesson learned from the Columbine High School shootings and other such episodes of community violence is the importance of having a mental health disaster plan in place *ahead of time*. Unfortunately, even when formulated, these plans often remain focused on single-intervention approaches, such as crisis debriefing groups. In catastrophic situations, well-meaning agencies and practitioners gravitate to prepackaged, structured approaches because they provide a sense of certainty and guidance when chaos reigns. As has been shown, however, certainty and structure are not the same as efficacy. This chapter has argued that a *multifaceted group approach at both the macro and micro level* is needed to prevent and intervene in chronic and acute episodes of community violence. Given the lack of clear empirical support for crisis debriefing groups, reliance on this single approach is both unwise and unrealistic. In particular, it is not appropriate or adequate for those victims who need more extensive services and/or who are exposed to chronic episodes of community violence.

Despite the best efforts of helping professionals, it appears that many people affected by disaster and trauma never seek or receive appropriate help. In the future, the challenges are to design, coordinate, and implement a flexible array of group approaches that penetrate many layers of the community's experience. Formally structured groups must also connect more directly to natural, spontaneous groups that develop in response to disasters. Groups are the way communities can provide organized and intense forms of social support to the victims of violence in order to mitigate its impact and to forestall its further spread. Groups are the way communities can begin to heal themselves.

RESOURCES

The following is a list of resources on violence, trauma, and disaster from major national professional or governmental organizations.

Crisis and Trauma

The American Academy of Experts in
   Traumatic Stress
368 Veterans Memorial Highway
Commack, NY 11724
(631) 543-2217
www.aaets.org

Baldwin Trauma Pages
David V. Baldwin, Ph.D.
Eugene, OR
(541) 686-2598
www.trauma-pages.com

Institute for Rural Health
Idaho State University
www.isu.edu/~bhstamm/tests.htm

Measurement of Stress Trauma and
   Adaptation
Edited by B. H. Stamm
Published by Sidran Institute
200 E. Joppa Road, Suite 207
Towson, MD
(410) 825-8888

www.sidran.org
sidran@sidran.org

National Center for PTSD
215 N. Main St.
White River Junction, VT 05009
(802) 296-5132
www.ncptsd.org

Psych Works/Managing Traumatic
   Stress
1515 University Drive, Suite 115A
Coral Springs, FL 33071-6084
(954) 344-2022
www.psychworks.com

Trauma Research Methodology
by E. Carlson (1996)
Published by Sidram Institute
200 E. Joppa Road, Suite 207
Towson, MD
(410) 825-8888
www.sidran.org
sidran@sidran.org

Disaster Mental Health

Center for Mental Health Services
Emergency Services and Disaster
   Relief Branch
5600 Fishers Lane, Room 17C-20
Rockville, MD 20857
(301) 443-4735
www.mentalhealth.org/cmhs/
   emergencyservices/index./htm

Federal Emergency Management
   Agency
500 C. St.. SW
Washington, DC 20472
(202) 566-1600
www.fema.gov

National Institute of Mental Health
Information Resources and Inquiries
 Branch
6001 Executive Boulevard, Rm. 8184,
 MSC 9663
Bethesda, MD 20892-9663
(301) 443-4513
www.nimh.nih.gov

Walter Reed Army Medical Center,
 Department of Social Work
6900 Georgia Ave, NW
Washington, DC 20307-5001
(202) 782-6378
www.wramc.amedd.army.mil/
 departments/socialwork/index.htm

Violence

Centers for Disease Control and
 Prevention
1600 Clifton Rd.
Atlanta, GA 30333
(404) 639-3311
www.cdc.gov

Minnesota Center Against Violence
 and Abuse
School of Social Work
University of Minnesota
105 Peters Hall
1404 Gortner Ave.
St. Paul, MN 55108
(612) 625-1220
www.mincava.umn.edu

National Center for Injury Prevention
 and Control
Mailstop K60
4770 Buford Highway NE
Atlanta, GA 30341-3724
(770) 488-4362
www.cdc.gov/ncipc

National Center for Victims of
 Crimes
2111 Wilson Boulevard, Suite 300
Arlington, VA 22201
(703) 276-2880
www.ncvc.org

National Organization for Victims
 Assistance
1757 Park Road, NW
Washington, DC 20010
(800) 879-6682 or (202)-232-6682
www.try-nova.org

UCLA/School Mental Health
 Project
Center for Mental Health in Schools
Department of Psychology
University of California
P.O. Box 951563
Los Angeles, CA 90095-1563
(310) 825-3634
www.smhp.psych.ucla.edu

REFERENCES

Abueg, F., Woods, G., & Watson, D. (2000). Disaster trauma. In F. Dattilio & A. Freeman (eds.), *Cognitive-behavioral strategies in crisis intervention* (pp. 243–272).
 New York: Guilford.

Beck, A., & Beamesderfer, A. (1974). Assessment of depression: The Depression Inventory. In P. Pichot & R. Olivier-Martin (eds.), *Psychological measurements in
 psychopharmacology* (pp. 151–169). Oxford: S. Karger.

Bradford, A. (1999). REBUILD: An orthopedic trauma support group and community outreach program. *Health and Social Work.* 24(4), 307–311.

Brener, N., Simon, T., Krug, E., & Lowry, R. (1999). Recent trends in violence-
 related behaviors among high school students in the United States. *Journal of the
 American Medical Association.* 282(5), 440–46.

Callaway, C. (2003). Peer networking to build resiliency among high school youth: A violence prevention group. In D. Capuzzi (ed.), *Approaches to group work: A handbook for practitioners* (pp. 64–73). Upper Saddle River, NJ: Merrill Prentice Hall.

Cannon, J., & Gingerich, E. (2002): Seeking alternatives to violence: A school-based violence prevention project. In S. Henry, J. East, & C. Schmitz (eds.), *Social work with groups: Mining the gold* (pp. 31–39). New York: Haworth Press.

Ceballo, R. (2000). The neighborhood club: A supportive intervention group for children exposed to urban violence. *American Journal of Orthopsychiatry.* 70(3), 401–407.

Centers for Disease Control and Prevention (1993). *The prevention of youth violence: A framework for community action.* Atlanta, GA: Author.

Curtin, D., & Aguilera, E. (2002, August 18). Feeling the pain. *Denver Post* (Section A), 1, 8–9.

Dattilio, F., Freeman, A. (eds.) (2000). *Cognitive-behavioral strategies in crisis intervention.* New York: Guilford.

Dembert, M., & Simmer, E., (2000). When trauma affects a community: Group interventions after a disaster. In R. Klein and V. Schermer (eds.), *Group psychotherapy for psychological trauma* (pp. 239–264). New York: Guilford.

DeYoung, M., & Corbin, B. (1994). Helping early adolescents tell: A guided exercise for trauma-focused sexual abuse treatment groups. *Child Welfare.* 78(2), 141–154.

Dulmus, C., & Wodarski, J. (2000). Trauma-related symptomatology among children of parents victimized by urban community violence. *American Journal of Orthopsychiatry.* 70(2), 272–277.

Fraser, M. (1994). Violence overview. In NASW's *Encyclopedia of social work* (19th ed., vol. 3, pp. 2453–2460). Washington, DC: NASW Press.

Gabriel, M. (1996). *AIDS trauma and support group therapy.* New York: Free Press.

Garbarino, J., & Kostelny, K. (1997). Coping with the consequences of community violence. In A. Goldstein & J. Conoley (eds.), *School violence intervention: A practical handbook* (pp. 336–387). New York: Guilford.

Glodich, A., & Allen, J. (1998). Adolescents exposed to violence and abuse: A review of the group therapy literature with an emphasis on preventing trauma reenactment. *Journal of Child and Adolescent Group Therapy.* 8(3), 135–154.

Goldstein, A., & Conoley, J. (eds.) (1997). *School violence intervention: A practical handbook.* New York: Guilford.

Harbert, K. (2000). Critical incident stress debriefing. In F. Dattilio & A. Freeman (eds.), *Cognitive-behavioral strategies in crisis intervention* (pp. 385–408). New York: Guilford.

Hopps, J., & Pinderhughes, E. (1999). *Group work with overwhelmed clients.* New York: Free Press.

Jagendorf, J., & Malekoff, A. (2000). Groups-on-the-go: Spontaneously formed mutual aid groups for adolescents in distress. *Social Work with Groups.* 22(4), 15–32.

Juhnke, G., & Osborne, W. (1997). The solution-focused debriefing group: An integrated postviolence group intervention for adults. *The Journal for Specialists in Group.* 22(1), 66–76.

Kayser, J., Silver, J., & Lyon, M. (2001). From the frying pan into the fire: Three advocacy tales in child and adolescent mental health practice. *Reflections: Narratives of Professional Helping.* 7(1), 48–60.

Kinney, J. (1995). *Violence at work. How to make your company safer for employees and customers.* Englewood Cliffs, NJ: Prentice Hall.

Klein, R., & Schermer, V. (eds.) (2000). *Group psychotherapy for psychological trauma.* New York: Guilford.

Levinsky, L., & McAleer, K. (1994). "Listen to us!" Young adolescents in urban schools. In A. Gitterman and L. Shulman (eds.), *Mutual aid groups, vulnerable populations, and the life cycle* (2nd ed.) (pp. 151–162). New York: Columbia University Press.

Melnik, T., & Baker, C. (2002, September 6). Psychological and emotional effects of the September 11 Attacks on the World Trade Center—Connecticut, New Jersey, and New York. *Morbidity and Mortality Weekly Report.* 51(35), 784–786. Available on-line: www.cdc.gov/mmwr/preview/mmwrhtml/mm5135a2.htm.

Mitchell, J. (1983). When disaster strikes . . . The critical incident stress debriefing process. *Journal of Emergency Medical Services.* 8(1), 36–9.

Mitchell, J., & Everly, Jr., G. (2000). Critical Incident Stress Management and Critical Incident Stress Debriefing: Evolution, effects, and outcomes. In B. Raphael and J. Wilson (eds.), *Psychological debriefing: Theory, practice, evidence* (pp. 71–90). Cambridge, UK: Cambridge University Press.

Muran, E., & DiGiuseppe, R. (2000). Rape trauma. In F. Dattilio & A. Freeman (eds.), *Cognitive-behavioral strategies in crisis intervention* (pp. 150–165). New York: Guilford.

Murphy, L., Pynoos, R., & James, C. (1997). The trauma/grief-focused group psychotherapy module of an elementary school–based violence prevention/intervention project. In J. Osofsky (ed.), *Children in a violent society* (pp. 223–255). New York: Guilford Press.

National Center for Injury Prevention and Control (2000). *Youth violence in the United States.* Atlanta, GA: Centers for Disease Control and Prevention. Available on-line: www.cdc.gov/ncipc/dvp/youth/newfacts.htm.

National Institute of Mental Health (2001). *Helping children and adolescents cope with violence and disasters: Fact sheet.* Bethesda, MD: Department of Health and Human Services.

Paine, C., & Sprague, J. (2002). Dealing with a school shooting disaster: Lessons learned from Springfield, Oregon. *Emotional and Behavioral Disorders in Youth.* 2(2), 35–40.

Perren-Kilingler, G. (2000). The integration of traumatic experiences: Culture and resources. In J. Violanti, D. Paton, & C. Dunning (eds.), *Posttraumatic stress interventions: Challenges, issues, and perspectives* (pp. 43–64). Springfield, IL: Charles C. Thomas, Publisher.

Rachael, B., & Wilson, J. (eds.) (2000). *Psychological debriefing: Theory, practice, and evidence.* Cambridge, UK: Cambridge University Press.

Regehr, C., & Hill, J. (2000). Evaluating the efficacy of crisis debriefing groups. *Social Work with Groups.* 23(3), 69–79.

Rose, S. (1998). *Group work with children and adolescents: Prevention and intervention in school and community systems.* Thousand Oaks (CA): Sage.

Rosenberg, M. L., & Fenley, M. A. (1991). *Violence in America: A public health approach.* New York: Oxford University Press.

Shahinfar, A., Fox, N., & Leavitt, L. (2000). Preschool children's exposure to violence: Relation of behavior problems to parent and child reports. *American Journal of Orthopsychiatry.* 70(1), 115–125.

Silove, D. (2000). A conceptual framework for mass trauma: Implications for adaptation, intervention, and debriefing. In B. Raphael & J. Wilson (eds.), *Psychological debriefing: Theory, practice, evidence* (pp. 337–350). Cambridge, UK: Cambridge University Press.

Silverman, E. (1986). The social worker's role in shock-trauma units. *Social Work.* 31(4), 311–313.

Stuhlmiller, C., & Dunning, C. (2000). Challenging the mainstream: From pathogenic to salutogenic models of posttrauma intervention. In J. Violanti, D. Paton, & C. Dunning (eds.), *Posttraumatic stress intervention: Challenges, issues, and perspectives* (pp. 10–42). Springfield, IL: Charles C. Thomas, Publisher.

Timnick, L. (1989, September 3). Children of violence. What happens to kids who learn as babies to dodge bullets and step over corpses on the way to school? *Los Angeles Times Magazine.* 6–14.

Ursano, R., Fullerton, C., Vance, K., & Wang, L. (2000). Debriefing: Its role in the spectrum of prevention and acute management of psychological trauma. In B. Raphael and J. Wilson (eds.), *Psychological debriefing: Theory, practice, evidence* (pp. 32–42). Cambridge, UK: Cambridge University Press.

Violanti, J., Paton, D., Dunning, C. (eds.). (2000) *Posttraumatic stress intervention: Challenges, issues, and perspectives.* Springfield, IL: Charles C. Thomas, Publisher.

Waldrop, D. (2001). *Critical incident stress management.* Washington, DC: Institute for the Advancement of Social Work Research. Available on-line: www.iaswresearch.org.

Weiss, J. (1997). Working with victims of ethnoviolence. In G. Greif and P. Ephross (eds.), *Group work with populations at risk* (pp. 121–133). New York: Oxford University Press.

Wilson, J., & Sigman, M. (2000). Theoretical perspectives of traumatic stress debriefing. In B. Raphael and J. Wilson (eds.), *Psychological debriefing: Theory, practice, evidence* (pp. 58–68). Cambridge, UK: Cambridge University Press.

Woodcock, J. (2001). Being, noticing, knowing: The emergence of resilience in group work. In T. Kelly, T. Berman-Rossi, & S. Palombo (eds.), *Group work: Strategies for strengthening resiliency* (pp. 5–17). New York: Haworth Press.

Ying, Y. (2001). Psychotherapy with traumatized Southeast Asian refugees. *Clinical Social Work Journal.* 29(1), 65–78.

Zilberg, N., Weiss, D., & Horowitz, M. (1982). Impact of Events Scale: A cross-validation study and some empirical evidence supporting a conceptual model of stress response syndromes. *Journal of Consulting and Clinical Psychology.* 50(3), 407–414.

Chapter 24

Group Work with
Employee-Related Issues

MURIEL GRAY AND MELISSA LITTLEFIELD

Issues of the workplace are of interest, in large part, because of the role of work in shaping the lives and identities of individuals and the impact of the nature of work on shaping the identities of nations. The workplace and its workers become increasingly important as the economies of nations become more interdependent and more dependent on work products and services.

From the worker's perspective, Studs Terkel (1974) considers the paradox of work by acknowledging that it is integral to personal identity but can also be degrading to the spirit. He quotes William Faulkner: "You can't eat for eight hours a day nor drink for eight hours a day nor make love for eight hours a day—all you can do for eight hours is work. Which is the reason why man makes himself and everybody else so miserable and unhappy" (p. xi).

Social workers have traditionally worked in a variety of host settings with a variety of populations; however, only recently has the workplace emerged as an appropriate practice setting for social workers (Gray & Barrow, 1993; Kurzman & Akabas, 1993). As a result, there has been a proliferation of creative efforts to use social work skills (Cherin, 2000; Root, 2000). This field of practice is commonly referred to as *occupational social work*.

According to Kurzman and Akabas (1993), the practice of occupational social work is different from more traditional fields of practice because "the auspices of this field-trade unions and employing organizations—are new, uncommon host settings . . . outside the social service

arena and not part of the formal human service tradition" (p. 3). Therefore, social work services in the workplace are typically provided by one
or a very few social workers, who are likely to be the only human service
professionals at the work site trained to deal with workers' psychosocial
issues. Hence, they may be called on to address anything that does not appear to be a personnel issue. While social work skills equip social workers
to perform many functions in the workplace, social workers function primarily in assistance programs (Gray & Barrow, 1993).

Historically, most employee assistance programs were "internal,"
whereby the social workers were employed by and staffed within the
workplace. Now, most programs are "external," in that the program is
provided by external contractors.

Assistance programs are commonly identified by the populations
they serve. They are typically employee assistance programs (EAPs)
when sponsored by management; member or labor assistance programs
when sponsored by labor alone; worker assistance programs when sponsored jointly by labor and management; faculty and staff assistance programs when sponsored by colleges and universities to serve those populations; and student assistance programs when sponsored by schools to
serve students.

THE SETTING

While basic social work principles and values are the cornerstone of such
practice, there are many nuances that make this setting different from the
more traditional social work practice settings. These nuances are often
reflected in the nature of the populations being served, the philosophy of
the programs, the manner of problem identification, and the types of issues being addressed. For instance, in this setting the social worker may
have multiple clients: individual workers, groups of workers, the work organization, and the labor union. Being effective requires an understanding of the broader cultural context of the workplace in order to address
both the needs of the worker and the needs of the organization. In some
instances, these needs may conflict with each other. At those times, Kurzman (1993) notes, occupational social work may present unique ethical
dilemmas and challenges. As in other settings, confidentiality is the cornerstone of clinical practice; however, in the occupational setting, the
perception of confidentiality is also critical. This can be quite a challenge
when resolution of a particular problem may require collaboration with
other systems within the workplace or when the worker has been referred
to the EAP by a supervisor who expects to collaborate with the EAP social worker.

The philosophy guiding the programs may also differ from that of
traditional social work practice settings. The philosophy of most assistance programs sees work as the goal of functional performance. These

programs typically assume that when workers have personal problems, these problems may affect job performance, and that job performance will improve as personal problems are resolved. Hence, work-related issues may be identified by the workplace and/or by workers. In some instances, individual workers may not be able to articulate a problem and may be unfamiliar with the assistance process because they may never have utilized the services of a professional helper. Moreover, since the services offered through assistance programs are not limited to a particular type of problem (such as mental health, substance use disorders, family), workers seek assistance for a variety of problems. Social workers in this setting have no idea what kind of assistance may be requested. Therefore, occupational social workers need to know enough about many concerns to perform a differential assessment. As in other settings, the assessment considers the person in the environment. In this instance, the environment is the workplace. Therefore, the assessment must consider the interaction between worker and work.

The types of problems or issues presented may also be different from those in the more traditional social work settings. In other words, many presenting issues may be those of the workplace and may require collaboration between supervisors, human resource managers, and occupational social workers.

Traditional approaches to human resource management utilized by U.S. corporations have focused on *individual* worker productivity; however, a global economy has resulted in management approaches focusing on work *group* productivity. Hence, many employee issues that were formerly defined as individual worker problems and addressed by social casework approaches may now be redefined as workplace problems and addressed by social group work strategies. Not only has there been a change in the approach used in managing human resources, there has also been a change in the nature and types of issues the workplace considers important to address. For instance, the editor of *American Business 2000* (1992) indicates that employers must adapt to the changing nature of work by replacing adversarial labor relations with a cooperative approach that recognizes the clash between workers' status as employees and their needs as individuals.

Hence, occupational social workers need to be mindful of the history of work groups and how the acceptance of group work may be associated with increased worker power and the resultant political ramifications (Bramel & Friend, 1987). Social workers need to be aware of the cultural context, political environment, and political implications when developing and applying group work strategies in the workplace. Of utmost importance is the role of labor (Molloy & Kurzman, 1993) and the nature of the labor-management relationship.

Finally, occupational social workers need to recognize that they are practicing in a culture that is primarily composed of groups but a culture that may not recognize that its day-to-day decisions (should) utilize basic group work principles. In other words, workers are so accustomed to working in an office or on a team that these work situations are rarely thought of as groups that require the application of group work principles.

These themes are a few examples of the nuances that may be unique to the workplace that social workers must be knowledgeable of if they are to be effective. In fact, Googins (1993) perceives social work's lack of familiarity with the operations and culture of the workplace as a deficit that must be overcome if social workers are to gain wider access to corporate management and labor.

The social and health issues of the employed population, and the tension of balancing the roles of worker and individual, have long been part of the social welfare tradition; however, contemporary assistance programs are characterized by a much broader array of services (Kurzman & Akabas, 1993). Increasingly, interventions are utilizing group methodologies.

The remainder of this chapter consists of an overview of selected work-related issues typically addressed by social group work interventions: brown bag seminar groups addressing life cycle development issues; post-trauma debriefing groups (also referred to as *critical incident stress debriefing*) addressing workplace violence; support and mutual help groups addressing issues of multiculturalism and diversity; and self-help and treatment groups addressing recovery from substance use disorders.

Note that in this chapter the term *worker* refers to an individual employee who may be employed by an organization or an individual worker who identifies himself or herself as a member of labor. *Worker* is therefore distinguished from *social worker.*

REVIEW OF THE LITERATURE

A review of the literature found that supervisor training and consultation (Akabas & Hanson, 1990; (Cherin, 2000; Googins & Casey, 1990), cultural diversity education (Gray, 1992; Gray & Barrow, 1993; Hood et al., 2001; Mor Barak, 2000; Van Den Bergh, 1998), drug-use-disorder recovery counseling (Gray, 1993) substance abuse prevention (Bennett et al., 2000) critical incident stress debriefing (Braverman, 1993; Michael et al., 1985), conflict management (Arnold, 1995; Jarboe & Witteman, 1996; Kellerman 1996), burnout prevention (Pouliot & Horne, 2001), and a variety of problems in living (Schopler & Galinsky, 1993; Sussal, 1985) are among the critical issues affecting employees that utilize social group work interventions. However, just as there are nuances in the workplace that require sensitivity, there are nuances that need to be taken into account when attempting to retrieve data on employee-related issues. For instance, the literature on employee-related issues is stored in several different databases under several different headings: employee assistance programs, human resource management, labor relations, business, social work, psychology, education, and training. In the workplace, the term *group work* is seldom used; however, the work group has long been recognized as an integral part of the workplace. Therefore, *work group* is a category that may result in an expanded computerized literature search.

While the study of work groups has long been of interest to scholars and practitioners of industrial psychology, industrial relations, and administration, it has not directly been the terrain of occupational social workers. However, with the presence of occupational social workers, the workplace has an increased expectation that these social workers are a resource to address directly the social dynamics that evolve within the work group. As a result, more information on practice in the workplace is appearing in social work literature and databases.

GROUP WORK IN THE WORKPLACE

In addition to working with individual workers and/or their families, occupational social work increasingly reflects various forms of practice in which the primary unit of intervention is the work organization itself (Smith & Gould, 1993) or special groups of workers (Arnold, 1995; Ford et al., 2000; Hood et al., 2001; Shaw & Barnett Powers, 1998).

To form groups in the workplace, the occupational social worker will need to be sensitive to resistance from workers who perceive themselves as self-sufficient and functionally capable. Therefore, promotional strategies that acknowledge self-sufficiency as a strength are often very effective.

While interventions with individuals may include clinical treatment, the purposes of most workplace groups generally include information exchange, training and consultation, self-help, mutual aid, support, and problem solving (Wegener, 1992). Only in rare instances is providing treatment the focus.

Workplace groups have been conceptualized according to their focus (Wegener, 1992) and may be generally categorized as

- groups formed to meet developmental needs or life transitions;
- groups formed in response to work-related needs;
- groups formed to address environmental pressures; and
- treatment groups.

The following section describes these workplace groups.

Groups to Meet Developmental Needs

Brown bag seminars offered during lunch hour are the most common types of information exchange groups. They are designed for special groups of workers to address issues in living and topics identified by workers as being of special interest (Vigilante, 1993). These groups may be offered as a series on family life education. Examples of topics include financial and legal planning, problems of adult children of alcoholics, parenting issues, elder care, child care, AIDS, and children of divorce. Most of these groups utilize a structured approach that includes a presentation on a specific topic, opportunities for questions and answers, information regarding additional resources to address the topic, and promotion of the EAP as a resource. These seminars may be conducted by the occupational social worker, or the latter may introduce a presenter with the needed expertise. Whether conducted by the occupational social worker or the informational expert, the purpose is to impart information that may (1) empower employees to address aspects of a personal issue of concern; (2) promote the EAP as a resource to help resolve a personal issue of concern; and (3) identify organizational problems.

Groups Formed in Response to Work-Related Needs

The focus of groups in this category is work related and addresses issues of the workplace or the individual as worker.

Social workers in the workplace may be called on to address a variety of work-related issues that are amenable to social group work approaches. These groups are typically self-help/mutual help groups, support groups, focus groups, training groups, or groups that have all of the aforementioned characteristics.

Self-Help/Mutual Help Groups. Self-help groups may or may not be developed by a professional. The focus is on the shared personal experiences of the participants. The group intervention is usually a standardized format with general procedures for sharing.

Such work-related groups are typically used in response to worker trauma (on or off-site) resulting from announcements of mass layoffs, corporate mergers, environmental accidents, natural or social disasters, or suicidal or homicidal violence. More recently, groups have been employed to assist workers with workplace stressors, including routine family separations (Van Breda, 1999) and workplace transformation (Cummins, 1995; Gladstone & Reynolds, 1997). Following a crisis readiness plan should be the typical workplace response to such crises (Everly et al., 2001). Defusing groups, deescalating groups, and debriefing groups are components of such a plan. Since the debriefing group is widely used, this chapter will highlight its format and content.

Posttrauma Debriefing Groups. The debriefing group, as previously mentioned, is one component in a larger crisis readiness plan designed to respond rapidly to a disastrous event. (Everly, et al., 2001). The crisis readiness plan is typically developed by management and a team of human service professionals that may include the occupational social worker. Following a traumatic event, the occupational social worker in conjunction with management, labor, and a crisis consultant identifies individuals who may be particularly affected by the event because of their connection to the event or their closeness to those directly involved in it (Braverman, 1993). Workplace trauma practitioners agree with Ephross and Vassil (1987) that experience is a good teacher when composing groups, and they have found it best *not* to include children or family members of trauma victims (Braverman, 1993).

Critical incident stress debriefing (CISD) groups are designed to assist individuals with their emotional reactions to involvement in traumatic events such as suicides, homicides, robberies, assaults, and traumas associated with losses incurred during natural disasters (Everly, 2000). These groups are typically led by a trained team of professionals. At the very least, there should be a management representative who is familiar with the event, the EAP social worker who is trained in posttrauma stress and familiar with the specific workplace culture, and the crisis consultant, who may be an external consultant. In some instances, the EAP social worker may also be the consultant. In other instances where the occupational social worker is external to the workplace, another workplace representative may be included. The main objective of the CISD group is to prevent post-trauma disorders. Like the regular CISD group, the debriefing for debriefers is to prevent post-trauma disorders, except in this instance it is to prevent trauma resulting from "vicarious" or "secondary exposure," through having heard the experiences of others who were directly involved in the traumatic experience.

To that end, debriefings should occur as soon as possible after the event but certainly within 24–72 hours in order to be most effective. Debriefing groups are very structured and may last for 2–6 hours, depending on the nature of the incident and its emotional impact on the group participants.

There needs to be a confidential, nonevaluative discussion of individual involvement, reactions, and feelings resulting from the incident (Boriskin, 1994). While debriefings have psychological and educational components, they are not therapy or treatment groups. They are often followed by individual counseling for those who have been identified in the group as needing additional help.

The Case of the September 11 Terrorist Attack: Debriefing the Debriefers

Following the World Trade Center attack on September 11th, 2001, a social worker was contracted to debrief a team of CISM debriefers returning from New York after debriefing employees working at the location at the time of the attack. In the plan that was developed, management scheduled a group meeting for the seven people during their work day, two days after their return. One debriefer had a death in the family and was not available to meet; he was offered an individual meeting at his convenience.

The EAP social worker began group facilitation by introducing herself and acknowledging that she knew what would take place because she had just returned from doing the same kind of group. It was also acknowledged that this CISD group would be slightly different from those that they were accustomed to in that group members would be recalling their reactions to descriptions of other people's traumatic experiences. The confidential nature of the group was emphasized and ground rules set. Then each member was afforded the opportunity to share his or her reactions, thoughts, feelings, and concerns. The social worker asked every one to prepare mentally to answer specific questions, such as: *How did it go? How do you think you did? What "ditzy" thing did you do? What themes emerged? Is there anything that you are worried about?* The social worker responded with empathy, validated reactions, and gave positive feedback on their work.

The next phase of the group meeting was the "response phase," eliciting comments on self-perception. This phase was guided by a discussion of the employee debriefing and included the following questions: *What did you say that you wish you had not? What didn't you say that you wish you had? How has this experience affected you? What is the hardest part of this experience for you?* Here the social worker is looking for self-blame or worry that they did something terribly wrong. This is also the time for the group to reassure each other that no major error occurred. The EAP social workers acknowledged the individual contributions to the debriefing process and the group discussed ways of handling problem issues.

The next phase which was the "teaching and wrap-up phase" was designed to help the debriefers prepare for the future and begin to take care of themselves. It was guided by the following questions: *What are you going to do to take care of yourself in the next 24–48 hours? What will it take for you to eventually "let go" of this experience?* The debriefing team was also offered the opportunity to process their feelings privately with the EAP social worker (who was also a licensed clinician) by scheduling an appointment to meet with her at her private practice. During the "wrap-up," the EAP social worker presented an opportunity for group members to say anything they had not said or to restate something already said. The group also accepted an invitation to schedule another meeting for the debriefers in the next month or two for an "emotional check-up".

The second group meeting—with the same EAP social worker and the seven debriefers—occurred three months later. Confidentiality guidelines and ground rules were again set. The purpose of the meeting was introduced as a "check-in," with the focus on emotional well-being, and three hours were allotted. The metaphor of "wellness as a journey" was the guiding theme. The EAP social worker acknowledged that there are different roads to wellness and allowed each debriefer to "check-in" using the following questions as a guide for discussion: *In relation to three months ago when we first met, where are you now on a scale of 1–5? 1 = in the same place; 3 = different place; 5 completely different place? Why did you place yourself there?* Following this "check-in" discussion, the teaching and wrap-up phase included a description of each person's wellness journey, guided by the following questions: *How would you describe your journey? What has sustained or nurtured you along the way? Any peak experiences? Any surprise discoveries about yourself? How do you feel about where the journey has taken you?* The "wrap up" phase was designed to help the debriefers continue on their wellness journey by developing individual plans for the future. It was guided by the following questions: *In order to be where you want to be emotionally—or to stay where you are—what do you need to start doing? Stop doing? Keep doing?* The social worker supported each individual plan. The meeting ended with an invitation for follow-up phone calls should individuals feel the need for additional support or have any other related concerns.

Evaluation Approaches. A study of strategies for coping with exposure to violent death (McCarroll et al., 1993) found that support systems in the work group seemed to facilitate effective coping in the short term, but the long-term results are unclear. Evaluation of CISD effectiveness raises the same questions as other primary prevention interventions regarding the extent to which the phenomenon would have occurred without the intervention. Therefore, it is difficult to determine the true impact of primary prevention interventions.

Groups Formed in Response to Environmental Pressures. Many workplace environmental pressures are experienced by workers. However, the U.S. Department of Labor (1988) cites the changing demographics of the workforce as a major challenge to the workplace and to its workers. Due to the compelling nature of this challenge, the use of groups to address cultural and ethnic diversity and to resolve interethnic conflict will be the focus of this section.

The emerging cultural diversity of the workplace creates an environment in which workers of various ethnic and cultural backgrounds need help in adjusting to and succeeding in the workplace and managers need help in creating an environment that is receptive to understanding and affirming differences among a diverse workforce (Ford et al., 2000; Gray & Barrow, 1993). Successful interventions result in a workplace that affirms diversity; however, conflict and the skills to resolve it are often part of this transformation process. While the conflict literature focuses mainly on intergroup conflict, Van Den Bergh (1998) notes that if diversity is affirmed, it is necessary for workers to be knowledgeable about many cultures and to be bicultural in individual transactions with each other.

For the most part, the traditional workplace has inadvertently used the work group for worker socialization; however, the progressive workplace *strategically* utilizes group work approaches for socialization. Gray and Barrow (1993) and Van Den Bergh (1998) identified the following foci as organizing principles of workplace groups addressing cultural diversity and multiculturalism:

- assisting employees in adapting to the workplace culture;
- assisting the workplace in affirming differences;
- assisting employees in acquiring workplace opportunities and rewards;
- helping to develop formal and informal networks and linkages among and between groups of employees;
- educating the workforce to cultural differences;
- reinforcing racial, cultural, and ethnic pride;
- protecting and advocating for group rights and concerns; and
- providing a vehicle for the resolution of intercultural and interethnic conflict.

Specific practice principles are determined by the focus of the group. For instance, Mondros et al. (1992) found that successful groups dealing with conflict must be structured, encourage a lot of participation, be coled by individuals who model the nature of the diversity in the workplace, and be contracted to focus on substantive issues rather than merely the ventilation of grievances. On the other hand, groups focusing on facilitating cultural and ethnic consciousness may utilize an educational approach while providing support and mutual aid for their members. Van Den Bergh (1998) points out that such groups may include topics dealing with strategies "for advancement and stress management." The occupational social worker may actually facilitate the group, or may broker or coordinate the planning of the group.

The Case of the African-American Managers

The EAP social worker for a large, predominantly white accounting firm observed that several African-American clients had utilized the EAP due to feelings of professional isolation and frustration because younger, more recently hired African-Americans were not receiving the professional training and mentoring that would allow them to be considered for future positions with the potential for advancement to the manager and partner levels. This observation led to the formation of a support group for all African-American employees who had an interest in career development and informal mentoring. The social worker served as the coordinator. In that role, he collaborated with the human resources manager to identify all African-American employees. A questionnaire was sent to all of these employees inquiring (1) about their interest in attending regularly scheduled group meetings focused on supporting and helping African-American employees develop strategies for career enhancement and promotion and (2) about convenient meeting times if interested. Twenty African-American employees indicated an interest. The social worker contacted his original clients, who agreed to facilitate these self-help support group meetings. The social worker scheduled the meeting place and time and notified all who had indicated an interest. He attended the first meeting, but only to market the EAP and to provide a brief program orientation.

Treatment Groups. In the workplace, treatment groups typically focus on recovery from an addictive disorder and prevention of relapse. They may have a support focus, a monitoring focus, an educational focus, or various combinations thereof. The most prevelant groups associated with relapse prevention are 12-step groups such as Alcoholics Anonymous and Narcotics Anonymous. While some workplaces may have 12-step groups on the work site, they are typically under the auspices of the group members, not the workplace.

The Substance Abuse Recovery Monitoring Group

The substance abuse monitoring group is another group that the occupational social worker may be asked to colead with a management representative. Monitoring groups are typically used by management for monitoring treatment plan compliance, identifying signs and symptoms of relapse, and determining the nature and quality of recovery. Membership is comprised of employees who have been diagnosed as having a substance use disorder and whose employment, or whose license to perform a particular type of work, is contingent on a contract of abstinence from alcohol and other drugs as regulated by external governmental agencies, licensing boards, or workplace policy. For instance, monitoring the recovery of airline pilots, drivers of vehicles carrying hazardous materials, physicians, nuclear power plant workers, and other groups of workers who perform safety-sensitive work is the responsibility of the employer.

In the organized workplace, this monitoring role typically involves collaboration between labor and management. Labor usually takes an active role because it has a stake in ensuring the continued employment of its members, whose job may be in jeopardy. In the labor assistance program, this group is part of the service delivery system offered by the union for its members with substance use disorders, although it may not necessarily be related to employment (Molloy & Kurzman, 1993).

The role of the occupational social worker varies according to the situation and setting. For instance, the on-site social worker employed by management or labor is likely to be the actual group coleader or the person responsible for contracting for the monitoring service; by contrast, the external social worker employed by an outside EAP company providing EAP services by contract is more likely to broker such services or to provide the services using a casework approach. In either event, this is a politically sensitive role that is expected to be performed in a neutral manner, respecting the concerns of both management and labor while ensuring that the focus remains on substance abuse recovery. This issue is also sensitive because in most instances group participants enter the group involuntarily.

In addition to group work skills, occupational social workers (as group leaders or as brokers of the service) are expected to be knowledgeable about substance use disorders, recovery, and relapse prevention models that recognize the importance of identifying factors associated with relapse (Lewis, Dana, & Blevins, 1994).

The monitoring group is a structured, open-ended group comprised of members in different phases of recovery. Its purpose is to maintain the positive changes that have occurred during a previous intensive treatment phase by

- encouraging compliance with the recovery plan;
- providing direct support;
- helping members explore other environmental supports; and
- assessing behavioral, cognitive, and affective coping strategies.

Most groups expect participation and provide an educational component based on shared experiences. Support and education are also components of the self-efficacy training that is the cornerstone of the meetings. This training helps group members identify their own high-risk situations of substance use and develop a strategy for addressing these situations before they are encountered. Members remain in the group until the group is certain that they are complying with the recovery plan and are not at great risk for relapse. In some instances, regulatory agencies may mandate participation for a minimum of 2–4 years, in addition to continued evidence of recovery. Often members voluntarily remain in the group to offer support to new members.

The Case of the Airline Pilot Monitoring Group

This ongoing group was co-led by the EAP social worker, the company physician, and the pilot union's EAP representative. The members were all pilots who had been "grounded" by the Federal Aviation Administration pending treatment and evidence of recovery from a substance abuse disorder. The group of 4–10 people met once a month for approximately 2 hours. After they were seated in a circle, each participant was asked to state the components of his recovery plan and to provide an update of his recovery activities.

Using the Checklist for Relapse Preventing Monitoring (Gray, 1990), the leaders asked questions to assess each member's cognitive, behavioral, and affective reactions to daily living situations, to being abstinent, and to the recovery plan. Other members offered supportive suggestions and comments on how they handled similar situations. After all members shared, the leaders asked what strategies each member had for handling upcoming holiday family get-togethers that might include alcohol.

CONCLUSION

Occupational social workers may be expected to help address a variety of anticipated and unanticipated needs in the workplace. Effective social work helps the workplace identify organizational as well as employee problems. The use of groups is helpful in identifying workplace issues of which management may not be aware. In this regard, the social worker may initiate the development of specific groups as a result of information about employee issues that may have been assessed from casework with clients or information derived from the ongoing process of assessing the organization. To this end, various types of groups may be used in addressing employee-related and organizational issues. The skills needed to address these issues may require continuing education and consultation. The resources listed below may be helpful.

RESOURCES

American Institute for Managing
 Diversity
50 Hurt Plaza
Atlanta, GA 30303
Phone: (404) 302-9226
Fax: (404) 302-9252
www.aimd.org

American Management Association
1601 Broadway
NY, NY 10019
Phone: (212) 586-8100
Fax: (212) 903-8168
Customer Service: (800) 262-9699
www.amanet.org

Employee Assistance Professionals
 Association, Inc.
2101 Wilson Boulevard
Suite 500

Arlington, VA 22201
Phone: (703) 387-1000
Fax: (703) 522-4585
www.eapassn.org

National Association of Alcohol and
 Drug Abuse Counselors
 (NAADAC)
901 N. Washington St., Suite 600
Alexandria, VA 22314
Phone: (703) 741-7686 or
 (800) 548-0497
Fax: (703) 741-7698 or (800) 377-1136
www.naadac.org

National Clearinghouse on Alcohol and
 Drug Information (NCADI)
11426-28 Rockville Pike, Suite 200
Rockville, MD 20852
Phone (800) 729-6686

www.samhsa.gov/centers/
  clearinghouse/clearinghouses.
  html

Employment Policy Foundation
1015 15th Street, NW, Suite 1200
Washington, DC 20005
Phone: (202) 789-8685
Fax: (202) 789-8684
www.epf.org

Society for Human Resource
  Management
1800 Duke Street

Alexandria, VA 22314
Phone: (703) 548-3440
FAX: (703) 535-6490
www.shrm.org

Society for Intercultural Education,
  Training, and Research (SIETAR
  USA)
573 Bayview Street
Yarmouth, ME 04096
Phone: (207) 846-9598
Fax: (207) 846-0763
www.sietarusa.org

REFERENCES

Akabas, S. (1993). Introduction. In P. Kurzman & S. Akabas (eds.), *Work and well-being: The occupation social work advantage* (pp. iii–v). Washington, DC: National Association of Social Workers Press.

American Business 2000. (June 23, 1992). The changing nature of work. 66–77.

Annis, H., & Davis, C. (1989). Relapse prevention. In R. Hester & W. Miller (eds.), *Handbook of alcoholism treatment approaches: Effective alternatives* (pp. 170–182). New York: Pergamon Press.

Bargal, D. (1992). Conflict management workshops for Arab Palestinian and Jewish youth—a framework for planning, intervention, and evaluation. *Social Work with Groups.* 15, 51–68.

Bennett, J. B., Lehman, W. E. K., & Reynolds, G. S. (2000). Team awareness for workplace substance abuse prevention: The empirical and conceptual development of a training program. *Prevention Science.* 1(3), 157–172.

Boriskin, J. (1994, February). On the front lines: EAPs battle workplace violence. *Employee Assistance.* 14–18.

Bramel, D., & Friend, R. (1987). The work group and its viscissitudes in social and industrial psychology. *Journal of Applied Behavioral Science.* 23(2), 233–253.

Braverman, M. (1993, Spring). Coping with trauma in the workplace. *Compensation and Benefits Management.* 58–63.

Cherin, D. A. (2000). Organizational engagement and managing moments of maximum leverage: New roles for social workers in organizations. *Administration in Social Work.* 23(3/4), 29–46.

Cummins, H. (1995). Group work on the factory floor—an experience of working with foremen facing redundancy. *Australian Social Work.* 48(1), 37–40.

Ephross, P., & Vassil, T. (1987). Towards a model of working groups. *Social Work with Groups.* 10, 13–23.

Everly, G. S. (2000). Crisis management briefing (CMB): Large group crisis intervention in response to terrorism, disasters, and violence. *International Journal of Emergency Mental Health.* 2(1), 53–57.

Everly, G. S., Flannery, R. B., Eyler, V. & Mitchell, J. (2001). Sufficiency analysis of an integrated multi component approach to crisis intervention: Critical incident stress management. *Advances in Mind-Body Medicine.* 17(3), 174–181.

Ford, M. E., Cochran, D. L., & Neal, E. (2000). African American Gerontology Network. *Health and Social Work.* 25(2), 153–159.

Gladstone, J., & Reynolds, T. (1997). Single session group work intervention in response to employee stress during workplace transformation. *Social Work with Groups.* 20(1), 33–50.

Googins, B. (1993). Work-site research: Challenges and opportunities for social work. In P. Kurzman & S. Akabas (eds.), *Work and well-being: The occupational social work advantage* (pp. 61–78). Washington, DC: National Association of Social Workers Press.

Gray, M., & Barrow, F. (1993). Ethnic, cultural and racial diversity in the workplace. In P. Kurzman & S. Akabas (eds.), *Work and well-being: The occupational social work advantage* (pp. 138–152). Washington, DC: National Association of Social Workers Press.

Hood, J. N., Miller, H. J., & Seitz (2001). Attitudes of Hispanics and Anglos surrounding a workforce diversity intervention. *Hispanic Journal of Behavioral Sciences.* 23(4), 444–458.

Kurzman, P., & Akabas S. (eds.) (1993). *Work and well-being: The occupational social work advantage.* Washington, DC: National Association of Social Workers Press.

Lewis, J., Dana, R., & Blevins, G. (1994). *Substance abuse counseling: An individualized approach* (pp. 169–190). Pacific Grove, CA: Brooks/Cole.

Lieberman, M. (1990). A group therapist perspective on self-help groups. *International Journal of Group Psychotherapy.* 40, 251–278.

McCarroll, J., Ursano, R., Wright, K., & Fullerton, C. (1993). Handling bodies after violent death: Strategies for coping. *American Journal of Orthopsychiatry.* 63, 209–214.

Michael, L. E., Russell, N., & Unger, L. (1985). Rapid response mutual aid groups: A new response to social crises and natural disasters. *Social Work.* 30, 245–252.

Molloy, D., & Kurzman, P. (1993). Practice with unions: Collaborating toward an empowerment model. In P. Kurzman & S. Akabas (eds.), *Work and well-being: The occupational social work advantage* (pp. 46–60). Washington, DC: National Association of Social Workers Press.

Mondros, J., Woodrow, R., & Weinstein, L. (1992). The use of groups to manage conflict. *Social Work with Groups.* 15, 43–57.

Mor Barak, M. E. (2000). Beyond affirmative action: Toward a model of diversity and organizational inclusion. *Administration in Social Work.* 23(3), 47–68.

Norman, A. (1991). The use of the group and group work techniques in resolving interethnic conflict. In A. Vinik & M. Levin (eds.), *Social action in group work: Principles and practice* (pp. 175–186). New York: Haworth Press.

Pouliot, S., & Horne, A. (2001). A support group to prevent burnout in the workplace. *Canadian Social Work.* 3(2). 36–42.

Pettigrew, T. (1987). Shaping the organizational context for black American inclusion. *Journal of Social Issues.* 43, 41–78.

Root, L. S. (2000). Education and training in the workplace: Social work interventions for the private sector. *Administration in Social Work.* 23 (3/4), 13–28.

Schopler, J., & Galinsky, M. (1993). Support groups as open systems: A model for practice and research. *Health and Social Work.* 18, 195–207.

Smith, M., & Gould, G. (1993). A profession at the crossroads: Occupational social work—present and future. In P. Kurzman & S. Akabas (eds.), *Work and well-being: The occupational social work advantage* (pp. 7–25). Washington, DC: National Association of Social Workers Press.

Sussal, C. (1985). Group work with federal employees. *Social Work with Groups.* 8, 71–79.

Terkel, S. (1974). *Working.* New York: Avon Books.

U.S. Department of Labor. (1988). *Opportunity 2000.* Washington, DC: U.S. Government Printing Office.

Van Breda, A. D. (1999). Developing resilience to routine separations: An occupational social work intervention. *Families in Society.* 80(6), 597–605.

Van Den Bergh, N. (1998). Managing biculturalism at the workplace: A group approach. In A. Daly (ed.), *Workplace diversity issues and perspectives.* Washington, DC: National Association of Social Workers Press.

Vigilante, F. (1993). Work. In P. Kurzman & S. Akabas (eds.), *Work and well-being: The occupational social work advantage* (pp. 179–199). Washington, DC: National Association of Social Workers Press.

Wegener, N. (1992). Supportive group services in the workplace: The practice and the potential. In J. Garland (ed.), *Group work reaching out: People, places, and power* (pp. 207–221). New York: Haworth Press.

Chapter 25

Group Work in Context: Organizational and Community Factors

ELIZABETH A. MULROY

Group work, as seen from an organizational perspective, is a method of practice set in larger systems of organizations and communities. Most groups, such as those for students at risk of dropping out of school, incarcerated mothers, people with mental illness, children of divorce, or people with HIV/AIDS, operate under the auspices of some type of organization or institutional structure. As a method of social work practice, group work is conducted within social programs that operate within, and are supported by, formal and informal organizations. Each program has specific goals, objectives, and outcomes. The success of a specific group depends in part on the viability of the overall social program; that program is itself dependent on the capacity of the sponsoring organization to operate *efficiently, effectively,* and *equitably.* To support its many programs, an organization needs to maintain financial stability, demonstrate program effectiveness through responsiveness to at risk clients, and demonstrate a commitment to social justice.

The dilemma for social work today is that many human service organizations are having trouble meeting these criteria. Whether they are public child welfare agencies, nonprofit settlement houses, YMCAs, or alternative feminist organizations, they operate in a "turbulent institutional environment" (Hasenfeld, 1992, p. 10) that also contributes to internal uncertainties and turbulence (Netting & O'Connor, 2003). Social programs and often entire nonprofit organizations have been, or are, at risk of being closed down. Group workers need a working knowledge of their organizations to best understand these external and internal dynamics and their role within the organization.

The purpose of this chapter is to examine some principles of organizations so that the beginning social worker can understand and appreciate the organizational context of group work and social work, and the effects of its community context on program implementation and service delivery.

THE ORGANIZATIONAL CONTEXT

A human service organization has a *transformative* purpose to help clients or consumers fulfill their unmet needs and improve their situations. Hasenfeld (1992) suggests that this transformative quality means human service organizations engage in "moral work" (p. 5), a powerful concept that adds to the complexity of operating human service organizations and measuring their outcomes. A first step in understanding organizations that exist to serve human needs is to know *sector* differences. *Public sector* agencies are governmental agencies that were established and continue to operate through legislative mandate. Some examples include federal, state, and county child welfare departments; family assistance agencies (formerly called public welfare); health; or education. Funding comes from legislative appropriations. *Nonprofit sector* organizations are nongovernmental, tax-exempt, and run by voluntary boards of directors. They are not profit-generating, and they exist to fulfill a particular mission, social purpose, or public benefit. Nonprofit organizations receive funding from a variety of sources, such as charitable contributions, government grants and contracts, fees for service, and fund-raising endeavors.

There is great diversity in types of nonprofit, socially oriented organizations. They may be large or small; highly structured, traditional bureaucracies or informal, nontraditional, alternative organizations; employ professional staffs or use only volunteers; have no geographic affiliation or be closely affiliated with and accountable to one neighborhood or community. Some examples include large, well-established child and family agencies, residential treatment facilities, YMCAs and YWCAs, settlement houses, crisis centers, shelters for the homeless, or relatively new community development organizations.

In contrast, organizations in the *for-profit sector* are commercial and form the backbone of the market economy (Netting & O'Connor, 2003). Their purpose is to make money and they pay taxes. While traditionally not social service providers, large multinational private firms such as Lockheed Martin, Andersen Consulting, and Electronic Data Systems have moved into human services delivery as a result of privatization. Some examples include for-profit residential treatment facilities, hospitals, or employment development agencies with job training programs.

Privatization

Human service organizations, irrespective of sector, have been affected by privatization—the contracting out of public services to nonprofit and for-profit organizations. Privatization has been operating for years in many public spheres, such as public works in which cities contract with private firms to pick up trash or plow snow; school districts that contract with private bus companies to transport students to and from public schools; transportation, in which counties contract with private construction companies to build or repair roads and highways; or social service departments that contract with private consulting firms to set up management information systems.

The implications of this development for nonprofit organizations and for social work became profound in the 1980s with the convergence of privatization in health and human services *and* deep cuts in federal spending for domestic social programs designed to help the poor. By the end of the 1980s, government contracts had replaced charitable contributions as the major source of funding for many large, established, nonprofit human service organizations such as child and family agencies, as well as for the vast majority of nonprofits that are small, community-based organizations (Perlmutter, 1984; Salamon, 1999). By the end of the 1990s, privatization had accelerated the commercialization of health and mental health care and shifted social work administrators in public agencies into roles of contract managers (Austin, 2000). Increased dependence on these fluctuating public grants and contracts weakened the financial base of small, community-based nonprofit organizations with social justice goals (Fabricant & Fisher, 2002; Gibelman & Demone, 2002). Some large nonprofits maximized opportunities in this environment and managed to grow and thrive. Privatization also enabled the for-profit sector to emerge as a major competitor in the provision of human services (Frumkin & Andre-Clarke, 2000).

With these politically turbulent environmental forces as a backdrop we turn the discussion to the five stages of organizational development.

Organizational Life Stages

Human service organizations adapt in response to the environmental changes just described, and their ability to do this successfully is influenced by their lifecycle stage of organizational development. This section will concentrate on the nonprofit sector because of its prominence in human service delivery, and because public agencies and private for-profit firms have different characteristics, roles, and functions. Very large, complex nonprofits, very small, grass-roots organizations, and nontraditional organizations with unique circumstances such as nonwestern cultures may find the following typology less helpful. It is a model for the majority of nonprofits.

Simon (2001), after conducting a thorough review of the organizational development literature, posits that organizations go through a journey of five life stages:

Stage One: Imagine and Inspire. This is the "I want to do a dream" stage, the inspirational beginning characterized by the enthusiasm and energy of a charismatic, entrepreneurial leader.

Stage Two: Found and Frame. In the start-up phase, the organization gets its official nonprofit tax status and becomes incorporated, formally establishing the organization. Some staff members may resist moving from an informal, participatory approach to decision making to a more formal arrangement.

Stage Three: Ground and Grow. This stage focuses on establishing procedures, growing the "business," and working through the challenges, opportunities, and choices that present themselves.

Stage Four: Produce and Sustain. Productivity is at its peak as workers are effective and procedures become routine. This has its benefits because systems are needed to keep the organization moving forward. Some employees, however may feel their creativity and opportunities for growth have slowed down.

Stage Five: Review and Renew. In this stage, managers of mature nonprofits engage in continuous surveillance of the organization's external environment (Mulroy, forthcoming) so that timely reviews and strategic decisions are made for renewal. It is argued that stressful conditions generate possibilities for new patterns of action to form. Thoughtful organizational self-assessment in Stage Five helps revisit the mission, vision, products, services, and structure to make major or minor changes as indicated. It may mean cycling back to earlier stages. For example, if changes to the basic mission and philosophy are needed, then the organization revisits Stage Two. If modifications in services or structure are necessary, then it revisits Stage Four.

Organizations generally move forward in a predictable path, but several factors influence where the organization is in its lifecycle: its age, its size, growth rate of its field or domain, social environment, and characteristics of its primary leader (Simon, 2001, p. 9). Younger organizations with few staffers and a small budget, for example, are in the early stages of the lifecycle. Those involved in a growth industry such as residential treatment facilities may move through the early lifecycle stages quickly. Welfare-to-work programs mandated by the Personal Responsibility and Work Opportunity Reconciliation Act of 1996 created market pressures for both nonprofit and for-profit organizations, and many nonprofits rushed through the lifecycle stages to capture these new federal funding streams.

Achieving success in each stage helps the nonprofit grow and thrive. In reality, boundaries between the five stages may blur, so that movement from one stage to another is not obvious. But problems can be expected to emerge in every stage, and a nonprofit organization can *decline and dissolve* in any one of them. The organization can become destabilized through the departure of a charismatic, highly respected founding executive director, loss of program funding, or staff turnover. This model does not predict an end-point for organizational life. "At some point the organization chooses to remain status quo, stagnate, regenerate, or dissolve" (Simon, 2001, p. 10). The extent of environmental turbulence suggests the need for continuous surveillance, review of impacts, and renewal of agency functions to keep the organization responsive and moving forward.

In order to do this well, managers must oversee a number of internal functions that exist in every lifecycle stage. These include:

1. Governance—the legal decision-making structure of a board of directors, agency policies and procedures
2. Staff leadership—the executive director's role
3. Financing—resource development and financial management of multiple grants, contracts, donations, endowments, and fund raising
4. Administrative systems—the equipment, office space, accounting, support staff, and technology needed to accomplish the mission
5. Products and services—the design and delivery of services, activities, and products needed to accomplish the mission
6. Staffing—the size, composition, and pattern of relationships among staff; pay schedules; and use of volunteers
7. Marketing—how the organization portrays itself to the public and to consumers.

In sum, we can see the complexity of organizational life and the importance of managing both internal and external factors that affect a nonprofit's well-being so it can be a healthy organization.

Social Programs

Programs are the heart of organizations because it is through programs that social policies passed by federal and state legislative bodies actually get implemented. In effect, social policies are translated into action at the local community level through programs with services that reach intended beneficiaries. Human service programs are concerned with *(1)* personal development of individuals and families through direct services such as education, training, counseling, therapy, or casework, and *(2)* social development in communities and with special populations through policy and advocacy, community organizing, planning, interorganizational collaboration, and network formation. The purpose of social programs, regardless of the methods used, is to enhance the well-being of clients or consumers, be they individuals, families, communities, or special populations (Lewis et al., 2001).

The effectiveness of health and human service programs has long been a concern of policy makers and funders. To address this concern, Kettner, Moroney, and Martin (1996) recommend that, before any new program is developed, social workers systematically take stock of the strengths and weaknesses of their organization's existing programs. Their eight-step effectiveness-based programming guide is outlined below. Primarily designed as a problem assessment tool, it is adapted here to include strengths and assets in the analysis.

1. *Define the Organization's Programs*—Learn how the organization defines and organizes its programs. Are they separated by type of client, by geographical region, by type of service provided, or by resources required?
2. *Problem/Issue Analysis*—How well is the issue understood? What is the condition the program seeks to address? Ideally, it should be grounded in a thorough review of research in terms of the type, size, and scope of the issue as it pertains to a target population, as well as historical precedents, community and policy factors, and theories of change on which the intervention is based.
3. *Needs and Assets Assessment*—How well is the need understood—as defined by experts, and as defined by those experiencing the need? What resources (assets) already exist in the community to address the need?
4. *Selecting a Strategy and Selecting Objectives*—Based on data from the foregoing analysis, a program hypothesis is developed. An hypothesis is a statement about what outcomes are expected if a person with the problems or issues outlined above receives the services about to be designed (Kettner et al., 1996, p. 20). This becomes the framework for the development of precisely stated goals, objectives, and activities. Examine existing programs to see how they accomplished this step.
5. *Program Design*—This important phase allows a social worker or a team of people to creatively assemble services (such as groups) or a combination of services and activities (groups, individual therapy, casework, community activities) that appear to have the best chance

of achieving program objectives. This is a critical step in the planning and management of programs because it is based on a carefully thought out assessment of the needs of a particular at-risk population *relative to* the needs and resources of the agency and the community.

6. *Management Information Systems*—To what extent did existing programs use agency resources such as the computer network to design and implement a database for their specific programs? A client data system is essential to produce data and information about the progress of clients throughout each episode of service, which helps determine service effectiveness at termination. When linked to other data sets it facilitates communication and coordinates services among several persons working with a client, while assisting management with its need to measure service effectiveness agency-wide.

7. *Budgeting*—Service delivery costs the agency money, so a social program needs to budget projected costs. An eight-session group could be less expensive to operate than an alternative service, such as one-on-one casework, and therefore more cost-effective. Social workers will want to use available data at an agency to calculate costs for items such as units of service (one group session for two hours), achievement of a measurable outcome (for a group), or achievement of a program objective.

8. *Program Evaluation*—In the final analysis the funders of a social program will want to know how successful the program was in meeting its objectives. Those who render direct services and those who manage the program need to provide evidence of how well the intervention helped achieve program outcomes. Assess the evaluation methods used by existing programs in.the agency, and draw lessons learned from their experiences. The point is this: Methods exist to evaluate an individual group; use them, but know that the group is not run in isolation. The group is also evaluated in the context of a social program, and the social program is evaluated in the larger context of the organization's mission and purpose.

Programs usually comprise a number of *services* designed to meet the needs of a population at risk. These services may be concrete, such as emergency financial assistance for rent and utilities for very poor families in public housing, or a transportation system that helps them get food at the food bank, or clothing and furniture at the Salvation Army thrift store. Or they may be less concrete, such as classes in financial literacy, job readiness training, volunteer training, crisis counseling, or leadership development. All of these services work together at various levels of need to keep families at risk of homelessness from being evicted from public housing. We will now turn to community issues because it is from the community that an agency and its social workers draw their clients.

THE COMMUNITY CONTEXT

Since a purpose of group work is to serve clients and the community, knowing the demographics of a community will help guide social workers in deciding who needs to be served by agency programs, what types of services and methods are most appropriate, and whether the agency mission statement is congruent with rapidly changing community conditions and needs. A community analysis can provide social workers with much-needed data and should be conducted before a new program or group is created. The following general framework can be used as a beginning point for a community analysis. I call this the *Reconnaissance* phase:

1. Use most recent census data to identify community characteristics of a geographically bounded area;
2. Identify a target at-risk population and its demographic characteristics within this area;
3. Determine resident needs and assets, and existing institutional resources available to meet those needs;
4. Identify leaders within the at-risk population if appropriate, and
5. Identify community structure, including presence of potential institutional partners and competitors inside the bounded area and outside of it (adapted from Netting et al., 1993).

Knowledge of the local scene is important. In very poor communities, residents often have more than one at-risk condition, as discussed in the six parts of this book. In a study of homelessness prevention in public housing, the households in the study sample identified as being at risk of homelessness typically had family members with multiple at-risk conditions at the same time—including health issues, adjusting to change, violence (as victims or perpetrators), substance abuse, or problems with institutions such as schools, the workplace, and the justice system (Mulroy & Lauber, 2002; Mulroy & Lauber, forthcoming). One of their most important shared conditions was being very poor and living in unsafe housing and neighborhood environments.

The extent to which the group worker is able to address these multiple layers of at-risk conditions in one group may depend on their organization's community-based orientation, a commitment to serve the very poor as reflected in the organization's mission statement, and their own cultural competence to respond appropriately. For example, the resident population living in the housing project described above was drawn from diverse immigrant groups. At least nineteen different languages were spoken. Increased diversity and multi-culturalism are central factors in many communities today and are predicted to become more important throughout the next decade.

Keeping close to the pulse of a community—whether defined as the public housing project, a particular neighborhood, or a whole city—opens up opportunities for group workers to serve the public interest.

One example can be found in immigration and refugee movement into cities and towns across America.

Immigrants and Refugees as At-Risk Populations

The international movement of displaced persons who are political refugees or immigrant workers—both legal and illegal—is arguably one of the greatest challenges facing the world, and it will be felt locally because it will alter the realities of diversity in our communities, organizations, and in civic life. Social workers on the front lines, particularly those skilled in group work, case management, community building, program development, and agency management, will be at the center of institutional and community problem-solving and change in the decades to come, as the following examples will illuminate.

The presenting problems for a school social worker, for example, may be how to mediate disagreements among students, or between teachers, administrators, parents, and students from many different cultures and religions in a high school beginning to bubble over with tension. Another need will be to work collaboratively and inclusively with all parties, including every immigrant and refugee group represented in the school district, to develop assimilation programs from kindergarten through 12th grade.

A social worker in an Employee Assistance Program of a large nonprofit or for-profit organization or other workplace setting will be asked to help solve misunderstandings and resentments that appear to be getting in the way of productivity and worker retention in its increasingly multicultural and multi-ethnic work force.

The medical social worker in the hospital emergency room sees an unmet need for trained multilingual staff to improve communication between the rapidly increasing number of immigrant and refugee patients and the medical staff. But the worker must define the problem and create the program with the cooperation and input from the at risk populations, then appear before several decision-making groups inside the hospital to re-frame the issues and offer concrete options that justify the increased costs in cost-cutting times.

City officials in places experiencing "sudden ethnic diversification" (Blais, 2003) are seeking out nonprofit organizations to collaborate in new and different ways. For example, city mayors are looking to nonprofit organizations to help refugees find affordable housing, health care, job training and jobs, help with business start-ups, and other programs—resources typically located in many different types of organizations, public, nonprofit, and for-profit. From the local government perspective, fresh ways of thinking and acting to resolve civic matters are needed on a *community-wide* basis, and these new approaches are being developed through coalitions and partnerships that must include leaders from the newcomer populations.

Communities with an influx of immigrant and refugee populations seek leadership and guidance in devising programs and services to assimilate newcomer populations. The social work profession's skills, values, and knowledge base prepare practitioners well to respond to these opportunities.

CONCLUSION

In conclusion, group work with populations at risk requires paying attention to community and organizational factors that will help guide and shape the direction of social work practice. With careful attention to organizational and community contexts, there is no danger of its being marginalized from the profession's social justice core value, an important consideration in the global economy.

RESOURCES

Alliance for Justice
11 Dupont Circle NW 2nd floor
Washington, DC 20036
www.alliance@afj.org

Association for Community
   Organization and Social
   Administration
www.acosa.org

Center for Community Change
1000 Wisconsin Ave.

Washington, DC 20007
(202) 342-0519
www.communitychange.org

National Community Building
   Network
8718 Mary Lee Lane
Annandale, VA 22003
(703) 425-6296
www.ncbn.org

REFERENCES

Austin, D. (2000). Social work and social welfare administration: A historical perspective. In R. Patti (ed.), *The handbook of social welfare management* (pp. 27–54). Thousand Oaks: Sage Publications.

Blais, P. The shock of the new: Lewiston, Maine, learns how to treat Somali immigrants like anyone else in town. *Planning.* February 2003, pp. 14–17.

Fabricant, M., & Fisher, R. (2002). *Settlement houses under siege.* New York: Columbia University Press.

Frumkin, P., & Andre-Clarke, A. (2000). When missions, markets, and politics collide: Values and strategy in the nonprofit human services." *Nonprofit and Voluntary Sector Quarterly.* 29(1) 141–163.

Gibelman, M., & Demone, H., Jr. (2002). The commercialization of health and human services: National phenomenon or cause for concern? *Families in Society.* 83(4) 387–397.

Hasenfeld, Yeheskel. (1992). *Human services as complex organizations.* Newbury Park, CA: Sage Publications.

Kettner, P., Moroney, R., & Martin, L. (1996). *Designing and Managing Programs.* Thousand Oaks: Sage.

Lewis, J., Lewis, M., Packard, T., & Souflee, F. (2001) *Management of human service programs,* 3rd ed. Belmont, CA: Brooks/Cole.

Mulroy, E. (forthcoming). Theoretical approaches to the social environment for management and community practice: An organization-in-environment approach. *Administration in Social Work—Special Issue: Educating Future Social Work Administrators.*

Mulroy, E., & Lauber, H. (2002). Community building in hard times: A post-welfare view from the streets. *Journal of Community Practice.* 10(1) 1–16.

Mulroy, E., & Lauber, H. (forthcoming). "An approach to user-friendly evaluation and community interventions for families at risk of homelessness." *Social Work.*

Netting, E., Kettner, P., & McMurty, S., (1993). *Social work macro practice.* White Plains, NY: Longman.

Netting, E., & O'Connor, M. K. (2003). *Organization practice: A social worker's guide to understanding human services.* Boston: Allyn & Bacon.

Perlmutter, F. (1984). *Human services at risk.* Lexington, MA: Lexington Books.

Salamon, L. (1999). *America's nonprofit sector: A primer.* New York: The Foundation Center.

Simon, J. S. (2001). *The five life stages of nonprofit organizations.* St. Paul, MN: Amherst Wilder Foundation.

PART VI

EVALUATING PRACTICE

Chapter 26

Using Evidence-Based Practice and Intervention Research with Treatment Groups for Populations at Risk

ANDREA MEIER AND EDNA COMER

As ethical professionals, social workers are obligated to seek out the most effective interventions for the individuals and groups whom they serve (National Association of Social Workers, 1996). To achieve this aim, they must make conscientious, explicit and judicious use of the best available evidence in making decisions about the care of the clients so that the treatments they offer have high odds of success (Fraser, forthcoming; Sackett et al., 1996). All across the health and human services system, the incorporation of systematically collected data and research evidence into clinical practice is commonly referred to as "evidence-based practice" (EBP). Another practical reason for social workers to become evidence-based in their practice is to respond to the pressure from policy makers and program funders who have called for increased accountability and evidence of treatment effectiveness in all kinds of human services and health settings (Meier & Usher, 1998; Nelson et al., forthcoming; Pollio, forthcoming; Pollio et al., 2000).

There are two major components of EBP. First, practitioners make systematic use of clinically relevant research to select accurate and precise diagnostic tests, identify prognostic markers, and assess the potential effectiveness and safety of different kinds of treatments (Sackett et al., 1996). Properly used, this type of information may support or invalidate previously accepted diagnostic tests and treatments, spurring practitioners to modify or replace them with new ones that are more powerful, accurate, and safer. Practitioners can acquire this knowledge by reading professional journals, attending conference presentations about specific populations, and by generating evidence through their own observations and research (Pollio, forthcoming).

The second component of EBP is that practitioners are expected to draw from multiple sources for information to inform their treatment decisions. That is, they should not use the "cookbook" approach relying on only one source of evidence (e.g., clinical trials). Instead, practitioners are called upon to think ecologically, taking into account findings about population characteristics and reports about the social environments in which their clients live (Bilsker & Golsner, 2000). They should try to integrate relevant research evidence, social science theory, and theory-based interventions with "practice wisdom" (Fraser, forthcoming; Sackett et al., 1996). Their diagnoses and treatment decisions should take into account clients' predicaments, rights, and preferences (Sackett et al., 1996). Practitioners are expected to discuss with their clients the range of treatment options and their associated risks and benefits, to the extent that they are known. Practitioners and clients work together to decide whether and how available evidence applies to their specific circumstances (Fraser, forthcoming; Sackett et al., 1996).

The aim of this chapter is to help social workers, particularly group workers, understand how best to use research evidence in their practice. We begin by describing general strategies for evaluating the quality of research evidence for treatment of individuals and groups. We then describe how to apply the principles of EBP in group work, and some means for carrying out this process within agency settings. We briefly describe some methodological reasons for the paucity of outcome research on group interventions that are needed for EBP. We propose an alternative research methodology, the developmental Intervention Research Paradigm (Rothman & Thomas, 1994), and discuss how social workers can use it to guide them in systematically modifying groups they are currently running or in developing innovative new ones. Finally, we describe where social workers can obtain information about EBP principles and procedures, find sources of research evidence related to their work with groups, and demonstrate ways to apply EBP principles in group work practice and research on their groups.

EVALUATING RESEARCH EVIDENCE

"What is the best evidence available for me to use in making my treatment decisions with my clients?" This is the key question underlying all discussions of EBP. Figure 26.1 lists the three main categories of research evidence: observational, systematic, and pre-processed. Within each cat-

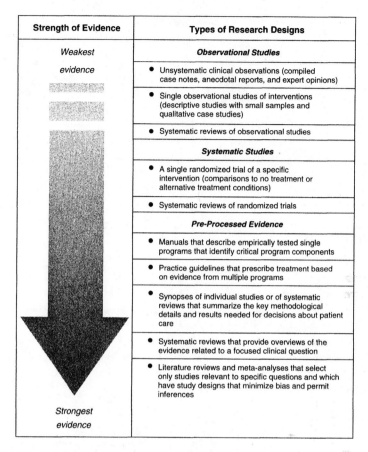

Figure 26.1. Types of Research Designs: Strength of Evidence for Treatment Decisions

egory, evidence ranges from weak to strong in the practitioners' confidence in generalizing study findings to a larger population, or to specific clients.

Observational Studies

It should be clear from Figure 26.1 that social workers have a wide variety of sources of evidence. The most common sources are unsystematic clinical observations, in which researchers simply observe the natural course of events and record the results without trying to influence them (Guyatt et al., 2000). For social workers, this type of evidence includes their compiled case notes, ancillary reports from colleagues and clients, expert opinions, qualitative case studies, and other descriptive studies that have used small samples.

Systematic Studies

In systematic research designs, investigators exert more control over the study variables, using sampling and treatment procedures that enable them to compare samples of participants who had a treatment with participants who did not (Guyatt et al., 2000). Researchers who are able to use these study designs can draw some conclusions about causal relationships between interventions and outcomes. The "gold standard" of systematic intervention research designs is the randomized clinical trial (RCT) that uses experimental designs. Here, participants are randomly assigned to a treatment or control group. When it is impossible to use the direct comparisons of an RCT, quasi-experimental research designs can approximate experimental controls by comparing the group that received a particular treatment to a similar sample of participants who were not exposed to the treatment.

Pre-processed Evidence

New resources are being developed to increase the efficiency of the clinical evidence–seeking process. New journals and database services are now made available that include "pre-processed" evidence (Guyatt et al., 2000). These reports vary in the level of detail they contain to support practitioners' assessments of the strength of the evidence. The particular usefulness to social workers of each type of information source is summarized below:

- Evidence-based treatment manuals, practice guidelines, and textbook summaries of specific practice areas are designed to support systems of care, to help practitioners identify the trade-off between treatment costs and benefits and guide them in their decisions through the treatment cycle (Hayward et al., 1995).
- Research synopses of individual studies and summaries provide information on key methodological details and results that practitioners need to apply research evidence to treatment decisions of individual patients.
- Systematic summaries of research evidence vary in their comprehensiveness and scope, but all include assessments of the methodological rigor of the studies contained in their reviews.
- Compilations of primary studies of specific issues are being compiled that include only those with study designs that minimize bias, enabling readers to have confidence in their clinical inferences.

When they apply research evidence to their treatment decisions, social workers should be mindful of the strengths and limitations of each of these types of evidence (Guyatt et al., 2000). When evidence was not systematically collected, there can be no certainty that it was effective. The apparent benefits of a treatment may be due to other factors: changes in the local environment where the intervention took place, placebo effects, or client and practitioner's expectations. Experts' opinions may be biased if they have not systematically considered the full range of options and possible outcomes. Observational studies may have larger samples and use treatment and non-treatment control groups, but apparent intervention effects may actually be due to differences in the characteristics of participants in each of the groups. Intervention effectiveness from observational studies is stronger when the effect size of a single group is very large, or when a systematic review of similar interventions shows comparable outcomes. Although evidence from clinical trials is considered the strongest evidence of intervention effectiveness, it, too, has its limitations. Recommendations based on those studies only reflect the characteristics of the "average client." Social workers who are able to find evidence based on RCTs should keep in mind that those findings might not be applicable to their individual client's particular circumstances.

Most descriptions of EBP principles reflect their historical roots in the medical profession, where EBP has been more fully articulated. In the medical context, evidence is used to characterize an individual patient's "clinical status" and guide the selection of treatments and the monitoring of patient progress. In this context, it is possible to use a very high standard of evidence. That is because more laboratories and randomized controlled trials have been done for medical treatments. Research on social interventions rarely achieves this level of rigor, because it is generally impossible to control most of the conditions of the research. This means that social workers must use the best-quality evidence available to them, recognize its limitations, and be conservative in their expectations about its applicability to specific clients or groups.

APPLYING EBP PRINCIPLES TO GROUP WORK

Group workers have many opportunities to incorporate research evidence to answer clinical questions that arise as they go through the phases of assessment, treatment planning, and intervention monitoring. Each question requires different kinds of evidence, and, as always, social workers have to adapt their decision-making strategies to the uncertainties inherent in each evidence type (Gambrill, 2000).

How are Client's Needs and Strengths Assessed?

"Does this client have a problem that can be solved?" This is the question that social workers must answer when they first meet a new client. Group workers use assessments for two purposes. They need to identify clients with the characteristics that would make them appropriate for a treatment group. Having done that, they must also determine the stage of development or severity of each client's problems in order to match them to groups composed of members with similar conditions. They begin to collect data and use that evidence from the moment they meet their clients. They draw on client intake information, biopsychosocial assessments, and, possibly, standardized psychological tests (Gambrill, 1997). The accuracy and validity of this information depends on the reliability and validity of the instruments used to collect data, the client's willingness to disclose truthful information, and on the social worker's skill in doing assessments and integrating information.

Social workers will not always be familiar with the types of problems their clients present. When social workers are uncertain about aspects of presenting problems, they should consult with more-experienced colleagues and refer to research for studies describing problem etiology (Gambrill, 1997). The worker can seek out reviews and practice guidelines describing alternative treatments for the client's identified problem and the range of probable outcomes for each type of treatment. Even experienced workers who specialize in a particular kind of clinical problem should check the research literature periodically to see if any progress has been made in their specialty areas.

After reviewing all this evidence, the social worker must decide whether or not any intervention is necessary. If an intervention seems advisable, his or her next question should be "What intervention or interventions can I use to solve it?" The social worker would then review the treatment alternatives. At this stage, the social worker must also take into account what services are available through the agency and within the community. Although a client may have characteristics that make him or her appropriate for group treatment, research evidence may suggest that individual counseling or psychotropic medication may also be effective. Or, a combination of a treatment group and other kinds of individual treatments may be helpful. The available information will help the social worker determine the best available treatment (e.g., group, group and some other treatment, or some other treatment rather than a group) for the client.

What evidence could a social worker use to determine whether participation in a treatment group could help remedy the client's problem? Group interventions are most often used to aid clients who are socially isolated, have difficulty with interpersonal relationships, and/or desire to develop their human potential (Toseland & Rivas, 2001). Groups are contraindicated when clients are intensely private, have problems that would be difficult for them to disclose to others, or behave in ways that other members might find intolerable.

In some settings, clients are court-mandated into a specialized treatment group, such as addiction treatment or anger management. These clients do not have a choice about being in a group, but they can make choices about whether and how they will take advantage of the group experience. Social workers need to help these clients understand how the group might help them in the short term. The social workers can also help clients understand that by cooperating in the group they may be able to reduce the time they stay under the court's supervision (Toseland & Rivas, 2001). There is evidence available to show that some kinds of mandated treatment groups can be effective with some populations, such as cognitive behavioral groups for multi-family juvenile first offenders (Quinn et al., 2002) and psychotherapy groups for incarcerated offenders (Morgan, 2002). By drawing appropriately on this research, social workers can instill hope in their clients for their ultimate success, while sustaining their own optimism about successful outcomes they can achieve when working with challenging groups.

What are the Desired Outcomes of Treatment?

After determining that the client is appropriate for group treatment, the social worker and client discuss what the client wants from treatment and how a group treatment could help achieve those goals. In general, the goal of treatment is to reduce the risk of harm or increase the number of protective factors—the resources and strategies the client can draw on to manage her or his problem condition most effectively. If the client has multiple concerns, the social worker needs to clarify which ones can be addressed through group treatment and which cannot.

Few clinical trials have been conducted to investigate the effectiveness of group treatments. Our knowledge of outcomes is founded primarily on consistent findings of many observational studies (Pollio et al., 2000). Overall, these findings indicate that treatment groups can alleviate clients' feelings of isolation, restore hope and, in some cases, empower them (Schopler & Galinsky, 1995). Groups can provide members with accurate information about areas of concern and ways to cope more effectively (Toseland & Rivas, 2001). Members may learn about cognitive self-management and practice new behaviors that improve their communication and social skills. They can develop greater awareness of their psychological processes and insight into their motivations.

What are the Risks of Each Treatment Alternative?

According to EBP principles, practitioners must help clients understand the possible risks associated with each type of suggested intervention, including costs, the likelihood of no improvement, and possible adverse effects. One reason that treatment groups are such a common type of service is that administrators and program funders view them as economical when compared to individual treatments (Crosby & Sabein, 1995), but this advantage must be compared to the relative convenience, effectiveness, and costs of medication or individual therapy.

Systematic studies of group intervention are scarce, making it difficult to judge in advance the likelihood of no improvements or other adverse effects. There is much more information available about the risks and benefits of individual therapy and psychiatric medications. The descriptive studies have, however, identified some of the risks that members run when they enter group treatment. Group leaders try to establish guidelines that will assure the safety and well-being of each group member. But group members are still at risk of experiencing unpleasant situations such as breach of confidentiality, or that other members may not respond to them in constructive ways (Corey & Corey, 1997). For example, a member may be scapegoated (Konopka, 1983). Observational studies suggest that some groups do not improve member psychosocial functioning but, instead, promote conformity and dependency. If a group has a few dominant or very talkative members, the group may focus on their needs and neglect those of more passive members (Yalom, 1995).

Is the Intervention Available to the Client?

Having reached agreement that a group experience is appropriate, the worker and client must then decide which type of group would most likely meet the client's needs and preferences. Their decisions regarding the choice of group will be based on the client's reasons for joining the group: social support, education on specific topics, therapy, emotional growth, or opportunities for socialization. To make it likelier that the client will receive the full group intervention, the social worker must help the client find a group with the appropriate objectives that is held at a convenient place and time, and make sure that the client has reliable transportation to get to the meetings.

Was the Group Conducted as Planned?

To judge the effectiveness of a group treatment, we must first know whether it was carried off as planned. Researchers refer to this concern as "intervention fidelity." By systematically collecting data from each session (Meier, 1999; Meier et al., 1995; Toseland & Rivas, 2001) social workers answer a variety of questions about intervention fidelity. What proportion of members attended all the sessions? To what extent and in what ways did members participate in discussions? Were the topics that were supposed to be covered actually discussed? How many members participated in group activities? Group leaders and supervisors, in consultation with group members, can use this information to decide whether and how the group's content or activities should be modified.

In group treatments, the group simultaneously provides the means for providing a service and the setting in which that service takes place (Vinter, 1985). To do this, the group must be viable as a social entity. Groups that function well usually achieve cohesion. Cohesion is not a stage in itself, but the result of all the forces acting on members that motivate them to remain in the group (Toseland & Rivas, 2000, p. 79). As groups progress toward cohesiveness over time, members shift psychologically from seeing themselves only as individuals to identifying with the group.

Of the group leader's many functions, one of the most important is to help the group achieve cohesion. To do this, the leader must plan and manage the group so that discussions and activities are aligned with the group's developmental processes (Toseland & Rivas, 2001). As members get to know and trust one another, they become better able to satisfy their individual needs for affiliation and to help each other in achieving their group's goals. They learn to communicate effectively, interact in constructive ways, and take on roles that are essential to reaching optimum treatment outcomes.

If group cohesion is so important in group treatment, what member behaviors should social workers watch for to determine whether their groups are becoming more cohesive? Group leaders should be familiar with the research describing these behaviors (Berman-Rossi, 1993; Northen & Kurland, 2001). For example, members openly express their satisfaction with the group. They become more willing to invest in and take responsibility for what happens in the group. They take more risks in their self-revelations. Members become more tolerant of individual differences, and are better able to resolve conflicts using consensus.

Group leaders select activities that they believe will encourage members to engage in these behaviors. In keeping with EBP principles, the group leader would also systematically monitor the group's development, documenting his or her observations of each session to determine whether those strategies helped the group achieve its goals (Toseland & Rivas, 2001). What leaders do in any session of their groups will vary according to the type of group, its stage of development, and their leadership styles and skill levels (Toseland & Rivas, 2001). Agencies should collect evidence about their social workers' leadership styles so that leaders will be appropriately matched to the type of group (Toseland & Rivas, 2001, pp. 126–128).

One variant in group formats calls for two co-leaders. From the EBP perspective, the presence of two leaders means that the group benefits from having a second expert. Co-led groups can offer greater flexibility in meeting members' needs, since leaders can decide whether they would be most effective by sharing the primary leader's role or trading off observer and primary leader roles (Toseland & Rivas, 2001). The co-leader's documented observations could offer additional evidence about intervention fidelity and group functioning.

How did the Client Respond to the Group?

Treatment groups are opportunities for individual members to learn new information, acquire cognitive self-management and social skills, and receive and give support. Assuming that their assignment to the group was appropriate to begin with, the benefits individual members receive from their groups will be related to how regularly they attend and how actively they participate in discussions and activities. Depending on the context of the service, information about individual members' participation in and reactions to their groups can be compiled from many sources. Group leaders' session report forms are likely to be the most accessible source. Group members' comments about their groups may also be found, however, in case notes of individual counseling sessions, or solicited in group discussions in which members are asked to give each other feedback.

How will Intervention Outcomes be Assessed?

In group treatments, social workers should assess process *and* behavioral change outcomes. In process evaluations of groups, we ask "To what extent and in what ways was the group satisfying to group members?" Here, social workers need to distinguish the sources of member satisfaction, (the attractiveness to the group of symptom relief), or some combination of both. In keeping with EBP, group workers may want to ask members' help in developing group self-monitoring procedures, including inventing their own measurement instruments and data collection methods. Or members could be consulted about the best ways to administer standardized measures. Members' reactions to being asked to complete particular instruments may help group workers interpret data collected using them. Group leaders need to document members' comments and incorporate this feedback when planning for future sessions and in assessing the manner in which the group influenced data collecting and analysis.

For a group to be viable, the group leader must be reasonably satisfied with the experience, too. In their session report forms, group leaders should document the challenges they faced as well as successes they achieved. After their groups are over, leaders can compare their own perceptions of how well the group worked to members' feedback on evaluation surveys. This evidence can be used as the basis for discussions in supervision sessions or other occasions when leaders need to reflect on their practice.

Individual-level Behavioral Outcomes

We measure individual outcomes when we want to discover whether an intervention had the desired effect on individual group members. Measures used to assess clients before starting the group (baseline) can be re-administered just after the group ends to discover whether or not there were measurable changes in desired behaviors, and the degree and direction of those changes. If social workers want to know how well changes are sustained over time, they can also administer the measure again at pre-specified dates.

Most readers should be familiar with these observational approaches to measuring individual client outcomes. They are variants of the single-subject research design commonly taught in social work programs (Faul et al., 2001; Gambrill, 1997). While very useful for understanding what happened in a specific group, findings based on this kind of evidence would be considered relatively weak. Due to the small sample size, these findings could not be considered representative of the population, and the group would have to have a very large effect in order to be detectable using statistical analyses.

By examining their agency's best practices, social workers can approximate a larger-scale outcome study of their group intervention (Epstein, 2001). This entails reviewing the records of all the clients who participated in past groups and comparing the characteristics and outcomes of the clients who completed a specific kind of group with those who did not receive any group treatment, or with those who did not complete the treatment. Other useful analyses would be to identify the types of clients who have completed their groups and then go on to complete other treatment or service plan goals.

Group-level Outcomes

When we want to know the overall effectiveness of a group intervention for all members, we can compile and average the differences between pre- and post-group scores of the measures administered to each group member. Here again, however, even if statistically significant changes have occurred, small sample sizes make it unlikely that they would be detected.

Social workers can overcome the problem of small sample size inherent in group treatment outcome studies by using wait-list control designs. This methodology is appropriate when it is impossible to randomly assign members to treatment and nontreatment groups (Rice, 2001). For groups routinely offered in an agency, social workers can take advantage of delays between the time that group members are recruited and when a group starts. In this approach, clients are assessed three times: at intake (Time A), just before the group begins (Time B), and at the end of the group (Time C). The amount and direction of change between Time A and Time B (no-treatment period), is compared to the amount and direction of change between Times B and C. This method enables practitioners to compare individual client outcomes when clients have not received any treatment, to the outcomes after they have. Doing wait-list control studies by accumulating data on groups that are routinely offered in an agency results in stronger evidence because findings are based on larger samples.

Thus far, we have devoted the discussion to descriptions of how EBP principles apply to treatment groups. Before going on, it is important to acknowledge social workers' work with task groups within organizations and social action groups. In these contexts, the desired outcomes of a group could be the team's completion of assigned tasks, or changes in organizations, communities, or policies (Toseland & Rivas, 2001). Although the application of EBP principles to task groups is beyond the scope of this chapter, social workers in macropractice settings should also be alert to the ways they could use evidence systematically. They can apply EBP principles by drawing on administrative data (Meier & Usher, 1998) and research in social psychology on social organizations (Seekins et al., 1984). This evidence can be helpful when deciding how to form teams and committees, facilitate team decisions, monitor team progress toward the achievement of their tasks, or assess the impact of their collective efforts within organizations, and communities, or on policy making.

THE INTERVENTION RESEARCH PARADIGM AND EVIDENCE-BASED PRACTICE

In the best of all possible worlds, social workers would have the skills they need to evaluate research and be motivated to seek out evidence of the best ways to treat problems. They would find the reliable and valid evidence based on systematic research that they need to guide their treatment decisions. As they begin working toward becoming evidence-based, however, they are more likely to encounter barriers instead of facilitative conditions, and gaps in the available information. For example, social workers' professional education may not have provided them with skills they need to use evidence competently (Fraser, 1994). Once on the job, they are unlikely to get experience collecting data systematically or using research evidence.

At present, social workers who are interested in applying EBP principles will find few reports of systematic research or treatment guidelines that apply directly to the kinds of work they do. Group workers, in particular, will have difficulty obtaining systematic evidence on the efficacy of small-group interventions. Most articles in social group work journals are devoted to descriptions of group programming and group dynamics. Outcome studies are relatively rare. Fewer still use experimental or quasi-experimental designs. Experimental research studies need standardized protocols. Because of the nature of the group's developmental processes it is difficult to maintain such high levels of control. Few studies achieve the statistical power needed to detect treatment effects, in part because researchers have problems obtaining and retaining large enough samples.

Given the scarcity of clinical trials on group interventions and the difficulty in conducting them, what can group workers do to systematically develop evidence to demonstrate the feasibility and value of their groups? One alternative is to employ a research methodology that better accommodates the realities of group work practice. The Intervention Research (IR) Paradigm offers such an alternative. Rothman and Thomas developed the IR Paradigm to provide an integrated perspective for understanding, developing, and examining the feasibility and effectiveness of innovative human service interventions (Bailey-Dempsey & Reid, 1996; Rothman & Thomas, 1994). Because IR methodologies take the uncontrollability of practice settings into account, this paradigm is more practical for testing innovative interventions than the social science research paradigm (Rothman & Thomas, 1994).

The conventional social science paradigm ascribes the greatest value to evidence from "black box" experimental studies that allow researchers to say with some confidence that changes in behavior are associated with participation in the intervention and not some other factor. They pay less attention to the intervention's specific mechanisms that may have caused those changes. The IR paradigm is founded on the principles of industrial research and development. In this context, interventions are seen as "social inventions" that must be systematically pilot-tested and modified until they work as planned under specified conditions. Here, an intervention's reliability and validity are primarily defined in terms of its feasibility under practice conditions (Thomas, 1985). In social work intervention research, social workers systematically test various aspects of their interventions using small-scale studies. Such pilot studies require relatively few resources. Early studies are conducted with abbreviated or simulated versions of the intervention and trial runs of data collection instruments. This design and development process (D&D) allows researcher/practitioners to determine whether their interventions are feasible and promising enough to be worth investing in full-scale field trials (Table 26.1).

In EBP, social workers are not expected to be researchers, but to draw upon research syntheses in making their treatment decisions (Fraser, forthcoming). In developmental intervention research, social workers are integral members of research teams. As in EBP, the IR approach embodies a collaborative approach. Practitioners and researchers work as a team, with group members providing vital feedback at many points in the intervention's development. Practitioners may take the lead in identifying problems about their groups that need study. Alternatively, researchers, from within or outside the agency, identify problems through their surveys of the literature and ask practitioners to collaborate in developing new groups. Researchers often (but not necessarily) take the lead in reviewing the research literature and bringing information (or the lack thereof) about population and community characteristics, assessment methods, treatment alternatives and monitoring strategies back for the team's consideration. People who are members of the intervention's target population may be asked to participate in the focus groups or other simulations to obtain their perspectives about whether and how the group works. Researchers and practitioners collaborate in developing the programming of the group's content, selecting activities, and developing ways to monitor group leader behavior and group development. Once the group is under way, practitioners and group members give feedback pe-

Table 26.1 Intervention Research (IR) Design and Development Activities for Group Interventions

PROJECT DESIGN AND DEVELOPMENT STAGE	Activities	
	REFINING AN EXISTING GROUP	INVENTING A NEW GROUP
Stage 1: Identify the problem.	Identify the aspects of the current group that are problematic.	Select the problem to remedy. Identify a range of possible strategies for achieving desired outcomes. Is a group a plausible intervention?
Stage 2. Characterize the problem.	Conduct literature reviews and analyze administrative data. • *To what extent and in what ways have the characteristics of the client population changed since the group was first offered?* Determine whether there has been new research to indicate that: • *the content or structure of the group should be modified, or* • *there are better ways to evaluate the group's effectiveness.*	Conduct literature reviews to see what researchers have done to determine the prevalence and severity of the problem, its causes and its etiology. Consult with professional experts, and other people who have lived with the problem to determine whether there are other perspectives not found in the research literature. Identify criteria for an appropriate and effective intervention.
	Integrate new information into the intervention design	
Stage 3. Specify the elements of the intervention.	Identify the changes to be made in the scope and sequence of the existing group's discussions and activities. Modify or design new materials and activity plans.	Decide on the scope and sequence of discussion content and the activities of the new group. Design materials and activity plans.
	Conduct feasibility studies of pilot version of the group.	
Stage 4: Pilot testing.	Modify or develop procedures for training and supervising group leaders. Modify or develop procedures for monitoring group processes to insure intervention fidelity. Select or develop evaluation instruments and satisfaction surveys. Analyze pilot-study data to identify the intervention's strengths and flaws. Modify group designs based on these findings to insure that the intervention is as accessible and satisfying as possible for participants. If the pilot study indicates that the intervention is feasible, conduct further small-scale studies to insure that all elements of the intervention can be implemented reliably under real-life conditions.	

Table 26.1 *Continued*

PROJECT DESIGN AND DEVELOPMENT STAGE	Activities	
	REFINING AN EXISTING GROUP	INVENTING A NEW GROUP
Stage 5: Experimental field testing.	Conduct full-scale, experimental, or quasi-experimental field tests of the interventions.	
Stage 6: Dissemination of information about the project.	Present preliminary findings from early studies at conferences and in publications. Make available manuals and other materials developed along the way to other researchers and practitioners so they can use them to learn how to implement the intervention. Present and publish on findings from the full-scale field tests.	

riodically on how the intervention design works. If it is not going well, researchers and practitioners work together to modify it to make positive outcomes more likely.

In design and development research on groups, group members are asked frequently for feedback that may, on occasion, prompt the research team to make "midstream" alterations in the group protocol in order to keep the group viable (Comer, manuscript submitted for publication; Meier, 1999). Practitioners/researchers are trained to view such modifications not as failures, but as opportunities to extend the understanding about interventions to new populations or conditions (Comer et al., forthcoming). At the end of the group, members are assessed to see if their participation in the group helped them achieve their desired outcomes. In addition, members and practitioners are surveyed to find out how satisfied they were with the group experience, and to allow them to offer suggestions about how to improve it. Practitioners and group members' suggestions are incorporated into each successive pilot study, thereby insuring the intervention's acceptability, appropriateness, and validity.

RESEARCH ON GROUP INTERVENTIONS USING DEVELOPMENTAL INTERVENTION RESEARCH METHODOLOGIES

There have been relatively few published reports of studies that explicitly incorporated D&D strategies to develop innovative group interventions (Comer et al., in press). The studies that have been done used D&D procedures to invent groups for varied purposes using face-to-face and technology-mediated communication channels. Face-to-face groups have been developed for people coping with chronic pain and sickle cell disease (Subramanian, 1991; Comer, 1998); and psychoeducational groups for HIV-affected people (Pomeroy et al., 1995). Telephone support groups have been developed for people with AIDS (Rounds et al., 1995) and family caregivers of people with AIDS (Meier et al., 1995). Meier has developed professionally facilitated, Internet-mediated support groups for social workers suffering from job stress (Meier, 2000b) and spouses of survivors of colon cancer (Meier, 2003).

In these studies, researchers used the early stages of pilot testing to investigate the appropriateness of specific elements of their research and intervention designs, such as recruitment (Meier, 2000a; Meier, 2003); data collection methods (Meier, 1999, 2003; Rounds et al., 1995); participants' comfort levels with the telecommunications technology used to conduct the interventions (Meier, 1999; Meier, 2003; Rounds et al., 1995); group discussion formats (Comer, 1999; Meier, 1999; Meier, 2003; Pomeroy et al., 1995; Subramanian, 1991; Subramanian et al., 1995); group development issues (Comer, manuscript submitted for publication; Comer et al., 1999; Meier, 1999; Meier, 2003; Subramanian et al., 1995); and participant satisfaction (Meier et al., 1995, 1999; Meier, 2003; Rounds et al., 1995). All these researchers used findings from their preliminary studies to improve their research designs and data collection techniques, and to clarify and extend intervention models.

DESIGNING AND DEVELOPING
GROUP INTERVENTION MODELS

Practitioner/researchers can use the design and development (D&D) procedures prescribed by the IR paradigm as a map to guide them in refining existing groups or developing new ones. But the map is not the territory. As with any journey, travelers may have to make unexpected detours not shown on the map before they arrive at their destinations. The stages shown in Table 26.1 are as if they were discrete and linear, but they are often cyclical and iterative. Practitioner/researchers should expect to make many modifications in their plans for their groups before completing any study. Practitioner/researchers often discover along the way that components in their interventions or their research designs need to be changed. In Meier's early studies of facilitated Internet support groups, for example, she discovered repeatedly that using the Internet as her only communication channel to recruit members was neither effective nor efficient (Meier, 1999, 2003). These findings led her to conclude that, in future studies, she should investigate whether the combination of face-to-face and on-line recruitment strategies will work better. In Comer's (1999) study of a face-to-face cognitive-behavioral group intervention for African-Americans with sickle cell anemia and depression, she discovered that group members felt the self-management tasks (recording and maintaining journals about their activities) were too burdensome. Because group leader observations and interim measures of members' depression levels showed positive trends, members were allowed to stop doing some of these tasks.

Whether the goal is to improve an existing group or develop a new one, researcher/practitioners who use the IR design and developmental procedures go through similar steps. The greatest difference in procedures for these two types of studies will arise during the early stages of problem identification and definition that precede the actual design or redesign of the intervention model. Table 26.1 summarizes the different starting points of their associated activities and (in stages 4 through 6 at the bottom of the table) shows where the tasks for both types of projects converge.

Modifying an existing group

Much of the preliminary work of modifying a group involves field work within the agency. If a group has been offered as a service for a long time, researcher/practitioners should consult coworkers and supervisors and agency records to reconstruct the group's history to answer the following questions: "When was the group first offered?" "Whom was it intended to serve?" "What changes have occurred that prompted the decision to modify the group?" The research team uses the information to clearly define the problem. Has it become more difficult to recruit and retain participants? If group leaders are reporting problems, what kinds of difficulties are they encountering? Are group members reporting low levels of satisfaction? Are group members not achieving their desired therapeutic outcomes? Answering these questions may illuminate several, interrelated problems that will impel changes in the intervention design.

For example, problems may arise from group composition. A group may stop working well if it was initiated to serve one type of client but was later opened to clients with other needs. In constructing the developmental history of the group, the research team needs to examine client records to see whether recent groups were still composed of members from the original target group. If not, the practitioner/researcher team may suggest reviewing treatment alternatives for the original target population. Alternatively, they may decide that their intervention research studies should focus on developing a group adapted to greater diversity among members.

As group members and group leaders change, so does group structure. Before attempting to modify an existing group, practitioner/researchers must have a clear understanding about how group leaders are running their groups. The research team reviews whatever documentation about the group is available and consults with the leaders. Group leaders are asked to describe the scope and sequence of the discussions and planned activities, their clinical rationales, and how the selection and sequencing of activities are related to group developmental processes. The team also needs to know what group leaders think works well—or badly—and their recommendations for changes. If several group leaders are running the same kind of group, the team may also decide to examine the evidence to see how similar or different the groups are in content and dynamics. Similarly, the team may review whatever data are available about member satisfaction. Afterwards, the team may decide to tap members' reactions to the group by conducting surveys or focus groups.

Practitioner/researchers must also discover what kinds of data have been collected on the group itself, and whether they have been collected systematically. For example, they need to find out whether and how intervention fidelity has been monitored. Are reports on each session required as well as notes in individual client records? If so, what aspects of the session are documented? When and how is this information reviewed? If group leaders or the agency do these kinds of reviews, how are the findings used in ongoing decisions about how the group should be run?

The practitioner/researcher team goes through a similar process to discover whether the client behaviors that the group is supposed to change are systematically assessed. If they have, when and how are these assessments administered? If standardized instruments have been used, are they reliable? Were they normed on the group's target population? Are they valid for use with this particular group, in that items on the instruments tap into the group's content?

Besides learning about the group intervention as it is currently used, the research team gathers the information they will need to help them decide how to modify it. As with EBP, they delve into the current research to update their understanding of the characteristics of the group's target population, the root causes and prevalence of the specific problem, the range of interventions available, and the expected outcomes. To focus this part of the search, practitioner/researchers may also decide to consult with experts in the field.

When they review local census and agency services data, the researcher/practitioner team may find that the community's racial or ethnic composition or its economic health has changed since the group was first offered. Alternatively, recent research on specific health and mental health conditions may suggest new causes of those problems or new opportunities for intervention. Updated information about client and problem characteristics may lead practitioner/researchers to recommend changes in group discussion content or activities. It may turn out that research indicates that a group intervention is no longer considered the most appropriate intervention for a given condition, or that combination therapy regimes, such as groups and anti-depressant medications, offer the most benefits. If there are no standardized baseline and outcome measures being used, or the ones that are do not appear to be reliable and valid, the literature review should include a search for better measures.

Inventing a New Group

In the previous scenario, the agency had already identified a problem and offered a group intervention to remedy it. Practitioner/researchers were prompted to modify the group because it was not working well in some way. In this second scenario, researcher/practitioners start from scratch, with the realization that there is a problem to be remedied. They must do preliminary investigations to determine its prevalence and severity in the community. Next, they must decide that the problem is significant enough to warrant investing the time and resources needed to develop and implement a new service. Finally, they must decide, based on research into problem prevalence and root causes, agency resources, and client preferences, that a group is the most appropriate intervention.

Designing and Developing the Group Intervention Model

In D&D Stages 1 and 2, practitioner/researchers use EBP strategies to decide on the group format and the information to be conveyed in their groups. In Stage 3, they begin to focus concretely on what group members and group leaders will discuss and do in each session of their groups, coordinating them with the parallel psychosocial group development processes. Group workers will be relying largely on their practice wisdom in this aspect of intervention design. Although experience tells us that the group is the vehicle for individual change through the support and challenge group members give each other, there is very little evidence available to help social workers understand how these processes and dynamics influence the group's outcomes (Northen & Kurland, 2001; Tolman & Molidor, 1994). Thus, group workers can make important contributions to our understanding of these relationships by systematically collecting evidence and reporting on their experiences with their groups in intervention research studies.

In Stage 3, existing program content is modified or new elements are created. For example, handouts used in sessions may be modified or new ones developed, videos, games or other activities are selected, and group leaders are trained to use them. Once all these elements are in place, the members are recruited for the initial pilot group. Because many aspects of the group are still untested, such pilots are often shortened versions of the full-scale version. These pilots are opportunities to get participant reactions to the discussion content, activities, and written materials, and data collection instruments. At this stage, practitioners and researchers are interested in getting a tentative answer to the feasibility question, "Can this group be run as planned?"

In Stage 4, practitioner/researchers draw on their experiences implementing the group to identify the group's strengths and flaws. If recruiting was not as successful as anticipated, service marketing and recruiting procedures may have to be changed or intensified. Group leaders may discover other things they need to know to be effective facilitators. If they are receiving supervision, they may also learn that a different kind of supervisory support will be needed. Feedback from participants may reveal that they would like a different type, number, or range of activities. Staff and researcher discussions on all these different issues can lead to decisions about what procedures should be modified, with the aim of making the group accessible to participants and the experience as satisfying as possible. If the intervention protocol was changed in response to member feedback, the data collection instruments used to assess outcomes may no longer tap into the group content, and new ones will need to be selected for the next pilot study (Meier, 1999).

Given all the ways that the intervention research plans can go awry, practitioner/researcher teams need to plan for multiple pilot tests of their groups to discover the most workable combination of elements for the research design and the intervention. Practitioner/researchers take advantage of opportunities to pilot different aspects of the group. They can try things out in the groups they run themselves, or collaborate with group workers whom they supervise. Sometimes, they can find small amounts of funding to conduct small studies. With each succeeding pilot, the evidence about what works accumulates.

Stage 5 calls for practitioner/researchers to conduct full-scale, quasi-experimental evaluations of intervention effectiveness. They only proceed to this stage after multiple pilot studies confirm that the intervention is feasible under practice conditions. Obviously, field testing for IR with groups can only be done if the funding and institutional resources for implementing a larger study are available.

In Stage 6, practitioner/researchers disseminate what they are learning about their interventions. In Table 26.1, dissemination is shown as the last step. Typically, researchers present findings from outcome studies of their projects at conference presentations and scholarly publications when the full-scale field testing has been completed. Researchers following the Intervention Research paradigm will also present and publish articles on preliminary findings from early studies. They also make available manuals and other training materials developed along the way, which other practitioners can use to learn how to implement the intervention.

RESOURCES FOR EVIDENCE-BASED PRACTICE AND INTERVENTION RESEARCH ON GROUPS

EBP and IR both call for social workers to go beyond their daily work routines, to learn more about their clients and interventions and how to improve their practice. Practically speaking, social workers face barriers that may deter them from even beginning. Heavy workloads are common. Many may not have the skills (Fraser, 1994; Fraser et al., 1993; Gambrill,

1999), or the practical experience (Kirk & Penka, 1992; Marino et al., 1998) to do either. Where can social workers acquire the knowledge they need to understand EBP and IR processes? How can they be efficient in their information searches? How can they get help to do IR with their groups? In this final section, we describe how to find help in understanding the principles of EBP, IR design, and development processes as they apply to group work.

Much of the early debate on EBP has taken place within the medical profession. Recently, social work researchers have also begun to express their views on the value and the applicability of EBP principles in social work (Fraser, forthcoming; Gambrill, 1997, 1999; Gibbs & Gambrill, 2002; Pollio, in press). As with all innovations, the response has been mixed. One of the strongest critiques has been in response to EBP's emphasis on the value of evidence from clinically controlled trials to identify best practices. Social worker critics have argued that this standard of evidence is inappropriate for social work, particularly for group work, where it is rarely available. Moreover, the uncontrollability of practice settings make it difficult to replicate experimentally validated interventions.

In this chapter we have advocated more realistic ways for social workers to incorporate research evidence in their decisions to use groups with their clients, and for systematically modifying or inventing groups. On-line databases are making the search for information about research evidence for social work practice more available through desktop computers. Social workers who do not have adequate access to the internet or the skills to use on-line data bases themselves should contact the libraries in their communities to see what resources and help they can offer. The impetus for EBP is leading to investments in the information infrastructure, such as the ongoing professional training and development of knowledge bases needed to support it. All of these developments will make it progressively easier for social workers to know about and take advantage of the evidence that exists when making treatment decisions. It will also support their efforts to conduct research on their groups. In this final section, we describe sources of information that social workers can use to support them in this effort.

On-line Training to Assess Research Evidence and Use Practice Guidelines

Social workers seeking to learn how to assess research evidence can find lots of help on-line. For example, the Center for Health Evidence (http://www.cche.net/) and the Netting the Evidence (http://www.shef. ac.uk/~shar/ir/netting/first.html) websites provide instructions and tools for appraising research evidence. The National Institutes of Health are funding a network of Evidence-Based Practice Centers to review and summarize research for a variety of medical problems, including mental health and substance abuse (http://www.ahcpr.gov/clinic/epcix.htm).

On-line Resources for Health and Mental Health Research Evidence

All social workers with internet access can now delve into numerous health and behavioral sciences research databases. One of the most fully developed is the PubMed website (http://www.ncbi.nlm.nih.gov/ PubMed/), a service of the National Institutes of Health's National Library of Medicine. This database provides access to over 12 million MEDLINE citations dating back to the mid-1960s and additional life-science journals, and links to other websites where users can download full text versions of many articles listed in the database (National Library of Medicine, 2003).

Social workers who have graduated in the past ten years will also be familiar with other social work–specific computerized or on-line databases, such as Family and Society Studies Worldwide, PsychInfo, Social Work Abstracts, and Social Services Abstracts. These databases are usually not available over the internet to users who are unaffiliated with a university or college, but they are likely to be available through university libraries. These databases do not currently include downloadable full text versions of the publications, but by reviewing the abstracts, users can use their time more efficiently when they go to the library to get copies of the articles. University libraries may also be able to offer social workers access to the Health and Psychosocial Instruments database, which provides information on measurement instruments, including questionnaires, interview schedules, checklists, index measures, coding schemes/ manuals, rating scales, projective techniques, vignettes/scenarios, and tests, developed for use in the fields of health, psychosocial sciences, and organizational behavior.

Computerized databases make it easy to identify many potentially relevant articles. The challenge is to decide which are the key research studies that address the most important questions and use the most rigorous research designs. In PubMed and the other databases mentioned above, it is possible to limit the scope of the search results by specifying the topic of interest and "reviews" as the publication type. This search strategy will select only review articles on the specified topic.

New databases composed of practice guidelines are under development. The Cochrane Collaborative has already developed reviews for medical treatments, including some in psychiatry and psychosocial group treatments for medical conditions. In 2000, following the lead of the Cochrane Collaborative members, a group of educators, psychologists, and social workers initiated the Campbell Collaboration (C2). Their goal was to develop the methodologies for conducting systematic reviews of research on psychosocial interventions that can serve as the foundation for such guidelines (Howard, 2001; Campbell Collaboration, 2003). Currently, C2 offers practitioners free on-line access to a database (C2-SPECTR) of publications containing over 10,000 randomized and possibly randomized trials in education, social work and welfare, and criminal justice. The goal of C2-SPECTRE is to develop a comprehensive database that supports C2's users and reviewers by including useful information about study methods, outcomes, and the rigor of the research designs. Systematic reviews of the education, crime and justice, and social welfare research are now in the early development stage. As of this writing (April, 2003) none had been put on-line.

Given their early stages of system development, it is not surprising that neither collaboratives' databases contain much that is immediately useful to social workers interested in group interventions. With the exception of cognitive behavioral group interventions for smoking cessation (Stead & Lancaster, 2003), Cochrane reviewers were unable to draw conclusions about the efficacy of other kinds of psychosocial group interventions. They could only find a few published studies using clinical trials. In most studies, sample sizes were small, or the quality of design and reporting was inadequate. While these conditions are not helpful for group workers who want to be "EBP-compliant," they should use the situation to motivate themselves to work on IR projects so they can create evidence about their interventions.

Collaborative Relationships with Researchers

Collaboration is strongly valued in EBP and the IR Paradigm. Many practitioners know how to design a group intervention, but they may feel less confident about their ability to conduct research on their interventions or analyze data. By developing collaborative relationships with colleges and universities, practitioners can gain access to needed expertise and resources that university faculty and students can provide. Such partnerships between the faculty and practitioners can benefit both groups. The faculty member might wish to collaborate with the practitioner in applying for research grants to develop group interventions or study group outcomes. For social workers, this would also provide opportunities to strengthen their EBP skills. They could get expert advice about what information to look for and how to do efficient literature searches. Social workers would be exposed to role models who could demonstrate and coach them in how to assess research evidence and apply it to the design of future projects and interventions. If these collaborative efforts result in research projects, social workers on research teams could also get experience in selecting appropriate measures and analyzing data.

Collaborative Relationships with Schools of Social Work

In agencies where social work students have field placements, students can be asked to participate in these collaborative research arrangements. Students who chose to join the team would have opportunities to learn about intervention design and development in the context of group work. For example, if the agency decides to modify a group, students could be asked to compile the information about the group's developmental history within the agency, or data on changes in community, population, and client characteristics. Students could help practitioners update their knowledge by identifying alternative interventions and new assessment tools. In the process, students would get to practice their skills with on-line research data bases. Since design and development work with group interventions usually extends over several years, these projects could provide an opportunity for a number of students to gain knowledge and training in IR research methodologies on a single project. Meanwhile, the agency would also benefit from the accumulation of data from a larger sample that would enable them to conduct rigorous analyses of their group's outcomes.

CONCLUSIONS

All scientific work is incomplete—whether it be observational or experimental. All scientific work is liable to be upset or modified by advancing knowledge. This does not confer upon us the freedom to ignore the knowledge we already have, or to postpone the action that it appears to demand at a given time (Hill, 1965, p. 300).

The many gaps in our knowledge about what makes intervention groups work makes using EBP and IR with groups challenging. We have much to learn about who benefits the most from what groups, and under what conditions. Clearly, filling those gaps using intervention research methodologies will be time-consuming and energy-intensive. Yet social workers' efforts to incorporate evidence in their treatment decisions and in conducting developmental research on groups are also intrinsically valuable. When they seek out the best available evidence to back their clinical judgements, or develop pilot studies on their groups, they are mining the knowledge bases that can help them better understand the people and communities they serve and the range of possible treatments they can offer.

REFERENCES

Bailey-Dempsey, C., & Reid, W. J. (1996). Intervention design and development: A case study. *Research on Social Work Practice.* 6(2), 208–228.

Berman-Rossi, T. (1993). The tasks and skills of the social worker across stages of group development. *Social Work with Groups.* 16(1–2), 69–81.

Comer, E. (manuscript submitted for publication). Integrating the health and mental health needs of the chronically ill: A group for individuals with depression and sickle cell disease.

Comer, E., Meier, A., & Galinsky, M. J. (1999). *Studying innovations in group work practice: Applications of the intervention research paradigm.* Paper presented at the American Association for the Advancement of Social Work with Groups, 21st Annual Symposium, Denver, CO.

Comer, E., Meier, A., & Galinsky, M. J. (forthcoming). Development of innovative group work practice using the Intervention Research Paradigm: Two cases. *Social Work.*

Comer, E. E. (1999). *Effects of a cognitive behavioral group intervention on the reduction of depressive symptoms in individuals with sickle cell disease.* Unpublished dissertation, University of North Carolina, Chapel Hill, NC.

Corey, M., & Corey, G. (1997). *Groups: Process and practice* (5th ed.). New York: Brooks/Cole.

Crosby, G., & Sabein, J. E. (1995). Developing and marketing time-limited groups. *Psychiatric Services.* 47(1), 7–8.

Epstein, I. (2001). Using available clinical information in practice-based research: Mining for silver while dreaming for gold. *Social Work in Health Care.* 33(3/4), 15–32.

Faul, A. C., McMurtry, S. L., & Hudson, W. W. (2001). Can empirical clinical practice techniques improve social work outcomes? *Research on Social Work Practice.* 11(3), 277–299.

Fraser, M. (forthcoming). Intervention research in social work: A basis for evidence-based practice and practice guidelines. In A. Rosen & E. K. Proctor (eds.), *Developing practice guidelines of social work interventions: Issues, methods and research agenda.* New York: Coumbia University Press.

Fraser, M. W. (1994). Scholarship and research in social work: Emerging challenges. *Journal of Social Work Education.* 30, 252–266.

Fraser, M. W., Jenson, J. M., & Lewis, R. E. (1993). Research training in social work: The continuum is not a continuum. *Journal of Social Work Education.* 29(1), 46–62.

Gambrill, E. (1997). *Social work practice: A critical thinker's guide.* New York: Oxford University Press.

Gambrill, E. (1999). Evidence-based practice: An alternative to authority-based practice. *Families in Society.* 89(4), 341–350.

Gambrill, E. (2000). The role of critical thinking in evidence-based social work. In P. Allen-Meares & C. Garvin (eds.), *The Handbook of Social Work Direct Practice* (pp. 43–63). Thousand Oaks, CA: Sage.

Gibbs, L., & Gambrill, E. (2002). Evidence-based practice: Counterarguments to objections. *Research on Social Work Practice.* 12(3), 452–476.

Guyatt, G. H., Haynes, B., Jaescheke, R. Z., Cook, D. J., Green, L., Nayolor, C. D., Wilson, M. C., & Richardson, W. S. (2000). *EBM: Principles of applying users' guides to patient care.* Centre for Health Evidence. Retrieved March 14, 2003, from the World Wide Web: http://www.cche.net/userguide/applying.asp

Hayward, R. S. A., Wilson, M. C., Tunis, S. R., Bass, E. G., & Guayatt, G. (1995). *How to use a clinical practice guideline.* Centre for Health Evidence. Retrieved March 3, 2003, from the World Wide Web: http://www.cche.net/userguides/guideline.asp

Hill, A. B. (1965). The environment and disease: Association or causation? *Proceedings of the Royal Society of Medicine.* 58, 295–300.

Howard, M. O. (2001). First Annual Campbell Collaboration Colloquium, Philadelphia, PA. *SSWR News.* 8, 12.

Kirk, S., & Penka, C. E. (1992). Research utilization and MSW education: A decade of progress? In A. J. Grasso & I. Epstein (eds.), *Research utilization in the social services* (pp. 497–421). New York: Haworth Press.

Konopka, G. (1983). *Social group work: A helping process* (3rd ed.). Englewood Cliffs, NJ: Prentice Hall.

Marino, R., Green, R. G., & Young, E. (1998). Beyond the scientist-practitioner model's failure to thrive: Social workers' participation in agency-based research activities. *Social Work Research.* 22(3), 188–192.

Meier, A. (1999). *A multi-method evaluation of a computer-mediated, stress management support group for social workers: Feasibility, process, and effectiveness.* Unpublished dissertation, University of North Carolina, Chapel Hill.

Meier, A. (2000a). Offering social support via the Internet: A case study of an online support group for social workers. *Journal of Technology in Human Services.* 17(2/3), 237–266.

Meier, A. (2000b). Offering social support via the Internet: A case study of an online support group for social workers. In J. Finn & G. Holden (eds.), *Human services online: A new arena for service delivery* (pp. 237–266). New York: Haworth Press.

Meier, A. (2003). *Colon cancer caregivers' online support group project: Research feasibility, and intervention feasibility and outcomes* (final report). Chapel Hill: University of North Carolina: Lineberger Comprehensive Cancer Center.

Meier, A., Galinsky, M. J., & Rounds, K. (1995). Telephone support groups for caregivers of persons with AIDS. In M. J. Galinsky & J. H. Schopler (eds.), *Support groups: Current perspectives on theory and practice* (pp. 99–108). Binghamton, NY: Haworth Press.

Meier, A., & Usher, C. L. (1998). New approaches to program evaluation. In R. L. Edwards & J. A. Yankey (eds.), *Skills for effective nonprofit organizations* (pp. 371–405). Washington, DC: NASW Press.

Morgan, R. D. (2002). Group psychotherapy with incarcerated offenders: A research synthesis. *Group Dynamics.* 6(3), 203–218.

National Association of Social Workers. (1996). *Code of ethics.* Washington, DC: National Association of Social Workers.

National Library of Medicine. (2003). *Entrez PubMed.* Retrieved March 3, 2003, from the World Wide Web: www.ncbi.nlm.nih.gov/PubMed/

Nelson, G. M., Meier, A., & Usher, C. L. (forthcoming). System reform and community practice. In M. O. Weil (ed.), *Handbook of community practice.* Newbury Park, CA: Sage Publications.

Northen, H., & Kurland, R. (2001). *Social Work with Groups* (3rd ed.). New York: Columbia University Press.

Pollio, D. E. (forthcoming). The evidence-based social worker. *Social Work with Groups.*

Pollio, D. E., Brower, A. M., & Galinsky, M. J. (2000). Change in groups. In P. Allen-Meares & C. Garvin (eds.), *The handbook of social work direct practice* (pp. 281–300). Thousand Oaks, CA: Sage Publications.

Pomeroy, E. C., Rubin, A., & Walker, R. J. (1995). Effectiveness of a psychoeducational and task-centered group intervention for family members of people with AIDS. *Social Work Research.* 19(3), 142–151.

Quinn, W. H., Van Dyke, D. J., & Kurth, S. T. (2002). A brief multiple family group model for juvenile first offenders. In C. R. Figley (ed.), *Brief treatments for the traumatized: A project of the Green Cross Foundation* (pp. 226–251). Westport, CT, Greenwood Press.

Rice, A. H. (2001). Evaluating brief structured group treatment of depression. *Research on Social Work Practice.* 11(1), 53–78.

Rothman, J., & Thomas, E. J. (1994). *Intervention research: Design and development for human service.* New York: Haworth Press.

Rounds, K., Galinsky, M. J., & Despard, J. R. (1995). Evaluation of telephone support groups for persons with HIV disease. *Research on Social Work Practice.* 5(4), 442–459.

Sackett, D. L., Richardson, W. M. C., Gray, J. A. M., Haynes, R. B., & Richardson, W. S. (1996). Evidence-based medicine: What it is and what it isn't. *British Medical Journal.* 312, 71–72.

Schopler, J. H., & Galinsky, M. J. (1995). Group practice overview. In R. L. Edwards & J. G. Hopps et al. (eds.), *Encyclopedia of Social Work* (vol. 1, pp. 1129–1143). Washington, DC: NASW Press.

Seekins, T., Mathews, R. M., & Fawcett, S. B. (1984). Enhancing leadership skills for community self-help organizatons through behavioral instruction. *Journal of Community Psychology.* 12, 155–163.

Stead, L. F., & Lancaster, T. (2003). Group behavior therapy programmes for smoking cessation (Cochrane Review). Oxford, UK: Update Software, Ltd.

Subramanian, K. (1991). Structured group work for the management of chronic pain: An experimental investigation. *Research on Social Work Practice.* 1(1), 32–45.

Subramanian, K., Hernandez, S., & Martinez, A. (1995). Psychoeducational group work for low-income Latina mothers with HIV infection. *Social Work with Groups.* 18(2/3), 53–64.

The Campbell Collaboration. (2003). *The Campbell Collaboration Homepage.* Retrieved March 2, 2003, from the World Wide Web: http://www. campbellcollaboration.org/

Thomas, E. J. (1985). The validity of design and development and related concepts in developmental research. *Social Work Research and Abstracts.* 21(2), 50–55.

Tolman, R., & Molidor, C. (1994). A decade of social group work research: Trends in methodology, theory, and program development. *Research on Social Work Practice.* 4(2), 142–159.

Toseland, R. W., & Rivas, R. F. (2001). *An introduction to group work practice* (4th ed.). Boston: Allyn and Bacon.

Vinter, R. (1985). Essential components of social group work practice. In M. Sundel, P. Glasser, R. Sarri, & R. Vinter (eds.), *Individual change through small groups* (2nd ed., pp. 11–34). New York City: The Free Press.

Yalom, I. D. (1995). *The theory and practice of group psychotherapy* (4th ed.). New York: Basic Books.

Index

441